Communists and Their Law

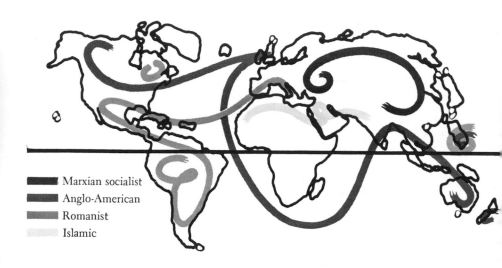

Marxian socialist
Anglo-American
Romanist
Islamic

*The Marxian socialist family of legal systems in the world
setting. Reproduced with permission of the Instituto de Derecho
Comparado of the Universidad Nacional Autonoma de Mexico*

Communists and Their

L A W

A Search for the Common Core of

the Legal Systems of

the Marxian Socialist States

JOHN N. HAZARD

The University of Chicago Press

Chicago & London

This volume is one in a series of
Studies of the Research Institute of Communist Affairs
of Columbia University

Standard Book Number: 226–32189–4
Library of Congress Catalog Card Number: 75–92770
THE UNIVERSITY OF CHICAGO PRESS, CHICAGO 60637
THE UNIVERSITY OF CHICAGO PRESS, LTD., LONDON

CONTENTS

PREFACE

When soviet troops, along with troops from Poland, Bulgaria, Hungary, and the German Democratic Republic, were ordered into Czechoslovakia late in the summer of 1968, the Soviet Communist party's *Pravda* denied as a malicious, provocative lie the charge that it was Soviet intent to foist upon Czechoslovakia a Soviet model of socialism.[1] Nevertheless, the editors made it clear that there was a core concept from which no member of the Marxian socialist community of states would be permitted to depart. They declared, "the destiny of the socialist gains of the Czechoslovak people . . . is not only the concern of the Communist party of Czechoslovakia but the common concern of the entire socialist community, the entire communist movement."

The dramatic troop movements clarified what had been noted by scholars of many lands during preceding decades, namely that considerable variation in political, social, and economic structure was to be countenanced within the Marxian socialist community, but that there was a limit to this tolerance of variation. From time to time efforts have been made in

[1] Pravda, 22 Aug. 1968. Eng. transl. in 7 Reprints from the Soviet Press, no. 6 at 1 (1968).

vii

scholarly circles to define this limit by determining the prime features of a common core of the political and legal system. One of the groups most interested is the international fraternity of legal scholars concerned with the comparison of laws. Members of this group had posed the question somewhat differently before 1968, but they were searching for elements of definition. They asked each other whether there were features within the legal systems of the Marxian socialist states that marked them off completely from other systems and whether variation from these features might reach a point at which the revisionist system would be read out of the family. They were also seeking to determine the limit of toleration, although they had not supposed that the point would be so important as to excite military pressures for conformity.

The legal scholars' conclusions were shown by the Mexicans in a map of the great legal systems of the world.[2] On this map there was a red swath originating in Moscow and extending westward into Eastern Europe and eastward into Northern Asia from Korea to Vietnam. This was the mapmakers' confirmation of what text writers had been saying for some years; that the principles of public order established by Lenin after the Bolshevik revolution of 1917 had given birth to a distinct legal family [3] comparable to the Anglo-American common law, the Romanist systems,[4] and the law of Islam.

There had been disagreement on what it should be called. Until Joseph Broz Tito was expelled from the Communist Information Bureau in 1948, analysts spoke of Lenin's creation in the singular. It was the "Soviet legal system," or, perhaps, the "socialist legal system." Within a few years after their ouster Yugoslav legal scholars demanded a new approach. They denied that the USSR continued to be a prototype. The appelation "Soviet" had become, in their view, wholly inappropriate, and

[2] Instituto de Derecho Comparado, Universidad Nacional Autonoma de Mexico (Prospectus) (n.d. cir. 1963) 11; reproduced as frontispiece to this volume.

[3] R. DAVID, LES GRANDS SYSTÈMES DE DROIT CONTEMPORAIN 22 (1964). For opinion to the contrary, see W. FRIEDMANN, LAW IN A CHANGING SOCIETY 91 (1959) and Lawson, Book Review, U. CHI. L. REV. 78 (1954).

[4] The term "Romanist family" is used throughout this study instead of the term "Romano-Germanic" or "civil-law system." European readers

even the title "socialist legal system" was inaccurate unless used in the plural.[5] A Polish scholar agreed, saying, "Polish law belongs to the great family of socialist legal systems."[6]

The argument ran that, although fundamental modifications were being introduced into the model developed by Lenin and Stalin in the USSR, the law of each of the Marxian socialist states remained within a distinctive legal family. The foundation of all was Leninism and socialism, albeit altered so that the identity with Stalin's public order system had been lost.

The Yugoslavs were not alone in their declaration of the right to innovate. Declarations within the family were hushed for nearly a decade, but they became audible to foreigners as Tito pressed his case. As early as 1957 Romanian scholars denied that there had been a "reception" in their state of the Soviet legal pattern. They preferred to call Soviet law only an "inspiration" to which the Romanians were adding their own ideas.[7] They did not find what they were doing comparable to Turkey's copying the Swiss civil code in 1924 without thought of its applicability to Turkish conditions.[8]

When the Romanians spoke, it had already become a commonplace to refer to the "socialist commonwealth of nations."

---

may object to omission of reference to the Germanic sources of some Western European law. Justification for simplification of the term is suggested by F. LAWSON, A COMMON LAWYER LOOKS AT THE CIVIL LAW (1953), who notes that since Anglo-American lawyers tend to find more similarities than differences in the French and German legal systems, a single source may be used in identification, namely the *corpus juris civilis* of Justinian. The designation popular among Anglo-American lawyers is avoided to escape confusion with the Romanist system's use of the term "civil law" to designate only private law, in distinction from public law.

[5] Blagojević, Some Characteristic Private Law Institutions in the Socialist Countries, a paper presented to a colloquium on the teaching of Marxist law in the United States. Parker School of Foreign and Comparative Law, Columbia University (1964). Mimeographed.

[6] Rozmaryn, *Le système de droit de la République populaire de Pologne*, in INTRODUCTION À L'ÉTUDE DE DROIT POLONAIS 61 (S. Rozmaryn ed. 1967).

[7] This phrase was used by the chairman of a group of scholars formed to meet with the author in the Institute of Law of the Academy of Sciences of the Romanian People's Republic, Bucharest, on 28 June 1957.

After the term was first uttered in *Kommunist* in 1955,[9] it gained wide usage, stimulated by Nikita Khrushchev's public statements following his unsuccessful attempt in 1956 to persuade Polish Communists to hew to the Soviet model. His successors seemed for a time to realize even more fully than he that the Communists of the USSR could no longer dictate a pattern from Moscow, at least not in minute detail. Communist parties everywhere began to demonstrate their freedom to formulate a political and social structure through revisions in law. Some of the boldest Communists, notably in China, even dared to say after Stalin's death that their Soviet comrades were guilty of retrogression—that they were opening the gates to capitalism.[10] Soviet ideologues answered that the Chinese had strayed so far that they could no longer claim even to have a legal system.[11]

The Sino-Soviet debate stimulated still more curiosity, both in Eastern Europe and in the rest of the world, as to what was fundamental to a Marxian socialist legal system—what contributed to its identifying characteristics. This curiosity was intensified as increasing numbers of Africans asserted their independence of colonial rulers and embarked upon the enactment of new law to create new political and social structures. Some of these leaders declared that Soviet rates of economic growth suggested the desirability of adopting Marxian socialist legal patterns for states in the process of development. Only economic planning as it had emerged in Marxian socialist states seemed to them capable of meeting their crushing problems.

Although the Marxian socialist model looked attractive eco-

---

[8] See *La réception des droits occidentaux en Turquie*, 11 ANNALES DE LA FACULTÉ DE DROIT D'ISTANBUL, no. 15 and no. 16–17 (1960). Also see 12 *id.* no. 18 (1962).

[9] *The Tie between Theory and Practice and Party Propaganda*, [1955] 14 KOMMUNIST 1 at 7. The Russian word *sodruzhestvo* has been translated as "commonwealth." See Z. BRZEZINSKI, THE SOVIET BLOC: UNITY AND CONFLICT 179 (1960).

[10] "Khrushchev has carried out a series of revisionist policies serving the interests of the bourgeoisie and rapidly swelling the forces of capitalism in the Soviet Union." See *On Khrushchev's Phoney Communism and Its Historical Lessons for the West*, [1964] 29 PEKING REVIEW 7 at 14.

[11] "In essence, the center of gravity in today's jurisprudence in China has been shifted to justifying and upholding arbitrary actions undertaken in the circumstances of the cult of the individual." Ilyichev, *Revolutionary*

nomically,[12] it lost its glow for many Africans as they saw in some of its elements the legitimation of Stalin's terrorism.[13] The Africans, although prepared to go far along the Soviet economic line, hoped to preserve in their African planned economies the political freedoms they associated with the legal systems they had come to respect as colonials studying in Paris, Rome, or London. They became interested in the variations on the Soviet model emerging in Eastern Europe and Asia as possible reformulations which could combine economic order with political freedom to serve Africa's needs.

Africans are not alone in their search for a legal system that can prepare the framework for social reorganization; many Asian leaders are similarly engaged. In Asia economies are more thoroughly developed. Cultures show clearer manifestation of historic patterns so deeply ingrained that only a brave leader insists on radical social change beyond redistribution of land, elimination of abuses in family custom, and construction of a viable system of basic industry. In spite of these differences the Asian politicians have considered the economics of development the first item on their agendas. For some of them the model presented in its variations by the legal systems claiming Marxian socialist inspiration looks attractive. In short, the developing countries are seeking legal institutions to be used to their advantage, either as a supplement to their traditional systems or as an almost complete replacement of their past. Contemporary Marxists seem to offer more suitable institutions than the more traditionally oriented common lawyers of the Anglo-American systems or the Romanists of continental Europe.

This study is designed to search for the common core of the

Science and the Present Day—Against the Anti-Leninist Course of the Chinese Leaders, [1964] 11 KOMMUNIST 12. Eng. transl. 16 C.D.S.P. no. 35 (1964) 8 at 14.

[12] Thiam, *Allocution*, [1962] ANNALES AFRICAINES 37 at 42 (Faculté de droit et des sciences économiques de Dakar, 1963).

[13] "In the Communist countries, the 'dictatorship of the proletariat,' contrary to the teachings of Marx, has made the state an omnipotent, soulless monster stifling the natural freedoms of the human being, and drying up the sources of art, without which life is not worth living." See L. SENGHOR, ON AFRICAN SOCIALISM 33 (M. Cook introd. and transl. 1964).

family of Marxian socialist legal systems. For the political scientists, the conclusions may be a guide to predicting the point at which the Soviet Communists will find it desirable to repeat the experience of Czechoslovakia. For legal scholars concerned with comparison of laws, the exposition of each of the various branches of law may serve as a guide to determining the outlines of what is being accepted in many quarters as one of the four great families of contemporary law.

The study is not a practicing law manual. It will not help a practioner find the solution to a case. It is an academic exercise, limited by the obvious necessity of fitting the materials into a single volume and also by the impossibility of exploring the vast body of detail which constitutes the law of the fourteen states which declare themselves members of the family of Marxian socialist systems.[14] To cope with the problem of quantity, a method has been adopted which focuses on the political, social, and economic structure of the USSR as reflected in its legal system, since that is the inspiration for the others within the family. Materials taken primarily from the Polish, Yugoslav, Czechoslovak, and Chinese systems are then introduced, along with lesser quantities of data from others within the family, to provide the basis for generalizations about the common core.

As with all studies of the Marxian socialist states, the search for motives for legal reform has had to rely primarily on sources within those states. The data found in judicial decisions and scholarly studies made within the countries concerned provide almost the only source from which applicability of the norms of the statutes can be determined. To the present the scholars in the West have had only limited opportunities to make their own studies on the spot in a manner which would provide satisfactory quantitative materials on which to base behavioral analyses.[15] Nevertheless, this limitation is no cause for despair.

[14] The Communist party of the Soviet Union distinguished the peoples accepted as building socialist society when it reserved for them the phrase "fraternal greetings" in the slogans issued on the forty-eighth anniversary of the Russian revolution. See Pravda and Izvestiia, 23 Oct. 1965 at 1. Eng. transl. 17 C.D.S.P. no. 43 (1965), slogans 16 to 28.

[15] The problems and possibilities for behavioral study have been analyzed and the literature set forth in Shoup, *Comparing Communist Nations: Prospects for an Empirical Approach*, 62 THE AMERICAN POLITICAL SCIENCE REVIEW 185 (1968).

Personal visits to all the European states except Albania and the German Democratic Republic and constant association over more than three decades with scholars from the area have provided some basis for evaluating Eastern sources. Revelations from the East when changes in policy have been made have suggested that a Westerner with such opportunities can become conversant with trends of thought and practice even though he may be denied access to the means of verification available to those who study Western Europe or North and South America.

ACKNOWLEDGMENTS

MANY INSTITUTIONS AND INDIVIDUALS HAVE STIMULATED AND helped to realize this study. Chronologically, the International Association of Legal Science provided the initial impetus through its colloquium on the rule of law in the East, conducted in Warsaw in 1958 by its Marxian socialist members.

Later activities included intensive research on Chinese traditional and communist law in Hong Kong; a winter at the Center for Advanced Study in the Behavioral Sciences at Stanford, during which an experimental seminar comparing Soviet and Chinese models was led together with Jerome Alan Cohen at the University of California (Berkeley); and a four-year seminar at Columbia University in company with Dr. Aleksander W. Rudzinski and Dr. Fu-shun Lin, financed by a grant from the Ford Foundation to Columbia's Research Institute on Communist Affairs. Publications by both scholars which developed from the Columbia seminar have been used liberally to determine features of Polish and Chinese law.

African comparisons emerged from a study conducted as Research Professor at the University of Dakar under a Ford Foundation grant to that university. Visits to Mali and Guinea in the following year enlarged horizons. A test of findings was made in a Romanist and an Islamic legal environment in 1966 during two seminars, one conducted at the University of Freiburg im Breisgau and the other at the University of Teheran. Finally a seminar on "development" conducted at the East West Center of the University of Hawaii in the company of several Asians suggested other comparisons.

'Throughout the past thirty years, association with Eastern European scholars has been constant, beginning with a period of three and a half years at the Moscow Juridical Institute under a grant from the Institute of Current World Affairs provided by the late Walter S. Rogers and the late Charles R. Crane, who thought it worthwhile as early as 1934 to initiate study of Soviet law soon after establishment of diplomatic relations between the United States and the USSR.

The relationships established in Moscow have been expanded over the years, largely while teaching with Eastern European scholars at the International Faculty for the Teaching of Comparative Law at Strasbourg. Western views of the communists' approach to law have been shared with colleagues at Columbia University in its Parker School of Foreign and Comparative Law, its Russian Institute, and its Research Institute on Communist Affairs. The latter has included the project in its distinguished series of studies and has provided a variety of indispensable assistance. Its seminar on comparative communism has been a constant source of insights.

The manuscript has been read wholly or in part by several scholars with expert knowledge of the matters discussed, namely Jerome Alan Cohen and Victor Li for China, Fred Warner Neal for Yugoslavia, Aleksander W. Rudzinski for Poland, and Isaac Shapiro for the USSR. My debt to them is large. Of course, none of them, nor the universities, institutes, foundations or centers who have supported the project or provided an opportunity for discussion and research, can be held responsible for the final product. The author must bear full responsibility.

Finally, in addition to expressions of gratitude due the late Messrs. Rogers and Crane, acknowledgment must be made of the debt due the two teachers who greatly influenced the author's early years and under whom he worked for the doctorate at the University of Chicago, namely Professors Samuel N.

Harper and Max Rheinstein. The encouragement of these pioneering scholars in Russian history and comparative law meant much at a time when neither discipline attracted wide interest in the New World.

Communists and Their Law

I

The Guidelines

COMMUNISTS FIND IT NECESSARY TO ESTABLISH GUIDELINES for those determined to create socialism and the legal systems designed to stimulate the process. Since so many statesmen claim that socialism is their goal yet reject much that has been attributed to modern manifestations of Marxism, criteria must be defined. If Marxian socialism is to retain its identity, standards must be enforced. To let matters drift while the developing world embraces socialism of varying content might subject the orthodox Marxists to double disaster. Not only might Marxian socialist leadership be rejected for want of an understanding in the very continents to which Lenin looked for success, but that leadership might be undermined on its home grounds by a dimming of the fervor which motivated Lenin and his comrades in the Russian revolution. This was the issue in Czechoslovakia in 1968 as seen from Moscow, which feared that the Communist party of Czechoslovakia was permitting itself to be undermined and the system to be subverted while thinking that the demand for reforms was under control.

The Communists of China had warned of just such dangers both at home and abroad well before the Czechoslovak issue came to the fore. In their opinion Yugoslavia was practicing capitalism in the guise of socialism.[1] Even Soviet society was seen as putting down deep social roots which provided a base from which domestic capitalist forces were "inundating" the Soviet Union.[2]

Individual scholars within the countries of Marxian socialist inspiration have been asking for some time how much of the principles and fervor of 1917 and of the revolution's legal techniques must be preserved to avoid degeneration into a socialism so revisionist that it loses all claim to be recognized by those who guard Lenin's mausoleum. What must be preserved, they ask, to avoid retrogression and an eventual loss of identity through amalgamation with an evolving Western European and Asian "welfare state"?

A Hungarian scholar has rebuked a Frenchman for supposing that a legal system is in the making which will constitute a convergence of the law of the classical capitalist states of the nineteenth century and that of Marxian socialism as put into practice by Lenin.[3] To the Hungarian there can be currently no middle way, no alternative to the model structured on social ownership of the means of production. He cannot see the "welfare state" engulfing the world.

The Hungarian's argument assumes that an impenetrable wall exists between the Marxian socialist legal systems and those of the "welfare states," whether they be of Anglo-American common law or a Romanist tradition. For the communists there is also a wall between the Eastern European systems and those of emerging African states, which have tended to follow the new social patterns of their old masters while clinging to the most revered of traditional African values.

In speaking of the family of Marxian socialist legal systems, no contemporary author in the field treats the family as monolithic. In practice, variations on the model are numerous, and they are accepted to the present by all except China as causing no need for exclusion from the family. There is, then, a frontier which can be identified. When expressed in terms of law, that

[1] *Carry the Struggle against Khrushchev Revisionism through to the End*, [1965] 25 PEKING REVIEW 5 at 8.

[2] *Id.* at 7.

[3] Eörsı, *Comparative Analysis of Socialist and Capitalist Law*, [1964] COEXISTENCE (Nov.) 139 at 151.

frontier is so sharply defined that the Hungarian thinks meaningful comparison between the Marxian socialist legal systems
and those of the West difficult, if not impossible.[4] In his view
they are different species whose relationship must be expressed
in such broad generalizations that it is scientifically meaningless.

If there is such a sharp difference between Western societies' systems of public order and their Marxian socialist counterparts, in what does it lie? Marxian legal scholars have begun to
search for the key to an understanding. The time is long past
when the leaders of the Communist International could tell the
shop stewards of England, as they did in 1920, that, although
they could admit theoretically the possibility of variation in
form depending upon the varying economic structures of different countries in a state of revolution, experience had given no
indications of the realization of this theory.[5]

A Soviet law professor seeking to explain the common core
to French-speaking European students in 1965 frankly admitted
that in the early years it lay in "socialisme à la soviétique"; but
today he sees a difference. He finds that Marxian socialists are
recognizing that the USSR has played a very important role—
has influenced others by its positive and negative experience—
but that the repetition of Soviet experience is no longer necessary to successful achievement of the goal set in general terms
by Marx and made concrete by Lenin.[6]

Adherence to Soviet legal forms is not, then, the criterion of
membership within the family of Marxian socialist legal systems. It is not the forms that currently define the boundary
between a Western welfare society and a Marxian socialist
society. The substantive ideas make the difference. Were it not
for the years when Stalin ruled the Marxian socialist camp, this
conclusion would not seem such a discovery. Passages in Lenin
support the concept and are now being written into texts to
support tolerance of variation. Even during Stalin's years every
Soviet student learned in his law institute that law was only a

---

[4] *Id.* at 145.

[5] THE I.L.P. AND THE THIRD INTERNATIONAL 44 (1920).

[6] Stated by Prof. Krutogolov in unpublished lecture to students of the
International Faculty for the Teaching of Comparative Law. Liège, 11
Aug. 1965.

superstructure resting on a social base defined not by techniques nor by legal terminology but by social factors summed up in the historic phrase "relationship to means of production." The implication of this theory was that it was the substance and not the form that mattered; yet when new Marxian socialist societies were planned, great attention was given to copying forms devised in the USSR. Current thinking is based on a return to fundamentals, in an escape from Stalin's "cult of the individual" under which only he could create a state structure with a pattern of law guaranteed to bring society to communism.

To express their rediscovery of the critical importance of substantive positions rather than legal forms, the twelve Communist parties in power in 1957, exclusive of Tito's Yugoslavia, met in Moscow to establish a catalog of principles for Communists who wished to be in good standing. It was only one year after the rebellions in Poland and Hungary and at the very time when the Chinese Communists were beginning to reject the tutelage of the men in the Kremlin. The declaration issued at the end of the meeting set forth what were called the "basic laws applicable in all countries embarking upon a socialist course." [7] Because of their primary character, they require statement in full:

> Guidance of the working masses by the working class, the core of which is the Marxist-Leninist party, in effecting a proletarian revolution in one form or another and establishing one form or another of the dictatorship of the working class; the abolition of capitalist ownership and the establishment of public ownership of the basic means of production; gradual Socialist reconstruction of agriculture; planned development of the national economy aimed at building socialism and communism, at raising the standards of living of the working people; the carrying out of the Socialist revolution in the sphere of ideology and culture and the creation of numerous intelligentsia devoted to the working class, the working people and the cause of socialism; the abolition of national oppression and the establishment of equality and fraternal friendship between the peoples; defense of the

[7] *Declaration of the Twelve Communist Parties in Power* (Nov. 1957) in D. Jacobs, ed., THE NEW COMMUNIST MANIFESTO 169 at 176 (3d rev. ed. 1961). Also in R. Braham, SOVIET POLITICS AND GOVERNMENT 74 at 82 (1965).

achievements of socialism against attacks by external and internal enemies; solidarity of the working class of the country in question with the working class of other countries; that is, proletarian internationalism.

These appear to be only generalities; but they were soon taken up by lawyers as a guide to action. A legal text produced in the USSR in the same year was obviously influenced by them.[8] It placed the essentials of a Marxian socialist legal system in three categories: political, economic, and ideological. The political was to be characterized by establishment of the authority of the toiling masses in the image developed in the USSR—under the leadership of the workmen and their vanguard, the Communist party. The economic requisite was to be liquidation of private capitalist property and the end of employment by private employers. The ideological focused on acceptance of the Marxist-Leninist view of world developments and the working out of a cultural revolution. The first two problems were to be the province of constitutional and civil-economic law. The third would influence domestic matters through criminal, family, civil, and labor law, and the world scene through manipulation of international public and private law.

The text writer further declared that implementation in practice would require that the Communist party lead in establishing a new state; that it create links between workers, peasants, and other strata of the toiling masses, that is the intellectuals; that it develop a social democracy, liquidate prejudices between races and peoples of different ethnic origin; protect the new state from attacks both from within and from abroad; and create brotherly solidarity with the working classes of other countries in the form of proletarian internationalism.

The economic policy would be implemented by law that would replace the liquidated private enterprise with public ownership of the principal tools and means of production, and that would introduce economic planning and improve the standard of living.

The legal implications were further elaborated in 1965 by

[8] INSTITUT PRAVA AKADEMII NAUK SSSR, GOSUDARSTVENNOE PRAVO ZARUBEZHNYKH SOTSIALISTICHESKIKH STRAN [Institute of Law of the USSR Academy of Sciences, Public Law of Foreign Socialist Countries] 3–4 (1957).

the same lecture to French-speaking students to which reference has been made. The Moscow professor expressed the belief that it was not the details of the Soviet constitution that required repetition in the constitution of a state claiming to be Marxian socialist, but the ideas that had inspired the draftsmen of the Soviet constitution. These he formulated as prohibition of exploitation of man's labor, that is, no private employment of labor for productive purposes; prohibition of private ownership of productive property exploited in a capitalist manner; basing of the economy on collective property, that is, the property of all of the people; location of power in the laboring class, with democratic participation by that class in government; material guarantees of liberty to citizens; denomination of duties as well as rights of citizens; and recognition of "socialist legality," that is, that the law must be obeyed, the most important being the law of the economic plan.

Within this framework there is room for considerable variation in the choice of means to achieve the goals, and the choices of the fourteen Marxian socialist states have been far from uniform, running from those of the Communists in the People's Republic of China on one geographical and philosophical extreme to the communist leaders of the Socialist Federal Republic of Yugoslavia on the other. Between lie the positions of the Eastern European states of Albania, Bulgaria, Czechoslovakia, the German Democratic Republic, Hungary, Poland, Romania, and the USSR; the Asian states of the People's Republics of Korea, Mongolia, and Vietnam; and the lone state in the New World—Cuba.

No mechanism currently exists to provide for unification of law among the fourteen. Agreement by treaty has been reached only on a unification of commercial law to govern relations between the European members of the family.[9] No courts with international jurisdiction establish uniform practice within the family. Conflicts of limited character, such as over commercial

---

[9] *General Conditions of Delivery of Goods between Foreign Trade Organizations of Member-Countries of the Council of Mutual Economic Aid*, 1958. Eng. transl. by Berman, 7 INT'L & COMP. L. Q. 665 (1958). Czechoslovakia and Poland created a Polish-Czechoslovak Commission for Juridical Cooperation in 1949. Its civil section drafted two parallel family codes, which were enacted, but the effort was then abandoned.

dealings, are resolved by arbitrators sitting in one or another of the states concerned, which does not help in the evolution of a strong uniform law of precedent such as is created by a permanently sitting international court with official records.[10]

Until the shock of Czechoslovak deviation in 1968, basic disputes of a political character were left to resolution by reunions of the Communist parties of the various countries under the 1957 twelve-party declaration. It had envisioned periodic conferences of the parties "to share experience, study each other's views and attitudes, and concert action in the joint struggle for the common goals." Such concert of the twelve parties materialized only once, in 1960,[11] for subsequent efforts to bring the original signers together were thwarted by the Sino-Soviet dispute.[12]

The 1960 meeting indicated the possibilities then envisioned of exacting conformity to fundamentals and the law that implements them, for it attacked the Yugoslav variation. Yugoslav leaders were accused of following a policy of international opportunism, which was called a form of right-wing opportunism, "which mirrors the bourgeois ideology in theory and practice, distorts Marxism-Leninism, emasculates the revolutionary essence and thereby paralyzes the revolutionary will of the working class, disarms and demobilizes the workers. . . ."[13]

In spite of this criticism the Yugoslav party was not read out of the family, nor was their law tabooed. Only the Chinese Communist party, in concert with its ally, the Albanian, continued to denounce in unequivocal terms the degeneration of Yugoslav communism.[14] The eleven other members of the Marxian socialist family patched up their quarrel with Tito,

[10] For details see K. GRZYBOWSKI, THE SOCIALIST COMMONWEALTH OF NATIONS: ORGANIZATION AND INSTITUTIONS, ch. 6 (1964).

[11] See *Declaration of the Eighty-one Communist Parties*, Moscow, Nov.–Dec. 1960, in D. JACOBS, *supra*, note 7 at 213, and R. BRAHAM, *supra*, note 7 at 86.

[12] For Chinese thoughts on the attempt to call a world meeting in 1965, boycotted by the Communist parties of Albania, China, Indonesia, Japan, Korea, Romania, and Vietnam, see *A Comment on the March Moscow Meeting*, [1965] 13 PEKING REVIEW 7.

[13] *Declaration, supra*, note 7 at 35.

[14] *The Degeneration of the Yugoslav Economy Owned by the Whole People*, [1964] 24 PEKING REVIEW 11, continued in 25 and 26 *id.*

although with some sharp expressions of distrust of the efficacy of what he was doing. He remained for the European Marxists, at least, a member of the family. So the matter stood until 1968.

The Czechoslovak events of 1968 introduced new elements. For the first time a Communist party was protected against its own lack of vision. There was no thought of expelling Czechoslovak communism from the community. The Czechoslovak leaders were forced to conform. But the enforcement of sanctions was not without preparation. Before the movement of troops, the other Eastern European members of the community, with the exception of Romania, Yugoslavia, and Albania, met to restate the common principles of the declaration of 1957, although in more generalized terms. In a declaration signed by six parties at Bratislava on 4 August 1968 it was said:

On the basis of historical experience, the fraternal parties became convinced that it is possible to advance along the road to socialism and communism only by being strictly and consistently guided by the general laws of construction of socialist society and primarily, by consolidating the leading role of the working class and its vanguard—the communist parties.[15]

Notice was again taken of possible variation, for the declaration added, "In so doing every fraternal party, creatively solving the questions of further socialist development, takes into consideration the national specific features and conditions." But there was to be a required common core in addition to the recognition of a Communist party's leadership. It was stated as "Unbending loyalty to Marxism-Leninism, education of popular masses in the spirit of the ideas of socialism and proletarian internationalism, irreconcilable struggle againsst bourgeois ideology against all anti-socialist forces."

Not until after the feared rebellion had been prevented did the newspaper *Pravda* provide more details on what the Czechoslovaks had done that was impermissible. These points will be introduced in subsequent chapters as the specific issues are treated within the confines of the Marxian socialist model, but

[15] Eng. transl. by Tass in Times [London] 5 Aug. 1968 at 12. Also in 6 REPRINTS FROM THE SOVIET PRESS, no. 5 at 42 (1968).

it is sufficient to say at this point that they amounted to no more than reaffirmation of the principles of 1957.

The principles of 1957 relate to the Communist parties themselves, but there has also been a guide to individual Communists in the form of codes of morals. Both the Soviet and the Chinese parties have adopted such codes, and they provide further evidence of the sharing of values by Communists of various systems.

The Soviet code was proclaimed in the 1961 program of the Communist party of the Soviet Union as a "moral code for the builder of communism." [16] No pretense of universality for citizens of all Marxian socialist states was established, but the code has had repercussions elsewhere. It finds expression in bills of rights inserted in the constitutions of the various states, some of which have adopted the Soviet constitution's bill of rights almost verbatim, even though draftsmen were free of Stalin's pressure for conformity.[17]

In the code of morals for the private citizen the Soviet party admonishes the member to show:

devotion to the communist cause, love of the socialist motherland and of the other socialist countries; conscientious labor for the good of society—he who does not work, neither shall he eat; a high sense of public duty; intolerance of actions harmful to the public interest; collectivism and comradely mutual assistance: one for all and all for one; human relations and mutual respect between individuals—man is to man a friend, comrade, and brother; honesty and truthfulness, moral purity, modesty, and unpretentiousness in social and private life; mutual respect in the family, and concern for the upbringing of children; an uncompromising attitude to injustice, parasitism, dishonesty, careerism and money grubbing; friendship and brotherhood among all peoples of the USSR; intolerance of national and racial hatred; an uncompromising attitude to the enemies of communism, peace and freedom of nations; fraternal solidarity with the working peoples of all countries, and with all peoples.

[16] Eng. transl. in J. Triska, Soviet Communism Programs and Rules 112 (1962).

[17] Constitution of the People's Republic of Romania, adopted 20 Aug. 1965, ch. 2.

Mao Tse-tung established a precedent for the Soviet code when he published a guide for his people in 1957. It was to help them in "determination of what is right and what is wrong in words and actions." He presented his conclusions as flowing from the principles of the constitution. In his view, words and action can be judged right if they:

(1) Help to unite the people of our various nationalities, and do not divide them; (2) are beneficial, not harmful, to socialist transformation and socialist construction; (3) help to consolidate, not to undermine or weaken, the people's democratic dictatorship; (4) help to consolidate, not to undermine or weaken, democratic centralism; (5) tend to strengthen, not to cast off or weaken, the leadership of the Communist party; and (6) are beneficial, not harmful, to international socialist solidarity and the solidarity of peace-loving peoples of the world.

He concluded, "of these six criteria, the most important are the socialist path and the leadership of the Party." [18]

The current loose relationship existing within the Marxian socialist family of fourteen states can only remind the historian of the situation existing before federation, at the end of 1922, of the various socialist Soviet republics permitted by Lenin to secede from Russia at the end of World War I and to become legally independent states. No common codes of laws, no common patterns of government were pronounced in 1917–18 to bring the system of social control within each republic into conformity with that of Russia. Nevertheless, there was considerable uniformity, exemplified by a telegram sent in December 1918 by the Bielorussian republic's judges to the Russian republic's Commissar of Justice to praise his People's Court Act. The Bielorussians even began to apply it as their own before it had been reenacted as Bielorussian law.[19]

The same phenomenon of copying occurred in 1922 when the Russian republic's Judiciary Act of 31 October was adopted by the sister republics.[20] When the Ukrainian commissar of

[18] MAO TSE-TUNG, ON THE CORRECT HANDLING OF CONTRADICTIONS AMONG THE PEOPLE, 1957 at 42. (Eng. transl. 6th ed. 1964.)

[19] J. HAZARD, SETTLING DISPUTES IN SOVIET SOCIETY: THE FORMATIVE YEARS OF LEGAL INSTITUTIONS 59, note 62 (1960).

[20] *Id.* 206.

justice published, on 4 August 1920, a circular defining criminal law, he made no effort to disguise his source as the 1919 circular issued in the Russian republic.[21] When federation was accomplished on 30 December 1922, the legal systems of the various republics within it had been brought into such conformity by the Communist party leadership of each that no revision was necessary for uniformity.

The federation's leaders, when their legislative organs began to operate in 1923, felt no need to proceed quickly with the enactment of fundamentals for the republic codes, as the constitution authorized. Not until October 1924 were the first fundamentals published, and then only for the judicial system, criminal law, and criminal procedure.[22] Uniform principles for land use were not established until 1928,[23] and those for collective farms waited until 1930.[24] Formal unification of civil law and procedure came last, with fundamentals not enacted by the federal government until 1961.[25] In short, common values were so firmly understood that the legislative intervention to assure uniformity envisioned by the constitution of 1923 was rarely required. Federal principles were written on the statute books at a leisurely pace, indicating the absence of any compulsion for speed.

There was one exception to this leisurely pace—the criminal law. Here Stalin indicated his perception of a need for speedy unification. He was unwilling to let the various republics continue to apply their varying codes, enacted in 1922 under Lenin's inspiration. He had his federal legislature adopt numerous specific articles concerning state security, and the republics were ordered to incorporate these into their criminal codes without change. Likewise, in 1934, when he felt that the republics' codes of criminal procedure restricted the practices of his security police, he required their amendment to incorporate a sim-

---

[21] *Id.* 113.

[22] Orders of 29 Oct. and 31 Oct. 1924, [1924] 23 Sob. Zak. S.S.S.R. pt. I, item 203 and 24 *id.* item 204.

[23] Decree of 15 Dec. 1928, [1928] 69 *id.* item 642.

[24] Decree of 1 Mar. 1930, [1930] 24 *id.* item 255.

[25] Law of 8 Dec. 1961, eff. 1 May 1962, [1961] 50 Ved. Verkh. Sov. S.S.S.R. item 525. Eng. transl. in SOVIET CIVIL LEGISLATION AND PROCEDURE (n.d. cir. 1962).

plified procedure dictated from the center.[26] This process was repeated in 1937 during the notorious purges.[27]

The key instrument in promoting legislative uniformity within the Soviet socialist republics before federation in the USSR was the Communist party. Its structure facilitated its work, for it was a highly centralized party without federal institutions of any character. Its centralist feature had been established after hot debate in 1903, at a time when the members from what was known as the Jewish Bund sought authority to unite in an organization which would maintain a semiautonomous position within a federated party.[28] Lenin insisted that federal-type bonds were too weak for the militant party he had in mind. In 1919 pressure was again exerted on Lenin to permit federation within the party to correspond with the measure of independence then granted to the republics as states. Lenin had his party congress adopt a resolution declaring, after rehearsal of the history of separation of ethnic groups into independent states, "But this does not mean at all that the Russian Communist party must in its turn be organized on the basis of federation of independent communist parties." [29] The party was centralized in 1903, and no departure from this cardinal organizational principle has since occurred.

Stalin seems to have anticipated the spread of the Soviet pattern to other lands as they were brought under Communist parties. The first region to be brought under Communist party domination outside the confines of what had formerly been the Russian empire was Outer Mongolia, previously a part of China. After its communist leaders proclaimed a people's government on 11 July 1921, they followed, as closely as their nomadic society permitted, a pattern similar to that espoused by Lenin. There was no formal tie making legislation of the USSR mandatory for its neighbor, but a Russian adviser was

[26] Decree of 1 Dec. 1934, [1934] 64 Sob. Zak. S.S.S.R. pt. I, item 459.

[27] Decree of 14 Sept. 1937, [1937] 61 id., item 266.

[28] L. SCHAPIRO, THE COMMUNIST PARTY OF THE SOVIET UNION 50 (1959).

[29] On Organizational Questions. Resol. 8th Party Congress, sec. A, par. 5, 1 KPSS V REZOLIUTSIAKH I RESHENIIAKH S'EZDOV, KONFERENTSII I PLENUMOV TSK [CPSU in Resolutions and Decisions of Congresses, Conferences and Plenums of the Central Committee] 443 (7th ed. 1953).

present to aid in drafting a penal law, and the first constitution was patterned on that of the Russian republic.

The Mongolian People's Republic, as it called itself, continued to follow Soviet models thereafter. Its second constitution of 30 June 1940 followed the style of the second USSR constitution of 5 December 1936.[30] Specialized Mongolian decrees, although not identical with those previously enacted by the USSR, showed Soviet inspiration. The law of land use of 6 February 1942 established the Soviet formula of state ownership and allocation of use in perpetuity to herdsmen for their privately owned herds of cattle. A labor law of 4 February 1941 and a social insurance law of 22 June 1942 followed the Soviet pattern. The distinctive Soviet concept of a procurator general was copied precisely.[31] All of this was done through close ties existing between the Communist parties of the two countries rather than through formal state relationships.

The successful influencing of Mongolian policy through the Mongolian Communist party suggests that Stalin felt he had a formula that suited his temperament. Without any legislative mechanism of coordination, he was able to direct a neighboring state's policy through its Communist party, just as Lenin had successfully directed the pre-1922 Soviet socialist republics through their Communist parties.

It is tempting to suppose that Stalin expected his formula to serve successfully after World War II, in the wake of Soviet troops advancing into Eastern Europe and Asia in pursuit of retreating German and Japanese forces. He had prepared the way, for during the immediate prewar years and during the war itself he had protected and trained in Moscow considerable numbers of Poles, Romanians, Czechoslovaks, Bulgarians, Germans, Hungarians, Yugoslavs, and Albanians on whom he relied for coordination of policies, not only on the international

---

[30] Comparison has been made in Hazard, *The Constitution of the Mongol People's Republic and Soviet Influence*, 21 PACIFIC AFFAIRS 162 (1948).

[31] G. Ginsburgs & R. Pierce, *Revolutionary Law Reform in Outer Mongolia*, 7 LAW IN EASTERN EUROPE 207 (1963). The distinctiveness of the Procuracy in comparison with counterparts in Western Europe is analyzed in Rudzinski, *Soviet-type Audit Proceedings and Their Counterparts*, 13 *id.* 287 (1967).

front but in structuring new societies. These men had learned his methods and had presumably become convinced of their efficacy. Even had they dreamed of some variations out of disgust for Stalin's brutality, they were forced by circumstances to conform, for none but the Yugoslavs were in a strong enough position to maintain power, after being placed in control, without the help of Stalin and his Soviet army.

The parallels between the pre-1922 experience of Soviet socialist republics emerging from the ruins of the Russian Empire and post–World War II experience in relations between the USSR and its weaker neighbors, where Communists needed Soviet support to retain power, might have extended to ultimate federation of all Communist-led states. There are those who thought that Stalin had this in mind, at least for Poland and Romania.[32] This would have meant incorporation within the USSR, in fulfillment of the prophecy made by the representative of the Communist International when the USSR was created in 1922. This representative had shouted at the constituent congress, "Long live the USSR of the World!" It is quite possible that many of his listeners then anticipated that the USSR would grow by accretion as neighbors came under the influence of Communist parties, which would ask for incorporation into the USSR. This technique had been used successfully in 1940 to bring the Baltic states into the USSR as constituent members, and in 1946 some Eastern Europeans feared that it would be used again as soon as their states had been sufficiently restructured to permit incorporation into the USSR without disrupting the Soviet Union's economic and political base.

Union of the Communist-directed states of Eastern Europe with the USSR, if it was ever contemplated, did not occur; for the model of subservience to Moscow's tutelage was to be cracked at its weakest point—Yugoslavia, whose communist leaders needed no help from Moscow to retain power. When Tito successfully resisted Stalin's attempt to discipline him—first by exclusion of his party from the Communist Information

---

[32] Two authors have concluded that early Soviet intentions were to integrate new Communist-led states into the USSR. K. Grzbowski, *supra*, note 10 at 1–6 and T. Kis, Les pays de l'Europe de l'Est. Leurs rapports mutuels et le problème de leur intégration dans l'orbite de l'U.R.S.S. 97 (1964).

Bureau, then by severance of economic ties, and finally by attempts at personal overthrow and, perhaps, destruction, which required the strongest security measures to thwart—the disciplinary system of the early postwar years reached a low point; but it collapsed even further in 1956. The rebellions in Poland and Hungary, and the severance of ties between the Chinese and Soviet Communists in 1957, indicated that Communist leaders in the USSR of that time had concluded that it was impolitic to attempt to maintain discipline by armed force.

After the Hungarian, Polish, and Chinese Communists demonstrated successfully that Moscow's discipline no longer needed to be feared, conviction alone maintained unity of state structure and law among party officials of Communist-led states. The fact that so much of the Soviet model was preserved in spite of the rebellions suggests that conviction had been a potent force even when Stalin loomed as a potential threat to those who refused to conform. Variation increased as fear of Soviet reprisals faded, but a common core remained. No one seemed to know just what it was in detail, but leaders of all of the states within the Marxian socialist commonwealth felt sufficiently within a family to remain in community. It was a time when a noted German comparatist began to talk of "style" as the determinant to be observed by classifiers of legal systems.[33] According to his approach, which offered no definition but claimed that legal styles were as apparent as artistic styles, the Marxian socialist states had reason to claim distinction. But this distinction was preserved by something other than compulsion.

Into this increasingly permissive system intruded the events of 1968. The Czechoslovak Communists had progressed so far in their determination of what variation might be permitted without arousing the ire of other members of the Marxian socialist commonwealth that they introduced considerable novelty and spoke of even broader measures. Even more important, they permitted some citizens to speak of such extreme change that the Soviet Communists and those of Poland and the German Democratic Republic became alarmed lest Czechoslovakia slip out of the commonwealth entirely. The response

[33] Zweigert, *Zur Lehre von den Rechtskreisen in* NADELMANN, VON MEHREN & HAZARD eds., TWENTIETH CENTURY COMPARATIVE AND CONFLICTS LAW: LEGAL ESSAYS IN HONOR OF HESSEL E. YNTEMA 42 (1961).

was vigorous—use of troops to support demands for a reversion in leadership and policies to patterns closer to the 1957 declaration. What had previously been an exercise for the imagination of scholars attempting to determine the common core became a matter of high politics. The conclusion was quickly drawn that the Soviet Communist party had changed its policy. The common core of the Marxian socialist system, as interpreted by the party, must be preserved on pain of overthrow of those responsible for excessive change. To this there was only the self-evident caveat, power. If the USSR's leaders thought a military adventure likely to fail, it would not be attempted. Under this caveat the Chinese Communists could continue to improvise, but less powerful parties had reason to think twice before departing widely from the common core required of the Czechoslovaks.

2

Leadership for the Elite

LEADERSHIP WAS GIVEN FIRST PLACE AMONG THE ELEMENTS OF
the common core established by the twelve Communist parties
in power in 1957. "Guidance of the working masses by the
working class, the core of which is the Marxist-Leninist party"
became the primary basic law to be observed in any country
embarking upon a Marxian socialist course.

To Soviet leadership since 1936 this principle has been the
cornerstone of the constitution, inscribed in Article 126. Before
that it was no less fundamental, although its legal premise had
been established by custom, or what might be called in British
terms "convention." For the Communist party had not only
led, it had provided a special kind of leadership in that it had
ruled alone. From the summer of 1918, when Lenin's limited
experiment with coalition government ended with the withdrawal of the Left Socialist Revolutionaries with whom he had
shared power, the Soviet system of government had been symbolized throughout the world as that of the "one-party system."

The special character of leadership in the Soviet Union has
been stated in precise terms in the manual entitled "Fundamentals of Marxism-Leninism," published in its second edition
in 1963, ten years after Stalin's death. Although many features

of government had changed in that decade, this feature had become fixed, for the manual declared, "As for socialist democracy, it is not directionless democracy, but *directed democracy*, that is, democracy directed by the party and the state to further the development of socialism and the building of communism." [1]

The Soviet definition is common to all Marxian-oriented leaders. Mao Tse-tung expressed his attitude similarly in 1957 when he told his people, after declaring his loyalty to the principles of freedom and democratic rights, "But this freedom is freedom with leadership, and this democracy is democracy under centralized guidance, not anarchy." [2]

Although adhering closely to the one-party system created by Lenin and mercilessly enforced by Stalin during his purges of 1935, when he arrested, imprisoned, and executed many of the former Socialist Revolutionaries and Mensheviks still living in the USSR, Stalin's heirs have been willing to recognize that the one-party system is not everywhere necessary to Marxian socialist government. In the 1963 Marxist-Leninist manual, the authors note that in Poland and Czechoslovakia the Communist party shares power with other parties, and in the German Democratic Republic the ruling National Front has included within its framework several bourgeois-democratic parties. [3] The authors might also have mentioned Bulgaria and China. The Chinese Communists have continued to permit small parties to exist, although they are relegated to an advisory position rather than being given seats in the National People's Congress, the formal law-making body.

The Polish People's Republic's Constitution of 1952, unlike the USSR Constitution of 1936, guaranteed the right of association without limitation of political activity to a single political

---

[1] FUNDAMENTALS OF MARXISM-LENINISM 599 (Eng. transl. 2d ed. 1963). (Italics in original.)

[2] MAO TSE-TUNG, ON THE CORRECT HANDLING OF CONTRADICTIONS AMONG THE PEOPLE 6 (Eng. transl. 6th ed. 1964).

[3] FUNDAMENTALS, *supra*, note 1 at 535. Only Albania, Hungary, Romania, and Yugoslavia followed the Soviet one-party model in Europe. For a listing of minority parties elsewhere see H. SKILLING, THE GOVERNMENTS OF COMMUNIST EAST EUROPE 65 (1966).

party.[4] The Polish constitution thus incorporated a practice under which the United Polish Workers' party, in which the Communist party has merged with the former Socialists, shares power with the United Peasant party, to represent the peasants, and the Democratic party, given the assignment of representing the non-Communist intellectuals, the petty bourgeoisie, and the artisans. Added to these is what is called an "interest group" designed to represent Roman Catholic elements of various political views without full political party status.

Polish Communists justify their variation on the Soviet model as the outgrowth of Poland's long history of vigorous multiparty government in its *sejm*. They even attempt some Marxist-sounding arguments to buttress their case, arguing that hostility to socialism was less strong in postwar Poland than it had been in Lenin's Russia in 1918. Finally, they seek to clinch their argument by noting that the Russians after Stalin's death had denounced the ideological basis for his policy of terror, which he had created in his speech to the Communist Party Congress in 1930.

Stalin had stated vigorously that during the advance toward a communist society the class struggle would become more acute, requiring creation of a very strong repressive force, which he called the "state." It was to be the strongest state the world had ever known.[5] Khrushchev denounced this concept of ever-heightening class struggle in what has become known as his secret speech of 1956, directed against Stalin's errors, and the manual of 1963 declares that "the experience of the Soviet Union and the People's Democracies by no means confirmed Stalin's thesis that the class struggle is bound to become sharper as progress is made toward socialism. On the contrary, during the successful building of socialism the general trend of the class struggle results in the positions of the socialist forces becoming consolidated and the resistance of the remnants of the hostile classes becoming weaker." [6]

---

[4] CONSTITUTION OF THE POLISH PEOPLE'S REPUBLIC, art. 72 (2). (Eng. transl. 1953).

[5] Stalin, *Report to Sixteenth Communist Party Congress*, 1930, 2 J. STALIN, LENINISM 245 at 342 (Eng. transl. 1933).

[6] FUNDAMENTALS, *supra*, note 1 at 535–36.

By their post-Stalin interpretation the Communists of the USSR have opened the way to introduction of a period of multiparty government without violation of orthodoxy. The common core acceptable to Soviet communism for adoption in the people's democracies, therefore, includes a multiparty variant, but with a difference from the Western multiparty concept. The Soviet manual says that the bourgeois democratic parties may be permitted to exist in a multiparty system "provided that the Marxist party of the working class occupies the leading position."[7] This caveat is observed in Poland. The statute of the United Polish Workers' party declares it to be "the leading political force of the Polish People's Republic." This rule is manifest in practice, for the number of seats in the parliament available to each party and to the Catholic interest group is determined in advance by the Communists in consultation with the leaders of the minority parties in what is called "The Front of National Unity," rather than by the voters. In the allocation of seats the Communists retain for themselves the preponderant majority, and they can veto nominations of candidates presented by the cooperating parties.

A Polish scholar has explained in a text prepared for readers in the West that the Polish system excludes the concept of parties in opposition.[8] The three parties and the Catholic interest group are considered as being parties cooperating in power, united in what might be considered analagous to a permanent coalition. The minority parties not only agree with the Communists on the number of seats to be held by them, but there is agreement on a single slate of candidates presented by all parties, not only for election to the *sejm* at the national level but also to the local people's councils.

Practice indicates that the persons listed on the ballots are usually more numerous than the seats to be filled from the district to be represented. This provides the voter a choice, but it is manipulated; the priority candidates upon which the parties have agreed are placed first. These are always elected, although not always in the same order, for the voters' choice may result in the lowering of a given candidate from his priority

[7] *Id.* at 535.
[8] S. Rozmaryn, La Pologne 73 (Comment ils sont gouvernés, vol. 8, 1966).

place to a place further down as a result of numerous scratches of his name, leaving him with fewer votes than his more popular colleagues on the preferred list. No case has been found by students of Polish elections in which a name on the preferred list was pushed below the line of those receiving the votes necessary to election. Thus, the final composition of the *sejm* remains from election to election what the parties have agreed upon, and the balance between them is held at approximately the same level. Only the personalities change because the names are not always re-entered for election on the expiration of a given deputy's term.[9]

Election of candidates on the preferred list has been explained by some Polish voters in private conversation as the result of three principal influences: inertia on the part of many voters, who drop the ballot into the box without scratching any of the preferred names; lack of information on the names listed after those of the preferred candidates because the alternate candidates are not given publicity by the press; or fear of official discrimination against the voter or his family because of his nonconformity.

The Bulgarian Communists have, like the Poles, permitted an agrarian party to function to win the confidence of the Bulgarian peasant.[10] This "People's Union of Bulgarian Agrarians" has been given a role to play in seating considerable numbers of deputies not only in the National Assembly but in the local people's councils. Thus, in the 1962 national elections, the Agrarians were allotted 80 seats of the 321 in the Assembly, and 44 seats were assigned to unattached persons. In the local elections, out of a total of 49,824 councillors elected, 9,798 were Agrarians and 7,937 unattached; the rest were members of the Communist party or the Communist youth league. The Bulgarian system, unlike the Polish, however, does not provide for a choice of candidates, all being allocated in advance to the seats for which they run.

At the outset the Chinese variation permitted several small parties, inherited from the period of coalition against the

[9] Ptakowski, *Parliamentary Elections in Poland*, 14 EAST EUROPE, no. 8 at 15 (1965).

[10] Spassov, *Representative Institutions in Bulgaria*, 11 REVIEW OF CONTEMPORARY LAW, no. 1 at 126, 130 (1964).

Kuomintang party headed by Chiang Kai-shek, to elect deputies to a People's Political Consultative Conference, at both its national and regional levels, so long as that conference existed; but as in Poland and Bulgaria, the minority parties functioned in consultation with the Communists and in union with basic communist policy. The provisional nature of the arrangement became apparent after the conference had completed its work in establishing a permanent government under the constitution of 1949, for the newly created People's Congress which became the supreme representative state body included no deputies named by minority parties. The major manifestation of political minorities in official positions thereafter was provided by the granting of ceremonial posts, such as those of vice president of the People's Republic, to those symbolizing the coalition. Some administrative positions, usually those of vice minister in technically oriented ministries, were also allotted to adherents of minority parties, but this may have been due more to their knowledge than to their politics.

Foreign students of Chinese communism have attributed the continuing existence of minority parties to Mao's desire during the early years of instability to attract to his policies groups that might otherwise have been hostile, or to symbolize in practice his theory that in his dictatorship over enemy forces within society he had joined those nonworking class elements in union with the Communists in their hostility to foreign-power domination of Chinese life.[11]

Mao added yet another reason for what he called the "coexistence of the various parties for a long time to come" [12] when he was courting all comers in 1957, and it was a practical one. At that time, before entering upon what was soon to become a violently partisan policy, he founded his coexistence on what he called "mutual supervision." This was defined as meaning "that the Communist party should exercise supervision over the democratic parties, and the democratic parties should exercise supervision over the Communist party." He justified such supervi-

[11] P. TANG, 1 COMMUNIST CHINA TODAY: DOMESTIC AND FOREIGN POLICIES 166–83 (2d ed. 1961).

[12] MAO TSE-TUNG, supra, note 2 at 44. For his theory that his new democratic republic differs from the socialist republic of the USSR type, see MAO TSE-TUNG, ON THE NEW DEMOCRACY 21 (Eng. transl. 1960).

sion as in the interest of Communists, "because for a party as
much as for an individual there is great need to hear opinions
different from its own." There was, however, to be a limit on
advice, for Mao added a word of caution. Advice and criticism
from other parties "will play a positive role in mutual supervision only when they conform to the six political criteria."

The six criteria chosen by Mao as limits to advice proved to
be, as he stated them, the six points of his moral code, already
quoted in chapter 1. To Mao the most pertinent was "recognition of the leadership of the party."

At the time, the limitation was not as restrictive as it
became when Mao moved down the road of the "cult of the
individual" which Stalin had previously trod. After he began to
exact loyalty not to the principles established by the Communist party as a whole but to those enunciated by himself alone,
the role of the minority parties became still more clouded. In
August 1966 his most fanatical supporters, his "Red Guards,"
even demanded that the minority parties be disbanded, but this
position failed to be adopted and was abandoned in November
of that year. Outsiders do not yet know why.

In its early years the Soviet model provided yet other means
of avoiding opposition—the weighting of votes against potential backsliders and the outright exclusion of presumed enemies.
This was achieved by the first constitution of the Russian
republic, of July 1918.[13] The votes of workmen were given more
weight in the election of deputies to local government agencies
than the votes of the preponderant peasantry, who might otherwise have controlled provincial and republic governments composed of delegates from the local bodies. Further, the vote, as
well as the right to run for office, was denied completely to
those who employed labor or were middlemen, as well as to the
clergy, the tsarist police and members of the former royal family.
Not until 1936, when the excluded elements were said to have
been reduced to less than 3 percent of the voters and when the
peasants were said to have developed a social consciousness like
that of the workers, were the restrictions removed.

[13] Eng. transl. in J. MEISEL & E. KOZERA eds., MATERIALS FOR THE
STUDY OF THE SOVIET SYSTEM: STATE AND PARTY CONSTITUTIONS, LAWS,
DECREES, DECISIONS AND OFFICIAL STATEMENTS OF THE LEADERS IN
TRANSLATION 79 (2d ed. 1953).

The Polish Communists have not found such constitutional exclusions necessary. Although their 1946 electoral law disfranchised over one million persons for having "profited from economic cooperation" during the German occupation, or for cooperating with the Polish underground guerrillas fighting the communist regime, they withdrew the exclusionary provisions from the electoral laws of 1952, 1956, and 1960. The Polish author previously cited indicates that by now his party has established a system that provides other guarantees against loss of communist leadership.

The Yugoslav Communists have introduced yet another variation on the formula for leadership. The constitution of 1963, like that of the USSR, states the primacy of the Communists, but in different words. It declares in its preamble that "Under the conditions of socialist democracy and social self-government, the League of Communists, with its guiding ideological and political work, is the prime mover of the political activity necessary to protect and promote the achievements of the Socialist Revolution." [14]

No other parties have been permitted to operate in Yugoslavia, but the Communists have attempted to unite with themselves citizens who are not acceptable for party membership, or who are willing to work for the new society although they refuse to join the party. To achieve this result, the Communists organized in 1953 a Socialist Alliance of Working People of Yugoslavia, which is said to have embraced "just about everybody and everything." [15] Unlike the Polish "Front of National Unity," the Yugoslav Alliance coordinates the work of individuals who constitute its membership and not of organizations. The Alliance's task is not only to put communist ideas into practice but also to reverse the informational flow by keeping the leadership informed of the general public's thought. Thus, in some measure it has become a channel of communication for interests not directly represented in the Communist party itself.

Some American students of Yugoslav politics who also have

[14] Constitution of the Socialist Federal Republic of Yugoslavia, Preamble art. VI (1963). See also Constitutions of the Communist Party-States (J. Triska ed. 1968).

[15] G. Hoffman & F. Neal, Yugoslavia and the New Communism 179 (1962).

wide knowledge of Soviet practice sense a contrast in intensity of party leadership in the two lands. The Yugoslav Communists seek to guide through education rather than by command, whereas Stalin preferred dictatorship and his successors still fear loss of party control if they relax discipline. The Yugoslav party is not so fearful, for it sees itself as only one among several of the forces leading society within the all-embracing Socialist Alliance.[16]

The variations on the one-party system which have been permitted to evolve in China, Poland, and elsewhere suggest the limits within which nonconformists may share the formulation of policy with Communists. In none of the variations has the Communist party risked loss of power. In no case has the vanguard position declared in the 1957 "basic laws" to be essential to the Marxian socialist system been abandoned. Some of the members of the family will not accept the Chinese and Polish experiments. This was made clear by the Romanian Communists in 1965 when they promulgated a second constitution for the Socialist Republic of Romania.[17] Its Article 26 maintains Stalin's traditional language of 1936 when it states, "The most advanced and conscious citizens from the ranks of the workers, peasants, intellectuals, and other categories of working people unite in the Romanian Communist party, the highest form of organization of the working class, its vanguard detachment." No provision is made in the succeeding Article 27 concerning the right of association for the formation of any other political party.

The one-party base remains in practice the cornerstone of Marxian socialist public law, although with variation held within strict limits. Under these limits noncommunist parties, if committed to socialism as a way of life and accepting Communist party primacy, may function, but only if conditions within society are such that some form of representation of interest groups through formal channels seems desirable for preserving public order with minimum expense.

The Romanian decision to reject variation, even though

---

[16] *Id.* at 185.
[17] CONSTITUTION OF THE SOCIALIST REPUBLIC OF ROMANIA (Eng. transl. 1965).

several members of the family of Marxian socialist states have found it desirable, suggests that, for the orthodox at least, the controlled multiparty system is not the structure of the future but only a transitional form made necessary in the spirit of temporary compromise with retarded social forces. It is not to be introduced by those who have successfully made the transition to the one-party system of the Soviet model.

Students of early Soviet history will be reminded of Stalin's position in 1922 against what he conceived of as "retrogression." At that time he was fighting the battle of federation, during which he was asked why some of the minority peoples, such as the Tatars, Buryats, and Yakutians, who had been incorporated into the Russian republic in 1917 and 1918 without insuperable opposition might not revert to independent status so as to join on a par with the Russians, Ukrainians, and Bielorussians in the new USSR. Stalin's reply succinctly expressed the communist aversion to what they believe to be political retrogression, for he said, "I think this would be an irrational and inexpedient method and that it is precluded by the very course the campaign is taking." [18] Clearly, once the smaller ethnic groups had been brought within the centralized framework he liked, there should be no reversal.

Abandonment by Romanians of the one-party system in 1965 in favor of the Polish variation might have looked as retrogressive to them as proposals for federal decomposition looked to Stalin in 1922. The Romanians probably do not stand alone, for other Communists, at least until the Czechoslovak upheaval in 1968, in spite of universal denunciation by Communists of Stalin's theory of ever-sharpening class struggle in socialist states, have evidenced their agreement with the Soviet premise. This is that any distribution of power, even in permanent coalition, can be no more than a compromise, to be abandoned when no longer necessary to the preservation of harmony.

This conclusion can be supported by reference to the reaction of the Soviet leadership to two quite opposite develop-

---

[18] J. STALIN, *Speech of Dec. 26, 1922 to All Russian Congress of Soviets* in MARXISM AND THE NATIONAL AND COLONIAL QUESTION (Eng. transl. 1935).

ments after Romanian reaffirmation of Stalin's constitutional formula for preservation of the one-party system. One occurred in Castro's Cuba in 1965 and the other in reform Czechoslovakia in 1968.

In Cuba Fidel Castro declared in October 1965 that his party had become a monopoly party with a structure similar to that of the Communist party of the Soviet Union during Lenin's years. And he adopted for it the name Lenin proposed for his Bolshevik wing of the Russian Social Democratic Labor Party in 1919—"Communist Party." In doing so Castro set forth his motives in expressive terms, saying, "We consider that we have achieved that stage of development in which once and for all we must clean out all shades of color and allusions to origin, distinguishing some revolutionaries from others, since we consider that we have achieved that phase of the development of our revolution when we can say that there is only one type of revolutionary." [19]

The Soviet party's reaction to this adoption of the Soviet model of the one-party state was immediate: a telegram of congratulations, saying that it "warmly congratulates you who are all members of a single party of the Socialist Republic of Cuba. . . . Together with you we look upon that most important political decision as a giant step in creation of a single party of the Socialist Republic of Cuba, as the vanguard of the Cuban people." [20] To the Communists of the Soviet Union, Castro's step along the path taken by Lenin in 1918 was progressive.

In Czechoslovakia, with the upsurge in the spring of 1968 of opposition to dictatorial practices of Communist party leaders who had followed Stalin's model, voices were heard widely calling for a return to a multiparty system which would function with independent parties liberated from the obligation to remain in permanent coalition with the Communists, but pledged to socialism. The old Social Democratic party which had combined with the Communists attempted to reassert its independence. No single factor aroused such fear of rebellion as this Social Democratic move. In *Pravda*'s editorial of 22 August

[19] *Our Aim—Communism*, Pravda, no. 281, 8 Oct. 1965 at 5.
[20] Pravda, no. 278, 5 Oct. 1965 at 1.

1968 asserting the reasons for Moscow's military suppression of Czechoslovak divergence, the declaration of a group of former Social Democrats that the merger with the Communists in 1948 was no longer valid received primary emphasis. To *Pravda* "There has in effect come into existence in the country a political opposition aiming to effect a capitalist restoration."

From the Soviet Communists' point of view the Czechoslovak Communist party had permitted the most telling blow possible to be struck at the Marxian socialist system. One of the primary elements of the common core was being challenged— that the vanguard role of the Communist party, as it had been created in the Soviet practice of the preceding fifty years, is the keystone of the system, obligatory for all members of the commonwealth.

Only four months earlier the rule had been reasserted in the latest of the constitutions within the family, that of the German Democratic Republic of 6 April 1968. The principle was placed at the very head of the document in Article 1 to read, "The German Democratic Republic is a socialist state of a German nation. It is the political organization of the working people of town and countryside, constructing socialism under the leadership of the working class and its Marxist-Leninist party."

Although the one-party system, with modifications to include the dominant party system, has become a cornerstone of Marxian socialist policy, Communists show no readiness to embrace within the family all modern one-party states, even when their avowed aim is the establishment of a socialist society, as in Africa and Asia. The single or dominant party must have a special character. It must accept Marxian socialism as developed by Lenin in practice, at least as to its main lines, and it must be structured as Lenin believed necessary to achievement of its goal. No cachet of the Marxian socialist family is being given to the Senegalese dominant party system, in which the general secretary of the party has found it possible to say, "What good is our independence if it is only to imitate European totalitarianism, to replace external colonialism by domestic colonialism? Dictatorship of the proletariat? That is simply gargling a formula: There would have to be a proletariat and a capitalism "at war" in our countries, to use Marx's language. In our Negro-Berber society, . . . there are no classes at war, but only social groups struggling for influence." [21]

Marxian socialist criticism of Africans seeking to create a socialism through a one-party or dominant-party system also takes issue with the concept of the African mass party, open to all citizens without restraint. Lenin faced just such a demand at the congress of his party held in London in 1903.[22] He opposed it on the ground that a party composed of sympathizers could not be the militant type of organization required to achieve victory in what he expected to be a struggle to the death. Under conditions as they existed in the Russian empire at that time, no parliamentary route to socialism was in prospect, as there was no parliament. He wanted a body of militant professional revolutionaries, willing, if necessary, to give their lives for his cause. Even within his own party at that organizational session, he was unable to carry the majority; but in 1905 he gathered his own forces separately from those who had previously defeated him and established the elite concept of the party. It has remained as a cardinal plank of Communist party policy ever since, not only in the USSR but in the other parties functioning within the family of Marxian socialist states.

In application of the principle, the Communist party of the Soviet Union has been limiting its members to militants screened through a process requiring recommendations from numbers of present members, and a trial period of candidacy. While its numbers had topped 12 million by 1965,[23] and 13 million by 1968 they were still but 8 percent,[24] a small fraction of the adult voters of the USSR, in contrast to the large parties emerging in Africa.

To these requirements of adherence to Marxism-Leninism

[21] L. SENGHOR, ON AFRICAN SOCIALISM 87 (M. Cook introd. and transl. 1964).

[22] For a history of the event, see L. SCHAPIRO, THE COMMUNIST PARTY OF THE SOVIET UNION 49–50 (1959).

[23] *The C.P.S.U. in Figures* (1961–1964), [1965] 10 PARTINAIA ZHIZN 8–17 (1965). Eng. transl. in 17 C.D.S.P. no. 29 (1965) at 14.

[24] The percentage of Polish participation in the dominant party is identical. See ROZMARYN, *supra*, note 8 at 66. The Chinese party, with 17 million members, is the world's largest, but this is a very small part of the population. See F. SCHURMAN, IDEOLOGY AND ORGANIZATION IN COMMUNIST CHINA 128 (1966).

and the elite concept must be added a third distinguishing feature—iron discipline. The post-Stalin era has witnessed some reduction in such discipline in all Marxian socialist countries. This has been so even in the USSR, where party rules permit no voluntary withdrawals; for figures now show a large number of persons dropped for nonpayment of dues, suggesting that a graceful exit is permitted those who lose heart or strength. The Polish Communists have gone further, for in 1959 they even amended their party's rules to authorize voluntary withdrawal without resort to subterfuge.

For those who remain members, however, discipline is strict under Lenin's formula known as "democratic centralism." This concept has been analyzed in so many texts that it requires no extensive definition. In brief, it means that discussion is permitted in party meetings, even to the point of lively debate since Stalin's death, but it cannot be permitted to expand into formation of factions within the party. Further, once a decision is adopted it binds all until the matter is again opened for reconsideration.

The 1965 rules of the Romanian Communist party,[25] which are the most recently adopted, preserve the principles inherited from Stalin's time in the USSR. By Rule 2 (c) every party member is obliged "to observe strictly party discipline, which is compulsory to an equal degree for all party members as strict observance of discipline is a principal condition of party unity," and by paragraph (b) of the same article it is stated, "The party does not admit the existence of factions in its ranks. Every factional activity is a crime against the party and is incompatible with the quality of being a party member." The Poles introduced a similar no-faction rule in 1959.[26]

The Czechoslovak Communist party seemed in Moscow's

[25] RULES OF THE ROMANIAN COMMUNIST PARTY (1965).

[26] Art. 22 reads, "Inner party democracy cannot be misused for purposes contrary to the interests of the party; in particular, membership in the party cannot be reconciled with any sort of activities of a fractional or group character, with any activities directed against the ideology of the party, its general political line and the unity of its ranks." Eng. transl. in THIRD CONGRESS OF THE POLISH WORKERS' PARTY, MARCH 10–19, 1959, CENTRAL COMMITTEE OF THE POLISH UNITED WORKERS' PARTY 583 (1959). The original statute did not necessarily require expulsion for factional activity, but it denounced misuse of internal democracy "for pur-

eyes to be threatening to legalize factions in 1968. *Pravda's* August editorial put the matter bluntly, saying, "In effect there came to be violated in the Communist party of Czechoslovakia the cardinal Leninist principles of the organization of Party life —the principles of democratic centralism and the ideological and organizational unity of the party. The party was on the verge of legalizing factions. . . ."

The Czechoslovak events of 1968 made evident beyond question that a cardinal point of the "style" of the Marxian socialist system, if not *the* cardinal point, is preservation of the "leadership" concept. It must be established by the public law of each member of the community, and the law must be enforced with rigor. Variation in methods of representing "interest groups" within society may be permitted if sufficient basis exists in Marxist-trained minds to identify a number of "classes," but the variation must be so structured as to avoid all challenge to Communist party power.

Since a "leadership" pattern is no part of the "style" of the Anglo-American legal systems or of the Romanist ones, some will challenge inclusion of this element within the determining features of any of the world's principal legal systems. To such a position there can be only one answer: the role of the Communist party is so fundamental to the inspiration, drafting, and application of law in Marxian socialist states that its inclusion among the criteria of classification is obligatory. Details indicating Communist party influence will be given in the chapters that follow.

---

poses contrary to the interests of the party and of the workers' class, particularly it cannot be misused for any factional activity."

3

Mass Participation in a State Form

ALTHOUGH THE COMMUNIST PARTIES REQUIRED IN THEIR DEC-laration of 1957 that society be led by a Communist party, they established no rule for the state apparatus through which the party would work. On the contrary, they exhibited tolerance of any form, for they professed willingness to accept the requisite dictatorship of the working class "in one form or another."

The 1957 approach to the state form was something new; the Moscow leaders had not always been so willing to accept variation. Indeed, until the events of October 1956 in Poland, outsiders could not have been accused of reaching hasty conclusions had they presumed from practice that Communists had a favored model. In every land where Communists had obtained power they established a special type of instrument to associate workers and peasants under Communist party leadership in making and administering policy. This ideal instrument had emerged from the Russian revolution as the "soviet," an assembly appropriating the ancient Russian word for "council" but infusing the old term with a new content.

Russian preference for the soviet as the ideal state form had been expressed forthrightly in 1920. In their letter addressed to English shop stewards seeking advice on what to do, the leaders of the Communist International have already been found to have praised the soviet type of government as proved in practice.[1]

The soviet form had faced its supreme test in communist eyes during the events of 1917, 1918, and 1919 in Russia and in central Europe. It had been a successful link between the Communists and the people in the interval from the eve of the tsar's abdication to the "October Revolution." It had been an instrument through which the masses were rallied to challenge and finally to overcome the Provisional Government headed consecutively by Prince Lvov and Alexander Kerensky. Proof of its universal value outside as well as within Russia was also found in events in Berlin from 9 November 1918 to 12 January 1919, during the life of the Berlin "Workers' and Soldiers' Soviet" and again in Bela Kun's "Hungarian Soviet Republic" between 12 March and 1 August 1919.[2]

The Russian Communists had been elated by the uprisings in central Europe, which they considered harbingers of the workers' revolution that they expected to become worldwide. Although some German socialist comrades had resisted what seemed to them inappropriate extensions to Germany of the Russian form,[3] this had not discouraged the Communist International's leaders. Their letter to the British a year later demonstrated their confidence in the exportability of the state form devised by the Russian revolutionaries.

Faith in the exportability of the soviet form was reasserted in China. In 1921 an author claimed that the Soviet Russian

---

[1] THE I.L.P. AND THE THIRD INTERNATIONAL 44 (1920).

[2] See the simplified account prepared for Russian schools, A. V. SHESTAKOV ed., A SHORT HISTORY OF THE U.S.S.R. 206–7 (1938). The readers were told that the Berlin soviet was betrayed by its Menshevik members, the Social Democrats.

[3] See the reminiscences of the veteran Social Democrat Philipp Scheidemann, quoted in FISCHER, STALIN AND GERMAN COMMUNISM. A STUDY IN THE ORIGINS OF THE STATE PARTY 61 (1948).

model was suitable for any country engaged in establishing a soviet system of government,[4] and a delegation attending a meeting in Irkutsk the same year was given opportunities to observe a local soviet in action. By 1928 the reception of the Communist International's favored form became official, for the Sixth Congress of the Chinese party resolved to spread the soviet form into the urban areas as a means of mobilizing the masses and helping them administer their affairs.[5] A Leninist definition of a soviet was included as a guide.[6]

The soviet had its Russian beginnings in 1905, but Lenin had found the prototype in events as early as the Paris commune of 1871. In the capital from which the troops loyal to the French government had been withdrawn in the face of the Prussian advance, a novel institution had been created to maintain the public services and organize the defense. In the fall of the Paris commune, Lenin read a lesson. In his view, missing elements had been strong leadership by a Marxian revolutionary party and representation of the peasantry, without whom the workmen could not obtain the necessary food; and the commune had failed to proceed uncompromisingly against the bourgeoisie.[7] The Russian soviet was not to be permitted to make the same mistakes. Years later, Mao Tse-tung reaffirmed briefly his faith in the Paris model when he thought the Chinese revolution betrayed by stultification of his people's committees because of expanding bureaucratic practices.[8] Like

[4] The incident has been described in Ilp-yong Kim, Communist Politics in China 33 (unpublished doctoral dissertation in Columbia University Library, 1968). Kim cites Chun, Lao-nung chih-tu yen-chi [A Study of the Soviet System] in [1921] 5 KUNG CH'AN TANG 33 (1921) [The Communists].

[5] Id. at 35, citing CHIEN-MIN WANG, CHUNG-KUO KUNG-CH'AN TANG SHIH-KAO 22–23 (1965) [Historical Materials on the Chinese Communist Party].

[6] Id. at 35, citing WANG at 173.

[7] For the steps leading to embracing of the Paris commune as a model, see E. H. CARR, 1 A HISTORY OF SOVIET RUSSIA 85–86 (1950). Lenin's comments are scattered throughout his works. See his Lessons of the Commune, 13 SOCHINENIIA 437 at 438 (4th ed. 1947) [Works]; Memories of the Commune, 17 id. 111 at 113 and Speech at Butyrskii District, 28 id. 24 at 26.

[8] The Great Lessons of the Paris Commune, [1966] 14–16 PEKING REVIEW (3 parts).

Lenin he sought to analyze the lessons of Paris and revive the revolutionary spirit of his party.

In outward appearance the soviet form is not startling, for it has elements closely comparable to a town or county council in England or the United States or to the government of a village "commune" in contemporary France. Still, there is at the same time a difference, which to the communist authors makes the soviet sui generis. This is to be found in the impact of its heritage even fifty years after the Russian revolution.

This heritage stems from the soviet's genesis in 1905 and its reincarnation in 1917 as a body representing solely working class elements in the population. Although this feature faded in 1961, when the program of the Communist party of the Soviet Union declared the soviet to have become representative of the people as a whole,[9] the revised status was not taken to mean the end of its class character. The party was saying only that with the transformation of society in the USSR from a multiclass structure into a composite of working-class elements, toiling in factory, office, educational institution and on the farm, the soviet as representative of society as a whole no longer had to be limited to representation of only a fraction of all the people. The "dictatorship of the proletariat," resting upon only one segment of the population, had evolved into a "state of the whole people" because there remained no nonworking classes over whom to rule. The class bias of the soviet as a developed instrument of the dictatorship of the proletariat continued to be a cardinal feature,[10] but it was no longer dramatically apparent, since "class" and "society" were now synonymous. The "segment" of 1917 had by 1961 engulfed the whole.

Although postwar Marxian socialist states in Europe and Asia have evolved in various forms, Communists of other lands have been influenced by the success thought evident in the steps taken to create and develop the soviet form in the republics emerging from the ruins of the Russian empire in 1917 and 1918. Eastern European events at the close of the Second World War proved this fact; for even before the military

[9] Program, pt. 2, sec. III.

[10] Chesnokov, *The Soviet State: Its Educational Role*, Pravda, 27 Feb. 1967. Also Chkhikvadze, *The Evolution of a Popular Substance of the Soviet State*, [1966] 10 Sov. gos. i pravo 3 at 15.

advance from the east, Czechs and Slovaks, together with Russian colleagues, hid behind the Nazi lines to set up "National Committees." Czechoslovak President Beneš, after his December 1943 conference with Joseph Stalin, noted that "National Committees in the Communist understanding are in fact 'Soviets.'" [11]

Following the arrival of Soviet troops in Balkan countries the pace quickened, and the pattern was almost uniform. It became clear that the script for Polish, Romanian, Hungarian, Yugoslav, and other Communists had been prepared, at least in its first draft, in the Moscow classrooms where many of them had been briefed before returning to their countries to assume leadership.[12] There was a precise idea of how much conformity the soviet model required. Variation was limited to the minimum required to meet local needs for compromise with tradition and facilitate the retention of power. Since the Russian model, constructed by study of the disappointments of 1871 and 1905 and of the successes of 1917, provides the base on which other Communists have built, it is well to note its principal identifying features. This is particularly true since the Yugoslav Communists after 1948 maintained that Stalin had perverted the Leninist form, to which Tito was determined to return after his liberation from Stalinism.

The 1905 soviets in Moscow and Petersburg comprised only workmen and those educated men who shared their interests, as their task was not to govern a state but to lead strikes among factory workers. They were organs of resistance, not of government. When their members were silenced by the troops of the tsar, they disappeared for just over a decade, to be recreated in "February" of 1917 on the eve of the tsar's abdication, but in a more popular form. Their base was broadened to include soldiers, without whose support the war-torn capital of the Russian

[11] J. Korbel, The Communist Subversion of Czechoslovakia, 1938–1948; The Failure of Coexistence 91, 131 (1959).

[12] A Yugoslav close to the situation explains, "The creation and development of local self-government were influenced by the political doctrine of scientific socialism and by experiences from the past (the Commune of Paris, local soviets, the local self-government known in Anglo-Saxon countries and so on)." Djorjević, *Introduction* to 2 Collection of Yugoslav Laws (The Local Government) 4 (Institute of Comparative Law, Belgrade, 1962).

empire could never have been seized. Within weeks peasants were added, making the soviet a representative of workers, soldiers, and peasants. The unsung heroes were the intellectuals, led after April 1917 by Lenin, just returned from exile in Switzerland. Lenin had maintained staunchly through a series of party congresses that intellectuals constituted not a class in themselves but a stratum attached to one or another class in accordance with its sympathies. He and his educated colleagues, therefore, required no revision of the formula to gain admission to the new elite, for they were "workmen" in political orientation. The only excluded element was the bourgeoisie and their sympathizers—excluded in application of the lesson in failure provided in Paris in 1871.

Lenin's policy took legal form in the first constitution in the new Russia, promulgated under his guidance in July 1918. The soviets became the instrument of state authority, with a class bias created by the electoral law.[13] Only the working classes could vote and hold office. Although this was the sole limitation created by law, another equally important one emerged almost immediately in practice as the second characteristic feature. The soviets became the implement not only of a single class, but of a single political party, as was indicated in the preceding chapter.

The third notable characteristic was the soviet's essentially hierarchical structure, embodying what is known in communist parlance as "democratic centralism." The subservience of the local level to the center, which is the core of the concept, was not easy to establish, for the socialist-minded peasants were parochial in their thinking, and they were joined in the early months following the revolution by many of the left-wing intellectuals. The socialism of the Bolsheviks was not their concept of the term, and at the outset of the new state they all fought hard against the desire of the Leninists to centralize authority, but to no avail. The dissolution of the Constituent Assembly in January 1918 by a resolute Bolshevik minority in league with the troops signaled their doom, and this was capped

[13] Constitution of the R.S.F.S.R., 10 July 1918, ch. XIII, notably art. 65 excluding the bourgeoisie from the vote. Eng. transl. in J. MEISEL & E. KOZERA, MATERIALS FOR THE STUDY OF THE SOVIET SYSTEM 79, 88 (2d ed. 1953).

at the Third Congress of Soviets, called immediately afterward, at which the soviet structure was formalized as the permanent pattern of government for the new Russia.[14]

The left-wing socialists of Lenin's early coalition government had wanted a state form respecting local autonomy, and they demanded it for the local soviets, but without success. They were strong enough to force a compromise with centralizing forces,[15] but the success was short lived. Their formula "All local matters shall be decided only by local soviets" went into the congress's resolution, but the constitution which followed in July destroyed what little had been gained in January. Article 62 of the new basic law established the right of superior soviets to "exercise control over the activities of the local soviets." This was expressed in concrete terms as the right of higher soviets to annul decisions of local soviets, subject to one proviso: notice to the central authorities in appropriate cases. The sweeping formula of the Third Congress of January, "Local soviets have authority to solve all questions of purely local importance" was placed in Article 61, but it lacked potency since the accent upon centralized control was made the rule of the article immediately following.

Centralism became a distinguishing feature of the soviet system during Stalin's dictatorial rule, and the principle was retained even after his death with only moderate erosion, in spite of centrally inspired campaigns, which reached their zenith in the Twenty-third Communist Party Congress of 1966, to strengthen the role of "mass participation" in government at the local level.

A fourth feature revered by Soviet political scientists in describing the soviet was summed up by Andrei Y. Vyshinsky in the late 1930s in the standard textbook on public law: "The Soviet structure from top to bottom is permeated with the general spirit of the unity of state authority." [16] Montesquieu's concept of separation of powers, which is distinctive of governmental structure in the United States and in some other lands,

[14] *Declaration of the Rights of the Toiling and Exploited People*, art. 1. Eng. transl. in *id.* at 57.

[15] G. Gurvich, Istoriia sovetskoi konstitutsii 2 (1923) [History of the Soviet Constitution].

[16] A. Vyshinsky, The Law of the Soviet State 300 (1948).

was roundly denounced as a bourgeois fraud. This rejection was manifest in the authority granted the soviet at every level of state structure to embody in principle all state power at that level: legislative, executive, and judicial, even though in practice it delegated some of these functions to others.

The soviet as an "assembly" functions as a policy-making body, a local "parliament," but it reserves to itself, in addition, the right to supervise every aspect of execution of policy performed by the departments made subordinate to its "executive committee," and to demand reports from the judiciary.[17] There is no theory of "checks and balances" limiting the authority of the assembly, for the executive is by law wholly responsible to it as the source of executive authority. The judiciary is likewise the creature of the soviet, being appointed and recalled by the deputies to the soviet at the level concerned, with one exception—that of relatively recent inauguration. Judges in the courts of first instance, the "people's courts," became elected rather than appointed officials on promulgation of the 1936 constitution of the USSR,[18] but judges at all higher levels are still named by the soviet at their level.

Although the concept of separation of powers is absent in some countries having no Marxist heritage, the most noted being the United Kingdom, there is a difference. The variant of unity of power adopted in the USSR has not yet, at least, become encrusted with "conventions" stripping the parliament, as in England, of the possibility of using to the full its un-

[17] USSR Constitution, 1936, arts. 101 and 108. Some Western scholars argue that since local soviets may not promulgate "laws," but only "orders," they cannot be called legislatures. This position overlooks the fact that the difference in terminology has been established to indicate hierarchical control within the system. It is not adopted to deny a policy-making function, which exists, albeit at a lowly level. This function can justly be called legislative to distinguish it from executive and judicial within the concept of political theory relating to separation or unification of powers. Note the praise accorded judicial reporting to the local soviet by Tikhomirov, *Division of Powers or Division of Labor*, [1967] 1 Sov. GOS I PRAVO 37, Eng. transl. in 5 SOVIET LAW AND GOVERNMENT no. 4 at 11, 17 (1967). Also note the report by the USSR supreme court to the USSR supreme soviet, [1967] 20 Ved. Verkh. Sov. S.S.S.R., item 262.
[18] No elections were held until after World War II.

doubted legal right to intervene to influence judicial discretion.

A fifth distinctive feature is the absence of popularly elected individuals serving as president of the republic, governor of a province, mayor of a city, or headman of a village. While individuals are sometimes introduced to foreigners by such titles, this is only to clarify their roles by providing some basis for comparison. In truth, the soviet system officially abhors individual leadership within the state apparatus. Everything of a state nature must be conducted by an assembly or by committees of the assembly. This means that individuals introduced by Western titles are actually chairmen of these assemblies. As such their ceremonial functions correspond to those of their counterparts abroad, and debate can be directed by them, but in no sense are they powerful executives on the presidential pattern, independent of the assembly. This follows not only from the absence of the concept of separation of powers, but from the fact that none of these men in the USSR is presented directly to the public for election as a presiding officer. Each is chosen by the respective soviet under Communist party guidance, and he can claim no popular mandate upon which to rely in subsequent assertion of personal power.

This is not to say that some of the men who chair the soviets have not wielded power approaching that of their foreign counterparts, but, if so, it has been not because of a personal mandate received at an election but because the powerful figure unites in his person both his authority as a holder of a government post and that of a high official of the Communist party. Still, the Communist party has frequently restated its position, never more strongly than since the Twenty-third Congress of 1966, that key party officials must not hold soviet chairmanships.

It is established that the chairman of the presidium of the supreme soviet, who is sometimes called in the Western press the "president" of the USSR, has a subordinate position. Although for purposes of international protocol he ranks as "head of state," his position domestically is lower not only than that of the first, or general, secretary of the party but also than that of the chairman of the Council of Ministers. Likewise on the local level no chairman of a provincial or city soviet challenges his colleague who is secretary of the provincial or city party committee, nor will he dictate in his own name as chairman to the body over which he presides.

Two additional characteristics of the soviets were also notable during the early years: the method of election and the term of office. Although neither characteristic now remains in its original manifestation, the ideas which inspired each live on; that the choice of candidates should not be left to the voters without party control, and that there should be frequent rotation of deputies in office.

As to choice: the original constitution of 1918 and its electoral law [19] made elections indirect and by employment groups rather than by geographical precincts. This meant that deputies to each soviet above the local level were named not by the voters of a general electorate but by the deputies to the soviet just below. The voting for the local soviet was by show of hands in groups assembled in factories, offices, educational institutions, and on the farms. This system made possible a choice by the party of candidates to be put forward for election, and it also tended to encourage selection of candidates who would have the same professional interest as members of employment groups, or at least be sympathizers with the groups.

Although the 1918 system was abolished by the 1936 constitution in favor of direct election of deputies to soviets at all levels in the hierarchy, its heritage lingers on: nominations of candidates still come from employment groups influenced by Communist party members rather than from political parties functioning within a geographically defined district; and choice of candidates is still limited to a single person approved by the Communist party for the ballot.

As to the term of office: Lenin set the term for the local soviets at three months,[20] and kept it at that short period until 1921. His expressed purpose was to provide for quick rotation in office so as to educate nearly every villager and many of the city people in the problems of public administration. Like Andrew

[19] For first Instruction on Elections of Village and Volost Soviets, see Order of 2 Dec. 1918, [1918] 86 Sob. Uzak. R.S.F.S.R., pt. I, item 901. For 1924 revision to include urban soviets, see decree of 11 Aug. 1924, [1924] 71 *id.* item 695.

[20] Constitution of the R.S.F.S.R., 1918, art. 57.

Jackson a century earlier in the nascent American democracy, he had confidence that an intelligent man or woman could learn to direct the affairs of state without expert training. He seems also to have been influenced by a desire to take a practical step toward Marx's goal of a disciplined society by creating a popular administration so firmly grounded that the state could wither away.

Although the terms of deputies were subsequently extended to two years at the levels below the republic supreme soviets and to four years for the supreme soviets of the republics and of the USSR itself, there was established in 1961, in reflection of Lenin's early concept, a rule of rotation in office which required that one-third of the deputies of each soviet be new in each election.[21] This introduced a constantly rotating group, few of whom could have obtained an expert knowledge of the representative function, but many of whom may have felt the thrill of sitting in highly dramatized state meetings.

Statistics show that from the first local elections of 1938 under the second federal constitution to 1966 almost 16,400,000 persons have served in soviets below the republic level, because the practice of rotation was introduced even before enactment of the formula.[22] About 70 percent of the deputies elected in the 1962 elections were newcomers.

The amateur status was reinforced by the circumstance that soviet assemblies at every level met only for short periods each year and were never in permanent or semipermanent session. Only the "executive committee" of the soviet, with the duty not only of preparing for the meetings of the assembly but of supervising the administrative department, had a professional standing. Although the formula for compulsory rotation was abandoned in 1966,[23] the soviet remains in conception a nonprofessional institution, offering large numbers of citizens a

[21] No statute or constitutional amendment established the rule. It appears only in the Communist party program.

[22] Paleckis, *Socialist Democracy in Action*, Izvestiia, 5 Dec. 1966. Eng. transl. in 18 C.D.S.P. no. 49 at 23 (1966).

[23] No statute was enacted. The Communist party's repudiation of its 1961 program on this point at its 1966 congress was taken as authority to drop application of a "formula" for rotation, while preserving in force the "principle."

chance to participate in the governing process beyond what would have been permitted them had the Communist party alone not guided and administered all aspects of political life.

Soviets became the hand of the Soviet political system while the Communist party remained the brain, conceiving of itself as an instrument one step removed from the administrative problems of everyday living. At the same time the soviets became a school for the preparation of activists in the administrative process. They must be looked upon, therefore, not only as what they are, but as harbingers of what is to come. They are not conceived as being the final administrative form.

Popular as the soviets are intended to be, they have tended in the mind of the communist leadership to become professional and bureaucratic in recent years, at least in their administrative functions. To counteract this tendency emphasis has been placed upon two features, one of long duration and the other of recent innovation. The longer established feature is the "standing committee," corresponding in some measure to the committees serving representative bodies in other countries by studying problems in advance of the full meeting of the assembly, by proposing the texts of appropriate resolutions, and by checking on the performance of the professional administration in the field of its concern.

The soviet "standing committee," created at every level of government, is novel among parliamentary committee systems in that most, though not all, include not only deputies but outsiders, known as "activists." So many of these outsiders have served that, included with the deputies, one out of every six or seven adults within the whole USSR is said today to have had some experience with soviet work.[24] These outsiders are specialists in the subject of committee concern, whether it is public health, sanitation, local schools, local construction, or street traffic. The outsiders share in the study and preparation of proposals and attend meetings of the assembly to hear what is said. By 1964 they numbered twenty million.[25]

The second, more unusual, feature designed to restrain the

[24] Paleckis, *supra*, note 22.
[25] A. DENISOV, NARODOVLASTIE I KOMMUNIZM 26 [Popular Power and Communism] (Narodnyi Universitet, Fakul'tet Pravovykh Znanii [People's University, Faculty of Legal Knowledge] pamphlet no. 10 (1965).

bureaucracy is an attempt to place unpaid individuals not only in the assembly as the policy-making body but also in the administrative departments of the local soviets. These persons have been given such functions in the administration of municipal housing that the Communist party program of 1961 anticipated the eventual elimination at the local level of all paid staff, except perhaps the departmental director.[26]

The use of unpaid volunteers in public administration has sometimes been justified, as were the short terms of deputies to the soviets in 1917–21, by reference to the need to prepare the public to administer things when the state has withered away. As attractive as the idea may be to a Marxist mind, it is not currently being pressed as a major desideratum, and it seems likely that the leaders have more in mind the practical advantage offered by costless utilization in public administration of pensioners and otherwise unoccupied capable people.

There are likewise two explanations for inviting large numbers of citizens to share as activists in the work of standing committees of soviets; preparing them for the day of withering, and giving them a sense of sharing in the system, since they have few other opportunities to share governmental functions with a Communist party which is limited in its enrollment policies.

Whatever the reasons, ideological or practical, these fringe features of the soviet leadership's penchant for "mass participation" have become ingrained within the system. They have increasingly become the subject of concern of foreign analysts as the Marxian socialist family has expanded, for "mass participation" is on the lips of the leaders of every one of the new states.

When one turns to the new states, it is striking that each of them, when freed from German or Japanese occupation after the war, was guided by its Marxist-trained leaders toward conformity to Stalin's model, not only in forming the leadership party but also in structuring the state apparatus. Thus the Polish Communists kept close to the soviet pattern, although they found it desirable to utilize some historic Polish forms to facilitate Communist rule, and the Chinese demonstrated, at

[26] Program, pt. 2, sec. III (1).

least before their Eighth Congress in 1957, that the soviet model was constantly before them. Even the Yugoslavs, although claiming real differences, presented a system identifiable as Russian-inspired until their split with Stalin in 1948.

The record of the Poles is exceptionally interesting because it suggests the outer limits of innovation permitted by Stalin himself during his most dictatorial period. There was no slavish conformity to the soviet pattern, but there was evidence of Stalinist "inspiration." Thus, local assemblies like those of the USSR were established as "people's councils" (*rady narodowe*) by the advancing "People's Council of the Homeland" as it moved in the wake of Soviet troops clearing Poland of Nazi soldiers. The prewar legislative organs at the provincial and local level were reshaped on the soviet model by the law of 11 September 1944,[27] but with this step the mimicry ended, for "executive committees" like those performing the administrative function in the USSR were not inaugurated. On the contrary, administration was left in the hands of officials appointed to fill the traditional Polish positions of *wojewoda, starosta, burmistrz,* and *wójt* (governor, county chief, city mayor, and village mayor).

Following inauguration of what was sometimes called "dual power," the old and new continued to coexist for some years, with the apparatus inherited from the past undertaking administration alongside the newly created assemblies patterned after those of the USSR. Both an inside[28] and an outside[29] analyst have concluded that this departure from the soviet model had one purpose: to aid Communists in consolidating power. A compromise to incorporate ancient administrative tradition was imperative at a time when reconstruction could not wait upon experiments with new forms of the executive.

The retention of prewar administrative forms was not the only Polish variation from the soviet model; deputies to the assemblies were chosen not by employment groups, as they had been in the USSR until 1936, but by organizations such as

[27] Jones, *Polish Local Government Reorganized on Soviet Model* 10 AM. SLAVIC AND E. E. REV. 56 at 58 (1951).

[28] S. ROZMARYN, LA POLOGNE 241 (Comment ils sont gouvernés, vol. 8, 1966).

[29] Jones, *supra,* note 27 at 58.

political parties, trade unions, and youth and social organizations. Although this difference in detail should be noted, it is less important than the result, for in both the USSR before 1936 and Poland in 1944 the concept of representation by deputies chosen in geographically defined electoral precincts was rejected in favor of representation of professional groups. The rejection of the common Western pattern facilitated leadership by the Communists, because political thinking can be influenced more easily among people who are all easily accessible to their professional associates than among the heterogeneous lot who appear at polling places established on the basis of geography alone.

Within six years the major Polish departure from the soviet model was erased, for by a law of 20 March 1950 [30] the pattern was made almost identical with that of the USSR. The executive functions of the independently appointed local executives were merged with those of the people's councils of corresponding level, and the system of voting for members was ordered changed.

The soviet model's hierarchical structure was also copied by the Poles. The 1950 law made each people's council responsible to the next higher council until the pinnacle was reached in the "Council of State." Here was adoption of Lenin's "democratic centralism," for higher levels were authorized to annul decisions of councils at lower levels and even to dissolve them if need be and call new elections. Duties of councils were made essentially those of the soviet model—to collaborate in strengthening state defenses, to preserve public order, and to implement the national economic plan.

At the top level the Polish *sejm* (parliament) was authorized to delegate authority to the "council of state" to issue decrees, and this it did so frequently as to establish a close parallel to the practice in the USSR, by which the major policy-making function has passed from the parliament to a smaller interim body which seeks ratification from its parent during the latter's brief sessions once or twice a year. Only after the Polish "October" of 1956 did the *sejm* regain its historic role of professional

[30] S. ROZMARYN, *supra*, note 28 at 243. Eng. transl. of text in Jones, *supra*, note 27 at 63.

legislature and introduce the concept of full-time deputies into the soviet-type structure. At that time the authority of local government was also broadened and the center's legal right to interfere restricted.

Whereas the Poles had to wait for liberation from Stalin's apron strings until his death, the Yugoslav Communists gained their opportunity in 1948 when Stalin expelled them from the Communist Information Bureau. By 1950 they had begun to innovate, although not without regard to their own earlier experience. Like their colleagues in other Eastern European states liberated from German occupation, they sensed the weight of influence created by Soviet assistance, but to a lesser degree. Even before the Soviet armies began to force a general German retreat, the Yugoslav Communists had shared in the formation of "National Liberation Committees" between 1941 and 1945 in regions brought under communist control. They came to be called "people's committees." These committees differed at the outset from the soviet model of Lenin's time because they were not limited in membership to the working classes. Since they were efforts to unite all forces in opposition to the Nazis, they drew to themselves other elements, and this left its mark. The base was worker, peasant, and worker-oriented intellectual, but there were also members from the middle class, the bourgeoisie, and the intellectuals sympathetic to the latter's cause.

Like the soviets of the USSR, but contrary to early postwar Poland, the people's committees of Yugoslavia united both policy-making and administrative functions, the latter authority being exercised, as in the USSR, by "executive committees." The first constitution of 1946 recognized these people's committees as the basic organs of the new state,[31] as had the earliest constitution in Lenin's Russia.

A key Yugoslav analyst later claimed that Yugoslavia's people's committees differed even at the outset from Lenin's in that the political structure of the Yugoslav state was built up from below rather than from the top down.[32] He also sought to

[31] Yugoslav Constitution, 1946, art. 6. Eng. transl. in 3 A. PEASLEE, CONSTITUTIONS OF NATIONS 522 (1950).

[32] Djorjević, Local Self-Government in Yugoslavia, 12 AM. SLAVIC AND E. E. REV. 188 (1953).

emphasize the difference created by their evolution as multi-class, anti-Nazi organs in contrast to Russia's one-class strike leadership committees of 1905 and early 1917. In this the Yugoslav analyst found a base of broader character than that created by the narrow class movement of revolutionary Russia.

Also from the outset, these committees—by law of 1946, but more noticeably by law of 1949, after the break with Stalin—began to reflect policies which were to become Yugoslav communism's post-Stalin trademarks; namely, local autonomy and mass participation in government. Although Leninist principles of democratic centralism are admitted to have been the inspiration for creation of the Yugoslav model in 1946, current comment sees a difference. It is that at the outset central authorities were authorized to annul acts of the people's committees, but only on subjects classified as general and on the basis of violation of law. They could not thwart local wishes on the grounds of unwise exercise of discretion. The new sacred principle was that local jurisdiction was to be held inviolate. What this meant in practice is hard to determine, but its presence on paper later provided the base for innovation of indubitable importance.

The year 1949 marked the beginning of review of the Stalinist heritage in Yugoslavia. Without Stalin's advisers to frighten them, the Yugoslav specialists concluded that practice had proved that the tail was wagging the dog. The executive committees were found to have violated their duty to serve only as agents of the people's committees, and to have become the homes of bureaucrats who looked to the assembly only for ratification of what had already been done by the executives. Further, the executives, as bureaucrats within a planned economy, tended to become subservient to the center in thoroughly bureaucratic fashion, so that local-level government became the agency of the central government and nothing more. This discovery is said to have led to experimentation in what has come to be known as Yugoslav "decentralization."

Yugoslav decentralization was manifested by the transfer from the federal government to the republics, which constitute the members of the federation, and even to their local committees of a number of administrative functions, and by reduction in the size of the administrative staff at the federal capital in Belgrade. A law of 1950 established management of what had been state-owned property as the concern of the workers in individual plants, and led eventually to development of the concept of "social ownership" instead of "state ownership." The details of this aspect of the reform will be treated in a chapter on property rights in productive enterprise, but its influence upon the structure of local government requires elaboration at this point.

The people's committees were reconstituted by a law of 1 April 1952 [33] to meet the new tasks placed upon them. As in the past they were to sit in rural counties (*opština*), towns (*grad*), and at the next higher level of "district" (*srez*), embracing from six to twenty counties. All were to be elected directly as they had been previously, rather than through professional and employment groups as in the USSR before 1936 and Poland in 1944, but an innovation was created to incorporate something of the same idea and probably to achieve the same purpose. The district and town committees were made bicameral; the first chamber was elected on the basis of population, which was predominantly rural, and the second as a "producers' council," elected not by general vote of all citizens but by employee groups. This smacked of the early soviet system, but there were differences, for the soviets in the USSR have never been bicameral, except at the federal level to give representation to the republics in a second chamber; and the Yugoslav variant, through its second chamber, provided a weighted vote for urban working elements.

This feature was established by the 1952 law through limitation of membership in the second chamber to groups engaged in producing material goods, although it was not a weapon to be used against private enterprisers. Groups could be represented whether they used state or private means of production. Only later were groups engaged in transportation and merchandising given representation, to provide a more inclusive pattern. At that point the second chamber had representatives of three groups: industry, farmers' cooperatives, and crafts, each group being represented in accordance with its contribution to the revenue produced in the area concerned. Much later, after the

[33] Off. Gaz. F.P.R. Yu., no. 22, 1952. Eng. transl. in 2 COLLECTION OF YUGOSLAV LAWS, *supra*, note 12 at 15.

adoption of the 1963 federal constitution which gave representation at the federal level to culture and health groups, representatives of these elements were added to the second chamber, which was renamed "chamber of working communities." [34]

The two chambers were given equal rights in economic matters by the 1952 law, and this principle has been retained. In some measure it permits a balancing of interests between town and country, for the working communities are preponderantly urban. In other matters the 1952 law left the population-based chamber to make decisions alone. Such matters were notably those of education, culture, health, and administration. But this unique authority was not to last, for deputies were added to the second chamber for education, culture, social welfare, and health. After 1963 some large communes added two other chambers, one to represent education and culture, the other to represent social welfare and health. Thereafter, the population-based chamber had to reach accord with the appropriate specialized chamber when matters within the competence of one of them were presented.

In further departure from Stalin's model for the state apparatus, the executive committee was abolished by the 1952 law, and its functions were transferred to a series of specialized committees to be created by the people's committee. These were to deal with local economy, municipal services, education and culture, health and social services, and internal affairs. They looked much like the standing committees of Stalin's soviets, but their difference was supposed to be that unlike Stalin's committees they had "executive" functions. They were not purely policy oriented.

Popularity was sought in Yugoslavia, as it has been sought in the USSR, by requiring rotation of membership in the specialized committees, not only among deputies to the people's committee of which they formed a part, but among outside specialists called in to help. The rotation was to be at three- or four-year intervals, depending on whether it was a rural or an urban people's committee. The chairmanship was to rotate

[34] Geršković, *Preface*, 12 COLLECTION OF YUGOSLAV LAWS (STATUTE OF THE COMMUNE OF POŽAREVAC) 14 (Institute of Comparative Law, Belgrade, 1965).

even faster, for its term was set at one year. To the Yugoslav Communists the merit of their innovation was the erection of a barrier against the curse of Marxian socialism in the Stalinist model—the bureaucratization and professionalization of the executive. Mass participation was to become real and not merely symbolic, as they thought it was under Stalin.

The Yugoslavs had a formula, but it had to be implemented by practical measures; for the specialized committees had to be staffed to keep papers moving, and at this point their system could slip back into bureaucracy. In an effort to create something new, they instituted an "administration" for each specialized committee, composed of a staff of technicians appointed by the parent people's committee.[35] This staff was to be organized by a chief clerk who functioned through a channel leading to the secretary of the people's committee. To reduce the likelihood of his becoming a bureaucrat, his term was limited to a period of four years with right of reelection, but for not more than twice in succession. His responsibility was to the chairman of the people's committee, an official conceived of not as a chief executive, but rather, as in the USSR, as the presiding officer of a committee, without independent personal authority. Because of this situation, the secretary of the people's committee had more prominence in practice than the committee's chairman, and the Communist party probably planned it so. As foreign analysts have noted, vigorous party members were given the role of "secretary" of the people's committee, thus providing the party with a means of leading local government effectively.

The next step came in 1955 when the numerous local governments were amalgamated to reduce their number from 357 to 95 districts, and from 4,000 opštine to 1,193 units of the same name, but given in official English translation the prestigeous name of "commune." These new communes were granted greater financial autonomy than had previously been permitted to local government units. They could levy a 2 percent sales tax on retail consumption and a tax of up to 20

[35] In this description, as well as in other matters concerning Yugoslavia, this account draws heavily upon writings and private conversations of Fred Warner Neal. See especially G. HOFFMAN & F. NEAL, YUGOSLAVIA AND THE NEW COMMUNISM (1962) and Neal, The Reforms in Yugoslavia, 12 AM. SLAVIC AND E. E. REV. 227 (1954).

percent on the purchases of local collective organizations, interpreted as being workers' housing, nurseries, and the like. Their financial autonomy, which the Stalinist model had always restricted by strict central budgeting, was further strengthened by authority to tax the income of their own enterprises as they chose. Funds from these sources were to become available for spending as the people's committee of the commune chose, although foreign analysts have noted that in practice higher levels in the governmental structure continued to exert considerable influence on decisions.[36]

Popular control, which Yugoslavs considered pivotal to their new attitude toward administration, was to be symbolized by town meetings, assembling all the voters of the village, and also by use of referenda. Candidates for the elections were to be nominated by the town meetings, and after election the town meetings were to watch the deputies' work and issue recalls if the trust was violated. Further, the public, through the town meeting, was to supervise in a general way through investigation of the work of the people's committee.

Whether the Yugoslav formula will bring public influence to bear upon the course of events has yet to be seen. Not all Yugoslav authors are sanguine, but even the doubtful ones hope that they have found a safeguard against reemergence of bureaucratic and despotic tendencies. If their hope matures to reality, their success will be notable, for it will represent effective use of an instrument which has found no supporters in the USSR, even since Stalin's death. The Soviet specialists, in their effort to meet the very same needs that the Yugoslavs have felt, turn to quite different methods: increasing the supervisory powers of standing committees of the soviets, recruiting non-professionals for service on administrative staffs, and experimenting with a hybrid bureaucratic-mass instrument which has gone through several metamorphoses—"popular control."

This last instrument now typifies the novelty of the Soviet effort to control bureaucratic practices. Built upon a model established by Lenin in the early 1920s to assume the duties of the traditional state auditors, it combines in one agency both professional auditors and great numbers of the rank and file in

[36] HOFFMAN & NEAL, *supra*, note 35 at 226.

the enterprise being audited. Stalin had by degrees restructured Lenin's instrument over his long period in power so that it became no more than a traditional bureaucratic ministry of professionals. Nikita Khrushchev had reversed this process in his reorganization of industry to involve four million nonprofessionals in its work.[37] Further, he combined it with the Communist party's auditing body to form a single "party-state control committee," empowered not only to audit accounts but to search for errors of judgment and simple refusal to humanize the administrative process.

On Khrushchev's dismissal, his successors again changed the agency. The 1965 statute separated the party auditors from the state auditors and changed the name to "popular control"; but the feature of mass participation was retained. Indeed, one Soviet historian has said that the change involved no more than a change in name.[38]

Still another novelty in state administration was introduced by the Yugoslav Communists in 1963. Also designed to prevent stultification of leadership, it focused on the highest political figures, not the rank and file administrators. It took the form of a constitutional requirement of rotation in office.[39] No one may be elected to the same chamber of the Federal Assembly for two consecutive terms. The rule reaches beyond the legislature to the federal state secretaries, the federal secretaries and some others. Although the rule may be relaxed on "special grounds for highly qualified individuals," to permit them to serve for a second term,[40] no such releases were issued when the question of retirement was first raised, on the occasion of the second elections after promulgation of the rule, with the result that some prominent Communists were required to step down. Among them was Edvard Kardelj. Only Tito was exempt, by exception written into the constitution; but after he dies or withdraws, even the office of president must rotate.

The Yugoslav rotation system is stricter than that which

---

[37] Ministerstvo Vyshego i Srednogo Spetsial'nogo Obrazovanie, Istoriia gosudarstva i prava, chast' ii [Ministry of Higher and Middle Specialized Education, History of the State and Law, part II] 488 (1966).

[38] Id. at 82.

[39] Art. 82.

[40] Art. 236.

Khrushchev introduced into the USSR in 1961, for no nationally distinguished persons have been required to step down from state office in the USSR. The Communists of the Soviet Union prefer to respect their rotation system in principle rather than in practice, for only the middle- and lower-level bureaucracy has been moved about in the USSR. Even the principle has lost some of its teeth since Khrushchev's ouster; for as has already been indicated, the 1966 party decisions revoked his precise formula for rotation of a certain percentage of deputies at each election, leaving the principle standing without any compulsory measure of its scope.

Chinese experimentation with local government began even before the Communists formally declared their people's republic, for large regions of China came under the control of guerrilla forces and even of de facto government by Communists in areas cut off from the reach of the Republic of China's Kuomintang. Foreign analysts still find in Chinese political life a strong tendency toward local autonomy and group decision-making.[41] Reflecting a condition of poor communication, the communist government, after its establishment in 1949, created six nearly autonomous administrative regions, each under the political supervision of a member of the politburo of the Communist party directed to form a people's government on the "soviet model." [42] Military-administrative committees perforce carried on in many areas until pacification was completed in late 1952, when the six regions were transformed into agencies of the central government. By 1954 they were eliminated as intermediate links in the administrative structure so as to permit direct subordination of the provincial governments to Peking; but something of the guerrilla period's tradition of regional autonomy and group decision-making still remained, although in subdued form, subject to centralized direction from above. It was to reappear in modified form with the creation in 1961 of six "regional bureaus" within the Communist party structure, following the abandoned boundaries of the former six administrative regions.[43]

[41] P. TANG, COMMUNIST CHINA TODAY 220 (2d ed. 1961).
[42] The system is discussed in *id.* 220 *et seq.*
[43] F. SCHURMANN, IDEOLOGY AND ORGANIZATION IN COMMUNIST CHINA 148 (1966).

The soviet model created by the Russian revolution was utilized to institute civilian government as soon as the military committees were no longer necessary to hold power. The structure became, therefore, that of an assembly, called "people's congress," at each level of the administrative structure, with an executive committee, called "people's council," at the helm of each congress. Until 1954 the delegates to the congresses were appointed by the military committees, usually in consultation with mass organizations, and the military committees continued to function alongside the new bodies to create a situation of dual power. Only gradually did the military groups fade from the scene, the assemblies becoming bodies of elected delegates, finally to be enshrined in the constitution of 1954 as the state organs of the people's republic. At the top level was placed a National People's Congress, with a State Council as its executive, and on the local level the "people's congress" was declared by Article 55 of the constitution to be "the local organ of state power."

Election to the people's congresses was established as it had been in the 1918 constitution of the Russian republic. This meant that at the bottom of the hierarchy, which was the rural district or the town, delegates were to be elected directly; but those sitting in congresses at the county and provincial level were to be composed of delegates chosen from members of the congresses at the next lower level. Thus, election for all congresses above the bottom level was "indirect." As in the USSR until 1936, the city dwellers were favored by a system of weighted representation, so that a delegate from a rural area to a county assembly represented four times as many citizens as one from an urban community. Functions of the deputies were similar to those of members of the soviets in the USSR. The people's council elected by each assembly to serve as its executive was responsible, as in the USSR, not only to the assembly which appointed and recalled its members but also to the next higher executive in the chain of command from Peking.[44]

---

[44] Constitution of the People's Republic of China, 1954, art. 62. Eng. transl. in A. BLAUSTEIN, FUNDAMENTAL LEGAL DOCUMENTS OF COMMUNIST CHINA 1 (1962). The work of the National Assembly has been analyzed in Ginsburgs, *Theory and Practice of Parliamentary Procedure in Communist China: Organizational and Institutional Principles*, 15 TORONTO L. J. 1 (1963).

Until 1958 no specialist conversant with the structure of the soviets of the USSR would have had trouble identifying its offspring in the People's Republic of China, but in that year innovation began. It emerged with what were called "communes" in characters translated by the Chinese into Western languages, but which in more literal translation meant "public society" or "popular grouping." [45] These communes bore no resemblance to those developed in Yugoslavia or to the agricultural communal administrations created in Soviet Russia at the time of the revolution in an attempt to demonstrate on a small scale the ideal society toward which the Bolsheviks were heading. They were unique in the Marxist family.

The Chinese communes' novelty lay in their combining of local government functions with those of local economic administration. For the leaders of the Soviet Communist party, separation of the two functions had always seemed desirable, partly because specialists in the agricultural process were considered to be too few to divide their time between the work of general local government and the exacting problems of management of collective farms, and partly because Stalin felt the need to keep a tighter hold on the agricultural production units than he thought possible through the sometimes unruly soviets, controlled by peasants in whom both he and Lenin lacked full confidence. The Chinese, however, were prepared in 1958 to reject the Soviet experience and to create a unified system of local all-purpose management, to be personified by a reorganized people's council serving as a managerial committee for all activity within the area delineated as the commune.

The Chinese innovation has been explained in part as a response to the shortage of personnel skilled in administration and also as a response to theoretical concepts centered in their expectation that the cooperative type of organization borrowed for the Chinese producers' cooperatives from the Russian collective farm model would give way swiftly to the state farm structure. Although the state farm model was also borrowed from Moscow as a means of advancing from a rural economy based on cooperative ownership to a rural economy based upon

[45] Schurmann attributes the choice of name to communist Chinese association of it with an armed population. This made it a symbol of "militarization of the peasantry," i.e., permanent mobilization of village life. See *supra*, note 43 at 478.

what was thought to be a "higher" kind of property, there was a difference in application. The Soviet leaders had moved slowly in the transition, and even fifty years after their revolution had no expectation of complete transition for years to come. Because of the timing, the Chinese saw no need to separate the administration of state property from that of cooperative property any longer, as the Moscow model required.

The transition to the commune type of local government has not been reflected in amendment to the constitution, and so the people's congress and the people's council still continue to be the legally established forms through which local affairs are conducted; but de facto the congress has become a "commune congress" which elects the Commune Management Committee absorbing the people's council.[46] The congress also chooses delegates to be sent higher to the county (*hsien*) congress. The amalgamation of local government and farm administration was cemented by union of the previously independent Communist party organizations of each.

Another difference between the model originally borrowed from Moscow and what emerged in the Chinese commune was the tendency of the Chinese to substitute officials, known by the French word "cadres," for the rank and file citizens chosen by the party to fill the seats in a large part of the assemblies at the various local government levels of the USSR.[47] The assemblies, perhaps because of this substitution, discontinued most discussion after 1954 and became largely inactive. The Chinese claim to have the same interest as Soviet politicians in public participation in government, but they desire to relate this general public, known as the "masses," to government in other ways. The most noted of the Chinese institutions is the organi-

[46] *Survey of a Commune II*, [1966] PEKING REVIEW, no. 11 at 18, 19. The commune surveyed had seventy-one delegates in its congress and fifteen members in its management committee.

[47] This was the thesis of Thomas P. Bernstein, now of Indiana University, set forth in an unpublished seminar paper at Columbia University. He has developed the comparison of China's powerful village leadership under numerous party cadres and well-trained village leaders in contrast to less thoroughly prepared Soviet leadership, often lacking local party officials as leaven, in his *Leadership and Mass Mobilization in the Soviet and Chinese Collectivisation Campaigns of 1929–30 and 1955–56: A Comparison*, [1967] THE CHINA QUARTERLY no. 31 at 1, 9–12.

zation created at the "street" level to give those who dwell along a given street an opportunity to participate in local administration.

While the Communists in the USSR have also utilized community groupings to maintain public order, particularly after 1957 when Khrushchev revived the moribund comrades' courts and encouraged the calling of "social assemblies" to castigate "parasites," the Chinese have gone further. Their agencies look "up the ladder" as well as down to the common man. They have relied on the street committees to play a part in monitoring the activity of local officials as they perform their duties, to make certain that extreme bureaucratic methods are avoided. They have also enlisted the street-committee members in campaigns of mass education and indoctrination, in the search for marginal resources in times of scarcity, in social control, and even in the performance of routine administrative tasks.

The Chinese have also sought to relate their officials to the public in other novel ways. They demand that officials live the spartan life of the masses without the special privileges which were accorded officials in the USSR during the times of shortage that marked the 1930s and which continue in housing even today. To make certain that the cadres keep their mass perspective, the Chinese leaders require them to serve at ordinary labor for sixty days a year. In policing these requirements of "simplicity," the street committees play their part. The Soviet leadership says such use of scarce technicians' time is wasteful, a form of false democracy.

Because of the increasing bureaucratization of the Chinese Communist party and state apparatus, Mao Tse-tung began in earnest in June 1966 to implement a slogan pronounced some months before—his "Great Proletarian Cultural Revolution." [48] While bureaucratization did not stand alone among the complex motives underlying this campaign, including those engendered by a struggle for power among those who hoped to receive Mao's mantle after his death, the issue of bureaucrati-

[48] This explanation was featured in *Decision of the Central Committee of the C.P.C. on the Great Proletarian Cultural Revolution*, Aug. 8, 1966, [1966] 33 PEKING REVIEW 6. See also *Carry the Great Proletarian Revolution through to the End*, [1967] 1 *id.* 8 at 9.

zation was surely in Mao's mind. This became evident as the "Red Guards," created by Mao from student radicals and supported later by large elements of the army, began attacks upon the Communist party bureaucracy, personified for them at Mao's bidding in the chairman of the republic, Liu Shao-chi.

New forms were in the making during 1966–68. For some months Mao called for a return to models inspired by the Paris commune of 1871, which he associated with "the people in arms." [49] By April 1967 he introduced in Peking the instrument of the new authority, a "municipal revolutionary council," composed of ninety-seven members selected from among workers, peasants, students, and the army.[50] This body took power from both the municipality's people's committee and its Communist party committee, combining in itself both party and state functions to become the sole governing force. Its stated goal was to lead the people ultimately to creation of a municipal government, patterned as nearly as possible on the Paris commune, interpreted as having been an institution lacking in professionalism and in bureaucracy, thereby becoming in Mao's view closely responsible to the people. To critics from the Soviet Union, nothing of the sort had happened. They saw in this creation the triumph of the army over the Communist party, with the aged Mao as a figurehead at the top to lend legitimacy and continuity, and the student Red Guards as a force utilized by the army to lend popularity.

Some credence was given to the Soviet charge of Chinese militarization of administration as it progressed into 1968. By April of that year the Peking model of 1967 had been installed as a "revolutionary council," in twenty provinces and by September in all. Most were headed by army commanders working in league with those Communist party cadres who had not been purged by Mao, and in some provinces the student Red Guards

[49] The most explicit statement to this effect is *The Great Lessons, supra,* note 8, esp. no. 16.

[50] The model was established on 25 Jan. 1967 at Kweichow and on 31 Jan. 1967 at Harbin. See *Birth of Provisional Supreme Organ of Power in Heilunkiang Province,* [1967] 7 PEKING REVIEW 12 and 14. See also P. H. Chang, *The Revolutionary Committee in China. Two Case Studies: Heilungkiang and Honan,* 6 CURRENT SCENE. DEVELOPMENTS IN MAINLAND CHINA, no. 9 (1 June 1968).

were also included. Mao no longer spoke of the Paris commune as his inspiration; and, indeed, he could not have done so, for the "people in arms" had been replaced by professional soldiers.[51]

Mao's local government also reflects some traditional Chinese forms, in that mediation has remained a prominent means of settling domestic quarrels. Through this mechanism marital and property disputes are settled out of court in accordance with a combination of principles established by current communist policy and traditional Chinese concepts of ethics.

This approach to dispute resolution is not solely Chinese; the Soviet leadership has also sought through the "workers' collective" to guide the wayward citizen toward marital peace and economic creativity. This unit, in which the individual comes into closest relationship with his fellows on the job, has looked ideal to socialist-minded authorities, but efforts to mobilize popular pressures have not been fully successful with the masses. The peoples of the Soviet Union have shown themselves less responsive to their much-advertised obligations as brothers' keepers than have the Chinese. In consequence, there emerged in the USSR after the ouster of Khrushchev in 1964 a tendency to restore to the organs of the state some of the functions of social control which Khrushchev had passed to employment groups in hopes that they would act out of a sense of communal responsibility to bring nonconformists into line with communist morals. This took concrete form in 1965 in a law undoing part of Khrushchev's system by depriving the "collectives" of the authority Khrushchev had given them to exile "parasites" to remote areas.[52]

Reviewing the experimentation with the state form which has occurred among Communists in various lands since 1917, the primary feature revealed is the incessant attempt to bring the general public into the process of government while at all times retaining control in the Communist party and the centralized state administration. Only during Mao Tse-tung's "Great Proletarian Cultural Revolution" of 1966–67 was this

[51] Grose, *Gain for Peking Moderates Seen in Provincial Regions* (including map). N.Y. Times, 19 Apr. 1968 at 5.

[52] Law of 20 Sept. 1965 [1965] 38 Ved. Verkh. Sov. R.S.F.S.R. item 932.

pattern upset, and then, apparently, because he had lost personal control both over the bureaucratic elements within the Communist party and over the central state administration. Elsewhere within the family of Marxian socialist states there was no such setback, although there was considerable experimentation, beginning with Stalin's loss of Yugoslav loyalty in 1948 in his pique over Tito's refusal to follow his leadership.

Yugoslavia and China have emerged as the most adventurous members of the family in their departure from the model established by the Soviet Communists. The Yugoslavs cut their government's apron strings by departing from the strict hierarchical administrative responsibility for which the Stalin's system was famous. They also sought to reduce the hold maintained by professional administrators over the administrative apparatus by abolishing the local assembly's executive committee and making technicians responsible to commissions functioning within the assembly.

The Chinese, on the other hand, increased the role of the professional administrators in local administration before the radical reforms of 1966 by giving them a near monopoly in the assemblies. The Chinese chose to make their play for public participation not where the European Communists had made it, in the assemblies, but by enlarging the activity of mass organizations, notably "street committees," charged with looking "up the ladder" to control the bureaucrats. The Chinese hostility to public participation in administration extended even to agriculture, where their collective farm law, which they had borrowed from the Russians, gave the farmers themselves, de jure, a voice in their own self-administration. The Chinese overturned this model by introducing the "communes," in which the administration of the farms was combined with that of local government and placed in the hands of "cadres." Mao Tse-tung's "Great Proletarian Cultural Revolution" set as one of its goals debureaucratization of the cadre apparatus, thus suggesting the extent to which Mao feared that the principle of popular participation had faded away and needed reassertion.

The evolution of the model developed for the state apparatus in the Marxian socialist family is dramatic, but it must not obscure the fact that major characteristics remain that distinguish the mechanism which has emerged in Communist-led states from that used to govern elsewhere. The theme of "class" continues to sound, even though it has been muted in the USSR since espousal of the concept of the "state of the whole people." Administrative centralization under the slogan of "democratic centralism" is widely proclaimed, although the degree of centralism varies. The Communist party remains the unassailable guide, except perhaps in China, where, since 1966, the army has been catapulted to a front-line position by Mao Tse-tung in his factional struggle with the professionals within the party. The separation of powers is everywhere rejected as a feature of governmental organization, to be replaced by the concept of unity of power in the assembly. Finally, nonprofessionalism in the performance of the representative function is hailed as a much-to-be-desired feature through which the deputy retains his relationship to his job. Only Poland adheres to the more traditional pattern of legislation by deputies devoting full time to their roles, and then only on the national level.

The Communists of the USSR, in reviewing the lessons of the fifty years after 1917, showed satisfaction with their creation. To them "the soviets as the form of the dictatorship of the proletariat and as organs of genuine popular rule of socialist democracy," have proved their value by the test of history.[53] This achievement was listed with items more closely identifiable with Marxian doctrinal pronouncements as a major feature of the Marxian socialist type of society. Although the idea was accepted that there may be variation in state structure, it became clear that, in the view of the celebrators of fifty years, a primary feature of the governmental system was the instrument from which the laws issue and in which is centered the mechanism of public administration.

Later, when loyalty to the model was put to the test in Czechoslovakia in 1968, nothing was made of differences in state structure between the USSR and the Czechoslovak republic. On the contrary, the editorial writers of *Pravda*, in their August editorial explaining why military measures had become necessary, chose this element as the major proof that the Soviet model of socialism was not being foisted on Czechoslovakia

[53] Resolution of C.P.S.U. Central Committee, 4 Jan. 1967. Pravda, 8 Jan. 1967 at 1. Eng. transl. in 19 C.D.S.P. no. 1 at 11 (1967).

from outside. The editors wrote, "It is common knowledge that the USSR and Czechoslovakia have different state structures, different methods of solving the nationalities question, and dissimilar systems of economic management."

In spite of this disclaimer an element of conformity was being enforced by the Soviet army. It was the aspect of leadership by the Communist party, which is nowhere so important as in the soviets. Were soviets to lose this feature, they would lose in Moscow's eyes their primary element of distinction and suitability to the task of creating a Marxian socialist society. As a careful student of the Marxian socialist system has concluded, "In concrete terms, the Czechoslovak intervention suggests that the Soviet Union will intervene when the following developments take place: . . . (4) the restoration of parliamentary government, whose power, responsibility and accountability would be to the electorate rather than the Communist party." [54]

The state form may vary, therefore, but never to the extent that the Communist party's leadership is lost. China's state form has been militarized beyond recognition as a variation on the USSR's model, although Mao Tse-tung has been struggling to recreate as an important, if not the primary, element a party responsive to his leadership as his prereform party was. The Soviet ideologues have been vitriolic in condemning these efforts as fraudulent. The editors of *Kommunist* have written, "The idea is to make the army, as well as the 'Red Guards' and the rebels who have shown their personal devotion to Mao Tse-tung, the backbone of the Party." [55] As to the state apparatus, the *Kommunist* editors say, "The Mao group has also adopted a policy of undermining state institutions of people's power. . . . Elected local organs of people's power have been disbanded and are being replaced by 'revolutionary committees,' cultivated by the Mao group."

The outsider can only conclude that the state form is not

[54] Aspaturian, *The Soviet Union and Eastern Europe: The Aftermath of the Czechoslovak Invasion*, New York University Conference on the Impact of Czechoslovak Events on Current International Relations. 6 December 1968 (mimeographed) 18.

[55] *On the Nature of the "Cultural Revolution" in China*, [1968] KOMMUNIST no. 7. Eng. transl. in 8 REPRINTS FROM THE SOVIET PRESS, nos. 3 & 4 at 3. (1968).

inconsequential to the Marxian socialist family's distinctive features. Wide variation is permitted by those who guard orthodoxy, but there is a minimal standard from which no member may depart. China's protection has been its size and strength. The hard truth is that its leader cannot be made to conform to a pattern laid down from abroad.

4

Flexibility versus Stability

No declaration on the nature of law or on its role in a Marxian socialist society was proclaimed in 1957 as a test of orthodoxy. Probably the leaders of the twelve Communist parties thought it unnecessary, for it could have been presumed to be a part of the socialist revolution in ideology and culture they were demanding in any state within the Marxist family. Certainly, no Marxist can fail to know the traditional Marxist attitude toward law. It has been stated simply enough since the beginning in all Marxist texts. Only the application of their theory was left unclear by the classic writers, and even that had been clarified by the experience of the Communists of the Soviet Union.

To begin with the texts, the most noted phrase distinctive of the Marxist approach to law is that of Lenin, "A law is a political instrument; it is politics." [1] His words, written just before the Russian revolution, epitomized rejection by Communists of a concept of law as a stable force beyond the reach of man. Law was seen as a flexible instrument of social engineering, to be used after a proletarian revolution to move society

[1] Lenin, *Concerning a Caricature of Marxism and Concerning "Imperialist" Economism*, 23 Sochineniia 36 [Works] (4th ed. 1949).

toward the goal of abundance and self-discipline set by Marx and Engels in their *Communist Manifesto* of 1848.

Marxists would have introduced nothing new had they stopped with a position which one natural-law philosopher has characterized as "but positivism pushed to its logical extreme." [2] Their much-heralded distinguishing ingredient was "class." To them law can be conceived only as a class instrument utilized to achieve a ruler's ends, since they believe that all societies are governed by their dominant economic classes.

Marx had put his idea in straightforward words in the *Manifesto* when he castigated the bourgeoisie of his day with the charge, "Your jurisprudence is but the will of your class made into a law for all." [3] Twenty years after the Russian revolution, Andrei Vyshinsky, as Stalin's legal philosopher, demonstrated the enduring nature of Marxist thought when he wrote, "Law is no 'enigmatic shape' but a living reality expressing the essence of social relationships between classes." [4]

Acting upon these principles, Lenin established an official position immediately after victory in 1917. He had risen to power with no time to blueprint a legislative program, for the months of 1917 after his return from exile, while the old regime was tottering, had been tumultuous. He had written his "State and Revolution" while hiding in a hut in Finland for fear of arrest by the provisional government, but he felt the urge to return to Petrograd to participate in the October revolutionary events rather than to complete his text. In consequence, at the time of the revolt he had only considered some important fundamentals. He had not decided how concrete meaning was to be given in practice to the concept of "dictatorship of the proletariat" during the initial years of proletarian revolution; and he did not know what ultimate impact upon the state and its law should be anticipated from Marx's expectation that with the achievement of communism the state must "wither away."

Lenin had no codes of any kind ready to introduce on the

[2] Wu, *Law* in THE CATHOLIC ENCYCLOPEDIA, Sixth Section, supplement II at 13, col. 1 (1955).

[3] MARX & ENGELS, THE COMMUNIST MANIFESTO, part II (1848).

[4] A. VYSHINSKY, THE LAW OF THE SOVIET STATE 38 (1948). Originally pub. in Russian in 1938.

floor of the Congress of Soviets when it met to legislate after the fall of the Winter Palace. He asked only for decrees declaring the principle of land socialization, the policy of ending the war, and the establishment of a new form of government based upon the soviets and utilizing as its executive arm a "Council of People's Commissars" to be chaired by himself.[5] Codification took five years for everything except the protection of the working man from his employer by a code of labor laws [6] and the establishment of a system of domestic relations that was freed from religious institutions and from feudal concepts of wifely subordination to a powerful husband.[7]

Meanwhile, a new system of courts loyal to the working class was created by the first decree on the courts, and was given instructions to apply the old imperial codes, but with caution.[8] No former law was to be enforced unless it corresponded to the requirements of the new society as established by the "revolutionary consciousness" of the judges. This formula made for "flexibility," and the principle was strengthened a year later by the People's Court Act of 1918,[9] which banned all reference to imperial law under any circumstances and directed the new judges to guide themselves by reference to such limited individual decrees as had been promulgated. For the rest they were to judge matters on the basis of their "socialist concept of justice." The judges were free to do as they wished in most matters, subject only to advice from the people's commissar of justice, who analyzed practice for them and noted decisions which deserved to be called good or bad. No appellate tribunal was created for some years to provide uniformity, although the "people's judges" of each district met from time to time to discuss problems and to concert their understanding of what was required in applying a "socialist concept of justice."

Lenin eventually found himself led by economic chaos to retreat from the stage of "militant communism" to a modified

---

[5] 1 S'EZDY SOVETOV V DOKUMENTAKH 1917–36 at 8–15 (1959) [The Congresses of Soviets in Documents].

[6] Decree undated. Printed in official collection, 10 Dec. 1918. [1918] 87–88 Sob. Uzak. R.S.F.S.R. pt. I. item 905.

[7] Decree of 22 Oct. 1918, [1918] 76–77 *id*. item 818.

[8] Decree of 27 Nov. 1917, [1917] 4 *id*. item 50, sec. 5.

[9] Decree of 30 Nov. 1918, [1918] 85 *id*. item 889.

form of capitalism operating under severe restraints and in a narrow sector of the economy. Only then did codification begin; but the concept of "flexibility" was still retained. In both the criminal [10] and the civil [11] codes, enacted in 1922, it was incorporated in important articles. The criminal code's Article 10 instructed judges to use the code as a guide in punishing "by analogy" to its specific provisions any acts deemed socially dangerous even if they were not so defined in the code. The civil code's Article 1 authorized judges to depart from the letter of the law when private rights were exercised in contradiction of their social and economic purpose.

By both the criminal and the civil codes of 1922 judges were invited to be "flexible" in application of the law, and the outside world came to believe that flexibility was such a cardinal feature of the new Soviet legal system that it put in question its very right to claim the respected status of "law." Of course Western scholars from the various schools of natural law took this position; but even positivists, who were prepared to recognize in law only the hands of the men who made it, considered such uncertainty a major qualitative departure from accepted standards. They found none of the stability and predictability which they deemed fundamental to even a positivist's concept of "rule of law." [12]

The 1920s witnessed frequent application of both the criminal code's and the civil code's flexibility bias. Studies of the period show that in 1922, courts applying Article 10 utilized its provisions to increase penalties above those prescribed by specific articles and even to define new crimes. Thus, the crime of "economic counterrevolution" was developed without legislative amendment of the code, as were other crimes for which no provision had been made. [13]

This expansion of the criminal code was the more remarka-

---

[10] Decree undated. Effective 1 June 1922, [1922] 15 *id.* item 153.

[11] Decree of 31 Oct. 1922, [1922] 71 *id.* item 904.

[12] See H. KELSEN, THE COMMUNIST THEORY OF LAW 193 (1955) in which the noted positivist declares Soviet legal theory deplorable because of its link to politics.

[13] VSESOIUZNYI INSTITUT IURIDICHESKIKH NAUK. MINISTERSTVO IUSTITSII SSSR, UGOLOVNOE PRAVO, OBSHCHAIA CHAST' 247–48 (4th ed. 1948) [All Union Institute of Juridical Sciences. Ministry of Justice of the USSR, Criminal Law. General Part].

ble because at the time of its enactment the People's Commissariat of Justice had issued a circular saying: "As a general rule punishment and other measures of social defense may be applied by courts only with respect to acts specifically indicated in the criminal code. Exceptions to this rule are permitted only in those special circumstances when the acts of the defendant are held by the court to be clearly dangerous even though not anticipated by the criminal code." [14]

An author of the time optimistically regarded this circular as a basis for excluding "the danger of Article 10's harmful impact in the sense of establishing the possibility of upsetting the organized step-by-step advance of the system of criminal law compulsion" and as a basis "for preserving all of its positive characteristics." [15] In spite of his confidence in the eventual evolution of a stable system of criminal law, the principle of analogy was restated in the second criminal code of 1926,[16] and expansion of the catalog of crimes proceeded swiftly in application of the policy of flexibility.

A climax was reached following Stalin's 1929–30 campaign to stamp out the "kulaks" as a class of rich peasants and to protect the newly favored collective farms from depredations. A law of 7 August 1932 [17] established the death penalty for thefts from collective farms, cooperatives, and state transport. Almost immediately the spirit of this extraordinary law radiated in several directions. Flexibility became the slogan of the times. Not only the legislature, but the Council of People's Commissars and the presidiums of the supreme courts of the USSR and of the Russian republic took a hand in extending the concept of death for property offenses.[18] Thus, the legislature declared it a

[14] This position was restated for many years. See Trainin, *Practical Commentary to Arts. 10 and 16–19 of the Criminal Code* of the R.S.F.S.R., [1940] 7 Sov. IUST 6.

[15] A. PIONTKOVSKII, UGOLOVNOE PRAVO RSFSR, CHAST OBSHCHAIA 215–16 (1924) [The Criminal Law of the R.S.F.S.R.].

[16] 22 Nov. 1926, effective 1 Jan. 1927. [1926] 80 Sob. Uzak. R.S.F.S.R. pt. I item 600. Eng. transl. as THE PENAL CODE OF THE RUSSIAN FEDERAL SOVIET REPUBLIC (1934).

[17] [1932] 62 Sob. Zak SSSR pt. I item 360.

[18] The measures given herein are taken from G. ROGINSKII & D. KARPINSKII, UGOLOVNOE KODEKS RSFSR, POSOBIE DLIA IURIDICHESKIKH VUZOV, SHKOL I KURSOV 97–99 (1936) [The Criminal Code of the R.S.F.S.R., Study Aid for Juridical Institutes, Schools, and Courses].

capital crime to distribute illegally the seed-grain reserve of the farm, to damage intentionally tractors or agricultural machines or to destroy horses, and even to falsify collective farm records on production of labor.

By joint party and administrative order, the law was interpreted as applying to theft of seeds from granaries, to intentional reduction of the sown acreage, or to intentionally poor work by a shepherd or sower. By R.S.F.S.R. court order the law was extended to those who clearly did not take measures to protect socialist property entrusted to their care; to those who mixed grain with substitutes in order to meet the weights of grain required as deliveries to the state; and to those who took without authority items of farm property which had become the property of the cooperative, if it was done to weaken the farm or was conducted in an organized manner or by a group. The USSR supreme court extended the law to thefts from the state savings banks by officials or by private citizens.

Flexible extension by analogy of the statute of 7 August 1932 by trial courts quickly went to such extremes that the People's Commissariat of Justice finally found it necessary to issue an order in November 1932 concerning errors in court work, noting application of the law to crimes not provided for, conviction of persons without sufficient evidence, retroactive application of the law in circumstances when neither the political importance of the case nor expediency required it, and its application to workers in insignificant cases.

Promulgation of the second federal constitution in 1936 brought a temporary lull in the application of the principle because Stalin introduced the draft to the constitutional convention with a demand for "stability of laws." [19] This was a surprise, coming from the man most responsible for instability, but legal authors thereafter seized upon his words to treat the new constitution as a watershed. The following year, discussions necessitated by the new constitutional requirement that federal codes be enacted to replace those of the republics opened the debate on the need for analogy under the new conditions. Some argued that the analogy concept negated the newly enunciated principle of stability, but others supported its retention on the

---

[19] Stalin, *On the Draft Constitution of the U.S.S.R.*, 1936., LENINISM: SELECTED WRITINGS 402 (1942).

ground that no such conflict existed. They felt that because the code had authorized application of the principle, and because judicial rulings in the late 1930s had subjected application to such severe limitations, there could be no real violation of the new principle of stability—in particular no increase in penalty beyond that prescribed in the code for a given crime.

The debate raged in the pages of the law reviews, but before action could be taken in the direction of stability, Nazi troops crossed the Soviet Union's frontier on 22 June 1941. The principle of analogy regained its vigor, but usually in increasing penalties for established crime rather than in creating new crimes. Thus, judges subjected theft of personal property from vacated apartments and home brewing of vodka to far heavier penalties than before the war because evacuations had enhanced the opportunities for theft and the war had increased the need for a sober labor force. The prosecutor general hailed the analogy principle as making possible quick changes of judicial policy without legislative action.[20]

Immediately after the war, an author reminded his readers that although analogy remained in the code, its application was limited to narrow circumstances.[21] He recalled Stalin's demand of 1936 by saying "otherwise it would lead to violation of the principle of stability of law." Nevertheless, the courts continued to apply analogy, usually to permit a sentence of death not for property crimes, as in the 1930s, but for sadistic murder, group rape, and especially malicious rowdyism, for all of which the 1926 code had established only prison terms. To take this step, the courts considered the crimes analogous to banditry, for which the code had long provided capital punishment because of the severe threat to public order caused by roving bands. Only later was the code amended by statute to incorporate what had become judicial practice.[22]

---

[20] Shargorodskii, *Questions concerning the General Section of Criminal Law under Wartime Conditions*, Uch. zap. vyp. 76. Trudy Iurid. fak. M.G.U., Kniga I. 100 at 104 (1945) [Scientific studies, issue 76. Works of the Law Faculty of Moscow State University, Book I].

[21] I. Goliakov, Ugolovnoe pravo 53 (2d ed. 1947) [Criminal Law].

[22] Decree of 30 April 1954, [1954] 11 Ved. Verkh. Sov. SSSR, extending to persons committing murder under aggravated circumstances the decree of 12 Jan. 1950 establishing the death penalty for treason, espionage, and wrecking.

Not until the completion in 1958 of the text of a new set of federal fundamental principles of criminal law [23] was the principle of analogy dropped from the codes, and then only after prolonged debate, resolved after the deaths of Stalin and Vyshinsky. By that time Stalin's political heirs had given support to the reformist law professors who had been arguing for years that analogy was outmoded in a legal system espousing stability.

The concept of analogy and the flexibility it sanctioned had been generally recognized by that time as the instruments Stalin utilized to establish his personal dictatorship through terrorist practices. The desire to preserve flexible application of law was finally brought to an end officially when communist leaders realized the futility and even danger of flexibly applied law in a society which claimed to have emerged from its turbulent stage and moved forward to a period of construction of communism.

This realization was expressed in Khrushchev's 1956 speech to his party colleagues in denunciation of Stalin's memory; but old attitudes die hard, especially at lower levels in the state hierarchy. This became evident as late as 1965 when the president of the supreme court of the Kirghiz republic reported from Central Asia, "We have not overcome the effort of some prosecutors and court workers to punish the guilty severely. To do so they do not hesitate even to qualify the crime under a law providing for a more severe penalty." [24] This was exactly what courts had done earlier in applying the principle of analogy. Clearly Central Asian practice had not yet caught up with the new times.

The transition from flexibility to stability was somewhat similar in the realm of civil law, except that the concept of flexibility faded faster as a desideratum of a Marxian-based system of law administered for the benefit of what was defined as the working class.

All legal systems provide for restraints on private rights being used to inconvenience neighbors unnecessarily, as in the

[23] 25 Dec. 1958, [1959] 1 *id.* item 6. The setting for change is described by F. FELDBRUGGE, SOVIET CRIMINAL LAW: GENERAL PART 77–78 (1964).
[24] [1965] 9 Sots. Zak. 77.

construction of a spite fence, the commission of a nuisance, or acting in bad faith. The legal system being codified by Lenin's lawyers in 1922 to meet the needs of a limited restoration of capitalist enterprise could have been expected to follow Western models in forbidding such abuse of right. The question that arose in the minds of foreign analysts of Soviet law at the time was whether the Communists intended to go further than Western jurists in applying the civil code's Article 1.

Lenin had set the stage for interpretation of his concept years earlier when he denied that civil law in the Soviet system would respect the ancient Roman concept of a sharp distinction between private and public spheres of law. He had declared that "all law is public," [25] by which he meant that there is a state interest in every transaction, even those traditionally private in nature, in which the major concern is an individual's transferring property or performing services by means of contract. He wanted to provide for annulment of contracts by state intervention if they appeared to run counter to the development of soviet society, especially if they took advantage of working-class elements. His New Economic Policy of 1921 permitted capitalists to function in the interests of restoring the devastated nation's economy, but they were not to enrich themselves at the expense of the working class. Article 1 was looked upon as more than the usual Western provision against abuse of right. It was to incorporate a "class" concept.

Judicial decisions soon began to apply the article. They were analyzed in the 1920s by authors both within and outside the USSR to determine whether a new form of flexibility had been introduced in practice to conform to the class line established by theory.[26] An order of the R.S.F.S.R. supreme court in 1924 indicated that the court thought the article was used excessively by the trial courts, for it warned against citing the article to avoid having to solve a difficult situation by quoting government statements of policy rather than appropriate articles of the code. In 1924 the supreme court again warned that the article was being used to simplify the courts' work by providing

[25] V. LENIN, 29 SOCHINENIIA 419 (3d ed. 1928–37). [Works].
[26] 1 V. GSOVSKI, SOVIET CIVIL LAW 325–26 (1948). Also see Greaves, *The Social Economic Purpose of Private Rights*, 12 N.Y.U.L.Q. 165 and 439 (1934–35).

a basis for arguing policy rather than analyzing the legal situation created by the facts in relation to the code. Excessive zeal in applying the code to permit confiscation of private property or renunciation of a lease was found by the supreme court in three decisions: failure to use tableware which was kept idle in a cellar; profitable private use of a mill leased from the local soviet, on the ground that a private lessee may not make a profit; and use of a leased mill so it became unprofitable for the local soviet under the payment provisions of the lease within one year of the making of the lease.

Application of the article was held to be correct by the supreme courts both of the R.S.F.S.R. and of the Ukrainian republic when the owner of productive property refused to use it. Thus, a mill owner lost his mill when he left it unused after refusing to pay the operation tax; lithographic machinery was taken from a nonusing owner; a storehouse was confiscated after lying unused for nine years; a small-factory owner was deprived of ownership when he closed the factory to avoid payment of a tax; a plant owner was ousted when he ran the plant at less than full capacity; a cattle-breeding ranch was taken away because it was not used for the purpose for which it had been denationalized.

Application of Article 1 terminated, however, along with the period of the New Economic Policy, and no decisions were recorded after 1930. This might have been expected, since large-scale productive property could no longer be owned. The five-year plans were inaugurated in 1928 to foster the development of state-owned production in accordance with a national economic plan, and the private owners of the 1920s were taxed out of existence.

With the change in circumstances, the question was raised years later whether Article 1 had a place in a Soviet civil code. Some thought its application should revert to Western usage, only to prevent chicanery and abuse of right, as in the building of spite fences around property to which an occupant had been assigned the right of perpetual use. Since the class enemies had been eliminated by 1936 through abolition of their base in the private ownership of productive property, flexibility no longer seemed necessary to the progress of the revolution. Those who felt this way argued that the article was unnecessary except in circumstances constituting violation of the ordinary rules of neighborliness.

A basis for such a view had been established by the second federal constitution of 1936. Not only was stability of law demanded as a new desideratum, as has already been indicated, but a principle was incorporated in Article 130 requiring citizens to observe the rules of socialist communal living. Some Soviet authors felt that Article 1 had taken on new meaning: protection of the constitution's Article 130 and no more. A distinguished professor of civil law argued that it was time to change even its terms to limit it clearly to the prevention of chicanery, and he proposed that its 1922 form be deleted from the proposed federal civil code.[27]

The war and postwar reconstruction prevented work on the federal codes for some years, but when the draftsmen again took up their pens, the necessity of incorporating the concept of Article 1 in fundamentals of civil law was raised again. Voices were heard against it, but the conservatives prevailed. The principle was restated in similar form in Article 5 of the 1961 fundamentals: "Civil rights are protected by law, except in instances when they are exercised in a manner inconsistent with their purpose in a socialist society in the period of the building of communism. In exercising their rights and performing their obligations, citizens and organizations must observe the law, and must respect the rules of socialist communal living and the moral principles of a society which is building communism."

No annotations to judicial decisions have been placed under this article in the commentaries that have appeared in the USSR since its enactment. In private conversation Soviet professors have suggested that retention of the concept of old Article 1 is by no means a sign that "flexibility" in the sense of the 1920s will be restored to Soviet civil law.

The trial courts have not been so sparing as the professors in their view of the utility of Article 5, however, citing it unnecessarily, in the view of a commentator, when one of the more

---

[27] Agarkov, *The Problems of Misuse of Rights in Soviet Civil Law*, [1946] 6 Izv. ak. nauk sssr, otd. ek. i prava 424.

specific prohibitions of the code would have sufficed to prevent the exercise of an otherwise legal right.[28] In order to provide guidance, two specialists have suggested limits to deflect judges from referring generally to Article 5 when a more specific article is appropriate.[29] Their hypothetical cases reveal academic thinking. Thus, they would prevent a homeowner who ordinarily enjoys the right to protect his personal property from erecting a charged electric fence around private orchards or vegetable gardens. They would apply the article to deny an author his otherwise legal right to protect the inviolability of his works if he demands the destruction of an entire printing because the editor made changes, if the changes are lacking in serious and significant distortion. The specialists argue that granting such a demand would deprive society of desirable literature. They would also deny an heir his otherwise legal right to prevent publication of his father's manuscript if it is deemed of substantial scientific significance and would be of considerable value to society if published. Finally, they would apply the article whenever a right is employed with the specific, morally condemned object of doing harm to another person.

It seems justifiable to conclude that Article 5 has meaning in the general Western European sense to prevent unneighborly acts, and that it is not to be applied as was Article 1 of the 1922 code in implementation of a policy of "class justice." Such a policy ended formally with adoption by the Communist party of the 1961 program announcing achievement of the "state of the whole people." With the new code Article 5 is designed to strike down not the class enemy but the citizen devoid of a sense of what is required of the good neighbor. If the Soviet code is novel in comparison with those of Western Europe, it is because of the definition of "neighbor." He is no longer only the man next door, or the villager who passes in the street. He is the citizen in general, the member of society as a whole, the reading public denied of its right to enjoy the literary produc-

---

[28] E. FLEISHITS, NAUCHNO-PRAKTICHESKII KOMMENTARII K G. K. RSFSR 17 (1966) [Scientific-Practical Commentary to the Civil Code of the R.S.F.S.R.]

[29] Ioffe & Gribanov, *The Limits of Exercise of the Rights of Parties in Civil Law,* [1964] 7 Sov. GOS. I PRAVO 76. Eng. transl. in 3 SOVIET LAW AND GOVERNMENT no. 4 at 31 (1965).

tions of its authors when they or their heirs seek to withhold publication for reasons that seem whimsical to the Soviet judges.

Although the Soviet experience of fifty years suggests that for Communists in the USSR flexibility is a principle of Marxist-inspired law to be fostered only during a turbulent period when social relationships are undergoing extensive reorientation, the experience in other Marxist-oriented legal systems presents conflicting evidence. On one side stand Poland and Yugoslavia; on the other is the People's Republic of China.

Polish Communists have from the beginning rejected a concept of flexibility in criminal law. They have refused to incorporate in their code authorization to punish by analogy. In private conversation Polish law professors declare such a concept counter to the Romanist tradition of which they feel themselves a part, in spite of their Marxist orientation. They are not alone among Eastern European lawyers, for the same view comes from their counterparts in Romania, Hungary, and Czechoslovakia. The record shows that no East-European Marxist-oriented draftsmen have followed the pre-1958 Soviet example to incorporate an "analogy" provision in the criminal codes.

Analysis of the extent to which flexibility has been and may still be a desideratum of Marxist-oriented lawyers cannot be limited to attitudes toward "analogy"; for flexibility can also be achieved through loosely drafted definitions of crime. The broadly stated crimes which in the USSR before 1958 were called "counterrevolution" provide notable examples. Their definitions will be discussed in subsequent chapters, but a word should be said at this point. Czechoslovak revelations in 1968 of the injustices committed against large numbers of innocent persons during the years of Soviet domination of Prague policies make the point that the law was not precise and inflexible. These same revelations bear witness, however, to the pent-up dissatisfaction even among the Communists with what was done in the past in the name of law and order. It is evident that unless reaction is forced upon them by Stalinist-minded leaders both within their country and outside, a trend toward stability of law will continue. No judge is to receive carte blanche to define crime as he wishes. His role is to be limited to interpretation. He cannot act as a legislator in determining the basic characteristics, objective and subjective, of criminality.

Although this rigid position has been increasingly favored in the people's democracies of Eastern Europe as they develop attitudes toward criminal punishment, the same has not been true for civil law. In this field, the Soviet pattern has been followed closely enough to suggest that a primary feature of the Marxian socialist legal family has been its emphasis upon preserving within the system some "flexibility." Herein may be found a qualitative distinction from other legal families, where flexibility plays a part, but in a more restrained fashion. The Polish situation provides an example.[30]

General provisions of civil law were adopted in Poland in 1950 [31] to guide the legal profession in applying the 1933 code of obligations, which was kept in force after the Communists seized power, unlike the situation in the Soviet Russian republic of 1917. The statute opened with a general statement that "rules of law have to be construed and applied in accordance with the [fundamental] principles of the structure and the goals of the People's State." Then followed in Article 3 a provision copied almost exactly from the Soviet code's Article 1, that "Rights cannot be exercised in a manner violating the principles of social communal living in the People's State." The principal difference between the two codes was that the Soviet code had required adherence to "socialist" principles, whereas the Polish code referred to the broader concept of "social" principles, perhaps because in 1950 Poland had no pretension to having achieved a "socialist" society. It was only on the road.

It was up to the courts to put meaning into this principle. Since the Polish courts with their Romanist tradition could have been expected to apply Article 3 in keeping with that tradition's practice, exemplified by the French courts, which refuse to enforce code-created rights in the event of abuse of right, the extent of Marxist influence is not easy to measure. The French author Léon Duguit argued in the early twentieth century that an exercise of right was an abuse and therefore

---

[30] Rudzinski, *Marxist Ethics and Polish Law*, 11 NATURAL LAW FORUM 48 (1966). Because Dr. Rudzinski's study may not be available in Europe, citations to the documents utilized by him are repeated here.

[31] Statute of 18 July 1950, [1950] 34 J. of L. Poland item 311.

illegal if it was contrary to its social function and social purpose and if if inflicted serious damage on neighbors or on the community. In keeping with this view Western courts refused to support code-defined rights when they were exercised to damage or annoy neighbors or others. This was labeled "chicanery," devoid of legal protection. Generally, however, the denial of legal protection prescribed by the code was limited in the mind of Western jurists to cases when the abuser lacked good faith.

Likewise, in Western Romanist systems, to merit enforcement under the code contracts have to conform to an ill-defined concept of *ordre public*, which is broader than "public order" as known to the Anglo-American common law in that it incorporates an element of commonly accepted ethics or *bonnes moeurs*.

Romanist tradition generally denies the protection of rights established by law only in the event of flagrant violation of those principles of ethics which society accepts. In general, law must be observed by a court resolving a dispute, and this is surely so when an express right is created by statute or code.

Polish practice emerged in the decisions of the new supreme court of the people's republic. Many of them concerned the claims of landlords for eviction of tenants who violated established provisions of the law. In all of these there was an element of class conflict in the Marxist sense, for the landlords who were still permitted to own real property under the new regime were considered hostile capitalists, even though they were tolerated by a system that was as yet unable to build and administer state housing. The right of eviction for failure to pay rent, which was sanctioned under statute law still in force, was terminated by a supreme court decision of 1952 applying Article 3.[32] The argument was that "Since the State exerts particular efforts to provide homes for everyone, no one may create a new need [for shelter] for the exclusive reason that he has a civil law claim for eviction." Although such a policy has been adopted in Western Europe in times of housing crises, it has been done by statute, not by court decision. In this lay the Polish contrast.

Polish civil law was brought into concert with Soviet law by

[32] Judgment of 21 Nov. 1950, C 345/50, [1951] Panstwo i prawo 741.

a decision terminating the awarding of pecuniary damages for physical pain and mental grief caused by the death of a spouse, child, or parent. Although the civil code's provision remained technically in force, the supreme court concluded in 1951 [33] that recovery of damages under such circumstances violated Article 3; but a curious provision was added that permitted the family of the deceased to demand that the party causing the death pay an appropriate sum to a social institution named by the family. Social communal living as understood by the new leadership in Poland seemed at that time to limit damages in the event of injury to purely material losses, as it still does in the USSR. Again, such a rule might have been established by statute without affecting the concept of stability, but when created by a court decision, it introduced an element of flexible application of the law for parties who could not have anticipated such a result when suit was brought.

The defense of homicide under stress of emotion was limited in practice in 1951, even though authorized by the Polish penal code then in force.[34] The court argued that Polish socialist morals were different from bourgeois morals. Poles were told that vengeance and jealousy must be regarded as base emotions because they arise from craving for power.

Class conflict was found in a suit for removal of a tenant's pigeon coop from the backyard of an apartment house. The tenant, a worker, argued that pigeon raising was a favorite working-man's hobby, and should be countenanced. The supreme court acted warily in this situation on request of the trial court for an opinion on whether Article 3 should be applied to prevent the landlord from exercising a landlord's right to determine how property shall be utilized.[35] The supreme court stressed the class character of the law suit, but preferred to avoid the question posed, remanding the case for further elucidation of facts. What happened subsequently was not revealed by the reports.

Divorce cases also gave rise to interpretations of Article 3. In

[33] Decision of 1/15 Dec. 1951, C 15/51, [1952] id. 877, reaff. by resol. of the full civil chamber, [1957] id. 1141.

[34] Decision of 23 Jan. 1952, [1952] id. 895.

[35] [1962] id. 351.

1951 the court found it possible to grant a divorce on that basis because of conflicting ideologies, saying, "Conflicting ideologies on political and social questions, especially if one of the spouses represents a progressive conception of life and the other, on the contrary, a backward one, justify divorce." [36] Not only were dissolutions granted in cases of marriage across class lines, but dissolution of adoptions was also permitted under similar circumstances.

Article 3 was even used to create a legal duty not established by statute. Thus, the moral obligation to work overtime for a trade union, youth organization, musical group, or sports club was changed by the supreme court into a legal duty in 1953 and in 1954.[37] The court found that a consistent refusal by an employee to participate in social work of this character was sufficient ground for termination of an employment contract. The guilty party was deprived of his job.

The socialized sector, composed of the state economic enterprises, received protection under Article 3 when in conflict with the private sector. In 1952 the court declared "An individual cannot use his right deriving from his private property in such an inconsiderate manner as to create serious difficulties in the implementation of tasks which according to the economic plan a unit of the socialized economy has to achieve." [38] In the same year, the court nullified those provisions of the civil code which contrasted with the statutes relating to state enterprises, even when relationships between private entrepreneurs were concerned, by saying that it was inconceivable that members of the private-enterprise sector should enjoy greater protection in law than the socialized sector's enterprises.

State enterprises were given by court decision rights not included within the statutes concerning them. Thus, in 1953 the court permitted termination by a state enterprise of an employment contract even through the management had not conformed to the requirement of the collective agreement that termination occur only with the consent of the labor union

[36] Decision of 11/29 Dec. 1951, [1952] *id.* 729.

[37] Decision of 29 April 1953, [1954] 6 Przeglad Zagadnien Spolecznych 54 and decision of 29 July 1954, [1955] 2 OSN 86.

[38] Decision of 16 Oct. 1952, [1953] Panstwo i prawo 821.

concerned.[39] Statutes at the time required that collective agreements be enforced as contracts between the parties.

Although flexibility proved to be the rule in practice in the early years of Marxist-oriented civil law in Poland, a change began even before the riots of 1956, which dramatically marked the end of the turbulent revolutionary period. Some trace of an attempt to limit the application of Article 3 is found in 1951, when extensive application of the concept of flexibility was still in vogue. The supreme court at that time refused to interpret Article 3 as a source of claims and rights,[40] ruling that it could be used only to defeat the claims of others based on statutes or acts deemed to have violated the rules of social communal living. In 1955 the court said that Article 3 was to shelter a debtor, not to serve as the basis for counterclaims against a creditor.[41]

In 1952 the court again attempted to limit excessive reliance on Article 3 when it said that the article should be applied only when the violation was clear and evident, when the sanctioning of statutory norms of law would clearly offend the moral sentiments of the toiling masses.[42] In 1953 the court moved to restrict flexible application of statutes adopted by the new state, saying that "the principles of social intercourse can never lead to a modification of explicit dispositions of socialist law in the People's State." [43] Under this ruling, Article 3 was narrowed in application to prevent enforcement of prewar statutes adopted, in Marxist terminology, by the bourgeoisie. Article 3 must become only a means of adapting old statutes to new purposes, not a means of decreasing stability in application of the new statute itself.

By 1956 resistance to Stalinism was in the air in Poland, even before the riots of October. The supreme court heralded the new emphasis when, in February 1955, its civil chamber adopted a plenary resolution stating, "People's legality means the duty of citizens to observe the laws in force. While impos-

---

[39] Decision of 30 Dec. 1953, [1954] 4 OSN item 84, quoted in [1961] 4 *id.* item 115 at 86.

[40] Decision of 17 April 1951, [1952] 2 ZOSN 179.

[41] Decision of 25 April/7 May 1955, [1955] 12 NOWE PRAWO 104.

[42] Decision of 13/27 Oct. 1952, [1953] 3 OSN 105.

[43] Decision of 5/19 Sept. 1953, [1954] 2 NOWE PRAWO 92.

ing this duty on the citizens it is not permissible to obscure the actual meaning of the law and to expose citizens to unexpected situations and surprises." [44] Later in the same year, the court repeated its position by saying, "A presumption exists that the provisions of law are in conformity with the binding principles of social intercourse." [45] After the October 1956 riots the court again stated the rule, saying, "Article 3 . . . cannot be applied when the statute itself provides in a concrete norm the legal basis for abolition or limitation of the right whose exercise the court is asked to consider as an abuse of right." [46] By these rulings the Polish court moved far toward the position adopted by the Soviet jurists when the turbulent period of the Russian revolution had passed.

Specific decisions thereafter indicated how firmly the new position was to be held. A landlord was permitted to evict a cooperative, even though cooperatives are favored forms of economic association in socialist states.[47] The court said, "A unit of the socialized economy does not enjoy in its relations with other persons any exceptional prerogatives not flowing from provisions of the law."

Class conflict between spouses no longer was cause for a decision against the bourgeois-oriented partner. A drunkard husband from the peasant class was denied protection against a suit for divorce and maintenance brought by his wife who had come from the landowning gentry, even though during marital quarrels she had called him a "churl," "yokel," or "shepherd." The court thought these outbursts justifiably provoked by the husband's flagrant behavior.[48]

In a prosecution for homicide, it was argued that the penalty should be increased because the victim of a motor accident was "an individual socially valuable in every respect." [49] The supreme court refused to accept the argument, and a professor later explained that life is sacred regardless of the social value of

[44] Resol. of the full chamber, 12 Feb. 1955, [1955] PANSTWO I PRAWO 290.
[45] Decision of 3 Nov. 1955, [1956] 2 OSN 74.
[46] Decision of 11 Sept. 1957, [1958] OSP item 229.
[47] Decision of 12 June 1961, [1962] 2 OSN 112.
[48] Decision of 10 Sept. 1957, [1959] 3 OSN item 72 at 52.
[49] Decision of 5 Jan. 1960, [1961] PANSTWO I PRAWO 1071.

the individual.[50] Had the court accepted the prosecutor's argument, it would have adopted a position similar to that of Soviet courts when they applied the analogy provision in absence of statutory authority to increase a penalty beyond what was provided in the code.

In applying Article 3, Polish judges returned, as had the jurists of the USSR with their Article 1, to the practice of Western judges applying the rule of abuse of right and chicanery. Thus, a court refused to enforce a son's demand for transfer of a plot of land from his father even though the son claimed that the father had promised to make the transfer before the son had erected a building upon it. The court found that the son had physically assaulted his father and insulted him and had been punished by a fine in a criminal court. Under such circumstances the court concluded that a suit to enforce his right to the plot would be an abuse of right.[51]

In addition, a suit for reinstatement in a job was decided in favor of the employee, even though the employer technically had the right to dismiss him.[52] The court found that the employee had been dismissed earlier without legal grounds, and a trial court had ordered his reinstatement. The state enterprise concerned had complied in reinstating the man, but on the same day had dismissed him a second time, apparently in keeping with its right under the letter of the law. The court decided that the second dismissal was chicanery and an abuse of right, even though technically legal, and gave the victim the right to reinstatement.

The draftsmen of the new Polish civil code, who published their labors in 1960, entirely eliminated Article 3.[53] They even excluded any general provision on abuse of right similar to Western models, presumably in reaction to what had previously been done to create flexibility, and hence instability, in the application of Polish law. Perhaps the draftsmen expected that courts, in exercise of their ancient right, would refuse to enforce the law in cases of flagrant violation of the morality accepted by

[50] See gloss by Igor Andrejew, *id.*

[51] Decision of 13 Jan. 1960, [1961] 3 OSN item 67 at 34.

[52] Decision of 29 Sept. 1960, [1961] 4 OSN item 115 at 85.

[53] Rudzinski, *New Communist Civil Codes of Czechoslovakia and Poland: A General Appraisal*, 41 INDIANA L. J. 33 (1965).

the community, and that no statutory authorization was necessary in the light of long-established judicial tradition.

Whatever the motivation, the draftsmen's decision was not to stand, for the code as adopted on 23 April 1964 [54] reinstated the concept of Article 3 as Article 5, but with an additional criterion for refusal to apply a provision of the code in the event of abuse. In the 1964 version an abuse of right is an action in contradiction of the principles of social communal living in the Polish people's republic, just as it was in the old Article 3; but an alternative criterion was added. The act would not be protected if it was in contradiction to the socioeconomic destination of the legal provision under which it was initiated. Here was language quite similar to that of Article 5 of the Soviet civil law principles of 1961.

Polish law today leaves to the court determination of the circumstances in which stability of law is to be sacrificed in the interest of conformity to the new morality and the needs of the economy. It is expected that in practice the circumstances justifying departure from the law will be few, but the possibility of flexible application remains and is lauded by two of the code's principal sponsors.[55] Flexibility is still a desideratum, in theory, of Polish socialist civil law, but in practice it is expected that, as in the USSR, the stability of law will be highly respected.

A large part of the debate between proponents of flexibility and of stability in the USSR and in Poland rests on the relationship between judges and the Communist party. As has been seen, in 1917 Lenin conceived of a court as an informal assembly deciding matters in a flexible way. This court would be presided over by a Communist or a locally respected elder who would, with the aid of local residents rotating as lay assessors, aid in resolving the disputes of the community by

[54] [1964] 16 J. of L. Poland item 93. For a French transl. see CODE CIVIL DE LA RÉPUBLIQUE POPULAIRE DE POLOGNE (1966). A Russian translation also exists. A Polish scholar has explained in private conversation that no English translation was undertaken because the terminology of common law could not convey the proper meaning.

[55] See Wasilkowski, *Metoda opracowania i zalozenia kodeksa cywilnego,* [1964] PANSTWO I PRAWO 745 and Rybicki, *Znaczenie kodyfikacji prawa cywilnego w okresie budownictwa socjalizmu,* [1963] NOWE PRAWO 617.

applying a "socialist conscience." The emphasis was on political orientation rather than on legal expertise.

The trend toward stability of law which began in 1922 with the enactment of codes of law designed to encourage the invest-ment of funds in the ailing economy by small capitalists brought a concurrent professionalization of the courts. Empha-sis was still upon political orientation of decisions, but the men who made decisions were gaining legal experience by practice. Furthermore, new men educated in the Marxist-oriented law schools began to assume judicial roles. Although legal education was not a prerequisite for the judiciary, a professionalism of sorts emerged because the presiding judge at each trial was a full-time judicial officer, appointed by the local soviet for the purpose.

To avoid professionalization of the judiciary, the system of lay assessors was retained, and these assessors were given the right to share with the judge in all decisions of fact and law and in determining the criminal sentence or the civil judgment. This effort to maintain a balance between legal expertise and the lay approach was heavily influenced by politics.

The Communist party laid great stress upon preservation of a political orientation among the increasingly expert full-time judges, as is evidenced by statistics compiled by Professor T. H. Rigby, which indicate the percentage of such judges who were members of the party.[56] Within a year after inauguration of the new codes in 1922, the presidents of the provincial courts (then called *guberniia* courts) were all members of the party. Ninety-seven percent of the deputy presidents were also party mem-bers, as were 76 percent of the members. Since these courts had become courts of appeal from trial courts' decisions, they were able to control the application of law to assure its proper political orientation. Further, under the procedural codes these provincial courts were made the trial courts in both civil and criminal cases of special social importance, so that Communist party concepts requiring flexibility of the new codes would be assured of application.

Communist party saturation of high judicial position was important to obtaining desired political results, since the peo-

[56] Statistics on the Communist party saturation rates have been taken from T. H. Rigby, Communist Party Membership in the U.S.S.R. 1917–1967 424–25 (1968).

ple's courts, which had original jurisdiction over the great majority of civil and criminal cases, were at the time still in the hands of nonparty judges. In January 1922 only 36 percent of the full-time judges in these courts were party members.

With the passage of years the percentage of Communist party judges at all levels increased. By 1925 81 percent of the full-time judges in the trial courts were Communists. By 1931 92 percent were Communists. By 1954 only 2.3 percent of the full-time judges were not members of the party and almost all judges at higher levels of the judicial system belonged to the party.

It has never been possible for the lay assessors to be so completely communized. Party membership policy designed to make the party an elite, not a mass, organization leaves too few Communists at the local level to serve as lay assessors. The rate of party membership among the lay assessors has therefore been low, but it has become approximately 50 percent since the Second World War, as the total number of party members has increased.

Figures like these indicate that an important element of the Marxian socialist legal system is the political orientation of its judiciary, and this inevitably and by design makes for decisions which conform to the party's policy of the moment. If the party wanted to reduce the stability of law through flexible application of the codes, it could do so swiftly by issuing a party order, which would be put into effect through official channels provided by the supreme court of the USSR and through the party's own committees, so that judges would be apprised of policy. The mechanism is there, but the party has chosen not to take such a position. On the contrary, party emphasis has increasingly been upon the stability of law. Individual party authors are writing papers for publication in the press of the supreme court and of the Procuracy urging abandonment of even the extraordinary procedures for review provided by the procedural codes to permit the reversal or amendment of both criminal and civil decisions after they have become final, on termination of the ordinary appeal.[57] Emphasis is upon stability, not flexibility.

---

[57] For a hint of the criticism, see *Procurators*, Pravda, 9 Jan. 1967. Eng. transl. in [1967] 19 C.D.S.P., no. 2 at 13.

A year after Stalin's death the party recognized the danger of intervention by Communist party secretaries in the court's work on individual cases, and in 1954 an order was issued prohibiting it.[58] Judges were expected to follow general Communist party policy as communicated in party literature and at meetings of the primary party organization to which they belonged. But they were expected to apply their legal knowledge and experience in solving concrete criminal and civil cases and were not to be influenced by the intervention of a party secretary without this technical knowledge. In short, party policy established without legal experience was undesirable. It encouraged arbitrary decisions without reference to norms set forth in codes or past judicial practice. Although the Soviet system does not revere judicial precedent, it has increasingly come to demand that courts adhere to the practice of the supreme court as shown in its decisions, and local party secretaries are not in a position to know that practice or to give counsel on whether it should be followed in specific cases.

Limitations placed on local Communist party leaders trying to influence individual court decisions are now so well established in principle that the then vice-president of the USSR supreme court was able to say in an article published in 1967, denouncing the growing efforts of some organizations to increase the influence of public opinion upon judges, "Public opinion cannot be placed in a position with respect to the court that is more privileged than that of other political institutions of the state, such as local bodies of authority and local party and public organizations, which, as is known, cannot interfere in the court's disposition of criminal and civil cases." [59]

Soviet judges are moving in the direction of the position taken by Romanist judges in Western Europe on stability of law, but with one difference: they are instructed by party officials in an official, generalized party position which they are required to support. Their counterparts in France, Italy, and

[58] Order of Central Committee, 1954, referred to in V. Radkov, Sotsialisticheskaia zakonnost' v sovetskom ugolovnom protsesse 152 (1959) [Socialist Legality in Soviet Criminal Procedure].

[59] Anashkin, *The Role of Law Consciousness and Public Opinion in Settling Punishment*, [1967] 1 Sov. gos. i pravo 42, Eng. transl. in [1967] 19 C.D.S.P. no. 9 at 8.

Germany have no such guide in their pluralistic societies. To be sure, most of them feel social pressures to conform to basic patterns of action, as studies of judicial behavior demonstrate, but these pressures spring from social attitudes rather than being dictated from above. There is a difference of degree so great as to force recognition of a qualitative difference in the judicial process.

Yugoslavs have shown more concern for stability of law than any other Communists, and for good reason. Their decision to strike a blow at centralized bureaucracy as the "cancer of socialism" by separating it from local government has multiplied the chances that legislation may be promulgated locally by a whim or even in spite. To reduce, if not eliminate, wide variation from general principles at the local level, the Yugoslavs have shown themselves unwilling to rely, as do their Soviet colleagues, on rectification of violations by a higher "soviet" following the protest of a procurator.[60] They have created a system of "constitutional courts" which are the first to be established within the Marxian socialist legal family.

The constitutional courts, created not only at the federal level but in each republic, were given the task by the Constitution of 1963 [61] of preserving "conformity of law with the constitution and conformity of other regulations and general acts with the constitution and law." The aim was to open to all an avenue through which stability could be assured. Under their several statutes [62] the courts are open not only to petitions by state organs including the procurators, but to those submitted by popular assemblies, the regular courts, working and self-governing organizations, and even by individuals. Proceedings may also be initiated by the constitutional courts themselves. In distinction from some other systems of constitutional review,

---

[60] For details on the work of the procurator, see G. MORGAN, SOVIET ADMINISTRATIVE LEGALITY, THE ROLE OF THE ATTORNEY GENERAL'S OFFICE (1962).

[61] Art. 150.

[62] Eng. transl. of the Law on the Federal Court, 31 Dec. 1963, the Law on the Republic Court of Croatia, 1964, and the Rules of Procedure of the Federal Court, 1964, see 14 COLLECTION OF YUGOSLAV LAWS (CONSTITUTIONAL JUDICATURE) (Institute of Comparative Law, Belgrade, 1965).

notably that in the United States, the courts will rule on a petition even before the petitioner has acted in violation of law to make a case.

Although they are designed to keep local sources of law and local administrators in line with national and republic policy as established by constitutions and superior statutes, the courts have review power over republic and federal legislation. This power was exercised only once in the court's first two years of activity following its opening in 1964. The case was one in which the Federal Assembly promulgated a law with the approval of only one of its chambers, thus violating the constitution. When the Federal Constitutional Court called this fact to the assembly's attention, the violation was remedied.[63] When laws of republics or lower-level bodies are questioned, they are suspended by the appropriate higher assembly until the decision of the court can be rendered. If the Federal Assembly's own laws are questioned the court acts, and the assembly is given six months to rectify its error. Only thereafter may the court issue a flat statement of "unconstitutionality" and suspend the law.

Practice during the first two years showed that most petitions were filed against local-level administration, as when a commune, after three months of discussion, gave farmers only three days formal warning to put their land to proper use under the Land Use Law or lose it. On the farmers' petition, the federal court restored title on the grounds that notice had been inadequate. In another case in which a municipality had ordered private owners of business premises to rent them or have them rented by the municipality, the court held that the action violated the owners' rights under a federal statute. Subsequently, when the Belgrade municipality attempted the same thing and refused to accept the previous case as precedent, the court held a public hearing, entered its decision against the city, and imposed severe penalties.

To contribute further to stability the federal court has used its right to present to the Federal Assembly proposals and opinions. One such was a recommendation to unify civil law in a new code to replace the confusing body of separate laws and

[63] Fisk & Rubinstein, *Yugoslavia's Constitutional Court*, 15 EAST EUROPE, no. 7 at 24 (1966).

regulations issued over the years in amendment of the prewar civil code. The court also proposed enactment of a law defining the responsibilities of civil servants.

The Yugoslavs indicate that they fully understand the threat to legislative power that they have created with their constitutional courts. Their theorists have grappled with charges that the new system upsets the typical Marxian socialist concept of "unity of power in the assembly" and substitutes the previously rejected concept of "separation of powers." In spite of such charges they have proceeded, arguing simply that they must avoid unconstitutionality if law is to be respected.[64]

An indication of caution on the part of the innovators lies in the appointments to judgeships. The federal court's president is a member of the executive committee of the party, and several members of the various courts are also prominent party members. Two American experts have concluded that this feature was designed "to establish the importance of the court and to ensure that its counsels would have ready access to the highest party circles." Also, they conclude that since the courts' presence is felt increasingly, legislation is enacted and implemented "with deliberate regard to the probable attitude of the court."[65]

The Yugoslav experiment is being watched by the lawyers in other members of the family of Marxian socialist legal systems. Their law reviews carry accounts of its activities, and there have been suggestions even in the USSR that a new constitution might well contain provisions for such an institution. Such is the craving for stability of law on the part of some legal technicians, who are not wholly content with what had previously been recognized as the Marxian socialist way to police a constitution, namely, through the Office of the procurator general.

To be sure, the procurator general, established by the constitution of every Marxian socialist state, was obligated to enforce constitutional principles throughout the entire governmental system; but during Stalin's purges the institution had notably failed to restrain the police. Indeed, after Stalin's death the

---

[64] Krivić, Foreword to CONSTITUTIONAL JUDICATURE, supra, note 62 at 5.

[65] Fisk & Rubinstein, supra, note 63 at 25, 28.

incumbents of the office disclosed secret files in which had been kept the record of the complete abdication of the procurator general, even when his own staff was accused of treason, leaving the police free to fabricate cases.

In the post-Stalin reforms the institution was given a new statute designed to reaffirm and strengthen its position as protector of legality, and the noted Soviet prosecutor from the Nuremberg anti-Nazi trials was placed in the post. Protests against illegal ministerial orders violating constitutional rights were reported in the press,[66] and the flow of protests against court decisions violating law attracted the attention of those who follow the work of the supreme courts of the republics and of the USSR. Still, this system of procuratorial defense of constitutional rights seemed to some Eastern European lawyers less adequate than the protection to be expected from a constitutional court. For this reason the Yugoslav experiment began to catch the attention of reform elements no longer prepared to equate the office of procurator general with a constitutional court, even though in political theory both procurators and judges should combine in their persons the same elements of political wisdom and technical competence.

Into this swelling current of demand for stabilization of law has come the People's Republic of China. A jarring note was introduced in 1957. For three years before that important date in the history of Chinese law, the progress toward stability in China seemed to be following the same course as had law in the USSR.[67] In the early 1950s there had been a start apparently similar to that made by Lenin in revolutionary Russia when he espoused complete flexibility; but the similarity may have been only apparent. Professor Victor Li [68] has noted that although Lenin had a diploma in law and even practiced for a time, and although many of his colleagues were trained in the law, China's revolutionary leaders were neither trained in law nor familiar with it. They accepted the idea of a legal system for the new China, but they did not understand its implications. They seem never to have been comfortable working in a legal context.

[66] G. MORGAN, *supra*, note 60.

[67] SHAO-CHUAN LENG, JUSTICE IN COMMUNIST CHINA 45 (1967).

[68] Statements at this point reflect private conversations with Prof. Victor Li of the University of Michigan Law School.

In view of this nonlegal orientation, the abandonment in 1957 of the Soviet-inspired trend should not have constituted the surprise that it did to many outsiders, including Soviet jurists.

Be that as it may, the record shows that China's revolutionaries started out on a program like Lenin's. By order of the Central Committee of the Communist Party, all Kuomintang codes were repealed.[69] Courts were instructed to apply the "new programs, laws, orders, regulations, decisions, and in their absence . . . the policy of the new democracy." [70]

Formal moves were made to prepare for law study. An association to study law was created by the party during the summer of 1949, soon after proclamation of the new people's republic, and this was followed in 1950 by the opening of a law school in the Chinese people's university.[71] But this proved to be only the prelude to reaction, which set in during 1952, so that by 1953 only Canton was listed as offering law degrees.[72] Even in 1954, on the eve of the new constitution, a "Guide to Higher Institutions" told prospective students, "those who are inferior seek after politics and law." [73]

The constitution of 20 September 1954 [74] was in some measure a promise of impending stability, but there were still gaping holes in the legal structure. There was no revocation of the 1951 regulation for the punishment of counterrevolutionary activities [75] in which the concept of "analogy" and "retroactivity" were specifically introduced.

The turn of the tide toward stability became unmistakable only in 1956, when Liu Shao-chi, holding the position of vice-chairman of the republic, rose at the Eighth National Party

[69] Directive of C.C. of C.P. China, Feb. 1949, art. 5. See Lee, *Chinese Communist Law: Its Background and Development*, 60 MICH L. REV. 439 at 449 (1962).

[70] See Lee, *id.* at 450, citing Ma Hsi-wu, *The Work of the People's Judiciary in the Shensi-Kansu-Ninghsia Border Area Based on the New Democratic Revolution*, [1955] CHENG-FA YEN-CHIU, no. 1 at 14.

[71] See Lee, *id.* at 464.

[72] *Id.* at 462.

[73] *Id.* at 463.

[74] Eng. transl. in A. BLAUSTEIN, FUNDAMENTAL LEGAL DOCUMENTS OF COMMUNIST CHINA 1 (1962).

[75] Arts. 16 and 18. See Lung-sheng Tao, *The Criminal Law of Communist China*, 52 CORNELL L. REV. 43 at 54 (1966).

Congress to declare an end to the period of "revolutionary legality" and to propose the establishment of a stable legal order. In reviewing the need for systematic enactment of law and law codes, he told his colleagues, "A complete legal system becomes an absolute necessity." [76] In November a criminal code was reported to be complete with 261 articles, and experimental practice in its application had been initiated. By June 1957 the journals announced that most of a civil code had been completed.

The Chinese Communists were moving along a path already well-trodden by the Soviet and Eastern European Communists. Soviet legal texts were being translated and used as the basis for textbooks prepared by the Chinese for teaching at the university. Liu's call for a stable order seemed to spell the end of flexible application of law; but then a new reversal began.[77]

An "antirightist" campaign was started in late 1957, apparently as a reaction to discovery of opposition, which had been expressed when Mao asked for criticism in the campaign known as that of the "hundred flowers." Lawyers were among those called to account, and in March 1958 many of them appeared as signatories to a "self-reform" pact in which they promised to give their hearts to the party. Among the signers was the ex-president of the supreme court. From that moment the drafting of codes was abandoned, and law was taught to a diminishing few, although teaching continued until the general closing of the universities with Mao's "Great Proletarian Cultural Revolution."

On 1 January 1965 the new president of the supreme people's court and the procurator general of the republic issued a report to the Third National People's Congress, reaffirming the principle that implementation of the party's line is the basic duty of the judiciary.[78] A party order required judges to confer

[76] Shao-chuan Leng, *Post-Constitutional Development of "People's Justice" in China*, 6 J. INTERNAT'L. COMM. OF JURISTS 110 (1965); also his JUSTICE IN COMMUNIST CHINA, *supra*, note 67 at 54, citing 1 EIGHTH NATIONAL CONGRESS OF THE COMMUNIST PARTY OF CHINA 82 (1956).

[77] The account that follows is taken from LENG, JUSTICE IN COMMUNIST CHINA, *supra*, note 67 at 54 *et seq.*

[78] The many party pronouncements on submission of judges to party leadership are chronicled in *id.* at 62–64.

with the judicial committee in the court, of which the party secretary was a member, before deciding each "important case." [79] Through this order the Chinese party emphasized that political considerations of expediency were to weigh heavily in every decision. Apparently the Chinese trend was to be in direct opposition to that of the European Marxist socialist states after Stalin's death and his denunciation by his heirs. This contrast was emphasized officially in 1963 by Chinese publication of criticism of the Soviet party program of 1961.[80]

The Chinese position became one favoring flexibility. It was denied that a Marxist socialist state could ever move beyond the dictatorship of the proletariat to a "state of the whole people," as the Soviet party program of 1961 claimed had occurred in the Soviet Union. Until the ultimate withering, the state would remain coercive along class lines. In the Chinese view class would remain a motivating concept of the legal system, and class justice would require flexible application of law rather than strict adherence to its letter.

The Soviet analysts interpreted the new Chinese position as just such a repudiation of stability, and the European Marxist states concurred in the interpretation. The Soviet party's ideological spokesman presented a conclusion which was representative of the whole European camp when he said, "The present-day splitters [the Chinese] are also revising in theory and practice Lenin's directives on the need for the strictest observance of socialist legality. To this day in China there are actually no codes at all. . . . The Chinese press asserts that articles of the law 'possess definite elasticity, and they may be called an elastic measure.' " [81]

The Asian members of the family were not prepared to be so critical. North Korea, as the "Democratic People's Republic

---

[79] Jerome Alan Cohen indicates the practice and notes one definition of "important case" as "cases of an important policy nature and of far-reaching implication." Another judge reported that he asked instructions whenever he proposed a sentence of "reform through labor." See J. COHEN, THE CRIMINAL PROCESS IN THE PEOPLE'S REPUBLIC OF CHINA 1949–1963: AN INTRODUCTION 38 (1968).

[80] Letter of C.C. of C.P. China to C.C. of USSR and reply, Eng. transl. in [1963] 15 C.D.S.P. no. 28 at 30.

[81] *Ilychev Speech Indicts Chinese Social Sciences*, [1964] 11 KOM-MUNIST 12. Eng. transl. in [1964] 16 C.D.S.P. no. 35 at 8, 14.

of North Korea," in contrast to China's rejection of the concept of codification, adopted a criminal code on the model of the Russian republic's code of 1922.[82] It enshrined in its code the concept of flexibility which the Chinese still consider essential to the Marxian socialist legal system, as the Russians did at that time. In Article 9 the Koreans took the early Russian thinking on "analogy" and made it their own, and they have held to this in spite of the Soviet legislators' 1958 rejection of the principle.

The Korean choice was a considered one.[83] Reformists rose at the time when the Soviet specialists were making their noted play for stability to argue for a similar move in Korea. They were overruled by the party's leadership, which said, as had the Soviet authorities of the 1920s, that no legislation can anticipate all the forms of danger to society which an evil man can devise, and that to argue for abolition of analogy was to foster the evil attempt to contain revolution within the restrictive frame of formal laws. The decision was subsequently sealed in a legal treatise reading, "Marxism-Leninism starts from the premise that formal legal rules must obey the laws of revolution and social development. . . . Revolutionary and socialist legality demands analogy."

Within two years after the Korean decision to adhere to the principle of analogy, the Chinese Communists loyal to Mao Tse-tung went further in their "Great Proletarian Cultural Revolution," most sharply attacking Liu Shao-chi for "revisionism." Although his sins were listed as many, readers knowing the record will recall that it was he who in 1956 had demanded stability of law. Chinese Communists began demonstrating in their new campaign that for partisans of Mao's school of thought there can be no room for stability of law. The concept of flexible application of law is elevated to a place among what

[82] The information on Korea has been taken from an unpublished paper by Pyong Chook Hahm of the Law Faculty of Yonsei University, Seoul, Korea. It is scheduled for publication in shortened form in AM. J. COMP. L.

[83] Prof. Hahm cites as source for the debate, KONGHWAKUK POPUN SAHWAECHUI KONSOLUI KANGRYOKHANMUKI 79–109 (1964) [The Law of the Republic is a Potent Weapon of Socialist Construction].

the Maoists believe to be the primary elements characterizing a Marxian socialist legal system.

Were it not for the development in East Asia, especially in the People's Republic of China since 1957, under Mao's leadership, the evidence would justify the conclusion that in Marxian socialist states "flexibility" is not a permanently distinguishing feature of the legal system, since relatively stable attitudes appear after the initial turbulent revolutionary period in each newly governed society. Since the Chinese and Korean developments are in contrast with what has happened in the European wing of the Marxian family since Stalin's death, however, such a conclusion cannot be put forward without reservation. Analysis of this point of distinction must end inconclusively.

5

Simplicity and Popularity

as Ideals

SIMPLICITY AND POPULARITY WERE BRACKETED WITH FLEXIBIL-
ity as major desiderata when Lenin drafted his first decree on
the courts immediately after victory in 1917.[1] He abolished the
imperial hierarchy of courts in all its manifestations, but the
void left by the abolition was only partially filled. His first
concern was for the masses in whose name he had led the
revolution. Matters pending in the empire's general courts were
left for later, since they had been largely the business of the
bourgeoisie.

The peasants and workmen of the empire had never been
closely concerned with the general courts except in the relatively few instances when some of them had committed major
crimes. For them the court routines of Nicholas II were person-
alized by inferior courts: those situated in the groupings of
villages known as the "volost" and those conducted in many of

---

[1] 27 Nov. 1917, [1917] 4 Sob. Uzak. R.S.F.S.R. pt.I item 50.

the urban communities by justices of the peace. The first were controlled during the declining years of the empire by the Ministry of the Interior and had jurisdiction over petty civil claims and criminal prosecutions among the peasants. The second heard court disputes of somewhat larger value and criminal prosecutions in which the penalty might be moderate fines or imprisonment up to eighteen months.[2]

Lenin's formula called for new inferior courts quite different from the instrument of the old regime. With the appealing new title "people's courts," they were to epitomize popularity. This was to be manifested by a bench composed of two elements: a single judge named for a term but usually without legal education, and part-time lay assessors, chosen in pairs to serve in rotation for each session of the court. These new courts were to replace the old inferior tribunals, but they had wider jurisdiction so that they might be for the most part the only court with which the citizen of the new Russia would have to deal.

No hierarchy of appellate courts was established. Decisions of the simple tribunal were to be final, except that if the judgment exceeded one hundred rubles or seven days' detention parties might ask for a review of the decision by a meeting of all the judges of the county or large city, called together as a "congress" from time to time for the purpose. This congress was never to re-try the case completely, as had been permitted by the empire's appellate procedure.

Procedural formality was to be a thing of the past. No statute prescribed a procedure, and each judge was left to establish what he wished. There was not even to be a professional prosecutor to aid him, or a bar to provide attorneys for the parties. Lenin's concept at the time called for placing on the bench either a wise elder or a more youthful man or woman with sound political orientation, aided by two lay judges or "assessors" and such public-spirited members of the community as might wish to serve as accuser and defender. Lenin expected this team, drawn from society itself, to determine the facts and mete out a popular form of justice without either procedural or

[2] The standard text is N. KORKUNOV, RUSSKOE GOSUDARSTVENNOE PRAVO 2 vols. (6th ed. 1908–9) [Russian Public Law]. See also S. KUCHEROV, COURTS, LAWYERS AND TRIALS UNDER THE LAST THREE TSARS (1953).

substantive legal provisions to guide them. For a time they were permitted to look at imperial codes for inspiration, but in no way were they bound by them. Revolutionary conscience and good sense were to be the major sources of inspiration governing the proceedings.

By degrees the vision of a simple court functioning without guidance from statutes and through the eyes of judges lacking in professional attitudes faded from the Russian judicial scene. Procedural needs were felt first, for as early as the spring of 1918 the Moscow judges found it desirable to prepare and publish two temporary instructions, one on procedure for the conduct of criminal cases, the other for civil cases.[3] By midsummer a first instruction on court procedure for the local people's courts was issued by the Commissariat of Justice.[4] In this instruction there reappeared a system clearly inspired by what had existed before. As such it looks familiar to those who know Romanist-type procedures. The trial of criminal cases was to be preceded by a complete investigation by a judge sitting alone, this being an investigation into all the facts, as presented not only by the accusers but also by the suspect in the manner of the *instruction* of the French examining magistrates. Further, the judge at the trial was to take the initiative in conducting the case. He was not to sit as arbiter between contending parties, as in the traditional Anglo-American court of common law. His task was to hear the factual statements of the parties making the complaint and to formulate them in simple legal terms. He would then call and question witnesses, and finally would decide what should be done to maintain public order.

Formality was excluded by an article of the instruction of the commissariat, declaring that "the court is not cramped by any formal considerations." The commissar issued an unofficial guide in July 1918, saying that the court was losing its formal structure, and that soon there would be no formality to which it would be required to adhere.[5] Court rules would be of a new

[3] For an account, see Cherliunchakevich, A *Report on the Activities of the Local People's Courts of the City of Moscow for the First Third of 1918*, [1918] PROL. REV. I PRAVO, no. 2 at 36.

[4] 23 July 1918, [1918] 53 Sob. Uzak. R.S.F.S.R. pt. I item 597.

[5] P. STUCHKA, NARODNYI SUD V VOPROSAKH I OTVETAKH (1918) [The People's Court in Questions and Answers].

type, no longer compulsory, but to be used only when the judge was convinced of their value. Judges were expected to develop imaginatively the purely technical parts of the trial, such as the means of summoning parties, gathering evidence, and investigating the facts.

From this early emphasis upon simplicity of procedure, taken at the time to be a major characteristic of Marxian socialist law, Communists initiated, or perhaps went along with, a slowly emerging recognition of the usefulness of formality. This change in attitude was influenced in part by the second decree on the courts,[6] designed to provide a means of clearing up cases left unresolved after abolition of the imperial general courts by the first decree. For these cases the second decree, of late January 1918, created a "district people's court," contrasting sharply with the people's courts of the first decree in that there were more judges on the bench and there was emphasis upon professionalism. The pretrial proceedings were heard by three professional judges rather than a single judge, and the trial itself was before three professional judges and four lay assessors, if a civil claim were involved, or before a single professional judge and twelve lay assessors with two alternates if it were a criminal charge.

No requirement of legal training was established for the judges of the district court, but judges generally had such training; and they needed it. Appeal in the old sense of retrial of the facts was prohibited, but there was to be created a system of review of the record—called in Continental tradition "cassation"—by a panel of judges elected from among their own number by all district people's court judges in each province. Remand for new trial was permitted, but only if substantial errors were committed, or the result was clearly unjust. Even here, where greater formality was the rule, there was to be no harsh adherence to form. Although the decree called for creation of a supreme court control, no such control came into being, and even the provincial review tribunals never met, partly because the local soviets distrusted what they feared to be

---

[6] No date, but later identified as approved 30 Jan. 1918. [1918] 26 Sob. Uzak. R.S.F.S.R. pt. I item 420 [misnumbered, as should have been item 347].

a return to formalities and professionalism in the district court system.

The commissar of justice at the time of the second decree was a member of the Left Socialist Revolutionary party and not a Bolshevik, because Lenin was trying to woo the peasantry by bringing members of their favored party into the government. Subsequent events in late 1918 after the coalition had been dissolved proved that the Communists were not happy with the second decree's return to some of the formalities of the past. The district courts were merged with the simplified people's courts, but the work of the Socialist Revolutionary commissar left its mark, for his bolshevik successor used elements of the second decree in preparing his procedural instruction of July 1918. Also, a system of court costs was established for the people's court in July 1918, and it was the same as the one established previously for the district courts.

Perhaps a major influence of the short-lived district courts was the impetus they gave to restoration of what amounted to the institution of prosecutor and defense attorney. Under the second decree, district courts had been permitted to call to their aid both professional accusers and professional lawyers, and an institution was created to provide them. These professional people were rigidly controlled, however, for they were organized in a college appointed by the local soviet from among those trained in the law and likely to be politically reliable. Parties were permitted to select attorneys only from the college, if a fee was to be paid, although they might avail themselves of the assistance of any private person acting without fee who might be willing to serve as accuser or defender.

The people's courts soon demonstrated that they too could use to advantage the help of professionals. In June 1918 the Moscow judges adopted a resolution [7] in favor of establishing a college of legal defenders, although they urged that care be taken to see that it included no one who would solicit legal business, and the rules permitted a local court to refuse to allow the appearance of lawyers in uncomplicated civil cases and in divorce cases. The measure of the change from prerevolutionary organization of the bar was also revealed in a growing move-

[7] 53 *id.* item 597.

ment to make the bar a salaried group maintained by the state rather than by clients' fees. This was to indicate dramatically that the lawyer was now accepted as a member of a judicial team rather than being treated as a "private hireling" of a client.

By the People's Court Act of 1918,[8] adopted in November, the district courts were abolished and the people's courts were expanded in jurisdiction to include all civil and criminal cases except those of a political nature, which went before revolutionary tribunals making no pretense of being courts of law. The bar became, as had been proposed, a salaried civil service, the same college also including persons who might be chosen by the court as accusers. The court could deny an application for an attorney, except when the accused was charged with attempt on life, the causing of serious harm, rape, robbery, counterfeiting of currency or bribery, or speculation in goods on ration or monopolized.

Procedural provisions were included in the act, similar to those of the rules published in July. Review was again to be only of the record, and no permanent reviewing court was created. It was still the congress of local judges, but now it was to be called a "council" and to be organized at the level of the province, not of the county or city. Emphasis was no longer upon immediate revision of the sentence but upon ordering a new trial in the event of error. For the first time violation of the forms of court procedure, was included as error although this violation had to be substantial to warrant retrial. The way was being prepared for what was to follow in later years: return to procedural formality.

The commissar of justice emphasized that the new courts would act quickly instead of slowly and that they would not decide mechanically. He still desired simplicity, and the Communist party reaffirmed that aim in 1919 in its first postrevolutionary program by saying, "The Soviet Government has replaced the former endless series of courts of justice, with their various divisions, by a very simplified, uniform system of People's Courts, accessible to the population, and freed of all

[8] 30 Nov. 1918, 85 id. item 889.

useless formalities of procedure." [9] The commissar jubilantly proclaimed that the Soviet court was in some ways analogous to the tribunal in ancient primitive law, for nowhere else did judges have such unrestricted authority.[10] In his view simplicity had triumphed and was a major characteristic of the new legal system.

With the introduction of the New Economic Policy in 1922 legal institutions were restructured and legal procedure was formalized in codes for criminal and civil actions, in keeping with Lenin's determination to reestablish confidence in the Soviet legal system so as to induce investment in the ailing economy both by foreigners and by those at home who might have capital.

In the years between 1918 and 1922, the court system had been subjected to some experimentation, and the 1922 codes built upon this. By the People's Court Act of 1920,[11] which had amended the act of 1918, the accusatory function had been separated from the defending function, and institutions had been created which were to lead to recreation of a prosecutor's office and of a conventional bar. The defenders had undergone the greatest change, for the concept of a paid staff had collapsed. In its place the 1920 act had created a panel of persons named by people's courts, revolutionary tribunals, provincial councils of judges, labor unions, and Communist party organizations to perform legal assistance as a labor duty, much as citizens perform jury duty in the Anglo-American common-law system. Judges were to choose their man, and if he refused to serve, he was to be prosecuted.

The system of 1920 was characterized later as a "telephone book" rather than a bar,[12] and it also failed; so the draftsmen of

[9] Eng. transl. of Program in W. Rappard et al., Source Book on European Governments, part V (1937).

[10] Kurski, The New Criminal Law, [1919] 2–4 Prol. Rev. I Pravo 24.

[11] 21 Oct. 1920, [1920] 83 Sob. Uzak. R.S.F.S.R. item 407.

[12] Ia. Berman, Ocherki po istorii sudoustroistva RSFSR s predisloviem N. V. Krylenko 37 (1924) [Sketches on the History of the Court Structure of the R.S.F.S.R. with a Foreword by N. V. Krylenko].

1922, in providing for the vigorous litigation they expected from property owners during the period of the New Economic Policy, felt impelled to recreate a professional bar. They formed a college of advocates, attached to the courts [13] but with sufficient autonomy to permit election of executives from its own membership, and with authority to collect fees. To prevent a relapse to the undesirable practice of the past when litigation cost too much for many workmen and peasants, the lawyers were required to provide services free of charge for those unable to pay, and a tariff was established to set limits on fees for paying clients.

In 1922 an institutional framework was instituted which was also mindful of the past and was formalized in an Office of the State Procurator, headed by a procurator of the republic, originally created within the Commissariat of Justice [14] but later made independent. He was to function at lower administrative levels through prosecutors responsible to their chief in Moscow, and without responsibility to local officials. On this point there was great dissension, resolved only when Lenin put the matter before the highest possible tribunal, the Political Bureau of the Communist party.[15]

For the courts themselves, the 1922 judiciary act [16] created three levels, each with appellate jurisdiction over the next lower level when that lower level had sat as a court of original jurisdiction. The supreme court had a supervisory or "audit" authority over appellate decisions, to be exercised after the normal appeal had become final. The audit authority permitted setting aside of the decision if there had been error or if high policy required a change. To provide experienced and educated judges in the more serious criminal cases and high-value civil cases as well as in civil cases in which the defendant was a state agency or official, the act placed original jurisdiction not in the people's courts at the bottom of the pyramid, but in the provincial courts serving as intermediate bodies below the republic's supreme court. To perform their new duties these provincial

[13] 26 May 1922, [1922] 36 Sob. Uzak. R.S.F.S.R. pt. I item 425.

[14] 28 May 1922, 36 *id.* item 424.

[15] Lenin, *On "Dual" Surbordination and Legality* in 33 SOCHINENIIA 326 (4th ed. 1951) [Works].

[16] 31 Oct. 1922, [1922] 69 Sob. Uzak. R.S.F.S.R. pt. I item 902.

courts, when sitting as courts of original jurisdiction, were reformed to place two lay assessors alongside the professional judge; but when they sat as courts of appeal, the bench consisted of three professionals. These professionals had to meet requirements designed to assure their skill and political wisdom, having not less than two years of responsible work in a state, public, professional, or Communist party position or three years as a people's judge. Appointment was for one year, but there might be reappointment. This permitted increasing expertise but left open an easy way to eliminate the politically or temperamentally unfit.

The court system was complicated by the creation of specialized courts with criminal jurisdiction in areas critical to the regime—military matters and transportation matters. These courts were made responsible to the republic's supreme court, and were conceived as less popular tribunals than those dealing with ordinary matters. No lay assessors sat upon them; all three judges were professionals. In addition, there were "land commissions" to hear disputes over use of the land, "arbitration commissions" to resolve disputes between state agencies in the commercial field, and a "labor session" of the people's court to try violations of the code of labor laws. The commissar was disappointed with this complexity, and he sought to apologize for it by explaining the necessity for these departures from what he hoped would become a simple unified and popular court system; but he had been outvoted. The party majority chose to proceed in the direction of complexity and expertise.

Soon after the 1922 reform came federation of the republics which had emerged within the former territory of the Russian empire, and this inevitably had an impact upon the legal institutions. A supreme court for the federation was created by the constitution of 1923,[17] along with a procurator of the USSR. This new court was charged with giving guiding instructions on the application of all-union law, with hearing protests brought

---

[17] For text see ISTORIIA SOVETSKOI KONSTITUTSII V DEKRETAKH I POSTANOVLENIIAKH SOVETSKOGO PRAVITEL'STVA 1917–36. (1936) [History of the Soviet Constitution in Decrees and Orders of the Soviet Government]. A Supreme Court Act was adopted 23 Nov. 1923, [1923] 10 Vestnik Ts.I.K., S.N.K. i S.T.O. item 311 and revised 24 July 1924, [1924] 2 Sob. Zak. S.S.S.R. pt. I item 25.

to it by the USSR procurator against decisions of the supreme courts of the republics violating federal law, with advising the federal parliament of federal legislation being violated by republic enactments, with deciding disputes between republics, and with taking jurisdiction over crimes committed by the federal government's top officials acting in their official capacities. A plenum of the supreme court was created to include the four presidents of the supreme courts of the republics, six of the judges of the federal supreme court, and a representative of the newly created agency of the security police, the G.P.U.

Cases not requiring a plenary sitting were heard by colleges of three judges, one of whom was to be a member of the plenum. All were to be professionals. The communist bias against the Montesquieu concept of separation of powers was reemphasized by a provision permitting the procurator to protest any decision of the supreme court's plenum to the Central Executive Committee, which performed the function of a legislature at the time, in spite of its name.

Procedure came to the fore with the erection of a complex court system, supported by professional prosecutors and bar. For some of the party die-hards, reemphasis upon procedure signified return to the formality of the past, and it took the old Bolshevik Mikhail Kalinin, serving at the time as president of the Central Executive Committee, to reassure them. In a speech to the specialists in law on 28 January 1922 he ridiculed those who thought that a return to formality meant a return to the bourgeois point of view.[18] He was prepared to admit that legality had suffered during the preceding four years, but "at the present moment it has for us a very great importance." He noted that other states enforce procedural legality, and concluded that it fixed in the consciousness of the masses respect for the court. He believed that such respect should be fostered by the Soviet leadership as well.

With sponsorship by the party, procedural reform advanced. The Russian republic's codes of 1922 and 1923 [19] were long and

[18] *The Speech of the President of the Central Executive Committee Comrade M. I. Kalinin,* [1922] 5 Ezh. sov. iust. 6.

[19] Code of Criminal Procedure R.S.F.S.R., 25 May 1922, [1922] 20–21 Sob. Uzak. R.S.F.S.R. item 230. Amended and revised 15 Feb. 1923, [1923] 7 *id.* item 106. Code of Civil Procedure R.S.F.S.R., 7 July 1923, [1923] 46–47 *id.* item 478.

technically detailed, but the commissar of justice, in presenting them for adoption, sought to cushion the impact by saying that they only systematized what had become practice in the courts. The principles could, therefore, be assimilated without difficulty.

The codes established a procedure essentially similar to that of France. Stages in criminal cases were: (1) initiation of proceedings, (2) short inquiry by organs of detention, (3) preliminary investigation, (4) transfer to court, (5) trial, (6) judicial review, and (7) execution of the sentence. But with the sanctification of formality, there were preserved some elements of the informal past. A judge might take the initiative in instigating proceedings, in setting the case for trial without the prior intervention of any other agency, in informing the accused of the charge against him, and in questioning him about his desires for his defense. Still, this simplification of procedure was to be used only in the exceptional case. Normally, there would be a preliminary investigation both by the police and by a special preliminary investigator, except in instances of crimes of no great consequence; and even when the judge acted alone, he had to issue a written reasoned decision explaining his assumption of authority.

Informality was also preserved by provisions that complaints could be filed by a labor union, a cooperative, or a citizen, but normally these went not to the judge but to the police, a prosecutor, or a preliminary investigator.

Great authority was left the judge to direct the trial, but this was not a communist innovation. Again, it sprang from Continental models, utilized also by imperial courts. No restrictions on the admission of evidence were set in the code, and the judge was left to his "inner conviction" to evaluate what was heard and seen; but so is a Continental judge. Proceedings in practice constituted a review of the folios placed on the bench by the preliminary investigator, and so the trial looked more like a verification of what had gone before than a hearing de novo; but again this is the procedure of Europe generally. The simplicity which is striking to one conversant with the complex rules of evidence of the Anglo-American common law, and which is sometimes taken as a distinguishing characteristic of Marxian socialist law, is in reality no such distinction.

Not only did the codes provide multiple stages of procedure

in the Continental tradition, but extensive practice in the courts indicated how often reversals of sentences and civil judgments occurred because of procedural violation. The 1922 code of criminal procedure provided the basis for court practice by defining what constituted a substantial violation requiring a new trial. Serious violations included an improperly constituted bench of judges at the trial; refusal of the trial court to terminate proceedings when circumstances required it (such as death of the accused, reconciliation in cases where there could be no prosecution unless the complaint was sustained, absence of any complaint from the victim when a complaint was required, laches, amnesty, absence of facts constituting violation of the criminal code); or a trial without the presence of the defendant or his attorney when his presence was mandatory.

Another article permitted the setting aside of a sentence because of clear injustice, and most appellate decisions based upon a review of the evidence have rested on this article. But a new trial had to be held so that the evidence could be heard again and evaluated by the trial judges. The appellate court was not considered capable of settling the matter finally through simple review of the record.

The return to formality worried some of the Communists who had been responsible for its introduction. The commissar of justice was himself unhappy about the increasing complexity of the law, noting that the People's Court Act of 1920 had included all that was necessary to establish court structure and procedure in 97 articles, whereas the new code of criminal procedure contained 450 articles and the code of civil procedure had 226. He assured students to whom he was lecturing that "our immediate task will be its simplification." [20] But his prediction was not to come true.

Procedural reform has followed procedural reform in the years that have passed. Stalin's efforts to bypass procedural complexity in political cases have been overturned by his heirs. His amendments to the code of criminal procedure during his purges of the late 1930s introduced the rule of no attorney at

[20] N. Krylenko, Sudoustroistvo RSFSR (Lektsii po teorii i istorii sudoustroistva). 161 (1923) [The Court Structure of the R.S.F.S.R. (Lectures on the Theory and History of Court Structure)].

the trial, no right to be present, and no appeal for "terrorists."[21] Counterrevolutionaries were to receive their indictment only twenty-four hours before trial, and were also denied the right to appeal.[22]

His creation in 1934[23] of administrative tribunals within the Ministry of Internal Affairs which were authorized to ignore the procedural code in banishing and imprisoning in work camps persons found to be "socially dangerous" was denounced in 1953 and the boards were abolished.[24] New fundamental principles of criminal and of civil procedure were adopted by the federal parliament on the initiative of the Communist party in 1958[25] and 1961[26] respectively, and later were incorporated in the codes of the republics belonging to the federation. They were refinements on the past, made to increase the likelihood of determining truth. Some elements permitting simplification of proceedings remained after the post-Stalin reforms, notably the exclusion of a defense attorney during the assembling of evidence by the preliminary investigator, which permits him to act without fear of restraint until he has prepared his indictment. Once the indictment is filed, however, procedural protections begin to operate, and the supreme courts of the republics and of the USSR have been assiduous in seeing that they are observed on pain of reversal.

This is not to say that Soviet procedure provides no contrast with that of Continental systems generally. The most notable difference is expansion of the right of the supreme courts, and even of the presidia of the provincial courts, to reopen cases for review and audit after sentence or judgment has become final, if

[21] 1 Dec. 1934, [1934] 64 Sob. Zak. S.S.S.R. item 459.

[22] 14 Sept. 1937, [1937] 61 *id.* item 266.

[23] 5 Nov. 1934, [1935] 11 *id.* item 84.

[24] The decree remains unpublished. For interview on the matter see Berman, *Law Reform in the Soviet Union*, 15 Am. Slavic and E. E. Rev. 183–85 (1956).

[25] Fundamentals of Criminal Procedure, 25 Dec. 1958, [1959] 1 Ved. Verkh. Sov. SSSR item 15. Eng. transl. in Fundamentals of Soviet Criminal Legislation, the Judicial System and Criminal Court Procedure. Official Texts and Commentaries (1960).

[26] Fundamentals of Civil Procedure, 8 Dec. 1961, [1961] 50 *id.* item 526. Eng. transl. in Soviet Civil Legislation and Procedure. Official Texts and Commentaries (n.d. 1962).

circumstances of justice or politics seem to require.[27] Here is an opening for reconsideration on whatever ground after the completion of a trial conducted with all procedural protections. It is a stage in proceedings which attracts the attention of judges of the Romanist system as violative of what they know as *res judicata*, and even Soviet legal writers have begun to attack this proceeding;[28] yet it remains. It is not, however, crucial to the Soviet legal system, or vigorously defended on theoretical grounds as fundamental. It seems, rather, to be a heritage from the early days when the party lacked confidence in its judges in the lower courts and preserved this method of reversing their decisions.

There is nothing doctrinal, therefore, in a system in which after exhaustion of procedural remedies devised during fifty years of practice a stroke of a pen may set aside all that has been done, because, in the words of the Russian republic's 1960 code, "A court of first instance has rendered an illegal or unfounded decision, or a higher court has without basis left unchanged, vacated, or changed previous rulings, decrees or the judgment in the case, or that in the consideration of the case in the higher court violations of the law have been permitted which have affected or might have affected the correctness of the ruling or decree rendered by it." [29]

Simplicity has not entirely disappeared from the minds of those who work in Soviet courtrooms, in spite of the erosion of principles designed to assure simplification of courts and procedures since 1917. In 1966 an author criticized proposals to replace the periodically elected lay assessors with a panel of citizens named permanently to the post.[30] In his criticism he

[27] For a comparison between European Marxian socialist and traditional systems of audit, see Rudzinski, *Soviet-type Audit Proceedings and their Western Counterparts*, 13 LAW IN EASTERN EUROPE 287 (1966). For China, see Ginsburgs & Stahnke, *The Genesis of the People's Procurate in Communist China* in two parts, [1964] CHINA QUARTERLY no. 20 at 1 and [1965] *id.* no. 21 at 53.

[28] Benin, *The Presidium is Not a Third Appellate Instance*, [1966] 16 Sov. IUST. 11.

[29] Code of Criminal Procedure, R.S.F.S.R. art. 379. 27 Oct. 1960, [1960] 40 Ved. Verkh. Sov. R.S.F.S.R. item 592. Eng. transl. in H. BERMAN, SOVIET CRIMINAL LAW AND PROCEDURE (1966).

[30] Razumnaia, *A Lay Assessor Writing about his Work*, [1966] 17 Sov. IUST. 16.

argued that "It would be wrong to draw the conclusion that it would be expedient to create a permanent cadre of people's lay assessors, since this might lead to an undesirable professionalism, a weakening of their keen perception of all that occurs in court proceedings."

Nor has simplicity passed from the minds of Marxist-oriented politicians at the top of the Soviet hierarchy. This became plain in 1959 when Nikita Khrushchev, as first secretary of the party, proposed that an institution inherited from the early days, and allowed to cease functioning during the war, be revitalized.[31] This was the "comrades' court," established by Lenin to provide a supremely popular and simple means through which social pressures might be brought to bear upon citizens who committed no crime but failed to conform to desired norms of social behavior. He was especially concerned with workers who were constantly late in arriving on the job, or inattentive to duties, and with citizens who made life unpleasant for fellows in crowded apartments because of their disorder. Khrushchev proposed to extend the work of these tribunals, and a statute of 1961 provided their new charter.[32] They were, as then envisaged, primarily social courts to be engaged in overcoming drunkenness, disorderly behavior, insults to women, abusive language, violation of apartment regulations, and petty destruction of communal quarters; but they might also hear civil claims if the amount demanded was small.

Their functioning pleased the leaders, and jurisdiction was expanded in 1963[33] to give them broader rights, even to punish for first offenses against the criminal code, when in the opinion of a prosecutor or of a people's court social pressures would be more effective than prison terms. Crimes for which such procedures might be adopted were intentional infliction of slight bodily harm not resulting in impairment of health, circulation of a libel, insult, theft of inexpensive articles of consumption and everyday life found in the personal ownership of citizens if

[31] Speech to twenty-first Communist Party Congress. Eng. transl. in L. Gruliow ed., Current Soviet Policies III at 67 (1960).

[32] 3 July 1961, [1961] 26 Ved. Verkh. Sov. R.S.F.S.R. item 371. Eng. transl. with annotations in Berman & Spendler, Soviet Comrades' Courts, 38 Wash. L. R. 842 (1963).

[33] Law of 23 Oct. 1963, [1963] 43 Ved. Verkh. Sov. R.S.F.S.R. item 750. Eng. transl. in [1963] 15 C.D.S.P. no. 47 at 7.

the victim and guilty person belonged to the same group, and the making of home-brewed liquor.

A Soviet investigator later disclosed that the comrades' courts were taking jurisdiction without statutory authority over petty thefts of state or cooperative property, theft of personal property, hooliganism, fraud on purchasers, misuse of official position or negligence in such a position, forgery of documents, and intentional refusal to pay maintenance of children and others.[34] In short, the system was being widely used to punish first offenders guilty of any but crimes of violence.

Civil jurisdiction of comrades' courts was likewise extended in practice, as was revealed in an answer to a question published in the journal of the Procuracy in 1966.[35] The editors replied that if a collective farm family consented, a comrades' court might resolve a dispute among its members over the division of the communally owned property when a member separated from the family. In doing so it was to be guided by the norms of civil law.

The comrades' courts reintroduced into Marxian socialist law in the USSR qualities of simplicity of procedure and popularity of personnel that had slipped away from the conduct of court business in the people's courts. No professionals were placed on the bench. The judges were three or more laymen, elected by their fellows for one-year terms because they seemed qualified as Lenin had wanted his first people's judges to be: primarily because they held prestigious positions in the community in which they lived and worked and had "good sense" as Communists understood it. Only a minimum number of rules for procedure were established by law; primarily that hearings be in public, that the accused be present, and that the court act promptly.[36] Judges in these courts were encouraged by Soviet jurists to attend brief courses in legal fundamentals at what were called "people's universities," or night classes,[37] but eyewit-

[34] Pavlishev, *Consultation*, [1966] 8 SOTS. ZAK. 90.

[35] *May a Comrades' Court Examine a Case on Division of a Collective Farm Household?*, [1966] 8 SOTS. ZAK. 83.

[36] On procedure in comrades' courts, see [1966] 7 Sov. IUST. 22.

[37] In Frunze district these classes expanded over a five-year period from 150 to 652 participants, including comrades' court members, lay assessors, members of the voluntary militia, and the lay section of the then-existing party-state control bodies. See [1966] 9 SOTS. ZAK. 73.

ness accounts by Soviet and foreign visitors indicate that legal education did not run deep.[38] Procedures were reminiscent of the simplicity established for the people's courts in 1917 and 1918.

Soviet jurists have not been entirely happy with the situation, for they note that many errors result from the absence of legal education.[39] The one means of control—supervision by the local prosecutors who are charged with attention to what they do—seems to have been ineffective; yet the tribunals have retained the confidence of the high party leaders even since the ousting of their sponsor, Nikita Khrushchev.

The Hungarian Communists preceded Khrushchev in reviving Lenin's system by installing comrades' courts in 1956.[40] As in the USSR, the courts developed in two stages: first they were limited in jurisdiction by the 1956 decree to breaches of labor discipline and damage to socially owned property, and to offenses against the rules of "socialist coexistence"; then they were extended by a 1962 decree to infractions of lesser importance referred to them by the local prosecutor or the ordinary court and to civil claims for defamation, slight personal injury, and property disputes not exceeding one thousand forints in value.

As in the USSR, the judges are responsible citizens, elected for two-year terms on nomination of trade union locals, or by the workers in a given enterprise or cooperative. No procedure is prescribed, but the decree and regulations establish the rules for constituting the bench, which has from three to five members, the speed with which action must be taken, the authority and duties of the president, the requirement that witnesses be warned to tell the truth, the right of all present to speak and to question, and the obligation to make public the testimony and any essential documentation.

Lawyers may not appear for parties, but relatives may intervene, as may fellow workers appearing either for the prosecution or for the defense. Decisions must be by majority vote and in writing, and there is an appeal: either to the trade union

---

[38] G. Feifer, Justice in Moscow 125–30 (1964).

[39] Kriger, *Inadequacies in the Practice of Transfer of Cases to Comrades' Courts,* [1966] 15 Sov. iust. 19.

[40] Gellert, *Comrades' Courts in Hungary,* 10 Review of Contemporary Law no. 2 at 45 (1963).

committee to whom the court is responsible, if the penalty is a reprimand, or to the police court if the penalty requires deduction of a fine or damages from wages. The police court may quash the proceedings, or refer the case to the higher criminal courts for consideration. Enforcement of a judgment expressed in terms of money is by the enterprise in which the court sits. It merely makes the deductions ordered from wages, never to exceed one-half of any pay envelope. The prosecutor has the duty, as he does throughout all Marxian socialist systems, to supervise proceedings for legality, drawing attention to defects and assisting in their rectification.

Three thousand such Hungarian comrades' courts had been set up by 1963, and all were reporting lively activity. As in the Soviet Union, the lawyers have been worried about their procedures, and a commentator says frankly, "A condition for the success of these courts is a proper appreciation of their purpose and principles and the forms of procedure which safeguard the due process of law." [41] To help in preserving legality, the lawyers have established, as in the Soviet Union, night-school courses to train the judges in legal fundamentals.

Whereas the Hungarian Communists were so enthusiastic about the potentialities of the comrades' courts that they even preceded Khrushchev in establishing them after Stalin's death, the Poles have been far more restrained. Some experiments were tried in Warsaw, Wroclaw, and Lodz at the same time the Khrushchev reforms were being popularized throughout the Marxian socialist countries, but legal periodicals gave them scant attention. Finally, on 30 March 1965 a statute authorized their creation on a regional basis, but left the initiative to local public organizations, which in practice meant the local party committees.[42]

The Polish model calls for workers' courts in industrial institutions, and also for "social conciliation commissions" among the residents of cities, towns, and villages. Their task, as in the USSR, is to hear charges of violations of the principles of social intercourse and social order, including violation of civic and family duties and minor infractions against social property.

[41] Id. at 55.
[42] [1965] 13 J. of L. Poland item 92.

Their authority is limited to imposing censure and to levying fines not exceeding three hundred zloty to be applied to a specified social purpose, and to judgment for damage which may have been done. The institution of these courts by formal statute has evoked no enthusiasm from legal authors, who have remained conspicuously silent in the law reviews. Evidently, as in other matters of Polish law, the current of formal court proceedings still runs deep. If there is to be simplification, the Polish Communists would prefer to establish it through the obligation created by the 1964 code of civil procedure,[43] which requires courts to seek conciliation at every stage of the proceedings "in cases where a settlement (composition) in court is admissible," [44] but not to the flagrant infringement of a well-founded interest of one of the parties, or in violation of the principles of social intercourse or law.[45]

Another simplified tribunal, introduced with Khrushchev's blessing in 1957 in the border republics of the USSR, had nearly a decade of experience before its abolition after Khrushchev's ouster. It was called in the first decree a "social assembly," assigned the task of banishing "parasites" from the communities in which they lived to remote provinces where they were expected to reform themselves by hard work, with the help of the local population.[46] After this experience, they were to return to their home towns to resume a useful productive life in the image of the communist code of morals.

These bodies, as their name suggests, were "assemblies" and not courts at all. No specific individuals were elected to make the decision and to accept responsibility for it. The assembly was a gathering of those who lived in an apartment house or along a given street, or those who worked in the same place of employment as the accused. The task of the group was to discover and condemn citizens who received income from unexplained sources. The group was called together by a community public-order committee, composed of Communist party or Komsomol members and other community leaders. Charges

[43] 17 Nov. 1964, [1964] 43 *id.* item 296.
[44] *Id.* art. 10.
[45] *Id.* art. 184.
[46] For an account and history of these courts, see Beerman, *The Parasite Law*, 13 SOVIET STUDIES 191 (1961).

were presented by the Komsomol, a labor union, or another public organization in accusation of "an antisocial, parasitic way of life." No definition was presented of the crime, and reports indicated that accusations even extended beyond cases of speculation to cases of listening to foreign broadcasts.

No procedural rules were prescribed, although a suggested order of activities was incorporated in regulations issued by the ministries: a tribunal was to be elected, including a president, but it was not a court like the comrades' court. It served only to guide the proceedings and add dignity. The decision on guilt and punishment rested with the whole assembly. Vote was to be by a show of hands. Although there was no appeal, the sentence had to be approved by the executive committee of the county soviet to avoid injustice that might be based on personal grudges. The accused had to be present, unless he refused to attend.

From the outset the new legislation was unpopular with legally trained Communists in the Russian republic, where they were numerous and had longer experience in the law. Opposition was registered in guarded terms on the basis that the general procedural reforms of 1958, designed to establish a new concern for legality, might be violated. The opposition was not without effect, for when the Russian republic's supreme soviet finally adopted a statute on the subject in 1961,[47] the assemblies became work collectives and their jurisdiction was narrowed. They could hear charges only against "parasites" who were fellow workers, performing their allegedly parasitic activities in their spare time. This excluded trials of persons with whom the members of the collective had no close relationship on the job. Further, no case could be heard unless the local prosecutor decided that the collective was more suitable for the trial than the people's court. Practice showed soon after that in most cases the prosecutor chose the people's court as the forum, although this forum in case of "parasites" acted with less formality than in its routine cases.

The 1961 statute of the Russian republic was accepted by all republics which had previously adopted more flexible statutes on the model of 1958. Press reports indicated that under the

[47] 4 May 1961, [1961] 18 Ved. Verkh. Sov. R.S.F.S.R. item 273.

new statute cases went to the collectives, but that there were referrals to the executive committee of the county soviet for approval of any sentence of banishment, as was required by both the 1958 and the 1961 statutes.

Opposition to this form of community action continued among legally trained Communists, but they seem to have had no further influence until after Khrushchev, the champion of the "social assembly," had been ousted. Then, on 20 September 1965,[48] these collectives lost their authority under a statute which returned to the courts in the great cities of Moscow and Leningrad and in Moscow Province exclusive determination of who was a "parasite," and gave the executive committees of the county soviets elsewhere the right to ascertain a breach of order without prior review by a collective.

In a sense the executive committee became an administrative tribunal for the purpose of identifying the offense, but it was of a different nature from the "special boards" of Stalin's time. The suspected "parasite" was given one month's warning to obtain legal employment or face the consequences. There was no secrecy in their proceedings, the accused was present, and the punishment was not confinement in a camp of exceptionally severe discipline. The culprit was not banished to a remote region to sit in a maximum security camp. Those subject to court jurisdiction might be banished from their home cities for from two to five years, but without confinement, although they were under supervision by local police charged with seeing that regular employment was provided. Those subject to executive committee jurisdiction were assigned to work within the province of their domicile.

Much literature has suggested that the system failed in its full mission under the pre-1965 law partly because there was no confinement, but also because the "parasite" continued to practice in his new abode as he had at home. Local residents showed no interest in those brought forcibly into their midst, and they did little or nothing to help in rehabilitation. The "parasites" were unwanted strangers.

Because of this experience the 1965 law placed responsibility for the supervision of convicted "parasites" arriving at their

[48] [1965] 38 *id.* item 932.

place of banishment squarely on the local police, who are now charged with putting them to work. If work is evaded, physical restraints may be imposed by the local people's court. If the convict attempts escape, trial and punishment for the crime are to follow.[49]

To legally trained Communists the whole episode of parasite legislation was distasteful because it smacked of violation of the spirit of the 1958 reforms, even though attempts to distinguish the two have been made. The apologists have argued that "parasitism" was not a "crime" but an administrative offense and, consequently, outside the provisions of the revised code of criminal procedure.[50] This distaste is noteworthy, for it marks the degree to which Soviet society's legally trained members have matured; but at the same time it is a reminder that the lawyers must still make compromises of their ideals with those who have more primitive concepts of "socialist legality."

Mass participation for contemporary Soviet jurists is in no event, even when "parasites" are concerned, to take the form that it has taken among the Chinese.[51] No crowds gather in fields before a stand on which the accused kneels, no mass voice raised in denunciation is palatable to those who now guide policy in the USSR. The vice-president of the USSR supreme court has even denounced the influence of public opinion upon judges in individual cases, except when it is channeled through public accusers and defenders in an orderly procedural form.[52] The final decision must be that of the judges. Sentences of the Odessa provincial court, and also of a court in the Virgin Lands, were denounced because the court cited "the demands of the public" as motivation for the punishment exacted of the convict in a number of cases. To this the vice-president said, "This formulation was rightly subjected to criticism in a survey

[49] This occurs under the Criminal Code R.S.F.S.R., art. 186 (escape from place of exile).

[50] Berman sets forth the Soviet argument and his criticism of it in his SOVIET CRIMINAL LAW AND PROCEDURE, *supra*, note 29 at 9–11.

[51] The Chinese "mass accusation meeting" is described in P. TANG, 1 COMMUNIST CHINA TODAY 272 (2d ed. 1961) and also by SHAO-CHUAN LENG, JUSTICE IN COMMUNIST CHINA 31 (1967).

[52] Anashkin, *The Role of Law Consciousness and Public Opinion in Settling Punishment*, [1967] 1 Sov. GOS. I PRAVO 42. Eng. transl. in [1967] 19 C.D.S.P. no. 9 at 8.

of the USSR Supreme Court's Criminal Cases Collegium as contradictory to the constitutional proposition on the court's independence. . . .''

Judges must not be separated from the emotions of society and public opinion, the vice-president declared, perhaps in reflection of the demands of Lenin's early formulation of what a court should be, but the public must be educated to understand the multisided, unemotional approach to the evaluation of phenomena and law violation which has become the current goal. The tables have been turned, for it is not the public which is to influence the judges emotionally, but the judges who are to influence the public in the direction of a judicial attitude.

This reformulation dramatizes the end of an era. Courts within the Marxian socialist family of states, at least in Europe, have moved progressively away from the simplified procedures and popularized forms chosen by Lenin in 1917 and glorified by the Communist party program of 1919. They have become institutions recognizable to any Western European jurist, even though they may still seem strange to some lawyers of the Anglo-American common-law system. Khrushchev's efforts to regain something of the spirit of the early days by popularizing subsidiary systems of tribunals has met resistance in his own country and even firmer opposition from the Romanist-oriented Marxists among his neighbors to the west.

No observer in a Soviet courtroom can say that all evidence of popularity has evaporated, even though procedural simplicity has clearly been a casualty of fifty years of experience. Judges now sit on elevated chairs with high backs and have carved great seals of state above their heads, but they dress without formality. Indeed, many appear still to be workmen or peasants, even those who have become professionals. Legal training and intellectualization of the working classes have gone far in the USSR, but these influences have not yet changed the appearance of those on the bench, nor have they eliminated all trace of the fraternity of participants in the court drama.

Soviet courts still look and act differently from those in Western Europe, but the contrast in personnel and procedures has been greatly lessened since the turbulent days of militant communism. Perhaps the changed situation has penetrated deeply into the consciousness of the Communists who drafted the 1957 declaration. The following chapter will demonstrate how far the change has gone in the states which started with Lenin's model as their ideal. But even before developing the detail, we can surmise that there were many sitting around the table in 1957 who would have thought reaffirmation of Lenin's goals unnecessary in the current era. It is noteworthy that no demand was made that those who accepted Marxist principles structure their judicial system on such simple and popular lines that courts could be compared in some measure with the tribunals of communally oriented primitive societies, as the Soviet commissar of justice thought possible in 1919.

6

The Erosion of Principles

THE EXPANDING PROFESSIONALISM OF COURTS IN LENIN'S
Russia gave rise to efforts to retain simplicity of procedure, at
least in resolving disputes between state economic enterprises.
The unsuitability of the people's courts for directing the economy was recognized as early as 1918 by a decree authorizing
state enterprise directors to refer to "state arbitration commissions" to settle their problems.[1]

No record exists to show whether there was much arbitration, and perhaps there was little, for not until the introduction
of the New Economic Policy in 1922 was there a real need.
Only then did Lenin demand that the state enterprises end
their wasteful inflationary practices and conduct their affairs in
accordance with the principles of business accounting.

Lenin's new policy made it necessary to allocate blame in
the event of loss so as to rectify the balance sheets of the
enterprises concerned. The only question was the choice of an
agency to perform the task. The 1922 statute's answer was to
create "arbitration commissions" attached to the local eco-

[1] 3 Feb. 1918, [1918] 28 Sob. Uzak. R.S.F.S.R. pt. I item 366.

nomic commissions.[2] Their purpose was to assure simplicity and flexibility, exceeding even that of the regular courts. To emphasize these features, appeal as of right was denied unless the amount claimed exceeded five million rubles. Popularity was never an issue here, for the arbitrators were to be economic experts, and their work was to be reviewed by specially experienced men on local economic boards and ultimately, if necessary, by a Russian republic Supreme Arbitration Commission in Moscow, which was conceived as an instrument of administration, not as a court determining right and wrong.

After federation, a Supreme Arbitration Commission of the USSR was created by decree of 6 May 1924 to hear disputes between economic agencies of "All-Union" concern or between enterprises located in different republics of the federation, and cases in which the director of a republic enterprise requested arbitration by the top body.[3]

The arbitration commissions betrayed the expectations of their creators. By March 1924 the key draftsman of the Russian republic's civil code reported to his colleagues that the arbitration commissions were becoming as legal as the courts, holding the parties to the strict rules of the civil codes.[4] He went so far as to propose merger, but his proposal was not accepted. Consequently, a separate system existed until 1931,[5] when in the general campaign "to strengthen the unity of the judicial system," the arbitration tribunals were merged with the regular courts, with one concession made to the proponents of a separate specialized tribunal. This was that the two lay assessors who sat with the professional judge were to be persons working in the economic organs of the state. To make the merger more palatable, a minister was authorized to settle disputes between enterprises subordinate to his own ministry without reference to court, but he had to act in person and alone.

Arbitration suffered loss of autonomy at the time not because of its utility but in the wide sweep of a new broom wielded by persons who feared that administrative boards would proliferate in other directions if arbitration were left to

[2] 21 Sept. 1922, [1922] 60 id. item 769.
[3] 6 May 1924, [1924] 62 id. item 618.
[4] Speech of comrade Goikhbarg, [1924] 12–13 EZH. SOV. IUST. 285.
[5] 4 March 1931, [1931] 14 Sob. Uzak. R.S.F.S.R. pt. I item 135.

follow its own course. This soon became evident, for the tribunals were recreated within a few months on 3 May, 1931,[6] and they appeared in a form which emphasized that they were not courts—not even specialized commercial courts. Although three levels of tribunals were created, there was to be no right of appeal by a disgruntled enterprise director from one level to another. The basis for jurisdiction of each level was to be the importance of the parties, the location of the place of business, and the size of the claim. The higher the amount sought the higher the appropriate tribunal, presumably to permit wiser and more experienced arbitrators to consider the matter, and also to prevent local prejudices from interfering with a decision when parties came from different republics or provinces.

The tribunals had been restored both to revive the features of simplicity and flexibility which had been fading away and to place the decision-making process in the hands of specialists who understood the activity of state enterprises. At the outset no lawyers were permitted to appear for their clients, and directors alone were to attend. This was to avoid pressures to reject conciliation for legal reasons. The duty of the tribunals was clearly stated to be to facilitate performance of the national economic plan. To this end the tribunals were to seek a formula which would obtain the desired production. The payment of damages was to be only a secondary consideration, and the severity of the penalty was designed not to permit the party wronged to make the profit he would have made in the event of performance, but to cause him to think twice before rejecting a settlement which would salvage most of the lost production.

Since speed was essential in salvaging production, emphasis was upon quick decision, not the determination of the absolute truth. A tribunal would be performing its task most effectively if it examined the facts promptly and found an acceptable solution rather than if it exhausted every effort to determine without question what had happened and then submitted the decision to a higher tribunal for reconsideration of its procedures and its judgment. "Expediency," not rigid adherence to law, either substantive or procedural, became the generally favored rule. To be sure, a minimum of procedure was necessary

[6] 3 May 1931, [1931] 26 *id.* item 203.

to an orderly review of the situation, but the arbitrators were left free to do what they wished to find the facts. They were subject to reversal not for excessive zeal, but only if their work was sloppy in omitting determinative measures they might have taken speedily.

The years changed even these arbitration tribunals in the direction of stability and formality. The arbitrators found the civil code and the code of civil procedure convenient guides to their action. The civil code was finally made applicable, subject to such flexibility of application as seemed necessary to achieve performance of the plan. The issue of stability and formality came to a head in 1960, after Stalin's death, when new sets of fundamental principles for civil law and procedure were discussed. The draftsmen of the civil code proposed to follow what had come to be practice and incorporate the rules for regulation of relations between state enterprises as well as between individuals in the new civil code. Some law professors argued that the issues were not identical. They thought it reasonable to create a special branch of law, called "economic law," to govern state enterprises. It would be less detailed and therefore would offer the arbitration tribunals more chance to apply principles of economic expediency to the resolution of disputes.

The debate between proponents of a new branch of law and those who favored extending the civil code to all civil disputes was complicated because in the late 1920s and early 1930s— when jurists still spoke of a relatively early withering away of the state and law, to be replaced by what Engels had called "the administration of things"—there had been a somewhat similar effort to create a flexible set of separate principles to govern state enterprises, also to be called "economic law." [7] That early effort had been denounced by Stalin in 1930 because it contributed to disorder and to a disrespect for legal obligations in general, and thus hampered his growing reliance on strict observance of law by his subordinates in order to strengthen himself as dictator. Those who proposed "economic law" in the early period had been ousted from their positions and in some cases executed. Consequently, the proponents of a

[7] Eugene B. Pashukanis led this school of thought. His thesis was set forth in his 1 KHOZIASTVENNOE PRAVO (1935) [Economic Law].

new "economic law" in 1960 felt it necessary to state that their proposals had nothing to do with any expectation that civil law would wither away in the near future. They claimed to be concerned solely with creating simple flexible rules to govern the relations of economic enterprises separately from the civil code, so that specialists could quickly decide disputes between state enterprise directors on matters concerning production under the plan.

As the dispute waxed hot between proponents of a new independent "economic law" and those who thought that it would introduce a trend away from the stability and formality which were post-Stalin desiderata of the civil law, Khrushchev referred the matter to a fellow member of the Communist party's Presidium, Alexei N. Kosygin—who later became president of the Council of Ministers after Khrushchev's ouster. After hearing the arguments from both sides he supported the proponents of a unified system of civil law to govern all aspects of the production process from enterprise to ultimate consumer, whether private citizen or state enterprise.[8] The issue was settled for the time being, but lip service was still paid to flexibility and simplicity. A leading specialist in civil procedure said in 1960, "Arbitration procedure is not, of course, civil court procedure." Yet he was able to add, "Nevertheless, in the event of gaps or incompleteness of norms of arbitration, those institutions of arbitration of civil procedure which are similar require application of the corresponding rules of the code of civil procedure." [9]

The trend away from simplicity in arbitration was accentuated by a decree of 1 July 1963 establishing new rules of arbitral procedure, with 133 articles framed like a code but emphasizing some vestiges of earlier attitudes.[10] Thus, its Article 8 requires the parties to attempt to settle their dispute before going to arbitration, and requires the tribunal to reject a suit if the plaintiff has made no attempt to settle peacefully. The code of civil procedure makes no such requirement, but in

[8] This account was given to me privately by some of the persons informed in the matter. All evidence points to its accuracy.

[9] A. KLEINMAN ed., ARBITRAZH V SSSR 15–16 (1960) [Arbitration in the U.S.S.R.].

[10] Eng. transl. in 2 Soviet Statutes and Decisions, no. 1 at 26 (1965).

its Article 34 merely permits the parties to withdraw a suit on settlement, subject to the court's determination that the settlement has not violated law. Further, the arbitration code requires the parties to exercise their rights in good conscience, to strive for a thorough, objective resolution of the dispute, and to manifest respect for the property rights and legal interests of the other party. The code of civil procedure makes no such requirement, and it requires the court to accept any complaint that is filed.

The arbitration code includes no rule for the evaluation of evidence, requiring only that the parties present whatever is necessary to support their case and authorizing the tribunal to demand more evidence or to exclude what is presented as irrelevant. The code of civil procedure contains the historic article already discussed, authorizing the judge to hear or see anything and to evaluate what he has heard or seen in accordance with his "inner conviction."

Complaints in the Soviet press indicate the extent to which legalisms have gained ascendancy since the adoption of the new civil code.[11] Lawyers now regularly appear for clients, often without the enterprise director or deputy director, and they are accused of refusing to compromise their cases. They refuse to recognize their client's responsibility, and some are accused of bringing unnecessary suits. They decide alone when suits are to be filed. Thus, if there is no money to be gained for their client they do not bring suit, even though the contract provides for penalties in the event of delayed performance. From their point of view, since the law puts 95 percent of the recovery of fines into the state treasury, the suit is unrewarding, and a busy lawyer should not spend his time in such actions.

Although some writers press for a return to the flexible and simple procedures of earlier times, some want even more stability and formality. Thus, appeals are being requested as they are found in the court system,[12] and this request is justified by the

---

[11] See Klement'ev, *Conflicts over Economic Inadequacies in Arbitration,* [1965] 10 Sov. IUST. 16; Khokhriakov, *A Higher Level of Organization and Culture in the Work of a Legal Adviser,* [1965] 4 *id.* 5; Brinykh, *For Effectiveness of Property Sanctions,* [1965] 23 *id.* 7.

[12] Dashkevich, *Make Effective the Structure of State Arbitration,* [1965] 16 *id.* 15.

claim that without the right of appeal no uniformity can be maintained in the law as it is applied by the tribunals in various provinces. These commentators are not content with the half-way measure permitted by the law, which forbids appeals as of right to disgruntled parties but nonetheless permits them to file a complaint with a chief arbitrator at a higher level. Although he is not required to respond, a complaint sometimes causes him to require rehearing to overcome obvious error and lack of uniformity.

The extent of transition to formality is shown in an *Izvestiia* correspondent's comment that since the arbitration system has lost its flexibility, claims for damages, at least, should be transferred to the regular courts, which would subject them to greater formality of procedure and to verification through appeal.[13]

State arbitration, under this proposal, would continue to exist solely to resolve those disputes which arise before a contract is concluded between parties who disagree as to what meets the requirements of the national economic plan. Courts have no precontract function; so some tribunal close to the administration must be the instrument of decision if such disputes continue to occur in state economic planning.

The future of state arbitration thus might seem assured, but, again, change is in the air in Eastern Europe. Voluntarism in the creation of economic relationships between state enterprises is part of the new post-Stalin economy in every Marxian socialist land. It is as yet in an early stage, and the plan still sets many basic relationships, but trials are being made of a system of planning which sets only primary goals. The enterprises are left to develop the details on the basis of what is beginning to be a form of consumers' choice. If this trend continues, precontract disputes will become a thing of the past because there will be no obligation to make a contract. State arbitration would then lose what currently seems to be its long-range reason for existence, and it would revert to being only an instrument for conflict resolution after breach of contract. As such it might become a specialized economic court, presided over by men

---

[13] Rcheulishvili, *The Arbitrator Is Mistaken*, Izvestiia, 10 June 1965. Eng. transl. in [1965] 17 C.D.S.P. no. 23 at 22.

who know administrative problems and administer inflexible law by strict rules of procedure. Verification of their action would be, as in the regular courts, by chambers of the supreme courts of the republics and of the USSR.

Yugoslav Communists have long since felt pressure for reforms of the state arbitration system along such lines. They have abandoned detailed economic planning for a statement only of broad policy goals. Administrative officials at the center have been reduced in number so that they could not, even if they would, exercise authority after decisions reserved by law to the local plant directors. The Yugoslav state arbitration was converted into an "economic court" in 1954 in response to pressures for revision of the Soviet model.[14] Disputes between enterprises, whether subordinate to state, commune, cooperative, or other collective body, are resolved by tribunals functioning under the rules of civil procedure applicable to courts and in application of the civil code. In short, the Yugoslav economic court has become a regular court, different only in that its judges have specialized knowledge suitable to the type of case they are called upon to hear.[15]

The Czechoslovak administrators are feeling the same pressures to stabilize a Soviet-type arbitration tribunal and its procedures when disputes between state enterprises come before them. Two authors have said, "Arbitration which has until now been conceived mainly as an organ of state administration should, in our opinion, take on more of the character of a judicial organ (perhaps something like a commercial court)." [16] They find it intolerable that arbitration may establish, modify, and annul legal relations which the parties have established, for they expect the role of law to be changed: "It will take on once more its classical nature which can be described by the formula,

[14] Law of 2 July 1954, [1954] J. of L. Yugoslavia no. 31. Eng. transl. in [1954] 3–4 NEW YUGOSLAV LAW 55.

[15] Prof. Branko M. Pešelj, a Yugoslav now a United States citizen, doubts that substantive change has occurred. He believes that the economic courts are comparable to the arbitration boards found in other Marxian socialist legal systems. See his *Socialist Character of "Jugoslav Law."* 1 REVIEW (Dorking, Eng.) 75 (1961).

[16] Boguszak & Jicinsky, *The Reform in Economic Management in Czechoslovakia*, 12 REVIEW OF CONTEMPORARY LAW, no. 1 at 66, 76–77 (1965).

'if certain given conditions are brought together, the organs concerned have certain given rights and obligations.' " Such stability requires formalization of procedures; and the authors draw this necessary conclusion, for they close, "It is therefore desirable that arbitration proceedings should become more like those of an ordinary court."

If the changes which have occurred in Yugoslavia and which are proposed in Czechoslovakia were made elsewhere in Eastern Europe, where the Soviet model of an independent state arbitration system exists—authorized to act speedily and with simplicity in resolution of disputes between state enterprises—it would generally mark the end in Marxist-oriented states of Europe of a prominent characteristic of the family of Marxian socialist legal systems. There might then emerge, as in the Western world, ad hoc arbitration established by the parties with or without the help of professional associations maintaining panels of arbitrators to resolve disputes outside the formal channels provided by state arbitration. This ad hoc practice has already begun in the USSR under an order issued by the USSR Council of Ministers in 1959, authorizing enterprise directors to choose third parties to resolve a given dispute if the parties are in the same city or in cities not far apart.[17]

In practice the new Soviet ad hoc arbitration has been placed in the hands of a fellow director who knows the parties and in whom both have confidence not only because of his wisdom but because of his expert knowledge. This method of resolving a dispute offers the advantage of saving time because the fellow director needs little explanation to understand the industrial process and local conditions which have influenced the performance, and he can realistically conclude what could be done to salvage production.

The trend in the USSR, Yugoslavia, and Czechoslovakia toward formality and complexity of procedures used in the resolution of disputes, not only in the courts but in state arbitration, is being paralleled elsewhere in Eastern Europe.

[17] Order of 23 July 1959, no. 824, [1959] 15 Sob. Post. S.S.S.R. item 105; also pub. in 1 ZAKONODATEL'NYE AKTY PO VOPROSAM NARODNOGO KHOZIASTVA 742, par. 4. [Legislative Acts on Questions of the National Economy]. See also Efimochkin, *For Further Democratization of the Work of Organs of Arbitration*, [1960] 6 SOTS. ZAK. 42.

Although Communists adopted the Soviet pattern for dispute resolution after the war when they established their states, they took the pattern as it had evolved by 1946, not as it was in the Russia of 1917. No one experimented with the informal tribunal created by Lenin to serve the community without codes of procedure or codes of substantive law.

In 1949 and 1950 Poland introduced by amendments to the 1928 prewar statute on court organization the Soviet model of two lay assessors to sit with the professional judge in all civil and criminal matters, and reduced to one the number of possible appeals.[18] Parties were not required to have an attorney. Other Marxian socialist states followed the same model for courts, prosecutors, and bar, but Bulgaria and Cuba introduced variations.

Bulgaria omitted the lay assessors in 80 percent of the civil suits, so as to call fewer people away from work, and required that only complicated suits be tried by the traditional Soviet type of bench.[19] Cuba's variation was really a carry-over from the past rather than an institution developed for the new conditions. Professional judges are appointed and function without lay assessors, but critics have already proposed democratization along the now-familiar Marxian socialist line.[20] The first steps were taken in the Province of Oriente to establish "people's tribunals," on which lay assessors sat alongside the permanent judges. These assessors were chosen, as elsewhere, from nominees proposed by workers in factories, mills, and farms. A Soviet commentator expects these new courts to be introduced elsewhere.

After the events of October 1956, Poland moved even further in the direction of formality by reemphasizing the professionalism and dignity of the court. By statute of 1957, graduation from a university law school again became a requirement for judicial position, and the candidate also needed two years'

---

[18] [1949] 32 J. of L. Poland item 237 and [1950] 38 *id.* item 347. For an account of the Polish system, see Jodlowski, *Organisation Judiciare* in INTRODUCTION À L'ÉTUDE DE DROIT POLONAIS 331 (S. Rozmaryn ed. 1967).

[19] Kulikova, *Exchange of Experience between Jurists of Socialist Countries,* [1965] 1 SOTS. ZAK. 38.

[20] Leonoi, *Revolutionary Jurisprudence of the Republic of Cuba,* [1965] 1 SOV. IUST. 25.

apprenticeship and had to pass a judge's examination.[21] The law of 1950,[22] which had authorized the Ministry of Justice to dispense with legal education and apprenticeship, and which entirely abolished the judicial examination, was repealed.

Judges, prosecutors, and attorneys were gowned in black robes, piped in purple, red, or green to denote courtroom function. The professional judge was again the bearer of the great seal of the judicial office, which he or she wore in the form of a golden pendant on a golden chain. Although not in itself a source of formality, judicial dress contributes to deemphasizing popularity. The officials in the courtroom are distinguished visually from their fellow citizens, as they generally are in the West. Thus, the robes of the Polish judiciary contrast sharply with the everyday clothes worn by the Soviet bench. The Soviet prosecutors, however, have been costumed since just before the war in military-type uniforms bearing epaulets denoting rank in the profession, which suggest a clear distinction between these officials and the masses.

It is against these trends in Eastern Europe that the Chinese Communists, and in lesser measure the North Koreans, have rebelled. Although the Chinese established their court structure, their office of procurator, and their system of advocates on the Soviet models, some observers now doubt that their provisional regulations of 1951 and their Organic Law of 1954 can be taken at face value. In the light of Chinese tradition, can they have understood the implications of what they were doing in trying to emulate the system developed by their Soviet comrades? Certainly the record since 1957 suggests that the commitments to the Soviet pattern, with its incipient formality and rejection of simplicity, were not firmly held even while they were being assumed.[23]

No change has been made in the formal structure of the court system since 1957. The supreme people's court continues to supervise inferior courts like those of the USSR. There are

[21] 29 May 1957, [1957] 31 J. of L. Poland item 133.

[22] 20 July 1950, [1950] 38 *id*. item 347.

[23] For an account of the trend toward stability and its reversal in 1957 see SHAO-CHUAN LENG, JUSTICE IN COMMUNIST CHINA 45–63 (1967). See also Tsai Huan, An Analysis of Peiping's People's Courts, 3 ISSUES AND STUDIES (Taiwan) no. 8 at 15–23 (1967).

both general and special courts, the latter hearing criminal charges related to military matters. Yet, although the courts have kept their initial structure, the same cannot be said of court procedures. The trend toward the formalities of the Soviet system which was evident in June 1957, after a very informal start during the early years, has not continued. The high point of Soviet procedural influence was in 1956, when the judicial committee of the supreme people's court issued a summarization of procedural law to be used on a trial basis in the people's courts.[24] This effort to introduce procedural order recalls what was done by the Commissariat of Justice in July 1918 in Soviet Russia, but the events since 1956 have not duplicated the experience of the courts of the USSR. On the contrary, many of the judges inherited from the past have been dismissed and their places taken by simpler persons.

In 1957 Chinese Communists denounced principles of procedure adopted by the Soviet code makers in the post-Stalin era as "theories of bourgeois jurisprudence." They declared that the post-Stalin Soviet procedures would protect the guilty from punishment and restrict the judicial organs and masses in their fight against counterrevolutionary and other criminal elements. Singled out for special attack were the principles being enshrined in the Soviet fundamentals—presumption of innocence, benefit of the doubt to the accused, and the free conscientious evaluation of evidence.[25]

Mao restored in more restrained form the mass line with which he had begun his purge of landlords when he seized power. This had been characterized by mass public trials in the fields, during which the peasants had chanted the verdict of "guilty" in response to a request from the tribune for their views. His "taking the courts to the people" was not done as it was in the USSR, where a hearing was held like that in a courtroom, differing only in locale. The Chinese concept included evoking public outbursts denouncing the accused, simplifying

[24] See LENG, supra, note 23, at 147, citing Kao Ko-lin (vice-president of the court), Work of the Supreme People's Court since 1955, New China News Agency, Peking, 24 April 1959.

[25] See LENG, id. 63, citing Wu Lu, Refute the View of the Benefit of Doubt for the Accused, [1958] 4 CHENG-FA YEN CHIU 59 and Chang Tzu-pei, Criticize the Bourgeois Principle of "Free Conscientious Judgment of Evidence," [1958] 2 id. 42.

procedure, and executing the sentence on the spot. Chinese commentators reported with pride that cases were adjudged within a day, and that more than 80 percent were tried outside the courtroom at the place where they would attract the persons most intimately concerned. There is marked contrast with the practice in Eastern Europe, where strict silence is enforced, except for rare, notable exceptions, as in the 1968 trials of Moscow protesters against limitations on freedom of expression.

Only in civil cases, and particularly those concerned with divorce, did the Chinese courts continue to exhibit respect for order, albeit with little success outside the capital. But, even in Peking the emphasis was upon conciliation and mediation far more than in other Marxist-oriented states.

Some Western authorities of Chinese origin explain this difference as stemming from the traditional Chinese view that the law's function is to protect the political and social order rather than to guard private rights and interests.[26] Interpreters without this background are asked to consider the influence of China's long experience in forming a moral climate in which illegal acts are restrained not by fear of law but out of respect for an ethic comparable to that taught by Confucius but today remolded by Mao.[27] Readers are reminded of the long history of the *li* as a system of propriety which has exerted a major influence on the resolution of conflict in Chinese society for generations. This contrasts sharply with the *fa*, which is the norm, comparable to a law, designed to punish illegal action after commission.

Whatever its origin, conciliation was institutionalized in pre-Marxist China through the creation of conciliation commissions, and the Communists recreated the institution in the Provisional Organizational Act of the People's Conciliation Commission, promulgated by the State Administrative Council on 22 March 1954.[28] The act establishes no compulsion to conciliate, nor does it make conciliation a precondition to suit, but it is widely used and is hailed as a means of educating the

[26] See LENG, *id.* 171.

[27] Lee, *Chinese Communist Law: Its Background and Development*, 60 MICH. L. REV. 439 at 440, 448 (1962). Also LENG, *id.* 172.

[28] Lee, *id.* 458, citing text in CHUNG-HUA JEN-MIN KUNG-HO-KUO FA-KUEI HSUAN-CHI 295 (1957) [Collection of laws and regulations of the People's Republic of China].

masses and reducing the length of crowded court calendars. In addition there are street committees in every residential area, with the duty of settling individual disputes before they reach such proportions that they lead to court. They have proved most effective in simple, immobile societies.

Although other Marxist-oriented states have also been seen to favor mediation and mass participation through comrades' courts in the resolution of disputes and the disciplining of social offenders, China has gone further. Some believe that Khrushchev appreciated the mass attractiveness of the Chinese trend and that China's lead was a factor in Khrushchev's revival of the comrades' courts in the USSR after Stalin had let them lapse. And they especially see Chinese influence in his development of the concept of the "social assembly" to try "parasites." [29] Although Khrushchev may have been trying to reduce the difference to avoid being typed as a "revisionist," events since his ouster have again increased it. As has been seen, the social assemblies have been abolished in the USSR, indicating that his move came from his own imagination and was not supported by the culture pattern which other Marxian-oriented Communists have developed over the years. China has been left to stand quite alone.

The emphasis upon simplicity has been made evident in China not only in doctrinal discussion and the espousal of mediation with ever-increasing fervor, but also in practice. Interviews conducted by Professor Jerome Alan Cohen with former Communist Chinese law-enforcement officers in Hong Kong indicate that low priority has been given to procedural safeguards even when they have been put on paper by the central authorities.[30] Chinese writers even supported this trend by insisting that the Soviet legal model was inapplicable to China and denounced those who relied upon Soviet practice as "making a set of troublesome procedures." [31] Severe police-imposed sanctions were perfected into a system, leaving the courts and procuracy with rights and duties which they were unable to

[29] O'Connor, *Soviet Procedures in Civil Decisions: A Changing Balance between Public and Civic Systems of Public Order*, [1964] U. ILL. L. F. 51 at 101, n. 214.

[30] Cohen, *The Criminal Process in the People's Republic of China*, 79 HARV. L. REV. 469 at 527–28 (1966).

[31] *Id.* 484, n. 27.

exercise, even if they wished to. Defense counsels became scarce, and the staffs of their offices slipped away. Judicial "teams" went to the villages to find offenders. Newspapers reported that these teams used techniques which had the advantage of smashing permanent rules, and judges were praised for showing the courage to innovate. Still, interviews have suggested that the move did not bring back a reign of terror like that of 1949–53.

The Chinese Communist party found it necessary, although fostering the mass line, to develop a better-ordered system of imposing sanctions than had been developed up to that time; for the party needed reliable determination of guilt. The Chinese Communists differ from their comrades to the West in their rejection of the latter's post-Stalin conclusion that reliability of proof may be found in the open trial conducted under codified rules of procedure and subject to reversal in the event of error. To the Chinese, truth is discoverable through secret inquisitorial procedures, conducted mainly by police and without what they identify as the delaying tactics used by hairsplitting lawyers seeking to take advantage of procedural guarantees. They are content to leave to the police the conduct of the entire proceeding, including the sentencing, in all but serious cases. Even when capital punishment is ordered, although they require judges to verify the work of the police to overcome the danger of accepting false confessions which could conceal the real criminal, they will not codify or foster professionalism to safeguard the principle that verification is designed to protect.

The North Koreans, as the "Democratic People's Republic of Korea," have taken somewhat the same position as the Chinese, although they have not extended it to such extremes.[32] With a cultural heritage which includes much of the same Confucian ethic, they have chosen to reject professionalism and to favor simplification of procedures, although, unlike China, they have adopted procedural codes. Their position is epito-

---

[32] Ch'oe Hakchu, *Kim Ilsong susang tongchi ui kyosi silchon ul uihan t'uchaeng kwa chongeso Pyongyangsi komch'alsoka otun kyonghom* [Experience Gained by the City Prosecutor's Office of Pyongyang in the Process of the Struggle to Practice the Teachings of Comrade Premier Kim Ilsong] [1959] 5 MINJU SAPOP 33–36, cited by Pyong Choon Hahm in unpublished manuscript scheduled to be published in shortened form in AM. J. COMP. L.

mized in their renunciation as a mysticism of professionalism among the judiciary. They require legal education neither in law nor in practice, even for the full-time judge in their people's court, for they think that legally trained minds are inflexible. As a consequence deference to procedure is slight, and this informal approach is enhanced by the procedural code copied from that of the Russian republic, which gives judges broad authority to discard formal rules of evidence, to avoid mechanical and formal interpretations of law, to continue or discontinue the trial as seems desirable, and to investigate the "whole man." The difference from the Soviet trend is that when Korean specialists attempted to introduce features like those of the 1958 reforms in the USSR, they were rejected by the Communist party, which preferred to retain the flexibility of earlier Soviet times.

The Chinese and North Koreans cannot be lightly dismissed as taking positions forever contrary to those gaining currency in Eastern Europe. Soviet jurists used the same arguments of utility in progressing up the first steps of their ladder of procedural reform. To a degree, the Soviet procedures still rest heavily upon police inquest or pretrial investigation to establish fact, but the burden is increasingly being put upon the court to reexamine the work of the pretrial investigators with great care. The Soviet emphasis since 1958 upon recognition of the presumption of innocence has exemplified the new attitude. Prosecutors have argued that such a presumption cannot exist, for it would be a vote of no confidence in the police and procuracy, who are charged with withholding a case from trial unless they are convinced of guilt. To this argument the highest Soviet judicial authorities have replied in sharp terms.[33] The court is not to take for granted that the police and procuracy are always correct, and an open trial including the participation of a defense attorney and applying rules set forth in a code of procedure now seems imperative to Soviet jurists not only to avoid convicting the innocent and leaving the criminal at large to commit further depredations, but also to implement a new concern for "socialist humanism" which began to emerge in 1958.

---

[33] Eng. transl. of the Soviet press reports in [1965] 16 C.D.S.P. no. 51 at 25 and [1965] 17 *id.* no. 4 at 11.

Again it is the difference in attitudes, and not solely in practice, which distinguishes the Soviet and East Asian approaches to the values of simplicity and popularity, which may still be taken in varying degrees as characterizing the family of Marxian socialist legal systems. If the Soviet position, supported also by the Communist-led states of Eastern Europe, were to be taken as characteristic, the gap between the Marxian socialist and Romanist families of law on attitudes toward simplicity and formality could be said to be narrowing; but when the Chinese and Korean attitudes are considered, it is wide indeed.

A final assessment of the distinctive procedure of Marxian socialist legal systems depends on an answer to two questions. Is the East Asian communist position only temporary, adopted solely for a period of violent revolutionary reform and directed no longer against the leading members of the former bourgeois society but against those who seem to Mao and Kim Ilsong to be turning too quickly to stability and formality and away from innovation? Or, should Mao's and Kim's positions be taken as heralding a permanently espoused hostility toward formality and complexity in the maintenance of social order? If it is the latter, the comparatist can but note a new element of style. If it is the former, there is only a time differential which, when overcome, will place the entire Marxian socialist legal family, in spite of variations in detail, very close to, if not within, the Romanist tradition of court structure and procedure.

A westerner may betray his imprisonment by the culture in which he lives when he concludes that it is the European trend which will become characteristic of the Marxian socialist states as a whole, and that even the Chinese will eventually conform to the pattern set by the European Communist leaders. Although it can be no more than a guess that modern society, wherever constituted, will require a more formally structured social order than the Chinese interpretation of Marxian socialist doctrine now permits, such a prognostication seems justified by the record in Eastern Europe. Certainly the Soviet leaders believe this to be the case, and their sharp criticism of the Chinese variation shows them to insist that stability and formality become features of the system in any Marxian socialist state as soon as the major opposition from the ousted regime and its partisans has been overcome.

7

Landownership and Land

Utilization

O WNERSHIP OF PROPERTY IS THE CRITICAL ELEMENT IN THE
Marxist criteria for classification of legal systems. The unique
place claimed for the family of Marxian socialist legal systems is
justified by nothing so much as its keystone concept: state
ownership of the means of production. On this principle all else
rests, particularly state economic planning, which Marxian socialists view as their major contribution to modern social organization.

With such a heritage of belief, the Communist parties in
power in 1957 could have been expected to place high upon
their list of "basic laws applicable to all countries embarking
upon the socialist course" the requirement that "public ownership" be substituted for capitalist ownership. Property law becomes, therefore, the key subject to be examined in determining
the Marxian socialist position on substantive law. The question
to be asked is, What does public ownership mean as a modern
criterion to be enshrined in a legal system?

To begin with the soil as the fundamental resource, the comparatist cannot overlook the wide variation that has emerged among the members of the family of Marxian socialist legal systems as they devise policies acceptable under the rubric of "public ownership." From Lenin's rule requiring monopoly of landownership in the state to the Polish and Yugoslav Communists' acquiescence in continued private ownership of peasant farms, there is a wide choice of formulas. Doctrine has not required that the Soviet model be followed, even in major detail, although there has been a pattern of use in the social interest which is the common denominator of all.

With his first two decrees on the land, Lenin established an attitude of mind which guides leaders in deciding what may be accepted in their countries. This attitude requires predominance of social interests, but is tempered by willingness to compromise with peasant mentality when refusal to compromise would inspire sabotage of the agricultural process by a disgruntled peasantry. Lenin's first decree expropriated only landlords and left the peasants in ownership of their plots.[1] He admitted frankly that he had compromised.[2] The Socialist Revolutionary party to which most of the peasants belonged was too strong and his Bolsheviks too weak to permit him to proceed as fast as he wished. It was not until the Constituent Assembly called to decide on a government of the new Russia had been dispersed in January 1918 and the peasant influence on politics had been greatly weakened that he felt able to take his second step and nationalize the land. With his decree of 19 February 1918,[3] landownership was monopolized by the state. No retreat from this position has since been permitted, even during the trying times of the Second World War when the peasants' loyalty was undermined by German attempts to woo them through the promise of a return to private landholding.

Lenin's strict principle was incorporated in early legislation and now is in Article 6 of the USSR constitution of 1936. This article became the rock on which land law has been built. Judging from what was done when Marxists first tested Lenin's

[1] 28 Oct. 1917, o.s., [1917] 1 Sob. Uzak. R.S.F.S.R. pt. I item 3.
[2] Eng. transl. of Lenin's statement in BUNYAN & FISHER, THE BOL-SHEVIK REVOLUTION 1917–1918 at 128 (1934).
[3] [1918] 25 Sob. Uzak. R.S.F.S.R. pt. I item 346.

formula elsewhere, with the advent of the Mongolian People's Republic in 1921, the formula was considered appropriate to any Marxist-oriented state, no matter how different. The first Mongolian constitution of 1924 also declared land to be the property of the state.[4]

Mongol patterns in emulation of the steps Lenin had taken to socialize the economy seemed to portend a similar program for other legal systems as they came under the control of Communists. Yet this prophecy was not to be fulfilled after the Second World War when states in Eastern Europe and Asia entered the new fold. Not one of them nationalized the land. Perhaps the long tradition of private ownership by peasant households made it perilous for would-be expropriators to proceed with such a scheme. Whatever the reason, all the postwar Marxian socialist leaders stopped their land reforms at a stage comparable to that established by Lenin's first decree, nationalizing only the great estates and exempting peasant households from socialization.

Yugoslav Communists are an example. In their first land law of 23 August 1945 they declared in Article 1 that "Land belongs to those who cultivate it." [5] Landlords employing labor on more than twenty-five to thirty-five hectares were deprived of ownership, as were absentee landlords on plots of any size, banks, joint stock companies, financial institutions, and persons not engaged in agriculture; but individuals who wished to till the land themselves could retain from twenty-five to thirty-five hectares, and the land obtained from the landlords was allocated to other individual households by a system of priorities which placed the poor peasants first, giving preference among them to veterans and to families of those killed in the war or by fascists. After allocation the land could not be sold, divided, or leased.

Yugoslav authors [6] claim that the policy, even though lim-

---

[4] Eng. transl. in CHINA YEAR BOOK 1926 at 795 (Peking, 1926). The historical background is set forth in P. S. H. TANG, RUSSIAN AND SOVIET POLICY IN MANCHURIA AND OUTER MONGOLIA 1911–1931 (1959).

[5] [1945] J. of L. Yugoslavia no. 64. Eng. transl. in 1 COLLECTION OF YUGOSLAV LAWS (THE LEGAL STATUS OF AGRICULTURAL LAND) 17 (Institute of Comparative Law, Belgrade, 1962).

[6] Vučković, Foreword, id. 5 at 6.

ited in the extent of socialization, had socialist features because the private employment of hired hands by landowners was prohibited, in conformity with the Marxist creed that exploitation of labor must be abolished. Also, use by cooperatives of peasants was encouraged. These features were accentuated by a second law of 1953 [7] on the agricultural land fund representing public property, which reduced the maximum private holding to ten hectares, with permission given to grant up to fifteen hectares in special circumstances of custom relating to religious or other ethnic considerations. Land acquired from expropriation under this policy was not allocated to private individuals as their own property, but was distributed entirely to agricultural cooperatives.

Two laws subsequently enacted, in 1957 [8] and 1959,[9] reemphasized the socialist features. Under the first every owner or land user is required to cultivate the land as other land is cultivated in the given district, and the propriety of the use is supervised by the people's committee of the region, called a "commune." Cultivable land which is not tilled within one year of the last harvest is to be taken temporarily from the owners or users and given to an agricultural organization or another individual farmer for use; but the cooperatives, as socialist organizations, are given priority in any such distribution. During the period of one to three years' temporary use, the user must pay rent to the owner if the latter is resident in Yugoslavia and if the owner's failure to cultivate was justified by old age, illness, or physical incapacity. On termination of the temporary use, the owner may reclaim the land from the people's committee of the commune, but it will be lost again if not cultivated within a period set by the committee.

The 1959 law requires every user, individual or cooperative, to use the land for agricultural purposes and in accordance with an approved plan, prepared with the help of technical commis-

[7] Law on the Agricultural Land Fund, [1953] J. of L. Yugoslavia no. 22. Eng. transl. in COLLECTION, *supra*, note 5 at 33.

[8] Law on the Cultivation of Uncultivated Lands. [1957] J. of L. Yugoslavia no. 12. Eng. transl. in COLLECTION, *supra*, note 5 at 45.

[9] Law on the Utilization of Agricultural Land. [1959] J. of L. Yugoslavia no. 43. Eng. transl. in COLLECTION, *supra*, note 5 at 51.

sions to assure maximum benefit through soil improvement. Those who refuse to follow the plan lose the land.

Although they follow a program of individual peasant farming, the Yugoslav Communists have not entirely abandoned their original pattern. In 1966 there were some two hundred state farms in operation, and some fifteen hundred agricultural cooperatives (*zadrugas*) owned land and machinery and had authority to rent land from peasants and to provide services on a contract basis.[10]

Only Poland has followed a pattern similar to that established by Yugoslavia, designed both to stimulate production by an individualistic agricultural population and to foster achievement of societal aims. Thus, restraints were initiated by the land reform decree of 1944,[11] limiting maximum holdings to fifty hectares in fertile central and eastern Poland, and one hundred hectares in less fertile and more thickly populated western Poland. Real-estate transactions in the newly created farms were forbidden unless permission was specially granted. Surplus holdings were expropriated by the state. Also, there was emphasis upon bringing the peasants together into various forms of cooperatives; but since they were liberated from domination by Soviet policy makers in 1956, the Polish Communists have ceased this pressure. On the contrary, most producing cooperatives were disbanded as members withdrew to resume traditional methods. By 1961 the land being farmed by private owners occupied 86.8 percent of the total area under crops, and accounted for almost 90 percent of the total production of Polish agriculture.

To restrain private owners to the benefit of the social interest under this new liberalized policy, however, measures were taken to limit the right to dispose. Although a 1957 statute[12] abolished all previous restrictions on sale, it required the buyer

[10] Freidmann, *Freedom and Planning in Yugoslavia's Economic System*, 25 SLAVIC REVIEW 630 at 638 (1966).

[11] 6 Sept. 1944, [1945] 3 J. of L. Poland item 13. See Stelmachowski, *Droit rural* in INTRODUCTION À L'ÉTUDE DU DROIT POLONAIS 241 (S. Rozmaryn ed. 1967). The author is also indebted to an unpublished study on Polish land law by Dr. A. W. Rudzinski.

[12] 13 July 1957, [1957] 39 J. of L. Poland item 172.

to submit a certificate, issued by the local administrative authority, evidencing his practical or theoretical qualifications to undertake farming; but no sale might exceed fifteen hectares for crop farms, or twenty for animal-breeding farms. Also, the Communist party, by resolution implemented by the supreme court in 1960, established a minimum limit to the size of farms distributed on death in accordance with age-old custom among heirs. Under 1964 regulations the resulting plot may not be less than two hectares in southern Poland, three hectares in central Poland, and four to five hectares in the other parts of the country. Also, heirs must qualify as experienced farmers, just as if they were purchasers.[13]

Use by private owners is also controlled, for they must plant according to plans set by county authorities to maximize production and must deliver grain, potatoes, and meat to the state under compulsory low-price deliveries covering about 60 percent of all produce acquired by the state. Private owners are encouraged to join cooperatives to purchase farm machinery on a communal basis,[14] and to make contracts with social organizations for delivery of their produce after they meet compulsory deliveries, although for these deliveries they receive open-market prices and technical assistance, seeds, and farm equipment.

Even Soviet land law has introduced some private overtones, in spite of strict adherence to Lenin's rule of state monopoly of ownership. Lenin was himself responsible for these overtones, and they were adopted to gain what he thought would be the advantage of incentives long associated with private ownership, without restoring title to the peasants. He adapted the institution of *emphyteusis*, used in the Roman law of the emperors, to create a "perpetual use" under which peasant households were allotted the use of land, all of which continued to be the property of the state. By the land code of 1922,[15] however, use was not ownership under another name, for severe restrictions of the right to dispose were instituted. There could be no sale,

---

[13] Civil Code 1964, arts. 160–67. The number of hectares permitted to an owner has varied. It is set by regulation in implementation of the code.

[14] Stelmachowski, *supra*, note 11 at 252 has summarized the law of 17 Feb. 1961, [1961] 12 J. of L. Poland item 61.

[15] 30 Oct. 1922, [1922] 68 Sob. Uzak. R.S.F.S.R. pt. I item 901.

leasing, or gift. Land as allocated by the village soviet's land department was to be used only for the purposes specified in the allocation, and if the user died or moved away, the use reverted to the land department for reallocation to those who could qualify.

Social features were also emphasized; priority in allocation was to be given to peasants organized in cooperatives of various forms. Not many of these existed, but there were enough to indicate the direction in which Communists expected the peasants to move. The simplest was the TOZ, in which farmers held their plots in their own names but combined to buy mechanized equipment and seeds. The second type was the *artel*, in which land use of the major fields was pooled, as was labor, but distribution of the income was on the basis of contribution in time and in accordance with skills. Each peasant family continued to own its home and a small garden plot near it. The third was the commune, in which all was pooled and distribution was made according to need. A fourth form of communal use was called the "state farm." It was designed in 1917 as a means of continuing the effective farming of former landed estates on which specialized types of agriculture required group effort under technical direction. Peasants on these farms received a wage and were considered on a par with laborers in a factory. Within the Marxist scale of values, this put them at the top of the favored class of "toilers."

When Stalin decided in 1929 to force the private peasant households into a socialized form of the cooperative movement, he chose the *artel* as the preferred type. The TOZ and the commune were transformed, and millions of private peasants were made to pool their land use in the *artel*, to which all uses were assigned in perpetuity. Although peasant resistance was so extreme that a halt had to be called to the campaign in 1930, it was later resumed, and the "collective farm," which became the colloquial name for the *artel*, arose as the symbol of the Soviet type of agriculture.

The model charter developed for the collective farm in 1930 [16] and revised in 1935 [17] established the legal status of land

[16] 1 March 1930, [1930] 24 Sob. Zak. S.S.S.R. pt. I item 255.
[17] 17 Feb. 1935, [1935] 11 *id.* item 82.

use by providing that use was assigned to the collective farm without limit of time, but it was not subject to sale or lease by the *artel*. Further, land had to be used for the purpose for which it had been assigned, so had to be maintained in good condition, with crops planted to meet a schedule of compulsory deliveries to the state under a price schedule which was lower than that obtainable on the open market. Easements were permitted to benefit users of land cut off from highways and water, but these easements were recognized only when they were necessary to production. There could be no gaining of an easement by long-uncontested use.

Although transfer by sale or lease was forbidden to those who received perpetual use, there was no limitation on transfer by inheritance. Inheritance presented no problem because the perpetual use was assigned not to an individual but to a household representing an extended family. Thus the death of any member, including the senior one, occasioned no inheritance. Usage continued in the family unless its ranks were so depleted that it could no longer till the land to full advantage, in which case it reverted to the land department for reassignment. This rule was extended to some of the land tilled by families entering the *artel*, for on their entry they did not transfer to the *artel* all the land which had previously been assigned to them. They were permitted to retain a small plot, varying in size with the fertility of the land, and this private garden passed from generation to generation under the rules applicable to households generally. If members leave the household a division may be permitted, but always subject to the consent of the land department authorized to decide whether it should be permitted.

Although nearly complete collectivization had occurred by the beginning of the world war, there remained some peasant households, usually in remote regions, which held the use of the land under allocations made in accordance with the principles of the 1922 land code. This has persisted, and as late as 1965 some 200,000 private households continued to use land outside of the collectives.

Withdrawal of perpetual use is forbidden without strict adherence to procedures designed to place the decision with high authorities removed from the influence of the local officials.[18] To require otherwise would make the right of perpetual use something less than perpetual, and nullify the purpose of its concept—to inspire in the peasant a sense that labor expended in improvement of the land will be rewarded and not lost through expropriation. Yet modern civilization must allow for industrial expansion, and farming land has to give way to the needs of factory and highway construction. To meet this situation, the law provides that if use is revoked, the perpetual users must be paid the value of structures and crops upon the land so that the fruit of their labors is not lost. Reports in the Soviet press indicate that the procedures to assure that land is really appropriated for industrial use have not been followed, and that local officials have nullified the value of the concept of perpetual use by depriving peasants of land use unnecessarily when alternative sources of land existed.

Practice also shows that collective farm managements often fail to appreciate their duty not to lease the land to others, or are bribed into violating the rule against alienation. Prosecutions of collective farm presidents are reported under various circumstances; for instance, one person, in return for services rendered as a shepherd to the members' privately owned cattle, was given the use of land belonging to the farm; and another outsider was falsely registered as a member and rented land in return for payments to the farm.[19]

Stalin had in mind rather quick but unscheduled conversion of the *artels* into state farms so as to place the peasants within a framework of mechanized farming comparable to mechanized industry. Just before his death, his final statement of goals made to the Communist party in 1952 called for transition to such forms, which he called "ownership by the commonwealth of the people." [20] Peasant resistance was strong, and after his death his successors moved slowly in the direction he had indicated.

---

[18] 1935 Charter arts. 2 and 3. The basic decree is that of 2 June 1938 establishing the requirement of high level authorization, but the procedures have changed as governmental structure has changed.

[19] Cases are presented in Dobrovol'skii, *Contract Relationships of Collective Farms*, [1961] 3 SOTS. ZAK. 39–40.

[20] J. STALIN, ECONOMIC PROBLEMS OF COMMUNISM IN THE U.S.S.R. (1952).

Their chance to foster the state-farm structure came in newly opened frontier lands in Central Asia. Instead of collective farms, state farms were created. Soon after this, truck-garden farms close to great cities, which had previously been structured as collective farms, were reorganized as state farms. Members became wage earners, and the land was assigned in perpetuity to the new enterprise. But again the pace proved too fast for the peasants, and after the ouster of Nikita Khrushchev in 1964, his successors called a new halt, promising to hold to current levels of *artel* farming.[21]

There has even been dramatic experimentation in some regions of the USSR with a system designed to increase production by stimulating private initiative. In the summer of 1965 parts of the land of a collective farm were allocated to a group of six farmers as their immediate responsibility for the summer season. A report indicated that yields increased six times, and that the farmers urged that the allocation be prolonged.[22] A Japanese scholar later interpreted the experiments as being a "gravedigger" for the state-farm–collective-farm system,[23] but few others see the innovation as more than a limited experiment to measure the production potential of peasants when incentives are appealing.

A more important trend is toward a state farm with a vestige of the collective farm's general meeting of members at the helm. This would constitute an attempt to avoid industrialization of agricultural management on the model of state factories, while introducing fixed wages, social insurance, and trade union affiliation as they exist for industrial workmen. In a sense it would extend to Soviet agriculture something like the Yugo-

[21] *Report of L. I. Brezhnev to CC of CPSU, March 24, 1965*, Pravda, 27 Mar. 1965 at 2. Eng. transl. in [1965] 17 C.D.S.P. no. 12 at 3, 9.

[22] Zhurin, *Who Are You, a Land Owner?*, Komsomolskaia Pravda, 9 Aug. 1965. See also endorsement of the experiment in editorial of Pravda, 10 Dec. 1966.

[23] Rinjiro Harako, *Proof of the Advantages of the Individual Peasant: Symptom of the Decay of the Soviet Collective Agricultural System*, SEKAI-SHUHO, 31 Jan. 1967 at 22–26 [World Weekly] quoted by Hiroshi Kimura in unpublished doctoral dissertation entitled Personal Property in the Soviet Union: With Particular Emphasis on the Post-Stalin Era: Ideological, Political and Economic Dilemma 105 (1968). In the Columbia University Library.

slav model of "social ownership" under "worker council" management, which will be explained in a subsequent chapter on the industrial enterprise; but it would not be a move in the direction of Yugoslav agriculture. No matter how serious the difficulties met in obtaining high yields from their farmers, the Soviet leadership shows no inclination to retreat to individual family farms like those permitted in the 1920s—much less to the private ownership of land as in Poland and Yugoslavia. The collective farm, with some modification, still stands as the primary structure through which the land is used.

The form of perpetual use has become standard for all types of land employment in the USSR. Thus, industrial enterprises and means of communication, even though exclusively state-owned, receive an allocation of land for use in perpetuity.[24] In these circumstances, the reason for Lenin's innovation—as a means of stimulating peasants' production without returning ownership to them—is absent. An enterprise director works for promotion and bonuses. He has no sense of being a proprietor. He would not work less because the land and plant might be transferred to some other enterprise when circumstances required. He needs no instigation comparable to that of a landowner. In view of this, the explanation for the allocation of perpetual use to an enterprise must be something other than stimulation of traditional peasant mentality. The conclusion is compelling that state enterprises receive perpetual use because of the convenience of conformity to a common pattern for all types of land use.

This conclusion is strengthened by discussion which arose after the war with regard to the allocation of land use to private individuals wishing to construct dwellings in the urban zones. Under the policy of the 1920s, established to encourage the private construction of homes to meet the housing shortage, individuals willing to invest in such construction were allocated use of the land for a term of years. With the passage of time, during which all urban dwellers were brought within the category of workers by virtue of the fact that all were employed as wage earners or in activities associated with wage earning, such as that of members of the bar, there appeared a movement for

[24] 1 Aug. 1932, [1932] 66 Sob. Uzak. R.S.F.S.R. pt. I item 295.

uniformity of land law among the law professors. It was argued that there was no longer any reason to have a form of lease for years, since house owners were now to be trusted in the main as workers.[25] If one or another should abuse his rights, the lot could be withdrawn under existing legislation relating to observance of the rules of socialist community living or under specific statutes permitting confiscation of property uneconomically maintained. The argument proved effective, and by decree of 1948 "for the purpose of establishing uniformity" citizens were authorized to buy or build private homes of limited size and to receive assignment of plots of land on the basis of use in perpetuity.[26]

There are positions midway between the Soviet and the Polish-Yugoslav solutions of the ownership question, and these have been taken by the Romanian, German, and Chinese Communists. For the Romanians, the land of everyone except the peasants was appropriated by the state and allocated to the use and administration of state enterprise and individuals free of charge as in the USSR, with only a minor theoretical difference. There was no declaration of perpetual tenure.[27] The major Romanian variation on the Soviet model was to leave the peasants with ownership, albeit with limitations against the hiring of labor. At the same time a campaign was mounted to induce peasants to enter cooperatives, structured like the collective farms of the Soviet Union. By 1958 this campaign had met with complete success in all areas where collectivization seemed feasible. Everyone except a few mountaineers lived under a regime in which the common farm lands were tilled by the cooperative's members, while the individual households retained the ownership of their home and a small adjacent garden plot.[28]

The Romanian system of land use appeared in practice to

[25] Venediktov, *On the Draft Civil Code of the U.S.S.R.*, [1947] 1 Sots. zak. 7 at 8.

[26] 26 Aug. 1948, [1948] 36 Ved. Verkh. Sov. SSSR 4.

[27] T. Ionasco & Bradeanu, *Le transfert du droit de propriété et de tout autre droit par l'effet de la transmission du tout ou d'une fraction du patrimonie*, Le droit et la propriété dans les pays de l'Est 53 (R. Dekkers ed. 1964).

[28] *Id.* at 52.

be identical with that of the USSR, but the legal status has been explained differently.[29] Whereas the Soviet state claims title to all land and allocates perpetual use to all users, including the collective farms and the peasant households, the Romanian state has kept title only to urban and industrially used lands, has transferred ownership of the rest to those who till. Thus, the cooperative "owns" the land used by it, and the individual family which is a member of the cooperative "owns" the plot on which its house and garden are situated. Yet in both cases the ownership is described as a "real property right of a new type." The cooperative's right is new because its ownership rights are limited. The state may withdraw title if the cooperative fails to utilize the land for the purpose for which it is assigned, or if the superior needs of the state require recovery. Otherwise the right is defensible against all. Further, the cooperative may not sell or mortgage the land, nor may third parties gain rights against it either in payment of obligations or as easements by prescription. The individual household's ownership is also of "a new type" because it may be replaced by collective exploitation if the general interests of the cooperative require.

The German Communists have gone even further to compromise with peasant sentiments, for not only does land remain in theory privately owned, but there is a benefit attached to such ownership. There has been the same emphasis as in Romania upon cooperative farming, and between 1952 and 1960 every peasant in the German Democratic Republic was brought into an agricultural producers' cooperative, in one of its three types. But in all three types individual members retain legal ownership of their land even after it has been pooled in the cooperative, and with practical effect.[30] Distribution of income from the cooperative after deduction of expenses is not based, as in the USSR or Romania, solely on the basis of work done. There is recognition of the amount of land brought into the cooperative by each owner. Thus, the income of the member who pools his land with that of the others is computed in part upon the amount he brought into the pool, subject to a limit. Only the

[29] *Id.* at 54–56.
[30] Heuer, *Agricultural Producers' Cooperatives in the G.D.R.*, 11 REVIEW OF CONTEMPORARY LAW no. 1 at 146, 158 (1964).

first twenty hectares are considered in the computation, unless the average holding of all members exceeds that amount. In such an event the owner's top limit for computation is increased to the average. The rate of computation on the basis of land ownership varies by type of cooperative, the highest rate being allowed in the least advanced type of cooperative and the lowest in the most advanced type, which corresponds in great measure to the legal structure of the collective farm in the USSR.

A form of restraint on ownership of land pooled in the cooperative is established by the statutes governing the various categories. No owner may alienate his land to anyone other than the state, the cooperative as a whole, or some other member. Peasant love of land seems still to be an important factor in making political decisions in the German Democratic Republic, for the constitution, in Article 24, provides, "On completion of the land reform the peasants are guaranteed the private ownership of their land." It is to conform to this politically desirable guarantee that the system of distribution of proceeds in accordance with ownership has been devised.

The Chinese Communists, probably because of the long history and deep understanding of the concept of landownership by peasants, have also found it expedient to refrain from total nationalization of land. Their constitution has guaranteed the right to own land [31] and left open the possibility of manipulating the concept of "title" in the interest of maximizing production among the peasants. Even before coming to power throughout the mainland, the Communists issued an Outline of Land Law on 10 October 1947 in which they stated their case in terms of transfer of ownership to the peasants.[32] Declaring that "some seventy to eighty percent of the land has been owned by landlords and rich peasants who have constituted less than ten percent of the rural population," the party's Central

[31] Art. 8, par. 1. Eng. transl. in A. BLAUSTEIN, FUNDAMENTAL LEGAL DOCUMENTS OF COMMUNIST CHINA 1 (1962).

[32] For an analysis of the "Outline," see SHAO-CHUAN LENG, JUSTICE IN COMMUNIST CHINA: A SURVEY OF THE JUDICIAL SYSTEM OF THE CHINESE PEOPLE'S REPUBLIC 20 (1967). The author is also indebted to an unpublished paper by Fu-shun Lin, Property System and Its Socialization in Communist China.

Committee characterized the lot of the farm laborers, and poor and middle peasants, as being one in which "they worked hard all year round and yet could hardly get enough food and clothes."

Having stated the problem in terms of "ownership" the Communists ordered that a "land-to-the-tiller" system should be put into effect. This was spelled out as recognition of landownership with the right to manage, to sell, and in certain circumstances to lease the land. Confiscation of landlords' lands and redistribution was decreed, but ownership by the middle and poor peasants was to remain protected.

Unlike Lenin, Mao Tse-tung came to the helm in 1949 subject to some strong influences which restrained him in formulating a land policy. One was the fact that Sun Yat-sen had preached "land-to-the-tiller" so vehemently that it would have been unpopular to introduce Lenin's solution of monopoly state ownership even if it had seemed theoretically desirable from the Marxist point of view. Another was the heritage of Communist failure with land reform in parts of China controlled by Communists at various times before the party had gained complete power. This experience dated from 1926 when the Chinese Communists were taking instructions from the Communist International in Moscow, which told them to introduce total confiscation of land wherever power was gained.

The early advice, based upon Soviet experience, caused violent opposition when it was tried in China, and led to a break in the cooperation between Communist and Nationalist forces in July 1927. Even with this loss of power, the Communists seem not to have learned; or perhaps they were as yet unable to free themselves from Soviet influence. The policy of expropriation was retained for a decade until the outbreak of the Japanese military adventure in July 1937. Thus, a Shanghai conference of regional deputies of the Chinese soviets, held in 1930, drafted what was called a "formal land law," designed to confiscate the lands of landlords and "counterrevolutionary" elements, and to make such lands the property of the state. Thereafter, the lands were to be redistributed only for cultivation, not for ownership. Their purchase, sale, lease, or mortgage was wholly prohibited.

Again hostility to the plan was great, even among the

middle peasants, whom the Communists found it necessary to woo. A revised law was adopted on 1 December 1931 by what was called the First Congress of Soviets of Workers', Peasants' and Red Army Deputies of China, held at Juichin.[33] It still called for confiscation of lands owned by landlords and rich peasants, but for the rest there was to be recognition of ownership, including the right to buy, sell, mortgage, and lease the land. Also, the previously stated goal of collectivization of land use was abandoned. The compromise policy was applied with success by the Juichin soviet until it was ousted by Nationalist troops in 1934.

With the Japanese attack, the communist tactic changed to a united front with the government of Chiang Kai-shek. In return for Chiang's promise to discontinue his effort to subjugate the Communists, the latter agreed to cease armed revolt and confiscation of landlords' lands. Emphasis thereafter was on reduction of rent and interest owned by peasants to landlords, and this was incorporated in a declaration issued by the Central Committee of the party on 28 January 1942. The declaration even provided a Marxist-oriented theoretical base by stating that the capitalist system of production was a progressive one at that time in China, and the capitalist class, including the rich peasants, was to be recognized as a progressive social element, indispensable to wartime production and victory over the Japanese.

With the need for compromise ended by triumph in the war against the Japanese, the Communists reverted in part to their earlier position. Land law was established by leaders in various provinces as these were brought under communist control.[34] Land of landlords was confiscated—an act justified as necessary against those guilty of treason, war crimes, and having been puppets of the Japanese. In an attempt to bring some order into this regional chaos, the Central Committee issued a directive on 4 May 1946 recommending death for traitors and common enemies of the people and confiscation of their lands. For lesser offenses, the land could be requisitioned and compensation paid according to the degree of exploitation. Each set of local authorities was to decide whether to confiscate or to requisition,

[33] LENG, *id.* 4.
[34] *Id.* 11.

and if the landlord was not to be killed, he was to be allocated a plot for his own maintenance. Land obtained in this manner was redistributed, the peasants being required to reimburse the government for half of the compensation paid to the landlord. Those who bought the land acquired ownership. Even the rich peasants were treated moderately, for the land cultivated directly was to be untouched, and only the leased portion was to be considered subject to requisition, depending upon the circumstances in each case. The policy was neutralization of the rich and solicitation of full support from the middle and poor peasants, so as to avoid antagonizing 95 percent of the rural population and thus cutting production.

The policy was unevenly applied by provincial leaders, and in many instances the middle peasants were antagonized. This necessitated the Outline of Land Law of 1947 to which reference has been made. It was still only a recommendation, as the Communists had not yet achieved universal power, but soon after their complete victory they enacted a 1950 Agrarian Reform Law [35] with two functions: "to abolish the landownership system of feudal exploitation by the landlord class" and "to carry out the system of peasant landownership." Emphasis was upon production above all, and so the law, although confiscating the land, farm animals, tools, and surplus food of landlords, protected other properties of landlords operated as industrial and commercial enterprises. They were even to be allocated land on which to feed themselves with their own hands. Under the law landlords were not to be exterminated physically but were to be deprived only of their feudal landholdings. In practice, however, many were put under severe restraints and some were killed.[36]

Rich peasants were not to be molested at all. Their land was to remain untouched, and they were even permitted to hire labor. They were to lose only land they had rented to others, if it was larger in size than the land they were tilling themselves with or without hired labor. Compensation was to be paid for requisitioned rented land. Again the effort was to neutralize the rich peasant and maintain production.

The familiar incidents of landownership were recognized by

---

[35] 28 June 1950. Eng. transl. in BLAUSTEIN, *supra*, note 31 at 276.
[36] LENG, *supra*, note 32 at 38.

the 1950 law—landowners being permitted to manage, purchase, sell, or lease their land without restriction—to stimulate the sense of proprietorship and thus to increase enthusiasm for production. Such provisions created conditions from which a new landlord class might have emerged, but this was avoided by the campaign for collectivization which, as it had in Romania, completely changed the concept of "ownership" without, however, eliminating it. The constitution of 1954 clarified the concept, as has been indicated, by authorizing the peasants to own land; but hostility to the rich peasants was clearly stated as, "The policy of the state towards the rich peasant economy is to restrict and gradually eliminate it." By Article 14 a general limitation is added: "The state prohibits the use of private property by any person to the detriment of the public interest."

Although they fostered private ownership to stimulate production, the Communists made no secret of their ultimate aim to collectivize. By resolution of 15 December 1951, the Central Committee of the party established a policy designed to encourage the formation of peasant cooperatives in the form of the "lower agricultural producers' cooperatives." [37] As in the 1920s in the USSR, the concept was declared to be one of voluntary association, so that little happened except encouragement to peasants to form "mutual aid teams." Not until pressure to join was initiated early in 1955 did things change. Then, the campaign was pushed with such vigor that by the end of 1955 some 70,000,000 peasant households had joined—60 percent of the peasants of China.[38]

These new Chinese cooperatives were something less than the Soviet collective farm because the concept of private ownership of land was recognized in various ways. When peasants entered the cooperative, they either retained ownership of their plot or received compensation for the land they brought with them; and if they withdrew, they had the right to their land or to compensation, if they had not already surrendered title. On entry, each household was permitted to retain a plot for private use not to exceed 5 percent of the average plot brought into the cooperative.

[37] *Draft Resolution on Mutual Aid and Cooperation in Agricultural Production*, [1953] PEOPLES CHINA, no. 13 (Supp.) 1 July 1953.

[38] For the dynamics of the pressures, see F. SCHURMANN, IDEOLOGY AND ORGANIZATION IN COMMUNIST CHINA 442 *et seq.* (1966).

The new cooperatives were only a first step, for a statute was adopted by the people's congress on 30 June 1956 [39] creating a model charter for an "Advanced Agricultural Producers' Cooperative." Even before promulgation of the statute, transition began. In this type, no peasant retained ownership of the plot he brought into the cooperative. Title passed to the collective without compensation. In the event of withdrawal, however, a peasant might regain his lot or demand allocation of another one of equal value and size. Again, each household retained a small vegetable plot by its home, not to exceed 10 percent of the average plot brought into the cooperative.

A renewed campaign for collectivization under the advanced type of cooperative was mounted, and during the short period of 1956–57 740,000 cooperatives were formed, comprising 97 percent of the peasant households of China. Under the pressures of the time membership became in effect compulsory, and withdrawals were unthinkable, even though permitted by law. Landownership acquired a new definition; for, in spite of the constitutional guarantee of Article 8, it could no longer be exercised by individuals in the traditional way. It had passed to the cooperative, subject to restrictions on use and disposition similar to those in the USSR and in Romania. The form of administration was patterned on that of the Soviet collective farm, but the concept of title was like that developed by legal theorists in Romania.

Events were soon to cause even further changes in the locus of title, for a third step was initiated in the campaign entitled "The Great Leap Forward" between August and November of 1958. A major feature was the formation of what was called the "commune." [40] The 740,000 advanced cooperatives were transformed into some 26,000 "people's communes," comprising 99 percent of the peasant households of China. [41] This meant the

[39] For Model Regulations of 17 Mar. 1956 and statute of 30 June 1956 in Eng. transl., see BLAUSTEIN, *supra*, note 31 at 411.

[40] Resol. on Establishment of People's Communes in the Rural Areas, 29 Aug. 1958. Eng. transl. in BLAUSTEIN, *id.* 442. The implementation is described in SCHURMANN, *supra*, note 38 at 476.

[41] In one region of Honan Province the 5,376 agricultural producers' cooperatives were amalgamated into 208 communes with an average population of 8,000 households. See SCHURMANN, *id.* 473. Later the communes were split into smaller units comprising about 2,000 households. *Id.* 487. For a diagram showing percentage of household participation in the lower

amalgamation of large numbers of villages under a single administration, and the divorce of the peasants from direct relationship to the management of land. In this lay its ultimate undoing.

Communes differed from Soviet collective farms in many ways, not only in size. They were more than central administrations for agricultural land; they were local government as well. Thus, the combination of local government functions with those of agricultural administration which had been broached but never accepted in the USSR became the rule in China. This meant that education, culture, commerce, local industry, and roads were concerns of the commune administration as well as agriculture, and such allied pursuits as fisheries, forestry, and side occupations were also brought within the purview of the administrators.[42]

The problem of ownership of land was raised again. At the outset, the procedure which had been followed in forming the cooperatives was repeated: the communes accepted transfer from the cooperatives of the title which they had held. But since industry, commerce, local banks, and construction enterprises also passed to the communes, they received what had previously been defined as "all-people's ownership" as well. This meant that they combined elements of cooperative ownership and what amounted to public ownership by state entities.

Soviet legal literature and the USSR constitution draw a distinction between state and cooperative ownership, although both are classified as "socialist ownership." Stalin expected, as has been said, that the cooperative form of ownership would eventually be transformed into whole-people's ownership, but he set no time schedule. Now, the Chinese were bringing the two types of property together forcibly before a form of combined management had been perfected. In practice this combination meant that peasants who still cherished the idea of direct participation in management of the land as co-owners, if not

and higher stage cooperatives on the eve of the communes, see Bernstein, *Leadership and Mass Mobilisation in the Soviet and Chinese Collectivisation Campaigns of 1929–30 and 1955–56: A Comparison*, [1967] THE CHINA QUARTERLY no. 31 at 1, 2.

[42] A chart demonstrating the administrative structure is reproduced in SCHURMANN *id.* 489.

more, were removed so far from management in the giant communes that they became, in effect, farm laborers devoid of all sense of proprietorship. They even lost ownership of and hence control over the use of the small plots reserved for their use close to their homes, as well as the land on which their houses stood, and no provision was made for compensation or withdrawal.

Peasants found themselves within an accounting unit which was the whole commune, where a remote, impersonal management decided upon the distribution of wages and goods to commune members. Only one measure of compromise was evident in this new scheme. The homes, clothes, furniture, trees around the house, small farm tools, and household animals and poultry were left in private ownership, as were bank accounts. Peasants were also permitted to conduct occupations on the side to gain extra income, such as the work of artisans, so long as this did not reduce the time available for the work of the commune; but the privilege was mostly on paper. They were kept too busy to engage in side occupations.

Incentive suffered, for peasants could not see a close relationship between their work and their reward. Villages and groups of villages within a commune received the same reward, with what seemed to peasants inadequate consideration of the extent of work contributed. Egalitarianism wreaked the same havoc as it had in the USSR in the 1920s, and management was too inept to improvise a system that would profit from economies of scale while making adjustments to meet local sensibilities. Coupled with this was the disruption of the rural market, which deprived peasants of a profitable outlet for what they might produce privately.

With dwindling production, concessions had to be devised, and they began to appear with the Lushan Conference held in August 1959.[43] The palliative was a shift in the *situs* of ownership. Title to land was taken from the commune and replaced in units corresponding to what had been the advanced agricultural cooperatives of some 240 peasant households, now called

[43] Dr. Fu-shun Lin has found no English translation of the Chinese text published in 10 Chung-hua Jen-min Kung-ho-kuo Fa-kuei Huipen 50 [Compendium of Laws and Regulations of the People's Republic of China].

"production brigades." The commune retained ownership only of the industrial, commercial, and other undertakings which were considered the public economy, and also such part of the profits of the production brigades as would be transferred to it as an "accumulation fund." For the rest, the title to land and machinery passed to the "production brigades." This left the small farm tools and draft animals unaccounted for, and title to these was placed even lower than the cooperative, in the village itself, which was now called a "production team," usually being a settlement of some forty peasant households.

Under the 1959 reform the "production brigade" became the basic unit of agricultural production and accounting. The commune management retained its supervisory and coordinating function for all the brigades within the commune, but it had no authority to command or interfere in the operation of the brigades. The brigade made work assignments to the teams, and after having paid its taxes and its share of the accumulation fund to the commune it was free to distribute its income among its members. The peasants were once again nearer the managerial process, and masters, in greater degree than in the original commune system, of their production plans and their income.

In 1960 another concession was made. Title to the small garden plots transferred to the communes two years earlier was returned to the brigades, which allocated their use to the households.[44] This was no return to households of title to these plots, but the change restored the peasant's managerial control over the land on which he worked to satisfy his immediate table needs.

The end of concessions was not yet reached, for peasants were still dissatisfied and insufficiently moved to produce to what the experts believed to be their potential. The communist leadership concluded that peasants still felt remote from control of their own destiny. This was indeed true. There was at this time an average of 4,800 peasant households gathered

[44] Dr. Fu-shun Lin takes this information from what is identified as "12 Articles Relating to the Work of Reshuffling Rural People's Communes" attributed to a defector found on Matsu Island. He believes its authenticity suggested by reference to it in a decision of the C.C. of the C.P. China, 20 May 1963.

together in a commune. With return to ownership by the brigade, the 240 peasant households of the brigade shared title and all that it signified in management rights. But the traditional unit of Chinese production had been the 40-household village, the "production team." Each team differed sharply from its neighbor in economic conditions and productivity. For this reason the brigade basis for management failed, for it did not take these factors sufficiently into account in distribution of work and profits.

Once again the matter of locus of title of land was raised, and in 1961 the journals began to propose that it be taken from the production brigades and placed in the villages, or teams. Evidence indicates that by resolution of the Central Committee of September 1962 entitled "Revised Draft Regulations on the Work of the People's Communes,"[45] title to land being used by the production teams was transferred back to them, subject to restrictions. It could not be rented to others, nor could the individual garden plots. This transfer of title carried with it the right to organize production and to maintain a separate system of accounting.

At the time of the transfer of title to land, ownership of draft animals, heavy farm implements and, machines was also transferred from the brigade to the various teams using them, and the commune and brigades were denied any further right to control their use. The team, in turn, allocated about 5 percent of its cultivated land to the individual households for their personal use. A final article reflected the chaos that had been caused by frequent change, for it provided that no further change should be made for a period of thirty years.[46]

The Vietnamese of the People's Republic in the North have been much influenced by the Chinese experience. They have

[45] Dr. Fu-shun Lin has found that the Nationalist government at Taipei has published the regulation, which has been kept secret by the Peking government of the people's republic, although reference to it appears in an article by Kuang Hual in [1963] 1 CHENG-FA YEN-CHIU 15. For further data on commune administration, see Liao Lu-yen, *Collectivization of Agriculture in China*, [1963] 44 PEKING REVIEW 7 and *Survey of a Commune* V, [1966] 14 *id.* 26 at 29.

[46] Art. 20 and pars. 1, 2 and 4 of art. 21 of the regulation, cited *supra*, note 45.

avoided experimenting with the Chinese commune, preferring to stop with the cooperatives.[47] At the outset they moved cautiously. Land was not nationalized, but was left in private ownership, as with the Chinese, although peasants were urged to pool their plots in cooperatives. The campaign started slowly at the start but then advanced quickly. By 1958 only 4.74 percent of the peasant households had joined the cooperatives established along the lines of the Chinese "first step." But by the end of 1960, 85.83 percent of the peasant households had been brought into agricultural cooperatives. By this time the Vietnamese Communists had established, in addition to the cooperatives of the "lower stage," a "higher stage" patterned on the second step initiated by the Chinese. Peasants were moving into the advanced type, for by 1960 11.81 percent of those in cooperatives had moved from the lower to the higher stage.

Reviewing the variations in land tenure existing within the States of the family of Marxian socialist legal systems, it is evident that full authority is now left with each Communist party to make whatever compromise it deems wise in establishing the principle of "public ownership" prescribed by the 1957 declaration of the Communist parties in power. Only the USSR and Mongolia have kept to the strict rule that public ownership of land can be manifested only in state ownership. Communists in other lands have been more imaginative. They have been able, without nationalizing land, to devise systems for peasants designed to bring them within the requirements of Marxism that there be no private employment of labor for productive purposes and that no profit be made out of activities considered violative of the labor theory of value. Within these limitations peasants may retain "ownership" in whatever measure their communist leaders think likely to be meaningful in creating incentive to maximize agricultural production.

In most of the postwar Communist-led states departing from Lenin's simplified pattern of total state ownership of land, a policy of collectivization of use has been installed. The result is a system of agriculture no less communal than what has been created in the USSR. This collectivization is not an end in itself

[47] Pham Thanh Vinh, *The Obligatory Nature of Planning Targets*, 12 REVIEW OF CONTEMPORARY LAW, no. 1 at 82, 83–84 (1965).

—it is declared to be only a prelude to an ultimate transition to the state farms which Stalin once claimed to be the culmination of "public ownership." From this policy Poland and Yugoslavia have diverged to an extreme position from which there may never be an advance—or so the Chinese think. Their leaders appear content to retain for very long periods of time private ownership of land and privately conducted agriculture, designed perhaps to lead eventually to collectivization, but without wide public acclaim of collectivization, much less of state farms, as the ultimate goal for all. At the other polar position is China. Although there has been a retreat from the original goal of the commune, the leadership, at least the adherents of Mao Tse-tung, seems unhappy with what peasant resistance to their policies has forced upon them.

Certainly individual farming and private ownership have no place in the Chinese Communist program, as they have in Yugoslavia and Poland. Even the cooperative form in China seems to be no more than a way station on the road to a structure which Mao interprets as representative of complete communism. Following the initiation of his "Great Proletarian Cultural Revolution" in 1966, intended to reaffirm nonpecuniary incentives and values, before the spring sowing of 1967 a readiness appeared to make still more concessions to the peasants, to induce a level of agricultural production necessary to avoid famine. Whether the concession was to be of more than brief duration was problematic, for the emphasis of Mao's message was upon escape from incentive systems as "bourgeois." Citizens were urged to move toward a social structure in which they would work from love of social contribution rather than for personal gain. If this attitude were eventually to be pushed to all activities, farming should be placed on a communal basis, where it could be justified on economic grounds with arguments based on efficiency of scale and on theoretical grounds as devoid of concepts of "ownership." There should then be no need to manipulate "title" to land in order to create incentive in the minds of peasants who lag behind their leaders in their willingness to absorb Marxist doctrines as preached from Peking.

8

Property in the Production Enterprise

T HE CONCEPT OF "PUBLIC OWNERSHIP" MUST BE IMPLE-
mented for industry as well as for land by all members of the
family of Marxian socialist legal systems under the 1957 declaration of the Communist parties in power, but there is no compulsory model to be used in implementation. As with land,
Lenin's early experience has been a guide, but there has been
much variation, especially since Stalin evicted Tito from the
Communist Information Bureau in 1948. Tito subsequently
defied the Soviet pattern as creating bureaucracy, which he
dubbed the "cancer of socialism," and to avoid this disease his
lawyers devised a new form which they called "social
ownership." [1]

Common to all members of the family is the principle
enunciated by Marx and Engels in their *Communist Manifesto*

---

[1] Djorjević, *A Contribution to the Theory of Social Property*, [1966]
24 SOCIALIST THOUGHT AND PRACTICE 73.

of 1848—that the bourgeoisie must be deprived of the owner-ship of productive wealth. Lenin introduced this quickly for agriculture with his two decrees on the land, but he moved more slowly with industry. He concluded that although peas-ants could be expected to produce crops even without guidance, workmen lacked the skills necessary to manage the complexities of industry. Nationalization of the industrial plants of the empire had to be initiated slowly enough, therefore, to avoid disruption of production. Owner-managers driven from the front offices by nationalization decrees could rarely be replaced, nor could employed managers of former private corporations be expected to remain to direct production if their new bosses were their former employees now personifying the state as the new owner.

Compromise with private owners became the rule of the day for Lenin. Workers' committees were established in their plants immediately after the revolution by decree of 14 November 1917 (O.S.) [2] as symbols of the revolution, but nationalization proceeded slowly. Only certain very large industries on which all eyes rested were nationalized by name in the early months. Not until 28 June 1918 [3] did a decree list the basic fields of industrial activity deemed to be the commanding heights and declare that these were nationalized without compensation. In practice there were delays in the assumption of management by state agents.

Smaller enterprises were left in private hands for two more years, until a decree of 29 November 1920 [4] established a crite-rion for nationalization: the state would take all enterprises having more than five workmen with mechanical tools or ten without. Contrary to what might be supposed, the rule repre-sented no careful determination of the point below which capitalists were no longer threats to power; it was a rule of convenience. The factory-inspection laws of the empire required registration of industries at that level, and as a result the authorities had a complete list only of such industries. To have nationalized smaller shops would have created administrative confusion.

[2] [1917] 3 Sob. Uzak. R.S.F.S.R. pt. I item 35.
[3] [1918] 47 id. item 559.
[4] [1920] 93 id. item 512.

Lenin discovered that even with precautions designed to induce skilled managers to remain, he had moved too fast, and he began his strategic retreat after the full extent of the economic disorganization caused by the 1919–20 civil war between "whites" and "reds" had been determined. His New Economic Policy of 1921 was initiated by steps designed to bring grain back into the market by permitting private trade, but it then moved into industry, for by decree of 7 July 1921 [5] private citizens were authorized to establish new small-scale enterprises employing not more than ten or twenty persons, as determined by each local soviet for each type of industry. Industries previously nationalized might also be leased to private entrepreneurs.

Lenin died in 1924, leaving the New Economic Policy in full operation. No one can say whether he would have permitted his compromise to continue for many years. History shows only that when Stalin came to the helm, he ended the concession as soon as he thought the public system strong enough to carry on without the private enterprisers. State planning was introduced in 1927, but it advanced slowly. Not until 1930 was a business tax upon private producers and merchants introduced, together with an income tax discriminating against them.[6] Soon most private entrepreneurs abandoned their efforts under the pressures, and those few merchants who remained were finally ousted through a decree of 1932 making the conduct of private merchandising a crime.[7]

Stalin's policy of exterminating private ownership in industry did not, however, prohibit all private activity, for the small producer employing not more than the limited number of workmen permitted by the 1921 decree was legal until 1936, when a licensing act reduced to one the number of employees permitted.[8] By December of that year, a new constitution prohibited all employment of labor for productive purposes,[9] which left legal only the artisan working alone or in partnership with

[5] [1921] 53 *id.* item 323.
[6] 2 Sept. 1930, [1930] 46 Sob. Zak. S.S.S.R. pt.I items 481, 482.
[7] 10 Nov. 1932, [1932] 87 Sob. Uzak. R.S.F.S.R. pt.I, item 385.
[8] 26 Mar. 1936, par. 1, note 1, [1936] 17 Fin. i Khoz. Zak., No. 11 at 17.
[9] Art. 9.

others as a producers' cooperative. In 1960 even the cooperative form was prohibited,[10] so that today only the single artisan may obtain a license to produce, and even he is rigidly controlled under a licensing act prohibiting specified types of lucrative production and limiting him generally to work upon raw materials supplied by clients.[11] This prevents him from violating the Marxist rule that no individual can be permitted to make a profit from purchase of materials for resale at a profit. His money income must represent no more than a return for labor, which alone creates value in Marxist terms.

The rule applicable today in the USSR was established by the constitution of 1936, whose Article 4 fixes the "economic foundation of the USSR" as "the socialist system of economy and the socialist ownership of the instruments and means of production, firmly established as a result of the liquidation of the capitalist system of economy, the abolition of private ownership of the instruments and means of production, and the elimination of the exploitation of man by man."

Other members of the Marxian socialist family have taken steps in the same direction, although some of them have halted their advance for longer than did Lenin and Stalin with their New Economic Policy. Poland is the most noted example, for private enterprise is permitted not only in agriculture, as has already been explained, but also in handicrafts, small industry, trade, and the provision of services. Yet reprieve has not resulted in great change from the Soviet model. The share of private industry in total net production in 1964 was less than 4 percent of the total value.[12] Before the Polish "October" of 1956, the national economic plan of 1950 anticipated the trans-

[10] Decree not published but referred to in Uriupin, *Improve Control of Service Enterprises and Taxation of Handicraftsmen,* [1960] 10 FINANSY SSSR 14.

[11] To the general rule established by art. 115 of the Civil Code R.S.F.S.R. are added a regulation on registration, dated 30 June 1949 (ISTOCHNIKI GRAZHDANSKOGO PRAVA 30 [1961]), and an Order of the Council of Ministers R.S.F.S.R., dated 4 Aug. 1965, listing the permitted professions ([1965] 18 Sob. Post. R.S.F.S.R. item 110).

[12] The information on Polish industry is drawn from an unpublished memorandum prepared by Dr. A. W. Rudzinski, entitled Private Nonagricultural Enterprise in Poland. His statistics are taken from ROCZNIK STATYSTYCZNY 73 (1965) [Statistical Yearbook].

formation of private handicrafts into socialist work cooperatives, and the 1952 constitution followed the Soviet model, so
that the events after 1956 represented a retreat from expectations rather than from actual levels of achievement. For two
years after the "October" there was a significant increase in
private handicrafts, industry, and merchandising; but after 1958
a harder line was resumed.

In 1963 the pressing needs for housing and consumer goods
resulted in a second reprieve for private enterprisers. Private
construction crafts were encouraged, and benefits were extended to private craftsmen. Tax reductions were introduced on
29 December 1964,[13] and on 29 March 1965 social security
benefits were extended to craftsmen on the same basis as to
workers and white-collar employees.[14] In May 1965 a special
social insurance fund for handicraftsmen was introduced.[15]

The economic plan for 1966–70 even devotes a special chapter to "Services for the Population and Handicrafts," assigning
to individual handicraftsmen the task of providing services to
the population and to agriculture and of producing articles for
export and for the internal market, to supplement and diversify
the production of socialized industry. The number of handicraftsmen is to rise from 255,000 in 1965 to 300,000 in 1970,
largely by an increase in the number of apprentices.[16]

As in the USSR handicraftsmen must be licensed, but the
restrictions are less severe than those of the Soviet act. Local
government issues the license after consulting with an advisory
body representing private industry and private trades and the
chamber of handicrafts, as well as the administration.[17] All
commercial and catering establishments require licenses, but
certain classes of handicraftsmen may function even without a
license: those requiring no materials from the socialized sector
of the economy, those providing services to the general population, and those which are traditionally performed in the villages, such as the making of folk and peasant art items. License
fees are high, reaching 50,000 zlotys for merchants and caterers

[13] [1965] 4 J. of L. Poland items 13, 14.
[14] [1965] 13 *id.* item 90.
[15] 19 May 1965, [1965] 26 *id.* item 173.
[16] [1966] 48 *id.* item 296, p. 461.
[17] 1 July 1958, [1958] 45 *id.* item 3224.

and 100,000 zlotys for wholesalers of fruits and vegetables. A subsequent regulation enumerated eighty-eight statutory categories of handicrafts, of which sixty-eight require no license, but the exemption applies only if not more than four persons are employed, not counting apprentices and members of the family.[18] Four types of private industry are exempted from the licensing requirement, but only if they employ not more than ten employees, not counting members of the family.

A ceiling is placed upon production capacity by private enterprise, even when a license is granted; so profit-making potential is always held within definite limits.[19] Also there is always an organization of the private enterprisers themselves to provide a measure of internal policing. Thus, the handicraftsmen must belong to "guilds" in traditional fashion, and these join "handicraft chambers" which are organs of economic and professional self-government supervised by a State Committee for Small Production created in 1958 to replace the Ministry of Small Industry and Handicrafts.[20] Private industrialists and merchants must also join semipublic, though less official, associations.

Statistics indicate that in spite of the provisions permitting private employment in the crafts and small-scale industry, the 1965 average number of employees in handicraft workshops was so small that slightly more than one of every two shops hired a hand, and in the larger private industries an average of only 1.3 persons was employed in each industry.[21]

Generally, private merchandising and industry are on the decline in Poland, except for private construction. The drop is illustrated by the private caterers, who increased from 500 in 1955 to 2,200 in 1957, but dropped back to 780 in 1964. In private commercial activities there has also been a drop, from 25,300 in 1957 to 15,380 in 1964.[22] It is obvious that Polish

[18] Ordinance of the Council of Ministers, 24 Sept. 1962, [1962] 62 *id.* item 296. For list of artisan categories, see Ordinance of 28 Feb. 1957, [1957] 33 *id.* item 145, amended 27 June 1963, [1963] 32 *id.* item 184.

[19] Ordinance of 24 Sept. 1962, [1962] 62 *id.* item 297.

[20] Statute of 11 Sept. 1956, [1956] 41 *id.* item 190.

[21] ROCZNIK STATYSTYCZNY, *supra*, note 12 at 59, 182, 531.

[22] *Id.* at 498.

Communists had only a certain type of New Economic Policy concession in mind when they gave private enterprise a reprieve in 1956. The private sector is tolerated more as a means of filling gaps in state production, to be replaced as soon as the state can fill the need, than as a permanent variation in Marxist-inspired society.

Chinese Communists alone departed from the Leninist model of expropriation of capitalist industrialists on assumption of power. They have innovated in pursuing a policy for which Mao has taken special credit, claiming it is less disruptive of industry than was Lenin's period of militant communism following the revolution. As early as 1947, before coming to national leadership, Mao established as one of his major economic aims the protection of the privately owned industry and commerce of what he called the "national bourgeoisie." [23] In his parlance, the national bourgeoisie were those who conducted their enterprises solely with Chinese capital and who had no interconnections with enterprises abroad. For those capitalists who could be identified with the "imperialists," his policy was confiscation and transfer of property to the new state as forces hopelessly opposed to the new regime; but he expected to be able either to neutralize the national bourgeoisie by his policy of toleration or to win them over to his side.

Mao's reason for toleration was strictly utilitarian. He made this clear when he explained that because of the backwardness of China's economy it was necessary to permit for a long time the existence of a capitalist sector and even to develop it as beneficial to the national economy.[24] A year later, Mao remarked in his often-quoted speech "On the People's Democratic Dictatorship" that the national bourgeoisie was by nature an exploiting class, though not a major one.[25] The Communist party had the task, he said, of educating and remolding them and eventually of transforming their capital into state capital.

[23] The information on Chinese law is drawn from an unpublished memorandum prepared by Dr. Fu-shun Lin, entitled Property System and Its Socialization in Communist China.

[24] *The Present Situation and Our Tasks*, 24 Dec. 1947. 4 SELECTED WORKS OF MAO TSE-TUNG 167 (1961).

[25] *Id.* at 419.

He thought it possible to do this without rebellion, and his prognosis proved correct; for many capitalists, especially in Shanghai, accepted the opportunity offered them to cooperate, thinking they could save their investments, at least for a time.

By the Provisional Regulations for Private Enterprises adopted after the Communist-led government came to power, the private enterprisers were required to submit their complete plans for production and sales to the government for approval.[26] Rules for distribution of income were established, first allocating to taxes 34.5 percent of net profits. The balance was then to be divided, giving 46 percent for reserves, 16 percent for welfare, and 38 percent for dividends.[27] All of this suggested toleration subject to strict limitation; but then began the campaigns to absorb the capitalists through social pressures not incorporated in law. Capitalist owners were constantly urged to contribute a large part of their dividends to causes recommended by the party. Some were charged for "back taxes," and their supplies and markets were controlled.[28]

Promulgation of the constitution of 1954 provided an opportunity to restate goals, and the preamble declared that "The general tasks of the state during the transition period are, step by step, to bring about the socialist industrialization of the country and, step by step, to accomplish the socialist transformation of agriculture, handicrafts, and capitalist industry and commerce." But by Article 10 the constitution provided, as no constitution of a Communist-led state following Lenin's model has done, that "The state protects according to law the right of capitalists to own means of production and other capital." Then followed provisions calling for control of negative aspects in capitalism and for eventual transformation of capitalist enterprise to a combination of state and capitalist economy.

This latter aspect was implemented by the Provisional Regulation for the Joint State-Private Industrial Enterprise,

---

[26] 29 Dec. 1950. Dr. Lin has found no transl. The text is published in 2 CHUNG-YANG JEN-MIN CHENG-FU FA-LING HUI-PIEN 1949–1950 at 539–44 [Compendium of Laws and Regulations of the Central People's Government].

[27] Pub. only in Japan, in CHUGOKU NO HO TO SHIKAI 167 (1960) [Law and Society of China].

[28] R. LOH, ESCAPE FROM RED CHINA (1962).

adopted 2 September 1954.[29] Under this all capitalist industrial enterprises were to be encouraged to join state enterprises. By 1956 the campaign was crowned with nearly total success, for 99 percent of all private establishments were reported converted into joint private-state enterprises. The same happened to commercial enterprises, so that by the end of 1956 the jointly operated or wholly state-operated enterprises accounted for 96 percent of all capitalist commercial enterprises as they had existed before the campaign.[30]

The concept of fixed interest was introduced in February 1956 under a regulation of 8 February limiting capitalists to a return of from 1 percent to 6 percent interest on their investment during the period of 1956 to 1962, later extended to 1965,[31] and permitted thereafter to run indefinitely. The discrepancy between various industries was erased in July 1956 by the establishment of a common rate of 5 percent return for all, said in 1962 to be the equivalent of 62.7 million United States dollars. By this decree the capitalists became, in effect, creditors rather than owners of equities. Even this creditor position was later undermined by increased pressure to contribute their interest to worthy causes. The capitalists, who in Shanghai alone numbered 90,000 in 1967,[32] were left only with managerial salaries, which were in many instances generous, but nevertheless were essentially wages for work done and in no way a return on capital.

Capitalism in its traditional sense was thus eliminated from the people's republic in the short space of fifteen years. This left as private enterprisers only the handicraftsmen of the villages, authorized to conduct such activities as sidelines to their participation in the tasks set by the commune, and such artisans as still ply their lonely trades in the urban areas, largely in the

[29] CHUNG-YANG JEN-MIN CHENG-FU FA-LING HUI-PIEN, 1954 at 65 [Compendium of Laws and Regulations of the Central People's Government].

[30] Cheng Chu-yan, COMMUNIST CHINA'S ECONOMY 1949–1962 at 72 (1963).

[31] Dr. Lin has found no translations. The 1956 text is in 3 Compendium, *supra*, note 26 at 282. The 1962 extension is in Jen-min jih-pao, 17 Apr. 1962 at 1.

[32] Gavrilov, *Capitalists on the Dole*, Izvestiia, 31 Mar. 1967 at 2. Eng. transl. in 19 C.D.S.P. no. 13 at 20 (1967).

service trades. They continued to enjoy the constitutional protection of Article 9, which is similar to the guarantees offered handicraftsmen and artisans in the European Marxian-oriented states, emphasis being upon encouraging them to form cooperatives.

The Vietnamese of the People's Republic in the North started their program of nationalization on the Chinese model, but by 1960 they had gone over to the Soviet pattern.[33] In 1958 industry was 36.4 percent state-owned, with a fringe group of 0.1 percent mixed state-private companies in Chinese style, and 3 percent mixed artisan enterprises. Commerce was 26.5 percent in private hands at the time, controlling 42.4 percent of the global volume of goods in circulation. The state controlled only 30.4 percent of the volume of goods transported by road and 15.3 percent of the goods transported by river in 1958. But by 1960, the picture had changed completely. All industry was state-owned and 98.9 percent of the private trading companies had been nationalized. 81 percent of the artisans had joined producing cooperatives. Vietnam had become a state-owned economy.

Fidel Castro moved in the direction of complete nationalization of private business, except for certain agricultural operations, when he pledged in March 1968 to "eradicate" all private business.[34] Thus, he went further than the Eastern European states, other than the USSR, which had been restoring private enterprisers in the service trades in 1967 and 1968 to meet the needs of a population discontented with the inadequacies of state enterprise in these fields. Castro moved against small bars, laundries, garages, and various family shops, and began to turn them into state-run services.

The record shows, in review of the policies adopted for industry in Marxian socialist states, that title has generally passed to the state soon after Communists have come to power. China's experiment with procedures designed to encourage former capitalist owners to continue to render skilled management services is a notable exception. Elsewhere, notably in Poland,

[33] Pham Thanh Vinh, *The Obligatory Nature of Planning Targets*, 12 REVIEW OF CONTEMPORARY LAW, no. 1 at 82, 83–84 (1965).

[34] *Cuba Begins Take-over of Small Businesses*, N.Y. Times, 15 Mar. 1968 at 20.

Hungary, Czechoslovakia, and Yugoslavia, the exception has been much less startling. These systems have adopted policies mindful of Lenin's retreat from militant communism in the early 1920s. Presumably, the leaders expect eventually to resume their march toward complete state ownership and operation of industry, the service trades, and distribution, as Stalin did in the USSR in 1928. Whether this will be possible remains to be seen.

Although attitudes toward capitalists present considerable uniformity within the Marxian socialist world, there is much debate over forms of management, and some of this is framed in terms of "ownership." Tito's denunciation of the Soviet system of industrial management as creating an intolerable bureaucracy was dramatized, as has been indicated, by Yugoslav coinage of a new concept, "social ownership."

Tito's position is a rejection of what has come to be known as "state ownership" in the USSR and the other Marxian socialist states. Under this system as devised by Lenin, the structure of management is the critical factor. This structure did not spring full-blown from Lenin's imagination. On the contrary, after achieving power he was content to utilize the traditional form then current in many lands of managing military production through arsenals run by ministries of war. He created as a special agency a ministry which he called the Supreme Council of National Economy, to which nationalized industries were transferred for management.[35] As with prewar state economic activity, this ministry received appropriations for the conduct of its activities, and when income was derived, it was returned to the state treasury, from which reallocation was required for the next budget period.

Although Lenin's system of financing was conventional, his management of the individual factories was intended to reflect the aspiration of the revolution, workers' control. This was personified by committee management, in which key members of various departments in an industrial plant shared in making decisions, subject to direction from the supreme council. No individual plant manager was responsible.

Lenin became disillusioned with his system in two areas:

[35] 5 Dec. 1917, [1917] 5 Sob. Uzak. R.S.F.S.R. pt.I item 83.

financing and management. The industries conducted like state arsenals on the basis of budget appropriations demonstrated no concern for costs. These mounted as inflation progressed and in turn contributed to that inflation. To be sure, accounts were audited in traditional fashion to hamper illegal use of funds, but there was no profit and loss statement relating income to expenditures from which it could be readily determined whether a given factory was costing more to run than the income it produced. Further, the workers' council form of management dispersed authority among members of a group, and Lenin discovered that no one could be made to accept responsibility. His effort to reduce this lack of responsibility by assigning charge of specific operations within the plant to each man on the council resulted in no beneficial change. His conclusion was that neither budget financing nor workers' council management had any place in his system. The reorganization of the economy made on the introduction of the New Economic Policy presented the opportunity he needed, and by 1923 he was ready with what became known as the "first decree on the trusts." [36]

This decree introduced two new concepts: (1) cost accounting by what amounted to an independent accounting unit, similar to a public corporation, to which assets would be assigned, and within which income would be attributed directly to expenditures without going through the process of budget allocation; and (2) one-man management instead of workers' council management. The first was called by a Russian word widely adopted in the Marxian socialist world—*khozraschet*— and the second by another Russian word, also widely used—*edinonachalie.*

Although both principles were presented at the same time, they were put into practice at quite different rates. The substitution of one-man management for the workers' councils took time, partly because there were not enough skilled managers, and also because the council forms of managing which had been introduced with the revolution could not be lightly abandoned by workmen who associated discipline enforced by one

[36] 10 Apr. 1923, [1923] 29 *id.* item 336.

man with hated capitalist management. Not until 1934 was it possible to do away with all workers' councils and to establish the manager as a single individual with full responsibility.[37]

The cost-accounting innovation was immediately effective, and it proved so successful that in 1927 the large units originally created as "trusts" in corporate form were split into their functional components under a "second decree on the trusts." [38] Each component was directed to operate economically under a system in which costs were computed with care and operations were held within income. The second decree also reflected the change in the economy which was occurring with the phasing out of the New Economic Policy and the introduction of state planning. At the time of the first decree, planning was yet a dream,[39] and private enterprises were thriving under Lenin's reprieve. State enterprise management at that time was directed to conducting operations with an eye to profits. These profits, when compared with those of private enterprise competitors, were expected to indicate the superior efficiency of state operation. In short, private enterprise motivation was utilized in state enterprise to measure efficiency.

By the time of the second decree there was no longer a competitive private sector, nor could the managers be permitted to conduct their operations primarily to make profits. The emphasis changed. Under the second decree the managers of state enterprises were directed to conduct their operations primarily to meet the requirements of the national economic plan, and secondarily to make profits, which would be used by the Ministry of Finance as indications of their efficiency. If profits

[37] 15 Mar. 1934, [1934] 15 Sob. Zak. S.S.S.R. pt.I item 103.

[38] 29 June 1927, [1927] 39 *id.* item 392.

[39] Planning began with creation of GOELRO (State Commission for the Electrification of Russia) in 1920; its first plan being approved 29 Dec. 1920, [1920] 1 Sob. Uzak. R.S.F.S.R. pt.I item 11. GOSPLAN (State Planning Commission) was created on 22 Feb. 1921, [1921] 17 *id.* item 106, but its only function was to gather statistics and to prepare general suggestions until it presented the First Five-Year Plan in 1928. When adopted on 28 May 1929, it was made retroactive to 1 Oct. 1928. [1929] 35 Sob. Zak. S.S.S.R. pt.I item 311. In preparation for planning a decree of 8 June 1927 made GOSPLAN's orders compulsory, [1927] 33 *id.* item 373.

were impossible, the state treasury would subsidize the key industries; but the effort should be made to cut costs to the bare minimum and to avoid waste.

Because of these two decrees a critical element of capitalist control, the measurement of profits, was introduced into state industrial management; but the position was stoutly defended that this was in no way a return to capitalism. It was explained as merely being the use of capitalist accounting methods to improve efficiency in state production.

By the time Eastern European states were brought within the Marxian socialist family after the war, the Soviet pattern of managing state property through public corporations operating on the basis of cost accounting and under a single responsible manager was well established. Trade unions and party organizations within the enterprises had been allocated roles subordinate to the managers. All vestiges of committee management had been terminated in 1937 when Stalin declared, under the pressure of necessity to produce for what seemed the inevitable war with Hitler, that the manager must be permitted to make decisions without countermands from trade unions or local party organs.

This had been the rule for years, but only on paper; for there had been developed what came to be known popularly as the "triangle," in which management met with trade union and party officials at the plant level to discuss common problems on an advisory basis.[40] In 1937 Stalin told these "triangles" never to meet again because they had in practice hampered management in taking bold decisions. This meant not the end of trade union and party representatives at the local level, but a change in their channels of influence. Although the representatives previously had threatened directors in their own offices, after 1937 they had recourse only to appeals to higher echelons in the trade union and party hierarchies. Their superiors, under this system, might complain to the industrial ministers, as the highest administrative level over the plant director, and thus try to set

[40] The relationships between the three institutions of the "triangle" were defined by the C.C. of the Communist party on 5 Sept. 1929. For text, see 1 SOVETSKOE KHOZIASTVENNOE PRAVO 83 (1934) [Soviet Economic Law].

right a faulty decision. But the manager was told not to wait for a decision from above but to proceed according to his own judgment until directed otherwise by his own superior. He knew that he was dependent on his minister, who appointed, promoted, and dismissed him.

Stalin's 1937 decision did not mean the end of trade union influence, much less Communist party influence, but it handicapped both institutions. Emphasis was upon speedy decisions in the interest of production, with subsequent rectification in the event of error. That was quite different from achieving concert of three interests before any decision could be made. Further, the likelihood of reversal was less than if the local officials of trade union and party could veto management's plans, for local prejudice would play no part in decisions on the ministerial level. This change meant that the local director had become supreme in his own plant.

On the ministerial level a similar supremacy of one man was established. Although a collegium was established to advise the minister, its members were department chiefs, subordinate to him in the hierarchy of the managerial organization chart and in no way capable of interfering with the decision.

One-man management was strengthened further during the war years. Production was needed without interference from trade union locals or from plant organizations of the Communist party, which were staffed with "generalists" not expected to understand the technical problems of production. The managers became an elite, and sociologists outside the USSR began to speak of a new managerial class which might, and perhaps already did, challenge the generalists of the Communist party.[41]

Stalin's model, enshrined in administrative law, became obligatory for the postwar Communist-led states, and all adopted his principles of cost accounting and one-man management of public corporations created to produce according to national economic plans. Even after Stalin's death, when his heirs put an end to personal dictatorship within the party with a return to

---

[41] The validity of this position is assessed in J. Azrael, Managerial Power in Soviet Politics (1966).

"collective leadership," there was an effort to avoid any change in the form of industrial management. The new leaders published pamphlets explaining that the abandonment of one-man rule in the Communist party did not require the abandonment of one-man management in industry.[42] These publications show the strength of a principle which had become enshrined in doctrine, a position held so firmly as to explain the continuing reluctance of the Soviet leadership to listen to arguments based upon what to them seems heresy—a return to committee-type management through workers' committees or councils.

The revolts in Poland and Hungary in 1956 forcefully emphasized the problem of management. The Polish and Hungarian rioters demanded that management be returned in one way or another to "workers' councils." They spoke for an institution devised by Tito in 1950[43] after his 1948 split with Stalin and currently enshrined in a Basic Law of Enterprises adopted in 1965.[44] Tito's scheme was designed to overcome the bureaucratic tendencies which he felt had emerged in Yugoslavia in applying Stalin's concept of what management was required in state ownership of industry. His aim was to permit workmen to share in managerial decisions and to serve as a control over tyrannical managers. To dramatize his change Tito declared that state ownership was being abandoned and his new system of social ownership was being substituted.

Tito's scheme authorized all the workmen in an enterprise to elect a council, which was given general responsibility for operations. The responsibility was extensive, for the council was to decide the items to be produced, their prices, the wages to be paid, the fund to be retained for investment, and the distribution of surpluses. To make the scheme realistic in view of the large number of workmen (fifteen to two hundred) in some of the councils, the councils elected executive committees of at

[42] E. Shorina, Kollegial'nost i edinonachalie v sovetskom gosudarstvennom upravlenii (1959). [Collegiality and One-Man Management in Soviet Public Administration].

[43] Neal, The Reforms in Yugoslavia, 13 Am. Slavic and E. E. Rev. 227 (1954).

[44] Pub. in [1965] 17 J. of L. Yugoslavia. Eng. transl. in 13 Collection of Yugoslav Laws (Laws of Enterprises and Institutions) 15 (Institute of Comparative Law, Belgrade, 1966).

least five members, responsible to the council. In small plants employing less than thirty, the entire work force formed the council.[45]

Elections to the council were annual until 1958 and thereafter were biannual. To assure rotation of the executive, only one-third might be re-elected for successive terms; and to assure participation by bench workmen, three-quarters of the executive had to be workers "engaged directly in production or otherwise in the basic productive activity of the enterprise."

The executive is powerful, for it oversees all daily operations, proposes to the workers' council the enterprise production plan, and sets wages and hours, although the council may reverse the decisions. If the shop is very large, each shop may be placed under a subordinate workers' council which may recommend action to the council for the entire plant.

The touchy subject of choice of director, which Tito found to be anathema in Stalin's model, was no longer left to higher adminstrative echelons. The director's appointment was assigned to a special commission formed by members of the workers' council and representatives of two other forces—the local governing body, comparable, in the measure indicated in chapter 3, to the soviet in the USSR, and the industry-wide chamber representing all workers' councils in the Republic in the same branch of industry. This three-way representation made the workers unable to exert their prejudices in the selection of a director. Representatives of the local populace, of which they were only a part, and of the workers in the industry as a whole, who knew conditions throughout the republic, were present to exercise a balance in favor of broader interests than those evident to a worker group emotionally biased over a local issue.

Competitive examinations are usually conducted to find candidates appropriate for the position of director, although outside observers have noted that the recommendations frequently come from party officials. Directors are ex officio members of the executive of the workers' council once they are chosen; so they can participate in discussions and often explain

[45] The description and evaluation of the Yugoslav system has been drawn from G. HOFFMAN & F. NEAL, YUGOSLAVIA AND THE NEW COMMUNISM 240–46 (1962).

away a grievance before it becomes a primary issue of confidence. But if they lose a vote of confidence, the workers' council may petition the local governing body, which again summons a special commission to decide the issue of dismissal and the appointment of a new director.

To assure serious thought about the petition of the workers' council, the law provides that if a decision is rendered by the commission against the petition and the workers' council continues to insist, the council is dissolved and a new election held, thus giving the full plant membership a chance to decide whom to support. If the newly elected workers' council continues its hostility to the director, he must be dismissed by the local governing body. In practice, charges brought against a director by a workers' council stand more often than not, even though both party and trade union representatives often oppose the workers' council on the request for dismissal.

The "social ownership" scheme was designed to dramatize the role of the workers in the plants as "owners," since they make the important production decisions instead of the central government's doing so through its appointed director. Although this feature is crucial to the scheme, the practical problem of maintaining strong leadership has required its modification over the years. The statute creating the workers' council system states that the director is the "highest employee" and "independently settles current problems." But it adds that he must do so "in conformity with decisions of the workers' council and its executive." He is not a prisoner of the council, however, for in certain instances he may appeal a decision of the workers' council to the local governing body, presumably to prepare his defense if the latter is asked to reassemble the special committee to decide on a plea for his dismissal.

Dismissals of directors appointed under the old bureaucratic system were numerous after the introduction of the new law, but they soon became stabilized. Curiously, most requests for dismissal were initiated not by the workers' council but by the local government organ.

The 1950 reform was accompanied by dissolution of the central industrial ministries in Belgrade, which had become symbols of bureaucratic control. There were substituted councils, boards, and committees with small staffs, incapable of intervening in many decisions but authorized to designate directors outside the workers' council system for a limited group of key industries. In 1953 even these higher bodies were eliminated, so that enterprises became self-governing under the workers' councils, subject only to the controls from local government and the industry generally which have been described.

The difficulties with enterprise autonomy came not from dismissals of directors but from votes for higher wages without corresponding increase in productivity, which caused widespread inflation. To put a halt to such votes, in 1954 enterprises were grouped in self-governing associations according to their type of activity, and these associations were assigned to chambers. Some of the large industries were given seats directly in the chambers. The chambers were directed to oppose the tendency of workers' councils to follow narrow interests, and they could lay down broad policies which, although they were not legally binding, came to have persuasive force. They could also represent the members before government bodies and obtain bank credit.

The chambers were strengthened in 1958 by the addition to their governing organs of representatives of the government. Although their own decisions were not binding, in some instances they were delegated by the government to prepare and enforce governmental regulations. If the government thought it necessary, it could suspend a decision of a chamber as illegal, and judicial review by the Supreme Economic Court could follow. Yugoslavs see these chambers as something other than the administration because they represent the workers as well, although in a controlled manner.

The Yugoslavs have faced the same problems as the leadership in the USSR in defining the relationship between managers, trade unions, and the party. In 1952 the Yugoslav party forbade direct intervention by local units in the affairs of an enterprise, preferring to work through the trade unions, whose national president is a member of the party. The party has few members on most of the workers' councils, except in very large plants. Consequently, in the absence of exceptionally talented leaders, it must rely for guidance upon the trade union local leaders who sit in the councils. This channel must curb, or attempt to curb, excesses on the part of the workers' councils.

Trade union control, however, seems to have been inadequate, judging by the outside restraints established to counterbalance the workers' councils in their basic decisions on choice of a director and wages.

Yugoslav experimentation with worker control has been reflected in all other Marxian socialist states, although to differing degrees.[46] Thus, the Polish Communists, after the October of 1956, introduced workers' councils and the directors of enterprises were named and dismissed by superior administrative organs on the advice of such councils. In 1958 the agencies of workers' auto-administration were emasculated to reintroduce the Soviet model.[47] In Czechoslovakia, Bulgaria, and Hungary, laws were introduced in 1958, 1960, and 1963 to permit the establishment of administrative councils named by the state but having representatives of social organizations including the trade unions. For a time, however, these councils were only consultative, the final decision resting with the director alone. Czechoslovakia was the first to break away from the Soviet-sponsored pattern and move in the direction of the Yugoslav solution. In 1968 it began to create workers' councils with far greater powers, including the choice of director. One hundred thirteen such workers' councils came into being during the summer of 1968, and many assumed broad powers of decision in the management of the firms. Judging from what happened when Soviet influence was reasserted through the use of troops, the Soviet Communist party's leaders must have become alarmed. On 24 October 1968 a government decree was adopted under vigorous Soviet pressure to stop the spread of such practices, and most of the councils returned to their advisory status. Only the council at the Skoda plant was determined not to be cowed; it published an advertisement asking technical experts to submit applications for the position of manager.

Even the Soviet leadership, in spite of its dislike of control by workers' councils, has found it necessary to make some concessions at home. It wants no return to the system of workers' councils which Stalin rejected in 1934 after years of

[46] Eörsi, *La gestion des entreprises* in LE DROIT DE PROPRIÉTÉ DANS LES PAYS DE L'EST 23 (R. Dekkers, ed. 1964).

[47] Starošciak, *Droit administratif* in INTRODUCTION À L'ÉTUDE DE DROIT POLONAIS 462 at 495 (S. Rozmaryn ed. 1967).

disillusionment with divided responsibility. Their alternative is a partial return to the position taken when the "triangles" functioned in industry. Pressure for departure from wartime policies of giving unrestrained powers to managers was in evidence as early as 1955, when the All Union Council of Trade Unions charged that managers were paying too little attention to production conferences with trade union members in their plants.[48] Soviet authors disclosed concern because the law on production conferences adopted in July 1929 had not been put into practice. The 1955 order was announced as being designed to revive a useful concept which Stalin had ignored after sponsoring its use.

After the Polish and Hungarian revolts the Communist party of the Soviet Union declared at a plenary meeting in December 1957 that it recognized the utility of the production conference and had decided to make it a permanent organ with wide participation by workers and technician-engineers.[49] By 8 July 1958 an order, issued jointly by the highest trade union body and the Council of Ministers of the USSR, approved a statute calling for the election of a collegial organ in enterprises having not less than one hundred workers.[50] The electorate was to be a general assembly of the workers, and the trade union factory committee was to organize the choice of its presidium of from five to fifteen persons.

The dominant, and apparently domineering, role being played by plant directors caught Nikita Khrushchev's attention, and on 2 July 1959 he demanded that the Communist party establish control over them. From this resulted a resolution of the party's Central Committee on 26 June 1959,[51] requiring the primary party organizations in each plant to create a committee to extend party control over the director. In 1962 the Central Committee of the party called for the further reform of trans-

[48] Order of 28 Sept. 1955 pub. in SBORNIK ZAKONODATEL'NYKH AKTOV O TRUDE 45 (3d ed. 1960) [Collection of Legislative Acts on Labor].

[49] 15 Dec. 1957. Order on the work of the trade unions of the USSR, *id.* at 25.

[50] *Id.* at 42.

[51] For text see ZAPISNAIA KNIGA PARTIINOGO AKTIVISTA 149 (1960) [Note Book of a Party Activist]. The statute on the control committee was approved 12 July 1959. See Pravda, 13 July 1959.

forming the permanent production conference in each plant into a committee,[52] which meant a permanent secretariat rather than an occasional gathering of a large number of persons to voice complaints and hear reports from management.

With this cascade of measures designed to restore the influence of the Communist party and the labor union in the plant, it was impossible to avoid the question of what was to happen to the one-man management principle; for it would be the rare director who would make decisions without approval of his colleagues.

The Communist party realized the danger, for the principle was reaffirmed in a 1965 Statute on the Industrial Enterprise [53] designed to reinforce the powers of the enterprise in the production hierarchy and to make it clear that the director spoke for the firm. Still, in practice his role remained obscure, and the Central Committee of the party found it desirable to restate the relationship between director, party secretary, and labor union leader in a resolution of December 1966,[54] resulting from a report of the Tula Province Party Committee. Restating the rule in the words "the principle of one-man management of production should be strengthened," in the very next paragraph the resolution calls for "raising the militancy of the primary party organizations, intensifying the party organizations' control over the functioning of the administration, heightening the role of the labor union organizations in protecting the workers' and employees' rights." This is language dating from the 1920s, and it is no wonder that it has left confusion and created erosion of the director's authority.

That this erosion has occurred is shown by the fact that, in spite of the reaffirmation of the principle of one-man manage-

[52] Resolution of C.C. of Communist party, 23 Nov. 1962 pub. in 4 SPRAVOCHNIK PARTIINOGO RABOTNIKA 191 (1963). [Reference Book of a Party Worker]. See also order no. 11 of plenum of Central Council of Trade Unions, 25 Dec. 1962, ordering creation of production committees, *id.* at 633, 638.

[53] 4 Oct. 1965, [1965] 19–20 Sob. Post. S.S.S.R. item 155. Eng. transl. in [1965] 17 C.D.S.P. no. 42 at 3. Also in 2 M. SHARPE ed., PLANNING, PROFIT AND INCENTIVES IN THE U.S.S.R.—REFORM OF SOVIET ECONOMIC MANAGEMENT 289 (1966).

[54] Resol. of C.C. of Communist party 22 Dec. 1966, par. 6, pub. in 7 SPRAVOCHNIK, *supra,* note 52 at 184, 189 (1967).

ment in the 1965 Statute on the Industrial Enterprise and the December 1966 resolution, one author was able to write in February 1967, "Every one knows that to this day the individual enterprise managers are sometimes unable to decide independently to drive a nail into the wall." [55] The author calls for a new reaffirmation of the one-man management principle and for educating enterprise directors to take initiative, but at the same time he emphasizes the counterweights of the party and of labor unions. He advises directors to call workers' meetings regularly and to utilize fully the production conference as well as the initiative represented by the working people's organizations. Clearly, a director needs skill in maintaining an acceptable relationship between the elements of what looks like a reinvigorated "triangle."

In 1956 the Chinese Communists rejected the system of one-man management as it was conceived by Stalin, even though in 1949 they had begun to emulate his system in establishing management for their own public corporations utilizing state property.[56] Professor Franz Schurmann has suggested that the Communist party rejected Stalin's scheme because it was out of accord with the party's historical experience with committee management, and because to the present it has felt it necessary in China to assert its leadership in administration at every level.[57]

In the Chinese experience, factories nationalized from private owners who were considered to be in league with foreign capitalists were first run by committees appointed by the communist military administration. When matters became more stable, the factories were transferred to factory management committees (*kungch'ang kuanli weiyuanhui*) composed of factory and section directors, military representatives, and the most skilled engineers. Usually a director was appointed to head the enterprise, but his loyalty was often doubted because of his past association with bourgeois owners. The factory committee tried to protect production from potential disloyalty on the part of

[55] Yeshtokin, *Party Life*, Pravda, 26 Feb. 1967 at 2. Eng. transl. in [1967] 19 C.D.S.P. no. 8 at 10.

[56] The information on China is drawn from SCHURMANN, IDEOLOGY AND ORGANIZATION IN COMMUNIST CHINA 250 *et seq.* (1966).

[57] *Id.* at 279.

directors, and the pattern of authority was unclear. Although some pressure was exerted for clear authority as in the Soviet model, often because of the participation of Soviet technical advisers who felt that Soviet experience had proved its necessity, the party maintained its participation in deciding details of operation. A further step leading to the breakdown of responsible management came with the organization under the factory director of functional staffs concerned with planning, technology, wages, finance, and accounting. These staffs often assumed considerable power in making decisions. "Multiheaded leadership" resulted and coordination was hard to achieve.

Books expounding the Soviet experience appeared in the late 1940s and well into the 1950s. Many were translated from Russian, but some were of Chinese origin. Soviet technicians, working under a Sino-Soviet agreement of 1950 to build a number of basic industrial units, pressed for reform and the Soviet managerial model was introduced by steps: first, the "system of responsibility" under which management and workers received specific responsibility for fulfilling production quotas and for maintaining equipment in their care; second, the system of "production sector management" under which each function within a factory was placed under the control of a manager and work teams were moved from place to place as their functions were performed.

The third stage of development of responsibility was the system of a single director (*ichangpchih*) for each segment of a factory. Factories were divided into shops and shops into segments, each under a chief having full authority and responsible only to his superior. The functional sections remained, but only as advisers without authority to issue orders to work supervisors in lower echelons. Their powers were exactly like those established in 1934 in the USSR when industrial management by ministries was reorganized on a production-territorial basis instead of a functional basis.

The Soviet model as introduced into China resulted in the gradual reduction in the authority of party committees in the factories, just as it had in Stalin's Soviet Union, and in that change lay its undoing; for Mao Tse-tung was not prepared to permit an emerging managerial class to defy the party at the factory level. Also, he may already have begun to fear Soviet penetration of his power structure, and adoption of the Soviet-sponsored system may have looked like such penetration. Some authorities think he expected the well-indoctrinated cadres to master management techniques quickly.

Whatever the motivation, the Fourth Plenum of the Party in 1954 called for increased observance of the principles of collective leadership by the party. There developed within the party a struggle over the question of unity of leadership in the industrial apparatus, and by March 1955 a purge began of those favoring the single-director system. But the system was eliminated slowly, since the party could not afford disruption of production. Not until September 1956, at the Eighth Party Congress, was the one-man management system officially replaced by a new system called "factory manager responsibility under the collective leadership of the party committee." The party committee was now to make decisions for the factory collectively. The director was responsible for implementation, but not for policy. In the words of a Chinese author, the director "must execute the majority decisions of the Party committee and be fully responsible to it." [58]

Disruption of the industrial process has occurred at times since 1956, as mass movements have been encouraged. Thus, during the Great Leap Forward movement of 1958–59 the mass movement in aid of production reached such frenzy that directors complained against sacrifice of what they deemed to be the traditional order required in the production process. Mao's response was to institute in 1962 what was called "independent operational authority," which Professor Franz Schurmann has defined as different from the Soviet model of one-man management and also different from Communist party management.[59] In his view, it can be understood best in comparison with the organization of the various divisions of General Motors Corporation in the United States.[60] But even this reform was not to last.

In 1966, at Mao's bidding, the Great Proletarian Cultural Revolution swept across China. In his effort to humble the

[58] Quoted by Hsiao, *The Role of Economic Contracts in Communist China*, 53 CALIF. L. REV. 1029 at 1049, note 123 (1965).

[59] SCHURMANN, *supra*, note 56 at 297.

[60] *Id.* at 303.

professional party cadres, Mao called upon the youthful Red
Guards to attack the conservative cadres in the factories, as well
as elsewhere. "Politics first" became the slogan in the factories,
and the mass line was restated, defined as everybody's taking a
hand, not as just a few persons' issuing orders.[61] Workers were
to take part in management as masters of the state alongside
the cadres. The masses were to put forth ideas, and the cadres
were to process them in a manifestation of democratic centralism. The leadership of enterprises was to be supervised by the
masses of workers and the staff members.

By January 1967, the Red Guards were going even further
and seizing power in the factories. A takeover in Shanghai was
hailed as emulating the Marxist principle of smashing the old
state machinery and establishing a new revolutionary order.[62]
The administrative post of workshop director was abolished,
and new men were elected to lead the production teams, with
emphasis upon revival of the ideal type of leadership: "not
sitting in front offices and giving orders, but making decisions
with the masses on the spot in the shops." Mao, in his determination to humble those of the party cadres who favored stability akin to that emerging in the USSR, was willing to return to
his earliest policies of favoring what he called "red" over "expert."

When the Red Guard movement in the factories began to
show adverse effects on production, Mao's advisers called them
off. The army was put into the factories to stabilize the production process. Presumably the army was returned to participating
in the decision-making process as it had during the early period
of military administration. At least, the Soviet Communist
party thinks so, in its criticism of Mao's policy of humbling the
cadres. In the party's opinion Mao has created a military dictatorship.

From the above it is clear that a common denominator in
all Marxist-oriented countries has been an effort to give industrial workers a sense of participation in the production
process. In the face of the exigencies of war Stalin moved far

[61] *Running Enterprises in Line with Mao Tse-tung's Thinking*, [1966]
9 PEKING REVIEW 2.

[62] *A Fine Example of "Taking Firm Hold of the Revolution and Promoting Production*," [1967] 9 *id.* 2.

away from mass participation and returned to a form of management which gave directors even more authority than the capitalist countries did, but since his death the pendulum has swung the other way. Tito has gone furthest in cutting down the director's power. His neighbors to the east have been more restrained, although since 1956 they have shown a determination to bring the plant workmen into the administrative process as advisers. The Soviet leadership has moved with the greatest reluctance, but even in the USSR there has been a trend toward worker participation in advice and review, though through the trade unions rather than directly through workers' councils. This has been accompanied by a strengthening of party controls. In China no real, lasting participation has been given the workers, even through labor unions, for the helm was taken first by the party, and then in 1967 by the army, after a costly interlude with the Red Guard concept of "mass participation."

Only in Yugoslavia is it claimed that ownership has passed to the workers, in what Tito calls a system of "social control." Elsewhere, the title to industry indubitably rests in the state. Even the public corporations who manage the property gain no title. Their right has been defined as one of "operational management," which has replaced the right of ownership in the traditional sense.[63] This new right is subordinate to the duty to use the property solely in accordance with the powers granted in the public corporation's charter, and in discharge of the obligation to fulfill the plan. Thus, the concept of invalidity of *ultra vires* acts is strong in Marxian socialist law; for if a public corporation uses the property assigned to it contrary to its charter, its acts may be set aside by a court or state arbitration tribunal.[64] To Marxist authors public corporations have a new form of property right, unknown in its novel details to the Romanist legal system, and hence of great importance in determining the uniqueness of the Marxian system.

In comparing industrial trends with agricultural trends in Marxian socialist law, it is evident that there has been strong emphasis in both fields upon mass participation in management; but there is a critical difference. In the land law, partici-

---

[63] Eörsi, *supra*, note 46 at 34.
[64] Dmitrov Camp of Gulag v. Zagotzerno, [1935] 20 ARBITRAZH 26.

pation has meant extending property rights to citizens through the cooperative form. Thus peasants, or "collective farmers" as they are more properly called, are in legal terms co-proprietors, no matter how restrained their use of jointly owned property may be. In its present form mass participation in land use is considered a concession to peasant mentality, a retrogressive step to be overcome as soon as possible by substituting the state farm as a symbol of ownership by the whole people for the collective, which symbolizes ownership by a group of co-owners.

Contrariwise, the mass participation in industry is not seen as a concession, except perhaps by a few of those in the USSR and abroad who feel themselves emotionally linked to Stalin's methods of centralized direction. Worker participation is looked upon as an element of worker democracy. As such it is seen as a step in the direction of the ultimate goal of a society in which the individual understands the social advantage of common ownership so fully, and has learned to discipline himself so well, that outside force to compel production is unnecessary. Visionary as this goal of the "withering away of the state" may be, it still lurks in the thoughts of many influential European Marxists, and in devising an industrial policy they keep this as an ideal. They want no military-type commander in a factory enforcing his word against a morose, uncomprehending body of workmen, and they are quick to criticize Mao Tse-tung for establishing what seems to them just such a military personage. They want no "boss" enforcing his rule through police and courts as during Stalin's time, arresting and penalizing those who come late to work or waver at the lathe.

The ideal for industry is a socially conscious collective of workmen, sharing decisions of a productive nature, including the dismissal of workers, and policing itself through social persuasion rather than through the courts. Because of this emphasis upon social understanding, attention has increasingly been upon informal social courts, to which sluggish and recalcitrant factory hands are brought for education in their social duties.

9

The Property Incentive

P RIVATE PROPERTY, IN THE SENSE OF OWNERSHIP OF THE MEANS
of production, is being legislated out of existence within the
family of Marxian socialist legal systems, but in every country
but China incentive to produce has been fostered mainly by
systems of widely differentiated wages. The Soviet party's leading theorist has justified the property incentive even on moral
grounds; in 1966 he told an election rally, "He who gives more
to his country has the right not only to the respect of society
but also to greater material benefits." [1]

To make the incentive effective, law has had to be formulated to recognize the right of ownership in the rewards distributed. From the earliest Soviet civil code, the citizen-owner has
found his charter in the formula common to Romanist legal
systems, "Within the limits set by law, the owner has the right
to possess, use, and dispose of his property." [2] What difference
the Marxian socialist legal systems have added to the Romanist
formula lies not in the complete abolition of property owner-

[1] Suslov, *Always together with the Party*, Pravda, 8 June 1966 at 2.
Eng. transl. in [1966] 18 C.D.S.P. no. 24 at 17.
[2] Civil Code R.S.F.S.R., 1922, art. 58, [1922] 71 Sob. Uzak. R.S.F.S.R.
pt. I item 904.

ship by individuals, but in the forms of its limitation. These have differed from the limitations established by legal systems in the nonsocialist states, and all Marxists and many of other philosophical persuasions find this difference to be qualitative.

Only Mao Tse-tung challenges the Marxist propriety of encouraging citizens to enrich themselves in nonproductive property.[3] He fears that property accumulation by individuals, even when subjected to various limitations and prohibitions, will corrupt intentions and reopen the gates to capitalism. In a letter of 1963 his Central Committee criticized trends in the USSR and Yugoslavia as creating bourgeois attitudes, which he expected to cause further retreats from proletarian-based society.[4] As the polemical furor engendered by these charges waxed, he permitted himself to take an even more radical position. His phrases, "it is frightful to think of the time when all people will be rich,' and "poverty is good" have been regarded by Soviet authors as efforts to make a virtue out of necessity because China is unable to emulate Soviet success in production.[5]

For Soviet leaders and the policy makers of all other Marxist-oriented states but China, the purpose of Marxist reorganization of society is to achieve "abundance," and this has meant satisfaction of creature comforts no less than elsewhere in the world. Indeed, it is claimed that the Marxist-oriented system will exceed the privately financed non-state-planned productive mechanism of capitalism in enriching the individual for several reasons. It is expected that state planning will prevent privately wealthy legislators from placing their own interests ahead of

[3] A Soviet author quotes Mao Tse-tung as saying on 29 April 1967, "The slogan 'to each according to his work' is bourgeois," and as adding that he had always been opposed to the wage system and to military rank, considering that "the system of rationed free supplies is the true Marxist style, a precondition for the transition to a communist mode of life." See Sladkovsky, *Threat to the Economic Foundations of Socialism in China*, [1967] 12 KOMMUNIST 92. Eng. transl. in 6 REPRINTS FROM THE SOVIET PRESS no. 5 at 3, 25 (1968). Exceptions were Mao's concessions to capitalist industrial managers, to overseas Chinese investors in the Chinese economy, and to inventors.

[4] Eng. transl. in [1963] 15 C.D.S.P. no. 28 at 3.

[5] Quoted in editorial *"On the Anti-Soviet Policy of Mao Tse-tung and His Group*, Pravda, 16 Feb. 1967 at 3. Eng. transl. in [1967] 19 C.D.S.P. no. 7 at 7.

socially oriented policies. And unprecedented enthusiasm should be expected from workmen who are convinced that higher production rates will benefit themselves and their government rather than private owners.

In the Marxist-oriented world outside China, quantities of privately owned nonproductive goods are expected to increase rapidly rather than to diminish during the period of socialism when full communism is still a distant goal. Civil law, as the instrument of protection and regulation of this ownership, becomes of vital concern in the legal system. Until all law has "withered away" with the achievement of abundance and the distribution of goods according to need, civil law is given a respected place.

It was not always so. Soviet jurists after the revolution took Marx and Engels to mean that the state and its law would wither away swiftly after the bourgeois captains of industry had been deprived of their property by the nationalization decrees. With these expectations the New Economic Policy of 1921 looked like a retreat, to be reversed swiftly when the economy had been restored to the minimum of order and wealth necessary to its development under state ownership and planning. The civil code of 1922 was announced as a concession to the capitalists, to give them enough confidence in the protection of private property in the new Russian republic to encourage ventures starting the new economy on its way.[6] When it had served its purpose, the code was to become progressively inapplicable as private ownership was reduced in scope. The code's legal framework would become only an empty shell with nothing to regulate. Then civil law could be considered to have "withered away." In keeping with this expectation, Soviet law schools of the early 1930s eliminated from the curriculum the course in civil law, and merely included a few lectures on the subject at the end of the general course on the administration of state-owned property. Likewise, textbooks relegated the matter of private ownership and its law to the end of studies on state property. It was only an appendage, to be dropped as the need for it disappeared.

All these expectations changed in the mid-1930s, when pro-

[6] *Speech to Fourth Congress of Persons Engaged in the Administration of Justice,* D. Kurskii, Izbrannye stat'i i rechi 69 (1948) [Collected Articles and Speeches].

duction became uppermost in the Communist party's hierarchy of tasks to be performed in the preparation of an abundant society. Stimulation of production by widely differentiated wage payments became a major policy. Those who clung to the position, popular with nineteenth-century socialists, that egalitarianism was a principle on which their societies were to be based were denounced as petty bourgeois utopians.[7] A sharp distinction was drawn between the use of property incentive as a means of satisfying creature comforts and its use as a source of private capital with which to make productive investments. Only the latter use was to be attacked. Marx and Engels were quoted from the *Communist Manifesto* in proof, for they had written, "The distinguishing feature of communism is not the abolition of property generally, but the abolition of bourgeois property."

To facilitate distinction, a new vocabulary was invented. What Marx and Engels had denounced in the Manifesto as "bourgeois" property came to be called "private" property, and property that was to be protected, not confiscated, was given the name "personal" property. This was property destined to meet the consumer's personal needs. But the line of demarcation was not easy to establish, for some goods can be either one. It was the task of the policy maker to draw the line, bearing in mind that the property right was recognized not only for doctrinal reasons but because it stimulated production. In a sense the task was to determine what items of property, even if they possessed an income-producing potential, might be left to unrestrained personal ownership; what items required specific prohibition of income-producing use; and how many elements of the right to use and dispose normally associated with private ownership might be recognized in law, even when there was no possibility of obtaining income, as with the inheritance of decedents' estates.

By 1936, when the second federal constitution of the USSR was promulgated, the answer to these questions was stated in a generally phrased Article 10 declaring, "The personal property of citizens in their incomes and savings from work, in their dwelling houses and subsidiary husbandries, in articles of personal use and convenience, as well as the right of citizens to inherit personal property, is protected by law." The lack of precision in the Soviet statement was intensified when the Chinese Communists enacted their constitution in 1954, for its Articles 11 and 12 say simply: "The state protects the right of citizens to own lawfully earned income, savings, houses, and other means of subsistence," and, "The state protects according to law the right of citizens to inherit private property." [8] Events since the enactment of the two constitutions, resulting in the public outbreak of rigorous debate and polemics of the mid-1960s between the Soviet and Chinese leaders over the application of these principles, indicate the contrasts in policy and legal formulation which are possible within the family of Marxian socialist legal systems in spite of commonly held fundamental beliefs.

Mao's differences with Soviet leaders have been accentuated beyond what might have been expected in a conflict of basic views over the place of personally owned property in a Marxist-oriented society because he has adopted the unconventional ideas on permanent flexibility which have already been analyzed. Thus, his rejection of the measure of stability established by codification of civil law in the USSR and in all other Marxian socialist states permits him to move quickly from position to position and to nullify the very aim of the other Marxist leaders—to establish in the masses a sense of confidence in their future and in the continuing protection of whatever property they may obtain through toil. Mao came closest to a position of stability of property relations when he had his legislators guarantee that the title to land when placed in the villages would remain untouched for thirty years. [9] For everything else, Mao's law may be changed from day to day.

Of course, all other Marxist leaders have also created rules from which they can depart without great difficulty because the

---

[8] Eng. transl. in A. BLAUSTEIN, FUNDAMENTAL LEGAL DOCUMENTS OF COMMUNIST CHINA 1 (1962). The Chinese use the word "private" because their system accepted continuation of the concept of private ownership of industry in contrast to the Soviet prohibition of such ownership.

[9] As to the problem presented in authenticating the source for this regulation, see chap. 7, n. 45 and 46.

Communist party domination of legislators makes it possible to amend the codes without strong opposition. Still, the long delays in the USSR and elsewhere in Eastern Europe when a code is to be amended suggest that since Stalin's death, at least, the publicly expressed attitude in favor of "legality," of which stability forms an element, militates against change without extensive discussion within the party, and on some matters among the general public as well. New restraints on the enjoyment of personal property are therefore introduced infrequently, usually only after such widespread public discussion of abusive practices among property owners that there is considerable demand for preservation of Marxist standards of ethics not only in the party-controlled press but in the corridors of offices and workers' clubs. Some examples of abuses and the legislation enacted to correct them will illustrate the point.

The major abuse of personal ownership rights has occurred with dwelling houses, because the housing shortage within the USSR has remained acute since the revolution in spite of extensive construction. The constitution sets no limitations, but guarantees the right to own "dwelling houses"; and many citizens do. One-third of all urban dwelling space in 1964 was privately owned, and the five-year plan called for the addition of 2,000,000 to 2,500,000 more private homes.[10]

In spite of this acceptance of the principle of private ownership of homes, there is recognition in law of the fundamental principle that citizens may not use personal property for the production of unearned income.[11] This principle has been implemented with precision by the civil code of 1964 for the Russian republic, and similarly by the civil codes of the other fourteen republics. These codes provide that a family whose members live together may own only one dwelling.[12]

Should a family unit receive by inheritance a second home, it must dispose of one or separate into two families.[13] If it fails to do so within a year, the property must be sold at auction by

[10] Semenov, *Your Personal Property*, Izvestiia, 18 Aug. 1966 at 5. Eng. transl. in [1966] 18 C.D.S.P. no. 33 at 7.

[11] Fundamental Principles of Civil Legislation, U.S.S.R., art. 20. 8 Dec. 1961, [1961] 50 Ved. Verkh. Sov. S.S.S.R. item 525.

[12] Civil Code R.S.F.S.R., 1964, art. 106.

[13] *Id*. art. 107.

the local soviet and the proceeds transmitted to the owner. This indicates no prejudice against the concept of private ownership, but rather the determination of the policy makers to prevent the use of living quarters to obtain income through rentals. There is no confiscation, only elimination of temptation.

The same elimination of temptation operates to specify a maximum size for the one house that may be owned.[14] By the civil code of the Russian republic implementing the Fundamentals of Civil Law for the USSR, not more than sixty square meters of living space may be created in a privately owned dwelling, unless special permission is obtained from the local soviet to build more; but even in such an event the precise area to be occupied must be established, and it must not exceed what the family could legally occupy if it leased buildings belonging to the local soviet. Thus, on each long-term change in the size of the family, there will be a redetermination of the space that may be owned.

The same principle prevents ownership of more than one apartment in a cooperatively constructed apartment house, and should the same family unit acquire ownership of both an apartment and a house, its members must elect to retain only one, or suffer forced sale if they do not dispose of one or the other within a year.[15]

Because it is understood that temporary changes in the size of a family, or the temporary removal of a family to another place of residence, may become necessary in performance of employment obligations, rentals are permitted; but if such rentals become systematic, "for the production of nonlabor income," the property may be confiscated after suit is brought in court by the local soviet to establish the facts.[16] The measure for determining "nonlabor income" levels on rental of privately owned premises is established by administrative order of the Council of Ministers of the Russian republic, dated 9 August 1963, at a maximum of 16 kopeks per square meter per month in cities. For vacation cottages in suburbs, which may be owned simultaneously with city house or an apartment, the rates vary with the locality. For Moscow and Leningrad, the rate set as

[14] *Id.* art. 106.
[15] *Ibid.*
[16] *Id.* art. 111.

maximum for the summer season is 3 rubles 60 kopeks per square meter for a fully insulated room; 3 rubles 24 kopeks for a "mansard" room; 1 ruble 44 kopeks for a glassed-in porch and 72 kopeks for an open porch. Rates elsewhere are designated in the order as lower.[17]

Sales of dwelling houses are subjected to controls to prevent illegal profit. This control is exercised by the state notaries, who are charged not only with authenticating the identities of the signatories, but also with verifying the agreement's legality.[18] They must refuse to approve sales designed to reap speculative profits; but they have not always done so. An author accuses a notary of approving the sale of two rooms in a four-room cement-block house built for 15,000 rubles. The sale, in the same year, netted 65,000 rubles, arousing the critic's denunciation of the seller for dishonesty and exploitation not only of the housing shortage but of the value of land.[19]

The latter charge needs explanation in a society where landownership is denied to all but the state. The argument is that the value of houses in suburbs mounts as the cities expand. Nothing has happened to increase the value of the materials in a dwelling: it has only become more desirable because it is nearer city transit and, therefore, jobs. In such instances, to a degree, a builder who sells his house at a higher price after a period of city growth regains more than the value of the materials and labor; he gains the value of the improved convenience of the location. A sale which would have been legal in the Western world has become illegal in the USSR, even though ownership rights in dwellings are constitutionally guaranteed, including the right of sale. The critic demanded more than notarial displeasure as an impediment to such profit-making. He wanted legislation with teeth.

Criticism is also aroused by sales of houses financed by loans

---

[17] The regulation is summarized in E. Fleishits, Nauchno-prakticheskii kommentraii k G.K. R.S.F.S.R. 354–55 (1966) [Scientific-Practical Commentary to the Civil Code of the R.S.F.S.R.].

[18] Instruction of Min. of Justice R.S.F.S.R., 1 Sept. 1958. Zakonodatel'stvo o notariate 13 (1960) (Ministry of Justice R.S.F.S.R.) [Legislation on the Notary's Office].

[19] Tarasenko, Concerning the Fight against Speculation in Individual Dwelling Houses, [1959] 7 Sov. iust. 52.

to the private builders from a state agency. On occasion an enterprise, to keep in its employ a valued specialist for whom increased wages are no incentive because of the shortage of consumer goods, will allocate to him scarce stocks of building materials and transportation for them. Cases have been reported of such dwellings' being sold immediately after completion of construction, at prices three times higher than cost, to persons unconnected with the state agency which made the sacrifice. Again, critics propose severe sanctions in the form of compulsory sale to the local soviet at cost price if the owner departs from the locality, with criminal prosecution for illegal dealing in nationalized property if sales are made otherwise.

The notaries realize the difficulties they face, and they have obtained for their own protection a ruling from the Ministry of Justice of the Russian republic forbidding sale of separate rooms in an owner's apartment unless the seller presents a certificate issued by the local soviet.[20] One notary argues that since he is not authorized to search out facts like a judicial official, he should not be required to certify anything whose legality cannot be determined from its face.[21]

Criminal prosecutions have been brought under Article 154 of the Russian republic's criminal code of 1961 for "speculation" when there has been a systematic practice of selling houses. Under the article the crime is defined as the "buying up and reselling of goods or any other articles for the purpose of making a profit," and it is treated as exaggerated when it is conducted as a form of business or on a large scale. In a 1961 case the attitude of the court was established in a decision on appeal affirming a sentence of seven years' imprisonment and confiscation of property.[22]

The accused was charged with systematically engaging in the purchase and resale of houses and automobiles. On appeal he claimed that he had not been doing so for speculative purposes, but the facts were taken to have proved the charge. Beginning in 1954 he had bought from private parties four houses and four automobiles, of which he had then resold three

[20] *Notarial Practice*, [1961] 4 Sov. IUST. 28.
[21] Eliseikin & Bel'glasov, *The Notary's Office and Prevention of Violation of Law*, [1965] 6 Sots. Zak. 40.
[22] Lebedinskii, [1961] 12 Sov. IUST. 28.

houses and three automobiles at higher prices. He had been attempting to sell the fourth automobile for 80,000 old rubles when he was arrested. The first house had cost 42,000 rubles. The accused had repaired it and sold it for 100,000 rubles, although he permitted the contract of sale to show only a price of 55,000 rubles. In 1956 the accused bought a second house for 115,000 rubles, repaired it, and sold it for 160,000 rubles. In 1960 he sold a third house, of undisclosed cost, for 220,000 rubles.

The automobiles were sold similarly after being purchased at lower prices. In 1958 he bought a car from a private owner for 16,000 rubles and resold it to a representative of a church for 42,000 rubles. Later in the same year he bought a second car for 32,000 rubles and in the following year exchanged it for a new car and the sum of 5,000 rubles. In October he resold the new car for 50,000 rubles.

For the automobiles there was no claim of contribution to value, but for the houses there was such a claim for repairs made by the owner. Still, this form of legal addition to value was not accepted as sufficient to explain the markup made by the seller, for nothing was said of it in the supreme court's opinion. The decision focused on the markup, which seemed large enough to the court to permit judicial notice that the profit exceeded what could have been contributed by repairs.

To avoid the resale of automobiles in the open market at high markups, in 1961 the Council of Ministers issued a ban, except when the sale was effected through state-run "commission stores." [23] In 1964 a second blow was struck at speculation by an instruction issued to state notaries not to register sale contracts of automobiles and large motorcycles, since all such sales were required to take place through the "commission stores," where prices were set in consultation with the store manager, with the store exacting a commission.[24] Simultaneously the civil code's Article 410 established the rule that

[23] Order of Council of Minister, no. 277, 23 Mar. 1961. Not pub. in printed form, but found in a Moscow library by Prof. Donald Barry. See his explanation in *Russia and Their Cars*, [1965] SURVEY (Oct.) 98 at 104, n. 14.

[24] 6 July 1964, [1964] 12 Sob. Post R.S.F.S.R. item 87, reprinted in [1965] 2 Sov. IUST. 34.

commission store sales shall be at prices not exceeding the state retail price for corresponding goods.

Speculation in houses was also attacked by the civil code of 1964 through the rule that a house may not be sold more often than once in three years, unless it has been obtained by inheritance.[25]

A rule of reason is sought, however, in applying the restrictive laws. Thus, a trial court which was too quick to convict for speculation found the procurator general intervening. The case concerned a conviction for sale of an automobile, against which the procurator general entered a protest on the ground that proof of sale to make a profit was lacking.[26] A similar intervention occurred when a trial court found facts which the procurator thought unsubstantiated. The court thought that the accused had bought a car from a state store in 1959 for 16,000 rubles and resold it the same year for 33,000; but the record showed that the purchase had been made five years before the sale, and that the automobile was sold not to make a profit but to obtain funds for a newer model, which the owner bought in 1960.[27]

Other extenuating circumstances overlooked by the trial court were an increase in the state retail price for such cars in 1957, and the absence in 1960 of the subsequently adopted regulation prohibiting secondhand sales except through the "commission stores." Further, the seller was a highly qualified machine-tool operator who had been a good example to his fellows by not following the usual practice of changing jobs frequently. He had remained in his factory for nearly thirty years. To the procurator, all these elements should have dictated acquittal.

When resale occurs at an advanced price, but after value is contributed through labor, and the price is no higher than the

---

[25] Art. 238.

[26] [1965] 4 Sots. zak. 93. The requirement of proof of sale in this case conflicts with the supreme court of the U.S.S.R. order of 20 Sept. 1946, as amended, for it permits conviction on the basis of well-founded belief that the accused contemplated resale. See Sbornik postanovlenii plenuma verkhovnogo suda SSSR, 1924–1963 gg. 299 (1964) [Collection of Orders of the Plenum of the Supreme Court of the U.S.S.R., 1924–1963].

[27] Dudarev, [1965] 6 Sots. zak. 79–80.

state retail price, a conviction for speculation may be set aside. This generalization is suggested by a case in which a truck driver was convicted for resale of two pigs, purchased from a collective farm while still piglets. They were fed for a year and then slaughtered and sold to a state dining hall at the state price. Encouraged by his success, the man immediately purchased three more piglets and fed them until they reached a weight of 460 kilograms. Then the police arrived. The supreme court set aside the conviction for speculation because the purchase had not been for quick resale at a profit, but to permit the owner to feed and slaughter the pigs for sale as meat.[28] The increased value could be attributed not to speculation but to labor. Probably the seller's conformity to the state price aided the supreme court in reversing the trial court.

The pig case presents some questions, for it contrasts with the sentences for resale of repaired houses. Also, no mention is made of the fact that the truck driver seems to have initiated a private business without being licensed as required by the provisions already discussed. Unlicensed private activity has sometimes resulted in prosecution.[29] Perhaps the acquittal merely indicates that the supreme court wanted to suggest leniency for those who contributed to the food supply in contrast to the supply of housing. Such a consideration is suggested by the civil code's Article 240, which exempts collective farmers from the general requirements of maintaining established state prices when selling agricultural products on the open market. Still, it seems more likely that the difference in treatment lay in the comparison of sums gained, for the money from pig raising was almost inconsequential, whereas the resale of repaired dwellings brought a large sum.

A similar policy of leniency was applied to save an owner of an automobile accused of conducting a taxi service.[30] After conviction by the trial court, he was released because the supreme court of the USSR found that he had carried passengers only twice, once from the center of Moscow to the subway

---

[28] Stefanov, *id.* at 80.

[29] Perlina. [1959] 2 Biull. Verkh. Suda S.S.S.R. 7. The conviction was reversed by the supreme court because of insufficient proof that dresses were made for sale.

[30] Dronevich, [1960] 5 *id.* 8.

station near his home, and once from that station to the railway station. In both cases he had accepted small amounts of money. The court concluded that he was not engaged in the systematic conduct of a business, and that the fact that the police found a railway timetable in his pocket when he was arrested was not sufficient proof that he systematically met railway arrivals.

Although the cases reviewed suggest that owners who lease or sell their property are subjected to restraints and to severe scrutiny by prosecutors on the alert to prevent speculation, another decision indicates that the freedom to alienate property as a gift remains absolute. This rule was tested by a disabled nephew who challenged his uncle's right to give his dwelling to another member of the family during the uncle's lifetime. The nephew argued that since he was unable to work, he would qualify as a dependent to receive the home under the civil code's provisions on inheritance should the uncle die, and that this was sufficient to prevent the uncle's disposing of the dwelling before it passed to the nephew. The court rejected the argument, affirming the owner's unrestricted right to make a gift.[31]

Yet the legal form of gift may not be used to mask some other type of transfer. This was established by an order confirming the right of a state notary to refuse to register a contract of gift of a dwelling when he discovered that the transfer was not in truth a gift, but was an element in an exchange of premises with a state slaughterhouse in Riazan.[32]

Private ownership carries with it certain duties, and if these are not performed, forfeiture without compensation is permitted. Thus, a private house owner must maintain the dwelling in good repair.[33] If it is left to become a ruin, the local soviet may begin a court action to determine the facts and to obtain an order transferring the premises to the local housing fund administered by the soviet. Protection is offered in that the owner must have adequate warning to permit him to make the repairs. The code's article rests on the rule that ownership must not be exercised to social detriment. The rule was established during the period of the New Economic Policy, and a number of court

[31] [1965] 7 Sots. zak. 87.
[32] *Notarial Practice*, [1966] 8 Sov. iust. 34.
[33] Civil Code R.S.F.S.R., 1964, art. 141.

decisions established the circumstances of forfeiture. These have been reincorporated into the practice to be applied under the 1964 code.[34] One decision is especially noteworthy: that no eviction from a house shall occur if the owner is a workman who lacks sufficient funds to make repairs. The house may be nationalized and transferred to the state fund, but the former owner must be continued as tenant unless the house is dangerous, in which case the local soviet must provide him with other quarters.

Also, the owner of property is under an obligation to use it for legal purposes.[35] Cases in which ownership has been lost because of illegal leasing have been discussed, but loss may occur if the property is used to commit other types of crime. A 1961 order provided for confiscation of automobiles, motorcycles, and other means of transport used to commit theft of state or public property.[36] This rule would be narrowly interpreted, however, under present policies prohibiting application by analogy of provisions of the criminal code. This is suggested by a case in which an automobile was used to attempt rape. When a trial court confiscated the automobile, the supreme court of the Armenian republic set aside the confiscation on the ground that it was permitted only in cases specified in the law, and that this was not one of them.[37]

Limitations on the quantity of property that may be privately owned are established not only for dwellings, but for livestock as well. The code establishes only a general rule authorizing such limitation,[38] and it is left to other acts to govern collective farmers, noncollectivized farmers, and city dwellers who keep barnyard stock. The scheme of limitation is related to personal consumption, as is evidenced by its following closely the various agricultural zones of the country.[39] Collective farmers in the fertile regions where the main activity

[34] See commentary to art. 141, FLEISHITS, *supra*, note 17 at 157–58.

[35] Civil Code R.S.F.S.R., 1964, art. 111.

[36] Decree of presid. of Sup. Sov. R.S.F.S.R., 7 Aug. 1961, [1961] 31 Ved. Verkh. Sov. R.S.F.S.R. item 427.

[37] Agaronian and Bagdasarian, [1959] 8 SOTS. ZAK. 94.

[38] Civil Code R.S.F.S.R., 1964, art. 112.

[39] Model Charter for Agricultural Artel, 17 Feb. 1935, [1935] 11 Sob. Zak. S.S.S.R. pt. I item 82.

is raising crops are limited to one cow, up to two head of young horned cattle, one sow with litter or two if the farm management thinks it necessary, up to ten goats and kids, up to twenty beehives, and barnyard fowl and rabbits without limitation. In regions where cattle raising shares equally with crops these limits for personal property are raised to two or three cows plus calves, with proportionate increase in other types of cattle. Where cattle raising is the exclusive activity, but the population is not nomadic, the rates are again higher; there may be four or five cows with calves, and proportionately more other animals, and for the first time there appear in the list one horse or milk-giving mare or two camels, or two donkeys or mules. For nomads, the limit on cows is increased to eight to ten plus calves, and goats and kids may number 150. Horses may number up to ten and camels five to eight.

During the postwar period when each collective farm was authorized to amend its own statute, reductions in these top limits were introduced in a burst of enthusiasm by management to conform to party demands for more intensive cooperative efforts; but with the Communist party's call in early 1965 for a return to measures which would not antagonize the peasants, the norms of the 1935 collective farm charter were ordered restored.

For noncollectivized farmers and city dwellers, the current limits were set by a decree of 13 November 1964.[40] They were: one cow or buffalo, and one calf, in addition to the calf of the current year; one sow with litter under two months of age or one boar in process of fattening; three sheep and goats over one year of age, not counting offspring; and in the absence of a cow or pig, not more than five sheep and goats over one year of age, not counting offspring. There is no limit on barnyard fowl or bees. The citizen who is able to work but is not engaged in socially useful labor is, however, under the decree subject to deprivation of the right to own any livestock, barnyard fowl, or bees on decision of the executive committee of the county or city soviet. Different norms may be established by local governments for the far north, central Asia, and regions where different types of livestock thrive.

---

[40] See commentary to art. 112, FLEISHITS, *supra*, note 17 at 130.

Resources used to purchase dwellings and vehicles were brought under scrutiny during Nikita Khrushchev's campaign against parasites. Thus by decree an owner of a house or vehicle found to have been purchased with funds obtained by means other than toil or inheritance may be deprived of his ownership on court order.[41] The supreme court soon found that so many confiscations had occurred under this decree that it issued an order calling for restraint and careful determination of the fact of parasitic practices.[42]

Parasitism does not extend, however, to those who entrust their savings to the state savings banks, which pay interest.[43] In this case, income received looks like a return on capital, but the return is established to induce citizens to deposit. In accumulating capital for economic development of the country, and in reducing the money in circulation to minimize inflation, the state policy makers early hit upon the idea of the savings bank deposit, and they added the state loan, on which interest was also paid.[44] With the passage of years the state loans have been altered to minimize their income-producing character by allocating to an account each year a sum of money representing the appropriate global income on the entire loan. From this fund lottery winnings are drawn. This may result in the transfer of a very large sum of money to an individual, which the recipient may, and usually does, use to buy a private dwelling. In a measure, this income is related to the recipient's toil, since the lottery drawing is paid as a reward for assisting the state in meeting its financial needs. The situation is not, therefore, regarded as a capitalist relationship; not as the receipt of unearned income. It is seen to be, rather, a reward for special services to the state in making personal savings available for the state's productive use.

Of the other Marxian socialist jurists, only the Czechoslovak

---

[41] Decree of 26 July 1962, [1962] 30 Ved. Verkh. Sov. R.S.F.S.R. item 464; extended to other consumer goods 28 Sept. 1963, [1963] 39 id. item 699.

[42] Order no. 14, 23 Oct. 1963. [1963] 6 Biull. Verkh. Suda S.S.S.R. 10.

[43] Statute on State Savings Banks, 20 Nov. 1948, par. 21. [1948] 7 Sob. Post. S.S.S.R. item 89.

[44] For example, see Order of 21 Feb. 1948, no. 441 on Terms for State 2% Loan of 1948, par. 9. [1948] 3 id. item 37.

draftsmen have sought to introduce Soviet practice directly into their civil code through novel phraseology. The deputy minister of justice, in explaining the code of 1964 to foreigners, emphasized this novelty, which he described as the requirement that the source of personal ownership must be honest, that is, derived mainly from work for the benefit of society.[45] He notes that this stark statement is only a development of the general principle enshrined in the earlier civil code of 1950, that ownership is not a relationship to a thing but a relationship between people—a social relationship. Hence, protection of personal property is granted only when society is to benefit. He claims that the new code's requirement is not a mere proclamation, but an operative provision, since anything obtained from an illicit source must be returned to the person who has been damaged. If both parties have sought to evade the social good, it must be surrendered to the state.

Objections were raised during the drafting process on the ground that a civil code can concern only the legal title to property and not the sources of its acquisition, but these objections were overcome because "in a socialist society it is natural that personal ownership, which is inviolable under the constitution, may originate only from honest sources."

An outside analyst has concluded that a further novelty of the Czechoslovak code, when compared with other Marxian socialist codes, is its departure from the conventional treatment of personal property owned by the state, cooperatives, or public organizations.[46] The Czechoslovaks treat personal property as a derivative of socialist property, and, therefore, as equally "sacred," but of limited protection; for an owner may rely upon the code only to the extent that the property satisfies his personal needs, for which, and only for which, it is permitted to exist. The analyst notes Article 130, whose second paragraph reads, "Things accumulated in contradiction with the interests of society in excess of the personal needs of the owner, his family, and household shall not enjoy the protection extended to personal ownership." The analyst wonders whether "an

---

[45] Kratochvil, *New Czechoslovak Civil Legislation,* 22 Bulletin of Czechoslovak Law, no. 1/2 at 1, 9 (1964).

[46] Rudzinski, *New Communist Civil Codes of Czechoslovakia and Poland: A General Appraisal,* 41 IND. L. J. 33 at 39 (1965).

owner of two or three wristwatches or a collection of rare
postage stamps is to be protected under the new Czechoslovak
code."

The Czechoslovak position suggests that in the draftsmen's
eyes there may be validity in Mao Tse-tung's argument against
permitting the individual to become "rich," if wealth is measured in terms of conspicuous consumption rather than ownership of goods which satisfy creature comforts. If goods only
cater to an individual's desire for social recognition and prestige, as displays of unusable wealth, will personal ownership still
be protected?

No suggestion that conspicuous consumption is beyond
Marxian socialist frontiers has ever come from Soviet draftsmen. What has worried Soviet legislators is that accumulation
of consumer goods beyond evident personal needs creates the
base for "speculation." It has been seen that houses may not be
accumulated beyond a family's needs because they may be
rented. Livestock may not be accumulated beyond a minimum
deemed appropriate to a family's needs because they become
the source of milk, wool, and meat for sale. In a sense accumulation of consumer goods gives reason to suppose that the goods
have passed from the consumption to the production category,
and so ownership is made illegal.

The wartime court practice on accumulations reveals the
Soviet attitude in depth. In various instances ownership in
quantities beyond needs has attracted the attention of prosecutors and courts. Examples will show the caution with which the
distasteful matter was approached, however. A man with 1,090
pairs of women's silk stockings was convicted of the crime of
speculation. While there was some testimony that he intended
to sell the goods, and also that he had no source of income in a
socially useful job, the trial court's conviction rested primarily
on the accumulation. The supreme court was not so forthright,
for it ordered a new trial to investigate further, presumably
because it wanted to find proof of sale, with which the trial
court had not been sufficiently concerned.[47] Later, a released
prisoner on his way home bought large quantities of pocket
mirrors, tobacco, cigarette papers, and some liquor, and was

[47] Eligulashvili, [1940] 9 Sots. zak. 72.

apprehended selling some of the items in a market. His defense was that he had no intention generally to sell the goods, but planned to give them to relatives and friends. On this occasion the trial court accepted the defense, but the supreme court ordered retrial because it sensed that there had been speculation within the definition of the crime.[48]

In two other cases, the accumulation alone was accepted as sufficient evidence to support conviction. In one, a citizen was found with 8 men's overcoats, 11 women's overcoats, 270 meters of cloth, and 115 spools of thread, when the family comprised only two males.[49] In another a sugar factory brigade leader had 209 meters of cloth, 8 pairs of new rubbers, 19 pieces of leather for shoe repairing, 57 spools of thread, 16 kilograms of sugar, and 7,761 rubles.[50] Witnesses testified that they had frequently seen the accused standing in lines to buy the goods and that he systematically made such purchases in quantities exceeding the needs of a family of three. In both cases the issue was not conspicuous consumption, but suspicious evidence of intent to conduct illegal trade.

By 1949 the supreme court of the USSR returned to the practice of requiring proof of sale to constitute the crime, and since that time the ownership of goods in excess of needs has not in itself been criminal.[51] Although accumulation will attract the comments of neighbors, and eventually bring on an investigation to determine whether the owner is a parasite, there is no violation per se of any Soviet law.

Chinese practice may be different. Since the Chinese have published no civil code, and since they do not make known to the outside world their court practice on property matters, there is no way for an outsider to compare them with the USSR. There is only the polemical literature to suggest that a sharp contrast in emphasis exists and that it is based on differing views concerning the desirability of stimulating production through the use of property incentives. There is also the fact that the wage system adheres more closely to early socialist concepts of egalitarianism than in the USSR. Plant directors

---

[48] Mintsberg, [1942] 1 Sud. Prak. S.S.S.R. 12.
[49] Kaveshnikov, [1940] 12 Sots. zak. 85.
[50] Levin, *id.* at 86.
[51] Kartsov, [1950] 1 *id.* 58.

are paid far less than Soviet plant directors in comparison with the bench workmen. The result is a condition approaching austerity even for the primary producers in the community.

As has been seen, the Chinese constitution of 1954 is simpler in phraseology but not different in substance from the Soviet constitution in its guarantees of personal ownership. The Chinese textbook on civil law, published in 1958 but written before the campaign against traditionalist lawyers, declared that no time limit was established or contemplated for the socialist transformation of personal property into some form of social property, and that even after full communism has been realized in China, so long as a legal framework remained, there would be no denial of protection to the ownership of consumer goods.[52] The constitution adopts the same position as that of the USSR, in that by Article 14 privately owned property may not be used to the detriment of the public interest, and it must be used solely for the purposes for which it exists—satisfaction of the material and cultural needs of citizens. It may not be used to exploit others, or to infringe upon their rights or lawful interests.

As in the USSR, the primary sources of personal property are wages, inheritance, and the part-time artisan activity of members of the people's communes. For the few remaining capitalists required to share ownership of their factories with the state there is the additional source of fixed dividends to which attention has already been given. Since none of the legal provisions in China represent the sharp departure in terms of austerity which Mao Tse-tung notes as distinguishing his system from that of the Eastern Europeans, the contrast must be created outside the civil law. One can only conclude, as has been indicated, that it arises from Communist party pressures to give up property, and to deposit savings, from the wage policies of near-egalitarianism, which reduce potential for accumulation of quantities of consumer goods, and also from production policies which currently place such goods under low

[52] Quoted by Dr. Fu-shun Lin in unpublished manuscript, citing CHUNG-HUA JEN-MIN KUNG-HO-KUO MIN-FA CHI-PEN WEN-TI 161 (1958). [Basic Problems in the Civil Law of the People's Republic of China] Eng. transl. as JPRS doc. no. 4879 (Washington, D.C.).

priorities. They simply do not exist in quantities sufficient to permit a citizen to display riches. Private dwellings alone constitute China's basic private property concern.

Examination of other members of the family of Marxian socialist legal systems indicates that the property provisions of the Soviet civil codes have become almost classic models for the draftsmen of Eastern Europe, except for Czechoslovaks. The Hungarians in their civil code of 1959,[53] and the Poles in theirs of 1964,[54] introduced no striking novelty. Each has maintained the conventional Romanist code structure, organizations, and terminology to implement Soviet-inspired ideas, albeit with limited variation.

The Hungarians, after listing what have become items of personal property in the Marxian socialist systems, namely family dwellings, furnishings, and personal effects, as well as agricultural tools used by a peasant household, state in Article 93, "The owner may dispose freely of his personal property to satisfy his personal needs." Subsequently this general statement is expanded by Article 98 to permit the owner to benefit from the right of possession and its protection; by Article 99 to use and take the fruits; by Article 112 to lease, pledge, transfer to another, or abandon; and by Article 115 to repulse any violation which prevents, restrains, or renders impossible the exercise of property rights.

In what has become standard Marxian socialist legal language, the Hungarians limit rights by an Article 5 which prohibits the abusive exercise of a right and defines such an exercise as abusive "when it leads to achievement of an aim incompatible with the social destination of the right and especially when it results in damage to the national economy, the vexation of citizens, an encroachment on their rights and legitimate interests, or the acquisition of unjustified advantages."

The Poles devote a second book of their civil code to property, following the pattern of the Soviet fundamentals of civil law. Personal property is not treated, as with the Czecho-

[53] Eng. transl. as CIVIL CODE OF THE HUNGARIAN PEOPLES' REPUBLIC (Paul Lamberg, transl., 1960). There is also a French transl.

[54] French transl. as CODE CIVIL DE LA RÉPUBLIQUE POPULAIRE DE POLOGNE (1966).

slovaks, as a derivative of social property, but rather as a category in itself.[55] As such it is given "complete" protection, not "special" protection. No quantitative maximum is established, except for housing. For this exception the Poles adopt the Soviet limitations on size, but they permit leasing within that maximum, as long as it is for good reason.

The Polish code also contains provisions on the private ownership of productive property, in contrast to the Soviet codes, but this is to provide rules applicable to a policy comparable in some measure to the Soviet law of the 1920s, when a degree of capitalist enterprise was permitted to restore a devastated economy. Limitations on the use of such property have already been sketched. For owners of property there is the rule, also already discussed, requiring that they comply with the social-economic destination and the principles of social community living, established in part by socialist ethics and not alone by statute.

In review of the law of "personal property," it becomes evident that all Marxian socialist states have found it desirable to create what they feel to be a novel and distinct category of property, whether it is derived from social property or not. It is a category limited in productivity and in quantity, but with an important part to play in the evolution of a Marxian socialist society. There is no expectation of the speedy substitution of communally owned consumer goods for private ownership, for this program faded from doctrine when Stalin abandoned his agricultural "communes" to put the entire weight of his Communist party behind the collective farm structure in 1929.

Communalization of property has never even been initiated in the urban communities of the USSR, and none of the people's democracies founded on the Soviet model have sought to introduce communalization experiments like those of the early years in Soviet Russian agriculture. Only the Chinese Communists with their Great Leap Forward in 1958 showed signs of moving in the direction of communal ownership of consumer goods, when they introduced the "communes"; but their experiment proved abortive and was dropped. Communal

[55] See Rudzinski, *supra*, note 46, for comparison of Czechoslovak and Polish treatment of property.

ownership of property was never introduced into the Chinese constitution or into the law. The guarantee and regulation of private ownership of consumer goods remained unchanged.

"Personal property" as a concept widely adopted by Marxian socialists evidently is justified because of its usefulness as an instrument stimulating production for the common good. Whether its place in the legal system will be recognized eternally is unclear. Presumably, in a condition of complete communism, when law has fully "withered away" as an instrument of compulsion, "personal property" will cease to exist as a concept protected by law. Presumably, also, consumer goods will, in a sense, be communally "owned." But it does not follow that the dress of the citizen will be returned to a communal wardrobe at the end of each day, or that all will live in communal barracks with no provision for family life and no sense of "mine and thine." Those in need are promised the distribution of consumer goods in response to that need, but once obtained, these goods can be expected to remain in the possession of the recipient for his individual and exclusive use. Fellow members of the community would be expected to respect that individual possession in the interests of good order. The obligation to respect will have been moved from the sphere of enforcement through law to the sphere of acceptance without the need of enforcement because it has become an element of communist morals. No Marxist preaches that communism brings a state of chaos in human relationships.

The conditions to follow the withering away of law remained of concern to Soviet jurists even as late as 1966, as is indicated by an editorial in their official journal. It reads: "It is not by chance that law will wither away on achievement of full communism, preparing in merited exchange for itself a more developed form of social regulation, a system of norms of communist communal living. Morality in communist society will not wither away; on the contrary it will grow in collossal fashion as a regulator of men's conduct." [56]

Although philosophers enjoy meditating on the distant future, and even the practical men who edit journals for Soviet judges and prosecutors find it appropriate to write about the

[56] *Law and Morals in Socialist Society*, [1966] 7 Sov. iust. 1 at 3.

withering process, it is the tasks of today that require primary attention, High among them is the task of meeting current expectations that the Marxian socialist system of social organization will soon usher in a more abundant society. The concept of "personal property" has a critical role to play in stimulating production and in providing a framework of order in the distribution and protection of possession. As such the concept has a practical reason to exist, and lawyers must concern themselves with its protection in law and practice.

To speak of such practical necessity to stimulate production is not to suggest that Marxist theory has been denied influence in the formulation of contemporary law on the ownership and use of personal property because the doctrine is impractical in treating this subject. On the contrary, the *Communist Manifesto*'s stand for continued ownership of consumer goods has practical value, and it provides convenient legitimation for the personal-property law of all Marxian socialist states. Marx probably intended his doctrine to work that way.

Further, the Marxist rule that "only labor can create value" has influenced the formulation of restraints on personal ownership. In varying degrees, depending upon the rate of progress of each Marxist state toward the goal of communism, restraints prohibit use of personal ownership to gain income classified as "unearned."

Finally, the Marxist rule that "property has a social function" is applied to prevent usage that is or might be harmful to the social edifice being erected by Communists.

Although all of this may be said with justice to Marxian socialist claims that the various Communist parties have been loyal to Marxism in formulating their policies on personal property, there are two elements of their policy that pierce holes in the fabric. One is the policy of paying interest on savings deposits and on state bonds, although the latter is somewhat softened by distributing the interest as lottery winnings rather than on the cutting of coupons. The other is inheritance. The first has been discussed in this chapter, emphasis having been given to its justification as a means of accumulating capital for state investment, without which there never could be the abundance required for communism, and as a means of controlling inflation. The second is the subject of the following chapter, for it is of such complexity as to require separate treatment.

10

Inheritance as an

Anachronistic Stimulant

Socialists GENERALLY HAVE LOOKED ASKANCE AT INHERITANCE as a means of perpetuating fortunes from generation to generation. Some have demanded its abolition as a source of wealth unrelated to a recipient's toil. The Marxian socialists have wavered while seeking its place within their doctrinal system.

The Russian Communists abolished inheritance soon after coming to power in 1917, but they now emphasize that they were then attacking only an element of the tsarist system, a means of perpetuating class domination resting upon fortunes invested in productive resources. They claim they had no desire to disinherit workers and peasants, and, to be sure, the first 1918 decree drew distinctions.[1] Estates not exceeding 10,000 rubles in value and comprising a dwelling, furnishings, and peasants' or workers' tools were to pass directly to surviving family members for administration and use. Only the excess was confiscated, but even then heirs retained an interest. Those defined as disabled

---

[1] 27 Apr. 1918, [1918] 34 Sob. Uzak. R.S.F.S.R. pt.I item 456.

relatives in a descending or ascending line, plus spouse and full and half brothers and sisters, had a claim thereafter on the local soviet for funds derived from administration of the property. In a sense the estates of the relatively wealthy became a social insurance fund administered for the indigent.

Interpretations of the law eroded its prohibitions. In 1919 working families having a communal economy were exempted from confiscation of the excess over 10,000 rubles in an estate.[2] This, in effect, restored unlimited inheritance to families of the rich peasants, although the shock was cushioned by explanations that peasant estates rarely exceeded the maximum. A later exception marked a more radical change, for it went beyond the working class. In the civil code adopted to implement the New Economic Policy, heirs, whether needy or not and regardless of their occupation, were permitted to inherit directly the property of a deceased person up to the value of 10,000 gold rubles.[3] The excess escheated to the state, but if it could not be segregated without economic disruption, it was to be administered jointly by the state agencies and the heirs, or the heirs might purchase the escheated portion from the state. The circle of heirs was redefined to exclude brothers and sisters, but to include any persons dependent upon the deceased for a year immediately prior to his death.

The rule of the new civil code was in part a concession forced by the need for administrative convenience, as the local soviets were in no way prepared to administer estates for the benefit of indigent heirs. It was easier to let the heirs take care of themselves, and it could be presumed that in the Russian extended family there would always be indigent persons whom the younger family members would be obliged by peasant custom to support during their old age or period of disability. In a sense the Russian family was an instrument of social security, as were the families of the other peoples inhabiting what had been the empire.

There was, however, another reason for removing restraint, and it lay in the philosophy supporting the introduction of the New Economic Policy. It was this: if the accumulation of property is to be an inducement to produce, as it was to be

---

[2] Ministry of Justice Instruction 21 May 1919, [1919] 20 *id.* item 242.
[3] Civil Code R.S.F.S.R., 1922, art. 416, [1922] 71 *id.* item 904.

under the new policy, the limitations upon the use of property accumulated through production should be at a minimum. Banning transmission of accumulated wealth to heirs would have reduced the alternatives open to the property owner for disposing of his property in a way that pleased him and would induce him to earn more. In short, inheritance provided support for the indigent bereaved, whom the impoverished state was in no position to care for, and also stimulated production by permitting workers to toil for their heirs as well as for their own consumption.

Having removed the top bars of the barrier against inheritance in the code of 1922, the policy makers found it necessary to lower it still further in 1926 because the administrators were unable to enforce the restrictions.[4] The minister of justice reported that property owners were disposing of property before death so there would be no excess to escheat. Since that date, no limitations in quantity have been introduced in any of the Marxian socialist states to prevent the heirs from receiving what the deceased has desired to leave to them. Such limitations as exist have concerned the choice of persons and organizations to which the decedent might pass his property and the right of the recipient to keep the property in the form in which it was transmitted.

All fourteen Marxian socialist states have adopted the same attitude toward inheritance. In none is recognition today considered as being a "creative extension," much less a violation, of Marxist principles. Although in some it is looked upon as a necessarily temporary solution to current problems of care of children and indigent adults, in others its long-term usefulness is not publicly questioned. To a Romanian academician the pertinent Marxist text supporting present policies is the founder's report to the second session of the First International in Bâle in 1869, in which Marx emphasized that it is not the right of inheritance which creates the possibility of abuse but rather the property right that is transmitted.[5] Restriction must be placed on what may be owned rather than what may be trans-

---

[4] Amend. to art. 418. Law of 15 Feb. 1926, [1926] 10 *id.* item 73.

[5] T. Ionasco & Bradeanu, *Le transfert de droit de propriété et de tout autre droit par l'effet de la transmission du tout ou d'une fraction du patrimoine*, Le droit de propriété dans les pays de l'Est (R. Dekkers ed. 1964) 51 at 65.

mitted. A Yugoslav law professor is more precise in quoting the pertinent passage of the debate with Bakunin in 1869: "As with other civil rights, the laws on successions appear to be not the cause but the consequence, the juridical product of the economic organization of society." [6]

The Romanian argues that since only consumer goods may be personal property and the subject of hereditary transmission, there is no danger in inheritance, since the items transmitted cannot become a means of exploitation.[7] Indeed, the right of inheritance, in his view, contributes to a continual increasing of the well-being of toilers and to strengthening personal property. This is so because it permits those who accumulate through toil to transmit what they have saved through economies to heirs, thus increasing their assets. Here is a contribution to achievement of abundance, the aim of Marxian socialism. Transmission also aids in meeting another aim, the strengthening of the family, because members of the family have the primary position as heirs.

Finally, to the Romanian, a third aim of socialist society is achieved by the inheritance law of the socialist states, and that is the strengthening of what he calls "social" property, since "there is a harmonious concordance between personal and collective interests." Without clarification of his meaning, it is impossible to interpret this with certainty, but he seems to imply that whatever fosters the desire to accumulate personal property also benefits the production of social property; for without such stimulation production would lag behind potential. In short, the possibilities offered by personal consumption of what is earned from toil are limited. The full potential of property stimulus under a differentiated wage system is achieved only when the wage earner can pass to his heirs what he does not need himself.

Although stimulation of production is avowedly a basic purpose, the importance of inheritance law as an instrument for molding a socialist family has also been clarified. The Yugoslav

[6] Blagojević, Les successions en droit socialiste. Lectures at Faculté internationale pour L'enseignment du droit comparé. Coimbra, 1966 (mimeographed) 2. An analysis of socialist inheritance laws by Western scholars is provided in 5 LAW IN EASTERN EUROPE (1961).

[7] Ionasco & Bradeanu, *supra*, note 5 at 66–67.

scholar provides detail in disclosing the nature of this relation-ship.[8] He notes that not only does inheritance law depend upon attitudes taken toward the family, the status of children born out of wedlock, the relationship of man and wife in society generally and in the family, and the content of connections between spouses, but "the institution of succession can also influence the development and the content of these and do so effectively." But the family is not alone concerned. He finds also that inheritance is interrelated with attitudes assumed by society on the nature of "liberty, equality, and conventionality." In short, inheritance law must take account of the changes which have occurred or which are about to occur in the different sectors of the social life of a country. It must follow these changes and translate them into concrete regulation of specific cases involving these values in the inheritance process, and at the same time it must play the role of an institution influencing the evolution of society in all its aspects. Thus, inheritance law is made responsible for safeguarding and making effective the various institutions established by society. In brief, the Yugo-slav is claiming for inheritance law a mission of critical, not secondary, importance, even though its major features are not its own but are defined by the laws of property generally and of the conjugal family, to which inheritance itself is only an appendage.

Inheritance law under Marxian socialism is currently found to be handicapped by long-standing traditions and customs, often not at all progressive. To the Yugoslav these influences are often underestimated, partly because they are often imper-ceptible and are regarded as "legal folklore" without serious negative effect. But he sees negative influences because policy makers are lulled into letting these folkloric tendencies con-tinue when efforts should be made to reduce their importance continually until they no longer have social influence. Some of these elements demonstrate, in his view, the survival of Ro-man-law influences which remain as a "burden" on the Marxian socialist legal system. Because of these relics of the past he finds it impossible to speak of a specific "socialization" of the law of inheritance. Its socialization is in its following the socialist

---

[8] Blagojević, *supra*, note 6 at 3.

development of property and family law rather than in any restructuring of its own provisions. Thus, the foreigner trying to find socialization in the inheritance law of the Marxian socialist states is warned by an expert from within the system that he will find little that is novel in its specific provisions. Socialist inheritance law's claim to uniqueness is in what it does and not in what it is.[9]

With such a warning, the foreign analyst seeking to find a common core to the Marxian socialist legal systems and to determine the extent to which a unique family of legal systems is emerging to take its place alongside the Romanist, the Islamic, and the Anglo-American common law systems might be advised to drop the subject of inheritance as providing no material useful to his quest. Still, inheritance plays an important part in the life of the conjugal family in the Marxian socialist states, and its implementation by officials of various legal institutions consumes a considerable part of their time— most especially the time of the state notaries, on whom the primary burden of administration falls, but also of the courts and of the advocates when disputes occur. Because of this, inheritance deserves more than to be dropped after explanation of its derivative character. The technical details contribute to an appreciation of the structure of Marxian socialist law, and of the way all branches of law are mobilized to serve a doctrinal purpose.

Of primary noteworthiness is the rule already stated that certain types of property when inherited must be transformed within a short period into other forms, so as to eliminate the possibility of their use for exploitation. This is notable in the law of dwellings. The USSR denies to a family unit the right to own more than one dwelling at a time, except for summer cottages.[10] Consequently, as has been indicated in discussing the law of personal property, the Soviet family which inherits a

[9] An Australian specialist recognizes the claim, saying, "There is now a Soviet law of inheritance, just as there is a French and an English law; no one reading the provisions of Soviet codes would be tempted to say that there is a socialist law as opposed to a capitalist one." Tay, *The Law of Inheritance in the New Russian Civil Code of 1964*, 17 INT'L & COMP. L. Q. pt. 2 at 472 (1968).

[10] See ch. 9, n. 12.

second dwelling must choose which house it wishes to retain and sell the other within a year on pain of forced sale. The details have already been discussed and require no repetition, but the principle introduces an element of novelty into inheritance law and thus bears repeating. The Czechoslovak civil code provides the same limitation,[11] although it permits the size of the single house to be double that allowed a family in the USSR.[12]

The Polish and Yugoslav Communists have also provided that a peasant family which inherits land exceeding the maximum permitted a household may not retain the excess.[13] This rule is extended to implement yet another policy of limiting distribution of land to tillers, for no distribution of land by inheritance will be permitted if the resulting plots would fall below the minimum deemed necessary for efficiency. Polish inheritance law must, therefore, implement both a land policy designed to improve efficiency and a general policy limiting the hiring of labor to an owner's advantage.

From these examples, it is evident that there is no limit on the money value of property that heirs may inherit in the USSR, Poland, Yugoslavia, and the other Marxist states. What is prohibited is possession not of quantity generally, but of certain types of property in amounts that would make possible unearned income from rentals or from hired laborers. The limitations can usually be overcome by gift or sale, and proceeds may be retained by the heir. In the USSR no taxation cuts into these proceeds, for there is no sales tax, nor is the filing fee charged by the state notaries sufficient to play any serious part in the redistribution of wealth after the decease of a property

[11] Czechoslovak Civil Code, 1964, art. 129. Eng. transl. in 22 BULLE-TIN OF CZECHOSLOVAK LAW no. 1/2 at 41 (1964).

[12] *Id.* art. 128.

[13] The Yugoslav author makes no distinction between Marxian socialist states, assuming that all permit an heir to sell, but the Polish Civil Code of 1964 provides otherwise. By art. 1068 land acquired by inheritance in excess of the maximum permitted to an owner "may be taken by the state without payment of value." The Yugoslav Law of Inheritance, 25 Apr. 1955, art. 153 provides for compensation. Cf. CODE CIVIL DE LA RÉPUBLIQUE POPULAIRE DE POLOGNE (1966) and 10 COLLECTION OF YUGOSLAV LAWS (THE LAW OF INHERITANCE) (Institute of Comparative Law, Belgrade, 1964).

owner. In Poland there is a tax on major purchases and donations.

Tradition heavily influences the techniques of inheritance. All Marxist states permit transmission by intestacy and by will, as does the rest of the world. Communists see no need to dictate to a wage earner how his property must pass, and indeed a major purpose of stimulating his production would be vitiated if he could not choose his heir and were forced to accept an arbitrarily designed system of intestate distribution. Still, appreciation of this was slow to develop in the USSR. Until 1961 testators were limited in free choice, for they could select only among the heirs who would have received the estate by intestacy had no will been executed.[14] This rule was once applied to strike down a legacy to a church, since it was not an institution authorized to inherit.[15] Even since extension in 1961 in the USSR of complete freedom in bequeathing property, testators are held to traditional Romanist rules of "forced heirship"— they cannot completely disinherit certain persons who could have inherited by intestacy in the absence of a will.[16] The rationale for the Romanist rule fits the communist book nicely, for it conforms to the policy expressed in the earliest Soviet decree—that inheritance must serve a purpose which the state was not yet equipped to serve, namely to provide an element of social security to the indigent. Thus minor children of the decedent and those among his heirs unable to work, as well as those dependent upon him for support, are given by the Russian republic's code the right to no less than two-thirds of the share they would have received had there been no will.

Other Marxian socialist states have established the same rules, although Yugoslavia permits a testator to exclude totally any heir who "committed a crime against the peoples' authorities or against the independence of the country or its defense

[14] Civil Code R.S.F.S.R., 1922, art. 422. The circle was enlarged in 1945 to add non-able-bodied parents unable to qualify as dependents.

[15] Hamlet Soviet v. Kichatova, case no. 1068. [1949] 1 Sud. Prak. S.S.S.R. 5. Yugoslav law excludes from inheritance by law or by will fugitives from justice or military service. See LAW OF INHERITANCE, *supra*, note 13 art. 131 (5).

[16] Civil Code R.S.F.S.R., 1964, art. 535. Eng. transl. as CIVIL CODE OF THE RUSSIAN SOVIET FEDERATED SOCIALIST REPUBLIC: AN ENGLISH TRANSLATION (W. GRAY & R. STULTS transl. 1965).

and socialist construction." [17] In all Marxist states a testator
may execute a will to modify the order of succession established
by statute, and he may transmit property by will to persons or
organizations who would not inherit by intestacy. Only in
Poland is there a limitation on his choice. Agricultural land
may be willed only to those who will work it.[18] This limitation
is to make certain that it does not become an item of
commerce.

Although the basic rule permitting transmission by testament is found in all Marxist states, the restraints on total
freedom of testamentary disposition vary. Whereas the Soviet
codes protect not only descendants, the spouse, and the testator's mother and father, but also dependents generally, the
others include no such dependent group outside the blood and
conjugal relationship. The Hungarian and Polish codes limit
those with rights of forced heirship to the surviving spouse,
descendants, and mother and father of the deceased. The
Czechoslovak code is even more limited, for the spouse is
excluded and only descendants have such a right. The Yugoslav
rule is broader but does not accept the Soviet concept of
dependents' rights. It adds to the group included by the Poles
and Hungarians all other direct ascendants and the brothers
and sisters of the deceased.[19]

Not all of those within the groups granted the right of
forced heirship may be able to exercise it, for quite different
conditions of acquisition are established by the various codes.
For the Hungarians, the Czechoslovaks, and the Poles, there is
no test other than the objective one of falling within the group
given the right. In the USSR certain members of the group
must establish their minority or incapacity to work, or inade-
quacy of resources necessary to subsist. For the Yugoslavs the
criterion is mixed. The objective test of falling within the
category is applied to descendants, spouse, and father and
mother of the testator, but other direct ascendants must meet a
subjective means test.

Wide variation exists in the size of the share that must be

[17] Law of Inheritance, art. 47 (3).
[18] Civil Code, art. 1065.
[19] Hungarian Civil Code, art. 611; Polish Civil Code, art. 991; Czechoslovak Civil Code, art. 479; Yugoslav Law of Inheritance, art. 30.

reserved for the heir who claims under the right of forced heirship. The Czechoslovak code grants to minor descendants the whole amount they would have received by intestacy and to the others two-thirds. The Soviet rule, as has been indicated, is two-thirds of the intestate share to a member of any protected category, and the Hungarians reserve one-half. The Yugoslavs, like the Czechoslovaks, indicate a different fraction for each category of protected heirs: one-half for the descendants, adopted children and their descendants, and the spouse, and one-third for the others. The Poles grant one-half to the protected categories, but this is raised to two-thirds if there is a permanent incapacity for work, or if the descendants are minors.

Concern for dependents is also manifested in a rule adopted by several of the Marxist states reserving the household utensils to members of the family of the decedent living with him at the time of his death. In the language of the Russian republic's code, "ordinary household furnishings and articles pass to the statutory heirs who have lived with the decedent for not less than one year prior to his death, without regard to their class or statutory shares." [20] Other Soviet republics are free under federal legislation to eliminate the one-year period of cohabitation. Since such furnishings are not counted within the estate for purposes of division between the various categories of heirs, an heir having the right to a statutory share by way of intestacy receives that share or fraction of share in other property of the decedent without regard to what he or she may already have received as household furnishings.

The Polish code gives to the spouse only the household right and the right to those household utensils which the spouses used in common or an item which the surviving spouse habitually used even though it was the individual property of the deceased. This right attaches to the spouse over and above his or her normal share in the succession, and is defensible against all heirs except the descendants of the deceased who also lived with him in the same common household at the time of his death.[21]

Since Marxist states also follow the Romanist principle of

[20] Art. 533.
[21] Art. 939.

passing title to inherited property directly to heirs, rather than the Anglo-American common-law rule of passing it first to a court-appointed administrator or executor named in a will and charged with payment of debts before distribution, the codes all provide that heirs must pay debts to the extent that they receive property by inheritance. While the Russian republic's code states this rule without specifying types of debts [22] (leaving to the Statute on the State Notary a listing in detail), the Czechoslovak code states that the payment of funeral costs is the direct obligation of the heir.[23] If there are several heirs, the funeral costs are to be shared in proportion to the value of the inheritance received by each. The Hungarians add to this the costs of insurance and expenses of administration incurred by the one who takes initial possession of the estate awaiting distribution.[24] Because of these onerous duties, all codes provide that an heir may reject the inheritance, but he is deemed to have accepted it if he actually takes possession of the property.

To facilitate collection of debts by creditors under such a system of direct transmission to heirs, the Russian republic's code permits a creditor to present his claim not only to the heirs who have accepted, but to the executor under a will, if the property is still in his hands, or to the notarial office which has jurisdiction over the inheritance.[25] The Czechoslovak code requires that creditors register their claims with the state notary on notice, if the estate is insolvent,[26] and thereafter no creditor who has not registered may recover from the estate, or from the heirs individually if no property remains after distribution to registered claimants.

The state notary's duties in payment of debts are illustrated by a case reported from the USSR. A mortician presented his claim to the notary for funeral expenses of a woman who died in Briansk on 18 November 1965. The claim was properly presented under the Statute on the State Notary, which provides that the notary shall pay from the estate four classes of

[22] Art. 553. The pertinent provisions of the Notary's Statute, art. 58, are pub. in [1966] 7 Sov. IUST. 34.

[23] Art. 470.

[24] Art. 677.

[25] Art. 554.

[26] Art. 471.

expenses: (1) those incurred in care of the deceased during his illness and for his funeral; (2) those incurred in immediate support, prior to final distribution, of citizens dependent upon the decedent; (3) those represented by claims for wages and claims equivalent to them; and (4) those incurred in summoning heirs, and in conserving and administering the property prior to distribution.

A dispute arose after the state notary had issued to the claimant an authorization to collect his charges from a life insurance policy in the amount of 300 rubles, taken out in June 1959 with the State Insurance Company for a ten-year term. The manager of the Briansk office of the State Insurance Company refused to honor the claim, saying that the benefits could be paid only to the heirs at law. The matter was taken to the main office in Moscow, where a ruling was made by the Department of State Insurance of the Ministry of Finance of the USSR in a letter of 4 January 1966 that the Briansk office should pay the claim on the order of the state notary in accordance with the requirements of the civil code, Article 549, and the Statute on the State Notary if the benefits under the policy were due to the heirs at law, since they were responsible for the debts of the deceased.[27]

To assure order in the distribution of that part of an estate other than the household furnishings, the Soviet state notary is obligated to issue at the request of an heir a certificate of heirship, which becomes proof of title.[28] It is, however, no more than evidence; if an heir fails to obtain the certificate, he is not forever excluded from claiming his rights on submission of other proof. The Hungarian code leaves no doubt of this right.[29] Generally the state notary is well fitted to perform his duties of establishing heirship, for he has drafted the will and supervised the execution before witnesses in a "signing party" conducted exactly as it is in all Romanist states. In consequence, he knows the parties who have been close to the decedent. It is rare that a distant relative long absent from the village returns to file a claim or that a dispute arises over the right of an individual to

[27] [1966] 7 Sov. IUST. 34 (back page).
[28] Art. 557.
[29] Art. 673. The Czechoslovak Civil Code, art. 483 makes the Notary's ruling in a dispute final.

claim as a dependent; but if such a dispute occurs, the courts have ultimate jurisdiction if the claimant is displeased with the notary's ruling. As has been indicated, the Soviet notary is not a judicial officer but a registrar. He must verify what he can establish from the face of the documents, but he is not obliged to determine the truth in the event of a dispute.

An example will indicate the Soviet procedure in resolving such a dispute.

An aged woman who was the last of her collective farm household died in 1959 leaving a house and its furnishings.[30] Her stepdaughter claimed as heir, and being denied a certificate of heirship by a notary, she brought suit in court, claiming that she had been the aged woman's dependent for thirteen years between 1918 and 1931, and that since that date she had assisted the decedent regularly in the conduct of household affairs. Although the plaintiff won at the trial and on appeal, the supreme court of the Russian republic on a review of the record concluded that the plaintiff was denied inheritance on two grounds: (1) as a stepdaughter she could not inherit, since this relationship was not within the circle of heirs by intestacy, and (2) she could not claim as a dependent because she had not proved, as the code required, that she had been a dependent of the decedent for at least one year immediately prior to death. The facts indicated that the plaintiff had property and was not in need; in fact she operated an independent household in another settlement, and only rarely visited the old woman to help in picking fruit and in repairing the house. This had no probative value as proof of dependency.

All Marxian socialist codes exclude from the circle of heirs those who have committed crime against the decedent or those close to him. For the Hungarians the exclusion is of one who is "unworthy" to succeed, defined as one who commits an attempt on the life of the decedent or potential heir or who prevents or attempts to prevent the testator's free expression of his desires.[31] For the Czechoslovaks the offender must have committed "a deliberate crime against the decedent, his spouse, children, or parents, or have acted reprehensibly against the

---

[30] Estate of Rogozhina, [1960] 13 Sov. IUST. 27.
[31] Arts. 600 and 602.

manifestation of the decedent's last will." [32] For the Russians the exclusionary language is "if they have promoted their inheritance through unlawful acts directed against the decedent or any of his heirs, or against the carrying out of his will as expressed in testamentary form, provided that such circumstances are confirmed through a judicial proceeding." [33]

This exclusionary provision inserted in the 1964 Russian republic's code marked no sudden change in Soviet law, for it had been established by judicial practice in 1926 to fill a gap in the code and had been reaffirmed in 1960 in a suit brought by two daughters against a sister to regain a family home bequeathed to her by their mother. [34] The claimants argued that the mother had been without legal right to the house at the time of her death because she had murdered their father, from whom the house had passed to their mother by inheritance.

The trial court had rejected the claim on the ground that the issue of murder had remained unmentioned for eighteen years after the father's death, during which time the mother had used the house. Under court practice, the court said, the daughters had forfeited their right to claim inheritance in application of a rule of laches. The supreme court's examination of the record produced evidence of a conviction for murder, and the decision was reversed in application of the 1926 decision against inheritance by a murderess. The court refused to accept the doctrine of laches in exclusion of such a claim.

The Polish draftsmen, with their evident penchant for detail, go further than the others in specifying the types of criminal activity which disqualify an heir. [35] Their categories of unworthiness include committing a deliberate crime against the decedent, eliciting by fraud or threat the drafting or revocation of a will, or similarly preventing the drafting of a will. They even include deliberate concealment of a will or its destruction, counterfeiting, or alteration, whether by themselves or by another.

Because Romanist legal systems generally know no such concept as the Anglo-American "trust," the Marxist-oriented

[32] Art. 469.
[33] Art. 531.
[34] Ermolaeva and Osokina v. Kozlova, [1960] 8 Sov. IUST. 27.
[35] Art. 928.

codes include no provision for such instruments of a testator's policy; but there have been minor inroads in some of the codes upon the policy of complete exclusion of the possibility of imposing duties upon heirs. The Czechoslovak code is not one of these, for it is in the strict tradition. It provides that "no conditions attached to the testament shall have legal effect." [36] Until the most recent enactments after Stalin's death, the Soviet codes took the same position, but the Russian republic's code of 1964 provides that "A testator may charge an heir under his will with the performance of any sort of obligation (testamentary duty) for the benefit of one or more persons (beneficiaries of a testamentary duty), who thereby acquire the right to demand its performance." [37] Then the article becomes specific in permitting a testator to charge a legatee to whom his dwelling passes with the duty of providing another person with the use of the house or a certain part thereof for life; and this charge continues against the house upon subsequent transfers.

The Russian republic's new code thus establishes an indirect means of creating the equivalent of a life estate, even though the concept of a life estate had been nullified by a 1960 decision declaring it illegal.[38] In the 1960 case the testator had attempted in his will to create a life estate in a part of a dwelling by providing that the dwelling would pass to a surviving spouse, but on her death must go to a son. In ruling that the restraint on the surviving spouse's ownership was illegal, the supreme court of the USSR had written, "the subordination of one heir to another, who survives the decedent and accepts the inheritance, is not permitted, because this would constitute a limitation on the right of ownership and a partial deprivation of the heir's right to deal with the inherited property; to bequeath it in his own discretion in accordance with law." The 1964 code provision does not categorize as an heir the beneficiary of a charge. His right is that of a creditor of the heir to whom the property has been willed subject to the charge, and suit must be brought against the heir in that capacity.[39]

The Hungarian attitude is similar, permitting a testator to

[36] Art. 478.
[37] Art. 538.
[38] Estate of Savenko, [1960] 2 SOTS. ZAK. 85.
[39] Tay, *supra*, note 9 at 22.

charge a legatee with duties and depriving him of his inheritance upon failure to perform the charge.[40] The Poles introduce
a more complicated arrangement creating a status comparable
to a life estate. Under a contract made by a mother and father
of a peasant household with a son, title passes immediately to
the son when he assumes an obligation to his retired parents,
including lodging (*dozywocie*) during their lifetimes.

Blood relatives and a surviving spouse are the heirs at law in
all Marxist states, but there is considerable variation in defining
blood relatives and in determining the priority of a surviving
spouse. Adopted children are universally included within the
blood group, but there is variation in the treatment of children
born out of wedlock. Marxists have prided themselves that a
natural-born child ranks with legitimate children within a father's circle of heirs. Only the USSR provides an exception,
because of its law of 1944 [41] repealing the previous procedure for
establishing paternity and the right to maintenance and inheritance.[42] This exceptional exclusion has long been an embarrassment not only to many Soviet jurists but to many Communists
abroad, and it was repealed for all except the offspring of casual
unions by a new set of federal family law fundamentals in 1968.
They will be treated in the chapter on domestic relations and
require no further comment at this point.

As to other blood relatives, the dispute has been over ascendants, for all favor descendants, providing that grandchildren and great-grandchildren shall receive the share that would
have passed to a deceased parent had he been a qualifying heir.
The problem of ascendants is raised with relation to the surviving spouse, and in some cases the spouse's rights are related to
descendants as well.

Thus, Hungary permits a surviving spouse to inherit only if
there are no descendants,[43] whereas the Soviet codes [44] and the
Czechoslovak code [45] include the surviving spouse with the

[40] Arts. 641, 642.
[41] 8 July 1944, sec. 20. [1944] 37 Ved. Verkh. Sov. S.S.S.R.
[42] Family Code R.S.F.S.R., 1918, art. 140, [1918] 76–77 Sob. Usak.
R.S.F.S.R. pt. I item 818. Family Code R.S.F.S.R., 1927, art. 29. [1926]
82 *id.* item 612.
[43] Art. 607, par. 4.
[44] Art. 538.
[45] Art. 475.

descendants in the first category of heirs at law. The Soviet codes favor the parents of the deceased more than do the other states because they give these persons the right to share equally with the surviving spouse and the descendants in the first category of heirs. The Hungarians permit the deceased's parents to take the estate only if there are no descendants or surviving spouse,[46] and the Czechoslovak code permits the parents to share with the surviving spouse and with persons who had lived with the decedent in a common household for at least a year prior to his death only if there are no descendants who qualify.[47]

Grandparents of the deceased have more difficulty: the Czechoslovak code excludes any ascending relatives above the parents.[48] The Poles give only the parents of the decedent an absolute right, but grandparents may demand of a testamentary heir that he support them up to the value of one-quarter of his inheritance if they are in straitened circumstances and cannot obtain resources necessary to subsistence from persons legally bound to support them.[49] This may help them in most cases if a collateral relative or stranger qualifies as heir. The Russian republic gives the grandparents on either side a right to inherit if there are no heirs in the first category, but they must share with surviving brothers and sisters.[50] The Hungarians place the grandparents in the line of succession, but even more remotely than the Russians, for they may take a share only in the absence of descendants, surviving spouse, parents, or descendants of parents.[51]

Collaterals are likewise treated quite differently in the various codes. The Soviet codes recognized no right of brothers and sisters to be included among the heirs until the Second World War, when entire families were destroyed and property would have remained untended and have become a public charge had the distant brothers and sisters not been permitted to inherit. Thus, by decree of 1945 the circle of intestate heirs was expanded to include brothers and sisters if there were no

---

[46] Art. 608.
[47] Art. 474.
[48] *Ibid.*
[49] Arts. 932, 935.
[50] Art. 532.
[51] Art. 609.

descendants, no surviving spouse, and no parents.[52] With the post-Stalin code revisions, this rule was introduced into the code so that in the absence of closer heirs, collaterals might share with the paternal and maternal grandfathers and grandmothers.[53] Their descendants have no right, however, to inherit. The Czechoslovak code takes the same position.[54]

The Polish code permits the brothers and sisters and their descendants to share with a surviving spouse and parents in the absence of descendants.[55] The Yugoslavs follow the lines of the Austrian civil code of 1871 and open the collateral group wider than any others. Their law on succession permits all descendants of the father and mother of the deceased, as well as the grandparents and great-grandparents and their descendants to inherit.[56]

The Hungarians in following the Austrian imperial code are likewise generous, declaring that in the absence of descendants and surviving spouse, and of father and mother of the deceased, or of either one of the latter, his or her descendants may succeed. If none of these qualify, the grandparents of the deceased succeed, and in their absence, their descendants.[57] If the grandparents of one line are incapable of inheriting, and have no descendants who may stand in their places, the entire estate passes to the grandparents of the other line or their descendants.

The conclusion is compelling that in the Marxian socialist states there is strong objection to escheat of an estate to the state, for a long list of heirs is now provided to which the estate passes in turn until there is no one left. It is a far different situation from that in 1917, when the first Marxian socialist state escheated an estate exceeding the bare minimum of the house and utensils used by the deceased and close members of his family.

Another change has occurred as the years have passed. The

[52] 14 Mar. 1945, 3 Sbornik zak. SSSR, 1945–46 at 163 (1947). [Collection of Laws of the U.S.S.R.].

[53] Art. 532.

[54] Art. 475.

[55] Art. 934.

[56] Arts. 13, 18, 19.

[57] Arts. 608, 609.

first Russian republic code provided for per capita distribution of an estate among the circle of qualifying heirs, so that grandchildren of the deceased shared equally with their uncles and aunts in distribution of the estate if their own father or mother had died before their grandparent, the decedent. In this way the maintenance characteristic of inheritance was emphasized, for these fatherless grandchildren had as much need, if not more, for the inheritance than their adult uncles and aunts. Not until the 1945 amendment broadening the circle of heirs to include grandparents and brothers and sisters of the deceased was there a revision in the per capita rule. Then, as if to emphasize in yet another way that the purpose of inheritance was no longer primarily maintenance, the system of distribution was changed to the more familiar *per stirpes* method, or descent by representation, so that all members of the same generation, living or dead, would share equally either for themselves or for their children if they had died before the owner of the estate being distributed. By 1945 intestate inheritance had become more a means of distributing the estate as the legislator thought the decedent would have provided had he left a will than a means of imposing the legislator's notions of how to provide appropriate maintenance for those in need among possible heirs.

All other Marxian socialist states apply the *per stirpes* method of representation in the event that an otherwise qualified heir dies before the estate owner, but probably do not follow the model created in the USSR in 1945. In the European cases, and in the Far Eastern Marxist states which received Romanist legal systems from Europe, the reason for such a rule is probably historical.[58] These states had not shared in the experimental thinking about socialized inheritance which immediately followed the Russian revolution. Inheritance had become an established feature of Soviet law by the time they emerged, and when each of the Eastern European legislatures sat down under communist direction to draft the law, most of them chose to continue with their old codes for a time and to provide only for flexible application in the event of distortion of

[58] For the Chinese heritage, see Van der Valk, *China*, 5 LAW IN EASTERN EUROPE 297 (1961).

socialist goals by the parties concerned. Inheritance remained as it had been before the Marxist epoch, except for the few restraints necessary to prohibit the accumulation of property in amounts which might have provided unearned income, and, especially in China, to permit women to inherit.[59]

When the legislatures turned, in the late 1950s and early 1960s, to drafting new codes in the Eastern European socialist republics, the social structure had become stabilized. Property incentives were an accepted way of stimulating production, and there was no doubt that the family was to be fostered as a key institution in formulating a system of communist morality in Marxian socialist society. An inheritance pattern tending both to stimulate production and to hold the family together through property transmission was useful. In short, there was no reason to alter inheritance law radically, and good reason to preserve it. In consequence the familiar Romanist rules were repeated in the new codes with patchwork such as might have been conducted by any legislature revising law to facilitate administration and eliminate isolated cases of injustice.

Reasons such as these may explain the tenacity with which Eastern European legal specialists adhere to the view that inheritance law is socialist for what it does rather than for what it is. It explains why they warn the foreign analyst not to expect striking novelty in the form of "socialization" of techniques. A look at the facts bears out the contention that there is no fundamental technical change, except perhaps the tendency to narrow the circle of heirs at law to those within the modern small conjugal family. Lawyers knowledgeable about Romanist systems will feel quite at home in the maze of detail which comprises the bulk of the law of inheritance in any legal system.

[59] The Chinese Communists' problem has been in insuring conformity to the principle of equality of the sexes, originally proclaimed by the Nationalist Government and restated as Article 6 of the 1949 Common Program of the Chinese People's Political Consultative Conference. See Van der Valk, *supra*, note 58 at 318–19. The law of inheritance in China is largely developed in application of only two articles of the Marriage Law of 13 Apr. 1950, namely arts. 12 and 14. For Eng. transl. see A. BLAUSTEIN, FUNDAMENTAL LEGAL DOCUMENTS OF COMMUNIST CHINA 266 (1962).

I I

Incentive to Imaginative Creation

MASS ENLIGHTENMENT AND MASS SATISFACTION OF NEEDS ARE
the major aims of the Communist parties of all Marxist-oriented states, for without success in both spheres communism is
no more than an unrealizable dream. Any hope of achieving a
society in which compulsion no longer plays a part rests upon
reaching a level of education so high that citizens understand
and enjoy performing their social duties, and a level of production at which goods may be distributed according to need. The
law of intellectual property has as its mission attainment of
both goals.

In a sense the name "intellectual property" is a misnomer,
inherited from the bourgeois world. In Marxist terms the law of
copyright and patent is more appropriately called the law of the
"author's right," for the writer and the inventor are given no
property interest in what they write or invent. They have a
special form of protection from which they gain definite benefits, including money payments, but this is not conceived as a

return on intellectual capital. It is only a special technique of paying deferred wages, made necessary by the peculiar nature of their work. In consequence, royalties due authors rank as wages whenever it becomes necessary to determine their priority in any payments system, and they are taxed in what is considered the honored and preferred category of wages rather than as less prestigeous income from private enterprise.

Although the 1957 declaration of "basic laws applicable in all countries embarking upon a socialist course" contains no specific provisions on the common core of the law of authors' rights, its strictures against capitalist ownership create a common base for this branch of law in all Marxist-oriented states. Exploitation of literary productions in privately owned print shops and production of inventions in privately owned enterprises are limited by the rules prohibiting or restricting private employment of labor, to which attention has already been devoted, and by limitations on reproduction. Even where licenses are granted to artisans to manufacture in their own small shops, none may be obtained for private reproduction of the written word in any form.[1] Consequently, the possibilities of personal enrichment through private exploitation of ideas are nonexistent with literary works, and limited to artisan manufacture of inventions within the limitations set by the laws of the specific socialist country concerned.[2]

Yet a policy of limiting the possibility of personal enrichment by private exploitation is not taken to prevent the use of property incentives to encourage artistic creation and invention. On the contrary, the law of the author's right, whether in publication or in production, has incentive as a major aim. Its provisions for stimulating creativity make it look so much like the law of capitalist states that a Czechoslovak socialist notes its "similarity" to the law of property, although it is not categorized as such.[3] It is unique in his eyes because of its other

[1] Regulation for the Registration of Non-Cooperating Artisans and Handicraftsmen, 30 June 1949. For citations, see ch. 8, n. 11.

[2] A limited opportunity to publish novels and other literary works apart from state printers exists in Poland, where the cooperatives may still operate publishing houses.

[3] Sodomka, La propriété intellectuelle in LE DROIT DE PROPRIÉTÉ DANS LES PAYS DE L'EST 75 at 76 (R. Dekkers ed. 1964).

features, which accent the interests of society generally, but without disregarding the requirements of personal pride and reputation.[4] The personal element must be balanced with the social benefit so that authors and inventors do not feel that they are wage-earning robots and cease to be creative and productive. After all, the party remembers that poets and novelists inspired the resistance in Poland and Hungary in 1956, and, as a party spokesman said in Moscow on the 49th anniversary of the Bolshevik revolution in 1966, "Literature and art are becoming an increasingly effective force in the country's cultural development and the communist upbringing of the masses. The Leninist Party has a deeply respectful attitude toward the creative work of the artistic intelligentsia." [5]

It is the peculiar balance established between social, moral, and pecuniary interests that creates the "style" of the Marxian socialist law of authorship. It is a composite, containing many of the same elements long fostered by law in Western European private-enterprise states, but distinctively recombined by all Marxist-oriented states, albeit with variation.

As in other fields of Marxian socialist law, the Soviet model has served as the inspiration, and its principles have become the core. Other Eastern European states have followed the pattern established by nearly three decades of experimentation in the USSR before Marxian socialist systems were introduced elsewhere.

In the words of the Czechoslovak specialist, this pattern is "a law of personal relationships rather than of property relationships"; but it is still a part of civil law although some aspects of labor law color it.

The public interest was brought to the fore in the first Soviet legislation on copyright, for in November 1918 the Commissarist of Education was authorized to declare as the property of the republic any published or unpublished scientific, literary, musical, or artistic production.[6] Here was a form of nationalization, but not the same as had occurred with land and industry. The state appropriated, but at a price. It would pay royalties in

[4] *Id.* at 77.
[5] *The True Leninist Path*, Pravda, 7 Nov. 1966 at 1. Eng. transl. in 18 C.D.S.P. no. 45 at 5 (1966).
[6] 26 Nov. 1918, [1918] 86 Sob. Uzak. R.S.F.S.R. pt. I item 900.

accordance with a fixed schedule to an author whose works were reproduced, and it left him his self-respect, for he could prevent editorial mutilation throughout his life, and for six months after through his heirs, although heirs received no royalties automatically. The decree reflected the spirit of the time which had abolished tsarist inheritance and substituted a system of public administration for the benefit of household members in need. Thus, to obtain funds, heirs had to prove their dependency upon the author before his death.

Patents were treated in like manner in 1919, for the Supreme Council of National Economy, which administered state industry, might on nomination of the Patent Committee declare any patent the property of the state.[7] Again there was no confiscation, for royalties were compulsory and heirs had rights similar to those of heirs of artistic works. Those whose patents were not touched seem to have been left free to exploit them, although during the years of militant communism and civil war an inventor could hardly have been expected to produce inventions in which the state had no interest.

As in all other fields of law, the initiation of the New Economic Policy in Lenin's Russia had profound influence. Copyright and patent took on capitalist characteristics to conform to the policy of stimulating production through property incentives, and many of these characteristics have remained to create the "similarity" with private enterprise systems to which the Czechoslovak refers. The first legislation on the New Economic Policy of 22 May 1922 [8] even went so far as to include copyright among the "property" rights to be protected. There was, then, at that time no thought of transforming such rights from property to personal rights. Likewise, the new patent law, adopted 12 September 1924,[9] established familiar principles inspired by the German law. It also declared an end to all patents formerly registered, and required owners of patents issued after 1 January 1910 to reapply for protection under the new law. This meant review for novelty, but it was to be novelty as of the date of the original filing. Patent life was limited to fifteen years from the date of the original claim, thus

[7] 30 June 1919, [1919] 34 *id.* item 341.
[8] [1922] 36 *id.* item 423.
[9] [1926] 9 Sob. Zak. S.S.S.R. pt. I item 97.

restricting enjoyment of royalties to only a few years for prewar owners.

A full-scale copyright law was adopted in 1925 [10] to create a base which has remained, with amendments, to the present day. It was a major concession for the time to capitalist sentiments, for it not only protected authors for life but also protected their heirs for fifteen years without limitation in amount. This was an exception to the policy then in force under the first civil code of 1922, restricting the transmissible portion of an estate to 10,000 rubles. Simultaneously the balance of interest was maintained with society, for the state was given the right to purchase any production without the author's consent, whether or not published, so long as it had taken concrete form. Not until the New Economic Policy was phased out did a new copyright law emerge to meet what were expected to become the conditions of socialism. From that point, patent and copyright entered upon complex programs of independent development designed to meet the needs of socialism.

In this setting the details of the years since the ending of the New Economic Policy provide the basis for contrast with other legal systems. To present those details the laws of patent and copyright must be separated, and discussion will begin with patents. The ending of neocapitalism required complete review of incentive to invention, and this was necessarily recognized with increasing intensity as state planning gained momentum. By 1931 a decree [11] was readied to set the stage, stating in its preamble, "The patent legislation existing up to the present time, preserving the interests of the inventor by means of allowing him exclusive rights to his invention, already is out of accord with the aspirations of the leading inventors, those who are conscious of their position as the builders of a socialist society." To meet the need for a change in fundamental principles, a new concept was created to rank alongside the old concept of patent. It was called the "author's certificate." Patents remained, but the new concept took such hold that no Soviet citizen asked for one. Before 1965 patents were primarily for foreigners who for prestige purposes wanted a Soviet patent,

[10] 30 Jan. 1925, [1925] 7 *id.* item 67.
[11] 9 Apr. 1931, [1931] 21 *id.* item 180.

to announce in advertising that an idea was protected throughout the world. In 1965 a change in the direction of Soviet international trade required a modification of practice, as will be shown below.

The "author's certificate" became symbolic of the socialist way of stimulating invention. It was adopted by the Chinese peoples' republic in 1954 [12] and by several but not all of the Marxian socialist states in Europe, although some of the Europeans link it with the issuance of a patent as well. Thus, in the USSR and Bulgaria the "author's certificate" not only provides evidence of the inventor's rights, but is the document giving state enterprises authority to exploit the idea on recognition of these rights, particularly the right to money payments.[13] In Poland and Romania, two documents are necessary to put an invention into production: an author's certificate indicating its novelty and the inventor responsible for the idea, and a patent issued to the inventor or to the state as represented by a specifically named organization. The difference is purely formal, and suggests only that in the states still clinging to legal forms inherited from the past and having a large foreign business in patent licensing, the lawyers have thought it desirable, if not necessary, to indicate that there are two steps involved: recognition of authorship and assignment of a right to use; for in strict logic the inventor does not assign recognition of the fact that he has invented a novelty, since that would be worthless. He can assign only the monopoly right to utilize the invention, and that is symbolized, as it always has been, by the document called a patent, which then becomes available for licensing by the state in foreign trade.

Although the alternative form of protection, the patent, has passed out of popular use in the USSR, it still retains vitality in some of the Eastern European Marxian socialist states, in which the exclusive right to exploit is granted to the inventor.

[12] Provisional Regulations, 6 May 1954. Eng. transl. in A. BLAUSTEIN, FUNDAMENTAL LEGAL DOCUMENTS OF COMMUNIST CHINA 523 (1962). Revised regulations were adopted on 23 Oct. 1963. Eng. transl. in SCMP, no. 3,117 (11 Dec. 1963) at 6.

[13] Sodomka, supra, note 3 at 83. I have drawn heavily on Dr. Sodomka's report and discussion of it at the Brussels conference to determine the law of Eastern European states.

In the German Democratic Republic, Hungary, and Czechoslovakia, change in the direction of the Soviet model is only beginning. The Germans have developed a "halfway" stage by placing in their law of 30 June 1963 two forms: an "economic patent," and a "patent granting exclusive rights." The "economic patent" is an approach to the Soviet "author's certificate," but with a difference. The state has no automatic right to utilize the invention; a specific authorization must be issued by the Inventions Office. The "patent granting exclusive rights" is in the classic tradition, however.

Hungary and Czechoslovakia, the latter only until 1963, preferred to retain old forms, and patent protection was offered only in this traditional form. Thus, the state could and did obtain exclusive rights from inventors by utilizing forms well known in the nonsocialist world. An inventor or his heirs could assign the patent to the state, or if the inventor was on the payroll of a state agency for the purpose of making inventions, or had developed his idea under contract with a state agency through which he received developmental funds, the state became the proprietor. In such cases the state's ownership was registered in the patent registry. In late 1963 Czechoslovakia undertook to introduce the author's certificate alongside the patent.

In explaining the vitality of the classic patent in Eastern Europe, other than in the USSR and Bulgaria, the Czechoslovak specialist indicates that it is a convenient and familiar means of exploiting Eastern European patents on the world market. Lawyers from other lands recognize the patent and negotiate licenses with Eastern European inventors, whereas an "author's certificate" would present them with an unfamiliar form and might raise questions as to what rights they could obtain by negotiating a license under its terms.

The USSR's ratification in 1965 [14] of the international convention protecting patents may introduce a similar practice into Soviet licensing, for it is evident that Soviet inventions are currently desired abroad and provide lucrative sources of foreign

[14] [1965] 7 Sob. Post. S.S.S.R. item 40. This order has not been available to me, but its substance and import have been communicated by Dr. Frank Arnold Nix, a German patent lawyer. He reports a new patent act in preparation.

exchange. Most probably the state, through its foreign trade monopoly "combines," will license patents, which have been issued directly to the state. There will be no need to refer in the document sent abroad to the author's certificate issued to the inventor. The Polish-Romanian system of two documents could be introduced and the foreign licensee would not have to ask questions about the unfamiliar document, which would never come his way.

Most states have followed the Soviet model in establishing a fifteen-year term for a patent, dating from the time of filing, but the German Democratic Republic sets the term at eighteen years and Hungary at twenty.[15] Also, all require that applicants establish novelty as against the whole world, and that the invention be useful. Different words are used in the legislation of each state to express this concept, but the result is the same. The Czechoslovak law speaks of a "new or superior effect"; the Soviet and Bulgarian speak of a "positive effect"; and all require that it open the way to technical progress. The Czechoslovak specialist combines the various requirements to include the provision that, in all Marxian socialist countries, an invention is "every progressive solution, previously unknown in the world, of a technical problem, and of utility at the moment or in the future." To him this definition introduces nothing new into the worldwide concept of invention: it is therefore not the concept but the manner of protection that is the socialist novelty; and the heart of this novelty is the author's certificate.

The author's certificate was conceived by the Soviet policy makers to avoid the evils of capitalism while utilizing property incentive to encourage invention. All inventors might have been placed on a payroll of a state enterprise with the task of invention, as is the trend in Hungary and Czechoslovakia. In this event, it would have been possible to abolish all forms of documentary recognition of the inventor, as the Hungarians have done. He would work like any other employee, and his product would become the property of the state. His salary level might be raised or lowered to reflect his inventiveness and thus stimulate his activity, as it is in many laboratories of great private firms in the capitalist economies, where staffs of scien-

[15] Sodomka, *supra*, note 3 at 82.

tists work under contracts which provide that everything they discover belongs to the firm.

Although such a system might look advantageous under Marxian socialism, it has not spread widely. Some distinguished professors who are members of the institutes of the Soviet Academy of Sciences, and also some experts on the payroll of Soviet enterprises, as men of demonstrated inventive potential, work in just such a way; but they are relatively few. The major source of invention seems still to be the individual working in a factory as an engineer on the production line who discovers in practice that a simpler form of manufacture is possible. Under the stimulus of promise of wealth, he works night and day to develop his scheme. Later, as part of his reward, he is given a post in a developmental institute, where he would never have been placed had he applied without proof of his skills. The scheme designed to find him has to be peculiarly fitted to conditions of socialism, in which private exploitation of invention will not be tolerated. The author's certificate was created as the solution.

The Soviet model, as established by the statute adopted in 1931 [16] and amended in 1941,[17] sets the socialist framework in its opening provisions. The right of exploitation of an invention can belong only to the state. Inventors to whom an author's certificate is issued lose control over their invention forever as soon as it is disclosed in an application. By accepting the certificate the inventor automatically assigns to the state all rights to exploitation, including the right to let the invention remain unused if circumstances suggest that it has no further utility. The inventor obtains only the right to remuneration, in accordance with a tariff, and to privileges set forth in the statute. This right may not be assigned, although the money remuneration may be inherited.

Remuneration was set by a formula calling for payment to the inventor of a portion of the savings or any other effect produced upon the economy by the invention or technical improvement. Further, tax exemption was offered on the first 10,000 rubles (about $1,000 at the time) and the inventor was

[16] *Supra*, note 11.
[17] 5 Mar. 1941, [1941] 9 Sob. Post. S.S.S.R. item 150.

given a priority in the allocation of housing and in appointment to positions available in scientific and experimental research institutions and enterprises. In this way the author's certificate served to identify geniuses for direct employment in laboratories maintained for invention.

The formula for establishing savings varies with the type of suggestion and the amount of the savings. An instruction issued under the statute established a scale of payments for three classes of activity: invention of a completely new tool, instrument, or process; a technical improvement of an existing tool, instrument, or process; and a proposal for "rationalization" of production. The inventor was to receive payments amounting to a portion of one year's savings to industry. The period chosen to compute the savings varied: for a "rationalization" it was the first year after its introduction; for a new tool, instrument, or process the inventor received an appropriate portion of the savings each year for five years, so that at the end of the period he had been paid the determined percentage of savings for the best year of the five. This scale recognized that savings appear gradually when something new is introduced. The 1941 formula represented a change in favor of the inventor, for under the 1931 statute, he had received a percentage of the best of only the first three years of savings.

The percentage of savings was set as follows: for those up to 1,000 rubles (about $100 at the time) in the year selected, 30 percent for new items, 25 percent for technical improvements and 12½ percent for rationalizations. For larger savings the percentage was reduced on a progressive scale so that at the top bracket, when savings exceeded 1,000,000 rubles, payments were to be at a rate of 2 percent on new items plus 21,000 rubles, but not to exceed 200,000, and for categories two and three the top receipts were limited to 100,000 and 25,000 rubles respectively.

Income tax was levied on these receipts, but at the rate for wage earners, which was the preferred rate; and, as has been indicated, the first 10,000 rubles was tax exempt. The opportunity for even greater revenue was offered in a 1942 instruction.[18] An invention opening up a new field of production or creating a new kind of valuable material, substitutes for nonferrous met-

---

[18] 27 Nov. 1942, [1942] 10 *id.* item 178.

als, or machines and instruments not previously produced in the USSR was to earn double the regular rates.

The 1941 law was replaced in 1959 [19] by the statute currently in force, and the substance of this act was introduced into the Fundamentals of Civil Law of the USSR in 1961 [20] and in the Russian republic's civil code in 1964.[21] The major change appeared in the instruction on rates of payment, which showed some reduction in the lower brackets. This may have been due in part to the change in tax policy soon after the 1941 law. The income tax brackets had been topped off in 1947 at 13 percent for all incomes, which meant that recipients of large payments had more after taxes.[22] In 1960, soon after the 1959 law, a first step was taken to abolish income taxation entirely; so even the 1959 reduction did not close the way to accumulation of considerable sums as savings. This abolition was later superceded, but the principle remains a goal. Although Soviet policy utilizes property incentives to stimulate production, it is not open-ended. In a socialist system there is a psychological limit to what a citizen, regardless of his contribution, may receive in relation to his fellows; and no outsider can predict what further reductions may occur. Since payments rest not upon any concept of the sacredness of property but on the necessity to induce invention, fluctuation in monetary return can be expected if a smaller payment will achieve the desired results. Returns might also be reduced to avoid an attitude which the Chinese Communists call bourgeois.

Although the right to protection of inventions is treated as a branch of civil law, the right to remuneration for innovations in the organization of production is considered a part of labor law.[23] Here there has been no creation of something wholly new, but rather an improvement of techniques or technology, a relative novelty attached to a local situation. This concept is developed in broadest form outside the USSR in Eastern Eu-

[19] 24 Apr. 1959, [1959] 9 *id.* item 59.

[20] 8 Dec. 1961, effective 1 May 1962, [1961] 50 Ved. Verkh Sov. S.S.S.R. item 525, part 4.

[21] Part 6 (arts. 520–26).

[22] Instr. Ministry of Finance, 27 Mar. 1949, 3 SPRAVOCHNIK PO ZAKONODATEL'STVU 111 at 122 (1949).

[23] Sodomka, *supra*, note 3 at 85.

rope, for the Soviet statute limits recognition of rationalizations to technical proposals. Bulgaria, Hungary, the German Democratic Republic, Poland, and Romania include within their systems of remuneration any proposals on the organization of production, and Hungary, Romania, and Czechoslovakia accept even proposals relating to organization of administration, which have nothing or almost nothing to do with technique. The reward for such proposals is wage increases and bonuses, rather than anything so formal as an author's certificate.

Since so much of the "style" of Marxian socialist law lies in the attitude toward "rights" adopted by those who make and administer it, the treatment of disputes over inventions helps reveal whatever novelty is in the system. There is considerable variation in the procedures to protect the inventor, and from these variations insight can be gained on the nature of his "right." Some of these procedures suggest that a right vests in him from the moment he has an idea, and should be protected by a court. Others suggest vesting only after a technical commission has determined whether he has a right. Still others treat the inventor who has been given an author's certificate as having something comparable to privilege, revocable at the will of an administrator, subject only to administrative review of his exercise of discretion.

Hungary is in the first category, admitting judicial review of all types of disputes: over novelty as determined by the technicians of the Inventions Office; over competing claims for remuneration from two inventors, both of whom think that it is their invention that has been utilized; and over computation of remuneration admittedly due. Still it must be remembered that in Hungary the patent owner is usually the state, which has employed the inventors in its shop and laboratories. The German Democratic Republic likewise permits appeal to the supreme court against denials of novelty by the Inventions Office as well as on decisions of the Inventions Office concerning remuneration under an "economic patent."

Romania, the USSR, and Czechoslovakia are in the second category although events in the mid-1960s suggest that the latter two began to search for ways to reduce the work of court review without denying it. For these three states the Inventions

Office alone has competence to decide the technical claims of novelty stated in the application and to create the right. From such decisions there is no appeal. Still, disputes over the identity of the inventor when a protected invention has been used, and over computation of remuneration, are for the courts. The new procedure introduced by the USSR and Czechoslovakia calls for preliminary review of claims based upon identity and upon faulty computation by an arbitration tribunal, created for the purpose by the trade union committee in the enterprise. This tribunal also hears disputes over innovations in organization of production and administration, which have become exceptionally numerous under Czechoslovak stimulation of such proposals.

Such a preliminary review on the spot may be of administrative convenience, because the contested issues are usually within the common knowledge of the workmen in the shop. A hearing of a disgruntled colleague's claim before the trade union tribunal may eliminate a large number of disputes before they reach a court.

Bulgaria is closer to the privilege theory. Only the Inventors Office may decide the matter of technical novelty, and even for disputes over remuneration there is no appeal to a court. The procedure is wholly administrative in that the dispute is treated as a labor dispute in the enterprise, to be heard by a grievance procedure. Appeals from this procedure may be only to the administrative superior of the enterprise, usually the ministry.

Poland prefers a system of administrative tribunals within the Inventions Office, although with a judicial atmosphere. Thus, objections to findings on novelty by the staff of the Inventions Office may be taken to a college of the office attended by representatives of the trade unions and of the technical associations. An appeal from this college goes to a Commission of Appeal attached to the Office, and its decision is final. The judicial atmosphere is provided in the college and in the Commission of Appeal of the office through the requirement that a provincial court judge or a supreme court judge preside. Disputes over the amount and means of payment of remuneration go to an arbitration commission which serves as a tribunal of final appeal from decisions of the enterprise and of its administrative superior. These commissions are also presided over by judges—those of the provincial court in the city of Warsaw.

Some judicial decisions from the USSR will illustrate how these rules are applied to concrete problems. The primary issue of novelty is brought to the courts, even though the 1959 law places jurisdiction over such claims solely in the Inventions Office. In 1961, the supreme court of the USSR found it necessary to issue an order on court practice to restate the rule that courts must not take suits over novelty, priority, or the issuance of author's certificates.[24] Trial courts had been violating the rule. A decision of the preceding year had perhaps stimulated the order, for a claimant had sued the Inventions Office of the Ministry of Agriculture to be recognized as the inventor of an automatic sowing machine to plant plots without use of measuring wire. He argued that although he had sent documents to the ministry in 1956, he had received no reply. In 1958 he had found in the ministry's journal an article by a fellow worker describing a similar invention as a novelty. The court, on reviewing the record, determined that registration of the invention as a novelty had been refused the claimant and said simply, "Consequently, since there is no item that has been invented, there can be no decision of a dispute over whether he is really the author." [25]

A suit over remuneration had been accepted, but was dismissed by the people's court because the accounting introduced in evidence had not been approved by the appropriate auditing agency. On review, the supreme court of the Russian republic found in the record the plaintiff's claim that there was an appropriate accounting but that it had not been produced, and so it remanded the case for new trial under instructions to determine whether the invention had really been used, whether the economic effect had been determined, and, if so, what it was.[26]

Another accounting was the subject of suit when an inventor claimed that the 3,000 rubles paid for use of his invention

[24] Order of 4 Mar. 1961, [1961] 3 Biull. Verkh. Suda S.S.S.R. 18.
[25] Mikhailichenko v. Invention Dep't. of the Ministry of Agriculture of the U.S.S.R. and Burenko, [1960] 4 Sov. iust 86.
[26] Zaitsev v. Factory, [1960] 5 *id*. 86.

for the preparation of food was by no means his share of an annual saving of 4,500,000 rubles in the resorts of Piatigorsk. The trial court, in application of the 1941 statute, rejected the suit as one to be heard only by administrative channels; but the supreme court noted that the 1941 statute was no longer in force, and the 1959 law had placed jurisdiction over such suits in the courts. It ordered retrial.[27]

Competing claims to recognition as the inventor of a hydraulic press, admittedly in use, elicited from the Russian republic's supreme court the response that there was assuredly jurisdiction in the court in spite of the enterprise's defense that the invention in use had been developed by a design agency and bore no resemblance to the plaintiff's tool. The supreme court remanded for new trial because the suit was over a civil right, proved by the plaintiff's possession of an author's certificate, and had been rejected in error by the trial court.[28]

Money is seen as a stimulus to invention in the Marxian socialist states, as it is in the capitalist economies, but Marxists do not forget that a day is planned when money will no longer circulate in society. The Soviet Union's Communist party still carries this plank in its platform,[29] as it did in 1919 when achievement of the goal was believed to be quite near. Today, no one expects speedy achievement of a no-money economy. Nevertheless, more socially oriented inducements are constantly being sought. A major one is social recognition, personified in the appropriate title and medal to symbolize achievement. In 1961 the Russian republic created the order of "Honored Inventor and Honored Rationalizer" and struck medals to be conferred on those recognized for contributing substantially to the national economy or for introducing a consequential step in the perfecting of production.[30] Under such a system, if it were eventually to replace the money system completely, an Inventions Office would still have to determine novelty, so that the proper man might be recognized, but no court suit would follow to establish the amount of remuneration. The "administration of things" which Engels anticipated as a substitute for

[27] Kravtsov v. Piatigorsk Administration of Resorts, [1960] 10 *id.* 27.
[28] Karpov v. Enterprise, [1960] 12 SOTS. ZAK. 74.
[29] Communist Party Program, 1961.
[30] 30 Apr. 1961, [1961] 16 Ved. Verkh. Sov. R.S.F.S.R. item 249.

law would end with determination of the inventor and conferring of the symbol of social recognition.

While awaiting development of such an advanced social consciousness, not only does the Soviet legal system elaborate a branch of the civil law to assure that money payments made as inducements are properly paid, but the criminal code has a role to play. Disclosure of an invention without the inventor's consent, misappropriation of his rights, and compelling him to accept co-authorship are all punishable by imprisonment for up to one year, by the assignment of compulsory tasks for the same period, or by fine up to 500 rubles.[31]

Artistic production presented some of the same problems of adaptation to a socialist society after the termination of the New Economic Policy as had invention. In this case the artistic pride of the author had to be reckoned with, for art is more than a matter of earning money. The West has been startled when its own painters have burned canvases rather than leave to posterity a work of which they are no longer proud, and composers and dramatists have refused to license the use of their works to grace causes for which they have no stomach. Socialist society knows the same emotions, and the legal draftsmen have had to accommodate them in a balance which gives to society the opportunity to know and enjoy the work, but which preserves to the artist-author control over the time of its public presentation, its editing after it has been given to the world, and even its use in circumstances lacking in overriding public interest.

To provide protection to both society and author, and also to induce creation, all Marxian socialist states have developed a system of rights and duties, focused on three concepts: rights of the state on the one hand, and moral rights and pecuniary rights of the artist on the other. The Soviet model of 1928 [32] is acknowledged as the inspiration. Under that model the state was authorized to take possession of a work through the Ministry of Education when the public welfare required, but only after the author had indicated by some form of public presenta-

[31] Criminal Code R.S.F.S.R., 27 Oct. 1960, art. 141. Eng. transl. in H. BERMAN, SOVIET CRIMINAL LAW AND PROCEDURE: THE RSFSR CODES (1966).

[32] 16 May 1928, [1928] 28 Sob. Zak. S.S.S.R. pt. I item 246.

tion that he considered it representative of his talents. In such circumstances the author retained a right to remuneration, and the right to prevent mutilation of the work through editing. For works performed upon a theatrical stage the law specifically permitted the state to act before printing and to license performances without the author's consent. For novels and poems the statute was less explicit, providing only that a copyright owner might be required to sell it to the state. No cases are known in which an unpublished manuscript which may have been read to a literary circle has been put into print against an author's will.

Social interest is also manifested in other ways, notably with regard to translation. The Soviet model was based on the assumption that the minority peoples of the USSR required literature in their own language, but that their limited numbers made distribution costs too high to permit paying both the author and the translator. In consequence, all translation was to be done without requesting the author's consent and without remuneration to him, although he was to have the right to see the translation and to determine whether it did justice to the work. Under this provision much has been translated from languages in use outside the USSR without payment to the authors, or with payment only in rubles deposited in a Soviet bank for use within the USSR.

When the copyright law was revised in 1961, with the enactment of a new set of fundamental principles of civil law, the attitude toward translation had begun to change. The Russian language had become a widely accepted medium of culture. And the Russian-language market within the USSR had become large enough to justify payments to authors of translated works. The fundamental principles of civil law permitted republics to do as they wished with translations,[33] and the Russian republic chose, in practice to provide for payment to authors when works in the languages of the national minorities were put into Russian, but not to require payment to Russian language authors when their works were translated into national minority languages.

Yugoslavia is not so severe in promoting the public inter-

[33] Art. 102.

est.[34] Although its law permits translation of foreign works under compulsory license, it does so only if the author has refused consent for ten years. Since Yugoslavia has ratified the Brussels Copyright Convention, it has had to introduce a reservation on this point. Yugoslavia conforms to the convention otherwise, for its publishers pay royalties to translated authors —in contrast to the USSR's denial of payment.

Other Marxian socialist states have adopted neither the Soviet nor the Yugoslav position on translations, largely because all of them are signatories without reservation of one or another of the international copyright conventions, under which the authors of translated works must be paid. They translate, therefore, only after obtaining the author's consent and on paying him. In other aspects of the protection of society's interests, however, these states follow the Soviet model; but they do so in terms of compulsory licensing of certain types of activity. The Czechoslovak law authorizes compulsory licensing for radio and television, and even for enterprises for which an author edits texts of a largely scientific nature. For radio or television use, royalties are paid. For the employee, however, no payment is made when the work is used within the employing enterprise. But if it is distributed outside, although the author's consent is not required, royalties are due even if the employee's task was to produce just such works.

The Soviet provision permitting the Ministry of Education to declare a work public property for general use has been incorporated in Czechoslovak and other Eastern European law, but in practice, according to reports, this right is almost never used. The Czechoslovak law establishes some limitations not set in the Soviet model of nationalization. It may be applied only to Czechoslovak citizens; the work must be of great social importance; and it must be impossible to reach an amicable agreement with the author. As in the USSR when nationalization occurs, royalties must be paid.

Certain uses are permitted without the consent of the author and without royalties under the USSR's 1959 statute, but these circumstances are about the same as are permitted under copyright law in the capitalist countries: to produce a new,

<hr>

[34] Sodomka, *supra*, note 3 at 92.

creatively independent production, but not a reworking into a play or scenario; to produce textbooks, scientific and critical works, and political education publications within limits established by each republic; to provide information in the press, radio, and films; to reproduce reports delivered in public and published productions of literature, science, and art; and to reproduce works of art in any form except mechanical copying by contact of works exhibited in public view, except in expositions and museums. The other states have added some points.[35] Thus, Bulgaria permits diffusion by radio without consent or payments, and Poland permits it without consent but requires payments. Romania permits compulsory licensing for radio and for phonograph records, but only on payment. For all of these the work must already have been published.

The effect of socialization upon copyright is to be found not only in the superior rights of the community established by statute—socialization colors the circumstances in which an author can enjoy the right. As with personal property, the Marxian socialist systems are alert to prevent utilization to obtain profits unrelated to earnings. Although an author's right is essentially the right to deferred earnings, it has, as the Czechoslovak specialist has stated, certain attributes which create a similarity to property, and these are controlled as property is. The limitations appear both on alienation and on inheritance.

As to alienation, it is forbidden to transfer a right to any private individual.[36] The author can license by contract only a state publishing house or an authors' association. Although the opportunity to bargain with private individuals is necessarily limited by the structure of Marxian socialist societies, which precludes publication by any but state agencies, Marxian socialist laws generally find it desirable to state formally the result of the situation that there can be no alienation to individuals. Perhaps the legislators have in mind the possibility of authors' negotiating with foreign publishing houses for publication in the capitalist enterprise countries. For such arrangements, the Marxian socialist systems offer the services of the state trading enterprises. Thus, an author of international appeal may appear

[35] *Id.* at 96.
[36] The Polish statute of 1952 provides an exception, permitting in art. 30 transfer of pecuniary rights to other persons in writing.

abroad; however, it is not he who negotiates the license, but the state agency to whom he has transferred his copyright. Violation of this rule has given rise in the USSR to celebrated denunciations and even criminal trials.[37]

As to inheritance, the law is complex and widely varied in the Marxian socialist states. The Soviet model of 1925 established a term of life plus fifteen years for copyright, and heirs were authorized to receive royalties without limitation on the amount. The usual inheritance laws of the civil code applied to permit an author to designate in his will those who might enjoy the fifteen years of payments, and if he failed to do so, the intestacy system of distribution applied. This pattern has remained to the present day, although with some variation between republics of the USSR. In its civil code of 1964 the Russian republic extends copyright protection for the same period on all types of works, but it limits royalties received by heirs to 50 percent of what the author would have received.[38] Some of the other republics, holding to a rule introduced by the statute of 1928, draw a distinction between types of works.[39] Thus, choreographic works, pantomimes, moving-picture scenarios, and photographs receive protection only for a specific term, usually ten years from the date of production, and heirs receive only what is left of the term should an author die before it has expired.

The Russian republic's code of 1964 has recognized for the first time in Soviet law the "literary executor," to whom an author may transmit the right to exercise the author's "moral rights" during the executor's life.[40] This individual exercises the right the author had during his lifetime to protect the integrity of the work against alteration by editors. If no such literary executor is named, the right of control as well as of remuneration passes to heirs for the fifteen-year term permitted, in association with the Writers' Association; and if there are no heirs, or after the expiration of fifteen years of control by heirs,

---

[37] Reference is to the 1966 trial of the writers Siniavskii and Daniel, accused of spiriting the manuscripts abroad through a foreign diplomatic pouch for publication deemed detrimental to the interests of the USSR.
[38] Art. 496.
[39] Sodomka, *supra*, note 3 at 96.
[40] Arts. 481, 496.

the Writers' Association functions alone. The usual rules on the ownership of marital property and its distribution on the death of a spouse are profoundly affected by the provision that royalties are part of the marital community only when received during life. Those payable after death are outside the community. This means that a surviving spouse has no direct right to one-half of them, but receives his or her share only to the extent that he or she could qualify within the circle of heirs by intestacy or will.

The length of the term of protection varies considerably with the other Marxist socialist states of Eastern Europe. To some degree this variation is the result of the persistence of tradition in societies which had adhered to international standards before socialization and which as yet see no need to change their rules. Thus Hungary and the German Democratic Republic continue to function under presocialist copyright laws, although they have introduced through contracts and ordinances a system conforming considerably in practice to those of other Marxian socialist states. Their major conformity to the past is extending the right of the copyright owner beyond the term of life plus fifteen years. For these two states and for Czechoslovakia and Yugoslavia, the term of protection is life plus fifty years. Czechoslovakia and Yugoslavia, however, introduce an exceptional term of only ten years from date of publication for films and photographs.

Other states within the Marxian socialist group have preferred to reduce the term to variations on the Soviet theme. Poland fixes the term at life plus twenty years,[41] but provides, as does Czechoslovakia, for a ten-year limit on protection of films, photographs, and choreography. Bulgaria's formula is novel in providing no fixed term of years of protection of heirs after the death of the author. The system is framed as an insurance measure during a period of presumed need, for descendants receive the royalties only during their period of minority, and the parents and surviving spouse of the author receive royalties for the life of each. Romania resembles Bulgaria in limiting inheritance by the aging ascending heirs to their lifetimes, but it is more generous to the youthful descendants, giving them

[41] Law of 1952, art. 26, par. 1.

the right of royalties for fifty years after the author's death. Other heirs, presumably collateral, if they should happen to qualify for inheritance, are limited to fifteen years' enjoyment.

All Marxian socialist states permit civil suit for damage and reestablishment of the violated right through press notice or otherwise and termination of the violation.[42] Only Yugoslavia permits suit for immaterial damage, in keeping with a tradition which other Marxian states have abandoned as unsuited to a socialist philosophy.[43] The Soviet Union also provides criminal sanctions, these being the same as those provided for misappropriation of inventions. To these rights of recovery of damages Czechoslovakia has added a unique right to follow the item into the hands of a purchaser, so that if he sells it at great profit, this profit must be shared with the creator. This right is of particular value to painters and sculptors and to their heirs, for the right continues throughout the life of the copyright. To protect such persons from a rapacious purchaser who might try to buy the right together with the work of art, it has been made inalienable.

Although the detailed variations in the protection offered by each state are extensive, the Czechoslovak specialist thinks that all tend toward unification, so that states having very close relationships may have a common legal language.[44]

Litigation in Soviet courts illustrates the implementation of the general principle. Several cases illustrate treatment of disputes over authorship. Thus, one co-author sued his colleague when he discovered that the latter had published the work in another district under his name alone. Recovery of damage was given, and further publication of the work without the name of the co-author was forbidden.[45] Two authors of a dictionary sued the authors of a new dictionary for copying their work. Experts were called by both sides, the plaintiffs testifying that four-fifths of the new volume was borrowed from the old, even to the extent of copying errors, whereas the defendants' expert

---

[42] Sodomka, *supra*, note 3 at 97.

[43] Poland provides a novel penalty: payment to the Red Cross for deliberate violation of a personal right, including copyright. Civil Code, 1964, art. 448.

[44] Sodomka, *supra*, note 3 at 98.

[45] Zinin v. Pomelov and Ustinov, [1961] 1 SOTS. ZAK. 86.

argued that all dictionaries were of necessity copies of preceding ones to some extent, but that in this case the copying was not over 25 percent, and that the reduction in size of the dictionary was in itself an original contribution. The trial court gave damages, but the supreme court decided that the compilers of the small volume had not exceeded the permissible borrowing.[46]

An author of a novel *On the Eve* was sued by a man claiming that he had written it jointly with the author under the title *Life*, and that the latter had changed only names and a few incidents from the original manuscript. The supreme court of the Ukraine dismissed the suit, finding that although the plaintiff had recounted his life to the author over a two-year period, there was no agreement as to co-authorship. Further, it concluded that "neither design, nor initiative, nor oral accounts, when not put into literary form, can be recognized as the plaintiff's creative participation in the preparation of the novel, and he gained no right to co-authorship." [47]

A series of cases arose over the rights of an employed author to royalties in addition to wages for his work. Thus, an employee ordered to write a history of the factory sued for royalties after his booklet was printed and distributed. An expert testified that it was not merely a factory report but an economic essay of original merit. The trial court gave judgment for him, rejecting the director's argument that there was nothing original, and that others had aided in its preparation as members of a team. But the supreme court reversed on the ground that the author, as manager of the factory, had been chairman of the team of writers; that he was obligated to prepare reports; and that no publishing contract existed to justify a conclusion that the work was not in line of duty.[48]

An employee of the State Bakery Inspection Office of the Ministry of Trade of the USSR likewise sued for royalties on a handbook on eliminating pests from grain. The brochure had been sold by the ministry. An expert testified that the brochure was not a manual of instructions, but a popularized brochure

[46] Saltanov v. Erasmus and Soviet Encyclopedia, [1937] 17 Sov. IUST 51.

[47] Emlianinov v. Stankevich, [1959] 1 Biull. Verkh. Suda S.S.S.R. 46.

[48] Vinogradov v. State Soap Rendering Candle and Chemical Factory, [1929] 1 Sud. Prak. R.S.F.S.R. 8.

about a scientific subject. The trial court rejected the testimony, concluding that the brochure had been written in the line of duty. The appellate court agreed, but noted that the author should be paid for the 150 copies promised him but not delivered.[49]

Computation of royalty payments came under court review when an artist under contract to illustrate a book claimed that he had received only half the royalties provided for in his contract. The publishing house argued that since it had dropped the book from its publishing plan, it was not required to pay the illustrator more than one-half the agreed royalties. The reviewing court determined that under the law full royalties were payable if publication did not occur within the period set by the contract, and ordered new trial under these principles.[50]

The close link between forms of copyright in Marxian socialist countries and in countries where private enterprise reigns is evidenced in several Eastern European countries which retain their old statutes. Draftsmen have felt the need to make only limited modification to meet the demands of socialism, and this modification is possible through contract even without change in law. In this is found an example similar to those offered in analyzing the law of personal property, where, in spite of radical change in the theory of protection, the legal core remains from the past. Only specific abuses must be eliminated from rights long associated with ownership. The changes in copyright form from presocialist times are not as dramatic as those in the field of patents, in spite of the acceptance of a theory of protection based on enjoyment of deferred earnings rather than on the traditional protection of property. The critical difference arises not from details of the law but from the substantive situation.

At the risk of unnecessary repetition, a fundamental element of difference bears restatement—the absence of an open market in which an author can shop for a publisher. This situation influences not only his monetary returns but the scope of his presentation. Since there can be only one client—the state—represented by publishing enterprises offering a form

[49] Sokolov v. State Bakery Inspection Office, [1929] 8 *id.* 7.
[50] Daran v. Publishing House "Sovetskaia Rossiia," [1960] 10 Sots. zak. 84.

contract and tied to realization of the same aims, there is a narrowing of the types of artistic taste to which artists, musicians, and authors may cater. A monistic society offers less variation in taste than a pluralistic one; so artistic works, whether painting, music, films, or literature, enjoy a paying public only when sponsored by enterprises whose tastes are governed by a uniform set of political considerations, often including, artistic considerations.

The Communist party of the Soviet Union has never concealed this. As recently as its twenty-third Congress in 1966, it adopted a resolution on literary creation which went from the general to the specific in saying: "The party expects creative new works that will win the reader by their depth and truthfulness and the high level of their artistic skill." Then, after this generality, the resolution states the direction a creation must take to receive patronage. Here is the substantive difference between copyright in a Marxian socialist system and in a pluralistic society. In the words of the resolution, the authors "must assist actively in molding the spiritual features of the builders of communism, and in inculcating in the Soviet people high moral qualities, devotion to communist ideals, a sense of civic pride, Soviet patriotism, and socialist internationalism." [51] A year earlier a *Pravda* editorial had set guidelines with the following words: "Our art has established itself as the art of the living truth, and hence it is optimistic in essence. . . . Only works that reveal persuasively and with deep feeling and eloquence the creative, constructive basis that determines the very essence of the life of our society, its drive toward communism, that implacably expose all that stands in the path of our progress, can become true contributions to the development of Soviet art." [52]

Not all Soviet authors have felt the urge to conform, nor have editors in state publishing houses interpreted the party's desires in the same way. A *Pravda* editorial in 1967 [53] found it

[51] Resol. on the Report of the C. C. of the Communist party, part III, par. 10. Eng. transl. in TWENTY-THIRD CONGRESS OF THE CPSU 279 at 307 (1966).

[52] Pravda reaffirms art policy of June 1963 plenum, 17 C.D.S.P. no. 2 at 4 (1965).

[53] Pravda, 27 Jan. 1967 at 2. 19 C.D.S.P. no. 4 at 3, 4–5 (1967).

necessary to take to task the editors of two principal literary journals—one for "underestimating the enormous historical experience and motive power of Soviet society," and the other for "underestimation of the fruitful advances that are now clearly apparent in the development of Soviet society and that represent the result of the restoration of Leninist principles and norms in all spheres of life." The first was accused of placing "exaggerated emphasis on the seamy side of life" and the second of "oversimplification." One author was accused by name for making an insufficiently profound appraisal of the change in reality as a result of the development of Soviet democracy and the strengthening of legality. His offense was glorifying in a novel the ringleader of a kangaroo trial and those who tried to conceal it from investigation.

Although there is, then, some variation in what authors can sell to state publishers, because of the inevitable variation in taste even among men pledged to achieve a single goal, this variation is less than in a pluralistic society, where editors have quite different goals and bid accordingly.

I 2

Law to Strengthen

the Family

A CLOSELY KNIT FAMILY, CENTERED ON A MUTUALLY ADORING couple married for life and charged with rearing children to respect communist morality: this is the goal currently proclaimed by all Communists.[1] Their legal systems are designed to foster this concept through property relationships, criminal law, and, of course, codes of family law as the key element in the process. Gone are the days when some of Lenin's colleagues used to argue that the family was an outgrown institution and that sexual relations should be of no more concern than drinking a glass of water.[2]

Although Chinese Communists gave the impression at the outset of their rule that they were drawing away from this common aim, their basic program has not differed from that of

[1] 2 SOVETSKOE GRAZHDANSKOE PRAVO 467 (1961) [Soviet Civil Law].

[2] Kollontai, *Communism and the Family* (1920). Eng. transl. in R. SCHLESINGER, CHANGING ATTITUDES IN SOVIET RUSSIA: THE FAMILY (1949).

the Communists of Europe. Their efforts to weaken the traditional extended-family "clan," which threatened the success of attempts to centralize authority in the state, are to be distinguished from their attitude toward the "conjugal family" of man, wife, and children. Not even the much-noted expressions during the "Great Leap Forward" period in 1958 of desire to quicken the pace toward a communal form of life for the village community can be taken as more than a dramatic interlude.[3] Even during the "Great Leap," the mass media and divorce courts urged marital fidelity, and legislation raised the marital age to one of presumed discretion to avoid ill-considered unions likely to result in divorce, as well as to cope with the population explosion.

The law governing the family relationship is as politically oriented as all other branches of Marxian socialist law. In an appreciation of that fact lies the key to interpretation of a course which has been dotted with abrupt changes in the fifty years since the Russian revolution, and which has undergone considerable variation since the emergence of Communist-directed states outside the culture patterns prevalent in the USSR. There was no early blueprint to guide those responsible for its formulation, nor has a blueprint been established by the 1957 declaration of "basic laws applicable in all countries embarking upon a socialist course." The declaration's most pertinent passage requires its signatories to carry out "the Socialist revolution in the sphere of ideology and culture." This makes the family a principal factor in "socialization," since it is a primary institution in any culture pattern, whether that of the Central Asian grasslands or the sophisticated urban center. But aside from this general command, Communists have left each group to its own devices in establishing the details of its system.

As with inheritance, family law has been profoundly influenced by the Romanist heritage of the legal draftsmen in the Marxist-oriented states. This is especially so in all European

[3] Prof. Franz Schurmann seems to suggest otherwise, arguing that the conjugal family was not attacked except during the campaign of the "Great Leap Forward" because "basically the regime did not see the usefullness of trying to destroy that almost inaccessible core of Chinese social organization." See his IDEOLOGY AND ORGANIZATION IN COMMUNIST CHINA 471 (1966).

Marxian socialist states where the base of family law is prerevolutionary tradition, into which have been introduced elements
designed to foster the revolution's values of equality of the
sexes, separation of church and state, and the primacy of loyalty
to society over loyalty to the family. This is partially so even in
the Oriental societies governed by Communists, for all had
been influenced in some measure by modernizing systems before the Communists came to power, and these systems had
been drafted on European models. Yet in the Oriental systems,
especially the Chinese, the Western influences upon the family
were paper thin, for quite different family traditions lay deep in
the system. This necessitated a different approach in introducing Marxist-oriented reforms; but the three values currently
sought in Eastern Europe are also sought in Eastern Asia. For
all, the words of Engels in his *Origin of the Family, Private
Property and the State* provide the currently revered doctrine.
Communists seek to avoid elements that their originator found
in the bourgeois family, which he identified as no more than
legalized prostitution in the buying or enticement of brides
with money, and a cover for polygamy among husbands who
were unfaithful to their first wives.

The desire to separate church and state and to make the
wife equal with the husband underlay the first measures taken
by Soviet draftsmen in 1917. At the time marriage and divorce
and even the maintenance of vital statistics were functions of
the religious communities.[4] These communities, in keeping
with the religious culture of some countries of the West and of
most of the Middle East, had tended to encourage feminine
subservience to the males of the family, especially in the Central Asian Islamic areas of the Russian empire. This attitude
had endured to the very eve of the revolution, except within the
homes of the enlightened intelligentsia. One has only to read
the Russian literature of the nineteenth century to grasp the
social significance of male predominance, even among the peasantry of the Orthodox church, and this was the heart of Russian
society. Even the factory workmen who emerged in ever-increasing numbers after the freeing of the serfs in 1861 reflected

[4] Berman, *Soviet Family in the Light of Russian History and Marxist
Theory*, 56 YALE L. J. 26 (1946).

peasant attitudes, remaining peasants at heart and returning to their villages for the harvest, in sickness, and in old age.[5]

Lenin's Bolshevism was designed to break the hold of religious institutions upon the community and to remold the family, particularly in liberating women from domination by husbands and sons. This motivation provided the thrust to the first family legislation—a decree on marriage of 18 December 1917,[6] followed the next day by a decree on divorce.[7] The ecclesiastical authorities were shorn of all power over the marriage relationship. Only secular marriage was given legal effect, and only secular courts were to have jurisdiction over divorce. Both decrees were combined with other materials on the child in a family code published in 1918 in the Russian republic.[8] Other republics appearing later within what had been the old Russian empire did likewise.

This first code established a principle of organization of the entire legal system which was to affect all Marxian socialist states that came after. Although family law is normally a section of civil law and a chapter of civil codes in states within the Romanist legal tradition, the Bolsheviks separated the two. Perhaps at the time there was no alternative, for they were by no means ready to draft a civil code in 1917; yet the need for restructuring the family was pressing. Still, the separation was later made a matter of principle rather than convenience to such an extent that it become a matter of dogma.

During the early 1920s, when the predominant idea was that civil law sprang from the marketplace and was a bourgeois form, to be cast aside as socialism became a reality, the argument was made that civil law and family law were incompatible. Marriage relationships could have nothing to do with market conditions of contract. Later, when this concept had faded, with repudiation of the "market-relations" theory as the source and continuing stimulus for the existence of civil law, the argument against union of the two codes became more general, but no less dogmatic. By 1967 an author contented himself with the explanation that the relationships of the fam-

[5] G. VERNADSKY, A HISTORY OF RUSSIA 195 (1929).
[6] 18 Dec. 1917, [1917] 11 Sob. Uzak. R.S.F.S.R. pt. I item 160.
[7] 19 Dec. 1917, [1917] 10 *id.* item 152.
[8] Oct. (undated) 1918, [1918] 76–77 *id.* item 818.

ily are quite different from those of the "general collective" regulated by civil law.[9] A Polish authority was more explicit. In his opinion the separation was necessary because the civil code was concerned "above all with the units of the socialized economy, in particular state enterprises and cooperatives." From this it followed that "since the content of these property relations are of completely different quality from the relations which are the object of Polish family law, these cannot in our view spring from civil law but represent a distinct branch of law."[10]

The dogma's strength had been tested in 1960 by Polish lawyers who tried to combine family and civil codes to return to the Romanist tradition, of which Poland had been a noted exemplar. The effort failed, primarily because laymen had become accustomed to the separation of family and civil codes during the preceding decade and feared that reconversion would transform the family code into a lawyers' law again.[11] The Polish family code was enacted separately on 25 February 1964,[12] the civil code following on 23 April 1964,[13] but both were made effective on the same date, perhaps to demonstrate unity. All other Eastern-European Marxian states have followed the same pattern of separation.[14]

Liberation of women was exemplified in various ways in the first Russian code of 1918, the most noted being abolition of the concept of grounds for divorce as these had existed in the ecclesiastical law of the Russian Orthodox church and in some other religious legal systems of the empire. Divorce was made available at the request of either party, although no petitioner had to appear in a people's court. This step was hailed as primarily a move toward liberation of a persecuted wife, of which there were said to have been many among the peasantry, although it also, of course, gave a disgruntled husband the same

[9] V. RIANTSEV, SEMEINOE PRAVO 13 (1967) [Family Law].

[10] Szer, *Droit et famille*, in INTRODUCTION À L'ÉTUDE DU DROIT POLONAIS 177 at 178, 179 (S. Rozmaryn ed. 1967).

[11] The author is indebted to Dr. A. W. Rudzinski's unpublished paper on the new Polish family code for the Polish materials, supplemented by Szer, *id.*

[12] [1964] 9 J. of L. Poland Item 59.

[13] [1964] 16 *id.* item 93.

[14] Knapp, *La nouvelle législation civile en Tchécoslovaquie*, 16 REV. INT'L DU DROIT COMPARÉ 753 (1964).

opportunity. Another provision was the strengthening in the cities of the imperial system of separation of marital property, so as really to free the wife from what had become the husband's traditional economic domination through management of marital property.

In providing a means for easy divorce Lenin had no intention of encouraging promiscuity. In later years this became evident when a specialist on family law disclosed that the requirement that divorce petitions be submitted to a court rather than to a registration bureau was an attempt to discourage frivolous dissolutions. He revealed that the Communists expected traditional reluctance to enter a courtroom to play its part in limiting petitions to those reflecting only exacerbated marital troubles.[15]

Establishment of state bureaus for the registration of vital statistics was designed as an indirect blow at the ecclesiastical authorities. Bolsheviks believed that the priests had exercised authority over their flocks not only through the requirement that marriage and divorce be regulated by the church, but also through the simple necessity of registering births and deaths with the priest; for this led automatically to christenings, religious funerals, and masses for the dead, from which the church derived not only income but prestige in the home. But registration served another purpose. It provided a checkpoint to enforce the new code's prohibitions on marriage of the underage, the nonconsenting, the feebleminded, and close relations.

Illegitimacy was another target of the first code, as a status incompatible with the revolutionary aim of equality for all. Children born out of wedlock were declared equal with those born of a marriage. This gave them the right to the father's surname, to maintenance, and to distribution of an inheritance. A criminal prosecution nearly twenty years later demonstrated the long-lasting nature of prejudice, however, for a mother of a child born out of wedlock killed her baby in desperation and shame after the father's desertion. In sentencing the woman the court refused to accept her argument that she merited leniency because "the crime was committed out of fear of the severity of

[15] This point was revealed in a conversation with the late Prof. G. M. Sverdlov at the University of Chicago conference on the rule of law, held in 1957.

her parents, her disgrace before them and her brothers, and also false shame before the neighbors." [16] To the court this attitude conflicted sharply with the new conditions of life, and with the expanding culture of the workers and collective farmers of the Soviet Union—the more so since the accused was economically independent of her parents and was sufficiently mature herself. To this explanation the court added a parting blow: "Such a sentence does not mobilize the masses to destroy the survivals of capitalism in the mind of man."

With the two 1917 decrees and the code of 1918 the Bolsheviks established a general model for the European people's democracies when their communist governments devised a policy for the family after the Second World War. Yet by that time, the social pattern in the Soviet Union had become more complex than that of 1917. In the intervening years there had been a period of experimentation with unregistered marriage and divorce, begun with the second family code, adopted by the Russian republic in 1926,[17] and continued in force until legislated out of existence by Stalin's unexpectedly strict amendments of 1944.[18] This experimentation had been so unsuccessful in practice that no leaders of Marxist states elsewhere tried it. A glance at the highlights will demonstrate the reasons.

Unregistered marriage had been ushered into the Soviet legal pattern by the 1926 code's provision that if parties established a joint household, they would be recognized as married for purposes of family names and patronymics, maintenance, family obligations, and inheritance.[19] Although registration was still possible and even favored in the interest of clarity of status in the event of the death of one of the parties, it was not required. The court was authorized to declare a union legally constituted if evidence indicated that a couple had lived together as man and wife. Numerous subsequent court decisions, especially over the right to inherit, found such cohabitation and established the right of inheritance, even when the parties had violated the code's prohibitions against marriage. All of these concerned women, and the measure was justified by

[16] Krivozubova, [1935] 22 Sov. IUST. 24.
[17] [1926] 82 Sob. Uzak. R.S.F.S.R. pt. I item 612.
[18] 8 July 1944, [1944] 37 Ved. Verkh. Sov. S.S.S.R.
[19] Art. 1.

stating that the primary aim of family law was to protect women from exploitation by men who thought only of satisfying their lust. To have applied conventional rules voiding marriages violating the prohibitions would have harmed the woman, who usually was innocent of these violations.

The code of 1926 might have occasioned no subsequent reversal of policy had it not applied the same principle to divorce.[20] Here it also recognized the right of a court to establish the fact of termination of a marriage relationship, even though neither party had availed himself of the convenience of the state registration bureaus, which maintained a divorce registry to keep the record straight. In a system where divorce was no longer a matter of contest, but merely a registration of a fact (permitted by the 1926 code to occur in a registration bureau rather than a court), there was no reason to consider the registration itself of legal consequence. Separation was the only determinant, and therefore it alone needed to be established.

In application of the rule of recognition of factual dissolution of a marriage, a party to the marriage could withdraw from the household, terminate the marriage without registration, and establish another household, without registration of the remarriage. The only inconvenience was to a court that might subsequently be asked to determine competing claims to the inheritance by two women. Certificates of registration of divorce and remarriage, had they existed, would have made the matter simple for the state notary to administer, but without these records, a court had to try the facts. Extensive litigation ensued, partly because under the inheritance law a will could not wholly disinherit a surviving spouse. In one such case a court found that the deceased had maintained two households until his death, and the inheritance was divided between the women.[21]

The 1926 revisions in the interest of recognition of factual, or what Americans would call common-law, marriage and factual divorce had a doctrinal base of some consequence. They marked in some measure the ending of state intervention in the marital relationship, which became a matter of socialist morals alone. To some of the commentators of the time, the experi-

[20] Art. 3.
[21] Annotation to Code of 1926 (1937 ed.) 43.

ment heralded the first stage in the withering away of law, since no enforceable rules limited marriage and none prevented its termination. Under the 1926 code parties emerged wholly free of legal compulsion in the culturally important sphere of family relationships, but it took some court decisions to reaffirm that such liberation was really the intention of the legislators; for the criminal code of 1926 continued the 1922 prohibition against bigamy.

In 1929 a trial court refused to recognize as valid a second marriage following one that had been terminated by separation alone. The court justified its opinion by saying that to hold the second marriage valid would have made the husband bigamous in violation of the criminal code. The supreme court of the Russian republic reversed the trial court, saying, "the refusal by the court to establish this fact [unregistered marriage following unregistered divorce] because the law forbids bigamy would not only be contrary to the law but contrary to simple logic." [22]

Those who thought socialist morality was already strong enough to establish conditions necessary to the withering away of legal restraints were to be disappointed. Promiscuity became widespread, and it was usually the woman who was exploited and left without maintenance or inheritance after having entered a relationship which she had been led to believe was to be permanent. Another consequence was the severing of parental ties with children when homes broke up. From this disruption of family relations Soviet society suffered the same disastrous results as have emerged elsewhere with broken homes. Rowdyism spread, and from this crime evolved.[23]

The remedy for the situation took several forms: establishing state institutions for homeless children; levying fines on parents of children disobedient to the police or participating in vandalism; instituting the right of suit for civil damages against parents whose offspring caused harm; [24] and finally orders to Communist party bodies and councils of ministers at the republic level to supervise the publication of children's books and to screen moving pictures to eliminate those harmful to morals.

[22] Gromoglasov, [1929] 20 Sud. Prak. R.S.F.S.R. 8.
[23] Nakhimson, *More on the Question of Struggling with Juvenile Crime*, 3 PROBLEMY UGOLOVNOI POLITIKI 81 (1935).
[24] [1935] 19 Sob. Zak. S.S.S.R. pt. I item 155 and [1936] 1 *id.* item 1.

Divorce practice also came to public attention in an effort to reduce juvenile delinquency. By law of 27 June 1936,[25] Both parties were required to appear at the registration bureau to register a divorce, to assure that a mutually satisfactory record of agreement on support of the children might be arranged more effectively. The amount of support required was set rigidly in terms of specific fractions of wages to be paid for each child, and imprisonment for two years was to be imposed on those who failed to pay. Although the child was uppermost in the minds of the reformers, he was not their sole concern, for they stated in their preamble that their purpose was "struggling with light-minded relations to the family and family obligations."

Presumably the draftsmen hoped by their 1936 amendment to discourage divorce by making a hot-headed spouse confront his partner before a state official in hopes that reconciliation might follow. But this was not to be the sole discouragement. The law took an unexpected tack, introducing a graduated scale of divorce fees. The first divorce was to cost 50 rubles, the second 150, and the third and subsequent ones 300. This was a startling reversal of policy, for it introduced a property qualification in direct conflict with the long-standing position taken against bourgeois systems on the ground that they favored the rich over the poor.

Although attempting to discourage divorce, the 1936 amendment took no step toward prohibiting it, for the registration bureau still entered the divorce at the request of either party. The absent spouse was merely served with notice, and if he or she failed to appear, the entry was made without the presence of both persons so long as the absent one made substituted appearance. If there was lack of agreement on support of the children, the matter was referred to a court for determination.

Other measures were taken at about the same time to encourage parental supervision of children and to create a homelike atmosphere. By the law of 31 May 1935 [26] establishing criminal penalties when a parent neglected his child, the Ministry of Education or the local police were required to notify the trade union at the parent's workshop of the neglect so that

[25] [1936] 34 *id.* item 309.
[26] [1935] 32 *id.* item 252.

social pressure might be brought to bear upon him; and if that failed, they were to raise the question of depriving the parents of rights under provisions of the code of 1926 and of installing the child in a children's home at the parents' expense.

Foster homes were found through publicity urging citizens to adopt homeless children under provisions of the 1926 code, or to establish a condition created in law in 1928 as "dependency," which differed from adoption in that there was to be no change of name or automatic acquisition of inheritance or rights of support.[27] The "dependent" can demand, however, if his natural parents die or have died or have insufficient means to support him, that his new family provide care and education as long as he is a minor or unable to work. He may even qualify as a dependent under the provisions of the inheritance law if he was completely dependent upon the deceased for a year before his death. Finally, in 1936 a new status, the "patronat," was created, under which a citizen might take a homeless child into his home under a contract with a state agency, by the terms of which the patron received a monthly payment from the contracting agency for the care of the child.[28] Since the child became no financial dependent of the foster parents, he could not qualify as a dependent under the inheritance laws to share in an estate on the death of either. The patron was made a guardian in other matters by the law, and was subjected to criminal prosecution if he left the child without supervision or support.

During the disruption caused by the Second World War, the number of homeless children increased by hundreds of thousands. Crime became an ever-greater menace among the waifs. Resources of the state were inadequate to provide all with homes, although some were housed under state care in institutions and children's colonies, and sons of soldiers and sailors killed in the war were placed in newly established academies named for heroes of the war with Napoleon. The only hope for the great mass, however, was reinvigoration of the family unit to protect the newly born and to provide shelter under the dependency, adoption, and "patronat" systems for those whom the state could place in foster homes.

[27] 29 Nov. 1928, [1929] 22 Sob. Uzak. R.S.F.S.R. pt. I item 233.
[28] 1 Apr. 1936, [1936] 9 *id.* item 49.

Nikita Khrushchev was given by Stalin the task of heading a group to review the situation and propose a solution. In his chairmanship is found an explanation for the remarkable shift in policy in 1944, and also for the long period during which that policy remained enshrined in law despite mounting opposition to its provisions on divorce and on children born out of wedlock. To many, the Khrushchev law of 8 July 1944 [29] looked reactionary. Its sponsor was blamed, after his ouster in late 1964, for permitting his peasant conservatism, extending almost to what might be called in the American tradition "puritanism," to dictate a policy totally at variance with the experimentation of the 1920s and 1930s in self-discipline as a means of preserving a home. The law abolished recognition of the unregistered marriage and the unregistered divorce. It even abolished the right of an unwed mother to institute proceedings to establish the father of her child so that the child might have an authentic patronymic—necessary, under Russian naming procedures, to self-respect, a surname, a right of support, and inheritance.

Although no opprobrium was intended, the children suffered. Women sought fathers for the children they craved from among men already married or from men without the desire to establish a family, and millions of children were born without legal rights against a father. By 1967 one out of every nine children was being born out of wedlock,[30] and complaints against Khrushchev's law multiplied. One writer said that a birth certificate without a father's name established for the child's whole life an "unerasable trauma" which conflicted with principles of communist morals.[31] Many complained of the maintenance problem, because the 1944 legislation, in depriving the unwed mother of her previous right to sue the father, gave her as a substitute only five rubles a month for one child, and even that was paid only until the child was twelve. For this reason great numbers of children were put in boarding schools or given away for adoption.

The widespread social revolution of 1944 was accomplished

---

[29] *Supra*, note 18.

[30] Beliavskii, *Caution—We're Dealing with Law*, [1967] 17 LITERA-TURNAIA GAZETA 11. Eng. transl. in 19 C.D.S.P. no. 17 at 19 (1967).

[31] [1965] 1 SOTS. ZAK. 31.

by the provision that a marriage not registered had no legal consequences. Thus cohabitation created no rights in the party subsequently seeking support or inheritance, nor did it place any offspring on an equal footing with children born of a registered marriage, unless a father later registered the marriage to legitimate the child's status. The sweep of the 1944 law seemed complete, but in 1965 a native of the Chechen-Ingush republic in the high Caucasus found that it did not protect him when he tried to return to customary practices of polygamy in his region.[32] When he was prosecuted for bigamy his lawyers argued that he could not have committed the crime because he had only one registered wife. A review of the facts showed that he had lived in registered marriage with one woman who had borne him two children. Later he concluded a second marriage in accordance with local custom with another woman, and brought her into his home with his registered wife, so that he lived as had been done from time immemorial with his two women. The court refused to accept the defense, noting that under the criminal code, Article 235, it is bigamy to cohabit with two women in a common household, and the code says nothing of the necessity of establishing two simultaneous registered marriages.

In taking this severe position against ancient family custom among peoples who had been primitively organized before the advent of the Soviet system, the court was in accord with a strict Soviet condemnation of all such custom. The Soviet criminal codes have long had a chapter on relics of local custom, prohibiting the purchase and abduction of brides, child marriage, the blood feud, and polygamy.[33]

The divorce provisions of the 1944 law were equally unexpected, for they not only gave jurisdiction over divorce to the court, but they required a hearing on the merits. Simple desire of one of the parties was no longer enough to register a divorce, nor was even the desire of both parties. The state alone, through the instrumentality of the court, had the right to decide whether a marriage would be terminated in law.

The new divorce requirements were not a complete return

[32] Datsaev, [1965] 4 Biull. Verkh. Suda. R.S.F.S.R. 8.
[33] Criminal Code R.S.F.S.R., 1961, chap. 11.

to prerevolutionary ecclesiastical conditions, without participation of the bishops, for the law listed no specific grounds for divorce. Judges were left free to decide whether the circumstances made evident the parties' inability to reestablish their common home. To emphasize the public desire for reconsidering the decision to separate, the law required the people's court to attempt reconciliation. Only if such efforts failed could a determined party take the matter to the provincial court with its more remote and experienced judges for a rehearing. Again an effort was to be made to reconcile the parties. But at this point, if it proved ineffective, the divorce decree was to be issued because of the presence of meritorious circumstance. Under this decree the courts were given the task of implementing vague public policy in living law.

Court practice under the 1944 amendments was guided by a general rule, established with some delay, but finally enacted by plenary decision of the supreme court of the USSR.[34] It required a finding that the "principles of communist morality" had been violated before the petition could be granted. Of course, suits had to be brought in large number before the formula was developed into a detailed guide. A few decisions will illustrate the trend that has emerged.

A wife obtained a divorce in 1959 because she proved that her husband was frequently drunk and had beaten her so badly that he had been sentenced by a criminal court to one year of "corrective tasks." In granting the divorce the supreme court of the Russian republic said, "Normal conditions for the continued cohabitation of the spouses and the proper rearing of children cannot be maintained. . . . The institution of the divorce action is provoked by profoundly thought-over and well-founded reasons, and continued preservation of the marriage would be inconsistent with the principles of communist morality." [35]

A year later a divorce was granted because there had been a four-year separation of the spouses, and the petitioner had taken

[34] 16 Sept. 1949, sec. 1. SBORNIK DEISTVUIUSHCHIKH POSTANOVLENII PLENUMA VERKHOVNOGO SUDA SSSR 1924–1957 g.g. at 86 (1958). [Collection of Orders of the Plenum of the Supreme Court of the U.S.S.R. Currently in Force 1924–1957].

[35] Vershinina v. Vershinin, [1959] 4 SOV. IUST. 87, case 12.

up life with another woman who had borne him a child.[36] In the next year the court accepted a petition when the wife proved bad treatment by her husband, jealous quarrels, and a conviction of her husband for insulting her mother, which was followed six months later by his arrest and detention for eight days because of rowdy behavior during a family quarrel.[37]

In 1965 a case with religious overtones emerged. A Central Asian provincial court refused to grant divorce even though it found that the husband had been drinking systematically, had beaten his wife, and had forbidden her to go to public places, probably in keeping with the Islamic custom that the woman should remain in the home out of sight of strangers. The supreme court of the Kirghiz republic set aside the denial of divorce, and in remanding the case for a new trial told the lower court to consider "that the defendant's conduct conflicts with principles of communist morals." [38]

Decisions in the other direction, when the divorce was denied, provide further clarification of judicial attitudes. A husband failed to obtain a divorce when the court concluded that discord arose primarily out of interference in their life by the wife's parents, not out of the wife's behavior.[39] For this reason the court decided that the family had not fallen apart. Another husband was denied a divorce even though he argued that he had met another woman and intended to marry her. The court said that he had produced no substantial proof of the spouses' inability to live together. On the contrary, they had resumed sexual intercourse even after beginning the proceedings.[40]

A divorce was denied even when a wife had been banished to a remote region of the country for four years under the law on "parasites." [41] This case contrasted with the others because it took a more formal position on the one point where formality

[36] Voropaev v. Voropaeva, [1960] 1 Sots. zak. 85.

[37] Grishakov v. Grishakova, [1961] 8 Sov. iust. 27.

[38] Kadyrova v. Kadyrov, Kirghiz S.S.R. Sup. Ct. 6 May 1965, summarized in *The Practice of Issuing Summary Orders in Civil Cases*, [1966] 2 Biull. Verkh. Suda S.S.S.R. 42 at 46.

[39] Arshipov v. Arshipova, [1959] 1 Sov. iust. 77, case 8.

[40] Ravilov v. Ravilova, [1960] 1 Sov. iust. 77.

[41] Mesheriakov v. Mesheriakova, [1961] 4 Biull. Verkh. Suda R.S.F.S.R. 6.

was possible. Under the stress of war and to speed decisions, an instruction had been issued by the Council of Ministers on 27 November 1944 interpreting the 1944 law's application to cases of an absent spouse.[42] Immediate granting of a divorce had been authorized if a spouse was absent, leaving no trace of whereabouts; if lost at the front during the war; if sentenced to a prison term of not less than three years; or if suffering from chronic mental illness, presumably in a hospital. In denying the petition in 1961 the Russian republic's supreme court held that since the banishment was not a prison term but rather an administrative measure designed to influence the wife's conduct, it did not fall within the interpretation of 1944. Perhaps the court was suggesting that her rehabilitation required her husband's presence at her place of exile in Siberia, and this was cause enough to resist his desire for divorce.

Appellate courts showed themselves quite ready to review a trial court's determination of grounds. The supreme court's plenum in 1949 demanded that the trial court's decisions be based on concrete facts and contain the grounds for the court's conclusion. There were even suggestions that the law should introduce absolute grounds in addition to those listed in the instruction on absence, but this was resisted by an author who argued, "It is not possible to include within the framework of some formal listing all the various occurrences of a lifetime in the sphere of the family and marital relationships of people." [43] He concluded that any such formal approach "is profoundly alien to Soviet law in general and to family law in particular." The view seems to be that the principle of flexibility, which was originally dominant in all fields of Soviet law but which has been yielding yearly to a desire for more stability, must be retained in family law as a particular exception to what is becoming a prominent trend.

Complaints against the strict provisions of the 1944 law

[42] The substance of the instruction was incorporated without specific reference to the source as annotation to art. 17 of 1926 Code of Laws on Marriage, the Family, and Guardianship R.S.F.S.R. in all editions subsequent to 1944. See also G. SVERDLOV, SOVETSKOE SEMEINOE PRAVO 84 (1951) [Soviet Family Law].

[43] Aniiants, *Codification of Soviet Law on Marriage and the Family*, [1958] 6 SOTS. ZAK. 49 at 51.

mounted following Stalin's death.[44] The people's courts reported that they had found it impossible to take the time
necessary to attempt reconciliation, and they asked to be relieved of this duty. Partisans of easy divorce noted that
hundreds of cases were coming to the courts after one or both
of the parties had established a new family without the benefit
of divorce and remarriage. In effect, the conditions of the
period of factual divorce which had been recognized between
1926 and 1944 were being recreated, without the benefit of a
law which would regularize them so that new wives or husbands
would have the rights of support and of inheritance, and children would be legitimate. In spite of a rising demand for
reform, nothing happened until after Nikita Khrushchev was
removed as first party secretary in 1964, leaving the way open to
reconsideration of policy.

Within a year a law adopted on 10 December 1965 [45] introduced a new policy, but it was clearly a compromise between
the conservative and liberalizing influences within the Communist party. The people's courts regained some but not all of
their authority because the right to grant divorce was returned
to them, but they were still admonished to attempt reconciliation before doing so. The requirements of the rather costly
publication of notice of the hearings in the local press which
had been introduced in 1944 were withdrawn. But beyond that,
no change was made. Courts were still to apply communist
morals in determining what acts justified a divorce decree, and
children born out of wedlock still had no claims for support, for
family name, or for inheritance from a father with whom their
mother was not registered in marriage. Soviet law remained a
law with strong emphasis on preservation of the home and
family as a font of socialist culture.

The theme of a strong socialist family was restated by the
Communist party in a 1966 resolution on the work of secondary

---

[44] Juviler, *Family Reforms on the Road to Communism*, in P. JUVILER
& H. MORTON, SOVIET POLICY-MAKING: STUDIES OF COMMUNISM IN
TRANSITION 29 at 52 (1967).

[45] [1965] 49 Ved. Verkh. Sov. S.S.S.R. item 275. The supreme court's
interpretation is in [1966] 3 Sov. IUST. 32. A journalist reports an 80 percent increase in divorce during 1966 after enactment of the amendment.
N.Y. Times, 24 April 1968.

schools.[46] Child rearing was to be discussed everywhere: in the local party organs, in trade unions, in the Communist Youth League, and even in industry. Parents were to be asked what they were doing and the schools were to be helped to influence neglectful parents. Study aids on the inculcation of communist morality were to be prepared for parents by the ministries of education in the republics.

Meanwhile the pressures against the rigid features of the 1944 law were building up. The legislative drafting committees were asked in letters to the editors of leading newspapers why they delayed introducing a new draft law, but nothing appeared until the spring of 1968. Then, after prolonged discussion, reputedly centering on the problem of the child of the unwed mother and on the continuing restrictions on easy divorce, new fundamental principles were published, discussed for some weeks, and enacted in June.[47]

The draftsmen had compromised with the various pressure groups. To placate the conservatives, registration of marriage and divorce was still required for legal effect, but there was a concession to the reformers. In the absence of registered marriage, a child might be granted, under limited circumstances, the same rights as those born "legitimately." Those circumstances were mindful of what had existed during the period when factual marriage was recognized. Legal rights were granted to offspring of unions which were as permanent as if registered. For such offspring the right of support was restored, as was the right to the father's name. This left outside the reform the child of the "casual" union, for the stated purpose of discouraging promiscuity.

Secondly, the draft sought to encourage second thoughts among those who wanted to rush hastily into marriage. For the first time in Soviet history a waiting period of one month was required before registration would be permitted.

The weeks of discussion of the draft forced still a third provision, a grave departure from the rigid procedures of the

[46] For summary, see Pravda, 19 Nov. 1966 at 1. Eng. transl. in 18 C.D.S.P. no. 46 at 6, 7 (1966).

[47] See draft, Izvestiia, 10 Apr. 1968. Eng. transl. in 20 C.D.S.P. no. 16 at 3 (1968), and law of June 27, 1968. [1968] 27. Ved. Verkh. Sov. S.S.S.R. Item 241.

late-Stalin years. The law as finally enacted introduced the concept of divorce without a court hearing if there was mutual agreement and if there were no offspring. Here was a return to registration of divorce by the state bureaus without any determination whatever of whether the parties' conduct conflicted with communist morals. It can be presumed that social pressures exerted by the Communist party and agencies controlled by its members will continue to encourage the maintenance of marriage bonds, but the door has been reopened to freedom of divorce, at least for those who have no children and agree that their union has been a failure.

In turning to the formulation of family law in the younger Marxian socialist states, the investigator finds that the Soviet experience has been the inspiration, but that each country has conserved its own cultural peculiarities and historical traditions. Unlike the Soviet policy makers, those who ordered codification in the younger states have provided no recognition for the customs of cultural minorities within society, even when the state structure provides for some recognition of cultural sensibilities. Thus, Czechoslovakia, in spite of duality of ethnic cultures, has only one code, and Yugoslavia has established uniformity in family law.

The influence of Soviet thinking is notable in the younger Marxist-oriented states when the law of divorce is examined. These states have entered the historical sequence not at the point where the Russian Communists began in 1917 with ideas of broad freedom of divorce, but at the point of restraint reached by the Soviet policy makers with their law of 1944. Thus, Czechoslovakia's 1963 code authorizes divorce without enumerating specific grounds, but establishes a rule of restraint through use of the following words: "The court may terminate a marriage by divorce on demand of one of the spouses when the relations between them have broken down so seriously that the marriage cannot fulfill its social purpose." [48]

The 1963 code's draftsmen showed their desire for rigorous scrutiny of reasons for divorce where children were affected, for

[48] Act no. 94/1963, sec. 25. A nearly similar rule requiring a finding of a "profound and lasting rupture" was incorporated in act no. 265/1949, art. 30, par. 1 at a time when family law was coordinated with that of Poland in identical codes.

Art. 24 requires courts to consider above all the interests of minor children in contemplating a divorce petition.

The rigidity of the rule has not overwhelmed the Czechoslovak courts, however, for a commentator reports that the judges rarely resort to this provision on children to reject a petition, but do lip service by explaining in the decision why the divorce seems not to be inimical to the minor's interests.[49] There is a feeling that an unhappy family background often exercises a more harmful effect than does a divorce on children forced to mature in an atmosphere of parental conflict.

The Soviet judiciary may also come to the same conclusion; a 1966 report from the All-Union Institute for the Prevention and Study of Crime shows that in a large sample of juvenile delinquents constant family quarreling and fighting was found in 50 percent of the cases.[50]

Yugoslavia provides more comparative interest than Czechoslovakia, since its culture patterns are more numerous and vary more from section to section. Although both Czechoslovakia and Yugoslavia share the influence of the Austro-Hungarian empire, only the latter was influenced by the Turks. In consequence, Yugoslav life still bears the heavy impact of Islamic culture in Bosnia and Hercegovina, and vestiges have been left even in Serbia and Macedonia. Croatia and the North, with their long experience with a secular regime even before World War I, have moved more easily into the Marxian secular system.

Although efforts were made between the wars by the Kingdom of Yugoslavia to unify the law and to introduce civil marriage and abolish the authority of the husband and paternal authority, they failed, largely because of the strong opposition of the religious communities.

On achieving power the Communists took immediate measures to alter family law, just as the Bolsheviks had done. Even before obtaining state authority, they made civil marriage op-

[49] Radvanova, *The Problem of Infants of Divorced Parents in Czechoslovak Legislation and Jurisprudence*, 11 REVIEW OF CONTEMPORARY LAW no. 1 at 163 (1964).

[50] Minkovsky, *Some Cases of Juvenile Delinquency in the U.S.S.R. and Measures to Prevent It*, [1966] 5 Sov. GOS. I PRAVO 84. Eng. transl. in 18 C.D.S.P. no. 30 at 9, 10 (1966).

tional in territories they occupied, and declared the equality of husband and wife. A Basic Law of Marriage was issued on 3 April 1946,[51] followed in 1947 by a Basic Law on Guardianship, a Law of Adoption, and a Basic Law on Relations between Parents and Children.

Yugoslavs declare that the purpose of these laws is to effectuate a series of policies: (1) to place the family, as an institution with a broad social function, under the protection of the state; (2) to equate males and females; (3) to give the state exclusive jurisdiction over the regulation and settlement of family relations; and (4) to make possible regulation of family relations within general policy lines by each of the Republics so as to take account of the special conditions of the area.[52]

Familiar features were placed in the new laws to protect health by denying marriage to close relatives, the insane, minors, and those who cannot exercise free choice because of compulsion or error. Civil marriage alone was recognized as valid, and had to be registered, of course, with the communal people's committee. Religious marriage subsequent to civil registration was permitted. All these points had been established by the first decrees in the Russian republic.

Laws were liberalized to permit divorce if the joint life of the spouses became unbearable,[53] but the spouse creating the situation may not sue for divorce. In practice this created what came to be known as the "extinct" marriage, which occurs when a marriage has been terminated in fact, but the innocent spouse refuses to sue for divorce, sometimes for revenge, to prevent the partner's remarriage. Much criticism was levied at this provision, and it is proposed that a guilty spouse be permitted to seek divorce after a long period when there is clearly no possibility of reconciliation.

The Yugoslavs, like the Soviet Communists of 1944, have sought to discourage divorce, but in a different way. They have not required that the court become objectively convinced of the impossibility of reconciliation. They take the parties' word for it if neither objects, but they require the guilty party to return

[51] Eng. transl. in 4 COLLECTION OF YUGOSLAV LAWS (THE FAMILY LAW) 15 (Institute of Comparative Law, Belgrade, 1962).

[52] Begović, *Foreword* to *id.* at 4.

[53] Art. 56.

gifts of major value, to pay the costs of the litigation, and even to provide indemnity on the demand of the injured spouse. The right of the innocent spouse to support in the event of poverty, incapacity for work, or lack of employment continues until the person enjoying it enters another marriage or is found unworthy by a court.[54]

Children born out of wedlock are treated as they were in the first Soviet code: they are equal to those born in wedlock, whether the union was permanent or "casual." [55] To permit a child to exercise his rights, a procedure is provided, as it was before 1944 in the USSR, to establish paternity. If that is successful, a putative father must support, care for, rear, and educate children born out of wedlock, as he must his legitimate children, until the age of eighteen or prior marriage, or even for longer in the event of extended schooling or incapacity to work.

In Poland, the legal problems inherited by the Communists resembled in some measure those of Yugoslavia, for the German, Austrian, and Russian civil codes dating from the time of the Polish partitions remained in force in large measure until the Communists came to power. These varying influences had to be considered and a common pattern introduced. The first four decrees on marriage, marriage property, the family, and guardianship promulgated during the winter of 1945–46 [56] introduced compulsory civil marriage and required that divorce be granted by state courts, as had been done by the first Soviet decrees, but with a difference. Divorce could not be granted at the request of a single party and specific grounds had to be established. Poland at that time was nearer to the reforms of family law made in Germany and France after the split with the Church than to the ideas of the early Bolsheviks, but by 1950 the wheel had turned.

Grounds for divorce were dropped by the second Polish family statute of 1950,[57] and the courts were given instructions like those of the USSR in 1944—to find whether a complete,

[54] Art. 70.

[55] Law on Relationships between Parents and Children, 1 April 1947, art. 3. Eng. transl. in 4 COLLECTION, *supra*, note 51 at 53.

[56] For enumeration see Szer, *supra*, note 10 at 179, n. 1.

[57] 27 June 1950, [1950] 34 J. of L. Poland item 308, amended 3 June 1953, [1953] 31 *id.* item 124.

permanent dissolution of the marital community had occurred for an important reason. The 1950 legislation enunciated only broad principles. The courts had the task of elaboration, which they proceeded to perform by decisions in concrete cases and by two general directives. The code adopted in 1964 [58] combines several influences: Marxist principles as enunciated not only in the USSR but in the other Eastern European states, to which credit is given by the draftsmen; the need to meet pressing social or economic needs defying solution in dogmatic Marxist terms, particularly population growth; and Polish tradition, considered by the overwhelming majority of the population as natural and firmly established. [59]

Marxist principles, or what Soviet doctrinaire authors have developed as such, have been applied in the USSR to draw a sharp distinction between the civil and family codes on the ground that marriage is not a purchase of a bride. The Poles, although accepting this doctrine, have nevertheless felt it necessary to indicate that "close connections existing between family law and civil law [are] beyond dispute," [60] and the timing of both codes to become effective simultaneously was to illustrate this harmony.

The physical separation of the civil and family codes on doctrinal grounds has legal consequences. For example, although civil law contracts are unquestionably voidable if executed under the influence of error, fraud, or duress, the question of the influences of these elements in a marriage has been debated. The Soviet courts took the position at an early date that these features should be discovered at the time of registration, to prevent the marriage. A subsequent voiding of a marriage which violates the prohibitions must be shunned, since it would usually be harmful to the wife, who has been taken advantage of. At the time of this rule divorce was easy to obtain; so no wife was forced by an indissoluble marriage to remain with an intolerable spouse. By upholding the marriage, even when it violated the prohibitions, a Soviet court would be

[58] 25 Feb. 1964, [1964] 9 *id.* item 59.

[59] These are Dr. Rudzinski's conclusions in paper, *supra*, note 11.

[60] *Id.* citing Proekt kodeksu rodzinnego i opiekunczego 42 (Codification Commission under the Ministry of Justice, 1962). [Draft Code of the Family and Guardianship].

assuring a wife or widow protection of her property interests in alimony and inheritance.

When the Polish supreme court was presented with the question of voidability in 1952, in the absence of any provision on the subject in the 1950 code, it decided against it.[61] The Polish court was not alone, for the Hungarians did the same. In a draft in 1952 they gave the answer, developed earlier by the Soviet authors, that divorce was always available as a remedy, and they added, to soften the change, that duress could not be expected under socialist conditions.[62]

The 1964 Polish code does not list error, fraud, and duress as among the reasons for annulment, and so the legislator's wishes are now clear. Grounds not listed are expressly excluded.[63] Family law is distinct from civil law as regards these features.

On the matter of divorce the Polish legislature has tended to follow the Soviet lead. In the 1950 code no grounds were stated, and Article 29 read, "If a complete and permanent breakdown of marital community occurs between the spouses for important reasons, each of them may demand that the marriage be dissolved by a court through divorce." The 1964 code omits the words "for important reasons" with the explanation of the Codification Commission that it is because such words suggest the existence of some objective criterion for determining importance, and "any fixing of a hierarchy of reasons for the breakdown of community would, therefore, lead to unjust decisions, and, in particular, to the artificial preservation of some marriages for the sole reason that a complete and permanent breakdown of marital life was caused in such a case by circumstances which in general do not result in such a breakdown." [64]

In devising this explanation the commission seems to have overlooked the probability that determination of "important reasons" need not require a fixing of a permanent hierarchy of reasons, but could be left to flexible judicial application of

[61] *Id.* citing S. Szer, Prawo rodzinne 37 (1957) [Family Law].

[62] *Id.* citing G. Sverdlov, Semeinoe pravo evropeiskikh stran narodnoi demokratii 65–66 (1961) [Family Law of the European Countries of People's Democracy].

[63] Art. 17.

[64] Draft, *supra,* note 60 at 45–46.

criteria changed from case to case. Whatever the motives, the removal of the words "important reasons" in 1964 indicates the Marxist-oriented legislature's fear of stabilizing divorce law in Poland. The more flexible formula of violation of "principles of social intercourse," interpreted as elements of socialist morality, was substituted in the 1964 code as the one to be followed by a court in granting a divorce.[65] As such the Polish code conforms to the Soviet practice under the 1944 law, but there is a point on which it goes further, at least in language.

Whereas the Soviet law of 1944 permitted a court to refuse the divorce if it believed that the rules of community morality had not been violated and there was a chance that the marital community might be reestablished, the Polish code of 1964 authorizes application of the "principles of social intercourse" as a barrier to granting the divorce.[66] This provision incorporates court practice between 1952 and 1955, which forbade divorce even when there had been complete breakdown of the marital relationship if the granting of such a decree would violate the principles of social intercourse. The Drafting Commission's report illustrated its members' desire by an example: "A wife has been afflicted with an incurable disease after a marriage lasting for thirty years and after having raised several children. Divorce will be refused the husband as contrary to morality." [67]

A similar concept of the requirements of communist morality emerges from a Soviet decision.[68] A husband sued his wife of thirty years for divorce after she had borne him four children. There had been quarrels, and he had rushed to court, saying that his wife was groundlessly jealous of him and had presented complaints at his place of work, from which quarrels had ensued. Although the wife opposed the divorce, the provincial court had granted it, but she then appealed to the supreme court of the Russian republic. This court ordered a new trial, saying that the quarrels did not mean that there was such a chasm between a husband and wife of thirty years with four children that it was impossible to preserve the family. The provincial court was criticized for not having explored the

---

[65] Art. 56, par. 3.
[66] Art. 56, par. 2.
[67] Draft, *supra*, note 60 at 46.
[68] [1965] 1 Biull. Verkh. Suda R.S.F.S.R. 10.

depth of seriousness of the husband's reasons, and, indeed, for not having determined why the wife had not appeared at the hearing; it had contented itself only with the husband's explanation and the record of the people's court hearing. It had made no effort at conciliation.

Polish practice has also been plagued, as has Yugoslavian, with the problem of the petition filed by the guilty spouse. Although the Yugoslavs have not yet found a way out of what they call the "extinct" marriage, which they cannot yet bring themselves to terminate legally, the Poles have devised as a solution the test of what is acceptable as an element of social intercourse or socialist morality. Before 1964 they denied, as do the Yugoslavs, the right to divorce to the guilty claimant unless the innocent spouse consented or unless, in the event of long separation, the social interest would support termination in the exceptional case. The 1964 code has a new approach, for it is now suggested that in special circumstances the refusal of an innocent spouse to give consent may be contrary to the principles of social intercourse as an abuse of right, or a form of chicanery.[69] This seems to suggest that if an innocent spouse behaves in such a spiteful or vengeful way toward a guilty one that the marital community would be wrecked were it to exist or be resumed, then a divorce should be granted.

Polish attitudes toward a child born out of wedlock have remained what they are elsewhere in the Marxist-oriented states, except in the USSR under its 1944 statute. A father is designated by the mother when the birth is registered, and he has six months from the birth of the child to deny paternity. The 1964 code, in the interest of equality of the sexes, grants a wife the right to deny the paternity of her husband within six months of the child's birth if she wishes to claim that an outsider is the father. If a man subsequently wishes to claim parenthood of a child born out of wedlock, the consent of the child's legal representative is required by the 1964 code in all cases where the mother is dead or deprived of parental authority or cannot be reached to give consent.[70] Another new provision

[69] Art. 56, par. 3.
[70] Art. 77.

authorizes a child, when he comes of age, to sue within three years for annulment of recognition of paternity if the man claiming parenthood is not his father.[71]

The child has protection both ways, for under Article 144 of the 1964 code he may sue the husband of his mother for support, even though he is not recognized as the father, if such a demand is thought by the court to correspond with the principles of social intercourse; and the child may even sue the wife of his father for support if she is not his mother (because he was born of an extramarital union).

Polish draftsmen have also been influenced by pragmatic factors having no relationship to doctrine. The most noted provision inspired by social need is the raising of the marriage age for men from eighteen to twenty-one[72] and the introduction of a waiting period before marriage. Like the Chinese, the Poles have found that youthful marriages often end in divorce, and also that they contribute to the population explosion. In consequence they and the Chinese have taken similar measures to prevent them. In doing so both have defied the traditional Marxist anti-Malthus position favoring population growth.

Although some Soviet authors have written in favor of provisions delaying marriages to induce contemplation, no such waiting period was enacted before 1968, perhaps because the Soviet policy makers had no interest in restraining the growth of population. On the contrary, it was state policy to encourage childbirth through bonuses to mothers of large families and even medals for "Mother Heroines" who bore ten children. The traumatic loss of twenty-one million people during the war was a factor, and it may be that pressure for population growth is still created by the new fear that a comparatively empty Siberia may look attractive to a China overflowing with people.

Traditional Polish influences may be found in Polish departure from other Soviet models. The old Polish obligation of children to obey their parents[73] reappears in the 1964 code, an obligation which has no statutory parallel in the USSR. The Poles had dropped this rule from the 1950 code, although it had

[71] Art. 81.
[72] Art. 10.
[73] Art. 95, par. 2.

survived the first socialist legislative changes of 1946, together with a limited right of parents to spank a child as long as they caused no physical or moral harm.[74] Restoration of parental controls apparently came with difficulty after the 1950 elimination, for a draft in 1962 also omitted the requirement of obedience. Perhaps the return to convention was facilitated by growing distress over juvenile delinquency, which was blamed in part on lax parental discipline. To cope with the problem they returned to tradition. Unlike the Russians, the Poles had no statue to Pavel Morozov, a young boy who had defied parental authority to report to the police on his father's anti-state activity; so they could unabashedly revert to the old law.

Likewise, in 1964 the Poles were able to take another bold step in reestablishing the duty of a grown child to contribute to the family's budget when he lived in the common household.[75] In their 1950 code they had followed Soviet patterns, which required a child to aid his parents only when they actually needed his help, and thus they had made the duty of support dependent on the financial circumstances of the parents. But even with their revision, they were not wholly out of step with a newly evolving attitude among their neighbors to the east, as is indicated by a Soviet case of a son with a high salary, a house, and an automobile who gave no help to his aged mother.[76] She was not, evidently, without funds, and for this reason the court denied support, but at the same time it issued a "warning" to the young man. This warning was then discussed by his co-workers in the mine, and he was severely criticized, after which he began to give his mother aid. His refusal to help was considered a violation of communist morals, if not of the law.

Alimony for the wife has also undergone statutory revision in Poland. The 1950 code had granted it on divorce only if a spouse "is unable to support himself by his own labor." [77] The draftsmen of 1962 thought this unjust to the innocent divorced wife and sought to introduce a provision that an exclusively guilty spouse be required to support the innocent spouse at the

[74] 1946 Family Statute, art. 25.
[75] Art. 91.
[76] [1966] 2 Biull. Verkh. Suda R.S.F.S.R. 45.
[77] Art. 34.

same standard of living as before the divorce.[78] Although this proposal met with favor during the public discussion of the draft, it was not adopted in full, for the final text of the 1964 code provides only for the satisfaction of justified needs. But these are generously interpreted, for alimony is to be paid even when the innocent spouse is not in straitened circumstances if the divorce results in a substantial deterioration in his or her financial situation.[79]

On the matter of paternity, the 1964 Polish code adopts a presumption of paternity in the husband of any child born during a marriage, but the presumption may be overcome if the mother also had sexual intercourse during the presumptive period with another man and circumstances indicate that he is more probably the father.[80]

Finally, on the matter of divorce by mutual consent, which has been much debated in the Soviet Union and which was accepted by legislation in 1968 only for couples without children, the 1964 Polish code goes halfway. The court may omit a decision establishing the guilt of one or the other of the spouses if both desire.[81] This means that in law both are innocent, and the minister of justice explained that this avoids dragging out, to the embarrassment of both parties, undesirable and strictly personal matters, not essential to a decision in the case.[82] To a degree this opens the door to divorce by mutual consent, in contrast to official opposition to the concept in most of the other Marxian socialist states. It represents a concession to public opinion, for a Polish Radio poll in 1962 disclosed that 31.8 percent of those questioned wanted divorce by mutual consent before a registration bureau and without court intervention.[83] The same result may be obtained by a Polish and Czechoslovak procedural device. When the respondent accepts the plaintiff's demand for divorce, the court may restrict evidence

[78] Art. 56.
[79] Art. 60.
[80] Art. 85, par. 2.
[81] Art. 57, par. 2.
[82] Rudzinski, *supra*, note 11, citing Rybicki, *The Draft Family Code in the Sejm,* [1963] PANSTWO I PRAWO (Aug.–Sept.) 197 at 202.
[83] *Id.* citing Podgórecki, *Divorce Law in Public Opinion,* WYDAWNICTWO PRAWNICZE 68 (1964).

to the hearing of the parties alone, without supporting witnesses.[84]

The Chinese Communists and their collaborators the Albanians, like Yugoslavia, their most criticized colleague in the family of Marxian socialist legal systems, have adopted a rule supporting divorce by mutual consent.[85] Yet in spite of this, in practice the Chinese are proudly demonstrating to foreigners divorce proceedings in which the judge makes a serious effort to reconcile the parties and to preserve the home.[86] They appear to think it desirable to create a family in the Marxist image of love and monogamy.

The attention focused by the Chinese Communists on their family policy over the years testifies to its importance among them. It has ranked with land policy in being given first priority on achieving power. Like the land policy, the family reform movement was begun as soon as the Communists controlled territory over which they could exercise authority.[87] In the Juichin constitution of the "Chinese Soviet Republic," adopted by the First All-China Congress of Soviets on 7 November 1931,[88] there was a guarantee of emancipation of women, including recognition of the freedom of marriage. Statutes [89] enacted on 1 December 1931 as the Marriage Ordinance (*hun-yin t'iao-li*) and the Provisional Marriage Regulations adopted soon

[84] Art. 442 of Polish Code of Civil Procedure 1964 and art. 239 of Czechoslovak Code of Civil Procedure, 1950, act no. 142. The German Democratic Republic's Family Code of 20 December 1965 rejected a proposal to return to the guilty party concept because "to do so would be to revert to individualism even idealism in marriage law." See BULLETIN OF INTERNATIONAL COMMISSION OF JURISTS, no. 32 (Dec. 1967) at 12. Art. 24 provides for divorce on complete breakdown of the marriage.

[85] Yugoslav Marriage Law, art. 56, par. 2; Albanian Marriage Law of 18 May 1948, art. 56, par. 2; Chinese Marriage Law of 1 May 1950, art. 17.

[86] F. GREENE, AWAKENED CHINA (1961).

[87] I am indebted to Dr. Fu-shun Lin for the information on Chinese family law.

[88] Eng. transl. in BELA KUN, FUNDAMENTAL LAWS OF THE CHINESE PEOPLE'S REPUBLIC 17 (1934).

[89] Dr. Lin has been unable to find Chinese or English texts of these statutes although he finds the essential features to be well known. See also S. L. Fu, *The New Marriage Law of Communist China*, 1 CONTEMPORARY CHINA 115 (1955).

after by the Central Executive Committee of the Communist party abolished the sale of women as wives and forbade child marriage, establishing the rule that a man of twenty could marry a girl of eighteen by registration at a soviet bureau, provided he was free of dangerous disease and was not lineally descended from the same grandfather. Divorce was to be granted by the local soviets if either party to the marriage requested it. Children born out of wedlock were protected on the same terms as those who were legitimate.

The Communists' retreat to remote northwestern areas in the face of defeat terminated the effect of these laws, and compromise with the Nationalist government after the outbreak of the Sino-Japanese war in 1937 brought a change in policy. A new Marriage Regulation of the Chin-ch'a-chi Border Area, adopted 21 January 1943,[90] stated that the source was the book of family law of the civil code of the republic of China, adapted to conditions of the Border Regions. Even with this Nationalist law, the regulation presented a sharp contrast with Chinese family tradition. The Nationalist code had been progressive, even though it was not always put into practice. The head of the family was denied his privileged position of control over the family members, and the extended family was terminated with the provision that the family was no longer of legal or moral significance, but was essentially a unit of private residence consisting mainly of a husband and wife and their children—a household of only two generations. The Nationalist legislation had also recognized equality between the sexes; freedom of marriage; no unilaterally established concubinage on pain of prosecution for crime; no need of parental consent if the woman was over sixteen years of age and the man over eighteen; divorce by mutual consent, but otherwise only if one of ten grounds is met and the action is brought by the innocent spouse.

With achievement of power, the Communists, in a 1950[91] law, revived the principles of the 1931 Marriage Ordinance. The code implemented a provision of the 1949 Common Pro-

[90] Eng. transl. in M. VAN DER VALK, CONSERVATISM IN MODERN CHINESE FAMILY LAW 68 (1956).

[91] 1 May 1950. Eng. transl. in A. BLAUSTEIN, FUNDAMENTAL LEGAL DOCUMENTS OF COMMUNIST CHINA 266 (1962).

gram adopted by the Chinese People's Political Consultative Conference, declaring the end of the feudal system; abolishing female bondage, and creating in its place equality in all fields.

Soviet models were admittedly used in drafting the new legislation; the chairman of the law compilation committee stated that not only had the theories of Marx, Engels, Lenin, Stalin, and Mao Tse-tung been studied, but the latest editions of the codes of Eastern Europe and Korea had been translated. This meant that the Chinese had before them Stalin's 1944 retreat from permissiveness.

By Article 1 the purpose of the marriage law was established as abolition of the feudal marriage system, based on the superiority of man over woman, and introduction of a new system based on free choice of partners, monogamy, equal rights for both sexes, and protection of the lawful interests of women and children. Article 2 prohibited bigamy, concubinage, child betrothal, interference with the remarriage of widows, and exacting money or gifts in connection with marriage. No doubt was left as to the kind of family desired. It was to be no more promiscuous than Lenin's ideal, for Article 8 read: "Husband and wife are in duty bound to love, respect, assist, and look after each other, to live in harmony, to engage in production, to care for the children and to strive jointly for the welfare of the family and for the building up of a new society."

Having established the goal, the code left its realization primarily to the parties, but not without stimulation to proper thinking by the propagandists. In short, it adopted the early Soviet attitude that the state should refrain from entering the relationship through law except to establish certain principles. Thus, the code set a minimum age, prohibited marriage between relatives within the fifth degree of kinship, and established the requirement of registration to enforce the prohibition. Equality of husband and wife is established with regard to the property of the family and to inheritance from each other. Children born out of wedlock are treated equally with legitimates, and since nothing is said of acknowledgment by fathers, it seems unnecessary.

Divorce may be granted without limitation, whether on mutual consent or on the request of either. No grounds need be stated, although many are implied. As in the USSR, reconciliation must be attempted before the decree is granted. In China this reconciliation is the duty in the first instance of the local government, and if this fails, of the people's court; but neither can do more than conciliate to reunite the couple. They are specifically forbidden to use compulsion, although constant reference to communist morals during the reconciliation attempt is known to make reconciliation far more compelling in China than in the West, or even in the USSR.

Although the code seems to be without restraint on the parties seeking a divorce, policy has been enunciated which makes the situation much like that in the USSR. The chairman of the drafting commission demands that the court render its verdict on the basis of the concrete situation, and he envisages that the court will consider whether reasons given are legitimate and indicate that the marital relations cannot be maintained. He declares that a court will reject the demand for divorce if there is no legitimate reason, but he gives no specific examples. When one remembers that a Chinese people's court gives no "important decision" without consulting the Communist party group of which the judges are a part, the conclusion is obvious that the Communist party will apply Mao's moral code, discussed in chapter 1, whose second point requires that acts of citizens be beneficial to socialist transformation. In short the Chinese, like their Soviet and Polish counterparts, are applying a standard called somewhat loosely communist morals. What precision can be discerned comes from Communist party pressures on society and a residue of traditional moral values making for restraint in breaking up the home.

Reports indicate that divorce was granted lightly at the outset, perhaps in reaction to the traditional strictness of the past, with the result that much promiscuity occurred; but since the early days the cords have been tightened progressively upon the family. The 1950 code established an important limitation on freedom of divorce to favor members of the revolutionary army.[92] It permitted no spouse to obtain a divorce from an army member unless he consented or failed to correspond for two

[92] Art. 19.

years. Since the concept of membership in the army was broad at the time, covering many government officials and party cadres, the prohibition was far reaching.

Property relationships between husband and wife have been manipulated in all Marxist states in an effort to achieve equality of the sexes. As has been indicated, in 1918 the Soviet leaders decided that protection of the wife in an urban family could be assured most easily if she enjoyed control over her own property. Separation of goods was expected to give her complete control over what she earned and to contribute to her liberation from male domination, if it could be enforced. The expectation proved false, and the rule was abandoned. In 1926 the concept of community property, or more accurately community of acquests, was chosen as appropriate to conditions which already reflected change in the woman's status. Under this decision the 1926 code declared that property gained during the marriage was to be held in common, and that owned by each individual before marriage was to remain his separate property.[93] Should the parties desire some other arrangement, they were to be permitted to institute it in a marriage contract so long as it did not disparage the rights of the wife.[94]

Practice of Soviet courts has developed a set of rules to protect each spouse. What is inherited or received by gift from outside the family during the marriage does not enter into the community but remains the property of the recipient.[95] A Yugoslav explains that the family community is a toiling community, so that only property acquired by toil is jointly owned.[96]

Although the principle is clear that toil alone creates a community interest, courts have had to intervene to settle disputes over the issue. Thus, a share in a gold watch and a bolt of cloth presented to a husband by his state employer when he completed twenty-five years on the job was denied to a wife

---

[93] Art. 10. For a survey of tsarist law and that of early Soviet Russia, see Johnson, *Matrimonial Property in the Soviet Union*, 16 INT'L & COMP. L. Q. 1106 (1967).

[94] Art. 13.

[95] But see Johnson, *supra*, note 93 at 1115 for a case in 1962 dividing lottery winnings.

[96] Blagojević, *Les régimes matrimoniaux* in LE DROIT ET LA PROPRIÉTÉ DANS LES PAYS DE L'EST 99 at 102 (R. Dekkers ed. 1964).

who claimed half on separation.[97] Had they constituted remuneration, both spouses would have shared their ownership, for they would have related to toil in a direct way.[98] To protect the wife who does not work outside the home but keeps it in order for her husband, the housework is considered contributory in the same degree as the husband's salaried job; for without her devotion to the home, he could not gain his income.[99]

To be treated separately from the community, however, gifts must come from outside the family. If a husband presents a wife with jewels on her birthday, they do not become her separate property. A court has found that it is only a display of the family's wealth, even though for the sole use of the wife.[100] The same is true of all items of "luxury" used by a single spouse but obtained with common funds. Decisions have been issued on a piano,[101] a shotgun,[102] and other such specialized items. A different rule has been enunciated, however, for items which are not considered to be luxuries, but necessary to the life of one spouse. In such a case, the item is automatically placed in the permanent possession of the one needing it, in the event of separation of the property on divorce or division of the estate on inheritance. Thus, the devices used by a blind husband to tell time and to write were his and his alone, regardless of the source of the funds used to purchase them.[103] This prevents their inclusion in the community for possible sale and division of the proceeds, which would produce less than was necessary for their replacement, assuming that replacements could be found.

[97] Case cited in SVERDLOV, *supra*, note 42 at 116. The author presented the details during the Stalin period in his *Matrimonial Property Law in the U.S.S.R.* in W. FRIEDMANN ed., MATRIMONIAL PROPERTY LAW 210 (1955).

[98] The result may be different if the gift is purchased from the wage fund. See Johnson, *supra*, note 93 at 1114.

[99] SVERDLOV, *supra*, note 42 at 111.

[100] Case no. 33,512, [1922] 23 Sud. Prak. Verkh. Suda R.S.F.S.R. 8. Johnson, *supra*, note 93 at 1115 concludes contrariwise that a husband's gift constitutes renunciation of his rights as co-owner.

[101] Case no. 33,512 *id.*

[102] Case no. 118 of Feb. 1940, cited by Reikhel, *Communal Property Relations of Spouses in Soviet Law*, [1940] 8–9 Sov. GOS. I PRAVO 109.

[103] Case no. 31,103, [1930] 9 Sud. Prak. Verkh. Suda R.S.F.S.R. 11.

The concept of community has an influence on inheritance, for its application prevents half the property from passing by inheritance on the death of one of the spouses. This means that one-half of the community is the property of the surviving spouse by virtue of his or her direct interest in it, and the inheritance law applies only to the other half, in which the surviving spouse will also have an interest, under the law of intestacy, or perhaps under a will.

An example will illustrate the complexity of the situation.[104] A case arose when a state notary refused to issue a widow a certificate of heirship to half of a house, but insisted that she take ownership by inheritance of the whole house. She resisted, arguing that she owned half of the house in her own right as her share of the community property, and she inherited only half by virtue of the provisions of his will. It made a difference in that if she received the entire house by inheritance she would have had to pay a notarial filing fee on the value of the whole house, whereas if she took only half, the fee would amount to only half of what the notary wished to charge.

The complexity of the case resulted from a dispute over the date of marriage. If the house had been obtained by the husband before marriage, he had owned it all, and inheritance by the widow would have been of the whole house. If he had obtained the house during the marriage by purchase with communal funds, the house would have been in the community and the widow would inherit only half. All agreed that the house had been acquired in 1922, and that the registration of the marriage had occurred in 1953. On the face of it, the widow had no case. The matter was taken to court, which established that the registration in 1953 had been dated back to 22 July 1920, when the spouses had entered into a factual marriage relationship, and had continued during the period after 1926 when such marriages were accepted as legal.

The court noted that under the 1944 amendment to the family code, persons who had entered into a marriage relationship before publication of the law might register under the decree indicating the length of cohabitation as man and wife. The parties had done this, and the record at the registration

<hr />

[104] [1966] 5 Sov. IUST. 32.

office bore the notation. The court concluded, "Under the circumstances there is no basis for refusal to issue a certificate on the right of ownership. Receipt of a certificate of the right to inheritance to the entire house under the circumstances is undesirable for Citizeness R, because she would have to pay a large sum as state tax, and this would also fall on property which belongs to her under the law, although under the documents it is attributed to the other spouse."

The court made no effort to clarify the legal result of a marriage in 1922 when registration was necessary to validity. Recognition of registered cohabitation as legal marriage became permissible only in 1926, which was four years after the date of acquisition of the house. The court seems to have interpreted the provisions of the 1944 amendment as permitting relation back to any date of factual cohabitation, even when it was antecedent to the date when unregistered marriage had first become of legal consequence.

Polish courts have likewise had difficulty determining what property is to be placed within the marital community. Although they function under a community property concept similar to that established by the Soviet code of 1926, their code of 1950 made no specific provision for salaries and wages received during matrimony. Unlike the Soviet courts, which decided that wages enter into the community regardless of their origin, the Polish courts held that they did not.[105] The 1964 Polish code has changed this to place wages and earnings of both spouses within the community,[106] although it exempts salaries and wages due but not yet received at the moment of determination, whether it be divorce or death. This provision was introduced into the draft at the last minute to prevent possible garnishment of the other spouse by creditors.

In review of what has been done in the Marxian socialist countries in the realm of marriage, it becomes clear that the law conforms generally to that of Romanist states in the West. The hard core of modern European law, whether in West or East, is to be found in the fact that marriage has been made secular, and that it must be monogamous. In both regions the parties

[105] Rudzinski, *supra*, note 11, citing Draft Law at 44.
[106] Art. 32, par. 2, sec. 1.

must choose freely to enter it, they must at all times be equal, and divorce is permitted, although with wide variation in grounds and procedures. These variations in both systems run the same gamut of possibilities; from legal and moral restraint to acceptance of no more than expression of mutual consent. Even those states in Eastern Europe which permit divorce by mutual consent offer nothing more libertarian than what is provided in a Romanist system like that of Mexico. The revolutionary days are gone when Soviet citizens could separate and be considered legally divorced without benefit even of civil registration.

Although the Eastern European and Oriental Marxist states provide in statutory law no enumeration of grounds for divorce, all establish grounds under a moral law and seek to conciliate and even to prohibit light-minded decisions to seek divorce, especially when there have been children. Some Marxist-oriented courts are now considerably more strict in the application of morals than are those Western courts which demand nothing more than a claim of incompatibility.

A search for a common and unique core to Marxian socialist law on the family cannot limit itself to an examination of what is currently law and practice of courts. It must review philosophers' statements of what the socialist family is to become. The nonagenarian Soviet philosopher Stanislas Gustavovich Strumilin wrote in 1961 that the home as presently constituted will wither away with the achievement of complete communism.[107] He and others hailed a program, established after the war and enlarged during the 1960s, to create rural boarding schools in which children might be placed by parents who wished to experiment or who found themselves too busy with state assignments to give full-time attention to the child's care. At the outset these schools were heralded as the wave of the future, when parents would be liberated of all family burdens and the state would assure the rearing of children with proper appreciation of the rigorous requirements of a system of communist morals. The Chinese "Great Leap Forward" in 1958 looked like a move to implement the same idea. Experiments in communal

[107] Strumilin, *Family and Community in the Society of the Future*, 2 THE SOVIET REVIEW, no. 2 at 3 (1961) transl. from [1960] 7 NOVY MIR 203.

living not only placed the children in day-care centers but gave night care as well.

The expectations of the Soviet and Chinese extremists have not been met. Reports indicate that Soviet boarding schools have cost unexpectedly high sums for what they have achieved.[108] The education offered by teachers has varied. Some have felt that the quality of instruction presented by teachers withdrawn from the intellectual stimulation of the urban environment has often lagged behind that of the city day schools. The students have too often come from broken homes rather than from a cross-section of society, and so the schools have taken on some of the character of colonies for the rehabilitation of delinquents or those on the verge of delinquency. This has not been without reward for the neglected child; one author notes that the schools have saved "literally thousands of children from the influence of bad companions and from the spiritual resentment very often connected with family troubles." Still, no one wants to make these schools corrective institutions to which children are sent by parents who have abandoned attempts to enforce discipline in a modern world of growing temptation and in a society offering abundance to sons and daughters of successful officials.

The boarding schools may also have been called upon to fill a void created by the 1944 law which released the father of a child born out of wedlock from all responsibility for his maintenance and upbringing. This situation has created some unexpected attitudes in Soviet society. For example, a mother is quoted in conversation with a boarding school principal as expressing hostility when her third child was denied admission after the other two were accepted, telling the principal that she had more right than others because she was an unwed mother and planned to have a baby every year to be placed in the school. In short, the schools are accused of having helped parents shirk their responsibility, thus increasing the number of unfortunate children rather than reducing them. Perhaps experiences such as this led the chief of a provincial department of education to remark on the relationship between school and home. He defined the different roles by saying: "While in

[108] Iziumskii, Just Like Home, Pravda 13 Nov. 1966 at 3. Eng. transl. in 18 C.D.S.P. no. 46 at 31 (1966).

questions of the quality of our children's knowledge the school plays the principal role, in questions of the development of the pupils' personalities all but the full weight of the burden falls on the family, and its role will steadily increase." [109]

Yet when there is no family to which the schoolchild can turn, the authors take a different attitude. A report of the All-Union Institute for Study and Prevention of Crime in 1966 noted the criticism of the boarding schools and the desire of many to transform them into extended day schools, and declared the criticism unsound.[110] The reason for the schools, in the institute's view, lay in what they were doing for children from broken homes, or from those with too many children for parents to provide care. The author of the report declares, "The extended day schools, for all their importance and promise, cannot replace the boarding schools where most of the youngsters without normal family conditions are now to be found." He provides data from sample investigations, showing that 40 percent of the boarding school pupils are children from incomplete families, either because of divorce or because the mother is unmarried, and 46 percent are from large families. To the reporter this is proof that any attempt to economize on costs of the boarding schools by abolishing or transforming them will lead only to juvenile delinquency and higher social costs.

The Chinese likewise have abandoned their short-lived communal experiments, but not for the same reasons. Resistance was met among those who wanted to maintain the home and disliked the barracks type of life. In consequence, the communes altered this feature of their organization.[111]

If communal living experiments and boarding schools were to replace the home and family completely, there would, of course, develop a radical contrast between the reforms of family law being developed in the West and the changes emerging in the Marxian socialist countries; for no one in the West contem-

[109] Zuyev, Not for a Whim, Pravda, 22 Jan. 1967 at 3. Eng. transl. in 19 C.D.S.P. no. 3 at 30 (1967).

[110] Minkovsky, *Some Causes of Juvenile Delinquency in the U.S.S.R. and Measures to Prevent It*, [1966] 5 Sov. Gos. i pravo, 84. Eng. transl. in 18 C.D.S.P. no. 30 at 9, 10 (1966).

[111] F. Schurmann, Ideology and Organization in Communist China 471 (1966).

plates the end of the family unit. Although much has been written on the subject among Marxists, the practice has gone toward strengthening the home. Only the Soviet and Chinese philosophers have indicated a desire to move toward communal care of children. The other Marxist-oriented societies seem content with what they have. Even in the USSR the boarding schools are becoming no more than what they are elsewhere— an aid to parents who for one reason or another find themselves unable to provide the home desired, or who wish to create a sense of independence in the child at an early age or to obtain tuition from teachers whom they expect to be more skilled than those available in their own community.

The Soviet boarding schools are not the wave of the future but a supplement to the present, in which the Marxian socialist family is the central institution of the culture pattern in circumstances designed to last for a long time. The conclusion is inescapable that communal living is not now, and is not likely to become an element of the core of Marxian socialist law.

13

Contract Law for

Nonmarket Economies

A MONG MARXIAN SOCIALIST STATES IN EASTERN EUROPE, Czechoslovakia alone has attempted to introduce new forms into the law of contracts. All the others have been content to continue with Romanist principles inherited from their pasts, making whatever changes seem desirable in the interest of justice to the worker or peasant caught in an unequal bargain and in the interest of economic planning.

The New Economic Policy introduced by Lenin in 1921 to revive a devastated economy may have proved reason for adhering to tradition. A neocapitalism centered on free sales in the marketplace was the heart of the new policy, and the first civil code of the Russian republic was drafted to give sellers and buyers confidence that their agreements would be respected in law. Flexibility was to be applied in the event that capitalists exercised the rights established in the code to the disadvantage of society. This feature, enshrined in the notorious Article 1, to which much of chapter 4 of this volume was devoted, was to provide a means of judicial escape from inequities which might result from strict application of the code. But aside from this instrument of proletarian justice there was not much in the first codes of each of the republics which emerged on the ruins of the Russian empire to attract the attention of comparative lawyers.

The New Economic Policy ran its course and passed from the scene under tax laws and criminal statutes, but its influence may still weigh heavily on the draftsmen in the Marxian socialist countries. Some Soviet jurists of the early 1920s thought that Soviet law had been permanently blighted by the market economy it was called upon to serve. Their hope was that it would soon wither away entirely as socialism replaced capitalism, and in its stead would emerge a new form of "administration of things." This analysis provided a happy rationalization for maintaining tradition, but not for all Bolsheviks. N. V. Krylenko, one of the architects of the New Economic Policy's legal system, was not prepared to make such a concession. He argued that those who saw the New Economic Policy as the font of Soviet law failed to understand what had happened in 1917. They interpreted the denial of bourgeois law as the denial of the utility of law in general. He declared that such people "had lost completely their balance wheel." In his view, "N.E.P. provided only the atmosphere, facilitating, it is true, and hastening the exposure of this inescapable phase of development of our court work, but it never did more than that. It never foreordained the content of our work." [1]

Be that as it may (and the analyst must admit at the outset that the question of whether civil law is new or merely refurbished tradition in the Marxian socialist legal systems depends in considerable measure upon the observer's philosophical approach to the impact of a legal system's aim upon its structure), the civil code first enacted in the Russian republic in 1922 served as a model for the other republics. Its imprint is visible even today upon the second round of codes, enacted after Stalin's death to implement a policy of increased reliance upon property incentives to encourage productive effort.

[1] N. Krylenko, Sudoustroistvo RSFSR (Lektsii po teorii i istorii sudoustroistva), lecture no. 12 at 159–60 (1923). [Court Structure of the R.S.F.S.R. (Lectures on the Theory and History of Court Structure)].

For most of the Marxian socialist states that emerged in Eastern Europe after the war, the denunciation of old codes and enactment of new ones seemed unnecessary in the light of Soviet experience; so they contented themselves with supplemental statutes introducing principles comparable to Article 1 of the Russian republic's code of 1922. Not until the late 1950s did new civil codes begin to emerge, and when they did, most of the chapters on obligations provided little that was new, except for some detail. Only Czechoslovakia was an exception, attempting to find a new basis compatible with socialist concepts and couched in quite new terminology.[2]

The major impact upon Marxian socialist contract law comes from nationalization of the means of production. The law of contracts has had to be drafted to fit two different situations: those arising when individuals deal in consumer goods, either between themselves or with a state agency, and those arising when both parties to a contractual agreement are state agencies. Whether both types of agreement belong within the category of what Romanists call the "civil" law, or whether they should comprise two categories, the latter a form of administrative law to be called "economic law," has been a burning issue in socialist legal circles since the 1920s. It has already been indicated that after Stalin's death a large school of thought opposed linking the two types of relationship on the ground that those in which individuals participated required stable law for their regulation, whereas those between state agencies required regulation by a more flexible law, expressed as broad principles without detail and applied by a special tribunal free to use its specialized knowledge and judicial imagination to resolve disputes.

The dispute between the specialists was resolved, as was indicated in chapter 4, by intervention of Khrushchev's colleague Alexei N. Kosygin, who was to become in 1964 chairman of the Council of Ministers of the USSR. He accepted the argument of those who saw in contractual relationships from producer to ultimate consumer a continuum to which civil law alone should be applied. In consequence the Fundamental Principles of Civil Law, adopted in the USSR in 1961 as a basis

[2] 26 Feb. 1964. [1964] J. of L. Czechoslovakia, act no. 40. Eng. transl. [1964] Bulletin of Czechoslovak Law, no. 1–2 at 43.

for enactment of the codes of the various republics, incorporate provisions relating to all types of contractual obligations, regardless of the nature of the parties.[3] Even state enterprises are governed by the code, being subjected to provisions which some Soviet jurists have thought so incongruous as to create a "rather complex draft . . . that cannot be satisfactory either to economic administrators or to citizens."[4] Jurists of other states among the Marxian socialist family of legal systems in Eastern Europe have followed this lead, except those in Czechoslovakia and, less so, in the German Democratic Republic, whose jurists see reason to separate civil and economic law.[5] In Eastern Asia there is a different approach. The Chinese people's republic has no civil code at all, but governs its economic enterprises by a series of special decrees, while it controls relations between citizens in application of "general principles" not yet enacted in a formal manner, which show a marked influence of Chinese tradition.

Contractual relations between citizens are today limited in the USSR to the exchange of consumer goods, for money or by barter. Several relations have already been illustrated—sales of dwellings, used automobiles and motorcycles, handicrafts made by artisans working alone, or food raised by peasant households on their garden plots, and payments in kind made to collective farmers by their farm administration. In no case may such sales become systematic, except for the artisans producing under license and the farmers authorized by general statute to sell

[3] 8 Dec. 1961, [1961] 50 Ved. Verkh. Sov. S.S.S.R. item 525. Eng. transl. SOVIET CIVIL LEGISLATION AND PROCEDURE. OFFICIAL TEXTS AND COMMENTARIES (n.d., circa 1962).

[4] Tadevosian, Comments on the Draft Fundamental Principles of Civil Law, [1960] 8 SOTS. ZAK. 47.

[5] The German Democratic Republic has at no time had a separate economic "code," but it early enacted a separate "statute" which its jurists treated as a law apart from the traditional German civil code which continued in force. Later, under pressure from Soviet jurists, East German thinking was reformed, but there remain specialists who would prefer to consider the law of state enterprise a separate category of law. Hungarian jurists debated the issue when revising law to provide for greater enterprise autonomy in 1967. They decided to amend the civil code rather than to draft an economic code. See Harmathy, The Reform of Economic Management and the New Regulation of Contracts in Hungary, ACTA JURIDICA ACADEMIAE HUNGARIAE, 10 at 215 (1968).

surplus upon the open market. A systematic private business invites prosecution for speculation, as does leasing surplus dwelling space at rates exceeding those established by law. Likewise, in no case may a contract be made to employ labor to produce goods for sale, for that would violate the Constitution's prohibition against "exploitation" of man by man. Only in those of the People's Democracies which still permit some small-scale capitalist enterprise, notably Poland, Hungary, Romania, Yugoslavia, and most recently Czechoslovakia, can contracts concern relationships of this kind.

Once the limits on contracts between citizens are understood, the legal provisions governing the narrow segment of economic life left to them become meaningful. In Marxist eyes they are novel because of the subjects treated, not because of their form. That which is not "exploitative" of man bears no relation to that which incorporates what Marxists identify as the basic characteristic of capitalism.

The first rule of contracts is for the Marxists what it is for jurists of all legal systems: voluntary agreement of the parties; [6] but after statement of this worldwide fundamental, attention must focus on a Romanist principle. Agreement need not be accompanied by what the Anglo-American common law identifies as "consideration" to make the agreement binding in law. It is enough that there be an agreement, as long as its manifestation is sufficiently clear to permit identification of its terms and hence its enforcement in the event of subsequent dispute. To facilitate proof, the 1922 code provided that an agreement must be in writing if it exceeded in value 500 old rubles.[7] This rule remains in the new 1964 code, with a doubling of the minimum to the equivalent of $110.[8] Oral testimony will be accepted in evidence for the small-value agreement. Leases must be in writing for a term exceeding one year.[9] For agreements relating to the sale of a dwelling, more than writing is required; the

[6] Civil Code R.S.F.S.R., 1922, art. 130, and Civil Code R.S.F.S.R., 1964, art. 160. Eng. transl. of the former in 2. V. Gsovski, Soviet Civil Law (1949) and of the latter in Civil Code of the Russian Soviet Federated Socialist Republic: An English Translation (W. Gray & R. Stults Transl. 1965).

[7] Art. 136.

[8] Art. 44, par. 2.

[9] Art. 276.

contract must also be notarized and registered at the land office of the local soviet.[10] This not only facilitates proof but brings into play the notary's function as policeman. He is instructed to deny notarization to any agreement that is in violation of the law.

A contract not requiring notarization need not be a single document. In keeping with modern practice throughout the world, the post-Stalin codes accept as meeting the requirement of writing an agreement manifested by an exchange of letters or telegrams, or acceptance of an order for performance.

The law of "offer" and "acceptance" that provides the pillars of all legal systems [11] concerning contracts conforms to the German rule. Thus an offeror is bound to hold open his offer for the time normally required to respond, if a specific time has not been indicated in the offer.[12] He has none of the advantage given by the Anglo-American common law, by which an offeror may revoke his offer until the offeree has placed his acceptance in a mailbox.

Since no involuntary agreement will be enforced against an individual, duress, and fraud vitiate a transaction as they do in any legal system; but to these widely accepted rules the Soviet code of 1922 added an additional provision which read: "When a person is induced by dire necessity to enter into a transaction which is to his obvious disadvantage, a court may at the request of the injured party or the appropriate state agencies or public organizations hold the transaction invalid or terminate it." [13]

A decision of a court following the end of World War II will illustrate application of this Article 33. The court that returned with the Soviet troops to Kiev, which had been occupied by the Germans under conditions of great privation, was asked by the daughter of a deceased couple to set aside a contract of sale of a dwelling to which she would have fallen heir had it not been sold. Her evidence proved that it had been

[10] Art. 239.
[11] For an exhaustive survey of the general principles of offer and acceptance throughout the world, see R. SCHLESINGER ed., FORMATION OF CONTRACTS: A STUDY OF THE COMMON CORE OF LEGAL SYSTEMS. 2 vols. (1968).
[12] Art. 163.
[13] Art. 33.

sold by her parents during a period of near-starvation for a small amount of food. The court determined that this contract had violated the provisions of Article 33 and set it aside.[14]

Although the provision sounds like an example of the impact of Marxian socialist principles, it is no more than an extension to Soviet law of the French rule of *lésion* (injury). It has not even survived in modern Soviet law, for its applicability to contemporary Soviet conditions was brought into question during the drafting of the post-Stalin codes. After discussion, it was excluded from the new codes as without contemporary pertinence. It was looked upon as a relic of the period of the New Economic Policy when the wily bourgeoisie was to be expected to act unjustly against the weak and infirm. Under Soviet conditions of the 1960s, achievement of relative abundance and inculcation of socialist morals make its preservation an anachronism in Soviet eyes.

Simple as the rules may appear, they have given rise to problems of interpretation in given situations. A court was asked to decide whether a contract had been brought into existence when three members of a family made what they believed to be a binding agreement with a state enterprise to construct a dwelling for their own use.[15] Under its terms, the three were obliged to contribute their labor, and the enterprise was to provide materials and sign over the house to them on completion. Before completion the enterprise made a second agreement with another workman on the same terms. One of the first group sued to set aside the second agreement as violating the first, but the trial court refused her suit on the ground that there was no contract. The appellate court elaborated the decision in affirming it, by saying that the agreement did not become binding until the plaintiff had "performed" the obligation to build, taking the view that "performance" could not be established until arrival of the date set for completion of the house. After reviewing the record, the civil college of the Russian republic's supreme court concluded that such a decision was erroneous. Members of the plaintiff's family had worked a total of 490 hours in construction of the dwelling at the time the enterprise made the second contract, and had thus per-

[14] Vitkevich v. Dziuba, [1948] 4 Sud. Prak. Verkh. Suda S.S.S.R. 9.
[15] Gus'kova v. Red Banner Plant, [1960] 11 Sov. IUST. 27, case 3.

formed 69.5 percent of the work-time stipulated in their contract.

The problem of revision of a contract came to a court on a charge that in selling a dwelling the seller had knowingly concealed structural defects. The buyer sought either an annulment of the contract with return of the purchase price or a reduction of the price by 10,000 rubles. The trial court refused to annul the contract, finding that the buyer had occupied the house for two months before purchase and had learned of all of the defects; but it gave judgment in the amount of 7,831 rubles, which it found to be the cost of repairing the floor, fireplace, window frames, and wall beams. The supreme court of the Russian republic reduced the judgment to 2,046 rubles, the cost of replacing only the beams.[16] For the rest, it noted that since the plaintiff had lived in the dwelling for two months before concluding the contract, he had received notice of all visible defects and must be presumed to have accepted them. The beams, however, had been concealed by wall paneling, and normal inspection would not have revealed their condition. Thus the contract stood, subject to this judicial revision.

Litigation has also arisen over contracts of gift. Since there is no doctrine requiring "consideration" in Marxian socialist law, such contracts have validity when agreement is reached to give and to accept. The code provides only some detail to avoid dispute, declaring that the contract is concluded at the time of the transfer of the property, but that it must be in special form if its value exceeds 100 rubles.[17] Contracts for between 100 and 500 rubles must be in writing, and those for over 500 rubles must be notarially certified.[18] Also, a gift of a dwelling must be registered at the local soviet as well as notarized. When some other special form is stipulated, the contract is concluded when that form has been complied with.

[16] Zavitov v. Lakhminov, [1960] 14 *id.* 26, case 2.

[17] Arts. 256–57.

[18] If notarization is required but not obtained, the contract is void and the object is returned to the donor. If notarization is not required but only a writing, the contract is valid even though oral, but the terms of the agreement may not be proved by oral testimony in the event of dispute. See commentary to art. 257 in E. FLEISHITS, NAUCHNO-PRAKTICHESKII KOMMENTARII K G.K. RSFSR 298 (1966). [Scientific-Practical Commentary to the Civil Code of the R.S.F.S.R.].

A donee brought suit in 1959 for a piano which he claimed his aunt had given him by contract of gift before her death, but which was sold by her daughter-in-law within three days after the aunt's death. The daughter-in-law defended, saying that the contract had been executed under fraudulent inducement by the plaintiff's father, and that the decedent had declared before her death that she wanted to leave her property to the daughter-in-law's children and had asked the plaintiff to return the contract. In evidence of her claim the daughter-in-law argued that the change of mind was the reason the piano had not been delivered to the plaintiff.

The trial court upheld the contract and ordered return of the piano to the donee and return of the purchase price to the purchaser by the daughter-in-law. The daughter-in-law and purchaser appealed, arguing that under the code the property must pass during the life of the donor, and that since that had not happened the contract should be held invalid. The Russian republic's supreme court dismissed the appeal, finding that the contract was in proper form, had been notarized, and was executed voluntarily as proved by the testimony of the senior notary certifying the document. The court also noted that five witnesses had testified that the deceased had said that she had given the piano to the plaintiff. There was no evidence of fraud or that the donor had tried to revoke the contract. Thus ownership had passed from the moment of notarization. As to the rights of the purchaser, the court concluded that he was not bona fide, for he had testified that he knew at the time of purchase that the daughter-in-law was not the owner.[19]

In a subsequent case in 1965 the Russian republic's court rejected an alleged contract of gift because it concluded that it was false.[20] The parties had tried to formalize a deal by which a woman would exchange her room in a building owned by a factory for ownership of a room in a privately owned dwelling. For some reason not stated in the opinion they wished to make the deal appear to be a gift of the private room. When the notary refused to certify the contract as a gift, court action was brought to compel certification. The Russian republic's supreme court upheld the notary, saying that the transfer was not

[19] Filatov v. Denisova, [1959] 9 Sov. IUST. 86.
[20] Romashchenko v. Notary, [1965] 3 Biull. Verkh. Suda R.S.F.S.R. 15.

a gift, since there was to be remuneration and gifts must be without remuneration.

False contracts of gift to cheat the law have been numerous with used automobiles. After enactment of the law requiring sales of used vehicles through state commission shops, owners sought to evade it by making contracts of gift, which were required in order to obtain a registration card from the Motor Vehicle Bureau, and then collecting money from the donee. In spite of the notary's duty to scrutinize such deals when a contract is presented for certification, the deals slipped by.[21]

Because the notary plays an important part in certifying the legality of contracts, a test was made of whether his certification could be attacked. The widow of one of two men who built a house sued for a share in the dwelling as heir. The co-builder argued that her husband had no property right in the house because a contract of gift had been executed to the co-builder by the man in whose name the plot on which the house stood had been registered at the local soviet. The contract of gift had been certified by a notary, and in that lay the co-builder's argument that it could not be attacked. Nevertheless, the widow argued that it was an invalid contract because the registered owner of the dwelling was not in fact the owner, but the recipient from the local soviet of the right to use the plot of land for construction of a house—a right which he had retained although he had never built the house. The construction had been performed by the co-builders.

The court concluded that notarial certification did not save a contract which was made by a man falsely claiming to be an owner. Consequently, in the light of other evidence, the property right was in both co-builders, and the widow of one builder had her usual widow's rights by inheritance.[22]

The thrust of contract law in most Romanist countries is toward specific performance of contracts,[23] and the Soviet system falls within the pattern. Damages are no substitute if

---

[21] Zile, *Law and the Distribution of Consumer Goods in the Soviet Union* in W. LAFAVE ed., LAW IN THE SOVIET SOCIETY 212 at 228 (1965). More recently owners have sought to disguise illegal sales by executing to the benefit of the buyer a power of attorney to use. See Pravda, 24 Jan. 1968 at 3.

[22] Filatova v. Ierokhina, [1961] 5 SOTS. ZAK. 89, case 2.

[23] Szladits, *The Concept of Specific Performance in Civil Law*, 4 AM. J. COMP. L. 208 (1955).

performance is possible. To induce an obligor to perform, the Russian republic's code, in keeping with Continental codes generally, provides that contracts may include clauses establishing the penalties for each day or other specified period of delay, and payment of such penalties has no relationship to damages which may be ordered subsequently.[24] Penalties are over and above damages, designed to enforce specific performance. Also, when a contract calls for transfer of a specific thing, the obligee may require transfer of the item to him if delivery is not made by the obligor. This right may be defeated only if the item has already been transferred to a third person who has a right of the same nature or if another person with a contractual right which antedates that of the plaintiff appears while the thing is still in the possession of the obligor.[25]

Specific performance is more difficult to enforce, however, if the obligation was to perform a particular task. All legal systems recognize this fact, and the Soviet system adopts the familiar rule of damages.[26] The obligee may either perform the task at the expense of the obligor or may demand compensation for damages he has suffered because of nonperformance. But even such payment does not free the obligor from performance in proper form if it has already commenced. In an article inserted in the general section of the code on contracts, but having importance primarily because of its relationship to performance on contracts executed in implementation of the national economic plan, the obligor is required to make specific performance unless the planned task implemented by the contract is no longer in effect.[27]

With the emphasis upon specific performance, rather than upon substitution of damages for specific performance, the Soviet legal system, since its 1922 code,[28] has adopted the rule that absence of fault will excuse an obligor.[29] Although this rule

[24] Art. 187.

[25] Art. 217.

[26] Art. 218.

[27] Art. 221. This rule is, however, limited to performance already begun. See FLEISHITS, *supra*, note 18 at 259.

[28] R.S.F.S.R. Code, art. 118.

[29] R.S.F.S.R. Code, 1964, art. 222. For a comparison of Soviet and English attitudes on fault, see Johnson, *No Liability without Fault—the Soviet View*, 20 CURRENT LEGAL PROBLEMS (London) 165 at 171 (1967).

in its unqualified form sounds unfair to an obligee, at least to ears familiar with the Anglo-American common law, which has traditionally held an obligor to damages regardless of fault and which has found it difficult, consequently, to develop a doctrine excusing performance even in the event of frustration of contract, it is a common rule of the Romanist legal systems. But the rule is not like that of the criminal code, for there is no presumption of innocence. On the contrary, the Soviet codes place the burden of proof on the obligor to prove absence of fault to avoid his responsibility.[30] In short, there is a presumption of fault in any breach, which the obligor must rebut to escape liability. Fault may be either intentional failure or negligent failure to perform. Soviet commentators indicate that intention is rarely present in failure cases, and if it is, there is usually reason to bring a criminal prosecution. The one exception to criminal prosecution for intentional refusal to perform is when an organization refuses to accept delivery of goods consigned to it under a contract, in which case the issue of civil fault is the only one present.

The rule releasing the faultless from liability sounds more extreme than it is, for qualifications have been introduced. Thus, an organization cannot escape liability for breach by proving absence of fault in the employee directly concerned with performance if other employees linked with the act, although not directly, were at fault. The organization must be considered as a unit. Although this would seem obvious to Western lawyers, it took a court decision to establish it in the USSR. In this case the chance of escaping liability through proof of absence of fault probably looked so attractive that the organization was induced to argue what seems an untenable position. The case was a suit against a railroad for damages on breach of a transportation contract when the goods arrived in a spoiled condition. The railroad argued that the spoilage resulted from a concealed defect in the cover of the manufacturer's container, and that since the railroad's shipping agent could not have discovered the defect, it was not at fault and not liable. In the trial it was proved, however, that the railroad had a statutory duty to examine all containers received for shipment and

[30] R.S.F.S.R. Code, *id.*

to make repairs needed to prevent damage. In consequence it was held responsible for the damages because some of its employees before the shipping clerk in the chain of shipment had failed to perform a duty.[31]

Liability cannot be escaped by absence of fault when an obligor fails to perform because one of his subcontractors has violated an obligation to him. In these cases the fault of the subcontractors has been imputed to the principal contractor in the practice of the state arbitration tribunals.[32] The same principle is applied to hold a manufacturer liable if his suppliers of raw materials fail him, even though he did his best to perform. The justification given for this rule is that in a highly complex industrial society, few items are produced solely by the obligor, and to deny the obligee a remedy in contract would be to leave him with no recourse in the event of breach. Thus, to establish absence of fault an obligor must prove not only his own innocence but that of his suppliers as well.

In some circumstances the law provides for strict liability, ruling out all opportunity to prove absence of fault. These are circumstances specified in the law on supply of goods by one state agency to another, as set forth in the statutes on the subject.[33]

Social interests pervade contract law as they do other branches of Soviet law, and it is to these that eyes turn to determine whether unfamiliar principles have been introduced into the Marxian socialist legal systems. The codes declare invalid two types of contracts: those that violate specific prohibitions of the law and those "concluded for a purpose deliberately contrary to the interests of the socialist state and society." [34] The first is, of course, relatively easy to identify, but the second raises questions of defending public policy, rooted in what is called socialist morality.

Under the first category a court struck down a contract which it found to be a concealed sale of a plot of land. A party who had received an assignment of perpetual use of a plot of land made a contract under which he transferred to another

---

[31] FLEISHITS, *supra*, note 18 at 259, n. 2.
[32] *Id.* at 262, par. 1.
[33] *Id.* at 262, par. 3.
[34] R.S.F.S.R. Code, 1964, arts. 48, 49.

party a segment of the land, and received in payment a part of the dwelling constructed upon the land by the transferee. The supreme court of the Russian republic concluded that the contract was in substance a sale of the land, and hence illegal.[35]

The penalty for innocent violation of the law is to return to each party that which has passed under the contract, or if that is impossible, to return its value in money; but if the act was concluded deliberately by both parties in violation of law, all that has been received or was to have been received by both parties is forfeited to the state.[36] If the illegal intent was that of only one party, the innocent party obtains the return of whatever he has delivered, but the guilty party's receipts or what is owing to him pass to the state. In a sense the law establishes a penalty of a fine in money or in kind.

Because of the possibility of absolution as an innocent party to an illegal deal, a woman accused of selling part of a plot of land assigned to her for use in constructing a dwelling resisted suit brought by the state for what she had received as purchase money.[37] She defended on the ground that she had not been criminally convicted of intent to violate the law. In review of the record, the Russian republic's supreme court found that the woman, as assignee of the building plot, had originally given her consent to formal transfer of a part of it to another, and the transfer had been registered. Everything looked legal, as of that moment; but years later, for no reason given in the opinion, the husband and wife who had received the allocation of the segment cut out of the original plot went to the prosecutor to complain that they had paid the original assignee 11,750 rubles to induce consent to the assignment. Proof established that payment had occurred in the circumstances claimed, but the prosecutor had refused to bring criminal prosecution against the original assignee because of the running out of the statute of limitations on the crime.

The case entered the courts when the prosecutor sued under the code of civil procedure to recover for the state the 11,750 rubles as unjust enrichment under an illegal contract to sell

---

[35] Ostanin and Lavrov, [1962] 10 Biull. Verkh. Suda R.S.F.S.R. at 10.
[36] R.S.F.S.R. Code, 1964, art. 49.
[37] Kirov Ward v. Melnikova, [1961] 4 Sov. IUST. 29, case 4.

land. The trial court gave judgment for the state, and the supreme court affirmed the decision in spite of the original assignee's defense that since she had not been prosecuted, she had not been shown to have intended to violate the law. In the supreme court's view, absence of a criminal prosecution brought to establish guilt was no reason to refuse to enforce the civil obligation to deliver to the state what had passed under an illegal contract.

Other illegal contracts have been found by courts in the review of attempts to lease collective farm land to individual peasants for their personal use, and also to pay collective farm members not in the established form of "labor days" representing a share in the year's net income of the farm, but in a percentage of the cash obtained by the farmer-salesman for the sale on the local market of produce belonging to the farm.[38] Such contracts were interpreted as "commission contracts" with middlemen, which are in violation of law.

The second category of illegal contracts, "concluded for a purpose deliberately contrary to the socialist state and society," rather than contrary to a specific prohibition of the law, present greater difficulty in identification. These introduce an element of undefined public policy into contract law. All legal systems have some such rule involving public policy. In Romanist systems, and in the Anglo-American common law, courts will not enforce transactions which shock the moral order upon which society is based even though there is no specific violation of statute. Some have said that the English and French traditions on this, although in agreement on the unenforceability of contracts in violation of public policy, differ in their base: French law is in a university tradition aiming at a rationalized and logically consistent body of law, and English law is in a professional tradition, more concerned with practical remedies and litigating procedures than with attempts to systematize the law in accordance with any formal scheme.[39] The practical result is that French judges apply a conception of public policy susceptible of philosophic justification. It pervades all law and is conceived to be a systematic body of doctrine, whereas the applica-

[38] FLEISHITS, *supra*, note 18 at 58.
[39] D. LLOYD, PUBLIC POLICY. A COMPARATIVE STUDY IN ENGLISH AND FRENCH LAW 147–49 (1953).

tion in English law is rare and haphazard; for English analysts believe that refusal to enforce a contract for public policy reasons is to some extent in conflict with the law rather than in integral union with it.

Since Soviet law is in step with the Romanist systems on many issues, the analyst would expect Soviet judges to take the French view, more so since Marxist philosophy permeates the entire legal system, and any philosophically based principle would presumably have to be in accord rather than in conflict with the specifically defined principles of the code. Still, the refusal to enforce contracts which violate moral principles has had no support in Soviet texts or commentaries unless there was clear intention to evade the law.

Although the principle of Article 1 of the 1922 civil code has been retained as Article 5 in the post-Stalin civil codes, its application is not encouraged. Its presence seems to be more obeisance to revolutionary tradition than a currently favored provision, and the same may be said of Article 49.[40] In the post-Stalin era the effort of Soviet jurists is to create a stable system of law in which parties may know in advance what prohibitions exist. Consequently, the public policy provision may be interpreted as applicable only in circumstances of last resort, should the unusual case appear in which a contract of dangerous implications cannot otherwise be voided. Until a practice is publicly reported, the outside analyst will be unable to find in this provision reflection of social conditions which are not well defined elsewhere.

Soviet draftsmen of contract law have conformed again to Romanist practice in setting forth in the code a series of chapters devoted to specific types of contracts. Unlike the Anglo-American common law, which looks upon contract law as providing a minimum number of generalized rules within which parties may reach agreement as they wish on a wide variety of subjects, the Romanist systems generally prefer to place after the code's general provisions some chapters with very specific principles governing each type of contract. This technique requires repeated restatement of many of the basic

[40] See a critical analysis of contemporary judicial practice as representing "unnecessary" reference to art. 5. FLEISHITS, *supra*, note 18 at 7, n. 1.

provisions, but it has validity in Romanist eyes because it makes it possible to specify without fear of confusion mandatory provisions for each type of contract, in contrast with those that may be included as the parties desire. The practice takes on special importance in the Soviet code because of the decision to include within it not only the law relating to contracts between individuals but also that relating to contracts between state enterprises. Although doctrine has required the draftsmen to include both types of contract within a single code, to manifest the unity of civil law, practical considerations require independent treatment of certain aspects of each type of contract.

This "diversity within unity" is achieved by including within the code separate chapters for each type of contract. Thus, a chapter on sales specifies what an individual may do if goods delivered are not up to quality,[41] and in a separate chapter on the "delivery" contract, a second article repeats some of the same material, such as the requirement that a claim must be filed within six months, but adds the provision, pertinent only in the latter case, that the goods delivered must correspond to state standards, technical specifications, and samples.[42] Likewise another chapter concerns contracts by an individual contractor to perform a service,[43] and a separate chapter covers the same work when performed by a state organization.[44] The chapter for the private individual restates the rule of the constitution that the contractor may employ no labor to help him.[45] The second, of course, contains no such limitation.

To a degree the socialist organization of the economy provides added incentive to separate into compartments the rules relating to each type of contract, because they incorporate elements of important difference when the parties are both citizens and when they are both state enterprises, but the principle of compartmentalization is Romanist, not socialist. The novelty is the use made of it in a socialist system. Further difference emerges from contrast in emphasis. The law of obligations in contract is restrictive in the socialist system of the

---

[41] R.S.F.S.R. Code, 1964, art. 245.
[42] *Id.*, art. 261.
[43] Ch. 30.
[44] Ch. 31.
[45] Art. 351.

USSR; that is, the parties are permitted to make only those agreements that are specified, in the manner specified,[46] whereas in a capitalist system the parties are left generally free to make whatever agreements they wish, subject only to a relatively few limitations established by the legislature in the interest of socially approved order.

The law of the USSR establishes no special category for contracts between citizens and state organizations, although they have become of great importance. Khrushchev's introduction of a policy of selling on credit through state stores, and of renting consumer goods to citizens, rather than selling them, to maximize efficient use of items in limited supply, greatly increased the number of contracts of a continuing nature. The familiar "over-the-counter" feature of the average contract between a state enterprise and a citizen, which gave rise to little more than consumers' claims for defective quality, was replaced in importance by the contract in which the state agency has a continuing interest as claimant. In consequence, in order to standardize practice, form contracts have been prescribed and published widely to implement the law and to bring forcefully to citizens' attention the rights and obligations of both parties under such agreements. No one need read the code, although the code contains, of course, chapters covering such agreements as well as some other popular ones such as "carriage" and "insurance."

In spite of the growing concern for agreements between state agencies and citizens, Soviet jurists have not attempted to innovate. Each type of contract is merely placed in its niche in the code, within the traditional book of the law of "obligations." There is no effort to create separate categories unrelated to tradition, although it is appreciated that there are distinctive features when a state enterprise is a party. One of these is that such a party has no choice but to make the sale or perform the service if the citizen qualifies.

When the other Eastern European socialist states developed their civil codes, they followed the Soviet model, which was

---

[46] Polish law, however, retains the traditional elements of freedom of contract, except in violation of law and morality. Thus, assignments, though omitted from the 1964 civil code, are considered valid.

generally in accord with their own traditional Romanist experience, and it was some years before a bold new approach took hold. Czechoslovak Communists provided the surprise when they introduced their new civil code to the world in 1964. Readers found that they had suppressed the traditional Romanist book of "obligations" and had created new terminology for some types of contracts—some being between state enterprises and citizens, and others between citizens alone. There were three new categories: "services," "civic aid," and "personal use." [47]

The "services" are those relationships by which state enterprises satisfy the material and cultural needs of citizens. They include, consequently, sales in shops; the "lending of things," which would under conventional terminology have been called "rentals"; the making of things to order; repairs; agency by a state enterprise; the provision of accommodations; the provision of transport; legal assistance by an organization of advocates; financial services, including the maintenance of bank accounts and the granting of loans; and insurance. In the debates preceding adoption, objection was made to abandonment of the traditional system of contracts for these services, but this was overcome with arguments that Roman law concepts did not meet the situations, as they are under socialist conditions.[48] Since these situations had come to be called "services" in practice it was decided to call them such in law.

The feature of "services" deemed characteristic and requiring specific statement in law was the guarantee of quality as it relates to the performance of all services, and of each service separately. The enterprise is made liable for the quality specified, and this liability cannot be contractually excluded or limited. The individual may demand removal of defects in service or cancel the contract, or he may demand completion if this is possible. In the event of defect, the individual may also

[47] I am indebted to Rudzinski, *New Communist Civil Codes of Czechoslovakia and Poland: A General Appraisal*, 41 IND. L. J. 33 (1965), from which much has been taken at this point. See also Wagner, *The Law of Contracts in Communist Countries (Russia, Bulgaria, Czechoslovakia and Hungary)*, 7 ST. LOUIS U.L.J. 292 (1963).

[48] Kratochvil, *New Czechoslovak Civil Legislation*, [1964] BULLETIN OF CZECHOSLOVAK LAW, no. 1/2 at 1, 13.

demand an appropriate price reduction. Details are provided on the term during which defects must be brought to the supplier's notice.

Although the legal institution is called a "service," it is also a "contract," but avowedly of a new sort. Article 224 reads, "Services shall be provided on a contractual basis or on the basis of other facts stipulated in legal regulations." The contract is not created on a voluntary basis, for "If the duties of an organization include the provision of a service, the organization shall have the duty to provide it at the request of an individual unless it is precluded by the scope of its operational possibilities." It is probably because of this compulsory feature that Romanist-trained jurists have had trouble with the inclusion of service contracts under the familiar rubric of contract, which in its original form requires that an agreement be voluntarily entered into to be enforceable.

The ancient rule of the common law placing on innkeepers the duty to receive all orderly guests, and the more recently adopted regulations requiring public utilities, even when privately owned, to provide service to all who qualify, have not upset the common-law mind. This is because of the Anglo-American rejection of legal conceptualism in favor of an approach favoring a step-by-step molding of the law to meet each social need as it is perceived, whatever it may be. Yet to the Continental, there has been a conceptual problem, and the new Czechoslovak code is an attempt to meet it by creating the new category. In addition the method provides a convenience to the citizen. In seeking a service he has a succinct, self-contained handbook of his rights in the given situation. He needs no lawyer to thumb through various parts of the code and interpretations to learn his rights. They are briefly stated in one place, ready to be framed and placed on the wall of the office to which he must apply. In this sense they meet one of the constant demands of socialists: that the law be simplified so the common man can use it to his advantage.

This aim is not unique with the Czechoslovaks, but coincides with that of the other Marxian socialists, who adopt no new language in their codes but continue to use familiar terms. The difference is one of draftsmanship. Take for example "transportation." This is relatively simple to define and provides a basis for quick comparison of legal principles. The Russian republic's code defines a "contract for carriage" by saying:

> By means of a contract for the carriage of a passenger, a carrier undertakes to carry a passenger to his destination, and, in the event baggage is given to it by the passenger, to bring such baggage to its destination and to deliver it to the person authorized to receive it; the passenger undertakes to pay the established fare for the passage, and, if baggage is given to the carrier, to pay for the transportation of such baggage.[49]

For the Czechoslovak draftsmen, the same thought is put into more verbose phrasing:

> The individual who uses a means of transport for the stipulated fare shall have the right to demand that the transport organization or another organization authorized to do so [the carrier] transport him to the place of destination properly and on time. The carrier shall be obliged to attend, during the transport, in particular to the safety and comfort of the passengers and in the case of mass transport to make it possible for them to use social and cultural facilities. If the passenger has luggage, the carrier shall transport it together with the passenger and under his surveillance or separately. If the luggage is transported separately, the carrier shall be obliged to attend to its delivery to the place of destination not later than at the same time as the passenger.[50]

In both codes provisions for liability, and for the transport of goods are set forth in subsequent articles.

"Civic aid" is a second novel category. Here is a set of obligations which the citizen must undertake "in keeping with the rules of socialist conduct." The concept is defined as "work carried out by one individual for another individual at the latter's request, a loan granted by one individual to another and other forms of help." [51] The distinguishing feature of the category is its emphasis upon the good-neighbor concept. Work is performed or a loan granted not to make a profit or to gain interest but to help a citizen in need. The good Samaritan is

[49] Art. 374.
[50] Arts. 307–9.
[51] Art. 384.

expected to perform with no more than reimbursement of his expenses, although provision is made that if agreement is reached on payment of interest within the statutory limitations of usury, it will be enforced.[52]

The owner of things lent is likewise protected by maintenance of the good-neighbor standard. Thus, if the item lent is designated generically, it must be returned in the same quantity and quality.[53] An agreement requiring return in greater quantity or other material benefits is invalid. If the item is designated specifically, it must be returned when requested, but without compensation for wear and tear unless it has been so agreed.[54] In any event, whether the item is designated specifically or generically, return must be on demand unless a fixed period was agreed upon. If the term was indefinite but indicated only in terms of a loan to meet a specific purpose, return cannot be asked for until the purpose could have been achieved by a good husbandman.

As a third category of special relationships established to replace contracts, the Czechoslovak code treats the subject of "Personal Use of Flats, Other Rooms and Land." The purpose is to provide in one place the rules to be applied in the allocation of land use and living space in state-owned dwellings. The Soviet code treats the use of land apart from the civil code, since it is state owned and its use allocated in perpetuity without charge.[55] Personal use is governed by provisions of the Land Code of 1922, which is currently in process of revision. The new code will not become a part of the civil code for doctrinal reasons, since it is devoid of all commercial implications.

Since the Czechoslovak draftsmen have already departed from the commercial implications which some Marxists see in a civil code, they have had no difficulty including the law relating to allocation of personal use of land in the civil code itself, although their decision to include the matter may have been facilitated because the use is established for pay. Even under former conceptions, this element would have justified inclusion

[52] Art. 387.
[53] Art. 388.
[54] Art. 389.
[55] See discussion, *supra*, ch. 7.

of the matter in a civil code governing relationships established for pay. Yet, apart from this payment feature, the principles of allocation of state-owned land are similar to those existing under the Soviet land codes: it is in perpetuity; it is limited in area; it is limited in use to the purpose for which it is assigned; it may not be contractually transferred; it is protected against trespass; it may be withdrawn only in the event of an important interest of society under conditions requiring payment; and it may be passed on by inheritance.[56]

Although the location of land-use law in various Marxist systems invites comparison because of contrasting theories, there is less to be said in examining the law of lease of dwelling space. Both the Soviet and Czechoslovak codes place the law in a specialized chapter of the civil code. The only difference is that the Soviet code includes in the same chapter leases by private individuals to other individuals and also those executed by housing authorities to cover apartments in buildings which belong to the local Soviets or Soviet enterprises where a tenant is employed, whereas the Czechoslovak code divides leases into two categories: those in public buildings and those in privately owned buildings.[57] The first is classified as a "service" and placed with other services provided by state agencies, whereas the second is a contract of nearly traditional Romanist form—a contract under which the right to occupy space for a term is transferred. As such it is placed in a catchall category including the other types of contract continued in traditional form without novelty[58] For this group there is no new conceptual treatment. Still, the contrast lacks practical reality because the lease of privately owned apartments is made subject "*mutatis mutandis*" to the same rules as those governing the provision of living quarters in public buildings.

There is good theoretical reason to place the right of occupancy of state-owned dwellings administered by a local soviet or Czechoslovak "people's committee" in a category apart from contract. The law of all the Marxist-oriented states derives from Soviet experience, begun in the 1920s and carried to the present

[56] Arts. 198–204.

[57] R.S.F.S.R. Civil Code, 1964, Ch. 27; Czechoslovak Civil Code, 1964, part III, Chs. 1–3.

[58] Part V, art. 390 and part VIII, art. 493.

day. The Soviet civil code of 1922 omitted consideration of type of occupancy, because it had not been formulated in law by 1922. The concept was developed subsequently through a series of statutes, housing regulations, and court decisions.[59] In these provisions a right was created in every citizen resident in Soviet administered, state-owned premises in the year 1924 to continue to occupy the space he held at that time. Marriages and births created rights to occupy the space in the persons brought into the family. In theory, health norms were applied to prevent overcrowding, but in fact the shortage of housing was so severe that families added to their numbers with no regard to crowding in the living quarters.

Under the regulations, the administrators were required to execute leases with the occupants, but in practice, since the right to occupy was established on the basis of status as occupant in 1924, or as an addition to the family subsequently, no written lease was executed in the great majority of cases. The law determined the rights and obligations of both the administration and the occupant, and there was nothing novel to be placed in the lease. Consequently, the right of occupancy came to be appreciated for what it was, a right acquired not by contract or lease but by status.

The right was so firmly recognized that when it became necessary to repair or demolish a building, the occupants could claim from the local soviet's housing department equivalent quarters elsewhere. When a divorce occurred, the divorced spouse had a recognized right to remain on the premises as a member of the family, even if a subsequent marriage introduced still another person. Few domestic relationships were not recognized as conferring the right of occupancy, a notable exception being that of guardian and ward. Neither gained the right to occupy premises with the other on establishment of the relationship.

The right could not be sold to another, but it could be exchanged, and state services were established to bring together occupants who might wish to exchange premises of different

[59] The historical development has been set forth in my SOVIET HOUSING LAW (1939). For an updating, see Rudden, *Soviet Housing and the New Civil Code*, 15 INT'L & COMP. L.Q. 231 (1966).

types or in different cities. Premises could be sublet only for brief periods of absence when the law provided that they would be reserved for the occupant's return. This was rare, occurring largely in circumstances of departure for military service, work in remote regions of the country, or service abroad. On death the premises passed to use of the other members of the family.

Rent had to be paid to the local soviet, but it was based not solely on the quality of the premises but also on the wages of the occupant. Thus the rent paid for premises would vary as the occupants varied or changed their wages. In reality, the rent was far less than the cost of maintenance, and at one early time in Soviet history, when the abolition of money was believed to be close at hand, there was no rent at all. Housing was provided as a public service. With the coming of the New Economic Policy in 1922 rent was reintroduced, but at a rate so low that the state had to subsidize maintenance. Even with the enactment of the 1964 code in the Russian republic, this concept of housing as a public service that ought to be provided free of charge remains, for Article 303 reads, "Until the introduction of free housing, a lessee is required to pay rent at the proper time."

Although by Stalin's death Soviet housing law had become a special branch of law, protected by the courts, in which housing and domestic relations became the two most litigated subjects, the draftsmen of the post-Stalin civil law decided to include it in the civil code. In consequence, it appears in the 1964 Russian republic's code woven into the chapter on "lease of property," where its provisions follow those on leasing by private owners of dwellings and by state enterprises which provide space in what is called "occupational housing" as a part of the perquisites of employment. Its unique character is evident, however, for the features developed over the years have been retained, especially the right of members of a family to occupy in perpetuity space allocated to a citizen, even if he was single at the time, subject to such transfers as may be necessary because of repairs or demolition. The code provides for the execution of a lease, for a term limited to five years, but the occupant has a right of renewal which may be contested only in a court, in the event that the lessee systematically fails to perform his obligations under the contract.[60] In effect, the lease creates or terminates no right. Putting the requirement in the code has done nothing but improve the likelihood that occupants will be informed of their position in law.

It is this evolution of housing law from a law of contract to a law of service that has sparked the imagination of the Czechoslovak draftsmen. Unlike the Soviet draftsmen, they have been unwilling to weave it into one fabric with leases of premises by private owners, which in their view retain their traditional form as contracts. Although they separate the two, the result is the same as that in the USSR because of the cross-reference in the code already described. This is evident from the Czechoslovak code's provisions. The provision of housing in publicly owned dwellings is a state service, and space is allocated to individuals for use without limitation of time.[61] Marriage creates a right to share premises with the spouse,[62] and on divorce the court must decide the housing right in the general settlement of the property.[63] On death the surviving spouse and heirs succeed to the space.[64] Should an occupant have to leave because of repairs or demolition, other quarters must be provided.[65] Rent must be paid.[66]

An occupant's right to occupy may be terminated only if he has abused it, and after warning, continues to violate grossly "the principles of socialist conduct"; if he fails to pay rent for over three months; if he has two apartments, leaves the space vacant without serious reasons, or uses it only occasionally; or if the space allotted becomes excessive under the local regulations.[67] Apartments may be exchanged,[68] but there is no provision in the code, as there is in the USSR, for sublease. As in the USSR, the lease is no more than evidence of a right allocated by the state organization administering the premises.[69] It is cer-

---

[60] Civil Code R.S.F.S.R., 1964, art. 238.
[61] Art. 153.
[62] Art. 175.
[63] Art. 177.
[64] Art. 179.
[65] Art. 186.
[66] Art. 168.
[67] Art. 184–85.
[68] Art. 188.
[69] Art. 190.

tainly not a contract in the traditional Romanist sense of conferring a right of tenancy.

At the end of the "parts" devoted to services, civic aid, and personal use of land and living space, the Czechoslovaks have placed what may be considered the traditional matters of obligations in contract in a Romanist type of system: sales, exchanges, donations, the leasing by an owner of apartments in a privately owned dwelling, the leasing of real property for temporary use, and attending to the affairs of others.[70] The heritage of the past is immediately evident when the words of Article 399 are read: "A contract of sale shall establish the seller's obligation to deliver the goods to the buyer and the buyer's obligation to take delivery of the goods and pay the agreed price to the seller." What socialist ring there is to the rule is in a second paragraph establishing price control to avoid speculation; but this has become a rule of many economies in times of scarcity, whatever their philosophical foundation. If novelty is to be found, it must lie in the reason for price control. Here temporary concern over the unsettling influence on currency values of a black market probably is secondary to the lasting determination of socialists to abolish what they consider to be unearned income gained from merchandising.

Although it is of the same vintage, the Polish civil code of 1964 [71] takes none of the steps favored by the Czechoslovaks to reflect the spirit of socialism. The Poles have generally followed the Soviet model, although they include fewer subjects. For drafting reasons they omit some of the subjects included by the Soviet lawyers in their new codes, namely, patent, copyright, and mortgages. They also omit the subjects of bills of exchange and checks which are traditionally included in Romanist systems, but so do the Soviet draftsmen, preferring to treat them in separate statutes. In keeping with tradition, the book on obligations in the Polish code is the largest, partly because it includes both the law of public enterprise and private contractual relations. This is because the Poles have accepted the Soviet position on the unity of civil law, as has already been indicated. But, because of this concept of unity, the Poles have shared with the Soviets the complexities of draftsmanship

[70] Part V, ch. 2.

[71] [1964] 16 J. of L. Poland item 93. See also Rudzinski, *supra*, note 47.

caused when two rather different types of relationship have to be treated in the same book. It is this that the Czechoslovaks have avoided, to the envy of some Soviet jurists, who cannot conceal their displeasure that the debate on the subject in the USSR went against them under Kosygin's arbitration.

Since the Chinese Communists have rejected the concept of codification of civil law, their law of contract has reverted to traditional Chinese practice modified by experience with the commercial law of the Republican period. Specialists note that traditional practice was built around mediation, and that disputes rarely reached the courts.[72] Mao has reiterated this approach with his 1957 admonition that disputes among the people be resolved, whenever possible, by "democratic methods, methods of discussion, of criticism, of persuasion and education, not by coercive, oppressive methods." [73] In consequence, it is the "people's mediation committee" in each community which usually resolves a dispute, utilizing residual concepts of what makes for a bargain and contemporary ideas of social order to guide them in bringing the parties to agreement.

Before Mao emphasized mediation, there had been some attempt to develop a law of contracts in the Western image, as modified by experience in the USSR.[74] This was revealed in a manual published at the very moment when the stable approach to law was rejected, apparently containing the lectures given during the preceding years by academicians prone to idealize the Soviet model.[75] If this manual has evidential value, which several Western specialists doubt because of the separation of Soviet-oriented academicians from the practice of the marketplace, Chinese law under communist influence was being constructed on a Romanist base.

In the teaching manual contracts are defined as voluntary

[72] Cohen, *Chinese Mediation on the Eve of Modernization*, 54 CALIF. L. REV. 1201 (1966) and Lubman, *Mao and Mediation: Politics and Dispute Resolution in Communist China*, 55 *id.* 1284 (1967).

[73] Cited by Cohen, *id.* at 1201 from Mao Tse-tung *On the Correct Handling of Disputes among the People*, 27 Feb. 1957.

[74] Pfeffer, *The Institution of Contracts in the Chinese People's Republic*, [1963] CHINA QUARTERLY, no. 14 at 153 and no. 15 at 115.

[75] BASIC PROBLEMS IN THE CIVIL LAW OF THE PEOPLE'S REPUBLIC OF CHINA (Institute of Civil Law, Central Political-Judicial Cadres School ed.) Eng. transl. in JPRS no. 4,879 (15 Aug. 1961).

agreements which are fair and reasonable in accordance with legal regulations. At the time, perhaps a bit more emphasis was placed on conforming to legal principles introduced in the interests of society than on the consensual feature. The manual criticized those who overemphasized the consensual feature as being "bourgeois rightists," inserting the "poisonous element of the bourgeois principle of 'autonomy of private law.'"

Like the Soviets, but perhaps with more emphasis, the Chinese sought and probably still seek to avoid illegality before a contract is concluded rather than undertaking litigation after its execution. Some have thought that the traditional Chinese desire to avoid courtroom litigation was influential in the emphasis placed upon state notaries as hurdles to illegality during the period of Soviet orientation; but the notaries were primarily instruments of control over private enterprisers in the early 1950s, and since that time they have passed from the reports.

Specific performance was a major aim in enforcing contracts, as it is in Romanist systems generally, for the manual notes that the people's court will normally compel a debtor to perform his obligation, although damages may be substituted in some cases—if the specific item which is the subject of the contract has been lost or destroyed; if performance is already without significance owing to the default of the obligor; and in circumstances specifically established by law. The payment of penalties was held to be no more a substitution for performance than it was in the USSR, for in both legal systems penalties were meant to stimulate performance and not to replace it.

Fault was given about the same importance in determining liability as in Soviet law, for an obligor was not to be absolved of liability unless his nonperformance resulted from a natural disaster, a military order, or a change in the economic plan. Damages, when payable, included not only actual injury but loss of benefits "which would otherwise be obtained under normal circumstances." Although this might sound like recognition of a right to recover expected profits, it may not have been so, for the example given in support of the proposition was that of an enterprise unable to perform because of delivery of under-quality petroleum products. It was authorized to recover only the purchase price and wages and expenses paid during the period of inactivity.

A notable feature of the manual was lack of interest in the relationship of contracts between private citizens and those executed by public entities in performance of the plan. No mention was made of the heated discussion in the European Marxist-oriented states about the theoretical desirability of maintaining a unified system of civil law covering both types of contracts, in contrast to the practical utility of separation. Although "consensualism" was stated as a major principle of contract law, not a word was written that raised the question of what should be done with this concept, when, under economic planning, it is excluded by the obligation forced upon the parties to contract in implementation of the plan.

Conceptualism seems to have had less interest for the Chinese legal scholars than for the communist Europeans who looked back upon a long tradition of legal scholarship and theorizing, inherited from their nineteenth-century forebears. In this difference may be found a reflection of what the Chinese legal historian John C. H. Wu finds in Chinese history —that the legal philosopher was never revered; in fact, the law was looked upon as outside the Confucian ethic and therefore was not a sphere in which philosophers of first rank wished to exercise their minds.[76]

Be that as it may, the Chinese Communists found it unnecessary to draw a sharp distinction in their teaching manual between contractual obligations assumed by private citizens and those assumed by state enterprises organized as public corporations. For them, there seems to have been no need to compose a separate chapter for each type of relationship, perhaps because contracts between private citizens were fading from the scene. For Europeans, however, there is such a question, and it carries over to the Vietnamese and Koreans, perhaps because colonial powers dominated their legal evolution more thoroughly than the imperialist powers dominated that of China. There is no escaping the fact that for European Communists contracts executed in implementation of the plan present distinctive theoretical problems. For many of them these problems have not yet been resolved.

[76] Wu, *Traditional Concepts of the Rule of Law in China and Problems Involved in the Reception of Foreign Law*, 9 ANNALES DE LA FACULTÉ DE DROIT D'ISTANBUL, no. 14 at 14 (1960).

Since the issues have been hard fought within the family of Marxian socialist legal systems, and provide more novelty than has been evident in the law of contracts between individual citizens or between a citizen and a state service enterprise, they will be treated in a separate chapter.

I4

A Law for State Planning

ALTHOUGH ECONOMIC PLANNING IS HERALDED AS MARXIAN socialists' gift to the world, it has no branch of law of its own. The norms under which the planners operate are scattered through parts of several branches: administrative, civil, labor, collective farm, and criminal. For the Czechoslovaks there is yet another category to replace civil law, namely, "economic law." To grasp the qualities of this multifaceted set of legal principles, on which a claim of uniqueness for the Marxian socialist legal system may well rest, requires analysis of a good many seemingly independent subjects which find their common denominator in the necessities of organizing a planned economy.

The 1957 declaration of the Communist parties in power has but a few words establishing the common core of the family of Marxian socialist legal systems on this score. It calls for "planned development of the national economy aimed at building socialism and communism, at raising the standards of the working people." How this shall be done is left to each Communist party. Variety has emerged, but some elements are common to the approach of all. First of these is the need to create a property base on which to plan, and second is the need to create a specialized novel apparatus to prepare and implement the plan. Marxian socialist jurists lay great stress upon the first element as prerequisite to the second. They believe it is quite impossible to plan for a society resting upon private ownership of productive wealth.

Although Marxists admit that many countries of the capitalist group, such as France, Japan, Belgium, the Netherlands, Sweden, Norway, and Italy, include elements of planning in governmental activity, they classify such planning as no more than "indicative." [1] It is not state planning as they mean it, for it does not employ directives issued from above and binding in some degree upon all who function in the economic mechanism. For indicative planners the instruments of implementation are economic levers, such as the credit system, rates of interest and loans, tax privileges and state subsidies, and sometimes licenses. In some states, such as the United Kingdom, France, and Austria, significant segments of the economic mechanism have been nationalized. In these segments the state plans directly, but to the Marxist the essential capitalist character of the economy prevents full planning, for the very "existence of private ownership in a considerable part of the instruments and means of production stipulates its indicative character." [2]

A legal editor in the Democratic Republic of Vietnam shows the tenacity with which contemporary Communists hold to these concepts.[3] He quotes Engels ("Anti-Dühring") in support of what he calls the original idea that for a socialist reconversion of society there are two essentials: the proletariat must "free the forces of production from the peculiarities of modern capitalism so that the social nature of these forces may develop most freely," and "then it will be possible to introduce social production according to a strictly drawn up plan." He notes that even after a year of reconstruction and three years of planning in his country, nonsocialist elements held important positions in the national economy, and that "In such conditions

---

[1] Khalfina, The Role of State Organs in Planning. General Report to Seventh Congress of the International Academy of Comparative Law, Uppsala 1967. To appear in the Proceedings of the Academy.

[2] Id. at 6.

[3] Pham Thanh Vinh, The Obligatory Nature of Planning Targets, 12 REVIEW OF CONTEMPORARY LAW, no. 1 at 82 (1965).

the implementation of the plan and its compulsory character are considerably restricted." He finds it impossible to draw up obligatory plans, and he comments, "If one restricts the obligatory character of the plan, one also restricts the true planned character of the socialist state." Clearly, to the Marxist, indicative planning is not enough; indeed, some of them would say that use of the word planning by capitalist authors to describe what is being done in their systems is only meant to confuse the workers into thinking that they already enjoy the rational direction of the economy promised them under socialism.

The measures taken to bring the national economy under state ownership or control vary among the fourteen Marxian socialist states. They have been reviewed in chapters 7 and 8. They run from complete "socialization" in the USSR, with expropriation of the capitalist owners in all fields (except for artisan production without the use of hired labor), to the compromises of China, where joint state-private enterprises provide a legal framework for utilizing those capitalists, who have no financial links with foreign capital. These men are placed in partnership with the state as "owners" of family industries, for which the state is not yet ready to assume full managerial responsibility. Midway between the extremes of the USSR and China are Poland and Yugoslavia, where there has been expropriation of capitalists in the industrial field, but where toleration of privately owned agriculture continues, subject to various control features, and where private production units employing small numbers of workmen are still in operation.

In all Marxian socialist countries the principle of state planning is elevated to the level of constitutional law. In the USSR the constitution of 1936 establishes in Article 11 that "The economic life of the USSR is determined and directed by the national-economic plan. . . ." The Czechoslovak constitution of 1960 declares in Article 12, "Management of the entire economy is implemented in conformity with the state plan of national economy. . . ." The Chinese provide in Article 15 that "By economic planning, the state directs the growth and transformation of the national economy in order to bring about the constant increase of productive forces. . . ." It is the same in the constitutions of the other Marxian states: Polish of 1952,

Article 7; Rumanian of 1965, Article 13; Bulgarian of 1947, Article 12; Hungarian of 1949, Paragraph 5; German of 1949, Article 21, and of 1968, Article 9 (3).

To distinguish state planning from indicative planning, it is declared to be "law," which means that it is obligatory for those to whom it relates. Violation of its provisions subjects the enterprise to civil suit for damages and, to the extent possible, for specific performance. In some instances criminal responsibility attaches to directors who have failed to perform. A 1958 decree in the USSR provided that "failure of managing and other responsible officials of enterprises, economic organizations, state farms, ministries and government departments to perform plans and duties to deliver production to other economic administrative regions or union republics and also for all-union needs is a grave violation of state discipline and shall incur disciplinary, property and criminal responsibility." [4] The decree listed the disciplinary fines as deduction of three months' pay from the wages of managers and other responsible officials who failed to perform plans and duties "without valid reasons." When managers failed to make deliveries destined for all-union needs or meant to pass across boundaries of republics or economic administrative regions, criminal responsibility was prescribed "as if they had committed the crime of malicious use of a responsible position."

The principle that failure to perform the economic plan is a crime was carried into the codes of several of the Soviet republics when new criminal codes were enacted in elaboration of the federal fundamental principles of 1958. [5] In those making no specific reference to the offense, the failure to perform may still be placed under the article on malicious use of a responsible position, in the view of Professor Harold J. Berman and of Soviet commentaries on which he relies. [6]

[4] Apr. 24, 1958, [1958] 9 Ved. Verkh. Sov. S.S.S.R. item 202.

[5] See Criminal Codes of Soviet Republics: Moldavian art. 155; Georgian art. 163; Uzbek art. 171; Kazakh art. 151; Armenian art. 157. Pub. in Ugolovnoe zakonodatel'stvo soiuza SSR i soiuznykh respublik 2 vols. (1963) [Criminal Legislation of the U.S.S.R. and of the Union Republics].

[6] H. Berman, Justice in the U.S.S.R. 147 (2d ed. 1963). Also Zile, *Law and the Distribution of Consumer Goods*, in W. Lafave ed., Law and Soviet Society 240, n. 142 (1965).

Other Marxian socialist states have been reluctant to prescribe criminal punishment for the offender who fails to perform. Even China seems not to have made failure to perform a crime. But although criminal law is not a favored medium, the offender is still punished. In the Chinese people's republic, interviews with refugees suggest to Dr. Gene T. Hsiao "that the usual Party and government disciplinary means serve to sanction delinquent parties. These disciplinary measures include criticism, self-criticism, demotion and dismissal." [7] To this he adds that dismissal from an official position usually results in unemployment, and under a state council decision of 3 August 1957 the unemployed are subject to "reeducation through labor."

European Marxian states would not go so far, although the manager who proves himself incapable is, as in the capitalist world, dismissed or demoted, and his responsibilities thereafter are fitted to what employment offices think of his capabilities. Gone are the widely publicized days when Stalin imprisoned or executed large numbers of managers for "sabotage" during the "purge period" of 1935–37 on the ground that failure to perform the plan created a presumption in fact, if not in law, that it was intentional. Personal confessions extorted, as Nikita Khrushchev was later to tell his party, by illegal methods utilized by the security police were accepted as sufficient evidence of intent; so few were able to rebut the presumption against them.

From this "purge" experience grew the movement among many Soviet law professors and judges, supported by some bureaucrats, to establish in law a presumption of innocence. This movement reached its climax in 1958 with revision of the code of criminal procedure to place upon the prosecution the burden of proving guilt.

Although all members of the family of Marxian socialist legal systems, except Yugoslavia, which will be discussed later, accept the rule that "the plan is law," and that this situation is necessarily accompanied by sanctions of one sort or another, there is wide variation in the method of planning. No states place the emphasis on centralized determination of economic

[7] Hsiao, *The Role of Economic Contracts in Communist China*, 53 CALIF. L. REV. 1029 at 1049 (1965).

detail that Stalin came to place during his declining years. All communist administrators have come to believe that Stalin's accent on centralized direction was too strong. Although his scheme called for reliance on local initiative to perform many tasks necessary to the success of the economy, leaving to local soviets at the province and city level, and even in the counties and villages, freedom to administer enterprises of local concern, his central planners were continually reaching into local territorial subdivisions to command specific production. This was especially so with the collective farms, which were authorized under their charters to make many locally important decisions, but which in fact were held to relatively rigid plans established from above. One of Khrushchev's measures after Stalin's death was to free the collective farms from much of this command system, even to the extent of depriving the Ministry of Agriculture of the administrative authority that it had possessed since 1932. In what looked like a symbolic gesture, its headquarters were moved to a village outside Moscow near experimental farms to which it was directed to devote its attention.

Khrushchev also sought to free industry from centralized direction by abolishing the central industrial ministries in the capital and substituting regional economic councils with operating control over the plants within their region.[8] The centralized planning apparatus remained, but in quite different circumstances; the compulsory indexes it controlled were reduced in number and for the rest "wide use was made of forms of economic stimulation founded on the operation of the law of value, as well as of economic levers, such as profit, price and encouragement of stimulating funds." [9]

Even after Khrushchev's ouster in 1964 and restoration in 1965 of the central industrial ministries, planning was not returned to Stalin's system. Although basic metals such as steel, copper, and aluminum were planned in minute detail so that every ton was allocated for specific use, subsidiary materials were placed upon a less rigidly controlled schedule. The use of some materials, such as gravel, cement, bricks, and lumber, procured locally on the initiative of local soviets, which was permitted in some measure under Stalin's system, was to be

[8] 10 May 1957, [1957] 11 Ved. Verkh. Sov. S.S.S.R. item 275.
[9] Khalfina, *supra*, note 1 at 9.

expanded. It was not to be centrally directed, but was included in the plan on the basis of estimates by local authorities who were left free to do the best they could with what was readily at hand.[10]

At the far end of the spectrum of socialist planning stands Yugoslavia. Although the plan is adopted by the legislature of the federal republic and by the legislature of each republic within the federation, it is not "law," sanctioned as obligatory for the subordinated organs.[11] In the main, planning is indicative only, and it could not be otherwise, since Yugoslav Communists permit the free exchange of commodities in the open market to play a prominent role in their economy. Thus, the state plan establishes only the basic "proportions" of economic development. The enterprises, owned by the workers within them under Yugoslavia's unique concept of "social ownership," work out with local government authorities and the branch representatives of the industry concerned production programs within these basic proportions, but have no sense of being commanded to conform.

Competition between socially owned enterprises is encouraged as a means of fostering initiative in the director and his council, but the state restrains the competition lest it impede implementation of the plans. For this purpose it manipulates both the distribution of public income available for capital investment and the terms of credits,[12] and it also fixes minimum wage levels so that competition cannot be at the expense of the workmen themselves. Still, local initiative sometimes results in the construction of enterprises deemed necessary locally, when on a national scale such use of resources is unjustified in comparison with needs elsewhere. A noted example was a resort hotel constructed on local initiative and with local resources in

[10] Kosygin, *On Improving Industrial Management, Perfecting Planning, and Enhancing Incentives in Industrial Production*, Izvestiia, 28 Sept. 1965. Eng. transl. in 2 M. SHARPE ed., PLANNING, PROFIT AND INCENTIVES IN THE U.S.S.R. 3 (1966).

[11] Balog, *Foreword* to 13 COLLECTION OF YUGOSLAV LAWS (LAWS OF ENTERPRISES AND INSTITUTIONS) 3 at 6. (Institute of Comparative Law, Belgrade, 1966).

[12] The central bank withdrew credits from local banks in 1967 to counter inflationary pressures. See Yugoslav News Bulletin, no. 398 (17 April 1967) at 10. Yugoslav Information Center, New York.

the foothills of the mountains of Bosnia, partly in expectation that tourism would increase in the area, but primarily to contribute to regional prestige. For some years it stood nearly empty until a construction project of very large proportions initiated by the federal government brought numbers of engineers to the city.

Lenin started slowly with planning, beginning with what he thought to be the key element—electric power. Then a state planning organization was created which devoted its first years to gathering economic statistics. Only in 1928, when the New Economic Policy was phased out, was state economic planning begun, with the first of the noted five-year plans. Leaders of other Marxian socialist states later followed Lenin's cautious example of the early years as they moved toward Stalin's type of centralized and detailed planning. The impression was given in the late 1940s and early 1950s that it was the goal of all to centralize increasingly and to plan more and more items, until all or nearly all had a place in the plan.

After this scheme of nearly automatic progression from stage to stage in economic planning, depending upon the extent of socialization of the means of production, Khrushchev's experiments signaled a revision which led everywhere to a change in attitude. Today the degree of centralization and complexity of an economic plan for any given state reflects its leaders' views on how to maximize production more than their perception of the presence or absence of restraints created by the level of socialization that has been achieved. Less dogma and more pragmatic experimentation are evident in the drafting of plans. Yugoslavia's position is the result of Tito's conclusion that bureaucracy is the cancer of socialism rather than the result of his sensing some technical inability of his engineers and economists to implement a detailed plan. Since he now has enough trained men to provide efficient management, his decentralizing is not due to fear of taking the reins. He decentralizes because he thinks that a centralized bureaucracy would lose the advantages of socialist planning in a confusion of procedures.

Tito's experimentation has not been ignored by his colleagues in the hierarchies of other Communist parties. Only the Chinese and Albanians say he has restored capitalism and betrayed the revolution. The others have understood his message, and although they are unwilling to go as far, they are willing to depart from Stalinist centralism and to experiment for themselves. In the words of a Soviet jurist, "The establishment of optimal correlation of centralized planning leadership and the initiative of the enterprises through the effect of economic stimuli is one of the key problems for the perfection of planning leadership. This correlation is not a firm one, nor is it permanent. It is dynamic." [13]

The common core of the family of Marxian socialist legal systems includes, it is evident, the concept of state planning as a basic element; but the amount of detail in the plan and the means of its implementation are not dictated for each member of the family by the Soviet Union, nor by the signatories of the 1957 declaration. The division of labor once anticipated for Communist-led states through COMECON, from which some dictation in formulating economic plans must assuredly have been felt, broke down in 1963 when Romania refused to accept the agrarian status assigned to her among the Marxian states of Eastern Europe. The communist leadership in each country is now free to plan as it will, without direction or criticism from other Communists. Only in the rare case of Chinese-Albanian criticism of Yugoslav goals and methods has it become evident that for these two groups of "leftist" leaders a point was reached where a Marxian could say that "quantity had changed to quality"; that the core had been lost because the methods used failed to meet the minimum of centralization and detail which they thought necessary within the family. Only in the Chinese-Albanian view had the Yugoslavs, in multiplying the circumstances in which managers could make independent decision, changed the system.

The plan has literally been law for Marxian socialists other than the Yugoslavs, although reform thinking may drive the East-Central European Marxian states nearer to the Yugoslav model. It is adopted as a statute by each legislature. To be sure, its general outline and even some of its detail spring from decisions of the Communist parties in the states concerned, but before it becomes obligatory it is passed through the legislature, often with changes found to be necessary by the technicians,

[13] Khalfina, *supra*, note 1 at 10.

who function more in the state apparatus than in the party discussion. Much is now made of the fact that the plan is developed from the bottom up, and in this is seen its democratic feature. This was so to a degree even during Stalin's most dictatorial period, for the USSR State Planning Committee in Moscow relied on the ministries, and they in turn relied on the managers in the field, to estimate what could be done in a given period. Stalin added to the estimates an increment designed to make the managers exert themselves, but this proved self-defeating. Knowing that the plan finally established would always exceed reported potential, managers and their staffs tended to submit figures lower than the achievement possible to protect themselves against an inevitable increase. A major revision of Khrushchev's regime was to restore reality to planning—to rely on the bottom to inform the top correctly and on the top to set goals that were realistic and not automatic additions to what the bottom had proposed.

In the USSR plans go through a second legislative stage. After they have been adopted on recommendation of the Council of Ministers of the USSR, they must be put into budgetary terms. For this purpose the legislature follows the enactment of the long-term plan "law" with an annual budget, which is also adopted as "law." These are the primary legal documents with which the apparatus of the State Planning Committee and the ministries works in distributing the established goals among the enterprises subject to their jurisdiction. Because the USSR is a federation, like Yugoslavia, not all enterprises are directly subordinate to the central authorities. For those which, for administrative convenience, are placed within the jurisdiction of the republics, a second set of laws must be passed: a republic plan and a republic budget, conforming, of course, to the overall federal plan and budget. On the basis of these laws, which establish detail not placed in the federal laws, the ministries of the republics issue directives to the republic-controlled enterprises establishing their concrete tasks.

But tasks are not established with full specifications for their performance. Since planning in detail is provided only for a few key materials and for capital construction financed by centrally controlled capital investment, as well as for systematic freight movements in large quantities, in relatively few cases does the task carry with it notice of the source of supply and the agencies to receive the product. For the rest of the transactions among the one million economic enterprises and organizations of the USSR,[14] the managers are free to establish their own relationships of purchase, sale, and transport. This has been so since 1928 when planning on a compulsory basis began. The major difference between Stalin's approach and that of the Khrushchev and post-Khrushchev period is that the number of key items rigidly planned has been reduced. In consequence, the managers are given less direction on implementation today than they received fifteen years ago. They are freer than before Stalin's death to decide with whom they wish to deal in performing the duties placed upon them by the plan.

What has given incessant trouble to Marxian socialist lawyers over the years in the implementation of the plan is this final step in its realization—the relationship of state enterprises engaged in production, transportation, and distribution to the public. Lenin established a pattern in 1923 when he created the first public corporations and directed them to compete with private enterprises on the market.[15] They were to use a form of contract to establish their relations, and to make the best deals they could. But this was before the beginning of detailed state planning. With the phasing out of the capitalist sector and the introduction of compulsory state plans, some administrators considered it wholly appropriate to abandon the contract form and to introduce the "administrative order" in its place. A state railroad would then issue to a steel plant an administrative order for the rails required by the plan, and the plant would produce and deliver.

The advantage of simplicity given by such a system was negated by the impossibility of planning all detail from above. No Moscow ministry, in implementing a planned task, could assemble sufficient detail to establish specifications, appropriate delivery dates, and shipping instructions. Stalin's administrators decided to continue to use the concept of contract to make it possible for the managers of each organization to negotiate the

[14] The figure is from Birman, *The Talent of an Economist*, [1967] 1 Novy mir 167. Eng. transl. in 19 C.D.S.P. no. 13 at 7, 11. (1967).

[15] First Decree on Trusts, 10 Apr. 1923, [1923] 29 Sob. Uzak. R.S.F.S.R. pt. I item 336.

details without referring to Moscow. In some instances, such as in the manufacture of a unique turbine for one hydroelectric project, the contract was a pure formality, for every detail was planned at the center and set forth in a production and delivery order. Some argued that contracts could be dispensed with in such planned relationships. But there were not many such unique items, and in the interest of uniformity the contract system was maintained even for them. For the great bulk of products the negotiation of a contract provided a convenient means of making terms precise, although the negotiators were not free to decide all questions as they might wish. In matters of quality and often of price they were held to state-established standards and tariffs. And most important, they were compelled to negotiate a contract, for to refuse was to deny the validity of the plan.

Here was the nub of the problem for the legal theorist. How could there be a compulsory contract, when by its traditional Romanist definition a contract is a voluntary agreement of the parties? A German professor has remarked, in commenting upon the declaration in the 1961 Fundamental Principles of Civil Law that civil rights and obligations arise from administrative acts and planning acts, "This probably is the first statutory formulation of the principle in legal history" and "no other legal system seems to have embodied such a principle in its Civil Code." [16] He explains that the classic civil codes know only of civil obligations arising from contract, or from "law," by the latter of which he means torts and unjust enrichment.

The introduction of compulsion into a framework designed for consensual agreement worried the Soviet jurists of the 1920s, and it has worried Romanist theorists in Marxian countries ever since. Some thought that contract was a concept created in the marketplace and, therefore, would be one of the first legal institutions to "wither away" with the achievement of socialism. This was one reason Soviet jurists wished to escape from civil law entirely and to create a new branch called "economic law" in which administrative orders could be recognized for what they were. They could not see why the recipients could not work out the details of delivery, specifications, and ship-

[16] Loeber, *Plan and Contract Performance in Soviet Law*, in LAFAVE, *supra*, note 6 at 128, 141, 142.

ment in a subordinate document to be attached to the order and thus avoid using a word whose traditional meaning they thought wholly inappropriate under the compulsory circumstances of the relationship.

The opponents of the contract form lost out in the debate, and those who thought like them foresaw only personal peril in raising the argument again until after Stalin's death. Their hearing was short, for they have been silenced throughout all East European Marxian socialist states, except in Czechoslovakia and to some degree in the German Democratic Republic, although there is now a difference in their treatment as defeated theorists. Grumbling still continues from the malcontents, even in the USSR, but it is no longer considered illegal or even impolitic. One can foresee that some day there will be a rehearing, but until then, the contract stands as a legal instrument with which Marxian socialist law is concerned in a mammoth way. Two hundred fifty million economic contracts are thought to be concluded each year in the USSR alone.[17] In every one lawyers participate as aides to the parties, and the negotiation or execution of many occasion disputes to which the principles of contract law apply.

Two Romanian scholars remark that too much emphasis has been placed upon technical convenience in negotiating contracts to specify elements which cannot be planned from the center.[18] They urge readers to look beyond convenience and see the educational usefulness of giving socialist organizations a certain freedom of initiative in establishing the relationships of contract. They find this of great importance, for although the decisions come from the central planning and administrative organ, they are completed by local initiative. They see in this "one of the most significant examples of socialist centralism and democracy brought together in an integral whole," and they find that "the deliberately incomplete nature of the planned target requires initiative." In short, the negotiation of a contract profits from classifying the matter under civil rather than administrative law, since there is still an element of voluntary agreement, limited as it is, and the managers of the enter-

[17] Id. at 131.
[18] Ionasco & Barasch, *The Obligation to Conclude Economic Contracts*, 12 REVIEW OF CONTEMPORARY LAW 51 at 55 (1965).

prises concerned will sense this and develop their initiative in its exercise.

In short, the contract, seen as establishing a civil-law relationship rather than an administrative-law relationship, becomes an exercise in managerial initiative. Without this Marxian socialists fear they will become entwined in bureaucratic strings emanating from the capital. In the post-Stalin era, especially since the measures introduced in the USSR in 1965 to encourage initiative by enterprise managers, the contract's role is enhanced. It becomes a major instrument for reforming attitudes, and a major means of bringing into play greatly expanded property incentives upon managers and workmen, who are encouraged to cut costs and expand profits, from which society will benefit in higher production at reduced unit cost.

Harmonizing the administrative obligation to contract with a policy fostering local initiative in negotiating contracts on a consensual basis is the task of state arbitration, whose structure has been described in chapter 6. The process is resolution of the "precontract" dispute. The very name suggests its novelty, for in the traditional capitalist system, where "contract" symbolizes voluntary consent to agreement, there can be no precontract dispute; for if there is basic disagreement there will be no contract. The parties will separate and go their own ways. But in the Marxian socialist systems the manager who is displeased with an offer cannot walk away if his colleague is not prepared to let him go. Although there may be alternative sources of supply, as when generic goods are obtainable locally or when specific goods are in surplus supply, a manager is keenly conscious of his duty to perform his planned task. If he thinks his colleague controls his only means of performing, he can turn to state arbitration to hear the dispute and to rule on its reasonableness.[19] No manager may take an unreasonable position to prevent another from meeting his planned task.

[19] Statute on State Arbitration in the U.S.S.R., 17 Aug. 1960, Sec. 3 (c). Text in A. KLEINMAN, ARBITRAZH V SSSR 184 (1960) [Arbitration in the U.S.S.R.]. Hungary created an exception to this general rule in 1967 while increasing enterprise autonomy. State arbitration was denied authority to oblige enterprises to enter into contracts or to determine the conditions of contracts. See Harmathy, *The Reform of Economic Management and the New Regulation of Contracts in Hungary*, ACTA JURIDICA ACADEMIAE SCIENTIARUM HUNGARICAE, 10 at 215, 220 (1968).

To facilitate review of the dispute, a buyer who objects to some proposed clause of a contract or even to concluding a contract at all drafts a "protocol of disagreement," which he presents to the supplier, who files his counterproposal with state arbitration.[20] If he fails to file within ten days, he is presumed to have agreed. Contracts of small value require no such formality, merely a refusal to accept a proferred order. If both parties are subordinate to the same minister, in keeping with the general rules on arbitration, resolution of the dispute is the task of the ministry's arbitration board rather than of the independent system of state arbitration.

State arbitration is not limited in the matters it may consider. It can decide not only matters of law but matters of operational expediency, such as when a supplier tries to force upon a buyer products he cannot use.[21] Since the arbitrator's first task is to support the plan, he must be alert to any proposal that would violate it; but beyond that he is expected to use his discretion in what he will require and what he will exclude. Some examples will illustrate his functions.

Several disputes arose in 1961 before conclusion of contracts between the enterprises that rework and bottle wine and soft drinks and various retail enterprises, over a clause proposed by the supplier relating to the quantity of empty bottles to be returned.[22] The suppliers wished to insert in the contracts as a standard clause the following: "Sound bottles, without defect, shall be returned to the supplier by the purchaser in an amount not exceeding 100% of the bottles filled with wine delivered to the given purchaser." The purchasers refused to accept the clause, saying that citizens returned more bottles to the retail stores than had been sold by the stores. In consequence, they wished to exclude the clause and substitute one permitting return of empty bottles without limit. Though the report gives no explanation for the discrepancy between the number of bottles sold and the returns, it is probably because bottles are taken from Leningrad to the surrounding resorts, or even farther afield. When empty, the bottles are not carried back to

[20] Loeber, *supra*, note 16 at 144.

[21] *Id.* at 146.

[22] *Precontract Request of Leningrad Provincial Arbitration for Advice*, [1961] 7 Sots. zak. 92.

Leningrad where they were bought, but are returned to the nearest state retail store.

Feeling that they could not decide so many cases without guidance, the provincial state arbitrators asked the USSR state arbitration in Moscow to give advice. The central arbitrator noted that nothing in the plan placed a limit on the return of bottles, and so the suppliers had no right to ask for what seemed an unreasonable provision in the contracts. Still, the central arbitrator could see eventual disruption of the plan if bottles accumulated in large surpluses where they were not needed, and he cautioned the provincial arbitrators to ask the planning organs in good time for direction as to how to dispose of such surpluses.

In another case a supplying enterprise sought advice on whether it might include in its contracts a limitation on its responsibility for delay in performing its shipping obligation at the end of each month, by providing that the producer would be given five or ten days' grace during which he could load products after the end of a month. In support of its request, it stated that the railroad ceases loading at 6 P.M. at the end of the month, but the supplier continues to produce until midnight, and it cannot with the best will in the world load the last six hours' production before the end of the month.

The chief arbitrator in Moscow explained that the delivery regulations for the type of product concerned indicate that the day of performance of an obligation to out-of-town buyers is the day the product is delivered to the transport organs, as determined by the stamp on the bill of lading.[23] Neither with the consent of both parties nor at the request of the supplier alone may this procedure be waived. In consequence, the proposed terms would be void if incorporated into a contract. The solution to the supplier's problem was not to insert a clause in the contract, but to plan his deliveries so that the carryover from the last six hours of production each month may be made available to meet contract deliveries scheduled for the following month.

The law of contract is prescribed by the civil codes of each of the republics of the USSR in a chapter on "Contracts of

[23] *Precontract Request of Enterprise in Voronezh Regional Economic Council for Advice,* [1961] 4 SOTS. ZAK. 91.

Supply" (sometimes translated as "Delivery Contracts"), which comes after the general provisions on contract and the specific provisions on contract of sale between citizens and by state agencies to citizens. The word "supply" is used to distinguish the two types quickly. Since the dispute over applicable law has been settled in the USSR in favor of a unified system of civil law governing all contracts, whether of sale or supply, there is a unity of principles governing both types, supplemented by the detail appropriate to one or the other alone.

A major general principle governing both is that specific performance is the rule and that the payment of penalties and damages does not release a supplier from performance. This principle, inherited from the Romanist systems generally,[24] is particularly suited to contracts of supply, because their purpose is to facilitate performance of the plan. Consequently, money damages would not be adequate, for in a planned economy, profits are not the goal of the contract system. Tons of coal must be delivered, and if they are not delivered, society suffers because the goods to be manufactured with the power generated by the coal have not been produced. The shelves of retail stores will be empty and the planned distribution of consumer goods disrupted. In extreme instances disorders and loss of confidence may result when the government is manifestly responsible for the failures in supply.

Likewise, fault is a factor in breach of contract, by a private citizen or by a state enterprise, and what has been said on this in the preceding chapter is applicable to the breach of a planned contract.

Some features of contract of sale differ, however, from those of supply. From the theoretical point of view the major difference is what is transferred by the two types of contracts. For the "sale," the expected consequence occurs, for the seller transfers "title"; that is, "ownership" in the thing which is the subject of the contract.[25] But for the contract of supply, no title is passed, for a reason important in theory. The supplying state enterprise cannot transfer title because it has none to transfer. All that it has under Marxian socialist theory is "operative management" of state-owned property. In consequence, the code provides that

[24] See discussion, ch. 13.
[25] Civil Code R.S.F.S.R. 1964, art. 237.

it transfers only "operative management" in accordance with a planning directive for the distribution of goods.[26]

Since the purpose of the contract is to obtain production and delivery, the law permits enforcement of a contract of supply in which not all essential points have been included.[27] In a contract of sale, such a provision would be unthinkable. But when the contract is in fulfillment of the plan, the essential points may be found in the plan; and if they happen to have been omitted from the contract, state arbitration will take them as meant.

In resolving disputes over breach of contracts executed to implement the plan, state arbitration most frequently has had to determine issues of "fault," since parties introduce innocence of fault as their defense against suit for performance and damages. The practice demonstrates that they are held to a severe standard. For example, a buying enterprise was sued for penalties for incomplete deliveries of cast iron. The metallurgical factory which was the supplier defended on the ground that it was not at fault since it had not received sufficient allocation orders from the regional economic council to which it was subordinate to permit it to contract for the raw materials necessary. Although it had complained in time, it had been unsuccessful. The state arbitrator decided that the producer was liable for the penalty since it was its duty to obtain the necessary allocations.[28]

In commenting on this case, Professor D. A. Loeber finds the decision harsh, but necessary in a planned economy. To release the supplier would have opened the gates to pleas of inability to supply. Units in the process of production could relax their efforts to procure planned material, and rely passively on the mechanism of planning. In this explanation is evident the less-than-perfect performance of plans which plagues Soviet production, a situation which has given rise to the employment of "pushers" in planning centers, who see that officials in the bureaucracy perform their duties promptly and fully. All economic systems have faced this problem, as became evident

[26] *Id.* art. 258.

[27] Loeber, *supra*, note 16 at 147.

[28] Stalingrad Office v. Alchevsk Metallurgical Plant, 1959. Cited in *id.* at 148.

during World War II even in the United States, where producers employed "expediters" in Washington to obtain from the lower-level officials in the War Production Board the allocations and priority orders which would permit them to perform on time contracts made in implementation of plans established by higher levels of the War Production Board.

All other Marxian socialist states have followed the Soviet model in the main in establishing a law for the formulation and enforcement of contracts of supply. Even the Chinese, without a civil code, have established, through a series of statutes and regulations, a system of contracts for the rendering of services and for supply of goods by one state enterprise to another.[29] Since Chinese planning has not been as extensive as that in the USSR, the contracts are limited to certain essential industrial products: steel and its by-products, lumber, equipment, and tools. The State Economic Commission annually issues a regulation defining the scope of distribution and a distribution plan. The first lists state organs and enterprises which may enter into contracts with their counterparts for the delivery of products. All others must purchase what they need from the Department of Commerce. The distribution plan is less precise. The State Economic Commission issues "control figures" to the central economic ministries and the provincial economic departments in accordance with estimates of demand and production. On the basis of these estimates each ministry and department prepares control figures for its subordinates and drafts plans for distribution of what it controls. Eventually contracts are executed between the producers and the consumers. In the event of a precontract dispute, the ministries supervising each enterprise make the decision either through direct negotiation or through negotiation guided by the "economic commission" at various levels of the state administrative apparatus, or, if need be, through an ad hoc arbitration board.

China's rejection of the Soviet practice, adopted in the other states except Yugoslavia, of creating a permanently functioning tribunal called "state arbitration," means that the settlement of disputes is relegated in most instances to negotiation between superiors of the disputants, or to guided negotiation

[29] Hsiao, *supra*, note 7 at 1029, 1045. Also Pfeffer, *Contracts in China Revisited*, [1966] THE CHINA QUARTERLY no. 28 at 106.

through the "economic commissions" or in rare cases to an ad hoc arbitration board. The Chinese way has been to prevent disputes, if possible, by establishing legal offices in state enterprises to aid in the preparation of contracts (although these have faded from view since 1958); by requiring supervision by state notaries of what has been done; by administrative supervision by superiors; and by financial supervision by the accountants of the parties and the People's Bank.

The bank and the accountants are authorized to withhold payment for performance which fails to conform to the contract or to the plan, and the bank may deduct payment from the buyer's account when it is due under the contract. Also party influence is brought to bear on a director by making performance a "political responsibility." [30]

Many of these same preventive measures are taken in the USSR; nevertheless, disputes reach the state arbitration in vast numbers. Professor D. A. Loeber estimates that the 130 state arbitration agencies in the USSR decide approximately 500,000 cases a year, and the arbitration boards within ministries, which hear disputes between enterprises under the jurisdiction of the same minister, hear between 400,000 and 500,000 more. These disputes concern claims totaling two billion new rubles a year, or $2,200,000,000, if the official conversion rate is applied.[31]

Even without a code of laws, the Chinese apply the same legal principles as other members of the family of Marxian socialist legal systems.[32] Paying a fine for delay or faulty performance does not release the obligor, for the plan must be performed. Alteration or termination of a contract may not be made by one party alone, but is possible only if the plan is altered or if the superiors of both parties agree. Some reported cases indicate that this rule is applied only flexibly. A Shanghai machine-tool factory failed to perform its contract and accumulated thereby a total fine of 150,000 yuan, which it should have paid in strict application of the law of the contract. It was released from its obligation to pay, however, because the ad hoc arbitrator concluded that enforcement of its obligation would

---

[30] Hsiao, *id.* at 1049.
[31] Loeber, *supra*, note 16 at 133.
[32] Hsiao, *supra*, note 7 at 1047.

seriously impede its production.[33] This case indicates that the general principle that contracts are executed only to implement the plan takes precedence over the law of the specific contract when a conflict arises between the two. A Soviet arbitrator might have taken the same position two decades ago, but under current conditions his attitude would be different. The emphasis is now more firmly upon inflexible application of law, even to the point of raising in the minds of some commentators the question of whether state arbitration has become nothing more than a specialized court rigidly enforcing law.[34]

The number of contracting agencies was greatly increased when the Chinese Communists began to shift "title" from the communes to the production brigades and then to the production teams in the manner discussed in chapter 7. This made the small villages the accounting units and increased the potential contractors to several millions. These units are subject to the vagaries of nature, which often make performance of contracts difficult if not impossible. Further, their status in law is not entirely clear, and there has even been a suggestion that title will be returned to a higher level,[35] in spite of guarantees that no change will be made for thirty years.

These factors, indicative of a flexible approach, tended to soften attitudes favoring legal sanctions administered by judiciallike bodies and to favor administrative and political methods even before Mao introduced his "Great Proletarian Cultural Revolution" in 1966, with its emphasis upon political pressures and ad hoc resolution of problems without adherence to established rules.

The legal principles enunciated in the teaching manual of 1958 were placed in the background at the outset of the "Great Proletarian Cultural Revolution." The emphasis changed, so much so that the Soviet Communists charged that the Chinese had abandoned "socialist legality" as practiced in the other Marxian socialist states. Time will tell whether the Chinese Communists choose to return to what has become elsewhere in

[33] Cited *id.* at 1048 from Jen Chien-hsia, *Strengthening the Work of Economic Contracts in Order to Promote the Successful Execution of the National Economic Plan*, [1957] 1 Cheng-fa yen-chiu 31–32.

[34] See discussion in ch. 4.

[35] Pfeffer, *supra*, note 29 at 123 and Hsiao, *supra*, note 29 at 1057.

the Marxian socialist world a standard pattern, although of a somewhat novel character, for utilizing and enforcing legal principles in obtaining performance of state economic plans.

What has been said up to this point relates to the planning mechanism for the distribution of goods and services necessary to the production process. It has not concerned the distribution of labor power, although men are as important as machines and materials to achievement of the plan. Planners in the USSR have been tempted to order the distribution of men, both in groups and individually, to participate in production, and for some years between the rise of Hitler and the end of the first period of postwar reconstruction, this policy was reflected in Soviet law. In its most severe form it became the law of 26 June 1940,[36] adopted immediately after the fall of France to Hitler's legions. From that moment Stalin began to prepare for a possible German attack upon his country, and the 1940 law was a primary instrument of preparation. It denied workers the right to leave their jobs without permission from the enterprise administration. Only if a worker was found to be in ill health or received notice of admission to a training institute or school which would enhance his technical qualifications could the administration be compelled to grant leave. Otherwise permission could be withheld at its discretion.

The 1940 law had severe sanctions. Previous measures of control over labor turnover occasioned by search for better pay or better living conditions had taken two forms: (1) political campaigns to educate workmen in the productive necessity of permanence at the job, and (2) notation in the employment record carried personally by each worker as his "labor passport" of reasons for termination of a job. The 1940 law provided a criminal penalty of from two to four months imprisonment on sentence by a court. To assure that no director would hire persons who had left previous jobs without permission, a penalty was also established against those who hired the culprit and concealed the fact.

The severity of the 1940 law was enhanced within less than a month by an interpretation issued jointly by the procurator and minister of justice of the USSR, declaring that the period

[36] [1940] 20 Ved. Verh. Sov. S.S.S.R.

of "unexplained absence" for which prosecution might be brought was shortened from one day to over twenty minutes' tardiness in the morning or after luncheon or over twenty minutes lost by early departure from work.[37]

Procedural simplification was established to speed prosecutions under the law by eliminating the usual preliminary investigation before trial, and by eliminating from the bench the two lay assessors required in all other court sittings. The full-time judge could sit alone.

After the Nazi armies invaded the USSR on 22 June 1941, an even more severe law was enacted within six months to consider those who left military industries without permission on a par with military deserters. For such culprits the penalties were established at from five to eight years.[38]

Whereas these two laws facilitated planning by holding at their jobs those already working rather than assigning workers to jobs in accordance with new needs of the plan, a decree of 19 October 1940 introduced the concept of assignment.[39] Engineers and technicians were required to accept transfer from one enterprise to another. If they refused to accept the transfer, they were to be prosecuted under the decree of 26 June 1940 for leaving the job without permission. This assured transferability of key personnel to meet planned assignments.

Within two years, as the Nazi armies rolled across the Russian and Ukrainian plains, great numbers of workmen were evacuated with their factories to remote sites in Siberia and Central Asia. Since the machinery was transported and set up in buildings erected at the new locations, the continuity of jobs was maintained. Workmen had to accompany the plants, and to remain thereafter in the remote regions under threat of prosecution, should they leave without permission to seek jobs elsewhere. In truth, they had no real choice at that time, as their homelands were overrun; they could not have returned. But the situation changed sharply at the end of the war. Ukrainians with great love for their native Ukraine refused to remain in remote, cold Siberia. Managers with an eye to rational distribution of labor were reluctant to permit them to

---

[37] Order of 22 July 1940, [1940] 13 Sov. IUST. 5.
[38] 26 Dec. 1941, [1942] 2 Ved. Verkh. Sov. S.S.S.R.
[39] [1940] 42 *id.*

leave, seeing no hope of replacing them in regions which were unappealing to the average workman from the European parts of the USSR. The question was raised in high Communist-party circles whether planning could require these men to remain even after the war emergency had passed.

The answer was equivocal. The law of 26 June 1940 was kept on the books, but under curious circumstances. It was removed from its accustomed place as an appendix to the criminal code of the R.S.F.S.R. in the edition of 1950. It continued to be printed, however, in the manual for trade-union activists, but without its operational clauses. In conversation with visiting foreign delegations of trade unionists, Soviet hosts stated that the law was not being enforced, and there is some evidence that it was secretly repealed in 1951.[40] Still, it remained on the books, and was not formally repealed until 1956, three years after Stalin's death.[41]

Public pressure to permit freedom of movement seems to have prevented application of the wartime "labor-freezing" law, and its reprinting without its sanctions in the trade-union activists' manual was to signify retention by the authorities of the attitude, if not the rule, that labor turnover was ruinous to state planning. Activists were supposed to urge men and women not to leave their jobs and also to explain the harmful consequences of labor turnover on the economy.

With repeal of the law, Soviet planning policy has returned to what it was before the wartime emergency: to direct the distribution of machines and materials through orders requiring the movement of goods, but to maintain for men the voluntarily accepted transfer. As had been learned a century earlier by the Russian serf-owners, whose serfs produced poorly in the factories emerging in the middle of the nineteenth century, so in the postwar epoch Soviet leaders came to appreciate again that men who are tied to a job by command are not as efficient as those who work because of inner-direction.

Since Stalin's death, planning of manpower needs is conducted only on the broad basis of estimates of need. When these have been established, men are encouraged to move to the

[40] H. BERMAN, SOVIET CRIMINAL LAW AND PROCEDURE: THE RSFSR CODES 45 (1966).
[41] *Ibid.*

areas of need by various forms of stimulation, some material and some political. The material forms are wage scales which are increased by specified percentages for the regions of the Far North and Siberia, joined with vacations longer than those available to workers in more healthful and more exciting climes. The political forms are appeals to Communist-party patriotism, like Khrushchev's campaign to open the "virgin lands" of Central Asia to agriculture. In the later 1950s more than 100,000 young Communists were encouraged to move to the nearly arid steppes to participate in an experiment in dry farming. Appeals were made to their patriotism, and their families were encouraged to urge them to go. In consequence, some went out of sheer enthusiasm for the idea and others went because their family and friends, particularly those of the older Communist-party generation who selected them as candidates, told them it was their duty.

Planning migration from surplus labor regions to areas in need of labor is evidently the goal of the planners, but it has not been working well. A demographer complains that "we have no valid, scientific system of regulating migration." [42] He notes that the population is ebbing away from Siberia in spite of the encouragement and inducements offered, and that it is flowing like a tide into Central Asia, where it is not needed in such quantities. He complains that, "The greater part of the migration in the USSR is of an unplanned nature," noting that masses of people were urged to leave the North Caucasus for eastern and northern parts of the country, but that fresh population then flowed into the evacuated areas. From his point of view statistics on which planning may be based are inadequate, because the census does not ask questions which would permit evaluation of population flow.

There remains one exception to the system of persuasion through wage differentials and appeals to love of country: the compulsory assignment of students. Stalin's heirs have continued to require students to go where they are assigned after completing specialized training at the university or technical school. Since education is planned to meet national needs and

[42] Perevedentsev, *Controversy about the Census*, LITERATURNAIA GAZETA, 11 Jan. 1967 at 13. Eng. transl. in 19 C.D.S.P. no. 2 at 15. (1967).

students are paid stipends to attend classes, the state demands that after graduation they serve in the places to which they are assigned by the placement commission. In 1933 the term of service was set at five years, but it was subsequently reduced to three, and Stalin's heirs have maintained that term.[43] A criminal penalty attaches to those who refuse to go or who depart before the end of the assignment. Under the rules, married students must be kept together and special consideration must be given to problems of health.

To enforce the rule, the USSR Council of Ministers enacted a supplementary decree of 29 May 1948 forbidding state enterprises to employ young specialists who have not been assigned to them by the ministries, and penalizing any executives who violate the rule.[44] This was introduced because it was discovered that considerable numbers of graduates were successfully evading their assignments and remaining in the large cities where they had been trained, in which the postwar reconstruction had opened up more jobs than there were young graduates to fill. The decree has remained, apparently, unenforced, for an author complains that no criminal prosecutions of directors have occurred, and he proposes that there be some civil action against them which would not be so hard to enforce.[45]

An additional practice has arisen under which enterprises pay for the education of their workers to improve their skills, obliging them by the terms of the grant to return after completion of the training. Although the system has been a boon to outstanding employees in the plants, it has sometimes resulted in personal tragedies; for the enterprises are adamant in demanding return, even when it means separation of a scholarship student and his new-found wife, or return to climatically unsuitable places when students have developed health problems. For these students the safeguards of the compulsory law on assignment of students do not apply, and there have been incidents

[43] 15 Sept. 1933, [1933] 56 Sob. Zak. S.S.S.R. pt. I item 356. Graduates of labor reserve schools were required by decree of 2 Oct. 1940 to serve four years on assignment. [1940] 37 Ved. Verkh. Sov. S.S.S.R.

[44] Decree of 29 May 1948, not published in official collection of Council of Ministers' Orders, but mentioned in Savichev, *Duty and Personal Wishes*, [1967] MOLODOI KOMMUNIST no. 3 at 78. Eng. abstract in 19 C.D.S.P. no. 18 at 32. (1967).

[45] Savichev, *id.*

like this. It is proposed that the system be abandoned and be replaced by contracts made with students during their last two years in school when their conditions and inclinations are clearer.[46]

Other Communist-led countries have preferred to use persuasion to meet planned requirements for labor force rather than to mobilize a labor army, subject to disciplinary rules and criminal punishments. The differences between them reflect the degree of militance of the several Communist parties. Pressures were lighter in Europe than they were in China, where Mao Tse-tung decided to foster his agricultural program by utilizing strong political pressure to force urban dwellers back to the farms.

Compulsion remains, then, a feature of planned population movement in some of the Marxist-oriented states, and there is need for comment on the impact of penal sanctions upon labor planning. During Stalin's time great numbers of citizens sentenced to confinement in labor camps by the special boards of the Ministry of Internal Affairs performed economically important work in the forests of Vorkuta, the gold mines of Magadan, and other remote regions to which no amount of political campaigns or wage bonuses had attracted large quantities of workmen. The same was true in the uranium mines of Czechoslovakia, in the swamplands of the Danube delta, and in other hazardous places within the states of Eastern Europe. Foreign analysts concluded that these mass movements of men and women, although made primarily to maintain social order by Communists fearing for the very lives of their political regimes, survived for some time beyond the moment of real peril because they met a planning need for personnel in remote but strategic areas of primary resources.[47]

Other analysts have doubted economic motivation because of the poor physical quality of the individuals condemned to such labor, and because of the hardship conditions maintained in the camps, which seemed out of keeping with efficient production. They have considered the camps what they seemed ostensibly to be: instruments of terror designed to subdue all

[46] *Ibid.*

[47] Crankshaw, *Forced Labour in Russia*, 35 NEW STATESMAN AND NATION 391 (1948).

resistance among peoples being led more swiftly than they were willing to go in the direction of a 100 percent state-directed and state-owned economy. According to this view the work performed by the hapless inmates of labor camps was secondary to the political reason for their incarceration. It was politics and not economics that explained the camps, for the economic return was only a by-product of the policy of terrorization. As impelling as has been the economists' analysis of the contribution made by prisoners to the development of remote regions, it is not convincing in the light of what happened after Stalin's death. The camps were cleared, the cases were reviewed, and recruitment to the forests and gold mines was restored to economic inducement and patriotic pressures.

Only relatively few, though no outsider knows how many, criminals convicted of offenses by criminal courts now serve terms in distant work camps. There is no mass emigration created by the secret activities of administrative boards run by the security police without the limitation of rules of criminal procedure, requirement of strict adherence to provisions of a criminal code, and concern for public detestation of security procedures smacking of terror. Such contribution as now may be made by prisoners to the realization of the plans is assuredly not motivated by economic necessity. It serves the purpose it does elsewhere: to keep the prisoners busy, and, it is hoped, to restore them to society with respect for work and with qualifications necessary for employment in the society to which they return.

Planning has also had repercussions upon the law of collective bargaining. Beginning with the first years of the revolution in Russia, Lenin established the principle that a major task of the trade unions was to spur the members to high productive efforts. Some of his colleagues wished to mobilize a labor army under discipline, which was later achieved during the Second World War through the 1940 decrees already discussed. But Lenin resisted this approach, preferring to utilize, to speed production, a trade-union movement in which workers had confidence because of the unions' part in opposing the evils of the tsarist system. He argued that there was still need of worker protection, but that there was no occasion for unions to fight management in nationalized factories. To do so was, under the theory of his revolution, to oppose a proletarian government, which was the workers' own.

The introduction of the New Economic Policy made the approach obsolete, for there were again many capitalist owners legitimately trying to minimize costs by cutting wages and spending as little as possible on safety measures and fringe benefits. The employers' excess zeal for profits could be controlled by establishing factory-inspection laws, minimum protection requirements, and minimum wage levels, but workmen were left to their own forces to increase their share in the net income of the capitalist ventures. In theory, the role of the unions in state-owned plants was to be different, but in operation it was hard for the trade-union organizations to appreciate that they must conduct two types of protective operations. They were asked to adopt different attitudes. Managers, whether private or state, were to be kept in their place, but in different degrees. The first were class enemies, whereas the second were "friends," even though they sat in the front office and looked much the same. Collective bargaining was the traditional instrument of pressure on both, even implemented by strikes.

With the end of the New Economic Policy, M. P. Tomsky, the Communist party leader who had headed the trade-union apparatus during the period of New Economic Policy, saw no need to change the union's role essentially. He agreed that state managers were representatives of the proletarian state, but he saw in their positions personification of a conflict of interest between management's objectives and workers' protection, and he wanted the unions to be "independent." Stalin could accept no such position, especially since state economic planning had been inaugurated. To permit the unions to exert pressure for increases in wages, shortening of hours, and improvement in working conditions seemed to him irrational. Pressure for change in these economic components meant distributing the national income on the basis of the interest of the group exerting the pressure rather than according to the rational decisions of economic planners.

The question was raised of the role of collective bargaining under conditions of complete planning. Stalin's answer was to change the function and the leadership of trade unions. The second was easier to change than the first, for Tomsky could be removed. He was replaced by Lazar Kaganovich, who had a reputation for disciplined obedience to the party leadership, particularly to Stalin. The change of function required several maneuvers. The unions were subjected to a campaign to show that wage increases were dependent upon the productivity of the workers. Strikes could only upset the planning whereas rationality promised the success of planning.

To symbolize the change, in 1933 the Central Council of Trade Unions was merged with the Ministry of Labor.[48] The council was chosen to be the instrument of the merged function. It assumed the administrative tasks formerly performed by the ministry, namely the labor inspection system and the on-job social-insurance system as it covered injuries and disease requiring brief absence but not total departure from the job. Both were close to the workman's heart and were activities which unions could administer to the benefit of their members, symbolicly replacing the old trade-union function of combatting management.

Collective bargaining required rethinking because of the changed function of the trade unions. Deliberation resulted in the termination of collective bargaining for most industries in 1933, and for the rest in 1935, although the textbooks continued to speak of the process. Not until 1947 was it revived.[49]

The termination of collective bargaining was facilitated partly because there was little left for negotiation between management and the unions. A policy of standardizing employment nomenclature, which had been initiated in 1925 with the services within the ministries, was expanded by degrees to other employment, until in 1938 an order required every ministry and central agency of the USSR to pay wages according to a fixed tariff, not only within the ministry but throughout the state enterprises subordinate to it, on pain of prosecution for violation.[50] Under this system the Second World War was fought. The unions had the task of making the workmen enthusiastic and obtaining maximum production in the national effort.

[48] 23 June 1933, [1933] 40 Sob. Zak. S.S.S.R. pt. I item 238.

[49] Order of 4 Feb. 1947, Izvestiia 19 Feb. 1947 at 1.

[50] Order of 4 June 1938, [1938] 27 Sob. Post. S.S.S.R. item 178.

Their task was the same as that of management, although with greater accent upon providing for recreation in workers' spare time and upon serving as a channel through which grievances could be aired and defended, if need be, against individual foremen who were unfair in applying pressure tactics.

With the end of the war, restoration of normal conditions led to an about-face. Collective bargaining was resumed in 1947, but not because of any change in the policy of fixing by statute all elements of the management-labor relationship elsewhere covered by such bargaining. Hours and wages remained fixed. Protection measures were set by statute and enforced by inspectors employed by the unions. There remained only a psychological element, and it was this that was seized upon to justify a return to collective bargaining. This element gave the union members a sense of participating in management decisions. Although the managers remain alone responsible under the principles of industrial management discussed in chapter 8, the unions were given even greater authority in conducting the grievance procedure, in sharing in any decision relating to the dismissal of a worker, and in ascertaining that management listened to proposals from members regarding rationalization of production and the use of inventions. The unions became a stimulus to improvement of production methods by managers who might be reluctant to innovate, and their protective features were enhanced.

Additionally, the unions were given the opportunity to share in decisions about the use of bonuses earned by the factory for overfulfillment of the economic plan. The law establishes the method of computing bonuses, but leaves to management and the union to determine how they shall be used. This feature has become the principal one to be negotiated. The workers are invited to decide, in consultation with management, whether they want recreation halls or kindergartens.

The collective agreements are long, containing many paragraphs on the obligations of management and unions, but only the distribution of bonus funds requires negotiation. The other provisions are those of the statutes, inserted in the agreement to give them publicity. Thus the administration obligates itself to perform the plan, and the union undertakes to call factory production conferences at stated intervals and to establish indicators of individual productivity from which individual wages may be computed. The administration agrees to inform workers of the conditions under which wages are paid, to post work rules to maintain factory discipline, and to operate sanitary facilities and keep them in repair. All these points are critical, but it would not require an agreement to establish them. They either are in the law or are logical implications of the law.

Other Marxian socialist states have adopted much the same procedures with regard to labor-union participation in collective bargaining, although in those states where workers may exert more direct influence upon factory directors, in the manner already discussed in chapter 8, than in the USSR the organized workmen are in a stronger position than that of the Soviet worker. The real nub of the problem is what mass pressures can be left to the union for enforcing collective agreements. In short, can the workers strike?

To all Communists a strike is unnecessary in theory because the workers, being the proprietors of the state, can change policy through the ballot box if they are not in agreement with it. Only the Yugoslavs admit the possibility of a strike, but if strikes occur they are treated as evidence of a temporary breakdown of the system, requiring immediate correction.[51]

It is the function and duty of the Communist party in each state to instruct the workers concerning the reason for any given element of policy so that they will accept its rationality. Here is the essence of the "vanguard role" played by the Communist party. The party teaches men and women what they need to know to make decisions, and in those states where the Communists have only recently attained power, or where the public is still somewhat irresponsible, it takes the reins until the citizens can be expected to participate rationally in the electoral process. Only in Hungary, Yugoslavia, and Czechoslovakia have the Communists indicated that they believe the time has come for open elections. In the spring of 1967 the Hungarian Communists permitted the voters a choice of candidates, although all were nominated with party approval. The Yugoslav Communists had permitted independent candidates to run for local office as early as 1957. In 1967 the Yugoslav Communists again

[51] G. Hoffman & F. Neal, Yugoslavia and the New Communism 398 (1962).

permitted independent candidates to run for office in local elections against those supported by the party, although the party's mass organization, the Socialist Alliance, was directed to guide but not "command" the nominating meetings.[52] By the spring of 1968 the Czechoslovak Communists were even speaking of permitting the minority parties to propose candidates for office in opposition to Communist choices, but Soviet military intervention in August ended all such speculation.

In such circumstances strikes occur only if the political system breaks down, as it did in Poland and Hungary in 1956. Opposition to communist policies was led by the workers of Poznan and Budapest, and the party could only accede to demands and make reforms. With Hungary, however, the Soviet army was rushed to the capital to prevent those reforms from going so far as to mean, in Soviet eyes, the abandonment of the Marxian socialist system.

With this background, it is evident why Soviet authors have said that the principal means of enforcing a collective agreement is moral suasion.[53] But there are other means to be used in extremity. Willful violation by management of provisions for the protection of labor is a crime, and since most of the protective provisions of the law are inserted in the collective agreement, violation of those provisions brings prosecution. Also the 1926 code in Article 134 and the 1961 code in Article 137 provided for prosecution in the event of "Obstructing the legal activity of trade unions or their agencies." These keep management in line. On the union side the code of labor laws provides specifically that the union shall not be held responsible in civil suit for any liability arising out of the agreement, and no criminal statute applies to the unions unless they intentionally attempt to wreck or disrupt the economic system. Under Article 69 of the criminal code of the Russian republic and of the USSR's fundamental principles of criminal law generally, this is termed "wrecking."

Marxists therefore find no need to place in their constitutions the right to strike. It is seen to be a revolutionary act

[52] *Assembly Elections*, 5 Yugoslav News Bulletin no. 398 at 2 (17 April 1967). Yugoslav Information Office, New York.

[53] ALEKSANDROV, TRUDOVOE PRAVOOTNOSHENIE 70 (1948) [Labor Law Relationships].

rather than a means of exercising pressure in collective bargaining, either at the negotiating stage or in enforcing the contract's provisions. Even Yugoslavia's draftsmen came to this conclusion in preparing their 1963 constitution, although they admitted the possibility of occasional strikes. After debate, the right to strike was rejected as being clearly in conflict with the Yugoslav system of influencing management through the workers' council.[54]

Economic planning has still another impact upon labor law, in that it bears the main brunt of implementing the right to work guaranteed in all Marxian socialist constitutions. Although the right is stated without limitation, it is supported in most Marxist-oriented constitutions by reference to economic planning. The Soviet constitution declares, "The right to work is insured by the socialist organization of the national economy. . . ." [55] The Chinese constitution states, "To ensure that citizens can enjoy this right, the state, by planned development of the national economy, gradually provides more employment, improves working conditions and increases wages, amenities, and benefits." [56] Only Yugoslavia's constitution of 1963 provides a more orthodox, Western-oriented guarantee, due probably to its minimal planning policy.[57]

In none of the Marxian socialist legal systems is the guarantee of a right to work implemented by a court order on an employment officer to provide a job, unless it is for reinstatement after illegal dismissal. The emphasis is rather upon maintaining a full-employment economy from which all are expected to obtain work. Lest there be any discrimination, the criminal codes punish managers who discriminate against applicants for reasons of sex or race,[58] and the procurator sets aside discriminating regulations.

No Marxian socialist state requires a state manager to take a worker when economic rationality will not permit it. Recruiting is the same as it is in modern capitalist states: on the basis of

[54] Pešelj, *Socialist Law and the New Yugoslav Constitution*, 51 Geo. L.J. 651 at 671 (1963).
[55] Art. 118.
[56] Art. 91.
[57] Art. 26.
[58] Criminal Code R.S.F.S.R. arts. 74, 139.

aptitudes and skills tested among individuals who appear voluntarily to ask for a job. Yet Marxists see a difference in the establishment of employment in the capitalist world and in their own. It lies in the concept of the individual agreement. Marxists deny that their agreement is a contract in the traditional sense. It is evidence, rather, of a social relationship.

By this difference in terminology, Marxists hope to indicate that they have advanced well beyond that stage in human relationships when a labor contract was looked upon as the purchase of a commodity, no different from the purchase of goods. Thus, they reject capitalism's "freedom of contract" because they think that that freedom is illusory on the worker's side of the deal. Under capitalist conditions they believe that workers are always subject to weighty economic pressure to sell their labor power without regard to the employer's onerous conditions. Capitalists of all lands would now agree that the old situation was intolerable, and everywhere limitations have been established on the employer's freedom, symbolized internationally by the conventions prepared by the International Labor Office and widely adopted. But Marxists think that this is not enough. They want to establish even more limitations, even against the state managers of the enterprises employing labor.

This current attitude was not represented in the code of labor laws adopted in the Russian republic in 1922 with the beginning of the New Economic Policy. In keeping with the spirit of the capitalist period it ushered in, the code defined the employment relationship in traditional terms as an "agreement between two or more persons, in which one party (the employee) offers his working power to the other (the employer) for wages." [59] The impact of this capitalist phraseology was reduced in some measure, however, by refusal to include the labor contract in the civil code. This refusal was intended to symbolize the fact that employment was not a sale of labor power in any commercial sense, but a new type of relationship, even though stated in conventional capitalist terms.

Years have passed since 1922, but the code of labor laws still remains in force in the USSR in spite of many amendments. A draft statute was published for discussion in 1959 but still

[59] 30 Oct. 1922, [1922] 70 Sob. Uzak. R.S.F.S.R. pt. I item 903, Art. 27.

awaits enactment.[60] By its provisions the labor contract becomes "an agreement between a toiler and an enterprise or office by which the toiler takes upon himself the duty to perform work of a given specialty, qualification or responsibility, and the enterprise or office obligates itself to pay him wages for the work and to assure conditions of work provided by labor law, the collective agreement and the labor contract." [61]

The major feature of the new labor contract is the same as that of the collective agreement: specification in law of all of its features. In consequence, workers have not signed written contracts with management, except in special circumstances, as when collective farmers have been recruited for work in the mines. To allay their suspicions that the jobs would not provide the protection and opportunities for which they left the farms, model contracts were published setting forth for easy reading what their rights and duties would be.[62]

In a measure Soviet jobs have all been placed under a civil-service system. They are classified, and wages are paid uniformly throughout the country according to the classification. The terms of dismissal are established precisely in the law. Those terms which are subject to interpretation, such as "lack of suitability," "systematic failure to perform," and "absence without acceptable reasons" have been placed within the jurisdiction of the peoples' court, although not until the remedies offered by the trade-union-directed grievance procedure are exhausted. Courts are burdened with litigation on these subjects, and reinstatements are often ordered because of violation of the law by management, even though with the consent of the trade union local, which is now required for all dismissals.

All Marxian socialist states but Yugoslavia, which has its special ideology on workers' self-government, adopt the same principles of protection on the job, and to these principles they credit, in part, their claim to a distinctive legal system. But it is not a claim based upon making jobs where none have economic reason to exist. The legal systems all permit termination of a labor contract in the event of liquidation of the enterprise, reduction in staff, or termination of the specific work for which

[60] For text, see [1959] 10 Sots. zak. 1.
[61] Art. 6.
[62] For text, see [1944] 12 Sob. Post. R.S.F.S.R. item 71.

the worker was employed.[63] Under the conditions of broadened property incentives introduced soon after Stalin's death and extended since 1965, emphasis is placed upon rationalizing production to eliminate unnecessary workers quickly, so that costs may be reduced. Managers who succeed in this receive bonuses, as do the remaining employees of the plant whose productivity has been increased.

Although managers, in theory, were previously free under the law to dismiss unnecessary workers, the accent was on retention, until the 1965 changes. Today the labor contract establishes less of a position of life tenure than was its prior practice. It has become more a manifestation of a relationship created solely for the production purpose. It is still a social relationship and not a sale of labor power, which means that the worker is to be treated humanely; but if dismissal becomes economically necessary, it is now to occur promptly. Then the state, through its employment retraining centers, is expected to prepare the man for other work. This is expected to become increasingly important with the progress of automation, which in the Marxian socialist countries, as elsewhere, is requiring constant relocation of workers who become technologically superfluous.

The exception for Yugoslav labor law is made necessary by the Yugoslav system of worker self-government. Since under the concept the workers "own" the enterprise, they are in a measure partners in the endeavor and not one step removed from ownership as employees of the state. They cannot be said to be subordinate to a "labor" relationship, but are subject to a social duty. They have been called "subordinate to their own work." [64] In practice, however, standards of employment have had to be established by law, to which management must adhere in the working relationship, and the effect on management and the individual worker is much the same as elsewhere within the family of Marxian socialist legal systems.[65] There must be pay-

[63] Code of Labor Laws R.S.F.S.R. 1922, art. 47.
[64] Baltić, *The Labour Relationship and the Rights of Management*, [1957] THE NEW YUGOSLAV LAW (Apr.–Dec.) 64.
[65] Law of 12 Oct. 1966. [1966] J. of L. Yugoslavia no. 43. Eng. transl. in 16 COLLECTION OF YUGOSLAV LAWS (LAWS OF EMPLOYMENT RELATIONSHIPS) 13 (Institute of Comparative Law, Belgrade 1967).

ment according to effort and product, no discrimination on grounds of sex, and protection through social insurance and old-age pensions.

In reviewing the breadth of detail provided by various branches of law in the Marxian socialist countries, the massive impact of state planning upon traditional legal institutions is evident, even to the extent of creating new branches. But, as with other fields, much of the difference between new and old is a difference in emphasis, in attitudes. Yet with the institution of the planned obligation, unrelated to voluntary agreement of the parties, a new element has emerged.

The novelty can be discerned only after noting that even legislatures in capitalist economies have introduced compulsion in the form of duties to contract, like the obligations placed on employers to bargain collectively and to make collective agreements, upon automobile drivers to buy liability insurance, and upon employers to contract for workman's compensation. All these compulsory features are thought necessary to provide justice to the victims of disaster and even to meet a newly felt obligation to society which pervades the capitalist world in varying degrees. Yet although this development provides a semblance of similarity in legal systems, these measures are only peripheral—patches upon the legal fabric inherited from the past and not the result of a complete reorientation of the economic process and the legal institutions designed to make it work. That is the novelty offered by the family of Marxian socialist legal systems.

15

Torts within a Social

Insurance Framework

N<small>EGATIVE</small> PROPERTY INCENTIVES PROVIDE THE RATIONALE OF tort law in Marxian socialist countries. Just as affirmative property incentives have been increasingly utilized in the USSR and elsewhere within the family of Marxian socialist legal systems to stimulate individuals to produce, so the threat of loss of property has gained popularity since the late 1920s as a means of stimulating individuals to take care in what they do. This is remarkable because socialist-oriented systems outside the Marxist orbit have tended to move away from such stimuli.

The trend in Western Europe and North America has been toward insurance, to which potential inflictors of injury are required to contribute, or toward extension of principles of strict liability to make the tort feasor an individual insurer of the victim. Dramatization of this latter trend is found in popularization of the concept of the irrefutability of presumed negligence, which one author has epitomized as "negligence without fault."[1] To protect the individual caught in the ever-expanding net of responsibility for harm, capitalist-oriented systems offer personal liability insurance, often made compulsory.

The Marxian socialist states, with a few variations by those longest associated with Western legal traditions, have rejected much of the Western trend. Personal liability insurance, except for foreign motorists, is not even allowed in the USSR.[2] The law of torts has not withered away in favor of social insurance, as socialists elsewhere have expected it to do. It has been strengthened so that a large number of suits in the civil law field are even brought to enforce a duty to aid those in peril. Tort law is made a major instrument of Marxian socialist morality. It must help to form the new socialist man.

The social-insurance concept generally favored by socialist thinkers at the time was introduced into Lenin's Russia soon after the 1917 revolution,[3] giving the impression that Communists planned to move along the same road as the non-Marxian socialists, but with one difference. There were to be no compulsory premiums from employees. The whole burden was to be placed upon the employer, whether private enterpriser or the state. But the treasury was impoverished, and it could not contemplate protection of property as well as life through a public insurance scheme at state expense. Even before enactment of the first civil code in 1922, the new people's courts were awarding damages to peasants for injury caused their crops by cattle wandering from neighboring fields.[4] Causation was established in traditional manner, and fault was presumed from the presence of cattle beyond the confines of their pastures.

With the introduction in 1922 of a new civil code to implement the New Economic Policy, the traditionalist Romanist place in the code was given to obligations incurred in causing injury, but with an emphasis which smacked of work-

---

[1] A. EHRENZWEIG, NEGLIGENCE WITHOUT FAULT (1951).

[2] Gray, *Soviet Tort Law: The New Principles Annotated,* in W. LAFAVE ed., LAW IN SOVIET SOCIETY 180 at 197 (1965).

[3] 31 Oct. 1918, [1918] 89 Sob. Uzak. R.S.F.S.R. item 906.

[4] Bazhenkov v. Vishivskii Village Community and Korinakov v. Vishivskii Village Community, mentioned in Kurskii, *Comments on the People's Court,* [1918] 5–6 PROL. REV. I PRAVO 19.

ing-class mentality. Rich persons who committed harm were to be held responsible to an impoverished victim even though not at fault, through an article reading, "In circumstances when the person causing injury is not required to repair the injury under the provisions of Articles 403–405, the court may, however, require him to repair the injury, taking into consideration his wealth and that of the injured party." [5]

Unclear drafting beclouded the meaning of the basic provisions of Article 403, taken from French law, but the draftsmen declared that they intended to make fault unnecessary.[6] Early court practice accepted their position, and the code was applied to require no fault and little causation to establish liability. Thus, a man who had conceived a child was held responsible for injury to its mother during a hospital abortion not performed by him, even though he had in no way been responsible for the hospital's fault.[7] Causation was found in the conception. The outsider is forced to conclude that for a Soviet court of that time a hapless victim of harm was given judgment, even if the court had to search through the community to find someone related in only a tenuous way to the chain of events that led to the harm.

Two American lawyers who analyzed judicial practice of the early years concluded that the courts applied a rule of liability without fault,[8] even though the code—in emulation of its French model—could have been interpreted, in spite of its vague wording, as distinguishing between acts, some of which occasioned liability in all events, and others of which subjected the actor to liability only in the presence of fault.

A former Russian imperial lawyer in search of an explanation of the no-fault tendency decided that the Soviet jurists had seized upon prerevolutionary Russian and Western European trends toward a concept of liability without fault and turned it to their own class ends.[9] Certainly, it was useful at the time as a

[5] Art. 406.

[6] Gray, *supra*, note 2 at 184. See also Rudden, *Soviet Tort Law*, 42 N.Y.U. L. Rev. 583 at 597 (1967).

[7] Citizen S, no. 339, [1929] 8 Sud. Prak. Verkh. Suda R.S.F.S.R. 5.

[8] Holman & Spinner, *Basis of Liability for Tortious Injury in Soviet Law*, 22 Ia. L. Rev. 1 (1936).

[9] 1 V. Gsovski, Soviet Civil Law 491 (1948).

form of insurance of the poor, financed by the capitalists of the New Economic Policy, who were hated in spite of Lenin's policy of toleration in the interest of economic revival. Such a conclusion could be supported by the code's provision that, "In fixing damages the court must in all cases take into consideration the wealth of the injured person and the wealth of the person who caused the injury." [10] Although this is sometimes said to be the bias of juries in the United States, no such stated principle is found in the law. In this lies the difference.

The trend of Soviet tort law in the mid-1920s toward no-fault liability to the poor, rather than in the direction of developing a new moral sense of obligation to take care, is remarkable because it accompanied an expansion of the social insurance and health systems. Seemingly, without specific legislation,[11] but as a result of an expansion of state sponsored health services, every citizen was given the opportunity, if not the "right," to obtain free medical care to cover his immediate needs after an accident. Also, social insurance benefits, initiated in 1918, were increased and extended to wider categories of people until they protected all who were employed, even if their injury or illness was not employment-connected.[12] The thought was fostered that with time even children, housewives, and collective farmers would be brought within the system.[13]

The phasing out of the New Economic Policy required a rethinking of the rationale for tort obligations. When all citizens had been placed in the category of wage earners, and differentiated wage schemes had been perfected, in abandonment of concepts of eglitarianism, those acquiring property enjoyed a respected place in society because they were a different kind of person from the capitalists of the NEP. They had bank accounts not because they had made money by employing laborers or selling merchandise, but because they had personally

[10] Art. 411.

[11] No statute has been found. The assumption stated was suggested by a conversation at the Faculty of Law of the University of Kiev, Sept. 1965.

[12] 76,900,000 persons were employed in 1967. Birman, *The Talent of an Economist*, [1967] Novy MIR, no. 1 at 167. Eng. transl. in 19 C.D.S.P. no. 13, at 6, 7 (1967).

[13] Eörsi, *The Adaptation of Civil Liability to Modern Needs*, 10 REVIEW OF CONTEMPORARY LAW no. 2 at 11 (1963).

contributed to the national welfare with their own toil in an important way, as measured by the wages they were paid. Those with money were now the favored citizens rather than the disfavored. There was strong national policy to avoid penalizing them for earning well by making them pay judgments for injuries caused without their fault.[14] Further, the moneyed individual was unlikely to become a potential tort feasor, for capitalist enterprise had been taxed out of existence. The state enterprise had become with the Five Year Plan of 1928 the major potential source of accidents, whether in production, in transportation, or in the dispensation of services.

Under the conditions of the 1930s the courts developed concepts in keeping with practice in the Romanist legal family. Fault was restored to prominence as a primary element of tort liability, and when the activity causing the harm was extrahazardous there was available for application Article 404, inserted by the 1922 draftsmen in emulation of the French model to protect the victim regardless of the inflictor's fault. Soviet tort law was becoming almost traditional.

What was happening in these developments of the 1930s? The conclusion is now inescapable that a major change in thinking had occurred. Instead of a gradual "withering away" of tort law with the expansion of social insurance, it had won a new lease on life because of the contribution it was expected to make in helping to create the new morality. Its primary function would be to enforce the duty to take care in all relationships from which harm could flow. The equivocally drafted Article 403 of the 1922 code, which had served during the early years as a base for establishing liability without fault because of the first of its two provisions, was turned to the new purpose because of its second provision, although not in the full Western sense. The difference was that the burden fell on the defendant to prove absence of fault. It was not on the plaintiff, as it is elsewhere, to prove that the accused had been at fault in committing the harm.

In developing the role of moral teacher for tort law, the courts had to relate its provisions to the social insurance system. Under the system employers were paying a tax, which appeared

---

[14] 2 SOVETSKOE GRAZHDANSKOE PRAVO 396 (1961) [Soviet Civil Law].

to be a premium for protection against suit by injured employees on the basis of whose wage line the tax was computed. This interpretation was given credence by Article 413, which read, "A person or enterprise paying insurance premiums to protect an injured person under social insurance, shall not be required to compensate for injury caused by the happening of the event against which the insurance has been purchased." But, the premiums paid by employers were not to give them absolute protection against suit on all causes of action, for a second paragraph of the article exempted from protection the employer guilty of a "criminal act or omission." No definition of "criminal" was provided.

In keeping with almost universally accepted rules of social insurance, the agency paying benefits to the insured for injuries caused by action for which the premium bought no protection had a right to sue the person causing the injury, by way of subrogation to the rights of the victim, to recover what it had paid as benefits.[15] This meant that for "criminal acts or omissions," when injury was caused, the social insurance agency could sue the person causing the injury, even though it was receiving premiums from him covering the workman's injuries, because the premiums did not cover that specific quality of wrongdoing.

The problem came, of course, with interpretation of the word "criminal." Did an inflictor of injury have to be prosecuted under a provision of the criminal code and found guilty before the social insurance agency could gain reimbursement in suit against the premium payer who had caused the injury? The answer finally came, and it was "No." A criminal prosecution was not necessary.[16]

Simply proving the existence of a protective regulation by reading it before a civil court and proving its violation met the test of "criminality" in the sense required by the civil code. Contrariwise, absence of violation of a protective regulation freed the defendant from liability. For the state enterprise engaged in manufacture or transportation, since most injuries were the result of a violation of a safety regulation, in practice

[15] Art. 413.
[16] Dobrovol'skii, *What's New in Judicial Practice in Tort Cases*, [1960] 8 Sots. zak. 54.

most injury could be classed under the heading of a "criminal act or omission," giving the social insurance agency the right to sue for the benefits it had paid. There were not many fault situations left to be covered by the premium, although it was by no means without value in some situations, as will be shown.

Social insurance according to the Soviet model is not, however, merely a means of making quick payment to a victim while suit is being readied by the insurance carrier against the wrongdoer. The system is framed to place the initiative in bringing suit upon the victim, not upon the insurance carrier which has paid benefits. This result is achieved by setting the social insurance benefits at a subsistence level, which is less than the average wage. Consequently, an injured workman who earned more than the amount of maximum benefits before the injury is forced by economic necessity, if he wishes to maintain his previous standard of living, to bring suit for damages against the party causing harm. The system offers the advantage of bypassing the social insurance bureaucracy when a moral lesson is to be taught to enterprise managers. The party most directly concerned brings the action, proves his loss, rebuts, if necessary, the defense of the defendant who has overcome the presumption of fault, and recovers his judgment. Thereafter, the insurance carrier, with no effort at all, files the judgment obtained by the victim as *res adjudicata* against the enterprise, proves the amounts it has paid and recovers an award from state arbitration in reimbursement.[17]

What has been said applies to the inflictor of injury who is the employer of the victim, and to the social insurance agency which has received premiums based on the victim's wages from the employer. But this is not the only relationship with social insurance which appears in tort. Suits are often brought by employed victims, insured under the social insurance system against state agencies which are not their employers, as when a truck driver slips on a grease smudge when entering a restaurant. Since the victim, like all employees, is protected by the social insurance system wherever he may be in the USSR, he immediately recovers his benefits. Thereafter, he may sue the inflictor of injury for such additional damages as he can prove,

[17] [1965] 11 Sov. iust. 24. State arbitration accepts claims once or twice a year and gives judgment automatically without review.

and the insurance carrier, by way of subrogation to the victim's rights, may also bring suit in state arbitration to recover the benefit. Since the premiums paid by the restaurant enterprise buy protection only from suits by its own employees, there is no need now and never has been need to consider whether the inflictor of injury was criminally at fault because criminally negligent. Recovery is possible in tort so long as fault of any kind is proved.

A large number of judicial decisions indicate that courts have been assiduous in their efforts to find fault before giving recovery. A sheet-metal cutter in a factory was injured when he tripped over the crane track and tore a ligament as he awkwardly stepped aside from an advancing crane. He sued, alleging negligence of the enterprise in operating the crane. Under the code, in keeping with usual Romanist practice, contributory negligence is no bar, so that negligence inherent in his awkward movements could not have excluded his action. On suit the enterprise attempted to meet the burden of proof of absence of fault by introducing the regulations governing movement of the crane. They required that a whistle be blown. The enterprise proved that the whistle had been blown. Since the suit was brought by a workman against his employer, the presence of "criminal negligence" had to be found to obtain recovery above social insurance. Although the trial court gave judgment for the plaintiff, it was set aside by the supreme court of the Russian republic on the ground that "disability cannot be blamed on the defendant"; and since it was an insured-against event, the enterprise had no obligation to compensate. The victim had to accept as his total recovery what he could obtain as social insurance, but in this he had good fortune. The court indicated that the usual maximum would be exceeded to cover his full loss.[18]

The fault principle was carried into the post-Stalin legislation of the USSR by the Fundamental Principles of Civil Law adopted by the federal Supreme Soviet in 1961, and subsequently extended in the civil codes of the various republics.[19] By Article 88 of the fundamentals, "The person who has caused

---

[18] Piskarev v. Factory, [1961] 2 Sov. IUST 29, case 3.
[19] Civil Code R.S.F.S.R. 1964 art. 444.

the injury may be relieved of the duty to compensate for it if he establishes that the injury was not caused through his fault."

The provisions relating to the rights of the insured and the insurance carrier which were in Article 413 of the 1922 code have been maintained, with one exception—that the protection to the enterprise paying the premium against suit by the insurance carrier to recover the benefits it has paid is given only if there is no fault at all on its part,[20] not, as in the 1922 code, in any case in which its fault was not "criminal." Whether this change in wording broadens in practice the responsibility of the insured inflictor of injury is debated, and seems still to be uncertain before the courts. The earlier downgrading of "criminal" fault under court practice in interpreting the 1922 code suggests that the difference is not as great as it may appear to be.[21] The new code may only have incorporated existing practice. As with the 1922 code, when the person who causes the injury is not one who has paid insurance premiums covering the employee concerned, there is no insurance protection to him, and the general rules of liability apply.[22]

The European members of the family of Marxian socialist legal systems have not passed through a period of enforcing liability on the rich regardless of fault, perhaps because they utilized their Romanist codes containing the usual rules until they had time to develop a new approach. Generally, they have adhered to familiar Romanist patterns even in their new codes, but there has been no uniformity on the question of burden of proof of fault. Some follow the Western European tradition and place it on the plaintiff. Others have gone over to the Soviet system. Thus, the draftsmen of the Polish code of 1964 preferred to adhere to the past, although not without debate as to the desirability of change. In their report, they declared their adherence to the old rule because "it made possible the retention in force of a rich body of judicial decisions which solve in accordance with social needs the many problems raised by the accepted provision." [23] The Romanians have felt likewise, but

[20] Fundamental Principles art. 91.

[21] Gray, *supra*, note 2 at 200.

[22] Fundamental Principles art. 92.

[23] Rudzinski, *New Communist Civil Codes in Czechoslovakia and Poland: A General Appraisal*, 41 IND. L.J. 33 at 59 (1965).

the Hungarians and Czechoslovaks have adopted the Soviet rule, perhaps with social justification.[24]

It is notoriously hard for an individual to prove negligence against a large enterprise, even when the judge is required, as he is in the Marxian socialist legal systems, to be active in helping the parties present their claims. It can be presumed that the enterprise will have good counsel and, being master of its own house, can present all pertinent facts. Further, the obligation to prove innocence of fault can be expected to stimulate the safety engineers in an enterprise to devise appropriate measures of protection and to make sure that they are in accord with whatever standards may exist nationally and locally through published regulations and general practice. Finally, there is little reason to fear that placing the burden of proof on the defendant will multiply litigation brought by men skilled as plaintiff's attorneys and functioning on a contingent fee basis under which they are paid only if they win. These practices, found in some countries of the West, are absent in the USSR, where attorneys are under stricter discipline than abroad and where citizens are discouraged from harassing state enterprise without rather sure chance of winning. This latter point is emphasized by legislation of 1961 requiring employees to seek redress from their employers for work-related injury before bringing suit, and requiring management to settle claims in accordance with principles of law as established by the code, if at all possible.[25] Litigation is further discouraged, for if the worker is dissatisfied with the settlement, he must ask the labor union shop committee to review the record before bringing suit. It is expected that managers will recognize their responsibility quickly when facts are presented and the award subjected to review by the labor union if the employee is dissatisfied. Likewise, an employee required to submit his complaints to the labor union before he takes the matter to court should think twice before he proceeds against the good judgment of his own union.

The 1964 Czechoslovak civil code makes the same provisions for relating recovery in tort to social insurance benefits,

[24] Hungarian Civil Code 1959, art. 339 and Czechoslovak Civil Code 1964, art. 421.
[25] 2 Oct. 1961, [1961] 41 Ved. Verkh. Sov. S.S.S.R. item 420.

requiring the victim to reduce his claim by the amount of the benefits he has received.[26] Nothing is said of the right of the insurance carrier to suit by way of subrogation to the victim's rights, but it may be presumed. The Hungarian code, in traditional form, is completely silent on the relationship between social insurance benefits and recovery in tort.

To the rule that fault alone creates liability a notable exception is found in the codes of all of the Marxian socialist states: the rule of strict or "absolute" liability in the event of injury caused by a source of increased danger. The rule is old both in the Romanist countries and in Anglo-American law, but no foreign analyst of Soviet law can find its justification under modern socialist conditions. Professor Whitmore Gray has called its existence a "paradox," [27] and indeed it is. Socialist states have none of the reasons for the emergence of the doctrine in the common law and in Romanist systems, where the owner of a source of increased danger was expected to bear the cost of human destruction arising from his operations and to pass on this cost to the consumer. In effect, the wear and tear on human life was to be amortized like that of the machine, so that the ultimately expended individual would be recompensed to the extent possible by money for loss of health or limb. The rule in the capitalist economies provided a form of compulsory insurance financed by the consumer and administered by the owner of the dangerous thing.

Socialism has its social insurance fund, so that the rule of strict liability can exist for no capitalist reason. This is realized and quite another explanation is given. The rule is explained as necessary to exact greater-than-normal observation of safety rules and to encourage the development of technological improvements to eliminate accidents.[28] Whatever the justification, and the one given seems inadequate to those who suppose that care is fostered only to avoid liability, the principle adopted from the French code to meet the needs of neocapitalism in Lenin's Russia in 1922 has remained with Marxian socialist systems since that time. It is restated in the 1961 Fundamental

---

[26] Art. 447.

[27] Gary, *supra*, note 2 at 197.

[28] Barry, *The Motor-car in Soviet Criminal and Civil Law*, 16 INT'L & COMP. L.Q. 56 at 73 (1967).

Principles of Civil Law of the USSR,[29] and in the new civil codes of her neighbors. Even the Czechoslovaks in their imaginative new code of 1964 continue to assert the principle, albeit in somewhat altered form. They place the emphasis upon transportation, stating that "Organizations engaged in transport shall be liable for damages caused by the special nature of their operations,"[30] and state that "The operator may not be relieved of his liability if the damage was caused by circumstances originating in its operation."[31] His only defense is "if he can prove that the damage could not have been prevented in spite of every effort that can be expected in this respect."

For the Soviet draftsmen liability attaches "unless they can show that the injury arose as a result of irresistible force or the intentional act of the injured party." To this was added in express terms in the 1922 code "or the gross negligence of the injured party." Although this qualification was removed in 1961 from the language of the strict liability article, it remains in force by virtue of the general provisions on fault of the injured party which establishes the rule of "comparative negligence," common to the Romanist systems. Gross negligence of the victim may be used, therefore, to reduce or deny full compensation if it contributed to or increased the extent of the injury.[32]

Since the existence of the strict liability rule is justified in Soviet eyes by the exaggerated care it is presumed to stimulate, no personal liability insurance is permitted to mitigate its effect, except for foreigners who will depart and from whom it might be difficult to obtain satisfaction of a judgment were there no insurance coverage. Czechoslovaks and Hungarians have not felt it necessary to go so far. They permit the owner of sources of danger to buy personal liability insurance, perhaps because he has always been permitted to do so,[33] and the concept of socialist justice to the citizen has come to include this old idea. Some Soviet jurists have come to feel the same way, as Professor

[29] Art. 90.
[30] Art. 427.
[31] Art. 428.
[32] Art. 93.
[33] Czechoslovak Civil Code 1964, art. 377; Hungarian Civil Code 1959, art. 560. See also Nagy, *Civil Liability for Industrial Injuries in Hungarian Judicial Precedents*, 10 REVIEW OF CONTEMPORARY LAW no. 2 at 86 (1963).

Donald D. Barry has demonstrated, but their complaints have fallen on deaf ears.[34]

To this prohibition of liability insurance there is an exception, namely for the state enterprise, operating an extrahazardous implement, which injures one of its own employees. The enterprise's insurance premium to the social insurance system protects it against suit by the employee and by the social insurance agency subrogated to his claim so long as there was no fault. This means that the rule of strict liability is mitigated for the premium-paying employer to a rule of liability under general rules of fault if the victim is his own employee.[35] For all others who may be injured by the extrahazardous implement, strict liability is applied.

The difference in treatment of strict liability between the various states of the Marxian socialist family lies not in fundamentals, but in the types of instruments treated as extrahazardous. The Russian republic's 1922 code listed them as "railways, tramways, industrial establishments, dealers in flammable materials, keepers of wild animals, persons erecting buildings and other structures, etc." The list was not exhaustive in the view of the courts, and it was augmented by a decision of the Ukrainian supreme court in 1925 to include the automobile. This decision was shocking to some jurists at the time, because in enacting the 1922 code the legislature had rejected the draftsmen's proposal to include the automobile as an extrahazardous instrument.[36] The 1925 judgment was never revised or supplemented by legislation, and it became a permanent fixture of the law. It was even put into the USSR codes by the 1961 fundamental principles.

The Czechoslovak approach, beginning as it does with the basic principle that the concept has primary validity as a measure against the organizations engaged in transport, lists in the group "the operator of a motor vehicle, a motor vessel, as well as the operator of an aircraft." [37] Then in a subsequent article the code opens the gate to court interpretation by saying simply, "Liability for damages due to the nature of an especially

[34] Barry, *supra*, note 28 at 74, n. 8.
[35] Gray, *supra*, note 2 at 201.
[36] Barry, *supra*, note 28 at 74, n. 9.
[37] Art. 427.

dangerous operation shall be borne by the operator similarly as in the case of the operator of a transport vehicle." [38] The courts are invited to analogize.

The Hungarians in their civil code of 1959 prefer the generalized formula, saying "he who engages in a particularly dangerous activity must compensate for the injury that results," [39] although they include wild beasts in a special article. The difference in phraseology between the states is immaterial, however, as the list is open even in the USSR and may always be lengthened by the court. [40] In some instances, as with aircraft, the rule in the USSR is included in the 1962 civil air code, but even more strictly than in the civil code; for, in keeping with the Warsaw Convention, there is no release from liability in the event of *force majeure*. Only the intentional act of the victim overcomes the airline's liability. [41]

Listing of an instrument as extrahazardous does not automatically confer strict liability if the instrument is not being used in a manner that is dangerous: thus a locomotive is considered extremely dangerous only when under steam, and an automobile only when moving, not when its door is slammed on a hand.

By far the greatest number of reported decisions pertain to automobiles and instruments of transport. For example, a collective farm's truck was destroyed while crossing a railroad track because the woman on watch opened the barrier to let the truck pass even though she knew that a passenger train was due. A criminal action was brought against the woman, and a civil suit for damages joined. She was found guilty and damages awarded, but as an impoverished woman, she was judgment proof, and the farm wanted to sue the railroad. In setting aside the civil judgment against the woman the Russian republic's supreme court reserved the right to the collective farm to bring suit for the value of the truck, noting that the railroad was a source of great danger, and so was responsible for the damage under Article 404. There was no need to prove fault. [42]

[38] Art. 432.

[39] Art. 345.

[40] Gray, *supra*, note 2 at 198.

[41] Air Code of the USSR, 26 Dec. 1961, [1961] 52 Ved. Verkh. Sov. S.S.S.R. item 538.

[42] Collective Farm v. Okuneva, [1959] 3 Sov. IUST. 83, case 4.

The notion of strict liability is so strong that it serves to make liable a collective farm whose driver used one of the farm's dump trucks during a drunken frolic and damaged an automobile from the pool of the Ministry of Foreign Affairs. Although the trial court gave judgment to the plaintiff, an appellate court reversed, saying that since the driver had used the truck on his own initiative after work to drive to town on a personal matter, the farm could not be held liable. The supreme court of the Russian republic set aside the reversal on the ground that the owner of a source of great danger is liable regardless of fault, although it notes a limitation: it remarked that the driver was not a thief of the truck, but an employee to whom the farm had entrusted the vehicle.[43]

The situation of a thief had arisen three years earlier, and the court was restating the rule of the case. An automobile belonging to a car-rental enterprise was stolen by unknown persons, who injured a pedestrian and fled. The victim sued the enterprise but judgment was denied since the car had been removed without its fault.[44]

Another limitation on strict liability is the gross negligence of the plaintiff, as has been indicated above. Some decisions will indicate the scope of the exception. First, a failure to find gross negligence: A passenger riding in the back of a truck was injured because it turned over when the drunken driver violated the speed laws. The trial court reduced the recovery on the ground that the plaintiff was himself negligent in riding in the back of the truck, presuming, perhaps, that he would not have been injured in the cab. The reduction in amount was set aside on review because the cause of the injury was the driver's drunken negligence, not the plaintiff's location in the back.[45] There was no suggestion, as there had been years earlier, that a victim had contributed to the situation because he had drunk in company with the driver and had not restrained him in his

[43] Motor Pool of Ministry of Foreign Affairs v. Collective Farm "Path to a New Life." [1960] 10 *id.* 26, case 2.

[44] Barry, *supra*, note 28 at 78, citing Kuznetsova v. Autobaza, SBORNIK POSTANOVLENII PRESIDIUMA I OPREDELENII SUDEBNOI KOLLEGII PO GRAZH-DANSKIM DELAM VERKHOVNOGO SUDA RSFSR 1957–1958 at 19 (1960) [Collection of Orders of the Presidium and Rulings of the Civil College of the Supreme Court of the R.S.F.S.R. 1957–1958].

[45] Kosartsev v. Auto Transport Office, [1960] 11 SOTS. ZAK. 86.

progress toward inebriation.[46] Perhaps that issue was not raised in the second case because it had already been settled by the court's earlier denial that sharing in drinking constituted gross contributory negligence.

A finding of gross contributory negligence occurred after a collision between a truck and a motorcycle. The driver of the motorcycle was found grossly negligent, and compensation reduced accordingly.[47] Gross negligence prevented recovery when a pedestrian stepped out in such a way that a driver could not avoid running her down.[48] But if the victim's injury was not directly the result of her fault, there may be recovery even if the driver could not have prevented the accident. Thus, when a woman was knocked into the street by the blow of an intoxicated man and was killed by a passing truck, recovery by her dependents was allowed. The owner of the extrahazardous instrument was held liable since neither *force majeure* nor intent on the part of the victim had been claimed. The court added that the enterprise could sue the drunkard to recover what it had been required to pay.[49]

Even *force majeure* is narrowly interpreted to exclude its use as a defense, as evidenced by a case involving a strong wind. A state enterprise engaged in lumbering sued the geological prospecting expedition sent out by the Northwest Geological Administration to recover damages caused by a forest fire touched off by the blasting of the geologists. State arbitration denied recovery because it found no fault, but the decision was reviewed on audit by the deputy chief arbitrator, and the case remanded for new trial on the ground that a blasting operation is a source of increased danger for which there is strict liability.[50] It made no matter that all possible precautions had been taken and that the expedition had followed the regulations. To the defense that the fire started quickly and was immediately

[46] Grishin, [1938] 10 Sov. IUST. 40, case 1.

[47] Barry, *supra*, note 28 at 81, citing case 1, in [1964] 1 Biull. Verkh. Suda R.S.F.S.R. 15.

[48] *Id.* citing case 3 in [1966] 2 Biull. Verkh. Suda R.S.F.S.R. 16.

[49] *Id.* citing case 1 in 8 Biull. Verkh. Suda R.S.F.S.R. 15 (1965).

[50] Lazoverski Forest Enterprise v. Murmansk Geological Expedition of the Northwest Geological Administration, case 401/1 for 1965, [1966] 11 Sov. IUST 31.

out of control as the result of the intervention of an insuperable force, the deputy chief arbitrator turned a deaf ear. He noted that it had been extremely dry weather, there had been a strong wind, and the blasting area had been covered with flammable bushes. "An insuperable force is an exceptional circumstance unpreventible under given conditions" said the deputy chief. He noted that the workers were aware of the high wind, and should have taken measures to prevent the danger.

No enterprise may utilize the labor contract to escape liability. The Hungarian civil code of 1959 establishes this principle, excluding contracts in which an employer seeks to avoid responsibility.[51] The Soviet rule is the same.

The measure of damages in Marxian socialist countries is the victim's earning power, although some of the countries most influenced by their traditions add compensation for other elements as well. Thus the 1964 Polish code retains the traditional Polish compensation for moral harm (*krzywda*), found in the event of deprivation of liberty or when a woman was induced by deceit, force, or abuse of dependent status to submit to a lewd act.[52] This right is personal, however, to the victim, and was denied to a widow and surviving children who would have recovered under pre-Marxist Polish civil law for moral harm and suffering. It was also denied to the victim of slander and libel, on the ground that recompense for such moral harm was not consonant with socialist morality. A compromise position was offered in that a victim of slander or libel, as well as of infringement of copyright or patent, was granted the right to demand that the wrongdoer pay an appropriate amount of money to the Polish Red Cross. In some measure the Soviet solution of a forced retraction of the libel or slander with appropriate publication and the levying of a fine is comparable,[53] although the required Red Cross contribution is peculiarly Polish, in that the payment is not exactly a fine but, perhaps, a source of moral satisfaction.[54]

The Czechoslovaks are also more generous to a victim than the Soviets, for their 1964 provision authorizes compensation

---

[51] Arts. 342 (1), 345 (1).
[52] Art. 445.
[53] Civil Code R.S.F.S.R. 1964, art. 7.
[54] Rudzinski, *supra*, note 23 at 60.

"for the pains suffered by the injured and for the resulting handicap in his social usefulness." If the damage was caused intentionally, a court may not only award damages necessary to restoration of the previous state of affairs, but also may "award the compensation of other damages if failure to award such additional compensation would be contrary to the rules of socialist conduct." [55] Thus, in contrast to Polish thinking, a Czechoslovak court's application of socialist morals may increase liability rather than provide a reason for its restriction.

The Hungarians are silent on reparations other than restoration of the *status quo ante*, either by payment of money or in kind, if the latter seems to be indicated as especially desirable.

Although the European Marxian socialist states, with a tradition of compensation in money for other than financial loss, have been reluctant to withdraw entirely from their past positions, there is no such reluctance on the part of the jurists of the USSR. For them, suit in tort can compensate only for financial loss suffered so obviously that it can be proved by the accountant's ledgers. Other types of deterrence, such as the criminal law to punish copyright and patent violators, or public retraction of a slander, seem to Soviet jurists more appropriate than recovery in tort to discourage antisocial conduct which results in no monetary loss and to satisfy the victim's desire for social recognition of his rights. One cannot speak of assuaging his desire for revenge, for under socialism such motivation is considered too base for satisfaction.

By the 1964 Russian republic code, the established rule of compensation for financial loss alone is restated in Article 459 as compensation "for wages lost as a result of his total or partial disablement, as well as for expenditures caused by the injury to his health (special diets, artificial limbs, special care, etc.)." To this is added the right of the person who pays burial expenses in the event of death of the victim to recover them. [56] Some doubts have been raised as to just what expenses beyond loss of wages may be included as damages, [57] for there have been efforts to recover the wages of baby-sitters required to watch convalescent

---

[55] Arts. 442, 444.
[56] Art. 469.
[57] Gray, *supra*, note 2 at 188.

children during the absence of a mother at work, and expenses for special diets. Generally, these expenses are collectible if prescribed by a doctor and if not too remotely related to the convalescence from the injury. The cost of a motor invalid-carriage may be included, but only exceptionally.[58] If an ordinary illness intervenes, unrelated to the fault of the inflictor of harm, as when partial loss of hearing results from an independent disease, there is no recovery for that supplemental disability.[59]

When the issue is one of property damage, the Russian republic's code[60] and those of other Marxian socialist states generally permit compensation in kind by delivery of an article of the same kind or quality, or by repairs. When the circumstances suggest it, compensation of full damages in money is required. Soviet commentators note a change in emphasis in 1964 from that of the 1922 code, which permitted the same alternatives but indicated preference for restoration of the previous condition, and specified money damages only as a supplementary remedy.[61] This change in emphasis provides one more example of the complete acceptance of money today as a convenient means of exchange. The explanation lies in the fact that the Soviet economy has expanded, and consumer goods are generally available to permit a victim to replace with his money judgment what has been destroyed. In 1922 a pocketfull of money might have been meaningless in the absence of adequate stocks of goods.

Since damages are to be computed in terms of wages lost following the accident and projected over the future, health examinations become necessary to determine the percentage of remaining capacity to work. The formula for extrapolation is to determine the workman's wage at the time of injury and to subtract the percentage of earning power that remains to him, on the assumption that he can earn at the reduced rate. This examination is conducted by social insurance doctors, and it is used to determine both the extent to which a social insurance

---

[58] FLEISHITS ed., NAUCHNO-PRAKTICHESKII KOMMENTARII K G.K. RSFSR 531 (1966) [Scientific Practical Commentary to the Civil Code of the R.S.F.S.R.].

[59] Dobrovol'skii, *supra*, note 16 at 54.

[60] Art. 457.

[61] FLEISHITS, *supra*, note 58 at 528.

pension should be paid and the amount of supplemental recovery to be adjudged in an action in tort. There is no comparison of the testimony of expert medical witnesses presented by the parties in court, for the certificate of the social insurance doctors is taken by the judges as proof unless they have doubts. In such an event courts have been permitted to seek expert testimony on their own initiative.[62]

If conditions change so that a victim can increase earnings or is unable to earn as high a percentage of his original salary as was expected, the medical finding may be reopened and a new determination made, which is then applied to readjust the judgment.[63] This revision is facilitated by the manner of payment of damages to be discussed below.

Since lost wages are the main measure of damages, and these are the wages at the time of the permanent injury or, in certain cases of temporary disability, the average wage over the two preceding months, a problem is presented in compensating young people who had not yet entered upon their full earning capacity when injured. The same is true of housewives who have no established wage. Before the promulgation of the post-Stalin codes, there was no legislative rule on the matter.[64]

Court practice established an approach in 1940 in the USSR. When a child sued the state street railway enterprise for loss of both legs, the court in giving judgment said it could reach no conclusion on the permanent rate of pension until the child reached his majority.[65] In another case at the same time a man injured in 1928 while he was a child and given judgment sued on reaching his majority for recomputation on the basis of the wages of a chief clerk, plus a lump sum for special diet, the wages of a constant companion, the purchase and repair of an artificial limb and shoes, and three years' residence in a watering place. The trial court gave all that he asked, but the supreme court of the USSR remanded for a new trial, partly because it thought the extra expenses insufficiently linked to the original injury, but also because it thought the wage of a chief clerk out of line with the youth's capacities. It proposed rather

[62] Shavshishvili v. Soiuztrans, [1939] 15–16 Sov. iust. 69.
[63] Civil Code R.S.F.S.R. 1964, arts. 466, 467.
[64] Fleishits, *supra*, note 58 at 538.
[65] Magradze v. Tibilisi Tramway Trust, [1940] 12 Sots. zak. 91.

that the wage to be used as a measure of damages be that of an unskilled clerical worker, for which the plaintiff's completion of the ten-year school presumably qualified him, whereas the position of chief clerk also required executive ability, for which schooling alone gave insufficient training.[66]

In an earlier case the court had held the defendant liable for maintenance of a child until he reached his majority at the age of sixteen, and then a review was to be held to determine for what the child was fitted, and on that basis the life pension would be computed.[67]

To settle the controversy over an appropriate measure of computation for minors, the 1964 Russian republic code established precise rules.[68] A child below the age of fifteen is to receive full compensation for "expenditures connected with restoration of his health" as determined by expert medical testimony before the court, and at fifteen a pension must begin, computed on the basis of the average wages of an unskilled worker in the particular locality. If the child happens to have been receiving wages before the age of fifteen, those wages are used for computation, but the compensation must not be lower than if the average wage of an unskilled worker had been used. If the child subsequently begins to work, a recomputation is made on the basis of his demonstrated capacities.

Since damages are paid in terms of lost wages, they take the form of a pension payable monthly. By law there may be no capitalization of this pension, except when a judgment is against a foreign inflictor of damages.[69] Even then, the victim is paid only a pension from the state insurance company, which receives the lump-sum judgment as a single premium on an annuity contract.

The rule of payment in installments rather than in lump sums may have some grounding in socialist principles and con-

---

[66] Revason v. Azov-Black Sea Railway, SBORNIK POSTANOVLENII PLENUMA I OPREDELENII KOLLEGII VERKHOVNOGO SUDA SSSR 233 (1960). [Collection of Orders of the Plenum and Rulings of the Colleges of the Supreme Court of the U.S.S.R.].

[67] Baltushkin v. Zapolsk Agricultural Artel, [1931] 3 Sud. Prak. Verkh. Suda R.S.F.S.R. 10.

[68] Art. 465.

[69] Art. 468.

ditions. A lump sum could not be invested in anything but the state savings banks or lottery bonds, so there would be no opportunity to live by income from skillful investment in any but limited fashion. Also a large lump sum might not remain in the hands of individuals having no experience with large sums of money. The cash might create an attitude of mind reminiscent of bourgeois approaches to wealth, although this possibility would be limited by the narrow opportunity for legal investment. It might even lead to criminal "speculation." Still, these socialist overtones to lump-sum judgments have little ground for credence, because some nonsocialist Romanist countries, such as Mexico, have adopted the installment method of payment of damages. The Soviet experience suggests, rather, that a pattern borrowed from abroad has been useful under conditions of socialism, but that it was not devised with those conditions in mind.

The fact that installment payment is a rule of convenience for citizens accustomed to wages is suggested by the Czechoslovak treatment, for in the 1964 code loss of earnings is compensated by a cash annuity, based on the average earnings of the victim before his injury; but the money award for pains suffered by the victim and for resulting handicap to his social usefulness is payable in a lump sum.[70] The Hungarian code of 1959 supports the theory of convenience also, for it permits payment of damages in the form of a pension "in the event that the indemnity is destined to furnish or add to the sustenance payments due a victim or those close to him and dependent upon him." [71] If sustenance is not the issue, the provision of the Hungarian code for payment in lump sums of money generally appear to permit it if the circumstances warrant.

The "sustenance" concept of damages is emphasized particularly when injury results in death and the matter of dependents is raised. The first Soviet codes, and the current 1964 Russian republic code, make clear that there has not been and is not now survival of a cause of action. At most, dependents receive damages because they need them to replace what they have been receiving or have a right to receive from the de-

[70] Arts. 444, 445.
[71] Art. 357.

ceased breadwinner. Thus, only "persons unable to work who were dependent upon him [the breadwinner] or had a right to receive support from him as of the day of his death, as well as a child of his born after his death, have a right to compensation." [72] The share of those qualified to receive payment is not the full wage of the deceased, but only such part as they received or had a right to receive for their support while he was alive.

Compensation ends for minors at the age of sixteen, or for students, at eighteen. Invalids receive compensation for the period of disablement. A spouse or parent of the deceased who does not work and is engaged in caring for children, grandchildren, brothers, or sisters of the deceased below the age of eight receives compensation regardless of age. The only other members of the dependent group who may receive compensation are women over fifty or men over sixty.

The 1964 code is more generous to dependents than the 1922 code, but it must be remembered that at the earlier time dependents received compensation only if they were in need. In 1922 the language of the code limited tort recovery to dependents who had been supported by the deceased and had no other means of support.[73] The 1964 code abolishes the means test, but in so doing it adopts a provision of the social insurance law which had been introduced in 1928 by instruction to facilitate administration.[74] The 1928 instruction had created a presumption of need in certain categories of persons authorized to receive social insurance payments in the event of loss of a breadwinner. The 1964 code, with very small changes in the ages defining these groups, makes this social insurance rule applicable also to the tort judgments for sums exceeding benefits from social insurance to those qualifying after the death of the victim.

The dependents of a victim of an accident are discouraged from bringing suit in court to obtain funds if their claim is against the former employer of their deceased breadwinner. The 1961 decree, already discussed as requiring presentation to the

[72] Art. 460.
[73] Art. 409.
[74] 4 July 1938, secs. 62, 88 pub. in KATS & SOROKIN, SOTSIALNOE STRAKHOVANIE 128, 132 (2d ed. 1936). [Social Insurance].

employer and audit by the trade union before suit is brought in court, applies also to dependents; [75] only if the claim is against a noninsurer of the victim may the dependents proceed directly to court.

Payment of damages to dependents is subject to the same rule of installment payments as applies to a permanently injured victim who survives. Thus a widow who brought suit to recover damages against the man convicted of the negligent killing of her breadwinner found her judgment in the trial court reversed because it was expressed in what was interpreted as a lump sum. She had sought to cover the maintenance of herself and her children, inadequately protected by the social insurance payments. The trial court framed its judgment in terms of a lump sum for damages to date and installment payments thereafter, but it had placed a ceiling upon the installments by ordering defendant to pay 33 percent of his wages until the total of 45,580 rubles was reached. The appellate court declared that the judgment should have stated the amount to be paid each time and over what period, the period being the entire period of need. [76]

The Czechoslovak civil code of 1964 adopts the same position as that of the Soviet draftsmen. A cash annuity is to be paid to cover the cost of maintenance of the survivors whom the deceased supported or was obligated to support. [77] The amount of damages is reduced, however, by what is received from social insurance. Average earnings of the deceased are used in computing the amounts, but if the death was caused intentionally, the court may award a higher amount "if failure to award it would be contrary to the rules of socialist conduct." Again, as in several other places in the code, the Czechoslovak draftsmen wish to reassert the possibility of exception when a court thinks it socially desirable.

Payment in installments presents a problem when a state enterprise is reorganized or liquidated. This is met by a provision of the 1964 Russian republic code, that claims are brought against its successor, or if there is none, against the superior organization or such other organization as is named in the

[75] FLEISHITS, *supra*, note 58 at 533.
[76] Kurbatova v. Pogodaev, [1961] 5 Biull. Verkh. Suda R.S.F.S.R. 15.
[77] Art. 448.

liquidation order.[78] If an outstanding judgment exists, the successor, if any, pays, but if there has been complete liquidation, "the payments must be capitalized according to the rules of state insurance and deposited with an insurance organization for payment in the prescribed amount and manner."

The penchant for enforcing a duty of care through tort litigation has driven Soviet courts, and finally the legislature, to accept responsibility even by governing institutions, such as ministries and soviets. As has happened in modern Romanist and Anglo-American common-law systems, the Marxians have demonstrated that their power to innovate has been limited by their inheritance of the ancient concept of immunity from suit for acts of *imperium*. The theory was so strongly held in the early years of Soviet legislation that it influenced the drafting of Article 407 of the 1922 civil code. Although Lenin made clear his determination to hold state economic enterprises liable through charter provisions established in accordance with the requirements of his first decree on the trusts, his civil code followed the traditional rule on acts of governmental authority.

Lenin's civil code sounded affirmative on the point: making governmental institutions liable for injury caused by improper acts of an official committed in performance of his duties. But then it added the decisive provision. Such liability was to exist only if established by specific laws.[79] Only five laws were enacted in the period up to 1961, when the rule was changed. Four of these were so specialized that they were never incorporated in the code, but one was incorporated: the liability of responsible agencies receiving deposits of property, including money, when made in accordance with some legal requirement or authorization.[80] The other four, being of little concern to the average citizen, remained in independent acts concerning administrations of merchant seaports, governmental maritime pilots, offices of requisitions and confiscations, and institutions having to do with the affairs of cooperatives.[81]

---

[78] Art. 470.

[79] Art. 407.

[80] Art. 407a.

[81] Barry, *Governmental Tort Liability in the Soviet Union,* 20 RUT-GERS L. REV. 300 at 314 (1966). I have also examined the detail in my *Soviet Law* in A. LARSON & W. JENKS, SOVEREIGNTY WITHIN THE LAW 268 at 277 (1965).

The courts remained traditional on state immunity at first, but by degrees they began to apply a functional test, holding governmental institutions, not organized as juristic persons, liable in tort when they performed a given economic function. Legislative acts of the soviets were held to be beyond the reach of damage suits, as when a resolution of the law-giving instrument of the Ukraine evicted a tenant from a government building.[82] Suit for losses resulting to an NEP capitalist from having to discontinue a business was rejected. Likewise, a claim against the Moscow Criminal Investigation Department for injuries to the plaintiff was denied. If, however, the injury resulted from negligence in operation of a streetcar, an automobile, or a ship, recovery was permitted.

The difficult cases followed. A test case was that of the Bureau of the Geological Committee, whose boring machine struck sparks which set a fire that destroyed the home and barn of a citizen. The bureau claimed immunity under Article 407, but the supreme court denied it on the ground that the bureau was not an "institution" within the meaning of the article, since it carried on definite activity, which, although directed to a scientific end, should be relegated to a scientific enterprise.[83] In short, it was closer to being economic than administrative in its scientific exploration.

The courts were moving, in the opinion of Professor Donald Barry, away from the test of determining the identity of the institution to ascertaining what it was doing.[84] The act was becoming determinative, not the actor, in spite of the language of Article 407. Still, the new approach was infirm, for when the Ministry of Health was sued for negligence committed in hospital treatment, it was excused not because of what it was doing, but because it was an "administrative" institution. This was thought to make it immune. Later the shaky foundation of the rule was demonstrated in two school cases, each decided differently when suit was brought for injury to children. One found liability and the other denied it because of Article 407.

Yet when a sign being erected on the roof of the Ministry of

[82] Barry, *id.* at 310–11.
[83] *Id.*, citing case 3561, [1925] 34 Ezh. sov. iust. 1151.
[84] *Id.* at 312.

Finance fell on a passerby, the ministry was held responsible,[85] and there was recovery from the Ministry of Defense when an army flare fell on a barn and destroyed it.[86] After these steps toward utilizing tort law to enforce a duty of care, even with regard to ministries, there was a hiatus for several years while Stalin conducted his revolution in law to oust the Pashukanis type of thinkers who favored creation of an "'economic law" to replace civil law. But after the civil law had been restored to full vigor, very few decisions on suits against government institutions were published—perhaps because the editor of the law reports did not wish publicity for the subject, but more likely because it was a time when the courts had little inclination to extend the law beyond its specifically stated principles. Article 407 remained untouched. When activity resumed after Stalin's death, there was variation in judicial treatment and sharp academic discussion, ending in enactment of a new statement of policy in the 1961 fundamental principles.

The 1961 fundamentals repeat the 1922 idea, but in reverse form, which changes its impact greatly. Instead of extending immunity to all governmental institutions unless a specific law provides for one or another of them individually, liability is extended to all unless a specific law extends immunity.[87] Such extension of immunity is anticipated by the code for organs of inquiry, preliminary investigation, the procuracy, and the courts. How far this will lead is as yet uncertain, for Professor Barry notes that Soviet authors differ even on the liability of hospitals since the adoption of the fundamentals.[88] Some expect liability to be unquestionable, but others take the contrary view.

There is a clue to future practice in a 1964 suit brought against the Soviet armed forces by the survivors of a deceased officer, killed while a passenger in a military automobile which collided with another because of gross violation of the traffic rules by the soldier driver. The military unit awarded pensions

---

[85] E. FLEISHITS, OBIAZATEL'STVA IZ PRICHINENIIA VREDA I IZ NEOSNOVA-TEL'NOGO OBOGASHENIIA 174 (1951) [Liability for Causing Injury and for Unjust Enrichment].

[86] Barry, *supra*, note 81 at 317, citing case 34381 in [1925] 50–51 EZH. SOV. IUST. 1551.

[87] Art. 89.

[88] Barry, *supra*, note 81 at 323.

to the invalid wife of the deceased and to his aged father, but both sued for additional compensation on the ground that the pensions were inadequate to their needs. The people's court gave judgment for them, but when it reached the supreme court, a retrial was ordered by the supreme court's civil college. The trial resulted in denial of the suit, on the ground that a special law governed obligations to military men.[89] It provided for pensions but was silent on suits. Thus, in the college's view the provisions of the civil code were inapplicable to the military personnel of the services. Sharp criticism of the decision indicated that the Soviet academic jurists are not receptive to this limitation of liability under the 1961 fundamentals.[90] They argue that the constitution extends to the military the full complement of rights of Soviet citizens and this principle supervenes the special law, or at least should apply when that law is silent. Nonmilitary citizens may sue the military services under ordinary rules.[91]

The Czechoslovak code of 1964 draws no distinction between various types of state organizations.[92] But as if to reinforce the obligation of organizations which receive goods for safekeeping, as with the 1928 amendment to the 1922 code of the Russian republic, the Czechoslovaks specifically define responsibility, subject to limitations on value.[93] Again the position taken is in accord with what that of the Soviet model has come to be.

The Chinese Communists offer in their treatment of tort law the same contrast offered in contract law and described in chapter 13.[94] As with contracts, the contrast springs primarily from differing traditions in Europe and in China. The Chinese preference for mediation over litigation leads them to seek an "arrangement" between hostile parties rather than the relatively

[89] Barry, *supra*, note 28 at 79, citing case 1 in [1964] 5 Biull. Verkh. Suda S.S.S.R. 34.

[90] *Id.* at 79.

[91] *Id.*, citing case 1 in [1964] 2 Biull. Verkh. Suda S.S.S.R. 15.

[92] Art. 421.

[93] Art. 433.

[94] I am indebted to Prof. Victor Li for suggestions as to an approach to the Chinese communist attitude toward the problem of torts. Li's own study of civil responsibility in the Chinese people's republic is in preparation.

black and white determinations of a court judgment. This traditional attitude is reinforced by Communists' belief that it is their duty to guide the people toward a new society in which all will have learned to live in harmony.

Beyond this foundation stone, inherited from the past and recut to correspond to the dreams of the future, there lies a secondary principle also created by tradition. It is the Chinese proclivity toward intermingling tort concepts with those of criminal punishment. This principle finds reflection in the Security Administration Punishment Act of 1957,[95] which allows the police to impose administrative sanctions for minor infringements of a citizen's personal or property rights,[96] and even to order payment of compensation to the victim for out-of-pocket medical expenses and property damage.[97]

The impetus to bring civil suit for damages is further reduced by some practical considerations, as it is in other Marxian socialist states. There is less reason to sue when victims can obtain free medical care and social insurance benefits.[98] Finally, the low income level of the average defendant would make a judgment no more than a right on paper.

In spite of these various factors militating against litigation in the manner of European Communists, Chinese lecturers at the Peking Institute of Civil Law found it desirable to set forth in their 1958 manual a chapter on civil liability for tort.[99] As with the subject of contract, the lecturers seem to have been seeking to create a body of doctrine similar to that of the USSR. The aims of tort law were stated as the same in both China and Europe, except for greater emphasis upon law as a

[95] Law of 22 Oct. 1957. Eng. transl. of pertinent pars. in J. COHEN, THE CRIMINAL PROCESS IN THE PEOPLE'S REPUBLIC OF CHINA 1949–1963: AN INTRODUCTION 205 (1968).

[96] Art. 2.

[97] Art. 29.

[98] See Labour Insurance Regulations of the P.R.C., 25 Feb. 1951, amended 2 Jan. 1953. Eng. transl. in A. BLAUSTEIN, FUNDAMENTAL LEGAL DOCUMENTS OF COMMUNIST CHINA 534 (1962). As in the USSR, protection is afforded only employees, with a maximum benefit of 75 percent of wages at time of injury.

[99] BASIC PROBLEMS IN THE CIVIL LAW OF THE PEOPLE'S REPUBLIC OF CHINA, ch. 21 (Institute of Civil Law, Central Political-Judicial Cadres School ed.) Eng. transl. JPRS no. 4,879 (15 Aug. 1961).

means of enforcing the dictatorship of the proletariat over "class enemies." The details of the law were the same, except for a lack of distinction between proved and presumed fault.[100]

The retreat from Soviet models after 1958, to which reference has been made in previous chapters, seems to have had an effect upon tort law. The Chinese legal literature of the 1960s has accentuated the tendency to differentiate between good citizens, categorized as the "people," and "enemies." [101] Coupling this fact with what is known of Chinese disputes with Soviet Communists over class conflict in a socialist society, the outsider can suppose, although he cannot yet prove, that the "enemies" are subjected increasingly to penal sanctions when they commit torts, while the "people" are urged to reconcile conflict through mediation rather than by taking the dispute to court.

Although tort law's major function in the family of Marxian socialist legal systems is seen to be the conventional one of enforcing the duty of care, it also has other purposes for some members of the family. These emerged after the USSR constitution of 1936 introduced two new articles creating affirmative duties for citizens. Civil-law actions in tort were joined with the criminal law for implementation, introducing an element of some novelty.

One of the new duties was specific and one general. For the specific one, tort law was early called into use, but for the general there has been, to the present, no legislative or judicial action, in spite of long continuing discussion of the desirability of some form of legal sanction. The specific duty is created by Article 131 of the constitution as the "duty . . . to safeguard and fortify public, socialist property as the sacred and inviolable foundation of the Soviet system, as the source of the wealth and might of the country, as the source of the prosperity and culture of the working people." In a second paragraph the constitution sets the basis for criminal sanctions by declaring persons committing offenses against socialist property the enemies of the people.

---

[100] They have been analyzed by Tsien Tche-hao, *La responsibilité civile délictuelle en Chine populaire*, 19 REV. INT'L DE DROIT COMPARÉ 875 (1967).

[101] For citation, see *id.* 878, n. 3.

Tort law's function in implementation of this specific duty has been indirect. It has not given the state the right to sue a citizen for loss suffered by the state because the citizen failed to perform his constitutional duty, but it has created circumstances encouraging his performance. Court practice, in implementation of the article and without any legislative guidance, developed through a series of cases the right of the citizen who performs his duty and is injured to recover his damages in tort.

The first of these cases arose when a claim was filed for damages suffered when a passenger on a train left the coach to assist in extinguishing a fire in a freight train nearby.[102] The court concluded that, although the civil code provided no recovery for the volunteer, the constitution had created a duty, and when it was performed, the citizen had a right to recovery. Judgment was entered against the railroad, whose property was in peril. A second case involved much the same sacrifice when a spectator at a sport contest helped save the property of the Dynamo sports club, a public organization, whose property is analogized to that of the state.[103]

From these two decisions Soviet commentators concluded that a right in civil law had been created, and the legislature confirmed the conclusion in enacting the Fundamental Principles of Civil Law in 1961. By Article 95, which was carried into the Russian republic's code of 1964 as Article 472, a citizen sustaining injury in rescuing socialist property from a threatened danger must be compensated by the agency benefited. General rules of tort law as set forth in the code apply, except for certain exclusions. The owner cannot escape liability by proving absence of fault, and the negligence of the rescuer is not to be considered under the ordinary rules of comparative negligence in assessing damages.

Commentators indicate that the rule serves to protect a rescuer not only of state-owned property, but also of the property of a collective farm or of another type of cooperative organization, as well as the property of a public organization, such as a trade union, the Communist party, or a sports club.[104]

[102] Martsiniuk v. Dzerzhinskii Ry. [1940] 22 Sots. zak. 1.
[103] Bychkova-Goncharenko v. "Dinamo," [1949] 10 Sud. Prak. Verkh. Suda S.S.S.R. 27.
[104] FLEISHITS, *supra*, note 58 at 543.

Of course, there must be a causal link between the attempted rescue and the injury.

The more generally phrased duty was set forth in Article 130 of the constitution of the USSR as the duty "to respect the rules of socialist intercourse." Soon after this duty was inserted in the code, legal writers raised the questions whether it required that citizens attempt to rescue those in peril, and whether those who made such an attempt could be compensated for injury, and those who failed to make the attempt could be sued by the survivors of the deceased for loss of a breadwinner who should have been rescued in accordance with the constitutional duty.

A textbook of 1938 took a strong position in favor of implementing the constitutional duty by creating in the individual who was not rescued or his heir the right to recover damages in tort from a citizen who did not make the attempt.[105] Still, the author realized that a good deal of courage was required on the part of a potential rescuer, and he surrounded his conclusion with conditions. The rescue could be demanded in performance of the constitutional duty of Article 130 only if the potential rescuer was in a physical condition suitable to making the attempt, and if the weather conditions were also suitable. Putting his proposal in the form of a concrete case, he felt that the duty existed if a strong swimmer on the bank of a stream which was not running fast saw a drowning man relatively close to the bank.

Subsequent authors were less brash. None gave a clear hypothetical case to illustrate his point, but all preferred to speak in general terms of instincts which should motivate the new socialist man to save his neighbor. Courts never rose to the occasion, perhaps because no suits were brought. Finally, a senior professor of civil law, in response to a question posed by an outsider, wrote an article to discuss the implications in tort of Article 130 of the constitution. After reviewing the situation and the absence of judicial decisions, he concluded that the obligation was moral rather than legal, and that as such it was within the jurisdiction of the comrades' courts rather that of the people's

[105] 2 Grazhdanskoe pravo 392 (All-Union Institute of Juridical Sciences ed. 1938). [Civil Law]. Prof. M. M. Agarkov was the author of the chapter concerned.

courts.[106] The first had to do with moral matters on which social pressures were exercised, whereas the second had to do with the written law and judgments for money damages.

The test came with preparation of the fundamental principles of 1961. Although Article 131 was implemented by the draftsmen in accordance with what had become judicial practice, no provision was made in civil law for implementation of Article 130. Only in criminal law, as revised in the Russian republic's code of 1961, were sanctions established. The matter seems closed in the USSR in the civil law field, but not so elsewhere within the family of Marxian socialist legal systems. The Yugoslav constitution of 1963 declares it to be "the duty of every person to render help and assistance to another person in danger," and implementation may be expected, as the matter is not closed.[107] The 1964 Czechoslovak civil code introduces the first sweeping provision in a European civil code, establishing the duty not only to rescue human life but, more broadly, to prevent any bodily injury, and even damage to health and property.[108] Although the duty extends to "everybody," it is not without limits. These are the same as those posed by the 1938 text writers in the USSR, for the code states, "He shall not be obliged to do so if he is prevented from doing so by a serious circumstance or if he would thereby expose himself or persons close to him to a serious danger."

Having created the duty to rescue in the civil code, the Czechoslovaks have established in the rescuer the right to damages by Article 419, reading, "Whoever was averting a threatened injury or preventing undue enrichment shall be entitled to compensation for costs actually incurred and damages suffered by him in such action also from the person in whose interest he had acted, but such compensation shall not exceed the amount corresponding to the averted injury." The rescuer is also excused from any liability for damage he may have caused in attempting the rescue, unless the threat could have been averted in another manner or unless the damage caused by the

[106] Orlovskii, *On the Question of the Competency of the Comrades' Courts in Settling Civil Law Disputes*, [1960] 2 VESTNIK MOSKOVSKOGO UNIVERSITETA, SERIIA X, PRAVO 15 at 19–20.

[107] Art. 59.

[108] Art. 416.

attempted rescue is obviously as serious or more serious than that which had been threatened.

Should a potential rescuer fail to perform his duty, he may be sued under Article 425, whose novel provisions read, "Any individual who failed to fulfill his duty . . . although its fulfillment would have prevented imminent injury, may be ordered by a court to contribute to the compensation for the injury to an extent appropriate to the circumstances of the case, unless the injury may be compensated for otherwise." The court is told to take into consideration what obstructed performance of the duty; the social importance of the damage; and the personal and material situation of the individual who failed to perform his duty.

Although the Czechoslovak code provision is the broadest in Europe, it is not the only one. The Portuguese, in their civil code of 1867, established a civil claim, although on a narrower basis, giving a person who is violently attacked the right to sue for damages an onlooker who fails to defend him.[109] Several states, France being the most notable, have established such a right of civil suit following enactment of criminal provisions punishing an individual who fails to perform a duty to rescue. The civil claim of the victim is joined with the criminal prosecution.

The German courts have extended to the rescuer the right to recover out-of-pocket expenses and bodily injuries suffered as a result of an action to save life. The Austrian civil code of 1811 provides likewise, and so does the Polish civil code of 1964, whose Article 438, like that of the Czechoslovaks, states that "One who suffers material damage involuntarily or even voluntarily in order to avert an injury threatening another person or in order to avert a common danger is entitled to claim compensation for losses proportionally from persons who profited therefrom." Dr. A. W. Rudzinski, as an expert on Polish law, indicates that the term "material damage" (*szkoda majatkowa*) also covers bodily injuries.

Clearly, some of the Marxian socialist countries interpret

---

[109] Rudzinski, *The Duty to Rescue: A Comparative Analysis*, in J. RATCLIFFE ed., THE GOOD SAMARITAN AND THE LAW 91 (1966). Also, Feldbrugge, *Good and Bad Samaritans: A Comparative Survey of Criminal Law Provisions Concerning Failure to Rescue*, 14 AM. J. COMP. L. 630 (1966).

socialist morals as including the duty to rescue and provide a system of criminal sanctions to enforce it, as well as some tort provisions to facilitate it. But this position is not taken throughout the Marxian Socialist family, nor is it unique to the family. Other states go as far, the main exceptions being those of the traditional Anglo-American common law, where the duty to rescue not only does not exist but is discouraged by holding the rescuer liable in tort if he fails to exercise due care in acting as a "good Samaritan." An aroused legal profession in the United States is now demanding that legislative action be taken, and a draft good Samaritan act has been proposed.[110]

Whether the common man is yet ready to honor his duty to rescue in the USSR may be doubted. In a discussion following prosecution of a group of neighbors for the failure to reenter a burning hut to save a group of children, various individuals gave what seemed to the newspaper reporters to be excuses.[111] One said in response to the question "Why didn't you wake up the neighbors?" "I lost my head"; but he took time to save all his belongings from an area not yet on fire. Another said when the question was put, "What! Do you think that my husband was supposed to go into the fire and risk his own life?" When the defense lawyer was asked her view on the matter she said, "Of course, from a moral standpoint this is ugly, but not within the purview of the courts." The trial court convicted, but the appellate court remanded for new trial to determine whether a causal link could be established between the children's death and the neighbors' inaction and whether aid could have been rendered without serious danger. In the opinion of the newspaper reporter, Russians have acquired from the long centuries of conflagrations of the Tatar-Mongol invasions the courage to enter the flames of burning huts, and this trait has been intensified by the experiences of the revolution and World War II. For these reasons entering a burning hut to save life is accepted as a civic duty, and the commentator thought it should be enforced.

In review of the Marxian socialist law of torts, the enforcement of the duty of care stands out as the common core of all members of the legal family. The element of distinction in

---

[110] For text, see RATCLIFFE, *id.* 279.

[111] Pushkar, *Into a Burning Hut*, Izvestiia 17 Nov. 1966 at 6. Eng. transl. in [1966] 18 C.D.S.P. no. 46 at 23.

comparison with trends elsewhere in the world's legal systems is the continuing Marxist reaffirmation of this function, in contrast with the trend away from it in the non-Marxian states, capitalist and socialist alike. While the non-Marxians desire to protect the victim under social insurance schemes, and are eliminating by degrees the necessity of establishing fault in a judicial proceeding, the Marxian socialist states have deliberately reduced social insurance coverage to a subsistence level to stimulate victims to bring actions and so police the careless possessor of state or personal property.

The desire to discourage negligence has become so extreme as to cause expansion of the concept of strict liability. Automobiles have been included among the instruments of great danger, following Austrian and German example, for it is argued that if the possessor of an automobile is held responsible in every circumstance, he will be cautious in previously unheard-of degree. In short, the Marxists argue that to reduce negligence in the use of some very dangerous instruments there should be no means of defending by proving absence of negligence. To psychologists in the non-Marxian countries the argument seems strained, but it is now firmly rooted in Eastern Europe. And this is not all. Even when ordinary negligence is necessary to maintain a claim for damage by nonhazardous implements, the burden of proof is transferred from the plaintiff in most Marxian states to the defendant, who is required to prove his lack of fault.

Tort law in two Marxist states is even given the task of enforcing affirmative duties to protect state property, and in one state, to induce citizens to act as good Samaritans in protecting the lives of those in peril. Although this function is not unique to the Marxian socialist legal systems, it is a colorful example of the role assigned to the law of torts in forming a new set of socialist morals. The aim of "carrying out the socialist revolution in the sphere of ideology and culture," as established by the 1957 declaration of the Communist parties in power, is sought in part by development of the law of torts. Its task is to contribute to the inculcation of a feeling of "mutual respect between individuals," and of "comradely mutual respect," in every citizen as required by the Soviet Communist party's 1961 code of morals.

16

Correction of Criminals in a
Renovating Society

DIVIDING CITIZENS INTO TWO GROUPS FOR PURPOSES OF THE
criminal law has been a hallmark of Marxian socialist legal
systems, although the basis of division has been articulated
differently. For Lenin, the division was made on class lines, as
determined by the Marxian definition of class origin. For Stalin,
it was ostensibly the same, but with the start of the "antikulak"
campaign in 1930, the distinction became increasingly more
flexible to put among the "enemies of the people" those who
opposed Stalin, with scant regard, if any, for origin. This approach led eventually to Stalin's great purge of 1935–37. For
Mao Tse-tung, the difference between "enemies" and the "people" has become even more flexible. The same person, in the
view of some specialists, might be categorized as an "enemy" on
one occasion and as one of the "people" on another, depending
upon the offense committed.[1] With the advent of Mao's "Great

[1] Fu-shun Lin, *Communist China's Emerging Fundamentals of Criminal Law*, 13 AM. J. COMP. L. 80 at 86 (1964).

417

Cultural Revolution" in 1966 many of the leaders of the Chinese Communist party were classed as bourgeois enemies, even Mao's former colleague Liu Shao-chi. Mao seemed to be going the way of Stalin in introducing as an element of the definition the measure of loyalty shown to him.

The distinction drawn between the two groups is of the utmost importance. It determines the approach of the penologist to the case. For those classified as among the "people," the approach is reeducation and restoration to society in a condition supposed to assure conduct becoming to a socialist man. For those ranked as "enemies," the formula is withdrawal from social relationships for long periods of time, for social defense, capped in the exceptional case by execution.

All Marxian socialist states can be placed somewhere along a continuum. At one end stands contemporary China, where "class enemies" are legion and are determined by standards which vary from time to time, and at the other end are the longer-established societies, notably the USSR of the late 1960s, where the "class enemy" has faded from society. This fading away creates a situation defined in theoretical terms in the Communist party's 1961 program as the end of the dictatorship of the proletariat and progression to a new form of state called the "state of the whole people."

For many bent on determining the characteristics of Marxian socialist law, the turbulent revolutionary period when leaders searched for the opponents thought to be lurking everywhere is a decisive one. This was the stage of "militant communism" in Lenin's Russia between 1917 and 1921, when he was able to say that for those who seemed to threaten his "Redarmymen," punishment was to be meted out whether the suspected attackers were guilty or not guilty. As a lawyer Lenin knew the challenge he was presenting to jurists of the world, for he added, "And let me be accused of any mortal sin whatever and of violating freedom—I admit myself guilty, but the interests of the workers will win out." [2]

To meet his needs Lenin supported two systems of tribunals: the people's courts to hear charges of crime among the "people," and revolutionary tribunals, which made no pretense

[2] 24 V. LENIN, SOCHINENIIA 241 (3d ed. 1935) [Works].

of careful deliberation. These were to rid society of those believed to be "enemies." Fidel Castro uses the same instrument in Cuba today. A Soviet observer has noted with satisfaction that the nine Cuban revolutionary tribunals "are typical bodies born of the revolutionary authority of the people." [3] The system is headed by a procurator of the Supreme Revolutionary Tribunal, performing his function through a subordinate in each provincial tribunal. Their mission is "class struggle" to prevent slipping back and to assure the internal security of the country by ferreting out counterrevolutionaries. They apply new laws, particularly the law of 17 February 1960, creating a new type of economic crime where the offender aims to upset the economy by burning sugarcane or halting the production of enterprises. Generally they apply "revolutionary law," this being the orders of the Council of Ministers supplementing the pre-Castro codes, which are kept in force, although subject to amendments, and scheduled for eventual complete recodification.

Not until 11 November 1922, almost five years to the day after the fall of the Winter Palace in Petrograd, were the Russians' revolutionary tribunals abolished to prepare the way for the judicial reform thought necessary to successful functioning of the New Economic Policy.[4] The lesser of the "enemies," measured in terms of wealth and influence, were given a temporary reprieve by the legislation of the New Economic Policy, introduced at the same time so that they might feel encouraged to aid economic reconstruction by enriching themselves.

With that reprieve the special tribunals for "enemies" were absorbed into a "unitary" court system, although by degrees the security police arrogated increasing power until the practice was routinized under Stalin to reestablish in fact a bifurcated system, one part treating criminals who were considered corrigible, and the other part "enemies," who had to be withdrawn from society at whatever cost. In 1934 Stalin established administrative tribunals called "special boards," sitting within the Ministry of Internal Affairs and authorized to banish from the com-

[3] Lesnoi, *Revolutionary Jurisprudence of the Republic of Cuba*, [1965] 1 Sov. IUST. 25.

[4] Judiciary Act of 1922, [1922] 62 Sob. Uzak. R.S.F.S.R. pt. I item 902.

munity and place in camps for hard labor individuals accused of no crime but deemed "socially dangerous." [5] Not until Stalin's death was the unitary system of courts reestablished for all in need of correction, as a first step toward what Khrushchev called the "state of the whole people."

The first criminal code of the Russian republic [6] was promulgated together with other codes for the period of the New Economic Policy. And since it reflected the determination of the Soviet leadership of that time to function with only a single, unitary court system, with jurisdiction over both categories of citizens, the "enemies" as well as those to be reeducated as wayward workmen were to be brought before it and tried under the same rules. In consequence, the code presents a curious mixture of principles, seemingly contradictory unless related to the dual purpose the code was to perform. There was unusual moderation in penalties for the common man, typified by a maximum penalty of ten years in a corrective labor camp for premeditated murder, and extreme severity for the political offender, who not only was warned specifically of what he might not do by articles defining capital offenses, but was also subjected to the terror of the unknown by the "analogy" article discussed in chapter 4. By this article, he could be executed for whatever action a court deemed exceptionally dangerous to society, even though the draftsmen had failed to anticipate the act in preparing the special part of the code. To indicate that this possibility was deemed of only temporary concern, and presumably would expire when the bourgeoisie were no longer a threat to society because of its restructuring along socialist lines, the death penalty was made "temporary." So it has remained to the present time, although the people for whom it was originally designed have long since passed from the scene, to be replaced by a new enemy of a different quality: the recidivist who seems to refuse to accommodate himself to the moral code of the new socialist man. He will be discussed below in chronological development of the theme.

Lenin's decision to stabilize law by codification, albeit with relative vagueness in the definition of crimes of "counterrev-

[5] 10 July 1934, [1934] 36 Sob. Zak. S.S.S.R. pt. I item 283.
[6] Decree effective 1 June 1922, [1922] 15 Sob. Uzak. R.S.F.S.R. pt. I item 153.

olution" and with the escape clause of analogy, has not appealed to the Chinese Communists. They have preferred to function without a criminal code for nearly twenty years since gaining power. Like Lenin in his precodification era, Mao Tsetung has issued decrees on a variety of separate matters to be treated as crime, some of them declared criminal in the 1920s when the Chinese Communists ruled in Juichin, but most adopted since 1949. Such are the Regulation on the Punishment of Counterrevolutionary Activities of 20 February 1951,[7] the Regulation on the Punishment of Corruption of 21 April 1952,[8] and the Provisional Regulation on the Punishment of the Undermining of the State Monetary System of 19 April 1951,[9] as well as a group of regulations on punishment of unlawful landlords.

The Eastern European Marxist states have shunned Mao's methods of governing without codes. On Stalin's death and denunciation their more moderate Communists seized the opportunity of liberation from his tutelage to reestablish more stabilized procedures in criminal correction and to abandon differentiation between categories of citizens. Although during the first years of shaky power all had adopted police tactics, under the direction of Stalin's security police, to round up and exile to hard labor presumed class enemies, few would accept Stalin's whole package. Most notable was their determination to preserve their intellectuals, although in subordinate positions and under mandate to absorb Marxism.

Yugoslavia had the first opportunity to change. Although Tito had included in his first criminal code of 1947[10] provisions copied from the Soviet codes, his second code of 1951 eliminated the article authorizing use of "analogy" to punish offenses not defined as criminal in the code.[11] The others in Eastern Europe had to bide their time until Stalin's death and his denunciation by his heirs, and even then, it took the courageous

---

[7] Eng. transl. in A. BLAUSTEIN, FUNDAMENTAL LEGAL DOCUMENTS OF COMMUNIST CHINA 215 (1962).

[8] *Id.* at 227.

[9] *Id.* at 233.

[10] [1947] J. of L. Yugoslavia item 106.

[11] [1951] *id.* item 13. Eng. transl. in CRIMINAL CODE (Union of Jurists' Associations of Jugoslavia, 1960).

rioters of 1956 in Poland and Hungary to clear the way for installation of more moderate communist leaders who chose not to emulate the Soviet model but to innovate as their own circumstances required.

We may trace the steps in the process of Polish communist revision of criminal law.[12] The Communists inherited the criminal code of 1932,[13] adopted between the wars, when politicians were moving to the right. Nevertheless, it was a code of considerable moderation compared to those emerging or about to be promulgated in Central Europe under Mussolini and Hitler. Although emphasis was upon crimes against the state and state authority, the categories were those found traditionally in the West as elements of "exterior treason": attempts on the state's independence and attempts to detach territory; attempts on the life and health of the president of the republic; service in an enemy army by a Polish citizen; undertaking armed action outside a foreign army against the Polish state in time of war. For this group the maximum penalty of execution was permitted. Otherwise, death was to be a rare penalty, for it was prescribed for only one nonpolitical crime: premeditated murder.

On achieving power the Communists decided to live with the 1932 code, but to supplement it with a "little criminal code," enacted 13 June 1946.[14] It took as its model the Soviet provisions on "counterrevolutionary" crimes, which were available in an ostensibly Polish source, a military code, adopted in 1944 as a means of establishing the new order in the forces of the Polish army accompanying Soviet troops in the purge of Nazi armies from Poland.[15] The "little criminal code" extended to civilians the crimes defined in the military code, and also provided that military courts would have jurisdiction over them. To some extent this introduced the concept of a special code

[12] Heavy reliance has been placed on Andrejew, *Droit pénal*, in INTRODUCTION À L'ÉTUDE DU DROIT POLONAIS 289 (S. Rozmaryn ed. 1967) and on an unpublished manuscript prepared by Dr. A. W. Rudzinski.

[13] French transl. in 3 LES CODES PÉNAUX EUROPÉENS 1471 (Centre français de droit comparé, 1958).

[14] [1946] 30 J. of L. Poland item 192.

[15] 23 Sept. 1944. In its amended version it appears in [1957] 22 J. of L. Poland item 107.

for "enemies" and a special court to try them, since the common man was presumed to fall under the 1932 code, as having no desire to unseat the new Polish Marxist-oriented state authority.

The four forms of treason established by the 1932 code were increased to twelve, or fourteen, depending on how the articles are read, and for all, the penalty of death was established as a possible maximum. Two of the definitions were directly pertinent to the four of the 1932 code: attempts to remove by violence the sovereign organs of the people and to assume their power by violence; and attempts to change the constitution by violent means. The others were quite new to Poland. A crime against security was established to protect from violent attack not only a military unit or person, but also a deputy to parliament, a member of a "people's council," a state official, a trade union representative or even an official of a political or social organization. This was considerably wider coverage of officials than the 1932 code's supreme protection on political grounds only of the president of the republic.

Economic crimes bearing the death penalty appeared for the first time, following the Soviet model. Thus offenses committed against the functioning of public utilities, transportation, and military defense became "sabotage." This crime was also to be found when faulty production of objects of military supply made them totally or almost unsuitable for use. Also punishable by death was the collection, production, or possession of arms, ammunition, or explosives without permission.

Espionage and counterespionage were the concern of the next group of definitions: accepting or seeking personal or material advantage from a person acting on behalf of a foreign state or an international organization in return for damage to the Polish state; the collection or keeping of documents containing state or military secrets; the furnishing of false or doctored documents to a Polish office; and concealment of simultaneous foreign service while performing Polish state services.

To these were added the peripheral crimes of counterfeiting Polish currency and conspiracy to commit or preparation to commit any of the above crimes, as well as failure to inform the authorities of knowledge of such preparation. Finally, there was the crime of violence in race conflict, for which the Soviet codifiers have always found a place among the most dangerous of antistate activities.

The events of 1956, when revolts throughout Poland ousted direct Soviet influence from Polish lawmaking, brought a change, but its immediate result was only restoration of civilians to the jurisdiction of the regular courts for all crimes except espionage, which remain subject to trial by military tribunals. This change, curiously enough, was also made in the USSR in 1958 when the Supreme Soviet enacted its post-Stalin judicial reform. It may be an early instance of what Soviet draftsmen have since acknowledged: the borrowing of models from Eastern Europe rather than the export of ideas which was characteristic of Stalin's time. The rest of the post-1956 reform was placed before a drafting committee, which vacillated for years before bringing forth the draft in 1963, only to have it rejected after heated discussion. A new drafting committee was formed and the work resumed *ab initio*. Not until 1968 was the draft returned to parliament for reconsideration before public discussion.

To the extent that an outsider can guess the reasons for the slow progress in reform of Polish criminal law, they lie in disagreement between those who were in favor of extending the moderate line which came to the fore with the events of 1956 and those who feared that the danger of retrogression was not yet over. Early drafts showed notable moderation, but the final product disappoints those expecting qualitative change, for it is militant in its protection of the state. Justification for the seeming triumph of the "hardline" may lie in the fact that bourgeois forces remain strong in Poland, under its type of economy, particularly its private-property based agriculture, and humanistic forces, nurtured for centuries, are still strong among the intellectuals, who have shown themselves restless under rigid discipline, even when they accept general principles of communist policy. To the Communist those forces seem hostile and require strict control.

To return from Poland, which provides an example of what has been happening outside the USSR within the Marxian socialist family, to the USSR, the main inspiration of Marxian socialist criminal law, attention must be directed to the theories that have evolved there with respect to correction of those who are to be categorized not as enemies but as members of the "people." It is because of those theories that Soviet draftsmen are also vacillating, in spite of the Supreme Soviet's adoption in 1958 of a set of Fundamental Principles of Criminal Law designed to last for a long time.[16] Within months they were being revised and amended, and the process has not yet been stabilized. There are critical questions still to be answered by high party officials before the draftsmen can settle upon a lasting policy, and the most critical is the cause of crime.

The answer to this question seemed easy to the men who made policy in 1922 when the first criminal code was in preparation. Marxist theory provided the clue. It explained crime in the capitalist world as a result of the inequities of the system and the emotions they engendered in the individual. Engels had traced the origin of the whole state apparatus of compulsion back to the dawn of history—to the cupidity of tribal chiefs who could not rest content with their share in the communal property.[17] In his view, these chiefs began to arrogate for their private use portions of this communal property, as it accumulated in considerable quantity after the division of labor between tribes and the initiation of barter and trade which this made possible. To formalize their right to possession they developed, according to the anthropology on which Engels relied, the concept of private property. This led eventually to the creation of a state apparatus of compulsion to protect it against members of the tribe who were discontented with the resulting unequal distribution of wealth and who sought to better themselves through revolts.

With the passage of millenia, during which, in Marxist eyes, there occurred a progression through social orders characterized by slaveholding, feudalism, and finally capitalism, there occurred again and again, with such regularity as to suggest a law of human behavior, ever-increasing enrichment of the few and impoverishment of the many, making necessary increasingly

[16] 25 Dec. 1958, [1959] 1 Ved. Verkh. Sov. S.S.S.R. item 6. Eng. transl. in FUNDAMENTALS OF SOVIET CRIMINAL LEGISLATION, THE JUDICIAL SYSTEM AND CRIMINAL COURT PROCEDURES: OFFICIAL TEXTS AND COMMENTARIES (1960).

[17] F. ENGELS, ORIGIN OF THE FAMILY, PRIVATE PROPERTY AND THE STATE.

forceful measures to preserve the property privileges of the few until the many revolted and set up a new regime protecting the property interests of those who had seized power.

Those who came after Marx and Engels studied meticulously their *Communist Manifesto* of 1848, in which the theory was summarized, and expanded the idea as it related to the cause of crime in their time. It seemed self-evident from the analysis that the private property system on which the power of the bourgeoisie during the capitalist epoch was thought to rest was the cause of impoverishment of the majority of the population and the cause of crime. Not only were the poor compelled to steal to eat, but in conscious or unconscious protest against the inequities of the system, from which there seemed no exit, they were emotionally compelled to murder their oppressors and rape their women.

A socialist system characterized by common ownership of property and administration by a state apparatus epitomizing the community logically seemed to promise an end to crime. There was to be abundance so great as to make possible eventual distribution of goods in accordance with need and participation by all in the process of governing. Protest against the system would have no logical foundation. Eventually compulsion of all sorts would become unnecessary, and the state would "wither away."

Although this was the hope for the long-range future, Lenin did not expect it during the first years after the revolution. Not only would class enemies try to unseat the new Communist-directed regime, but so long as citizens from the working classes saw few increases in production levels, because the state was not yet organized to meet all needs, and so long as they procrastinated in accepting their new responsibilities, and in exercising their new opportunities, they could be expected to continue familiar practices. Crime would, therefore, remain for some time a problem for Soviet penologists.

Lenin's formula for eliminating crime was production and education, and, for the working people who committed crime, rehabilitation. For such people the period of restraint must become a "road to life." The theatrical stage, the romantic novel, and the screen were called upon to dramatize this program, and so was the language of the 1922 criminal code.

The concept of "guilt," long a feature of pre-Marxist criminal law and having its roots in medieval religious morality, had no place in Soviet legislation, nor did the concept of "imprisonment," which suggested, because of the experience of tsarist times, incarceration without efforts of any kind at rehabilitation and eventual restoration to society of a whole man. Both words were suppressed and in their place new words were sought. They were found in the vocabulary of a popular contemporary Italian school of penology, that of Enrico Ferri and his positivists and sociologists.[18] "Guilt," as a concept identifying a man for correction, would be replaced by the one test that mattered in the new society, the test of "social danger"; and "imprisonment" would be replaced by the concept of "deprivation of liberty," which suggested a brief period of removal from society during which a man would be fitted to assume his responsibilities. To Ferri's sociology, the Marxists added their own concept of "class conflict." This meant that to Ferri's despairing determinism, based on the theory that social and physical circumstances conditioned the actor, Lenin's penologists added the hopeful expectation that as socialism achieved its wonders in mitigation and eventual elimination of class conflict, man would become a free agent as he had not been since his tribal days. He would then choose to conform to social necessity, and criminal codes would have no further function to perform.

Since the new Soviet man was to be a free agent, no longer the prey of economic circumstances driving him to crime, the first code of 1922 and its successor in 1926,[19] in spite of new terminology, expressed the basis of criminal responsibility in conventional terms as direct intent or its equivalent, "criminal negligence," understood in the classical sense of negligence of such reckless character that it amounts to intent. In keeping with the new philosophy, intent or criminal negligence created no "guilt" in the moral sense. They were important not as measures of degree of violation of a moral law, for which retribution was necessary in expiation of sin, but rather as

[18] H. Berman, Soviet Criminal Law and Procedure: The R.S.F.S.R. Codes 30 (1966).

[19] 22 Nov. 1926, [1926] 80 Sob. Uzak. R.S.F.S.R. pt. I item 600. Eng. transl. in The Penal Code of the Russian Federal Soviet Republic (1934).

measures of degree of danger to society. A man who intended to upset the social order of Marxian socialism was standing in the way of swift progress along the road of historical inevitability, and the same could be said for a man who acted with complete disregard for what he ought to have recognized as the logical consequences. As social dangers, such actors needed to be deprived of liberty, not to be punished but to be reformed, if possible. If this seemed out of the question they were to be executed, if their act was threatening to the foundations of the new social order.

To these general principles, the draftsmen provided exceptional alternatives, some already discussed at length. Thus, to repeat, if a man committed an act not defined in the code as a crime, but found by a judge to be socially dangerous, he might be removed from social intercourse in application of the principle of "analogy." No Soviet penologist thought it necessary to argue whether "intent" or "criminal negligence" could be present when an actor had not been put on notice of what the codifiers considered so dangerous as to require isolation of the actor. The "class struggle" duty of the judiciary also made it possible for a judge to impute hostile intent when it was hard to prove but could be suspected from the circumstances, especially when the actor's class origin was not that of peasant or worker, or friendly intellectual.

The exceptional measures were not, however, only to permit the court to move in the direction of severity. Some permitted an opposite move.[20] The court was authorized to measure the danger in objective terms, even when intent to cause harm or criminal negligence was clearly present. It could reduce the period of isolation from society below that prescribed for the act by the code, or even waive it completely, using as a basis for such variation its own assessment of the situation or any legislation which might have been passed between the time the act was committed and the sentencing. This authority cut both ways, for if legislation established new policy, by increasing the period of isolation beyond the term stated in the code or even by creating new definitions of socially dangerous acts, it could be applied retroactively. As the architect of the code was to say

[20] Arts. 6 and 8.

later in proposing a revision, a code must not be looked upon as a bill of fare in a restaurant.[21] The court must not be held to fixed penalties on the theory that the accused made a bargain with the state when he committed the dangerous act to pay only the price listed in the code.

Judicial decisions applying the principle of analogy have already been presented in chapter 4, but those on intent and criminal negligence bear examination to determine the extent to which they conform to practice outside the Marxian socialist family. They most often reach the judicial reports when they involve complex situations where there is a dispute over the nature of the intent. In 1931 a court found a young man guilty of counterrevolutionary intent when he persuaded a young girl whom he had seduced to set fire to a hayfield, destroying the crop. No direct evidence was presented of the counterrevolutionary intent, but it was imputed because the accused was the son of a rich peasant who had been banished during the antikulak campaign begun the previous year and had been refused admission both to the collective farm and to the Young Communist Youth League because of his ancestry. Causation was established by proof that he had used threats to persuade the girl to set the fire.[22]

A man who murdered a state official visiting in his village was found to have had counterrevolutionary intent, and thus to be subject to execution rather than to ten years' deprivation of liberty, because the evidence showed that he was without a profession, had a criminal record for arson, for making illegal liquor, and for keeping firearms. He had shadowed the official on his arrival at the village and followed him to his host's home, stabbing him, in the early morning, when he was ordered to leave the house.[23]

Although these decisions demonstrate the extent to which the courts were prepared to use their judicial discretion to establish severe measures of social defense in cases where clear proof of intent was lacking but might be inferred from the circumstances, other decisions indicate the moderating influ-

[21] Krylenko, *The Draft of the Criminal Code of the U.S.S.R.*, 1 PROBLEMY UGOLOVNOI POLITIKI 3 at 19 (1935).

[22] Kholkin, [1931] 8 Sud. Prak. Verkh. Suda R.S.F.S.R. 9.

[23] Savelev, [1931] 17–18 *id.* 8.

ence possible in exercise of this discretion. Two young sons of clergymen found their severe sentences reduced by the supreme court of the Russian republic even though they admitted that in breaking a windowpane in a clinic they had intended to harm the Soviet state. The penalty was reduced below that prescribed by the code because the court concluded that the damage had been minimal. The crime was reclassified from counterrevolutionary destruction of state property to what was then the relatively minor offense of willful destruction of property belonging to state institutions.[24] At about the same time some peasants were given only a conditional sentence when they started a riot in attempting to prevent the arrest of their village priest. The supreme court noted that they were of poor and middle-class origin; that all were ignorant and illiterate; that all were old; and that no serious consequences had resulted from their efforts.[25]

Criminal negligence has concerned the court in a wide variety of factual situations, from which some effort to establish objective criteria has arisen, the most frequently used criterion being violation of work rules. Thus, when the driver of a truck for a state enterprise knocked down a railway flagman while crossing the tracks against the signal, it was considered a serious crime committed under circumstances of criminal negligence because the work rules on driving across railroad tracks had been violated.[26] But when two bank clerks failed to note a forgery of a check on which money had been paid out, they were acquitted because they had violated no work rule. Their audit followed the payment of funds, and even if it had not, the court suggested that they would not have been sentenced because there was no evidence to suggest that auditors should have the special knowledge necessary to detect a forgery.[27]

In the absence of objective measurements such as work rules, the court's task is more difficult. Two nearly identical cases twenty years apart will indicate the judicial process. In each the trial court read the evidence to support a conviction of

[24] Shanev and Beziaev, [1930] 11 *id.* 9.
[25] Iakunin et al. [1929] 1 *id.* 10.
[26] Sergienko, [1940] 23–24 Sov. IUST. 37.
[27] Hodareva and Gogia, [1944] 6 Sud. Prak. Verkh. Suda R.S.F.S.R. 18.

intentional killing, and in each the supreme court reduced the penalty because it found simple negligence. In the first, in 1939, a young man threw a stone high into the air while watching a street fight between his brother and an assailant. On its descent the stone killed the assailant. The supreme court reduced the penalty to five years' deprivation of freedom on the ground that there was no direct intent, nor was there criminal negligence resulting in death, as no one would have anticipated death from such an act. But since the thrower should, in the court's view, have anticipated causing bodily harm, he should be treated accordingly.[28]

In the second case a newspaperman with a camera without apparent reason approached a drunkard standing before a tree. The drunkard, thinking he was to be shamed by a photograph, cursed the newspaperman roundly and spat in his face. The newspaperman became enraged and struck the drunkard with his fist, causing him to fall backward, hitting his head against the tree so hard that he died within a few minutes of a brain hemorrhage. The trial court convicted the newsman of intentional killing with base motives, but the supreme court reduced the sentence from ten years' deprivation of freedom to three years' on the ground that he should have anticipated that the blow would cause the drunkard to strike his head on the tree, but that he never intended to kill him.[29]

Having established the crucial importance of finding intent or criminal negligence before sentencing to deprivation of liberty, the draftsmen faced all the familiar problems of absence of intent which appear in any legal system with mistake, self-defense, insanity, drunkenness, and minority. All of these have been resolved by the Soviet codes and judicial practice in conventional manner. The insane were to be removed from society for treatment in a medical institution.[30] Since the purpose of removal from society was not to punish but to protect, it did not matter whether the accused was rational when he committed the offense and subsequently became insane. Drunkenness was declared to be no defense.

Minors presented a special problem, owing in part to the

[28] Azhoichik, [1939] 1 Sov. IUST. 73.
[29] Antonov, [1960] 2 SOTS. ZAK. 87.
[30] Criminal Code R.S.F.S.R. 1926, art. 11.

split of opinion in the USSR, as elsewhere in the world, on the age at which a child matures so he can understand fully what he is doing. The general rule was clear-cut: minors are not to be subjected to the measures of social defense prescribed for adults, and should be exonerated completely below a certain age. When they can be expected to know the meaning of their acts but are still immature, they should be placed in the care of medical-pedagogical institutions. In the 1922 code the age of fourteen was set as the age of responsibility, but the special form of treatment had to apply to delinquents to the age of sixteen. During the juvenile crime wave of the 1930s these ages were reduced in 1935 to make minors responsible and subject to adult measures at the age of twelve years if they committed serious crimes.[31] Authors thought that experience had proved that many had matured sufficiently to know what they were doing and to realize its social unacceptability, and even to use their knowledge of the special treatment reserved for them to commit crimes with impunity. To avoid abuse of the provisions on minority the age was lowered, but always with the provision of the general part of the code that minors under eighteen might not be subjected to capital punishment.[32] In effect, they were presumed always to be corrigible.

Mistake has presented the to-be-expected complications regarding intent, and its utility in measuring social danger. Thus, when a purchaser of firewood entered the forest to transport his purchase to his home and took by mistake the pile set aside for use of the state school, the supreme court released him from responsibility as having no intent to commit a crime.[33] But when a man shot his own brother by mistake, thinking him to be an opponent with whom he had been quarreling and whom he intended to kill, he was subjected to the full penalty for intentional killing.[34] The court declared that he must have been conscious that death would follow from his shooting, and the lives of the man he intended to kill and of his brother "are of equal value." Social danger is here measured by intent to kill a human being, and it did not matter that the actor's intention

[31] 25 Nov. 1935, [1935] 1 Sob. Uzak. R.S.F.S.R. pt. I item 1.
[32] Art. 22.
[33] Kurtiashvili, [1942] 1 Sud. Prak. Verkh. Suda S.S.S.R. 12.
[34] Shiganov, [1961] 7 Sov. IUST. 30.

with regard to a certain man was thwarted because his brother came to the window rather than his enemy.

The problem of the accessory's intent when his principal exceeds what had been agreed upon also has been brought to the law reports. Since intent is important in assessing danger, an accessory who helped a thief enter a dormitory but who did not anticipate that he would use a knife to cut a watch off a man's wrist was held responsible only for the entering with intent to rob, and not for the more serious crime of theft with a dangerous weapon.[35] And a young man who participated in the preparations for an act of highway robbery was released from responsibility for the crime because he withdrew before it was committed. He was, however, held responsible for the lesser crime of failure to inform the authorities that it was to be committed.[36]

A line is drawn, however, between accessories and coparticipants, some of whom may not have shared in striking the fatal blow or in all of the crimes committed by a group. Two cases illustrate the approach. In one, six persons participated in a drunken fight, during which three caned a participant after he had been felled by a fourth. Death resulted from the injuries. The trial court sentenced the man who struck the first blow to death and gave the others three years' confinement each. The supreme court of the Russian republic thought the discrepancy in penalties unjustified and ordered retrial of the three who were lightly sentenced, demanding punishment of them all for complicity.[37]

In the second case, three men participated in a band, organized by V and K in the autumn of 1960 and joined by Z in December of that year. The group committed a series of armed robberies on state enterprises and retail stores, although not all were present on each occasion. Lawyers in defense of K and Z, who had not been present on all occasions, argued for a reduced penalty, but the supreme court of the Russian republic supported the trial court's decision, saying, "From the evidence, it has been established that K and Z were active participants in an armed band organized by V. K was a member of this band from the beginning in the autumn of 1960 and Z from December

[35] Pleshivtsev and Starodubov, [1960] 5 *id.* 89.
[36] Zharkov, [1960] 4 *id.* 89.
[37] Rybkin et al., [1961] 4 Biull. Verkh. Suda R.S.F.S.R. 7.

1960. Therefore, the court had reason to place on K and Z responsibility for all crimes committed by the band for the period mentioned." [38] In short, intent was imputed to all, even though on occasion some were absent.

The self-defense cases have also raised no specifically "socialist" principles, although they have given rise to a discussion of whether a socialist man should be penalized for defending himself when he might have fled. Some trial courts convicted individuals who remained to fight on the ground that they had exceeded necessary measures. The dispute has been resolved by the USSR's supreme court in favor of the accused on the ground that flight from attack is "foreign to the principles of Soviet morals and socialist legal concepts." [39] Numerous judicial decisions apply the rule to complex facts. Thus a husband whose wife was beaten and threatened with a knife by a thief during the night was acquitted of crime when he mutilated the thief's knife-wielding hand after warning that he would shoot unless the assault was stopped. The trial court thought the measures exceeded the bounds of permissible self-defense, but the supreme court held that "the character of the act, its intensity and the degree of danger from the point of view of reality of the threat justified the means of defense." [40]

When the events were even more complex, the court had greater difficulty in sorting them out to determine blame. Thus, when a drunken man went on a rampage in a railway terminal restaurant, swinging an ax, and when thrown out of the room was followed by a group of patrons, one of whom he struck with the ax, he was held responsible in spite of his plea of self-defense. His argument had been that the man he struck with the ax had approached him with a stone in his hand, and there was no alternative to self-defense. The court concluded, "it is evident that G caused severe bodily harm to M not in self-defense, but at the moment when he himself was the attacker." [41]

[38] Vishnevskii et al., [1961] 2 *id.* 8.
[39] Order of Plenum of Sup. Ct. U.S.S.R., 23 Oct. 1956, in SBORNIK POSTANOVLENII PLENUMA VERKHOVNOGO SUDA SSSR 1924–1963 at 178 (1964) [Collection of Orders of the Plenum of the Supreme Court of the U.S.S.R. 1924–1963].
[40] Chaplia, [1960] 2 SOTS. ZAK. 87.
[41] Gerasimov, [1958] 1 Biull. Verkh. Suda S.S.S.R. 25.

This treatment of attempts provides what little novelty is to be found in the establishment of intent, for they are subjected to the same measures of social defense as the committed crime. Perhaps the explanation is the Soviet sense of danger, which seems more easily aroused than that in longer-established social orders. Although the Anglo-American common-law judges have been impressed by the problem of proof of intent in the absence of completion of the crime, or by the fact that intent might change at any moment up to the completion, and have in consequence set penalties below those for the completed crime, Soviet draftsmen have felt no such restraint. Only recently has there been an indication that considerations similar to those in more settled societies may now be expected to appear. Thus, a man charged with attempt to kill was acquitted even though in attacking his wife he had shouted, "I'll kill you!" He had not completed the crime, for she had shouted back, "Who will take care of the children?" The shock of his own looming responsibility may have overwhelmed him. The decision does not reveal his motive, but only says that he withdrew from the attack. In rejecting the indictment the court said that this was not an attempt because the accused stopped of his own volition and not because of outside intervention.[42]

The moderation of the court's decision in 1965 is representative of the change in attitudes which has captured those who create and administer the Soviet legal system since Stalin's death and denunciation. Adoption of the fundamental principles of 1958 marked the zenith of the movement, which began with some measures taken immediately after Stalin's death, the most noted being the abolition of the special boards of the Ministry of Internal Affairs in September 1953 and formulation in practice of the rule, later incorporated in the 1958 principles, that "criminal punishment shall be applied only by judgment of a court."

The 1958 principles set about undoing the worst of Stalin's excesses, but they carry in their terminology a lasting memento of his purge policies of the 1930s. Gone is the hostility to use of the word "punishment" which motivated the draftsmen of 1922

---

[42] Kulikov, [1965] 2 Sots. zak. 90. The sentence was reduced to one year's deprivation of freedom for premeditated light bodily injury.

and 1926 to adopt the term "measure of social defense." Gone is hostility to the word "imprisonment," which had been replaced in the early years by "deprivation of liberty." Although some of the terms of the 1920s continue to be used throughout the 1958 principles, they are paired with the prerevolutionary vocabulary, which during Stalin's regime lost its previously unwanted connotations.

Stalin had reintroduced the word "punishment" into his law of treason in 1934 at the moment when he was conducting a campaign to convince the public that a good society was near at hand. "Imprisonment" was restored to the vocabulary for the most serious crimes in 1936, at the time of adoption of the second federal constitution. The restoration of old, hated terms at the dawn of a new socialist era looked out of place, but it was for a reason. The new Soviet society, with the achievement of socialism, could hardly explain crime as caused by capitalism, for the 1936 constitution, with its official proclamation of socialism and prohibition of employment for personal gain, required some other explanation.

The solution was to place the blame on corruption of individuals to such an extent that they were beyond rehabilitation. A 1937 statute spoke of inflicting "suffering" upon the criminal.[43] Finally, Stalin spoke up in 1939 to the Eighteenth Congress of the Communist Party and laid the blame on foreign powers who kept capitalism alive in the minds of men and sought to utilize this to subvert his government.[44]

For the Communist who resisted Stalin's program, and the recidivist who continued to commit murder or rape after periods of deprivation of liberty and rehabilitation, "imprisonment" and "punishment" seemed to be appropriate terms. Without a background as members of the bourgeoisie they could not be considered class enemies, but they could be and were considered enemies of the people, even though reared among the people. Two authors, one a noted Soviet authority on constitutional law, published a paper at this time to denounce the thief, the bandit, the embezzler, and the counter-

[43] [1937] 66 Sob. Zak. S.S.S.R. item 297.
[44] J. STALIN, *Report to Eighteenth Party Congress*, in LENINISM 434, 474 (Eng. transl. 1942).

feiter as beyond the reach of exhortation and demonstration.[45] Such offenders were no longer to be pitied for their poverty or their ignorance, for the state had provided the opportunity to escape both. In a sense they were "guilty" in a novel meaning of this word when they killed or stole; guilty not of violating a moral law established by Moses or Mohammed, but of violating their obligations to a new society. There was occasion to reintroduce the word "guilt" with a new social, nonreligious meaning. No one suggested restoring the concomitant of "retribution" in the sense of punishment in the hereafter, but it seemed wholly appropriate to the jurists of the time to take measures of social defense which were at the same time a measure of "punishment" for those who refused to be corrected.

Stalin's outburst against foreign states took place in 1939. The Second World War soon engulfed the USSR, leaving no time or occasion to argue causes of crime in circumstances of wartime hardship, poverty, and social chaos; but the writers resumed their discussion after the war, with the same theme. Professor Viktor Chkhikvadze came forward to write of the role of the court in overcoming the relics of capitalism in the minds of men.[46] He considered the recidivists bad citizens, if not enemies, for they would not respond to efforts at rehabilitation. He proposed that they receive their just deserts: repressive measures to restrain them from intervening with socialist construction of a new society on the new economic and social foundations that had been laid. But the old explanations persisted. As late as 1952 Georgi Malenkov, as Stalin's principal henchman and prospective heir, reported to the party that there were still foreign powers seeking to undermine the Soviet system by subverting its citizens.[47] Within months of this congress Stalin was dead, and the stultifying influence of his simplified explanation of crime was lifted, although it took time for the

[45] Denisov & Merkushev, *The Draft of the Criminal Code of the R.S.F.S.R.*, [1939] 3 Sov. IUST. 4 and 4 *id.* 5.

[46] *The Role of the Soviet Court in Overcoming the Relics of Capitalism in the Minds of Men*, [1949] 2 Sov. GOS. I PRAVO 17.

[47] Malenkov, *Report to the Nineteenth Party Congress*, Part I, sec. 2. Eng. transl. in L. GRULIOW ed., CURRENT SOVIET POLICIES: THE DOCUMENTARY RECORD OF THE NINETEENTH COMMUNIST PARTY CONGRESS AND THE REORGANIZATION AFTER STALIN'S DEATH 102 (1953).

theorists to brave tradition by suggesting a new approach based on something other than "capitalism in the minds of men."

The 1958 fundamental principles were drafted by jurists determined to escape the terror that Stalin had imposed, but who were not yet prepared by theoretical work to sponsor a new penology. Penalties were reduced all around, even for the traditional "counterrevolutionary" crimes, and these were renamed, to conform to worldwide practice, "crimes against the state." The concept of "analogy" was removed, along with its companion, the right to apply criminal legislation retroactively. The range of punishments was narrowed to exclude banishment from the USSR, deprivation of civil and political rights, and denomination as an "enemy of the people." The maximum period of confinement was reduced from twenty-five to fifteen years. Exile and banishment within the USSR were limited to five years. Confiscation of property was permitted only for crimes against the state and for a few serious crimes with mercenary motives. Finally, the concept of parole was liberalized.

The new charter of liberty was a single article of two paragraphs, the first declaring that "Only a person guilty of committing a crime, that is, who intentionally or negligently commits a socially dangerous act provided by law, shall be subject to criminal responsibility and punishment," and the second prohibiting in language already quoted any restoration of Ministry of Internal Affairs tribunals.[48]

The fundamentals were related to socialist society, as legislative tradition probably required, by the definition of crime. Article 7 declared that "A socially dangerous act (an action or an omission to act) provided for by the Special Part of the present Code which infringes the Soviet social or state system, or the political, labor, property, or other rights of citizens, or any other socially dangerous act provided for by the Special Part of the present Code which infringes the socialist legal order, shall be deemed a crime." Then followed definitions of intention and of criminal negligence, and authorization to a court to depart from the formal provisions of the code to excuse from punishment one who acted or failed to act if, because of

[48] Art. 3.

the insignificance of the action or failure to act, no social danger was threatened.

Although flexibility in application of the fundamentals was renounced with abolition of the concept of analogy, the vague language of some of the definitions of crimes against the state left open the possibility of pursuing and punishing enemies of the old, class kind. Although they could not be expected to appear in their original guise, since they no longer had a base in capitalism, the idea that capitalism lingered in the minds of men made the draftsmen wary of any language which would limit a court in ferreting out the socially dangerous individual who through some wily maneuver might avoid falling within the wording of a precisely phrased article. Stalin's influence was not wholly dead, as the section on crimes against the state indicated, but it was on the wane.

Although the lingering remnants of the original militant class approach of the revolution still attract the attention of the outside world, for the Soviet jurists they are of diminishing concern. These remnants remain in the codes to catch the man or woman who may be subverted by foreign money or propaganda to attempt to undermine the Soviet regime. To this extent they are "anticapitalist" clauses and easily explained as such to Marxist audiences. But the acute problem is presented by the social offenders who have not availed themselves of the opportunities to improve their lot and to whom no foreign money or foreign propaganda can be traced. Why do they continue to commit crime, and what should be done to rectify the situation?

Definition of the Soviet state as "the state of the whole people" by the Communist party in its program of 1961 opened the door to free discussion of causes of crime and rectification of the criminal. Professor Sergei Golunskii, shortly before his death in 1961, opened the discussion by saying that the concept of the state of the whole people requires that there be an end to study of legal problems in a formalistic and dogmatic way.[49] He urged jurists "to risk their reputations" as none would have dared to do during Stalin's time, so that new ideas might be presented for debate. He denounced what had been common

[49] [1962] 11 Sov. gos. i pravo 3.

practice: the repetition of formulas taken from Marxist classics. This was an open invitation to make suggestions and to do research without being limited to discovery of remaining forms of "capitalism in the minds of men."

Some of Golunskii's colleagues have taken up his challenge. In 1963 Dr. B. S. Nikiforov was willing to say, "To pretend to explain anti-social acts and all other human conduct uniquely by social factors would be a simplistic generalization." [50] He argued that individuals are not automatons; that they have a certain freedom of choice; and that this choice relates to traits of character, to temperament, and to ability to adapt to changed situations. He concluded that the causes of crime are no longer those created by a capitalistic society, but are excesses owing to individual character. These excesses can be eliminated with improvement in material and cultural conditions and in education, and with the appearance of a new social conscience.

A realistic appraisal appeared in a leading article in the journal of the Procuracy in 1965.[51] It established three general causes of crime: the consequences of the past war; inadequate educational work in the family and school; and shortcomings in ideological work among certain categories of citizens. By the latter it meant failure to teach Marxism-Leninism and the moral values of that system. Then it approached some more specific reasons which could be subsumed under the generalities. Educational shortcomings included failure to conduct individual work with carriers of alien views, presumably those who still held capitalist ideas within their minds. The consequences of the war were still reflected in the shortages of certain categories of goods. Other consequences even went back to prewar times. Some violations of the party rules and of state law establishing a socialist legality had their origin in dictatorial procedures tolerated, if not authorized, during the period of Stalin's cult of the personality. Finally, the editorial listed what it called violation of socialist principles in the conduct of the economy, especially in agriculture. By this it probably meant brutality in administration dating from forced collectivization and Stalin's subsequent refusal to take into consideration the

[50] [1963] 4 *id.* 60.
[51] [1965] 4 Sots. zak. 2.

opinions of peasants and workers in drafting his severe disciplinary laws.

Although the 1965 editorial emphasizes reeducation, as all Soviet penologists have done since Lenin's time, it is realistic in its analysis because it does not look only to the mind; it looks to material conditions in society, especially to shortages of goods, which education cannot remedy.

To make studies of the new, broad type, the Soviet leadership established an All-Union Institute for the Study and Prevention of Crime, and sociological research was begun, although it was hampered by the paucity of statistical studies. Some long-standing Marxist attitudes still motivate authors who criticize new men who are bold with their research. Thus, when a geneticist indicated his impatience with explanations that crime will be eradicated by a change in social conditions and explained findings of research with twins to show that quite different individuals can emerge from similar upbringing, and sometimes one twin will commit crime, one of the senior criminologists in the USSR took him to task in a paper entitled "Biology Has Nothing to Do with It." [52] Arguing that "such maxims are contrary to the Party Program, V.I. Lenin's basic dicta, and the fundamental tenets of Soviet jurisprudence," he declared that the author should have familiarized himself with "Soviet criminological literature and the appropriate tenets of Marxist-Leninist theory." The position expressed was considered patently reactionary. Assertion that there will always be violators of laws is noted as being "contradictory to one of the fundamental tenets of Marxist sociology and the theory of the state and law." The author proceeded to say, "As is known, in a communist society a process of the withering away of both the state and the law, and hence of juridical legislation, occurs."

Having reestablished some traditional limitations on research, the noted author points out that the causes of crime are diverse, but are of a social nature, having no relation to biological heredity. One of the most prominent causes, in his view, is ignorance of the law. He quotes a study of letters asking for information on legal matters, showing that about 60 percent of

[52] Gertsenzon, Izvestiia 26 Jan. 1967 at 4. Eng. transl. in 19 C.D.S.P. no. 4 at 27 (1967).

25,000 letters, as well as 5,000 oral questions asked at evening sessions devoted to propagandizing law, showed the participants did not know the law. Consequently, in his view, one cause of crime is ignorance, and he recommended that legal education be given in the schools, noting that although the fundamentals of jurisprudence were taught in prerevolutionary secondary schools, they have been excluded from the Soviet curriculum. Also, in his view, newspapers seem to publish stories on sensational violations of law rather than to campaign against them. He proposed a new legal magazine for the mass reader.

Not all of this critic's colleagues would stress ignorance of law as a cause of crime. Most note the high incidence of intoxication among criminals, and measures are proposed to limit access to liquor. Statistics were presented in 1960 to show that over 90 percent of the persons convicted of rowdyism and 70 percent of those convicted of intentional killing committed these crimes when drunk.[53] A 1959 report demonstrated alcohol's influence in 96 percent of the cases of rowdyism, 70 percent of the murders and 67 percent of the rapes. Still, studies are only beginning on why people drink.

Sex offenders have been studied by an investigator who denies any desire to generalize, but who notes that the majority of these crimes are committed by youths and adolescents and that their victims are usually girls twenty years old or younger.[54] His investigations demonstrated that among both accused and victims "everything was mixed up, everything was encrusted with licentiousness and cynicism, bravado and indifference, thoughtless imitation and ordinary boorishness." He concludes that the girls were often as responsible as the boys, leading them on until the rape occurred. His prescription for the malady was threefold: open the doors of trials for sex offenses so that the public may know the social causes of these offenses; encourage parents to give sex education to their children, so they will not seek it in the gutter, and increase education in the great and immortal examples of love through reading of the

---

[53] Panchenko & Ostroumov, *On Criminal Statistics*, [1960] 2 Sots. zak. 45.

[54] Shpeyer, A *Difficult Subject*, Literaturnaia gazeta, 2 July 1966 at 2. Eng. transl. in 18 C.D.S.P. no. 28 at 10 (1966).

great literature so that youth will not relate love only to the sex act.

While this sex study was admittedly only the impressions of a single investigator, albeit one with long experience, the reports of the All-Union Institute for the Study and Prevention of Crime show careful sociological research. In analyzing the causes of juvenile delinquency the director of the department in the institute reports several causes: [55] survivals of the past in economics, ideology, culture, and everyday life; shortage of material resources; parental neglect of children; incorrect upbringing by parents who set bad examples; mere lip service by families to Soviet ideology, accompanied by Philistine talk among parents and dishonest doings; heavy drinking; school deficiencies; lack of moral tempering of the personality; shortcomings in job placement; frequent changing of jobs; and slow action by the police in arresting juvenile delinquents. These conclusions result from findings such as these: about half the crimes occur after 10 P.M., for parents do nothing to bring their children home; lawbreakers from families where there is only one parent vary in number in different places, but they appear from 50 percent to 200 percent more frequently than those from unbroken homes; mothers who work have little time to tend children, for statistics show that they spend up to forty hours a week on housekeeping after completing their daily jobs; juvenile delinquents come from homes where in 25 percent to 30 percent of the cases the parents are heavy drinkers; in 50 percent of the cases there is constant family quarreling and fighting; in 90 percent of the cases where crimes are committed by employed juveniles who were intoxicated, the youths had learned to drink at home before becoming employed; 85 percent to 90 percent of the delinquents are from two to three years behind their coevals in educational level, being grade repeaters or dropouts; the proportion of nonstudying and nonworking youngsters among the criminals is 15 percent to 20 percent greater than the proportion of such youngsters in control groups.

Inasmuch as the emphasis has been placed for decades upon

[55] Minkovskii, *Some Cases of Juvenile Delinquency in the U.S.S.R. and Measures to Prevent It*, [1966] 5 Sov. GOS. I PRAVO 84 (1966). Eng. transl. in 18 C.D.S.P. no. 30 at 9. (1966).

education and rehabilitation, the draftsmen of each code since the first of 1922 have sought to create some typically socialist measures of social defense to facilitate the process. Something other than capital punishment or long terms of imprisonment is necessary if the methodology of reform is to be tried. Of course, shorter terms of confinement could present an opportunity to rehabilitate, if accompanied by educational measures, but this had not been deemed novel enough. Throughout Soviet history the desire has been to establish a situation in which the offender would be subjected to the influence of his colleagues while held under some form of restraint. Three forms of "social defense" were developed in 1922, and they have remained in Soviet codes ever since, reappearing in the fundamental principles of 1958. None involve confinement, for in application of all three the convict remains at large in a community of his peers, presumably performing socially useful labor. These three are: exile, banishment, and compulsory labor without deprivation of freedom, sometimes translated as the assignment of "correctional tasks." [56] Each is justly a novelty, although the first two were used by the tsars, without the mass influence component.

Exile is defined in the 1958 principles as "the removal of a convicted person from the place of his residence, with obligatory settlement in a certain locality." [57] Under this type of sentence the convict is taken to a remote region, usually Siberia or Central Asia, in which he is required to remain for the term of the sentence. He is subject to periodic report to the local police, who are in some measure responsible for launching him in a new career, although complaints indicate that this is not always done well. On his new job the convict is brought to the attention of the labor union, which is responsible for organizing measures to bring him into the life of the workers' collective of the factory or farm in a meaningful way, so that he will feel that he is again a member of a community to which he owes socially suitable conduct. Reform through work is the principle applied, with varying success. Some repeat their offense on return to their home community as soon as their term has been served.

[56] This is Berman's preferred language, see *supra*, note 18 at 151.
[57] Art. 25.

Banishment is a method of applying the same technique, while placing upon the convict fewer restrictions than constitute exile.[58] The convict is removed by the sentence from his place of residence, and is prohibited from living in certain localities, usually those which have been extensively urbanized. The penalty may be the basic one or may supplement a period of confinement, providing in this case a form of transition from confinement to complete freedom. It can be applied only when authorized by the penalty clause of the specific article of the criminal code that has been violated. It may not be meted out to minors who were under the age of eighteen on commission of the crime, to pregnant women, or to women who have dependent children under the age of eighteen years. In principle the penalty, since it leaves the convict considerable freedom of movement, is not thought appropriate to youths whose crime was probably caused by insufficient maturity, suggesting that they still need supervision, nor is it suitable to women during pregnancy when they need a stable place of residence, nor to women with children, for the children would be required to accompany their mothers to indeterminate new homes. Still, for men and older women without small children banishment is thought to afford a chance for rehabilitation in a workers' collective while they are kept away from the type of urbanized community in which the original crime was probably committed.

The third and most commonly used of the three novel penalties is compulsory work without deprivation of liberty.[59] It is limited in duration to a year, and is almost always performed at the job held at the time the crime was committed, although it may be served elsewhere if the court directs. During the period of the penalty, the convict is required to remain at the job to which he was assigned, whether his former one or a new one. The time served is not counted toward job seniority under the code of labor laws, and so pensions are affected, but if the tasks are so well performed as to receive commendation by the collective in which the convict works or by the labor union, the time served may be restored to the seniority record. Dur-

[58] Art. 26.
[59] Art. 27.

ing the period of work, a deduction from wages is payable to the court at such rate as may be set, becoming a form of installment fine.

Again, as in the case of exile and banishment, the group within which the convict works is supposed to help him move toward rehabilitation by bringing him into group activities and by emphasizing to him his social duties. If the convict evades working as required, the court may confine him under terms of a sentence of deprivation of liberty, and his unserved term is transposed into a new term of confinement at the rate of one day of confinement for every three days of unserved compulsory labor.[60]

It is primarily the third form which has a "socialist" ring, although all three, in emphasizing community attention, provide an element prized by socialists. Its pertinency to socialism is that only under state ownership of employing enterprises can it be supposed that the personnel manager could be induced to take the convict for employment on such terms. Also, only under a system in which the labor union is closely related to the state could a court require it to assist the convict toward rehabilitation.[61] Perhaps only under a system of disciplined one-party leadership epitomized by that of the Communists could the whole community be enlisted in a program of assisting convicts to help them prove their worth and thus regain social favor. Elsewhere campaigns can be conducted in the press and through religious institutions, trade unions, and social organizations such as the Rotary or the Lions, but there are very different qualities to the voices that urge community participation in the Marxist and the non-Marxist worlds.

Soviet authors take pride in pointing out that compulsory labor without deprivation of freedom is the form of penalty most frequently applied.[62] In 1954 it constituted 38.4 percent of

[60] Art. 28.

[61] Confidence in the therepeutic potentialities of labor unions and other social organization has also resulted in development of a form of supervision of mild offenders under which they are bound over to the organization for supervision and guidance (peredacha na poruki). It might be called "social parole."

[62] N. BELAIEV, PREDMET SOVETSKOGO ISPRAVITEL'NO-TRUDOVOGO PRAVA 11 (1960). [The Subject of Soviet Correctional-Labor Law].

the penalties given all convicts, and since that time it has increased in popularity with judges. Still, as late as 1960 it was a matter of complaint that scholars had not done research on the subject. There had not been the renewed interest expected after Stalin's days, during which it fell into disuse, particularly during application of the restrictive labor discipline law of 1940, which forbade workmen to leave their jobs without permission, except under very limited circumstances related to health and education. At that time the penalty had been meaningless, as nearly all citizens were required to remain on their assigned jobs. Under such conditions of a "labor freeze," the penalty constituted no more than an installment fine, which could have been ordered as the sentence without the additional feature of compulsory supervised work.

At the time of the reforms of 1958, it seemed to Soviet jurists that the time had come to place maximum emphasis upon rehabilitation and upon devising penalties that made such an approach feasible, but soon after the reform came retrogression to an attitude of the past: discouraging crime by terrorizing potential criminals with the threat of death. In spite of the fact that most of the penologists of the world had reached the conclusion by that time that threat of death does not deter the would-be criminal, the Supreme Soviet, under Communist party guidance, amended the 1958 principles for several crimes to restore the death penalty as a maximum threat.

The amendments began to appear in 1961 and continued until 1965, although the bulk came in 1961–62.[63] Fifty-two articles in the Russian republic's code of 1960, redrafted from its 1926 form to incorporate the 1958 fundamental principles, were amended in 1961 and 1962 alone. Ten new crimes were defined, but most of the changes were increases in penalties for existing crimes. The amendments of 1961–62 added six other crimes to the ten peacetime crimes and twelve wartime or combat crimes for which capital punishment had been authorized as a maximum penalty in 1958. For the seventh (taking or attempting to take the life of a policeman under aggravating circumstances) the penalty of death is not a maximum but the only prescription. The six whose penalties were increased were

---

[63] The statistical count is taken from BERMAN, *supra*, note 18 at 62.

actions disrupting correctional labor institutions, counterfeiting, violation of rules on currency transactions, stealing state or social property on an especially large scale, group rape, and the taking of a bribe by an official. One of the crimes, violation of rules on currency transactions, was noted especially because the increases in penalties were made in two stages which were applied retroactively, in violation of the 1958 principles. Special authorization was provided by the legislature, which, under the Soviet concept of no separation of powers, is all-powerful and cannot be held by the judiciary to a principle previously announced.

Second thoughts on the utility of the threat of capital punishment are now coming to the fore. The vicechairman of the USSR supreme court, who presides over its criminal college, has written that "an individual who is not sufficiently versed in criminology will sometimes assume that intensification of judicial repression is sufficient to eliminate crime completely. This is the result of feeble legal propaganda." [64] His words suggest that experience set forth in the United Nations reports denying the effectiveness of the threat of death as a preventive of crime is being confirmed in Soviet sociological research. The judge then cites a resolution of the USSR supreme court of 26 August 1966 on combatting crime as indicating that there is a sharp difference between the two categories of criminals: first offenders, for whom deprivation of freedom should not be ordered but rather penalties designed to aid reform without isolation from society, and dangerous criminals and malicious individuals, for whom the courts will permit no laxity.

The Chinese Communists, before their sharp break with Soviet legal tradition in 1957, followed the Soviet pattern of Lenin and Stalin. Although the court decisions are few, they have permitted Professor Lung-sheng Tao of the United States to conclude that "the class enemies have been denied the equal protection of the law." [65] This is what happened in the USSR in its years of instability. Dr. Tao's cases illustrate the point:

[64] Anashkin, *The Role of Law-consciousness and Public Opinion in Settling Punishment,* [1967] 1 SOV. GOS. I PRAVO 42.

[65] Lung-sheng Tao, *The Criminal Law of Communist China,* 52 CORNELL L. REV. 43 at 47.

One Chao, a high-school teacher who had been a landowner before his property was confiscated by the state, conspired with a factory worker to steal coal from the state factory at Hanyan, Hupeh Province. The trial court found the worker guilty of the relatively minor crime of theft, but it convicted the teacher of the most serious offense of counterrevolutionary crime in violation of the Anticorruption Act and sentenced him to twenty years of prison for labor reeducation. The court explained that Chao's "previous records, background, ideological quality, and class composition," enabled it to presume counterrevolutionary intent in committing the crime.[66]

The bias against hostile class elements went so far in two cases as to read crime into acts in which there had been no intention to commit harm. In one, the Fukien people's court convicted a man discovered to have been in communication with his relatives in Taipei of the counterrevolutionary crime of "maintaining a link with the imperialists and betraying his motherland." Nothing was found in the letters to indicate such an intention.[67] In the other, a landlord who took communally owned property thinking it was his own was executed by order of an administrative bureau. The people's court was not even given a chance to hear the case.[68]

One case having to do with violation of work discipline contrasts with early Soviet practice. It is an illustration of the application of the Chinese espoused doctrine that the situation may establish the "enemy" classification of a criminal, even when there was no intent to upset the regime by an act, and when there was no history of bourgeois class origin. The criminal branch of the Antung higher court sentenced a worker to life imprisonment as a counterrevolutionary when he negligently violated a safety regulation and caused an accident which was fatal to another worker. In the decision it was noted that the negligence occurred in a factory where production was unsatisfactory and the rate of accident high.[69]

A similar act of negligence causing a fatal accident resulted

[66] Cited by Tao as *The Hupeh Higher People's Court*, HSING EH TSE, case 281 (1953).

[67] Cited by Tao from *id.*, case 175 (1952).

[68] See Tao, *supra*, note 65 at 60.

[69] Cited by Tao from HSING TUNG TSE, case 1207 (1953).

in a suspended sentence of two years' imprisonment because the act was committed in a factory where production was high, work efficiently managed, and the accident rate low.[70] Dr. Tao concludes that the decisive element in differentiating the penalties was presumably not the gravity of the harm, nor the nature of the act as expressed by the *mens rea* of the defendants, but the desire to suppress bad elements and to deter potential criminals in that area.

What can be said in comparison of the Soviet and Chinese approaches to the correction of criminals? Both believe in correction through education, if at all possible. Both believe that individuals with bourgeois backgrounds are less likely to be reformed than are those with proletarian backgrounds. Both have established special procedures to overcome the danger believed to lurk in the bourgeoisie, the Soviets having introduced the revolutionary tribunals in 1917 and the special boards in 1934, and the Chinese the mass public trials before enraged peasants of 1949 and 1950.

The divergence between the Chinese and Soviet approaches has come within the past decade, and was brought to a head with enunciation in the Soviet Communist party's program of 1961 of the concept of the "state of the whole people." Under that concept, there was no more class struggle, and, consequently, there could be no more class enemies. Stalin's heirs had been moving in the direction of equal treatment under law for all social offenders ever since the dictator's death, but 1961 marked the formal announcement of their position.

The Chinese Communists have chosen this point as the major difference between them and their Soviet colleagues. For them there can be no end to class conflict until complete communism is achieved throughout the world. In consequence, they cannot for theoretical reasons accept the application of the doctrine of state of the whole people to criminal law. They believe that in the Soviet Union there are citizens who have demonstrated class hostility through theft of state property, and that they should be treated as class enemies, which means with less, if any, procedural protection and formal application of law. To this line of reasoning the Soviet penologists have called a

[70] Cited by Tao from *id.* case 819 (1953).

halt, and in doing so have marked a sharp difference between themselves and the Chinese.

As has been indicated, the Soviet penologists recognize "enemies" in society, but they are not "class enemies," and this theoretically based position has legal consequences. The Soviet penologists are severe in the penalties they prescribe for those who demonstrate that they cannot be reformed, but the trial they are given differs in no way from that accorded first offenders. They are not second-class citizens. For the Chinese such offenders are second-class citizens, and, therefore, deserving of less consideration than those who by their actions demonstrate that they deserve to be classed among the "people."

What looked until 1961 like a common core of policy on correction of criminals in Marxist-oriented states, with variation caused only by degree of stability of the Communist-guided regimes, has vanished. The Chinese have gone their own way in prolonging indefinitely and as a matter of doctrine a position which leaders of Eastern European Marxist states abandoned as soon as they felt strong enough to do so.

I 7

Types of Crime in the

Absence of Capitalism

THE FAMILY OF MARXIAN SOCIALIST LEGAL SYSTEMS TAKES FOR granted that definitions of crime shall include those tested by time as necessary to social order. Lenin's early rejection of Russian imperial codes as guides did not mean that murder had been legalized, even though the new government took no formal measures to define crimes against the person until it prepared its first criminal code in 1922. The Chinese Communists have been of the same mind. Of course, in the Eastern European Communist-led states where there was no rejection of pre-Marxist codes in their totality, as there was in Lenin's Russia and Mao's China, the definitions of crimes against the person remained what they had been. Only patching here and there added a new political component, as in Poland, where attacks against the person of state and party officials were elevated by the "little criminal code" to the level of serious political offenses. Otherwise murder, rape, and robbery remained what they had been.

The continuation of pre-Marxist policy which has universally made attacks upon a person and his property criminal seems to have caused Lenin's commissar of justice no philosophical concern whatever. When he faced the issue in the law journal of his commissariat in 1919, he took it for granted that such acts were upsetting to social order and should be subjected to measures of social defense.[1] His government had been defining crime by individual decrees for some time, but it had not included acts dangerous to the individual citizen. Its focus was on instigation to treason, counterrevolutionary activity, refusal to answer a call to military service, bribery of state officials, refusal to till the land in accordance with orders from local authorities, violation of the rules relating to the use and distribution of metals, trade in monopolized goods, or refusal to report surplus grain. All these acts were manifestly of major concern to a fledgling state struggling for its life. Only four were of economic concern, and even these economic measures could have been adopted by a non-Marxist society suffering from such severe shortages that rationing and compulsory production were necessary.

How could actions dangerous to the person be called crimes? There was no legislation on the subject, nor was there any formal carryover from the past of the tsarist code, which became only a temporary, limited guide to thinking. Judges were directed to apply their socialist consciousness of law, and this they had been doing during the early months to protect society from those who committed acts dangerous to the person, unless they had justification in Marxist eyes as revolutionary actors against landlords and capitalists. Self-help was not encouraged by the Bolsheviks. The revolutionary tribunals were established to channel acts of violence against the bourgeoisie through party-influenced bodies; but in remoter areas it was condoned. Thus, if one worker murdered another, the act was as criminal as before. This was made clear by the commissar of justice in his article listing on four pages the separate statutes adopted during the first seventeen months of the new regime, as if they had been chapters of a criminal code. Among them were

[1] Kurskii, *The New Criminal Law*, [1919] 2–4 PROL. REV. I PRAVO 24.

crimes against the person, with a citation to the People's Court Act of 1918 as justification for their inclusion.

To a casual reader making no reference to the cited act, the inclusion of attempts on life, the causing of serious bodily injury or mutilation, rape, and robbery under a general rubric which the commissar called "crimes against the individual" could cause no surprise. But to those who looked behind the citation, the commissar seemed to be taking liberties, for the act of 1918 created no such crimes. The only reference to them is in the description of the members of the court necessary to try such charges. Other members of the commissariat were not as sure as the chief that crimes against the individual were defined in law. One author writing in the same issue of the journal bemoaned the fact that the decrees of the new government had not included acts against the individual and acts against property among the crimes specifically defined.[2] In his statement these were "two types of criminal activity representing a significant part of all crime," and as a result of inaction by the law-making authorities they remained without regulation. His explanation was that policy, not accident, explained the situation. The local authorities were to be left free to develop themselves by establishing the new rules.

Perhaps Lenin surmised that a local judge faced with determining what types of activity were to be treated as criminal and having no guidance from above would become a more responsible man if he thought out for himself what was necessary for social order. In a measure the policy could have been linked in Lenin's mind with preparing man for his eventual liberation from compulsion, for it would place the community's leaders in a position where they would show the way toward creating self-discipline, without which the state could never wither away. They, at least, would consider what was necessary to create foundations of social order, and having reached their own conclusions, rather than having been directed from above, thousands of them would provide nuclei around which a new social consciousness would form.

[2] Berman, *On the Question of a Criminal Code for a Socialist State*, *id.* at 49.

The outsider is tempted to conclude that the new Marxist leaders were applying "natural law" to augment their list of types of crime. They had found it necessary to define specifically only those acts which were not by nature criminal. For the rest, which were included in the law of nature as the wisdom of the ages or the subject of divinely inspired writ, it could be assumed that local judges, no matter how illiterate in formal law, would know that measures of social protection were required. Had the issue been presented to them, the early leaders might have admitted that they expected this. But surely they would have added that the list of crimes had been lengthened to include these unwritten crimes not to "punish" sin, but to protect society. In this, they would have seen a vast difference.

This conclusion is reinforced by Chinese experience forty years later. No provision for crimes against the person was included in the acts defining crime in the People's Republic of China; yet they were treated as such. A Peking Law School textbook on criminal law had this to say in 1957, in what was almost identical treatment with that of the Soviet commissar of 1918: "Criminal homicide, robbery, and rape, for example, are acts which the state does not have to proscribe by penal statutes, because the seriousness of these acts is obvious." [3]

For whatever reason, the acts directed against the individual were given a place in Marxian socialist law in 1918. With codification in 1922 in the Russian republic and in the other republics arising beside it on the territory of what had been the empire, official sanction for their inclusion within the area of prohibited action was provided. It was not the statutory definitions, but the prescribed measures of social defense that were notable. This has been discussed in the preceding chapter.

Crime against the individual was conceived of as within the sphere where education and rehabilitation were effective. If it lacked political motivation, it could better be eradicated by teaching the citizen its danger to social order than by terrorizing him through threat of death into living peacefully with his neighbors. The preceding chapter has traced the disintegration

[3] CHUNG-HUE JEN-MIN KUNG-HO-KUO HSING-FA TSUNG-TSE CHIANG-I (1957) [Lectures on the General Principles of Criminal Law in the People's Republic of China]. Eng. transl. in JPRS no. 13331 (U.S. Gov't. Pub. no. 10317, 1962). Lecture no. 46.

of the educational approach when it met the problem of the repeater and the evidently incorrigible offender, and there is no need to repeat. But to understand the characteristics of the family of Marxian socialist legal systems one must appreciate that the crimes defined around the world as those against the person also appear in the definitions established by Communists, and the list of such crimes is not closed.

The process of expanding the list is well illustrated by Stalin's sudden inclusion of sodomy among the prohibited offenses. Apparently, at the time of drafting the first codes, it was assumed that the new socialist man had already abandoned such practices. Only the Uzbek republic had begun to sense the danger when it established in 1929 a new crime of homosexual corruption of minors and the conduct of schools of homosexual activity. Not until 1933 did official attitudes change at the center, reportedly because Joseph Stalin learned with disgust that the practice was spreading beyond the Moslems of Central Asia, about whom he probably, as a Georgian, knew a great deal. His reaction took the form of a federal decree enacted under the permissive provisions of the 1924 fundamentals of criminal law authorizing federal definition of new crimes "when the USSR thinks it necessary to follow a single line through establishment of a single court practice."

The crime was defined by the decree as homosexuality of men.[4] It was not then, and has never since been, extended to women. It established two grades: the act in simple form, and a more dangerous form when the act was accompanied by taking advantage of the dependent status of the victim, or when force was used or payment made, or when it was conducted as a profession or publicly. Penalties were for periods of up to five years' deprivation of liberty for the first grade and up to eight years' for the second. Although republics were directed to amend their criminal codes to introduce the crime, they were instructed that they were not to eliminate other articles under which they punished sexual perversion, pimping, seduction, and maintenance of brothels.

The definition was changed by amendment within three months to simplify it by eliminating from the second grade

[4] 17 Dec. 1933, [1934] 1 Sob. Zak. S.S.S.R. item 5.

reference to payment, professional activity, and public perform-ance.[5] Penalties were also altered to establish minima. All re-publics but three conformed to the amendment, but the Ukraine held to the first version in all detail; the Tadzhik republic kept the first definitions, but adopted the new minima; and the Uzbek republic, although it adopted the new form, retained its provisions against homosexual schooling of youths.

So the offense continued to be defined until after Stalin's death, but with the reforms of 1958 sodomy was no longer a federally defined offense. The republics regained their pre-1934 right to define it or not as they willed. All have included the offense among the definitions of their post-1958 criminal codes,[6] but there has been considerable variation in penalty and some variation in description of the exacerbated form. All have re-vised the 1934 wording, although the Russian republic's drafts-men chose to retain the principal features of the 1934 decree, and the Bielorussian republic has followed their example in every detail.

For the other republics there is wide innovation: the Ka-zakh, Lithuanian, Latvian, Kirghiz, and Estonian republics have retained the title of the crime but established no definition for the first grade, the simple act. As to the second grade, most republics have introduced variety to exclude reference to threats, but to include exacerbating circumstances as a catchall phrase. Penalties were varied for the first grade from a one-year minimum to upper limits of two, three, and five years; and for the second, between minima of two or three years and maxima of three, five, seven, and eight years, plus, in some republics, exile or banishment thereafter.

The newer Marxian socialist republics outside the USSR have felt free since their inception to adopt wide variations from the Soviet model in their criminal codes. Although, as indicated by the Polish "little criminal code," there was borrow-ing in some detail to define new crimes against the state, the crimes against the individual have been kept as they were or

[5] 7 Mar. 1934, 15 *id.* item 110.
[6] The criminal codes of all republics of the USSR are published in UGOLOVNOE ZAKONODATEL'STVO SOIUZA SSR I SOIUZNYKH RESPUBLIK 2 vols (1963) [Criminal Legislation of the U.S.S.R. and of Union Re-publics].

expanded as new circumstances required in the light of local cultural conditions.[7] Taking the crime of sodomy, which has been examined as its definition emerged in the republics of the Soviet Union, even more variation is seen in the criminal codes of the family of Marxist legal systems outside the USSR.[8] Some of these republics establish no such crime, these being Romania, Albania, and Bulgaria—unless the latter's Article 159 punishing compulsion of another to commit or consent to commit something against his will can be regarded as a basis for prosecution of the exacerbated form. Albania's Article 160, which punishes sexual relations established by force, by threat, or by exploitation of the helplessness of the victim, might also be used to strike down the socially serious form of the act.

The Hungarian and Czechoslovak criminal codes punish women as well as men for the homosexual act, but the Hungarian code punishes only if the act was compelled or achieved by exploiting the helpless condition of the victim. The penalty is raised if the victim is a minor. Yugoslavia limits the crime to men, with penalties only up to one year unless force or threat of direct bodily harm is used, when the maximum penalty is ten years. The German Democratic Republic adhered until 1968 to the old German code of 1871, which punished unnatural relations between men with a prison term and deprivation of the rights of a citizen, and increased the penalties if the victim was a minor or if force was used, or if homosexuality was conducted as a business. Mitigating circumstances might reduce the penalty to three months' imprisonment.

Although crimes against the person present no real novelty in Marxian socialist definition, except as they attain elevation into the category of crimes against the state when committed for political motives, the same is not true of acts directed toward the economic foundations of the new society. And it is here that most of the novelty lies in the criminal law of

---

[7] Poland's prewar criminal code of 1932 punished homosexuality only in the event of solicitation for mercenary reasons (art. 207).

[8] Russian translations of the codes of Eastern European People's Democracies were published in Moscow in 1961 and 1962 in a series entitled UGOLOVNOE ZAKONODATEL'STVO ZARUBEZHNYKH SOTSIALISTICHESKIKH GOSUDARSTV [The Criminal Legislation of Socialist States beyond the Frontier].

Marxian socialist states. Many of these have already been indicated in the discussion of the fundamentals of the law of the economic base. The alienation of property removed by the constitution from private ownership and trade becomes a crime, novel in the breadth of its subject matter. It is far more than the punishment of the sale of prohibited goods, such as the pornographic materials condemned by all societies. It particularly reaches the attempt to sell land.[9] It prevents even its leasing, by individuals or by collective farms.

Chattels, whose ownership for consumption purposes is permitted, and whose sale is legal by artisans or collective farmers under prescribed conditions, become the *corpora delicti* when sold as a business.[10]

Economic planning has left its mark in the crime of failure to perform the plan not only quantitatively but in conformity with state standards of quality.[11] Engaging in a prohibited business becomes a crime, and the offense becomes qualitatively different from that in other lands because prohibition falls on all business which hires labor for personal profit.[12] Discrimination by state personnel directors in hiring practices is criminal,[13] as is hampering labor unions in the performance of their functions.[14] Finally, the constitutional duty to work[15] is enforced by the "parasite legislation," which during the height of its popular application provided the basis for banishing many to remote regions to work out their salvation in hard labor, even though the offense was not technically treated in the Soviet Union as established by penal legislation.[16]

By far the most serious of economic crimes defined in the 1958 law on state crimes was "wrecking."[17] Its definition is the

[9] Criminal Code R.S.F.S.R. 1964, art. 199. Eng. transl. in H. BERMAN, SOVIET CRIMINAL LAW AND PROCEDURE: THE R.S.F.S.R. CODES (1966). Translations of the articles used herein are taken from this text.

[10] *Id.* art. 154.

[11] See discussion in ch. 14.

[12] Criminal Code R.S.F.S.R. 1964, art. 162.

[13] *Id.* arts. 74, 139.

[14] *Id.* art. 137.

[15] U.S.S.R. Constitution 1936, art. 12.

[16] See discussion in ch. 14.

[17] Law on State Crimes, 25 Dec. 1958, art. 6. [1959] 1 Ved. Verkh. Sov. S.S.S.R. item 10.

vaguest one remaining since the reforms of 1958. In a measure it is currently the major reminder of Stalin's great purge, when untold numbers of enterprise directors, engineers, and common workers were sentenced to death under its severe classification as "counterrevolution." [18] The 1958 reforms have reduced the impact of this offense upon evaluation of the distinctive features of Marxian socialist law, for the maximum penalty for its commission has been reduced from death to fifteen years' deprivation of liberty with confiscation of property, with or without additional exile from the home community for a term of from two to five years. The offense still remains, however, in the federal law on state crimes, and, therefore, in the codes of all Soviet republics, although it is probable that few individuals, if any, are now brought under its provisions. Capital punishment was not restored as a penalty for the offense in 1961–62, as it was for many offenses where violations were frequent. It is defined as:

> An action or omission to act directed toward the subversion of industry, transport, agriculture, the monetary system, trade, or other branches of the national economy, or the activity of state agencies or social organizations, for the purpose of weakening the Soviet state, if such act is committed by making use of state and social institutions, enterprises, or organizations, or by obstructing their normal work.

In the economic field, another contrast with practice in the non-Marxist states is the differentiation in treatment between misappropriation of state and personal property. Since the Soviet Union is a socialist state, its constitution, like those of all other members of the family, declares "socialist property" to be the economic foundation of the state,[19] and the courts are given as their first task the goal of protecting it from any infringements.[20] Protection of personal property rights is placed in the second category of goals. This same differentiation in importance is reflected in the criminal codes.

[18] Criminal Code R.S.F.S.R. 1926, art. 58 (7). Eng. transl. in THE PENAL CODE OF THE RUSSIAN SOCIALIST FEDERAL SOVIET REPUBLIC (1934).

[19] Art. 4.

[20] Law on Court Organization of the R.S.F.S.R., 27 Oct. 1960, art. 2 (a). Eng. transl. in BERMAN, *supra*, note 9 at 429.

Crimes against personal ownership are placed in chapter 5 of the Russian republic's criminal code, in the usual configuration of theft, open theft, robbery, swindling, extortion, intentional and negligent destruction, for which penalties vary from compulsory labor without deprivation of liberty to fifteen years' deprivation of liberty without exile for robbery under exacerbated circumstances. Crimes against socialist ownership are placed well forward in chapter 2, immediately following crimes against the state, and the same offenses are assigned penalties ranging from compulsory labor without deprivation of liberty to death, the latter being applicable to the stealing of socialist property on an especially large scale, regardless of the manner of the stealing.

Under this provision, introduced in 1962, scores of individuals caught in various schemes to steal and sell state and cooperative property have since been executed, to the accompaniment of bitter criticism from outside the Marxian socialist family. Professor George Kline, in denouncing Khrushchev, says, "He has steadily enlarged the class of capital crimes and, for the first time in modern Russian history, made crimes against property punishable by the firing squad." [21] Although Kline, in his reference to "modern" history, overlooks the fact that the law of 7 August 1932 was applied to authorize execution of thieves of state property right up to general and brief peacetime repeal of the death sentence in 1947, his expression of shock is an example of Western philosophical evaluation of the novelty of Soviet attitudes toward economic crime.

Also typically Marxist is that part of the criminal code that treats of religion, for Soviet leaders accept without qualification Marx's denunciation of religion as an intolerable superstitution, an "opiate of the people." Still, in the first constitution of the Russian republic at the moment of separation of church and state a guarantee of freedom of conscience was included.[22] This, of course, influenced the course of criminal legislation on the subject. A chronicler of the drafting process in 1918 has reported that the wide guarantee, which then authorized not only

[21] Kline, *Socialist Legality and Communist Ethics*, 8 NATURAL L.F. 21 at 32 (1963).
[22] Constitution of the R.S.F.S.R. 1918, art. 13.

the practice of religion but also its propagation, was contrary to the aims of the Russian Social Democratic Labor party, which was later to become the Communist party. Nevertheless, the guarantee was inserted. He explains that it was necessary to win adherents to the Bolshevik cause at a time of difficulty.[23] The constitutional guarantee has remained in subsequent constitutions, but in truncated form, since the right to propagate the faith was removed by amendment in 1929, leaving only the right to worship. In that form the guarantee was placed in the 1936 federal bill of rights, alongside the broader guarantee given to atheists to propagate their position.[24]

In spite of the broad constitutional guarantee of religious freedom in the 1918 constitution, discrimination was introduced in the very same document in its electoral provisions. The right to vote and hold political office was denied to priests, as it was to the members of the former royal family, the old police, and the bourgeoisie.[25] In 1921 a stop was put to religious education of youth and children, in spite of the constitution's guarantee, for a criminal statute prohibited the teaching of religion to children under the age of eighteen in public or private schools.[26] Another statute forbade the collection of a tax for the benefit of the church, which had been the custom before the revolution.[27] Another forbade religious ceremonies outside the church, or the placing of religious emblems in state, trade union, or cooperative offices.[28]

Various civil law features hampered the church, such as denial to the congregation of the privilege of creating legal entities.[29] This meant that the church could not receive bequests in wills. It was also denied the right to own the church buildings, vestments, or religious utensils, all of which became the property of the state on assignment to the elders of the

[23] Gurvich, Istoriia sovetskoi konstitutsii 79 (1923) [History of the Soviet Constitution].

[24] Art. 124.

[25] Art. 65.

[26] Gsovski, *The Legal Status of the Church in Soviet Russia*, 8 Ford. L. Rev. 1 (1939).

[27] *Ibid.*

[28] *Ibid.*

[29] Criminal Code R.S.F.S.R. 1926, art. 122.

parish, who were held responsible individually for their preservation until dissolution of the parish and return of the property to the state. Finally, administrative regulations were applied to demolish edifices which stood on islands in the middle of main streets, in their customary place as the most prominent buildings of medieval Russian towns. The pretense was that city planning required the opening of broad boulevards through central locations.

Within this atmosphere of discouragement, which did not end in 1936 when the prohibition on priests' voting and holding political office was withdrawn, the criminal law has continued to play its part. It has appeared to protect the faithful, as when it penalizes those who obstruct the performance of religious rites, but at the same time it has opened wide avenues of legal restraint by placing a qualification conducive to broad interpretation on the rites; for they must not violate public order or be accompanied by infringement of the rights of citizens. Court practice has built on this qualification over the years.

The Russian republic's current criminal code, which became effective in 1961, includes for the first time an additional provision, appearing to increase protection to parishes. It penalizes those who commit crimes against the property of associations not constituting socialist organizations.[30] This would include religious organizations, except that they have very little property of their own, other than their collections during mass. Also in the new code was a further restraint on the priests; the prohibition of "teaching" was extended by specifying that it is now a crime to draw minors into a group which, under the guise of religious teaching, causes harm to health or sexual dissoluteness.[31] This provision would present no novelty were it not for the framework of judicial determination as to what is such harm, for other legal systems restrain religious practices on health grounds, as the United States does with the prohibition of bigamy and the use of dangerous narcotics as part of the religious experience. One state of the United States, in its effort to ban alcohol from the community, has forbidden its use even for the Eucharist, although this state statute has not yet been

[30] Art. 151.
[31] Art. 227.

tested before the Supreme Court of the United States. Some Soviet judicial decisions will indicate how the prohibition of Soviet criminal law is enforced.

Judicial practice has established what appears to be intolerance of the sects which have existed for centuries in Russia alongside the Orthodox church, although subject to severe repressions. Many of their strictly orthodox interpretations of the Bible lead to terrorizing their members with threats of hell for the sinful, and to religious ceremonies in expiation of sins which lead to flagellation and other forms of penance. It is these to which the criminal courts have directed their attention in more recent years. The clergy of the Orthodox church, the mosque, and the synagogue have been discouraged in other ways on the expectation that their congregations will sink into an inevitable desuetude as they are deprived of any chance to teach youth, and as this youth is saturated with vigorously presented atheistic propaganda. The departure of Stalin's daughter from the USSR in 1967, partly because she felt her opportunities for religious expression limited, may change this situation, but at the moment it is the sects which are brought to court.

A religious case came before a comrades' court in 1961 when a leader of a sect called the "fiftyites" was brought before the tribunal for conducting the sect in such a way that some members were alleged to have lost their health; neighbors were kept from sleeping because of the loud wailing of prayers; and a young girl was terrorized by her mother into staying away from the activities of the communist children's organization, the Pioneers. Questions from the bench and the audience brought forth quite customary responses from the sect leader. He sounded like one who practices full orthodoxy anywhere in the world. He appeared as a reformed dissolute man. When taunted with his past, he replied, "The Father forgives everything. I repent of my sins." When taunted with a comment, "Do you know, Nezbritskii, that the root of your faith is propagated in the capitalist countries which are alien to us?" he replied, "God himself leads me." To the charge that he had subverted many, he said, "No one is dragged into the sect. All my free time I read the gospels. I pray, I repent of my sins."

After hearing the testimony of a teacher that a young girl

had been kept from participating in social activities at school and the testimony of a hospital that two members of the sect were undergoing psychiatric treatment, and after hearing neighbors complain of insomnia because of the noise of the cult, the court issued a severe reprimand to the accused, and warned him that if he continued, he would be prosecuted for establishing groups harmful to the health of citizens.[32]

When in 1961 a similar group of "fiftyites" was held to have made an elderly member feel so remorseful that she committed suicide, the article was applied to close it down and penalize its leaders.[33]

The case is remarkable for what it reveals to Westerners of the fanaticism of some Russian sects. The leaders were charged with preaching systematically that in thankfulness for the gift of eternal life and the kingdom of God, the sect's members should be prepared to make any sacrifice. Allegedly under their influence, a weaver, mother of four children, tried to kill her infant by throwing him under a truck, but the alert driver stopped in time. Later she tried to drown the baby in the river, but the intervention of another citizen prevented drowning. Her inability to sacrifice the child led to mental depression, and in this condition she committed suicide, throwing herself under a train. The leaders were also accused of influencing another woman to do likewise.

One of the defendants was accused of calling K to him on 21 July 1960, and in an effort to obtain absolute obedience, of accusing her of disclosing secrets of the sect and of sending her daughter to a Pioneer camp for training in communist morals. He asked her to repent of her sins by sacrificing her daughter, and to report to a subsequent regular meeting of the sect what she had done. Since she was afraid, she only told of her sins and then informed the group of what she had been asked to do to her daughter. In this way the fact became known. The group of four leaders was convicted and sentenced to various terms, ranging from two to five years, to be followed by a two-year period of banishment. The sentence was affirmed on appeal.

In 1965, however, prosecution under the same article failed

[32] Nezbritskii, reported in Andreeva, *The Court is in Session: Behind Closed Shutters*, [1961] 10 Sov. IUST. 20.

[33] Afonin, et al., [1961] 4 Biull. Verkh. Suda R.S.F.S.R. 8.

under quite curious circumstances.[34] Four persons were brought to trial in Kazan for conducting services in private homes and communal apartments and for distributing leaflets. All four were convicted and sentenced to five years' confinement in a labor colony of the "general regime." On appeal the supreme court found that the group had left a Baptist Christian congregation in Kazan because of disagreement with its new governing council, and the new statute on Baptist-Christian union, adopted in 1960. It was because of this disagreement that they ceased attending church and began conducting services in private homes and apartments.

The case had been brought to the supreme court by the procurator general of the USSR on the ground that departure from the established church constituted no crime punishable by the state, since church and state were separated by the constitution. Consequently, the state does not enforce church discipline. The court said in its opinion that since the constitution guarantees freedom of conscience, the accused had a right to conduct religious services in private homes and apartments. It noted also that the distribution of leaflets is not a crime. The only crimes are causing harm to health, urging citizens to refuse to perform social activity or civil duties, and involving children in the group. By this decision, the limitations on the application of the article were drawn more narrowly than had been done previously. But the decision makes it clear that distinctive features remain in the USSR law on religion.

In spite of the practice of discouragement, religion lingers on in the Soviet Union, as is indicated by a report of the Moscow state university's sociological laboratory.[35] In a survey of a Ukrainian village in which all social groups were presented in proportions typical of rural localities throughout the country as a whole, it was found that icons adorned the homes of 60 percent to 75 percent of the elderly nonworkers and pensioners, 47 percent of the families of collective farmers actually working upon the land, 30 percent of the families of workers and employees in state enterprises functioning within the village,

[34] Terentev et al., [1965] 2 SOTS. ZAK. 89.
[35] Arutiunian, *The Social Structure of the Rural Population*, [1966] 5 VOPROSY FILOSOFII 51. Eng. transl. in 18 C.D.S.P. no. 25 at 20, 24. (1966).

and 21 percent of the families whose heads were employed in state institutions as civil servants. A similar study among families of the Orel collective farms indicated that 36 percent of those questioned were religious believers.

Perhaps because of the tenacity with which peasants hold to old beliefs, the Soviet policy-makers have struck one more blow. A 1966 order prohibits not only the conduct of religious schools, but also any social activity in the church which is not precisely related to worship.[36] Athletic games under church auspices, picnics, sewing circles, and the many other activities which encourage the fellowship fostered by religious organizations in other lands, and to which religious communities in the USSR seem to have been turning, have been outlawed in the USSR. In this legislation lies the major contrast between Soviet law and the restrictive rules of all legal systems limiting religious practices harmful to health and public order.

Discouragement of religious practices has not gone as far in other member-states of the family of Marxian socialist legal systems. In several states, where under pre-Marxist law priests were paid in part by the state with taxes collected for the purpose, this practice continues. Buildings are not molested. The attention of the world has been focused on the dispute in Poland between the state and the church, where there has been strong antichurch legislation, tempered, however, by a sense of restraint lest persecution of the Roman Catholic church weaken the loyalty to the Communist-led state of a militantly religious population. This fear accounts for departure from the extremely militant Soviet models, as when the Polish constitution of 1952 omitted any guarantee of antireligious propaganda.[37] The Polish Communists preferred to take a position like that of the Russians in 1918 rather than the one the Russians had reached by the time the new Polish state was brought into being by the Communists. They wanted to avoid unnecessary stimulation of opposition through official attacks on fundamental beliefs.

This sense of restraint did not, however, cause them to stay their hand entirely. Soon after achieving power the Polish Communists decreed penal sanctions for those using compul-

[36] Order of 18 Mar. 1966, [1966] 12 Ved. Verkh. Sov. R.S.F.S.R. item 219.

[37] Art. 70.

sion, including psychological pressure, to enforce participation in religious activities. Their decree of 5 August 1949 [38] also punished priests who refused church burial to members of the Communist party and who preached sermons against state regulations. Prosecutions occurred under the decree.

At the same time, in emulation of Soviet policy, they sought to avoid unnecessary confrontation between churchmen and stupidly inept hotheads. The decree made it a crime to insult publicly an object of religious worship, such as a crucifix or a place devoted to religious rites.

When they felt stronger, they went further in their attack. By 1961 the teaching of religion was banned in state schools, and by 1966 the pope was prevented from visiting Poland for the celebrations in honor of the millenium of Christianity in that land. Polish Communists have demonstrated their ability to advance and retreat as the situation requires.

Stalin established a precedent for such moderation in the face of adversity during the Second World War. [39] He terminated the activities of his League of Militant Godless after the Nazi invasion of the USSR in 1941. He courted the bishops of the Orthodox church and obtained from them and their priests spiritual and even material support for defense of the motherland. In 1944 he consented to the restoration of organized religious instruction, but only for those who planned to be priests. Parents were authorized to permit the priest to give individual religious instruction to children, but never in groups or schools. A formal channel was established within the Council of Ministers in 1943 for the approach of religious leaders to the state when grievances required a hearing, and the Orthodox church was permitted to elect a patriarch and even to publish a periodical for the first time since 1929.

With the end of the war, policy reverted to its former basis. A Society for the Dissemination of Scientific and Political Knowledge was created to preach atheism, and antireligious museums were reopened for official visits of school children as well as the casual inspection of those who dropped in. Although historic churches have been repaired and repainted, they are

[38] [1949] 45 J. of L. Poland item 334.
[39] For details of the era, see J. CURTISS, THE RUSSIAN CHURCH IN THE SOVIET STATE (1953).

treated as state architectural monuments, and in few of these monuments are there religious services. Within the Communist Youth League there has been firm reassertion of the rule that no one may join who professes a religious faith. Attitudes toward religion appear constant among the Communist militants. It is only the tactics that change. Among those tactics the criminal law plays a minor part. Emphasis is upon formal antireligious education; upon public pressures to conform to an atheistic point of view and upon discouragement of the faithful by limiting promotion to positions of leadership to those who profess atheism.

The Chinese Communists present a contrast, for their policy is to remold religious institutions rather than to destroy them. In consequence their emphasis is not upon punishment of priests and destruction of temples on one excuse or another. They conduct study conferences at which the militant antiparty elements are denounced, but the great majority of the Moslem imams and Buddhist monks are guided through programs in which they are urged to "surrender their hearts to the party" and "resolutely to take the road to socialism." [40]

The Chinese approach implements the conviction that Chinese religious institutions are not firmly rooted, since the culture reveres ethics more than religion of a formal, organized type. The Chinese religious institutions are not militantly organized, except for the Christian churches, and these latter represent only the infinitesimal few. Consequently, the Communists feel that they can wean the clergy to their new programs and let the institutions of the religious bodies die. The official attitude is much like that toward the partnership with capitalists. Except for those tied to the great corporations of the West, the capitalists can be utilized and won over until they become an anachronism and disappear. So also the techniques of propaganda and change of conditions can win over the religiously oriented.

The Chinese placed in their constitution of 1954, when they were still greatly under the influence of Soviet models, a guarantee of freedom of religious belief, but they omitted any mention

---

[40] Quoted from Chinese sources by Lee, General Aspects of Chinese Religious Policy, with Soviet Comparisons, [1964] THE CHINA QUARTERLY no. 19 at 161.

of atheistic propaganda.[41] Unlike the Poles, they probably did so not because they feared arousing unnecessary hostility by a frontal attack, but because they preferred their way of persuasion. Unlike the Russians, they saw no need for militancy. Dr. Rensselaer W. Lee III contrasts the expectations of Chinese and Russian Communists.[42] In his view the Chinese confidence in the natural death of religious institutions over time is quite unlike the Russian belief that only militant atheistic propaganda and vigorous social discrimination can prevent believers from adhering to their faith and hampering communist plans for social development.

Lee is, however, cautious in his predictions. He foresees the possibility of a change in the policy of toleration if religion should prove to be an insuperable impediment to achievement of the Communists' goals, for he thinks the Chinese as capable of mounting a frontal attack as the Russians if there is no other way to clear the road ahead. Both Communist parties adhere to traditional views of religion as a superstition and a brake on social reform.

The Yugoslav, and more recently, the Czechoslovak Communists also show signs of becoming tolerant toward religion, although they do not share the Chinese expectation that it is moving toward a natural death. They seem to feel that coexistence is possible between church and state, even though the relationship is devoid of mutual trust. Both have gone through periods of persecuting the religious communities in emulation of the models established by Lenin and Stalin. Tito showed himself as ready as the Russians to attack the clergy in his early years. In 1946 he attacked the Roman Catholic church in Croatia as a supporter of fascism during the Second World War. He tried, convicted, and sentenced to sixteen years in prison the Roman Catholic archbishop of Zagreb, Aloysius Stepinać, and subjected the Orthodox and Moslem clergy to severe restraints and even arrests.[43]

By 1953 the attack lessened, and a law regularized church-state relations: guaranteeing to the religious communities inter-

[41] Art. 88.

[42] Lee, *supra*, note 40.

[43] G. HOFFMAN & F. NEAL, YUGOSLAVIA AND THE NEW COMMUNISM 94 (1962).

nal autonomy and the right to conduct seminaries and publish
religious materials.[44] Partial subsidies were to be paid to the
priests as in the kingdom of Yugoslavia, and penalties were
established for self-appointed fanatics who interfered with religious services. Church marriages were permitted following those
conducted by civil registrars. But the battle was not over, for in
1954 the Orthodox metropolitan of Montenegro was convicted
of antistate activities on the charge that he had sought to
interfere with local state elections. But he was the last high
prelate condemned. Only lesser clergy were imprisoned in later
years, when they aroused the Communists' anger by political
activity.

With Archbishop Stepinać's death in 1960, following his
release from prison in 1951 and his elevation to cardinal, relations with the Roman Catholic church improved. The acting
archbishop was decorated with the People's Order of Merit, and
a new primate was named.[45] Finally, in 1966 a concordat was
signed with the Vatican, but one issue of conflict remained. As
in other European Communist-led countries, the Communists
had created clerical associations to which they sought to attract
the clergy. In Yugoslavia, membership provided the clergy their
only opportunity to obtain social security benefits, and many
joined. The Roman Catholic bishops have sought to discourage
the use of these associations as channels between church and
state, and have urged the state to deal only with the Council of
Bishops.

Peaceful coexistence may be in the making in Yugoslavia,
for the Communists' hostility now rests primarily on a desire to
limit political opposition. The Marxist theoretical position on
religion as a dangerous superstition appears to have been relegated to the back of the Yugoslav Communists' minds.

Philosophers and sociologists in many Marxian socialist
states of Eastern Europe have been called upon to attack
religion in a way more effective than the frontal assault of the
past. A conference of directors of research institutes held in
1967 heard a report from the director of the Philosophy Institute of the Ukrainian Academy of Sciences noting that the

[44] *Id.* at 403.
[45] *Ibid.*

institute was giving much attention to research on ways and means of overcoming religious survivals in the minds of men.[46] During the discussion it appeared that nearly all the institutes represented were concentrating on studies of atheism together with alternatives to religion in establishing humanitarianism and ethics on other bases.

Criminal law has still another role to play in Marxian socialist legal systems, to which many analysts have turned in defining major contrast with other systems. This is the discouragement of seditious expression by severe penal restraints. Of course all modern political systems discourage and penalize seditious expression in one way or another. Some which have no Marxist base whatever have achieved widespread notoriety for severe restraints. Because of this apparent similarity, and the emergence with increasing frequency of patterns of like sort in fledgling states liberated from colonialism after World War II, analysis must be made in some depth to determine whether there is any Marxist distinction, related to Marxist concepts of socialism.

Attention was focused in the preceding chapter upon the influence of the Marxian class-warfare approach upon attitudes toward penology. It makes for division of citizens into "people" and "enemies" in all Marxian states, although with different degrees of distinction. The system of classification creates sharp differences in treatment of suspected criminals, especially when the charge is seditious expression, for the "class enemy" is often presumed to intend disruption of society, whereas a citizen classed among the "people" is given the benefit of the doubt. But this is not the focus of this chapter. Here the definitions of crime are examined to determine whether they reflect any peculiarly Marxist features.

The definitions of the USSR's fundamental principles of 1958 are not strikingly novel. Most are found in non-Marxist legal systems. They define as crime the use of forms of expression to overthrow or weaken the government. In the words of the fundamentals, the crime is "agitation or propaganda carried on for the purpose of subverting or weakening Soviet authority

[46] Korzheva, *Conferences of Directors of Philosophy in the European Socialist Countries*, [1967] 2 VOPROSY FILOSOFII 146. Eng. abstr. in 19 C.D.S.P. no. 18 at 27 (1967).

or of committing particular, especially dangerous, crimes against the state, or circulating for the same purpose slanderous fabrications which defame the Soviet state and social system, or circulating or preparing or keeping, for the same purpose, literature of such content." [47]

Materials to help determine whether application of this principle conforms to something like the "clear and present danger rule" of the United States Supreme Court are scant. This is because precensorship rather than postcensorship has been the Soviet rule. For many years the oral word has been controlled under a license system, requiring that conferences receive approval from levels of government corresponding to their coverage. Thus, all-union conferences have to be licensed by the Council of Ministers of the USSR; republicwide conferences by the Council of Ministers of the republic, and lesser area conferences by the executive committee of the Soviet at that level. [48]

For the printed word the controls have been even tighter. No individual will be licensed under the business licensing act administered by the Ministry of Finance to operate, even without hired labor, a handbill press, whether typographic, engraving on glass, photographic, or lithographic, or a letter foundry, nor is anyone to be licensed to produce multigraph machines of any kind, or even to make metal or rubber stamps, punches, or letters for typewriters, or to engage in the engraving or optics trade. [49] Violation of the regulations is a crime. [50] If it is on a small scale and without the hiring of labor, the penalty is mild: a fine for the first time, with the option to the judge of raising the penalty to compulsory labor without deprivation of liberty. If it is on a large scale or with employed labor, the penalties may be as high as four years' deprivation of liberty with or without confiscation of property.

Since the prohibition of private printing leaves only state printing establishments available to the individual wishing to spread the printed word, there is precensorship of what is to be

[47] Art. 7.

[48] 15 May 1935, [1936] 26 Sob. Zak. S.S.S.R. item 209.

[49] Regulation for the Registration of Non-cooperating Artisans and Handicraftsmen, 3 June 1949, discussed and cited in ch. 8, n. 11.

[50] Criminal Code R.S.F.S.R. 1960, art. 162.

distributed because he must obtain the approval of the editor of the publishing house. For many years there was an official censorship agency, called *Glavlit*, to which editors had to submit manuscripts they had chosen for publication. Under its statute, the agency existed to put into effect all types of political, ideological, military, and economic controls over items prepared for publication or for distribution in the press, over manuscripts, pictures, and drawing, and also over radio announcements, lectures, and exhibitions.[51] The office was in the Ministry of Education.

Khrushchev claimed that the agency was abolished after Stalin's death, with the state editors left to their own good judgment as to what to publish, guided from time to time if that judgment seemed faulty to the writers' union and the propaganda section of the Central Committee of the Communist party. Nevertheless, a truncated *Glavlit* seems still to exist to review the doubtful case, for in a record published in Paris and purportedly made during a trial of two authors, Siniavskii and Daniel, in 1966, there is reference to a refusal by the *Glavlit* to license their productions for publication.[52] Also, Soviet authors in a 1967 meeting protested its continued existence, and indeed there seems to be a Chief Administration for the Protection of State Secrets in the Press, functioning within the Council of Ministers' Committee on the Press.

Whatever the present status of the censorship, there are acknowledged limitations on publication at the publishing house, and this has reduced the likelihood of prosecution for violating the criminal code by publication within the USSR. Prepublication censorship effectively eliminates the necessity of postpublication prosecution.

The oral word, spoken outside licensed meetings where agendas are prepared under the scrutiny of moderators who either come from the ranks of the Communist party or are attuned to its wishes, has rarely been prosecuted in the courts,

[51] 6 June 1931, [1931] 31 Sob. Uzak. R.S.F.S.R. item 273.

[52] M. HAYWARD ed., ON TRIAL: THE SOVIET STATE VERSUS "ABRAM TERTZ" AND "NIKOLAI ARZHAK" (1966). An outsider claims that the censorship continues to exist within the Ministry of Education, directed informally by the Committee on State Security. A. BUZEK, HOW THE COMMUNIST PRESS WORKS (1964).

probably because in Stalin's time the special boards banished the speaker before he had had an opportunity to arouse his neighbors. To this there has been one exceptional case, of which much has been made among foreign commentators on Soviet law—the case of K.[53] The speaker was prosecuted during the war for "counterrevolutionary" crime, as it was then defined by the code, of systematically uttering anti-Soviet opinions.

K was acquitted by the trial court, and the acquittal was supported at higher court levels. It was found that K was by no means a systematic agitator. He was accused of saying something calumnious to a soldier he was drilling. The record makes no clarification other than to say that it violated the constitution. Perhaps it was a slur on the soldier's race, made under the tension of the drill field. The supreme court thought the testimony far from convincing, as the witnesses changed it in court from what they had said during the preliminary investigation. Also K's personality was such that the court thought it incredible that he might wish to harm Soviet society. On the contrary all evidence showed that he wished to strengthen military discipline, for he was a man who had served in Soviet army units since 1917, had been sentenced to death when captured by Admiral Kolchak during the civil war, and had never conducted himself negatively. The supreme court thought it unnecessary to remand the case for new trial in view of the record, and left the acquittal standing.

Were it not for the trials of various authors, including Siniavskii and Daniel in 1966, there would be no recent court material concerning application of the article punishing anti-Soviet agitation.[54] Siniavskii and Daniel evaded the censorship by sending their manuscripts abroad in a diplomatic pouch. They also evaded quick identification by using pseudonyms. When they were tried, it was for circulating slanderous fabrications. They were convicted and sentenced under the 1960 code of the Russian republic, even though to do so hostile intent had to be imputed from the circumstances. The issue, some Soviet authorities believed, was only one of the equivalent of "clear and present danger," even assuming that their acts fell under the

[53] 3 Feb. 1944, [1944] 3 Sud. Prak. Verkh. Suda S.S.S.R. 9.
[54] HAYWARD, supra, note 52.

text of the code's article. In the view of these moderates, the danger to the state in Siniavskii's and Daniel's action was insufficient to warrant a trial which could be expected to attract worldwide attention and possibly make their writings known to many who had not previously heard of them. The majority of the Central Committee of the Communist party were not, however, of this view, and the trial was held. Because of limitations on the persons permitted to attend, there was worldwide criticism of the lack of real publicity, and this was heightened by the failure of the authorities to publish a record. Only the purported record to which attention has been drawn was published abroad.

The decision to go to trial indicates that, as of that moment in 1966, the element of danger to the state perceived in publication of literary material portraying society in the USSR in a derogatory light was too great to remain unnoticed. The Central Committee's majority were taking notice of the unrest mounting among Soviet authors, and they seemed to be notifying their intellectuals that there was a definite limit of tolerance beyond which they could not tread. This conclusion was heightened in 1968 when other citizens were tried for exceeding permissible bounds of expression and were exiled to Siberia.

The Soviet Central Committee's concern extended in the same summer to Czechoslovakia. Of the various elements stimulating the Soviet Communist party to make its decision to intervene in Czechoslovak domestic affairs, the issue of freedom of expression stands out as of major importance. *Pravda*, in its editorial of 22 August 1968 justifying military intervention, had this to say: "In short, a situation was brought about in Czechoslovakia in which it became possible for Right-wing elements openly to come out in the press with antisocialist statements, to stage demonstrations and rallies under their own counterrevolutionary slogans, while statements in which the situation in the country was assessed from Marxist-Leninist positions were shrouded in silence and their authors persecuted."

When Soviet influence had been reasserted, the Czechoslovak Communist party was required to reestablish censorship and to dismiss many of the editors who had established the press and radio policies to which *Pravda* had referred. It was made clear that at least in the current stage of development of the Marxian socialist commonwealth, severe restraint on freedom of expression is a prominent element of the common core of the family of Marxian socialist legal systems, although the restraints are less militantly enforced than they were in Stalin's era.

Mechanical means of transmitting the oral word have come under control in the USSR as these new techniques have been invented. Thus, radio transmitters may be operated only if licensed, and violation is subject to fine,[55] but this restraint exists elsewhere to avoid cluttering of the air waves. More meaningful was the prosecution of an individual who manufactured a sound-recording instrument and phonograph records.[56] This was treated as a forbidden business. Such a restraint would not have been imposed in an open economy, and to this extent the offense is purely Marxist in its economic implications. Whether it is Marxist in its political implications is harder to say, although when viewed in the light of other cases of public expression, it falls into the pattern of precensorship to which the Marxian socialist states seem committed.

In summary, the contrast between Marxian socialist definition of crime and that of non-Marxist lands suggests that novelty appears primarily in the category of "economic crime." There are notable differences in attitude toward the social role of religion, but the difference here is primarily in emphasis. Marxian atheism leads its proponents to see danger to health and morals when other states also desiring to protect health and morals from excesses would not prosecute.

Crimes in the political sphere also reflect differences in attitudes, and there is a limit of toleration which no member of the socialist commonwealth will be permitted to exceed if the USSR and those who think likewise can prevent it. The Marxists have demonstrated that they are prone to sense seditious motives sooner than are those who preserve public order in societies further removed from their revolutionary pasts. Their fear derives from various sources, but especially from their persistent belief that capitalist societies will not, and perhaps cannot, coexist with those of Marxian inspiration. They fear

---

[55] 7 Apr. 1960, [1960] 6 Sots. zak. 85.
[56] Ustinov, [1960] 14 Sov. iust. 29.

also that such societies still exert great power over weak men and women lacking in determination to accept present privation in the expectation of ultimate achievement of previously incredible abundance.

The Czechoslovak events of the summer of 1968 emphasize the pervasive nature of Communists' fears for their future and the extent to which they are willing to go in suppressing opposition. As long as this fear persists, criminal law will exhibit, as one of the major aspects of the Marxian socialist legal systems, a proclivity for restraint of expression. Perhaps in the long term, current fears will abate as maturity and stability are achieved. If self-confidence results, the contrast in definitions of crime between the various legal families will narrow, leaving "economic crime" as the major hallmark of the systems within the family of Marxian socialist legal systems.

18

The African Sibling

THE COMMON CORE OF THE MARXIAN SOCIALIST FAMILY OF
legal systems has been sought in preceding chapters through
analysis of materials taken from the experience of the states
proclaiming themselves members of the family. The offspring
of the Russian revolution, whether they were guiding policies in
Poland, China, Czechoslovakia, or Yugoslavia, demonstrated on
gaining power their desire to follow closely the Soviet model in
establishing their political parties, their state organization, their
economic base, and the legal system generally. What variation
they introduced was held to Lenin's formula, which recognized
that historical experience had necessitated some concessions to
national sensibilities. Only after Stalin expelled Tito from the
Communist Information Bureau in 1948 did broad innovation
occur within the principles of Marxism-Leninism.

Although Tito's Yugoslavia was the first to start down its
own distinctive road to socialism, it proved to be by no means
the last. The movement toward imaginative development of
Marxist principles gained speed after Stalin's death in 1953.

Permission to reprint in this chapter part of a paper previously appearing in 77 *Yale Law Journal* 28–69 is gratefully acknowledged to the
editors and Fred B. Rothman & Company.

The pace quickened after the revolts in Poland and Hungary in 1956 and became alarming to Stalin's heirs when Mao Tse-tung rejected Nikita Khrushchev's advice in 1957 and developed his "Greap Leap Forward" in the face of the Russian's prediction of doom. Nevertheless, in spite of expanding freedom of innovation, the Marxian socialist family was held together by argument and persuasion until the Czechoslovak deviation in 1968. Common elements believed essential to continuing membership within the family were many, as comparison has shown, although the Chinese variations were raising questions in the minds of Soviet leaders intent upon preserving their concept of orthodoxy.

A test of membership within the Marxian socialist family of legal systems can be made not only by examining the fourteen states within the family, but also by studying those just outside. The Republic of Mali is the prime example of the latter, for its leader, Modibo Keita, took pride in his Marxian socialism from the moment of independence in 1960 until his ouster in November 1968. One of his first acts, after separating from Senegal to create for himself a completely free hand, was to opt for socialism.[1] He turned to the Soviet Union in search of a model, although he proposed no complete reception of Soviet political and legal institutions. His 1960 constitution, suspended on his downfall, established the guidelines in vague terms, saying that the republic was "to organize the conditions necessary to the harmonious evolution of the individual and the family within the bosom of modern society and with respect for the African personality." [2]

Keita showed some independence from the start, for he told his people on the first anniversary of their independence, "Our socialism will not be for us the manifestation of a tendency to copy servilely what others have done." [3] When he visited his friends in Moscow a year later, he made this clear in his banquet toast, saying, "Like you, we are sure of the triumph of socialism. That is why we wanted to visit the sources of this idea, to see with our own eyes, the life of your country and your

[1] See DEUXIÈME SEMINAIRE DE L'UNION SOUDANAISE–R.D.A. BAMAKO LES 5–6–7 Sept. 1962 at 23 (Bamako, n.d.).

[2] Law no. 60–1, 22 Sept. 1960, [1960] 65 JORM at III.

[3] M. KEITA, DISCOURS ET INTERVENTIONS 43 (1965).

successes." Yet as an African he was not to be overwhelmed, for he added, "still, your actual conditions and your methods would differ somewhat from ours." [4] He was for "assimilation" of the Soviet experience, but not for outright adoption. His aim was to achieve the end set by the Soviet leaders, but to do so in his own way.

Although Keita's creed, like that of his neighbors in Guinea and Senegal, called for a combination of socialism and the African component, it was not identical with them; and in that fact lay its peculiar suitability for comparison with the fourteen states within the Marxist family. Keita rejected President Léopold Sédar Senghor's argument that socialism can be combined with an African culture to create a mutation of Marxism to be called "African socialism." [5] Keita also rejected President Ahmed Sékou Touré's picking and choosing in the Marxist arsenal to create what Touré calls Guinea's "noncapitalist way." [6] For Mali's Marxist leaders, there was no mutation, and no partial acceptance. Their socialism was for them the traditional Marxist variety, the "universal truth," even though integrated into the realities of Mali's African context. One of Keita's ministers once said, "We do not pretend to have invented socialism in the twentieth century, but simply to have subjected it to the needs of our country." [7]

To analyze Keita's system in comparison with that of the countries reviewed in the previous chapters, his political and legal measures will be taken one by one and measured against the standard presented by the orthodox states. This requires beginning with the leadership component, which was predominantly necessary, according to Lenin, in establishing a pattern that would avoid the disappointments of the Paris commune of 1871. It is the point at which the twelve Communist parties then in power required conformity when they made their declaration of 1957 on the core principles of their system and the major cause for intervention in Czechoslovakia in 1968.

---

[4] *Id.* at 128.

[5] See Milicent, *Senegal* in AFRICAN ONE PARTY STATES 87,134 (G. Carter ed. 1963).

[6] 13 S. TOURÉ, L'AFRIQUE ET LA RÉVOLUTION 168 (Conakry, n.d., distributed in 1966).

[7] DEUXIÈME SEMINAIRE, *supra*, note 1 at 73.

Mali's social architects accepted only part of the rule on orthodox leadership. They permitted no opposition. Although the constitution declared that normally suffrage was to be expressed through parties and political groups, the "Union-Soudanaise—R.D.A." had monopolized political power. Its only opponents, the "Parti Soudanaise Progressiste," which was an affiliate of the French socialist party, and the Parti du Regroupement Soudanaise, were absorbed in 1958 even before Mali's complete independence.[8] When some of the former opposition leaders reappeared on the political scene in 1962, they were charged with plotting subversion. After confessing guilt, the three key men were sentenced to death.

Although the party demonstrated its conformity to orthodoxy on the monopoly rule, it departed from the Soviet model on the point deemed critical by Lenin in 1905 when he was finally able to organize his Russian Social Democrats as he wished. Mali's party rejected the orthodox requirement that it include in membership only the elite. It was called by its political secretary "the party of all the people," [9] thus dramatizing the fact that membership was not limited by class considerations.

In other respects Mali's party followed Lenin's prescriptions. Its members, whatever the extent of their commitment on entry, might not remain mere sympathizers. By party rules they had to promise to serve militantly within its ranks,[10] and party recruiters were advised that "placing party cards is not an end in itself." [11] They had to explain not only that membership meant total engagement and sacrifice, but also that "formation of the militants in political theory is an imperious necessity." [12] These provisions on militancy were sufficiently similar to Len-

---

[8] For histories, see SAMIR AMIN, TROIS EXPÉRIENCES AFRICAINES DE DÉVELOPPEMENT: LE MALI, LA GUINÉE ET LE GHANA 21–75 (1965) and F. SNYDER, ONE PARTY GOVERNMENT IN MALI: TRANSITION TOWARD CONTROL 9–79 (1965).

[9] SIXIÈME CONGRÈS DE L'UNION SOUDANAISE R.D.A.—BAMAKO LES 10–11–12 SEPT. 1962 at 107 (1963).

[10] Rule 3. For Rules, see id. at 107. Eng. transl. in SNYDER, supra, note 8 at 134.

[11] SIXIÈME CONGRÈS at 118.

[12] Id. 123.

in's to weaken the contrast provided by rejection of the elite feature.

The party had to be avant-garde, and its members were expected to be models of selflessness. Keita reaffirmed the importance of this rule in 1966 when he told the party's youth, "I must again put the party on guard against the embourgeoisification of customs and the tendency to live beyond means." [13]

The concept of a party as the "party of all the people," which had been the Malian formula since the party's early days, would have been unthinkable in other Marxist-oriented societies until the Soviet Communist party's adoption of the same phrase in its program of 1961. Before that time Communist parties had to be "proletarian class parties" to meet the test of Marxian orthodoxy. Although the Chinese party is now vitriolic in its criticism of Nikita Khrushchev for sponsoring the new formula, Khrushchev justified his change by referring to the ending of class struggle in the Soviet Union with the complete elimination of capitalism and classes. The resulting absence of class enemies in society left the party free to evolve into a party of all the people, but this did not require that it be opened to all. The new formula only excluded the class conflict from membership requirements. That part of the elite concept characterized by limitation to activists was preserved as a cardinal element of the leadership role which the Soviet party continued to play.

Keita's unorthodox characterization sprang from his belief that Malian society could skip the historical period of class struggle: "The question of class is quasi-nonexistant." [14] Malian Marxists admitted to different strata in their society, but "there are absolutely no violent contradictions between them, no relationships of exploiters to exploited." Nationalism was, therefore, "neither in feudal nor bourgeois form, but it is veritably a nationalism of the whole people."

Not only was there no capitalism in this view, but there was no need to develop capitalism as a predecessor to socialism. Keita's party supported this conclusion by quoting Lenin's 1920

[13] Speech on the Sixth Anniversary of Independence, 22 Sept. 1966, L'Essor, 26 Sept. 1966, at 4, col. 4.
[14] Deuxième seminaire, supra, note 1 at 74.

address to the Communist International, in which he argued that the capitalist stage was not indispensable for backward countries moving to socialism after the First World War. Mali would follow this direction, moving to socialism without passing through capitalism, and without class struggle.[15] Thus, the monopoly party required no class component to fight its battles. It did not even think it necessary to follow Guinea's example in attacking that fringe group of capitalists, the merchants. Even these could join the party if they shared its goals.

In organization the Malian party was orthodox. Thus, "democratic centralism," as prescribed by Lenin, was a focal point, and in traditional form: "Acceptance of the law of the majority within our organization; acceptance by the minority which has taken a position on a given subject of the duty to defend the solution adopted by the majority." [16] This rule was accompanied by all the familiar Marxian prescriptions: "the spirit of discipline is the base principle; a decision once taken must be accepted by the militant even if he has proposed a different solution. No one may conduct a campaign for the candidacy of a militant before the latter is invested with the status by a competent organization. The party may take sanctions running from warning to exclusion." [17] Contrariwise, every member was left free to express his views, so long as he refrained from organizing a faction to support them.

Only on one point of party discipline was there a striking contrast with the Soviet model. "Our party has erected as a fundamental principle freedom of religious opinion." [18] This concession went further than that of the Soviet constitution, which has been seen to extend a guarantee of freedom of conscience to the citizen: it included party members as well, for there was no requirement that a party member be an atheist. On the contrary, atheism was expressly rejected by Keita in a 1962 speech to the students of journalism. He asked, "How then, it is said, can religion and socialism be conciliated? I say that the question rests on heresy. If in the Republic of Mali religion had been an instrument of oppression and domination,

[15] *Id.* 75.
[16] Sixième congrès, *supra*, note 9 at 128.
[17] Deuxième seminaire, *supra*, note 1 at 15.
[18] *Id.* 17.

if it had made itself the agent of the colonial system, or even if in our remote past it had been an instrument of the feudal system, if it had played the role of poison, as a factor making for resignation, then the struggle could be justified." [19]

After dissociating Mali from conditions cited by Marx to justify his conclusion that religion is the opiate of the people, and by Lenin to order destruction of religious institutions in Russia as instruments of the tsarist state, Keita went even further to claim Islam as socialism's own. He declared, "There is no religion more socialist than the Moslem religion, because it teaches among its principles that the rich must give to the poor, must divide their goods in order to relieve the suffering of others." [20]

Party structure in Keita's Mali was reminiscent of that of the Communist party of the Soviet Union. There was the familiar pyramid, resting on the *comité* at the level of the village, the city *quartier* and the nomadic *fraction*. Above was the *sous-section* in the geographically defined *arrondissement* and above that the *section* at the administrative level of the *cercle* in the state apparatus.[21] Above these was the Party Congress, which elected its National Political Bureau. Each level was directed by an executive committee, which looked upward for guidance as well as to its parent body.

What variation on the Soviet model there was came from the fact that Mali's party originally established no organization in the factories and ministries on production lines. Lenin had insisted on this, but only after a resolution of 1962 was there a trend in this direction in Mali. It authorized creation of "political groups," designed to play a role as a "brigade of socialist labor" in factories and shops,[22] but it differed from the Soviet model in that it was not a membership base unit but a coordinating unit for those belonging to *comités* in different *quartiers* who worked together in the same place.

The Malian variation from Lenin's pattern in party base may have been the result of three factors: (1) a dissimilar history, for Mali's *comités* were not conspiratorial groups cre-

[19] M. KEITA, *supra*, note 3 at 107–8.
[20] *Id.* 108.
[21] SIXIÈME CONGRÈS 144.
[22] *Id.* 180.

ated by workers, as they were in Russia, to fight the regime from as secure a position as possible; (2) the absence of more than a very few industrial units until recently; and (3) the result of emphasis upon all the people rather than a class base, making organization by class groups unnecessary.

Supporting youth organizations followed Soviet models, except that after 1962 the top leadership of Malian youth had been abolished, out of fear lest its chief become a political contender for power. Direction was passed to the National Political Bureau of the party to assure conformity to policy.[23] The Soviet model calls for indirect control through overage members of the party in the youth organization's various levels. With Keita's 1962 decision, the overage method of control was abolished by the establishment of a maximum age limit of twenty-five for all members.[24]

Smaller children belonged, as in the USSR, to the "Pioneers," which enlisted children from the ages of seven to eighteen. Its mission was the same as that in the Soviet model: to educate youths in all fields—political, economic, civic, cultural, social, and artistic.[25]

Women, who have always been fully integrated into the party structure in the USSR without a separate organization, were provided with their own organization in Mali. Emphasis under Malian conditions had to be on separate organization of women in the light of long custom.

The collegial system of leadership was espoused at all levels in the Malian party,[26] as it is in principle in the USSR, but Malians faced some of the same temptations of power and some of the same necessities of strong leadership as have been faced in the Soviet Union. Personalization of leadership forced Modiba Keita to the fore and his personality left a strong imprint upon the party. He was so greatly praised that one outside observer concluded that Mali had built a "cult of the personality" around him.[27]

Readers of the party's newspaper, L'Essor, could see the

[23] Id. 180.
[24] Keita before his ouster was contemplating an age limit of thirty.
[25] SIXIÈME CONGRÈS 147.
[26] Id. 180.
[27] F. SNYDER, supra, note 8 at 5.

resemblance to Stalin's *Pravda*, but there was no Malian "Stalinism." Keita demonstrated qualities more like those of Nikita Khrushchev until near the end of his regime, ranking as a first among equals. Perhaps this was because he thought he had to share power with members of a Political Bureau chosen from large ethnic and regional groups, for whom they could speak.[28] Credence was contributed to this supposition in 1967 when Keita narrowed his leadership circle on his return to the Franc bloc to avoid financial collapse. He suspended, as Stalin had done during his crisis of World War II, the functioning of the Political Bureau and created a "Military-revolutionary Committee" to formulate policy.

The concept of the party as a party of all the people, open to all, did not bring its leaders to conclude, as has Sékou Touré in Guinea, that there could be a merger on the village level of state and party authority. For Keita's Malians the party "conceived" and the state "executed." The Council of Ministers, as the supreme executive, had the duty of guiding the administrative apparatus in execution of tasks set by the party. Lenin's admonition that there must be a minimum of crossing of lines was maintained by a rule that no party official or organization should substitute himself or itself for an administrator.[29]

Administrators, like their Soviet counterparts, were reminded that their duty was to seek advice from responsible political officials, because all administrative acts had political repercussions.[30] Party people were to advise when it seemed necessary. Keita faced the same problem of balance as had been evident in the USSR, particularly during the war and under Khrushchev's policy of direct concern with agriculture. Mali's party people found it hard to resist putting their hand to the wheel in addition to putting their pen to paper, but the rule was stated in three principles of orthodoxy, expressed by the

[28] See DuBois, *Mali Five Years after the Referendum*, AMERICAN UNIVERSITY FIELD STAFF REPORTS SERVICES, SIXTH WEST AFRICAN SERIES, no. 3 at 5 (1963).

[29] DEUXIÈME SEMINAIRE, *supra*, note 1 at 18–19.

[30] An African professor from Dakar concludes that in Mali constitutional organs are subordinated to party organs more than in Guinea. SEYDOU MADANI SY, RECHERCHES SUR L'EXERCICE DES POUVOIRS EN AFRIQUE NOIRE: CÔTE D'IVOIRE, GUINÉE, MALI 165–66 (1965).

slogan, "primacy of politics, non-meddling and politico-administrative coordination." [31]

Further, militancy of administrative officials was required, at whatever level the official served. "His first duty is to apply the principles of the party." [32] As in the Soviet system, there was no concept of the apolitical civil servant above the political fray. The party said that no administrator, for lack of political acumen, could be permitted to shake public confidence, to make the public regret the passing of the colonial regimé, or even to remind it of the old methods.

Although leadership was stressed, it was not to the exclusion of mass participation; but this desideratum was not pressed as strongly in Mali as in the Soviet Union. The claim was made that "the practice of democracy goes well beyond classic democracy," [33] just as the Soviet party claims, but the fact belied the theory. There was always a veto at the center. At the village there was mass participation through a village council. [34] Elected by universal suffrage, it might include women as well as men. [35] It served as a deliberative organ, but emphasis was upon its role as conciliator. It was to resolve disputes over land and property matters, administration of the common fields, ponds, rivers, forests, and quarries, and it must regulate economic problems concerning the whole village community. It was also to seek to maintain public order, protect individuals and their property, and administer the local police, health matters, the streets, trails, and diverse financial matters.

At this point similarity with the Soviet model ended, for whereas the village soviet in the USSR elects its own executive committee, the Malian village council could only nominate the "village chief." His appointment was by the central government. His dependence upon the center was more direct than that of the executive of the village in the USSR, although the system of dual subordination developed by Lenin provides for subservience in execution of central policy by the executive

[31] Deuxième séminaire, *supra*, note 1 at 19.
[32] *Id.* 29.
[33] *Id.* 30.
[34] Organized within the République soudanaise by Ordinance no. 43, D.I. 28 Mar. 1959 and continued by Mali.
[35] Law no. 63–32 AN, 31 May 1963, [1963] 147 JORM 132.

committee of the next higher soviet in the hierarchy as well as responsibility to the soviet from which the local executive committee's authority stems.

The Malian village councils were called "a marvelous school for apprenticeship in democracy and administration of public affairs." [36] Lenin conceived of his soviets similarly. Being a man who placed the party first, he could have said with the Malian minister of the interior, "Alongside the village council, organ of administration and execution, is the political apparatus of the community, elected by all the militants of the village: the village *comité*." [37] The *comité's* function with relation to the village council was stated in orthodox terms as, "first of all the role of mobilization in the bosom of the masses, which they are charged to educate." As has been seen, the current Marxist-Leninist manual in the USSR calls this "directed democracy," and this manual was on the library shelves of the Ecole national d'administration in Bamako.

Municipalities also were governed as a "commune" through a municipal council, popularly elected. [38] The mayor and his deputies were chosen by it from its members. Varying in size from seventeen to sixty-one in accordance with the city's size, its life continued unless dissolved by the National Assembly, although its activities might be suspended by decision of the Council of Ministers for periods up to three months. This represented mass participation, but with restricted authority, for it could only give advice and express wishes. To make these operative the minister of the interior had to give his consent, if the subject was one of nine critical ones. Large expenditures and borrowing of any size had to be approved by the Council of Ministers itself.

The Soviet model was departed from at intermediate levels, for here the Malian masses could not participate at all. There was no presence in the form of an assembly. Mali's system above the village placed a "chief" between the village and the *cercle*, in what is called the *arrondissement*, [39] in continuation of

[36] Deuxième séminaire 31.

[37] *Ibid.*

[38] Law no. 66–9 AN, 31 Mar. 1966, [1966] 218 JORM at vii.

[39] Constitution art. 41. See also Deuxième séminaire, *supra*, note 1 at 32–33.

French terminology. Named by the central authorities and directly subordinated to the commandant of the *cercle,* these 226 officials were indubitably the center's men. They replaced the traditional "chiefdoms," which were eliminated, except in the nomadic tribes. Their critical political importance was evidenced by the rule that they had to be political figures of proved responsibility. This was necessary because they could not only administer but share in the political education of the party's *comités* within their district. Thus, they combined formally in their persons both party and state lines of authority as was never the case in the USSR. They would seem superfluous to the Soviet party, since they sat in an area in which there was already a *sous-section* of the party, capable, one would suppose, of political education of the *comités* in the *arrondissement.* These remarkable figures, heirs to the old chiefs, had an additional function of conciliation. Disputes between villagers or villages cutting across village lines had to go to them for conciliation in both civil and commercial fields.

The commandants of the forty-two *cercles* were similarly conceived. Named by the governor of the next higher unit, the *région,* they represented central authority, but they maintained a special relation to the party at their level, being ex officio members of the political bureau of the party's *section.*[40] Through this device Keita attempted to maintain what in the USSR is sought through the medium of the county assemblies of the soviets, namely close coordination between administration and the desires of local residents on economic, social, and cultural matters.

At the regional level the same administrative pattern was repeated, although there was a trend toward closer similarity to the Soviet system. The six regional governors were named by the center, but were instructed to work closely with the party organs in the *région's cercles, arrondissements,* and villages, but without ex officio membership in any of these.[41] The governors' primary function was formulation and execution of the economic plan for the *région,* and to aid them they were given in

[40] DEUXIÈME SEMINAIRE 35.
[41] *Id.* 37. Law no. 65–22 AN, 1 Apr. 1965 on the powers of regional governors was not found.

1962 a commission to regulate financial matters. It was composed of the party's responsible officers in all *sections* of the *région*, of the National Assembly deputies resident in the *région*, and of the commandants of the *cercles* of the *région*.

The financial commission was to be expanded eventually into a regional assembly to be elected by universal suffrage in the manner of provincial assemblies in the USSR, but this assembly had not been instituted at the time of Keita's ouster, perhaps because it might have provided a means of undermining the governors' power, at a time when centralization was thought necessary to stability.

At the top, under provisions of the constitution, was a National Assembly and a Council of Ministers, presided over by a president, elected by the assembly at the opening of each five-year term.[42] This official served as chief of state, and bore the title "president of the republic"[43] in a pattern described by a French specialist as "profoundly original" in French-speaking Africa.[44] The post of vice president of the council of ministers, originally established, was early abolished to avoid confusion of authority.[45]

The president of the republic was responsible with his government to the assembly, but the assembly was automatically to be dissolved, as in France, if within twenty-four months two ministerial crises occurred. Dissolution occurred in 1967 during a financial crisis, without awaiting an adverse vote. The eighty deputies of the assembly were elected on a single list prepared by the monopoly party, and none was assigned to a specific district.[46] This system was designed to focus the attention of all on national rather than on regional interests.

Suffrage was open to all, except those excluded for crime, as could be expected under the Malian nonclass approach. Thus, there was no effort to exclude bourgeois class elements, as was

[42] Constitution, art. 7.

[43] Constitutional law no. 65–9 AN, art. 6, 16 Apr. 1965, [1965] 195 JORM 167.

[44] 1 D. LAVROFF & G. PEISER, LES CONSTITUTIONS AFRICAINES 164 (1961).

[45] Law no. 61–25 AN, 20 Jan. 1961, [1961] 80 JORM 245.

[46] Ordinance no. 65 bis on the electoral law, 24 Nov. 1960, [1960] 73 *id.* 1.

done under Soviet constitutions before the current one adopted in 1936.

Party concern with the details of state matters was increased in 1966 by creation of five committees within the Central Secretariat of the party: for politics, for economic and financial matters, for administrative and judicial matters, for social and cultural affairs, and for the press. These committees were charged with making profound studies of all matters interesting both party and state. In a sense they assumed some state functions, for they were described as "veritable departments at the level of the National Political Bureau; functioning with well-tried cadres, they must be veritable instruments of affirmation of the primacy of the Party." [47]

In a speech two days after formation of the commissions, Keita reaffirmed the purpose by saying, "I should remind you once more of the primacy of the party over the administrative and legislative organs, which is embodied in the right of all levels of the Party to conceive the whole policy of the country (economic, social and cultural) and by the right to see to the execution at the same level of that which has been conceived and whose execution is the task of administrative and legislative organs." [48]

Dramatic evidence of the interrelationship was provided by a protocol ranking of party and state officials,[49] issued as a guide to foreign diplomats and others needing to be informed of precedence of rank when both party and state officials were present on the same occasion.

Since Marxian socialists' greatest pride is state economic planning, Mali's leaders began immediately after independence to construct a typical system. By the constitution the National Assembly was given authority to fix the fundamental principles of the organization of production.[50] A Committee of Economic Direction was established in 1960, to which the Ministry of Economic Direction submitted proposals.[51] A Planning Minis-

[47] *Session Ordinaire du Bureau Politique National*, 20 Sept. 1966, L'Essor 26 Sept. 1966, at 8 col. 4.

[48] Speech, *supra*, note 13.

[49] Decree no. 271 PG, 26 Nov. 1962, [1962] 133 JORM 932.

[50] Constitution, art. 24.

[51] Decree no. 268, 12 Oct. 1960, [1960] 68 JORM 853.

try was set up, within which were formed a Planning and General Statistical Service [52] and an "Action Rurale" to aid in forming cooperatives and in drafting legislation on the subject.[53] The first compulsory plan was inaugurated 1 July 1961 to run for five years, but it was subsequently revised frequently, for example by a revised investment program for economic and social development adopted by the National Assembly in 1964.[54]

The year 1966 brought further revision of the plan in the direction of retrenchment. The 1966 budget sought equilibrium between needs and means through limitation on imports destined for current consumption on the one hand and increase in production on the other. Agriculture was favored so as to expand the essential base of the economy, but the budget for industrial equipment was cut proportionately on the basis of completing operations in the course of construction, absorbing losses on projects which had miscarried, and including within the total scheme industrial projects financed from abroad. It was called a "budget of consolidation."

In emulation of Lenin's strictures on the need for control of credit, Mali's leaders established exchange control immediately after separation from Senegal.[55] This measure was followed by regulation of private insurance companies, requiring investment of 5 percent of their 1960 premiums in Mali under a program to be approved by the Ministry of Commerce and Industry.[56] Thereafter all profits, after deduction of the required reserves, had to be reinvested in Mali.

Banking came under control of a Malian Credit Council, charged with the broad duty of establishing a credit policy for the republic, and of coordinating banking and issuing cur-

---

[52] Law no. 61–65 AN, 18 May 1961, [1961] 90 *id.* XXII, reorganized by Decree no. 46 PG, 4 Apr. 1964, [1964] 169 *id.* 358.

[53] Law no. 61–66 AN, 16 May 1961, [1961] 90 *id.* XXII.

[54] Law no. 63–95 AN, 25 Jan. 1964, [1964] 162 *id.* 104.

[55] Ordinance no. 13 PC 17 Sept. 1960, referred to in Seydou Madani Sy, *supra*, note 30 at 51. Exchange control regulation 20 Nov. 1960, [1960] 73 JORM IV.

[56] Decree no. 139 PG, 6 Apr. 1961, [1961] 83 *id.* 381. Foreign insurance companies were regulated further by decree no. 32 PG, 9 Mar. 1964, [1964] 167 *id.* 263.

rency.[57] A savings bank system to be administered within the post offices was created at the same time.[58]

Foreign banking was struck an incisive blow in 1962 by a monetary reform and creation of a central bank.[59] National enterprises had been financed since 1960 by the "Banque populaire du Mali," a state bank created for the purpose.[60] Another bank, known as the Banque Malienne de credits et de dépôts was a mixed company, whose capital was provided jointly by the state treasury and the renowned French bank "Crédit Lyonnais." [61] Thus, even before 1962 the state was assuming the role of principal banker to the economy.

The year 1962 brought the end for what was to be a five-year period of the link with the Franc zone by severance of the monetary relation with the Banque central des états de l'afrique de l'ouest, which supported the French African Community francs previously in circulation as Mali's currency. The Malian franc replaced the "C.F.A." notes, and the new bank assumed the issuing function.[62] Keita went before the National Assembly to explain the necessity for this radical step, saying, "Dear colleagues, as far as we go back in time history teaches us that political power always and necessarily is accompanied by the royal power to coin money; that monetary power is inseparable from national sovereignty; that it is the indispensable complement of it, the essential attribute." [63]

History was to prove that Keita had moved too fast in emulation of Lenin's model. With a swiftly deteriorating economy, without Russia's natural resources, and without massive economic aid from outside, Keita found himself forced to return to France for stability. The link between the Malian and French francs was restored in 1967, and French advisers were

[57] Decree no. PG 155, 6 Apr. 1961, [1961] 83 *id.* 383.

[58] Decree no. 171 PG, 20 Apr. 1961, *id.* 404.

[59] Law no. 62–55 AN, 30 June 1962, [1962] 120 *id.* 1. The Central Bank was expanded in 1964 to include the Central Office of Mutual Agricultural Credit. Law no. 64–2 AN, 14 May 1964, [1964] 172 *id.* 434.

[60] Seydou Madani Sy, *supra,* note 30 at 51. The statute has not been found.

[61] Deuxième seminaire 63. The statute has not been found.

[62] Law no. 62–54 AN, 30 June 1962, [1962] 120 JORM iii.

[63] Speech to the National Assembly, 30 June 1962, in M. Keita, *supra,* note 3 at 141–42.

invited to help in bringing order to the economy. The political shock was great to those who thought they had gained independence from French economic power. As has been indicated, Keita felt it necessary to solidify power, first by suspending the activity of the party's Political Bureau and later by dissolving the National Assembly.

Although retreat was necessary in fiscal policy, there was no comparable abandonment of industrial policy. Mali's socialist-minded leaders sought to capture and retain permanently the commanding industrial and commercial heights, as have all orthodox Marxists. By the economic plan of 1 July 1961, development of all new industries operating as textile factories, slaughter houses, refrigeration plants, petroleum refineries, canning plants, and sources of construction materials are monopolized by the state.[64] Even before new construction in these fields was monopolized, the state was reaching into existing private enterprises. An important company exploiting navigation and associated activities in the Niger River valley was recreated in 1960 as a mixed company to which the government and the Société des messageries africaines contributed the capital.[65] The government's shares were made nontransferable, as were the private company's shares for the first two years. Later in 1962 the private shares were bought by the state and a new company formed as a public corporation.[66]

A model statute for public corporations was enacted in 1963,[67] and existing statutes were reissued in the new form, beginning with a preamble in Marxist language, reading:

Born in the struggle for economic independence of the country, the national enterprises are a decisive victory of the toilers of the Republic of Mali. These enterprises belong to the entire Malian people; they are the people's property. The exploitation of man by man is abolished in them once and for all, and a new type of labor is beginning to develop in them. In these enterprises the toilers work for all of society, for themselves. To

[64] SAMIR AMIN, *supra*, note 8 at 77–78.
[65] Law no. 60–25, 8 Aug. 1960, [1960] 62 JORM 700.
[66] Law no. 62–11, 15 Jan. 1962, [1962] 110 *id.* 115.
[67] 26 Jan. 1963. Statute not found but identified by SEYDOU MADANI SY, *supra*, note 30 at 49.

protect and increase continually the property of the People in these enterprises is, therefore, the duty of every toiler.[68]

In the same pattern the state assumed in stages responsibility for the Bamako airport, Air Mali, electric and water services, railroads, posts and telegraph, petroleum exploitation, canning, brickmaking, hotel management, and public works. For all of these the pattern of organization was the public corporation, created in the image of the enterprise developed on the base of Lenin's experimentation begun in 1923, and since adopted as the standard operating unit for state economic activity throughout the Marxian socialist states.

Mali's leadership was concerned only with commanding economic heights, not with the entire economy, as the USSR model requires. This was made clear by a 1962 law establishing the terms for private investment.[69] The Ministry of Planning was authorized to sign conventions with "all enterprises whose activity presents a special interest for the Malian economy and whose creation or investment program concurs with the provisions of the plan of economic and social development of the Republic of Mali."

Limitation of investment to production was established by a clause excluding commercial enterprises from the regime. The Malians were showing typical Marxist aversion to the middleman as a noncontributor to value, but they were also acting out of fear. The merchants were considered a potential challenge to the regime, and history proved the fear well founded. On 20 July 1962 public demonstrations developed in the Bamako market, of such magnitude that the police found it necessary to make 250 arrests, and the former leaders of preindependence opposition were tried for inciting the merchants to treason.

Under the investment code any enterprise with which a convention was signed had the right to retransfer the investment, but on the expiration of the term buildings and installations were to revert to the state without indemnity. A model convention was attached to the statute. Profits could be limited by operation of a clause permitting state representatives to share with the enterprise's owners in establishing the produc-

[68] Law no. 63–65 AN, 26 Dec. 1963, [1964] 162 JORM 112.
[69] Law no. 62–5 AN, 5 Jan. 1962, [1962] 110 *id.* 112.

tion plan and in fixing prices. In practice, foreign companies were permitted to repatriate annually 25 percent of their profits, but the remaining 75 percent had to be reinvested within Mali in keeping with the provisions of the economic plan.

Fear of merchants also led to a policy of control of commerce at the point that had always been vital in Mali—import and export. Pharmaceuticals were immediately placed in the hands of a public corporation,[70] and a public corporation named SOMIEX was created within the Ministry of Commerce and Industry to monopolize the exportation of the primary export product, peanuts, and the importation of basic products, including cement, salt, sugar, oil, soda, jute sacks, tobacco, matches, flour, and concentrated milk.[71] Rural cooperatives were required to sell and buy only through it.

Within the Niger valley monopoly powers over the export of agricultural products from the valley was passed to the "Office du Niger," which was charged with valley development.[72] In 1964 the sale of hides was made a monopoly of another public corporation, SONEA.[73]

Apart from monopolization of the importation and exportation of basic commodities, Malian policy called only for price control and licensing of those private merchants who were to function in domestic markets. A 1961 decree [74] regulated prices in an all-inclusive manner, saying, "The importation, exportation, circulation, manner of fixing prices; the detention, declaration, and control of inventories; the use; the putting up for sale; the advertising of prices for all products and articles of merchandise of whatever origin and source are regulated by decrees."

Merchants had to obtain licenses under a statute of 1964,[75] designed to assure stability and open dealing. Although many of the Lebanese formerly doing business chose to leave Mali rather

---

[70] Ordinance no. 18, 15 Oct. 1960, [1960] 67 *id.* 808.

[71] Ordinance no. 33, 29 Oct. 1960, [1960] 69 *id.* 899.

[72] Ordinance no. 49 PGP, 18 Nov. 1960, creating "Office Du Niger," [1960] 70 *id.* 948.

[73] Decree no. 12 PG, 2 Feb. 1964, creating "Sonea," [1964] 163 *id.* 181.

[74] Decree on 185 PG, 2 Mar. 1961, [1961] 86 *id.* 1 as amended decree no. 225 PG, 6 June 1961, [1961] 89 *id.* at 1.

[75] Decree no. 189 PG, 24 Dec. 1964, [1964] 188 *id.* 31.

than to remain under the restrictions, retail trade remained in private hands, limited though these were as to sources of supply and level of prices.

When special knowledge was required, Mali's policies permitted private enterprise, but in the form of a mixed company. Thus a Society for the Exportation of Animal Products was chartered in 1965.[76] The state owned the majority of shares, but equal distribution of seats with the private investors, known as the "Group Mothes," was provided on the administrative council of six members. The state kept the key places, however, for of the six, the posts of president and director general were reserved for the state, and the private group had only the deputy director's place. Further discrimination was exercised by a requirement that the private directors deposit at least fifteen shares as a guarantee of honest direction, whereas the government's directors were required neither to own nor to deposit shares.

Likewise the radio electric industry was placed in the hands of a mixed company in 1965 with 4,000 shares, of which the state was required to hold 60 percent. Again, an equally divided administrative council of four members was established, of which the president must be Malian.[77]

Keita explained his policy on private enterprise in 1963 as maintenance of equilibrium in the state's balance of payments, which required control of foreign commerce so that it would conform to the provisions of the economic plan. As to merchants, he added:

I know that some merchants are experiencing difficulties in the exercise of their customary pursuits; but since evolution necessarily creates selection, it is indispensable that those who lack their own resources and who lived under a system of mercantilism during the period of the colonial regime, and who were accomplices in the exploitation of the rural masses by the great foreign companies reconvert themselves to become more useful to themselves and to their country.[78]

[76] Law no. 65–28 AN, 2 July 1965, [1965] 202 *id.* 387.
[77] Law no. 65–36 CP–AN, 13 Sept. 1965, [1965] 207 *id.* 525.
[78] New Year's Speech to the People of Mali, 1963, in M. KEITA, *supra*, note 3 at 201–4.

He demanded that all renounce fraudulent trade, but assured merchants who conformed to Malian laws that they could count on the party's desire to sacrifice no stratum of the population, albeit holding it indispensable that the favored strata understand their duty and renounce their surplus so that others might live and develop.

Mali's leader was declaring no such merchant's war as Sékou Touré has declared in Guinea, but he was giving private merchants only a limited role to play under the watchful eye of the party and of a security apparatus intent upon avoiding a repetition of the rebellion in the Bamako market in 1962. This position was reaffirmed in 1967 at the time of devaluation of the currency. The merchants were castigated for smuggling, but the attack was not upon them as a class. Those who had remained honest were given the government's praise for their proper civic conduct.[79]

Land law was in process of revision even before Mali's separation from France. A decree of 1957 had established a socialist theme by providing that in territories especially designated by decree "lands acquired by concession and which were not put in a condition contributing to their value under the law of 3 May 1946 within five years could be wholly or partly transferred to the national domain." [80] An indemnity amounting to the original cost revalued to conform to the increase in living costs, plus the registration fee and the value of any improvements not "sumptuous," was to be paid.

The new Malian government built upon this policy early in 1961 to enact a law providing that "every building or plot of land whose title has been registered but which has been abandoned for six consecutive years shall be considered as vacant and incorporated in the national domain." [81] The commandant of the *cercle* was to establish vacancy in a hearing on notice, and opponents were given three months to establish their case. No indemnity was to be paid, because the theory of reversion was based on loss of rights by prescription.

[79] Speech of Louis Negre, 5 May 1967, Quotidien d'information du Mali, 9 May 1947, no. 946 (mimeographed).

[80] Blanc, *Chronique foncière: Quelque lois Guinéens et Maliennes récentes*, 72 RECUEIL PENANT 297 (1962).

[81] Law no. 61–30, 20 Jan. 1961, [1961] 79 JORM 208.

Fairness in transactions involving land transfers or mortgages was the subject of two accompanying decrees of January
1961. By the first, transfers of land, whether by sale or gift, as
well as any act creating an interest in land by mortgage, usu-
fruct, or long-term lease, had to be submitted on pain of nullity
to preliminary approval of the government.[82] The accompanying decree suspended provisionally all existing law on the sale of
land by forced expropriation.[83] In May a new procedure requiring governmental approval of sales on court execution was
introduced.[84]

Customary rights in land posed a potential obstacle to
development. To overcome it, state enterprises needing such
land could address a request to the minister of rural economy,
who examined the customary claims and then issued a decree of
acquisition and registration in the name of the state.[85] The
procedure was made more favorable to the tribes in 1962 by a
decree requiring that the notice of hearings on acquisition of
tribal land for public use be published to permit interested
parties to exert their rights.[86]

Mali made no effort to follow Lenin's example of nationalization of all land. Her leader's policy was to respect existing
rights, limiting their exercise only for purposes of assuring that
no poor Malian debtor be treated unfairly. The policy of payment of indemnity when the state acquires real property was
extended by decree of 31 May 1963,[87] covering unexploited
buildings of commercial or industrial use. The decree charged
officials with making an effort to reach a friendly accord with
the owner on value before establishing an indemnity unilaterally and ordered that if the building were ever returned, the
owners should be paid damages as estimated by a state commission, if any had been suffered.

Subsoil rights of value were monopolized by the state, represented by the Mining Bureau.[88] Precious metals and gems

[82] Decree no. 41 bis, 26 Jan. 1961, [1961] 77 *id.* 139.
[83] Decree no. 40 bis, 26 Jan. 1961, [1961] 77 *id.* 139.
[84] Law no. 61–67 AN, 18 May 1961, [1961] 90 *id.* xxiii.
[85] Law of 22 May 1959, discussed by Blanc, *supra,* note 80.
[86] The procedure was applied in "Avis de demande d'immatriculation,"
[1962] 121 JORM 447.
[87] Law no. 63–53 AN, 31 May 1963, [1963] 147 *id.* 387.
[88] Law no. 61–68 AN, 18 May 1961, [1961] 91 *id.* xxiii.

might be prospected for and commercialized only by public authorities,[89] although these might be cooperatives of prospectors as well as state enterprises,[90] and the state enterprise was not required to undertake the prospecting and commercializing itself, but might assign its rights to private companies.[91]

Use of land left in private ownership was treated as in Romania and Czechoslovakia; it was subject to a policy of collectivization of agriculture, but steps were taken cautiously. An Institute for Rural Economy was established in 1960 to elaborate a base for agricultural planning.[92] Basic crops were to be purchased only at prices established by the state.[93] Emphasis was early placed upon cooperatives with organization of the *Action rurale*, charged with aiding farmers to form cooperatives and to draft laws on cooperatives.[94] Similarly, in 1965 emphasis was placed upon organizing cooperatives among the fishermen with creation of a National Fishing Committee as well as regional fishing committees.[95] The commercialization of cereals was made a monopoly of the cooperatives.[96]

The cooperative movement was fostered primarily to provide services to farmers. There was nothing comparable to Stalin's campaigns to spread agricultural producers' cooperatives in the form of collective farms. Yet this was envisaged, for each village was encouraged to expand the size of the "common fields," tilled since time immemorial to meet community needs. Keita suggested in 1961 that these common fields be expanded until they averaged one hectare for each family in the village by the end of the five-year plan in 1966, and every village was to establish a "permanent team for labor" to spend one or two days a week working in rotation on family plots.[97] Presumably

[89] Law no. 20 PG, 25 Feb. 1964, [1964] 166 *id.* 236.
[90] Cooperatives are formed under decree no. 15 PG, 3 Feb. 1964, [1964] 163 *id.* 177.
[91] Law no. 64–3, 4 May 1964, [1964] 172 *id.* 435.
[92] Ordinance no. 59, 29 Nov. 1960, [1961] 74 *id.* 3.
[93] As an example, see order no. 225 AE-CP, 4 Mar. 1961, [1961] 80 *id.* 259, fixing the purchase price of rice from growers.
[94] Law no. 61–66 AN, 18 May 1961, [1961] 90 *id.* xxii. Name changed to Direction nationale du développement rural, Law no. 63–48, 31 May 1963, [1963] 147 *id.* 386.
[95] Decrees no. 89 and 90 PG, 6 Aug. 1965, [1965] 203 *id.* 423.
[96] Decree no. 167 PG, sec. 2, 24 Nov. 1965, [1965] 211 *id.* 671.
[97] M. KEITA, *supra*, note 3 at 79.

the additions necessary for expansion of the common fields were to come from plots privately tilled, but no one explained how such transfers were to be encouraged, or whether it was expected that virgin land would be brought under cultivation.

At the end of the plan, Keita revealed more of his thinking in his sixth anniversary speech in October 1966.[98] He was prepared to say that agriculture had to be transferred from small individual and archaic family production to large socialist production "in giving it gradually by stages new adequate structures which will permit better equipping and staffing." He thought that the creation of rural groups and their development as a process of progressive collectivization would meet his objective. This sounded like a move in the direction of the Soviet collective farm.

Cooperatives not only were to be fostered in agriculture, they were chosen as the desired form for expansion of production by artisans and handicraftsmen.[99] Although large numbers were still to be seen working independently in Bamako, they were told in 1962 that "their true interest resides in reality in their association in cooperatives of production." The state established demonstration centers for artisans willing to innovate, where they set examples with modern machinery for crafts. Others were induced to join cooperatives by the offer of state loans to permit them to buy such machines. The result was expected to be development in a "semisocialist manner," such as Lenin used to predict in the early 1920s.

Like those of other Marxist-oriented systems, Mali's leaders showed no haste to revise the law of privately owned property. The civil code remained that of France, modified formally only by deletion of the chapters on marriage and the family to establish a new family code. This left in force the important chapters on obligations in contract and tort, and the chapter on inheritance.

How much the code was changed in application is hard to say, although Malian lawyers claimed that socialist ideas had influenced the courts. The major such influence, as in other Marxian socialist legal systems, was to be found in the with-

[98] Speech on Sixth Anniversary, *supra*, note 13 at 4.
[99] Sixième congrès, *supra*, note 9 at 101–2.

drawal from the sphere of the code of the previously important subject of privately owned productive property, which became the business of the state or of cooperatives. A second influence with regard to obligations was a tendency to aid the debtor by protecting him from any sharp practices on the part of those with whom he had to deal. Such limitations by statute included the general freezing of rents [100] and the fixing of rents for new premises in accordance with quality.[101]

The new Code of Marriage and Guardianship was substituted on 3 February 1962 [102] for the provisions of the civil code. Marriage was declared valid only if executed as a secular act, and a fine was imposed if a religious marriage preceded state registration. The primary target of the draftsmen was the arranged marriage, and consent was made requisite to validity. Still, tribal custom had to be met halfway, and Article 2 read, "Every request for marriage of a woman or young girl pledged to another with her consent is non-receivable." The fiancé under the betrothal agreement had the right to oppose marriage of his fiancée to another until his expenses had been repaid, and judges were authorized to fix the damages. Under tribal custom the gifts on the occasion of betrothal were great, and repayment could cause severe hardship.

Again, custom was met halfway in provisions that permitted the giving of gifts on the occasion of marriage, but by Article 3 a "dowry," which in Mali is a gift to the bride's father or head of family on the occasion of marriage, was not to exceed 20,000 francs for an unmarried girl or 10,000 francs for a previously married woman. Return of the gifts and dowry could be demanded by a husband in the event of divorce on ground of a wife's torts, and vice versa. Exceeding the prescribed limits on gifts subjected the culprit to prosecution under the criminal code.[103]

Marriages contracted in violation of the prohibition of polyandry, or polygamy for those husbands who chose monogamy

[100] Decree of 24 Dec. 1960, [1961] 57 JORM 67.

[101] Order no. 331 AE-CP, 11 Apr. 1961, [1961] 83 *id.* 400.

[102] Law no. 62–17 AN, 3 Feb. 1962, [1962] 111 *id.* 1. Also pub. in RÉPUBLIQUE DU MALI, MINISTÈRE DE LA JUSTICE, LA JUSTICE EN RÉPUBLIQUE DU MALI 362 (1965).

[103] Mali Criminal Code, art. 185.

at the time of marriage, subjected the culprit to prison terms and fines, unless a woman enjoying the option for monogamy agreed to amendment of her marriage contract. The option was designed to permit Moslems to follow Islamic custom if they desired, but they too would be subjected to criminal penalties if they exceeded the Koranic prescription of four wives. Officials who ministered to prohibited marriages were to be punished with the same penalties.

The woman's role under the code followed custom in part, for she was required to obey her husband, but enjoyed his protection in return. A new feature was to give her civil independence with regard to her property, unless she chose community property in the marriage contract. She had the duty to live with her husband as "chief of the family," but he had a corresponding duty to receive her.

Custom was defied on divorce in that repudiation of the marriage was outlawed. Dissolution was permitted only in the event of death or pronouncement by a court on grounds stated to be adultery, personal excesses, cruelty, or serious injury rendering conjugal life impossible; condemnation of a spouse to a severe and degrading penalty; inveterate alcoholism; and impossibility of intercourse. In addition, the wife alone had the right to demand divorce if the husband refused to meet her needs for food, clothing, and housing, or to pay the dowry at the end of the period of delay set in the marriage contract. In the latter case there might be criminal prosecution of a husband who refused with evil intent to perform his obligation.

A Malian author explained the reform by saying that "polygamy exists and cannot be rooted out without upsetting the social structure, the economic base of the country communities." [104] The legislature could do nothing but correct excesses. Under customary law a husband who could not endure a wife selected by his parents was required to retain the family collectivity by giving her to another of its members. Moreover, the wife could be inherited by one of the brothers on the death of her husband. The code had to be framed within this context, and thus a woman remained a charge on the family to which

[104] Dicke Ousmane Boubou, *Le mariage et le divorce au Mali*, 75 RECUEIL PENANT 319 (1965).

she was married. On the other hand, her emancipation was aided by introducing separation of marital property, and women were given the right to administer the home in the absence of their husbands. She was protected against the intervention of the clan or the family collectivity. In short, in his view, "Malian law concerning marriage and divorce draws its originality from the fact that it found a way to conciliate the exigencies of social life with the evolutionary current of the modern world." [105]

Labor relations were, in the French tradition, kept apart from the civil law of contract. Mali inherited a liberal labor code, based on the French model, and this code required only revision and reenactment in 1962 to meet conditions of socialism.[106] The code rested on the constitution's preamble, which recognized in the French manner "for all men the right to work and to rest, the right to strike, the right to join cooperatives or trade unions of their choice for the defense of their professional interests."

The usual Marxist approach was followed in that the rights were paired with the duties, so that the preamble provided that "labor is a duty of every citizen, but no one can be forced to perform any specific work except to perform an exceptional service in the general interest, equal for all under circumstances established by law."

Mali's placement of these provisions in the preamble rather than in a bill of rights in the body of the constitution followed French rather than Soviet models, for to the Soviet mind preambles are not enough. Still, the contrast was lessened by the fact that neither the Soviet nor the Malian government accepted the responsibility to provide specific jobs to those who become unemployed. Rather, the promise was conceived to be limited to directing the economy toward full employment. Jobs derived from that, not from court orders on a government employment office. In Eastern Europe and in Mali the right to work was essentially a reaffirmation of the right to protection against discrimination in employment.

The labor code established a forty-hour week and the basic

[105] *Id.* 486.
[106] Law no. 62–7, 19 Aug. 1962, [1962] 128 JORM 708.

provisions of the employment relation, leaving little to the individual or collective contract. The right of dismissal was limited to instances of the laborer's fault, or to circumstances provided in the contract. One to three months' notice had to be given on termination of contracts without limit of time, depending upon the importance of the position held, except when there had been serious fault. Damages were payable to the victim of abusive termination, and an employer who had induced breach was held responsible jointly with the worker for damages caused. Even if there had been no inducement to breach, the second employer was liable if he knew of the contract or continued employment after learning of the breach.

Collective bargaining followed French rules: mixed commissions were formed by the minister of labor on demand of a labor union, the most representative employer, or the workers themselves. Specified matters listed in the code had to be settled by the agreement. After conclusion, it might be extended, as in France, to the same branch of industry generally. Damages were recoverable in the event of breach by either side.

Labor disputes might be submitted either to the labor inspector of the Ministry of Labor or directly to the Labor Tribunal. The inspector's task was to conciliate, but in the event of failure, he transmitted the case to the tribunal, which was a creature of the Council of Ministers, named on proposal of the Ministry of Justice, after notice to the Ministry of Labor. Representatives of employers and labor union sat as assessors under a chairman who was a magistrate.

Hearings were public, and parties might be represented by members of the bar, trade associations, or labor unions. As usual under Romanist procedures, the chairman bore the burden of questioning and confronting the parties with witnesses. Reconciliation was desired before proceeding to decision, and appeals were prohibited, except to the president of the system, when the amount in dispute was less than 100,000 francs. The line of appeal for the cases of higher value was through the social chamber of the court of appeal to the supreme court, but only on matters of law.

Disputes arising under the collective agreement had to be

transferred to the labor inspector, who had to attempt reconciliation. On failure, the Council of Arbitration was seized by the minister of labor. This body, having a magistrate of the court of appeal as chairman and two representatives each of employers and labor associations, accompanied by two civil servants with consultative voice, one from the Ministry of Commerce and one from the Ministry of Labor, decided the case on the basis of both law and equity. If the parties refused to execute the award, the matter was taken to the Council of Ministers for a political decision, if the matter was of national concern. Strikes and lockouts were illegal during the period of attempted conciliation.

The state services were subject to a special statute on organization and recruitment, enacted in 1963,[107] and revised to form a "code" in 1966.[108] It was a civil service act, fixing classification for all categories of service.

Although the right to strike was enshrined in both the constitution and the labor code, party policy opposed such methods of attempting to influence results. A party political commissar in reviewing labor union policy in 1962 described the unions' tasks as explaining to workers "the need to increase productivity and production; to freeze wages and prices; to initiate the monetary reform; and eventually to raise the work norms which are susceptible to change on the initiative of the unions themselves." [109]

To open other channels of influence to the unions, the commissar noted that the party had already placed labor union representatives on the administrative councils of the central bank and of the import and export company (SOMIEX) and that such representatives would soon be placed on the councils of all public corporations.[110] A few days later, labor union participation was made a feature of the party's political secretary's report to the sixth party congress.[111] The party promised to raise higher than ever the unions' position in all their social

---

[107] Decree no. 247 PG, 21 Dec. 1963, [1964] 161 *id.* 48.
[108] Announced in L'Essor, 8 Aug. 1966 at 1, col. 1.
[109] Deuxième seminaire, *supra*, note 1 at 104–5.
[110] *Id.* 101–3.
[111] Sixième congrès 105.

activities, so that they might fulfill their role as a "true school of administration of the national economy." [112]

The unions were criticized for having decided on their own initiative to vote no in de Gaulle's referendum, whereas the party had advised a vote of yes. Since the party's recommendation had been accepted by the voters, the party commissar concluded that the "battle for the primacy of policy over the unions had been won." [113]

Mali's party appeared to have demonstrated more successfully than had Lenin's in 1920 its ability to gain acceptance within a short time of the principle that the role of labor unions changes greatly after a Marxian revolution. Mali tried to sweeten the pill for unions that found their task changed from pressing for advantage to executing plans established by the party by enhancing the unions' place in enterprise administration. Yet even here the role of the unions was subordinate, for Lenin's model, which Mali's leaders had accepted, calls for predominance of the enterprise director. It is he who is responsible for success or failure.

The charter of the Office of Agricultural Products of Mali (OPAM) provided an example of the relationship between directors and the unions in plants.[114] By Article 20, "The Director is personally responsible for direction, administration, accomplishment of all tasks and for development of the enterprise." The labor union's role was on the five-man Council of Direction, with members of the administration, and a delegate of the party. The pattern was mindful of Stalin's "triangle" of administration, labor union, and party, which was abolished in 1937 under threat of war and the need for quick and unencumbered administrative decision, but which reemerged under Nikita Khrushchev as a "permanent production conference."

Labor's position was further enhanced in Mali by enactment of a law on pensions [115] and one on social security,[116] without which no state, socialist or not, can today meet the demands of its people. French models were followed in drafting

[112] DEUXIÈME SEMINAIRE, *supra*, note 1 at 102.
[113] *Id*. 97.
[114] Law no. 65–7 AN, 13 Mar. 1965, [1965] 195 *id*. 177.
[115] Law no. 61–70 AN, 18 May 1961, [1961] 90 *id*. xvii.
[116] Law no. 62–68, 19 Aug. 1962, [1962] 128 *id*. 749.

these two statutes. The problem became not a legislative one, but the financial one of obtaining the economic resources to pay the bill.

The draftsmen of the new criminal code felt the need for novelty, and to indicate what they had done they introduced their code of 3 August 1961 [117] with an unusual report as a preface, saying, "The draft criminal code submitted to the National Assembly constitutes a veritable renovation in the application to our population of the law on repressive matters." Their task was conceived to be filling the gap left with the departure of the French, while recognizing that the conditions of life, morals, and traditions were greatly different from those of the French.

Noteworthy modifications selected for comment were: placing the husband as well as the wife under threat of criminal penalty for adultery or abandonment of the conjugal domicile (previously only the wife had been subjected to punishment); raising criminal penalties for political crimes and offenses, but eliminating the penalties of deportation outside the country and of detention in a fortress (Mali had no outside territory, and she preferred employing convicts in useful public works to long-term imprisonment); elimination of the French exception to the provisions on theft, excluding thefts within a family (Malians prefer an ultimate court sanction in such cases, knowing that a family brings a case to court only in despair of any family solution).

Other new offenses were the crime of aggravated alcoholism, outbidding of other offers of dowry to obtain a desired wife, and failure to pay a debt in bad faith. New definitions were given to vagabondage and begging, and the age of majority for criminal responsibility was reconsidered.

The new attitude toward the criminal code was summarized in these words: "It must be a tool for peace, for prevention of social trouble—not an instrument of degradation of the social climate because of application without knowledge of its provisions."

No evidence of a desire to find inspiration in the Soviet

---

[117] Law no. 99 AN, 3 Aug. 1961, [1961] 98 *id.* 1. Also pub. in LA JUSTICE EN RÉPUBLIQUE DU MALI, *supra*, note 102 at 51.

models, either of the early period or of the later revision, was to be found in Mali's criminal code. There was no reference to "social danger" in place of "punishment," no espousal of "analogy," no declaration that capital punishment was a measure of temporary expediency, no graduation of penalties on the basis of who owns property, no introduction of new definitions of crime related to economic planning, and no prescription of rehabilitating techniques such as leaving a convict on the job to be subjected to the restorative influence of his fellow workers.

Mali's penologists have ignored all of this, even avoiding an introductory article comparable to that of the Soviet codes declaring the codes' purpose to be the protection of socialist society. Mali's criminal code remained a French type of document, both in form and substance.

Some may think a few of Keita's innovations attributable to socialist influences, but examination shows them to be minimal. The most likely examples of a new force in the draftsman's mind were to be found in the code's definition of "vagabondage" and in a 1964 amendment introducing the concept of "economic crime." [118]

The vagabondage article opened with the phrase, "Labor is the duty of every Malian. In consequence vagabondage is an offense." This had a ring like that of the USSR's constitutional requirement that everyone work, but its treatment differed from the Soviet model, for there was nothing novel in the enforcement of the principle, as there has been in the Soviet Union. There was no provision for a social court to apply measures of social opprobrium to the man who avoided work, much less of a social assembly authorized to banish an offender to remote parts of the country for an experience in a new environment. Keita held to the conventions of criminal law, providing for punishment of vagabonds like any other criminal —by court trial in the ordinary way.

The 1964 amendment creating the concept of "economic crime" may have been more directly inspired by the Soviet model. Fraud, contraband, and other voluntary and deliberated infractions committed against economic, financial, and banking institutions were made subject to punishment, but in a form

[118] Law no. 63–92 AN, 1 Feb. 1964, [1964] 162 JORM 91.

milder than in the Soviet Union. There was to be ten years' loss of civil rights, confiscation of property, and prohibition against employment in state agencies for ten years. Malian draftsmen shunned imprisonment for the offense and showed no tendency to classify such offenses, as Stalin did, under the crime of "sabotage," for which the penalty might be death.

In sum, the socialist influence on criminal law was nominal in Mali under Keita's rule. The major character of the criminal code was the retention of French practice, modified slightly to meet Malian conditions as outlined in the code's preface.

French influence was again paramount in the structure of the judicial system with regard to the three major institutions: courts, prosecutors, and bar, and also in the allied institution of the state notary. The constitution set the stage with the conventional declaration in Article 42 that "the Republic of Mali assures and guarantees the independence of judicial authority, guardian of individual liberty and charged with the application in its own domain of the laws of the Republic." What difference there was in the approach to the judiciary was in attitude, not in legal terminology. Thus all state officials, including those serving in the judicial system, had the duty to be militant in their espousal of policies established by the party, of which they were members.

An African author, writing from Senegal, saw in Mali's approach to judicial officials an imitation of the approach of certain socialist republics, and found it possible to conclude that "the judicial power in the western sense of the term has no existence of its own but is absorbed in the executive power." [119] Such a conclusion probably requires modification after the events of 1965, to be discussed below, but it establishes a mood which must not be overlooked in evaluating Marxian influence upon the mechanism that administers justice.

Clearly, there had been a conflict of view in Mali between two schools on the role of the judiciary. Although both favored political militancy for judges, one school thought that a political court was necessary apart from the judicial system to attend to political matters such as the conduct of referenda and of

[119] M. JEOL, LA RÉFORME DE LA JUSTICE EN AFRIQUE NOIRE 141 (1963).

elections, the constitutionality of drafts presented to the legislature and of administrative acts, and claims filed by civil servants against the state. The other wanted to merge what had been a jurisdiction similar to that of Napoleon's Conseil d'état with the regular court.

The political school won the first round and established their court by constitutional provision as a Cour d'état, but a concession was made to the other school in that appeals from the claims section went to the supreme court. By 1965 the overlapping jurisdictions had caused such confusion that the party found it necessary to discuss the matter. Proposals were made to abolish the supreme court and substitute the Cour d'état for all supreme decisions, but the final decision went the other way. The three sections of the Cour d'état were added to the supreme court and the court abolished as evidence of the triumph of the men of the law.[120] The merger was, in fact, easier than it had seemed possible, because the claims section had never heard a case. There was, therefore, no pending business to be transferred, only a staff of twenty-nine persons who were absorbed without difficulty.

The merger established a single unified court system. Even the customary law tribunals existing as a separate entity under the French were no longer separate, but customary law problems went before the regular courts, with the addition of lay experts on the law to assist the career judge.[121] The system was composed of justice of the peace courts with civil and criminal jurisdiction, courts of first instance for more serious cases, a court of assizes in the French manner for capital offenses and those of great seriousness, a court of appeal, and a supreme court of the republic.

No effort was made to copy the Marxian socialist model in popularization of courts. Thus, no lay assessors sat in the courts, except when required by French custom in the court of assizes,

---

[120] Constitutional Law no. 64–1 AN. [1965] 195 JORM 167, amending the constitution to combine the Cour d'état with the supreme court; Law no. 65–2, 13 Mar. 1965, [1965] 195 *id.* 168, reorganizing the supreme court appropriately.

[121] For the organization of the judicial system, see Law no. 61–55 AN, 15 May 1961, [1961] 90 *id.* II, also pub. in LA JUSTICE EN RÉPUBLIQUE DU MALI, *supra*, note 102 at 6.

the labor court, and as expert assessors on customary law. No judges were elected, as they are in the USSR, but all were appointed for life as career judges, except for the supreme court, where the term of appointment is five years. Malians explained that because of the scarcity of trained men, appointment was the only efficient way to use manpower.

Procedure, both civil [122] and criminal [123] was reenacted in new codes, but on the French model. Malians said the influence of socialism in the procedural field was to be found in the fact that courts were made more readily available to the average man than before, and in the reduction of costs. Thus, whereas before independence, the court of assizes sat only once a year to hear all accumulated cases of severe crime, it was convened in Keita's Mali at least every four months, and more often if needed. Also, before independence the nearest court was in Dakar, in what is now Senegal. After independence a man was tried in a sitting relatively near his home, for the court went on circuit. Defense attorneys were assigned without charge to the accused, and procedure was simplified for certain types of cases. All trials were public, even those for treason.

Departure from the Soviet model was especially marked during the preliminary investigation before the trial, called the *instruction* in accordance with French practice. As has been seen, this state of the proceedings is conducted in the USSR by an official appointed by the prosecutor, admonished by the code to hear evidence from both sides impartially but nevertheless considerably influenced by his administrative subordination. In Keita's Mali, as in France, this official was a magistrate, responsible to the rules applicable to the judiciary, and in no way subject to the prosecutor's control. Further, as in France, the person under suspicion was given the benefit of counsel during the preliminary investigation, whereas in the USSR counsel is admitted only after the indictment has been presented to the accused.

When Malians engaged in the apparatus of justice were asked in 1966 to indicate the socialist features of their legal

[122] Law no. 101 AN, 18 Aug. 1961, LA JUSTICE EN RÉPUBLIQUE DU MALI, *id.* 146.

[123] Law no. 62–66 AN, 6 Aug. 1962, [1962] 126 JORM 581, also pub. in LA JUSTICE EN RÉPUBLIQUE DU MALI, *id.* 208.

system in addition to those in procedure, they reaffirmed what was self-evident: that the major influence of Marxist thinking was in the shift in emphasis to state industry and economic planning. So long as the private enterprise sector remained, there was of necessity a body of law of familiar Romanist type to regulate it, but Lenin's proposition that all law becomes public in a proletarian state was also revered in Mali. This meant that the state's paramount interest had always to be recognized in legal relationships. Thus, in registering a contract a notary checked not only the form but the substance to determine that no provision contrary to law was included. Also, the *procureur général* might intercede to protect the state's interests even if they appeared in litigation concerning the private sector.

Yet French influence remained strong, and there remained also African features of importance. Although Keita's Malians rejected the idea that a new type of socialism was being created in Mali because of this African influence, they were proud in noting departures from the Eastern European form of Marxian socialism to meet African requirements. The most notable Malian feature, in their view, was the rejection of Eastern European attitudes favoring flexible application of law, especially during the early years following their Marxist-oriented revolution. Malian Marxists wanted stability of law, and to prove that this was a motivating factor they pointed to the 1965 solution to the conflict between the supreme court and the Cour d'état, decided in favor of the men of the law. They pointed also to the concluding article of each of the new procedural codes, which sought to minimize the vagueness which might arise if there were gaps in the legislation. Thus, the Code of Civil Procedure concluded with a provision that "matters not regulated by the present Code remain governed by the texts in force so far as their dispositions are not contrary to those of the Code." A nearly similar provision ended the Code of Criminal Procedure.

A balance struck in favor of stability was the concern of an editorial printed in the party's newspaper, *l'Essor*, on 1 August 1966.[124] The editors wrote: "Without doubt there is a civic duty

[124] *Notre fait du jour*, L'Essor, 1 Aug. 1966, at 1, col. 4–5.

to speak a word regarding the manner in which justice is rendered, but this duty stops right there, and must not push any one to dispute the social necessity of having a judicial organization."

Although the balance was struck in favor of stability, it was not one to make unnecessary constant consideration of the societal approach. The editors made that clear a few lines later in their editorial, by stating, "It is certainly good to concern oneself with the fate of the delinquents, but to move from this position to one in which one forgets the fate of the victims, and that of society in general, is to fall on the worst of abberations. It is to support the guilty against society. That is never to be countenanced."

Indubitably, under Keita's guidance, Malian law became a complex fabric of customary, French, and Marxian socialist influences. His ouster in 1968 proved that the weakest of these three was Marxism, for on his ouster there was speedy collapse of what he had introduced. The monopoly party disintegrated; the agricultural policy was switched from a trend toward the Soviet type of collectivization to a return to tradition; merchandising reverted to private enterprise. Only the concept of great state industries was retained under pressure from the trade unions, which could not conceive of returning to a private-enterprise industrial system. Keita was proved to have erred greatly in thinking that he had successfully introduced the foundations of a Marxian socialist polity.

The collapse of Keita's regime without the firing of a shot, when he accepted his arrest by his army successors, provides a clue as to why Mali was not included within the Marxian socialist family of states as a fifteenth member. Its Marxian socialism was only skin deep, and the USSR was too far away to help Keita retain power until he could consolidate the system. The protectors of the socialist commonwealth may well have doubted that circumstances warranted assuming a commitment to a pattern of organization and a way of life which had not yet progressed far enough in the direction of Marxian socialist models to acquire stability. It lacked essential ingredients, particularly an elite party of disciplined members, and without this element Keita's society could not be shored up from abroad.

Keita's ouster seemingly added a new criterion to those a

country must meet for inclusion within the family of Marxian socialist states. The system must have a lasting quality. It must be more than a formal structure which cannot be maintained under strong attack. This requires either a strong political party determined to maintain its vanguard position at all costs or a geographical location which permits other members of the family to utilize pressures, including military pressures, to preserve the regime against forces determined to reverse permanently the progression of historical eras from tribal communism to Marxian communism. Mali failed on two counts: its domestic regime was unable to maintain power, and its geographical position made its leaders inaccessible when their hour of doom approached.

19

The Common Core

V ARIATION HAS BECOME THE RULE AMONG THE STATES GOV-
erned by what is claimed to be the novel family of Marxian
socialist legal systems; yet Marxists see a common core, and the
Soviet Communist party has demonstrated its determination to
preserve it, if at all possible. A sharp distinction is drawn
between states within the family and those outside. This has
been made manifest by the Soviet party in times past by its
ranking of countries of the world in terms of progress achieved
toward Marxian socialism. At the time of the most recent
ranking in 1967, only fourteen were found to have met the test
of "building socialism." [1]

Even Mali, which at the time was thought to be establishing
a system conforming to many of the criteria of the Marxist
systems, was placed below the dividing line. Its category was
shared by Guinea and the Congo (Brazzaville), as the group
"building independent, national, democratic states and struggling for social progress." Clearly, there has been a real differ-

[1] C.P.S.U. Central Committee Slogans for May Day, Pravda, 18 Apr.
1967, at 1. Eng. transl. in [1967] 19 C.D.S.P. no. 16 at 12. Subsequently
issued slogans for the fiftieth anniversary of the Russian revolution on
7 Nov. 1967 and for May Day 1968 made no ranking of states.

ence in Marxist minds between states above and below the salt. This has been so even though for the outsider it has been hard, if not impossible, to determine the precise nature of the contrast between some states kept within the official circle by the Soviet Communists and those left outside.

Although there is an official circle of fourteen states meeting the test, in Moscow's eyes they have not done so in the same degree. Neither the Chinese nor the Albanian Communists have been ranked as meeting the supreme requirements. The Moscow guardians of the socialist commonwealth have drawn a line semantically between the twelve that maintain among themselves "eternal, indestructible friendship and cooperation," and the Albanian and Chinese peoples, who are said to exist only in a state of "friendship and cooperation" with the others. The Chinese would rank the same group in reverse order, placing Yugoslavia outside the family and the USSR in the position of a state on its way out.

The contrast within the family is not simply in tactics of spreading the Marxian socialist system to other lands, although the literature suggests that this issue plays a large part in the dispute between China and Albania and the others. The contrast is also in the domestic policies of the disputants, and it is on those domestic policies, and their reflection in the legal and political structure of the Marxist-oriented societies, that this study has been focused. Justification for omission of foreign policy as a factor of analysis lies in the fact that a legal system is territorial in its application. If it is to be categorized on a map of the world's legal systems, such as the one published by the Mexican experts, its characteristics must be sought in its structure in the homeland, and not in foreign-policy aims of those who manipulate the state.

Traditional methods of comparing legal systems fail the analyst who seeks to establish the distinguishing features of the family of Marxian socialist legal systems. The methods of finding and applying law have been the criteria of the comparatists for nearly three-quarters of a century. The Anglo-American and Romanist systems have usually been distinguished by differing concepts of sources of law and by contrasting attitudes of judges, clustered around the core concept of the role of the judicial decision in the legal process.[2] The Islamic, Hindu, and Hebraic systems have been distinguished by concepts of sources and attitudes of judges, but clustered around a different core concept, the role of holy writ. Judged by these criteria the family of Marxian socialist legal systems offers no novelty. Its method is the method of the Romanist, although to a distinguished Islamic scholar, skilled in the comparison of laws, there is also an element of holy writ technique in the Marxist systems.[3]

Because the family of Marxist systems offers no novelty in attitudes taken toward sources of law or in attitudes shown by judges toward these sources, it has lost the interest of some professors of law engaged in the comparison of legal families as such. It has attracted the attention, in contrast, of political scientists, of economists, of philosophers, and of sociologists who look upon the law not as a technique but as a reflection of social values and as an instrument of social change. There is reason for this wide interest, as will be evident to readers of the record. Some will charge that this volume is not a book about the "law," for it treats of political theories, of political structures, of economic techniques, and of social problems blended in such a way that some readers can be expected to deplore the obfuscation of pure lawyer's law.

Critics imbued with such an attitude must, however, acknowledge that the family of Marxian socialist legal systems has points of distinction, so long as they are not confused with definitions of "law." No one doubts that the family is notable because of the law's conscious and purposeful involvement with politics, economics, and social organization. Of course, all legal systems show such elements of involvement to a degree, as is symbolized by European law faculties which teach law along with political science and economics, within a single building and under a single dean. In contrast, English and American practice establishes a separate law "school," usually physically

[2] R. David, Les grands systèmes de droit contemporain (1964).

[3] This was the position expressed by the former dean of the Teheran Faculty of Law, Dr. Hasan Afchar, during a seminar in comparative law conducted at his faculty during the autumn of 1966. He has since published his views in Farsi.

separated, and often emotionally apart from the rest of the
university in which it functions. To the Anglo-Americans, then,
the emphasis of the family of Marxian socialist legal systems on
nonlegal features presents more of a barrier to understanding
than it does to Continentals, and this has been reflected in the
various studies of aspects of Marxian socialist law that have
been published throughout the world.

Romanists have found it easier to categorize their counterparts to the east than have the common-law lawyers. Not only
has there been a correspondence of legal techniques, but there
has been an appreciation of the need to note law's involvement
with other disciplines. The contrast for the European is not on
these issues between West and East but in values, perhaps best
epitomized in the words of a noted French-trained African
commenting upon his neighboring president, who seemed to be
building on the Soviet pattern in establishing the structure of
his new state.

President Léopold Sédar Senghor of Senegal, in contrasting
the system he hopes to institute with that of President Ahmed
Sékou Touré of Guinea, lays emphasis upon values. For Senghor, deeply imbued as he is with French culture, the accent in
his value scheme must be on humanism and socialism in combination, whereas he accuses his neighbor of thinking of socialism
as an instrument taking the form of production terms and
preoccupied with the standard of living.[4] In his view, the contrast between them lies in emphasis upon the cultural rather
than upon the economic. It is in appreciation of the elements
of Senghor's definition that this study opened with an analysis
of codes of morals, for it is they which determine in European
eyes, both Western and Eastern, the differences in legal systems
between those functioning in the purely Romanist half of
Europe and those in that half where the Romanist base has
been remolded to achieve the purposes of a system of Marxist
morality.

Readers willing to accept comparison which goes beyond
legal techniques to codes of morals, and to political, economic,
and social structures, will note that the institutions commonly

---

[4] Thiam, *Allocution*, [1962] ANNALES AFRICAINES 37 at 49 (Faculté de
droit et des sciences economiques de Dakar, 1963).

known as those of the law have undergone change in Eastern Europe and even in those parts of Asia where Marxist ideas prevail. The accent has been placed vigorously upon the economic. Organization for production within the confines of a state planning system is superimposed upon the Romanist civil-law system inherited from their predecessors by all Marxian socialist states, even China, although admittedly, the latter's period of prior Romanist practice was relatively short and of limited geographical spread. The civil-law relations in their traditional Romanist form have been pushed to the fringes of social relationships somewhat like the first settlers, the aborigines who now live on the Indian reservations of the United States or in the mountains of Japan and Taiwan. These traditional "aboriginal" relationships remain, but they stand on the verge of becoming museum pieces. The original outlines can be identified by an expert using methods akin to the techniques of the anthropologists searching for remnants of tribal law in Africa, but they have been permeated with the new culture. There are few, and some would say none, that remain in their aboriginal form.

The first mark of distinction emerges, therefore, as an economic factor marking the difference between Marxian socialist and welfare state frameworks for legal systems. It is evidenced by the degree of involvement of all elements of society and of its institutions in the operation of a fully state-owned and planned economy.

The second mark of distinction is political: a structuring of society to assure strong, even unchallengeable, leadership, fortified by law in maintaining its dominant position, but relying upon its members' skills both as organizers and persuaders to make leadership effective. Again, as with comparison with welfare states on the economic front, the drawing of precise distinctions is made difficult by the fact that there are non-Marxist systems which fortify leadership in an unchallengeable position. Authoritarian systems of government and law abound in the West and in Asia and Africa. The studies are legion which seek to distinguish between them and those of the Marxists, focusing usually on contrasts in degree of total social involvement in the political process. It is here that the economic situation and the political situation are related, for an authoritarian system functioning without the advantage of state ownership of all productive resources cannot command such obedience as a system which rejects a pluralism founded on alternative sources of power. In this feature many have found the contrast between authoritarian and Marxist-inspired systems, and to be sure, the legal arrangements in each differ.

But total social involvement rests on more than abolition of the economic base which provides the strength of pluralism. It rests upon political and social organization, utilizing the state economy but going beyond it into every aspect of life. What the Marxian socialist family of legal systems has done to regulate the conjugal family and to establish social duties such as those called the "duty to work" and the "duty to rescue" is a part of the mobilization for total social involvement. Perhaps only the sociologist can measure the degree of change in attitudes in these areas, especially in view of the French law on the "duty to rescue," but the legal analyst can note the importance of comparing social attitudes in determining the distinguishing features of the family of Marxian socialist legal systems.

The criminal law has many conventional features in defining what will not be permitted to nonconforming citizens, but it goes beyond the normal confines in an attempt to create a new "socialist man," aware not only of the rule that "thou shalt not kill," but also of the rule that "he who does not work shall not eat." Ancient moral law established by holy writ has been utilized as inspiration for the community of total involvement which Marxists seek to erect by compulsory means.

Coupled with economic, political, and social change stands also the elusive Marxist concept of the "withering away of the state" as a mark of distinction of the legal system. Soviet legal philosophers say today that the accent is not now being placed upon this concept, as it was in Lenin's time or even during the early period following Khrushchev's succession to power. This is evident in legal literature from all the Marxian socialist states; nevertheless, the concept plays a part in the determination of policy. It lurks in the back of the Marxist-oriented mind as an ideal requiring that in some manner the general public be brought into the process of administration of the state, and eventually into the process of making policy. Still, evolution toward mass participation must not upset the concept of strong leadership, without which Marxists expect the public to slip back to the way of least resistance.

There is a groping evident in all legal systems of the Marxian socialist family for a new type of electoral law which will permit choice of candidates, with its inevitable impact upon policy, without endangering maintenance of key positions thought by the Communist party to be necessary to economic growth. In the opinion of Mao Tse-tung, the people must not be permitted to abandon by popular vote the rule of austerity which he has sanctified as a rule of Marxism. To the others, the goal is abundance, and this should always be kept in front of the people as the ultimate value to be sought. Nevertheless, measures of austerity are still required, and for this, leadership capable of exacting sacrifice from the people is thought to be essential.

A satiated, enlightened public is the declared goal. It becomes the task of production to meet the economic need. Law is given a clearly defined and relatively simple role in aid of production; but education is to create "enlightenment," not only through formal schooling but through participation in government. It is here that communist leaders and their lawyers do not yet know what to do, and their confusion provides the dynamic for the evolution of their constitutional law.[5]

Discussion of "class" is slipping from the pages of Marxian socialist law books as the economic base of socialism is firmly laid. In the USSR, where there is total state ownership of productive resources and undoubted stability of Communist party leadership, the concept of "class" has lost its base. The 1961 Communist party program has dropped the terminology entirely, and courts do not use it, except in explanation of goals of criminal policy. "Capitalism" must be erased from the minds of men, but this no longer requires separate institutions to determine social danger and to punish offenders, as it did in 1917 and under Stalin's reign of terror. For some European Marxist states, the concept of "class" is still discussed because private enterprise is still permitted, albeit with severe limitations. But a separate system of courts or revolutionary tribunals

---

[5] The search for new forms of public participation in the political process is well represented by V. M. CHKHIKVADZE, GOSUDARSTVO, DEMOKRATIIA, ZAKONNOST' [State, Democracy, Legality] (1967).

for the class enemy and a flexible standard to be applied in law enforcement has disappeared since the revolts in Poland and Hungary in 1956.

"Class," as an element of distinction of the family of Marxian socialist legal systems, in establishing different yardsticks for the application of law to the "people" and the "enemy," seems to become of decreasing importance as the Communist-led regimes stabilize themselves. Cuba is an example of the unstable state in which revolutionary tribunals on Lenin's model still function, to deal with the "enemy" on a kangaroo court basis.

In no place except China is the "class" approach, as represented by separate treatment for "people" and "enemies," hailed as a permanent mark of distinction of the Marxian socialist legal system. Other states have their new "enemies," but these are not "class enemies." They are treated to the full severity of the law as incorrigibles, but they are not placed in a "class" apart. Their trials do not differ from those of the first offenders. It is the penalty and not the procedure which is distinctive, whereas under the "class" approach it is characteristically the procedure which is primarily affected.

With the increasing variation which occurred among members of the family of Marxian socialist states and their legal systems after Stalin's death and denunciation, there seemed so little conformity to core concepts that some foreign analysts concluded that communism was dead—that there had come an end to its ideology and the institutions that protected it. This position cannot be supported by the developments chronicled in this volume. The elements of distinction, the universals, remain, and the events of 1968 support such a conclusion. Modibo Keita's failure in Mali and the intervention of the Soviet military in Czechoslovakia suggest the criteria that must be met to gain entrance into the Marxian socialist family and the standards that must be maintained, in Moscow's view, by those who have been granted admission.

Keita met a good many of the tests. To the extent possible within a very much underdeveloped economy, he restructured both agriculture and industry so as to move as quickly as possible, without inspiring revolt, from a traditional African tribally oriented village structure to a centrally directed, planned economy functioning through the collective farm and the state-owned enterprise for production and distribution. He recognized the need for strong leadership, structured to implement Lenin's concept of democratic centralism. In short he moved as fast as a primitive society can be expected by Marxists to move; but he did not receive the Soviet Communist party's cachet. His ouster from the presidency in November 1968 laid bare his failure, and the outsider can conclude that this failure was feared, if not anticipated, by the Soviet party. He had been unsuccessful in creating a strong, disciplined political party dedicated to a Marxian socialist solution to Mali's developmental problems. He had violated the first rule established in the declaration of 1957, to which all Communist leaders in power had pledged their allegiance. Keita's experience confirms the keystone position of this requirement.

The Czechoslovak events of 1968 point in the same direction. It was the failure of the Czechoslovak Communist party to maintain its distinctive role that was singled out by the Soviet party in primary justification of its intervention.

Mali and Czechoslovakia had one shortcoming in common. The vanguard party failed to perform the duties assigned it under the 1957 model because of lack of discipline. For the Africans there was no such tradition, and by opening membership to all Keita compounded his difficulties. He threw away the opportunity Lenin had seized of centering power in a small group of militants which could be developed into a governing elite. The Czechoslovaks had had too long an experience with multiparty parliamentary democracy to repress the desire for a pluralistic system. Millions of Czechs and Slovaks believed it possible to revert to their traditions as long as they retained a commitment to an ill defined "socialism," and even the leaders of the Czechoslovak Communist party thought themselves capable of maintaining control while acquiescing in the demands. It was the task of the Soviet Communists to correct their misapprehension of what the keepers of the Marxist-Leninist legacy deemed essential to the common core prescribed for all.

In brief, there are universals found in all fourteen of the

Marxian socialist states which provide reason to conclude that the legal systems of those states, in spite of a wealth of differences and a vocabulary and even a "grammar" inspired by the Romanist systems, constitute a distinctive legal family which the Soviet Communists intend to preserve to the extent of their power.

ABBREVIATIONS AND CITATIONS

THE SYSTEM OF ABBREVIATION AND CITATION USED IS THAT recommended by the Council of Europe and accepted by specialists in the United States for works on the family of Marxian socialist legal systems. It is set forth in A *Uniform System of Citation*, 11th ed., 1967, copyright by the *Columbia Law Review*, the *Harvard Law Review, University of Pennsylvania Law Review* and the *Yale Law Journal*.

Information recommended by the system has been reduced in some cases where it seems unnecessary for judicial decisions and statutes.

The Cyrillic alphabet has been transliterated into the Latin alphabet in accordance with the system recommended by the United States Library of Congress.

For titles not included in the recommended system, the following abbreviations have been adopted for the notes.

Arbitrazh   Arbitrazh, Organ Gosarbit-
                              razha pri SNK SSSR
Biull. Verkh. Suda RSFSR   Biulleten' Verkhovnogo Suda
                              R.S.F.S.R.

Biull. Verkh. Suda SSSR	Biulleten' Verkhovnogo Suda S.S.S.R.
CDSP	Current Digest of the Soviet Press
Ezh. Sov. Iust.	Ezhenedel'nik Sovetskoi Iustitsii
Fin. i Khoz. Zak.	Finansovoe i Khoziaistvennoe Zakonodatel'stvo
JORM	Journal Officiel de la République du Mali
JPRS	Joint Publications Research Service
J. of L. Czechoslovakia	Sbirka Zarkonu
J. of L. Poland	Dziennik Ustav
J. of L. Yugoslavia	Služben. List
OSN	Orzecznictwo Sądów Polskich
OSP	Orcecznictwo Sądow Polskich i Komisyj Arbitrazowych
SCMP	Survey of the China Mainland Press
Prol. Rev. i Pravo	Proletarskaia Revoliutsiia i Pravo
Sbornik Zak. SSSR	Sbornik Zakonov SSSR i Ukazov Prezidiuma Verkhovnogo Soveta SSSR
Sob. Post. RSFSR	Sobranie Postanovlenii i Rasporiazhenii Pravitel'stva Rossiiskoi Sovetskoi Federativnoi Sotsialisticheskoi Respubliki
Sob. Post. SSSR	Sobranie Postanovlenii i Rasporiazhenii Pravitel'stva Soiuza Sovetskikh Sotsialisticheskikh Respublik (with issue no. 5 for the year 1946 the title became Sobranie Postanovlenii i Rasporiazhenii Soveta Ministrov Soiuza Sovetskikh Sotsialisticheskikh Respublik)

Sob. Uzak. RSFSR	Sobranie Uzakonenii i Rasporiazhenii Rabochego i Krestianskogo Pravitelstva (with issue no. 1 for the year 1925 the title added the words, Rossiiskoi Sotsialisticheskoi Federativnoi Sovetskoi Respubliki)
Sob. Zak. SSSR	Sobranie Zakonov i Rasporiazhenii Raboche-Krestianskogo Pravitel'stva Soiuza Sovetskikh Sotsialisticheskikh Respublik
Sots. Zak.	Sotsialisticheskaia Zakonnost'
Sov. Gos. i Pravo	Sovetskoe Gosudarstvo i Pravo
Sov. Iust.	Sovetskaia Iustitsiia
Spravochnik po Zak.	Spravochnik po Zakonodatel'stvu dlia Sudebno-Prokurorskikh Rabotnikov (pod obshchei redaktsiei G. N. Safonova. Izdanie 2, Moscow, 1949).
Sud. Prak. Verkh. Suda RSFSR	Sudebnaia Praktika RSFSR pod redaktsiei Predsedatelia Verkhsuda RSFSR
Sud. Prak. Verkh. Suda SSSR	Sudebnaia Praktika Verkhovnogo Suda SSSR
Ved. Verkh. Sov. SSSR	Vedomosti Verkhovnogo Soveta Soiuza Sovetskikh Sotsialisticheskikh Respublik
ZOSN	Zbiór Orzeczén Sądu Najwyzszego

BIBLIOGRAPHICAL NOTE

Literature in the languages of the states within the family of Marxian socialist legal systems is voluminous. Much of it has been scanned in preparation of this study, as is indicated by citations in the notes. Literature in Western languages is primarily in periodicals, although the number of books is increasing, especially those explaining and analyzing the legal systems which have existed for long periods, particularly that of USSR. Pertinent articles have also been cited in the notes.

Comparative studies of the political and legal systems of members of the Marxian socialist family are rare. Most focus upon the constitutional and institutional structures, and none treat in any detail the elements of what has traditionally been called "private law."

In the belief that materials in the languages of the Marxian socialist states are of value for reference rather than general reading, they have been indicated only where necessary to support statements in the text. These reference materials are not listed again in this bibliographical note, nor are the various periodical articles in Western languages which support a single point. This note is designed for general readers of the English language who seek background studies of the countries treated and translations of documents. In a few cases where there are no comparable English language studies, reference is made to French texts and translations.

For those who wish to delve further, a selective list of general bibliographies is included.

General Bibliographies

C. Szladits. *A Bibliography of Foreign and Comparative Law: Books and Articles in English.* Parker School Studies in Foreign and Comparative Law. 3 vols. New York: Oceana, 1955, 1962, 1968. Annual supplements.

UNESCO. *A Register of Legal Documentation of the World.* 2d ed. rev. and enl. Prepared by the International Association of Legal Science and the International Committee for Social Science Documentation. Paris, 1957. 422 p. [3d ed. forthcoming in 1970].

UNESCO. *World List of Social Science Periodicals.* 2d ed. rev. and enl. Prepared by the International Committee for Social Science Documentation. Paris, 1957, 209 pp.

U.S. Library of Congress, Slavic and Central European Division. *The U.S.S.R. and Eastern Europe, Periodicals in Western Languages.* 3d ed. rev. and enl. Comp. P. L. Horecky and R. G. Carlton. Washington, 1967.

Bibliographies by Country

Blagojević, Borislav T. *Bibliographie juridique yougoslave.* Belgrade: Institut de droit comparé, 1959. (Supplement for 1960 and 1961. Belgrade, 1962.) (2d ed. in preparation.)

Butler, William E. *Writings on Soviet Law and Soviet International Law: A Bibliography of Books and Articles Published since 1917 in Languages Other than East European.* Cambridge, Mass.: Harvard Law School Library, 1966. 165 pp.

Czachórski, M. W., ed. *Bibliographie juridique polonaise 1944–1956.* Institut des sciences juridiques de l'Académie polonaise des sciences. Warsaw: Panstwowe Wydawnictwo Naukowe, 1958.

Horecky, Paul L., ed. *Russia and the Soviet Union: A Bibliographic Guide to Western-Language Publications.* Chicago: University of Chicago Press, 1965. 473 pp.

Knapp, V. *Bibliography of Czechoslovak Legal Literature 1945–1958.* The Institute of Law of the Czechoslovak Academy of Sciences. Prague: Publishing House of the Czechoslovak Academy of Sciences, 1959.

Kolarz, Walter, ed. *Books on Communism: A Bibliography.* London: Ampersand, 1963. 568 pp.

Lin, Fu-shun, ed. *Chinese Law Past and Present: A Bibliography of Enactments and Commentaries in English Text.* The East Asia Institute, New York: Columbia University, 1966. 419 pp.

USSR Academy of Science, Institute of State and Law. *Literature on Soviet Law: Index of Bibliography.* Moscow: Publishing House of the USSR Academy of Science, 1960.

Constitutions

"The Constitution of the German Democratic Republic, April 9, 1968": *Law and Legislation in the German Democratic Republic.* Special ed. Berlin: Association of German Democratic Lawyers, 1968.

Peaslee, Amos. *Constitutions of Nations.* 3 vols. 1st ed., Concord, N.H., Rumford Press, 1950; 2d ed., The Hague: Nijhoff, 1956.

Triska, Jan F., ed. *Constitutions of the Communist Party States.* The Hoover Institution of War, Revolution and Peace. Stanford: Stanford University, 1968. 541 pp.

Codes and Statutes

People's Republic of Albania:

Revised Penal Code of the People's Republic of Albania. Tirana, 1959.

United States Department of Commerce. Joint Publications Research Service. *Laws Governing Albanian Agriculture and Finance.* Part I: Doc. no. 7,584, 27 March 1961; Part II: Doc. no. 9,099.

People's Republic of Bulgaria:

United States Department of Commerce. Joint Publications Research Service. *The Laws Governing the Transition from Socialism to Communism—Bulgaria.* Doc. no. 11,764, 3 January 1962.

People's Republic of China:

Blaustein, Albert P., ed. *Fundamental Legal Documents of Communist China.* South Hackensack, N.J.: Rothman, 1962.

Revolutionary Government of Cuba:

Leyes del Gobierno Revolucionario de Cuba. Vols. 1–59. Havana, 1959–65.

Czechoslovak Socialist Republic:

The Penal Code. Act no. 140/1961. *Bulletin of Czechoslovak Law,* no. 1–2. Pub. by Jednota Ceskoslovenskych Pravniku [Union of Czechoslovak Lawyers], 1962.

The Act concerning Judicial Penal Procedure [The Code of Penal Procedure]. Act no. 141/1961. *Ibid.,* no. 3–4. 1962.

The Civil Code. Act no. 40/1964. *Ibid.,* no. 1–2. 1964.

The Code of Civil Procedure. Act no. 99/1963. *Ibid.,* no. 3–4. 1965.

The Economic Code. Act no. 109/1964. *Ibid.*, no. 1–2. 1965.

The Labour Code. Act no. 65/1965. *Ibid.*, no. 1–2. 1966.

Act no. 97/1963 concerning Private International Law and the Rules of Procedure Relating Thereto. *Ibid.*, no. 4. 1964.

German Democratic Republic:

Law of the Agricultural Producers' Cooperatives, 3 June 1959. *Law and Legislation of the German Democratic Republic,* 1961. No. 1/2, p. 118.

Model Statute for Agricultural Producers' Cooperatives Type I. *Ibid.*, p. 125.

Labour Code, 12 April 1961. *Ibid.*, p. 81.

Decree on the Operation of District and County Labour Courts, 29 June 1961. *Ibid.*, 1962. No. 2, p. 82.

Decree on the Promotion and Direction of the Movement of Innovators, 31 July 1963. *Ibid.*, 1964. No. 1, p. 51.

Law on the Procurator's Office, 17 April 1963. *Ibid.*, 1964. No. 1, p. 53.

Decree on the Establishment of Semi-state Enterprises (Excerpts), 26 March 1959. *Ibid.*, 1967. No. 1, p. 75.

Directive on the Establishment and Activities of Arbitration Commissions, 21 August 1964. *Ibid.*, 1966. No. 2, p. 83.

Family Code (Excerpts from Draft) *Ibid.*, 1965. No. 2, p. 47.

Law on the Contract System in Socialist Economy, 25 February 1965. *Ibid.*, p. 61.

Hungarian People's Republic:

Lamberg, P., trans. *Civil Code of the Hungarian People's Republic*. Budapest, 1960.

Lamberg, P., trans. *Criminal Code of the Hungarian People's Republic*. Bupdapest, 1962.

Mongolian People's Republic:

United States Department of Commerce. Joint Publications Research Service. *Laws and Legal Documents of the Mongolian People's Republic*. Doc. no. 27,051. 23 October 1964.

People's Republic of Poland:

Czarchórski, W., ed. *Code de la famille et de la tutelle de la République populaire de Pologne*. Trans. M. Szepietowski. Warsaw, 1966.

Szepietowski, M., trans. *Code civil de la République populaire de Pologne*. Warsaw, 1966.

Union of Soviet Socialist Republics:

Berman, Harold J. *Soviet Criminal Law and Procedure: The RSFSR Codes*. Trans. Harold J. Berman and James W. Spindler. Cambridge, Mass.: Harvard University Press, 1966.

Gray, Whitmore, and Stults, Raymond. *Civil Code of the Rus-*

sian Soviet Federated Socialist Republic. Ann Arbor, Mich.: The University of Michigan Law School, 1965.

Hanna, George H., trans. *Fundamentals of Soviet Criminal Legislation, The Judicial System and Criminal Court Procedure: Official Texts and Commentaries.* Moscow, Foreign Languages Publishing House, 1960.

Sdobnikov, Yuri, trans. *Soviet Civil Legislation and Procedure: Official Texts and Commentaries.* Moscow: Foreign Languages Publishing House, n.d. circa 1962.

Triska, Jan F., ed. *Soviet Communism: Programs and Rules: Official Texts of 1919, 1952 (1956), 1961.* San Francisco: Chandler Publishing Co., 1962.

Socialist Federated Republic of Yugoslavia:

Institute of Comparative Law. Collection of Yugoslav Laws (1962–1967) Belgrade:

    I. The Legal Status of Agricultural Land
    II. The Local Government
    III. Nationalization and Expropriation
    IV. Family Law
    V. The Execution of Criminal Sanctions
    VI. The Status of War Veterans and Victims of War
    VII. Constitution of the SFR of Yugoslavia
    VIII. Constitution of the SR of Serbia
    IX. The General Usages of Trade
    X. The Law of Inheritance
    XI. Criminal Code
    XII. Statute of the Commune of Pozarevac
    XIII. Laws of Enterprises and Institutions
    XIV. Constitutional Judicature
    XV. The Legal Status of Religious Communities
    XVI. Laws of Employment Relationships
    XVII. Laws on Joint Investments of Enterprises

Studies by Country

Triska, Jan F., ed. Integration and Community Building among the Fourteen Communist Party-States (Hoover Institution Studies):

Aspaturian, Vernon V. *The Soviet Union in the World Communist System.* Stanford: Stanford University, 1966. 95 pp.

Doolin, Dennis J., and North, Robert C. *The Chinese People's Republic.* Stanford: Stanford University, 1966. 68 pp.

Paige, Glenn D. *The Korean People's Democratic Republic.* Stanford: Stanford University, 1966. 60 pp.

Rupen, Robert A. *The Mongolian People's Republic*. Stanford: Stanford University, 1966. 74 pp.

Triska, Jan F., ed. Integration and Community Building in Eastern Europe:

Hanhardt, Arthur M., Jr. *The German Democratic Republic*. Baltimore: Johns Hopkins Press, 1968. 126 pp.

Morrison, James F. *The Polish People's Republic*. Baltimore: Johns Hopkins Press, 1968. 160 pp.

Pano, Nicholas C. *The People's Republic of Albania*. Baltimore: Johns Hopkins Press, 1968. 185 pp.

Zaninovich, M. George. *The Development of Socialist Yugoslavia*. Baltimore: Johns Hopkins Press, 1968. 182 pp.

Ginsburgs, George, and Mathes, Michael. *Communist China and Tibet: The First Dozen Years*. The Hague, 1964. 218 pp.

Jaworskyj, Michael. *Soviet Political Thought: An Anthology: 1917–1961*. Baltimore: Johns Hopkins Press, 1967. 621 pp.

Schram, Stuart R. *The Political Thought of Mao Tse-tung*. New York: Praeger 1963. 319 pp.

Schurmann, Franz. *Ideology and Organization in Communist China*. Berkeley: University of California, 1966. 540 pp.

Starr, Richard F. *The Communist Regimes in Eastern Europe: An Introduction*. Hoover Institution Publications. Stanford: Stanford University, 1967. 387 pp.

Legal Studies

Berman, Harold J. *Justice in the U.S.S.R.* Rev. ed. New York: Vintage, 1963. 431 pp.

Cohen, Jerome Alan. *The Criminal Process in the People's Republic of China 1949–1963: An Introduction*. Cambridge, Mass.: Harvard University Press, 1968. 706 pp.

Leng, Shao-chuan. *Justice in Communist China*. Dobbs Ferry: 1967. 196 pp.

Romashkin, P. S., ed. *Fundamentals of Soviet Law*. Moscow: Academy of Sciences USSR, 1961. 526 pp.

Rozmaryn, Stefan, ed. *Introduction à l'étude du droit polonais*. Warsaw, 1967. 588 pp.

Comparative Studies

David, René. *Les grands systèmes de droit contemporains*. Paris, 1964. 630 pp. [Eng. transl. as David and Brierly, *Contemporary Legal Systems*. London and New York: Collier-Macmillan, 1968].

Halász, Jozsef. *Socialist Concept of Human Rights.* Budapest, 1966. 309 pp.

London, Kurt, ed. *Eastern Europe in Transition.* Baltimore: Johns Hopkins Press, 1966. 364 pp.

Skilling, H. Gordon. *Communism National and International: Eastern Europe after Stalin.* Toronto: University of Toronto, 1964. 168 pp.

————. *The Governments of Communist East Europe.* New York: Crowell, 1966. 256 pp.

INDEX